THE MONSTERS KNOW WHAT THEY'RE DOING

COMBAT TACTICS
FOR DUNGEON MASTERS

KEITH AMMANN

SAGA PRESS

LONDON SYDNEY **NEW YORK** TORONTO NEW DELHI

SAGA PRESS
AN IMPRINT OF SIMON & SCHUSTER, INC.

1230 AVENUE OF THE AMERICAS, NEW YORK, NEW YORK 10020

Copyright © 2019 by Keith Ammann
Cover illustration by Lio Pressland
Interior illustrations by Jen C. Marshall

First Saga Press hardcover edition October 2019

SAGA PRESS and colophon are trademarks of Simon & Schuster, Inc.

For information about special discounts for bulk purchases,
please contact Simon & Schuster Special Sales at 1-866-506-1949
or business@simonandschuster.com.

The Simon & Schuster Speakers Bureau can bring authors to your live event.
For more information or to book an event, contact the Simon & Schuster Speakers
Bureau at 1-866-248-3049 or visit our website at www.simonspeakers.com.

Interior design by Michelle Marchese

Manufactured in the United States of America

7   9   10   8

Library of Congress Cataloging-in-Publication Data
Names: Ammann, Keith, author.
Title: The monsters know what they're doing :
combat tactics for dungeon masters / by Keith Ammann.
Description: First Saga Press hardcover edition. | New York : Saga Press, 2019. |
Includes index.
Identifiers: LCCN 2019026607 | ISBN 9781982122669 (hardcover) |
ISBN 9781982122676 (paperback) | ISBN 9781982122683 (ebook)
Subjects: LCSH: Dungeons and Dragons (Game)—Handbooks, manuals, etc.
Classification: LCC GV1469.62.D84 A66 2019 | DDC 793.93—dc23
LC record available at https://lccn.loc.gov/2019026607

ISBN 978-1-9821-2266-9
ISBN 978-1-9821-2268-3 (ebook)

CONTENTS

PREFACE

In 1979, as a precocious ten-year-old with a yen for puzzles, I was always excited to get my hands on a copy of *Games* magazine. The September/October 1979 issue, though, seized my attention like no other had, because it included a feature article that described an entirely new kind of game—one involving maps, monsters, and hunting for treasure—called "Dungeons & Dragons." I showed the article to my mother, and before long, I had the Dungeons & Dragons Basic Set in my hands. It contained a rulebook, an adventure module called "The Keep on the Borderlands," and a set of the exact same hard polymer polyhedral dice I'd seen advertised in my mom's teacher supply catalogs.

We sat down to play it, and . . . neither of us could figure out what to do.

It sat on my shelf for a long time.

Later, in high school, I got together with a group of friends who had figured it out and were playing D&D along with other roleplaying games such as Villains & Vigilantes and Call of Cthulhu. Four of us formed a tight group that played D&D, taking turns as Dungeon Master, starting with my friend Julian. I was last in the rotation, so I got to see three different examples of how to be a DM before taking on the job myself.

In those years, I didn't think of what we were doing in our D&D games in strategic or tactical terms. None of us did. We had plan A (*"Get 'em!"*) and plan B (*"Run!"*), and that was the extent of it.

That group disbanded when, one by one, we stopped coming home from college over the summer. I kept playing D&D for a year or two after that in college, but I'd begun to lose interest in the high-fantasy roleplaying genre; then early adulthood hit, and multiple intercity moves in pursuit of work, and I never managed to find another gaming group that I clicked with. Eventually, I returned home to Chicago and reconnected with Julian and some other players—but by that time, they'd moved on from D&D as well. They were playing GURPS (the Generic Universal Role-Playing System), which worked with *any* genre, including fantasy.

Everything changed in 2015, when my wife came home from work one day and asked me whether I could help get a D&D game going with some of her coworkers. (Someone at her office had referred to a client as "someone who looks like he'd play Dungeons & Dragons in his mother's basement," to which one of the aforementioned coworkers had replied, deadpan, "I would *totally* play Dungeons & Dragons.") My first thought was to run a fantasy campaign using GURPS, but my wife said her coworkers wanted to play *D&D*, and she prevailed on me to stick with the biggest name in roleplaying games.

I hadn't played D&D since shortly after the second edition of the game came out, and I hadn't kept any of my books, so I went to a friendly local game store and bought the D&D Starter Set. The timing couldn't have been better: Wizards of the Coast, which had bought the rights to D&D from its original publisher, TSR Inc., had recently released the fifth edition of the game. This edition had taken a hulking gallimaufry of accumulated rules and options and streamlined it into a tight, consistent system that treated all its core functions—attack rolls, saving throws, and ability checks—the same way, reducing a plethora of lookup tables to simple calculations, while preserving the game's high-fantasy soul. The more I got into it, the more I liked it (even though I still favored anchored fantasy over wild, fantastic, superheroic fantasy). I also began to recognize certain emergent properties of some of fifth edition D&D's mechanics—properties with tactical implications.

As a young person, I'd always been interested in strategy games, but I'd also never been particularly good at them, because I never learned to *think* strategically. What really drove this fact home for me, a couple of years before discovering fifth edition D&D, was playing the computer game *XCOM: Enemy Unknown*. Over and over, I kept getting massacred, even on the easiest levels. What was I doing wrong? I had no idea. However, by that time, after many hard years, I had finally learned *how to learn*. And I figured out that I was failing at *XCOM* because of something I hadn't known I didn't know: specifically, small-unit tactics. When I started reading up on them, my *XCOM* game changed overnight.

As I ran a fifth edition D&D campaign for my wife and her coworkers, I began to think something was missing in how I was running monsters and non-player characters in combat. Reflecting back on my *XCOM* experience, I decided I needed to understand those monsters and NPCs more deeply and to come up with action plans for them *before*, rather than during, our game sessions.

Once I'd come up with these plans, it seemed selfish to keep them to myself. So I created a blog, *The Monsters Know What They're Doing* (themonstersknow.com), where I analyzed the stat blocks of monster after monster for the benefit of other DMs, figuring that what was helpful to me might be helpful to them as well.

I began writing *The Monsters Know What They're Doing* in August 2016. Six months later, I noticed a spike in my traffic, seemingly driven by Reddit. Users of D&D-related subreddits were answering "How I do I run [monster *x*]?" questions by sharing links to my blog. Eventually, I realized that a growing number of other DMs were visiting my blog as a routine step in their combat encounter planning. The comments rolled in: "I love what you're doing here." "This resource is fantastic!" "Thank you for doing this. It's saved me a lot of work."

I now have the honor of presenting *The Monsters Know What They're Doing* to you in book form—consolidated, revised, in some cases corrected, and supplemented with additional material, including analyses of monsters not examined on the blog. Note well: This is not a substitute for the *Monster Manual* (or any other D&D core book); for the actual abilities, traits, and other stats of D&D monsters, as well as the official lore attached to them, you'll need the *Monster Manual*. But if you want advice from a D&D veteran about what to do with those abilities, traits, and other stats when the fur starts to fly, *The Monsters Know What They're Doing* is the book for you.

*A*ny creature that has evolved to survive in a given environment instinctively knows how to make the best use of its particular adaptations.

That seems like a straightforward principle, doesn't it? Yet monsters in Dungeons & Dragons campaigns often fail to follow it.

No doubt this is largely because many of us begin playing D&D when we're teens (or even preteens) and don't yet have much experience with how the world works. Or we come to D&D as adults with little or no background in evolutionary biology, military service, martial arts, or even tactical simulation games, so we don't consider how relative strengths and weaknesses, the environment, and simple survival sense play into the way a creature fights, hunts, or defends itself. Consequently, we think of combat as a situation in which two opponents swing/shoot/claw/bite at each other until one or the other goes down or runs away. Not so.

Primitive societies may fight battles by charging out into the open and stabbing at each other, but trained soldiers don't. They use ranged weapons and shoot from cover. They strive to occupy high ground, where they can see farther and from which it's easier to shoot or charge. While one soldier or fire team moves from cover to cover, another stays put and watches for danger; then they switch. They've learned this from centuries of experience with what wins a battle and what loses it. They know what they're capable of, and they make the most of it. This is what makes them effective.

What makes the predators of the natural world effective is evolution: behavior fine-tuned into instincts over countless generations. Lions, crocodiles, and bears are all potentially deadly to humans. Yet lions and crocodiles don't charge at us from out in the open. They use cover and stealth, and they strike when they're close enough that we have little chance of running away. This is their most effective strategy: A crocodile isn't fast enough to give chase over land, and a lion will tire itself out before catching an impala or wildebeest if its prey has enough of a lead. Black and brown bears, which are also deadly up close—and are more than fast enough to chase a human down—use stealth hardly at all. Why? Because, by and large, they don't hunt. They scavenge, forage, and fish. Their environment is different, and their diet is different, so their habits are different.

In a game of D&D, what distinguishes goblins from kobolds from orcs from lizardfolk? In many campaigns, hardly anything. They're all low-level humanoids who go, "Rrrrahhhh, stab stab stab," then (if the player characters are above level 2) get wiped out. They're cannon fodder. Only the packaging is different.

Yet the simple fact that they have different names tells us there should be differences among them, including differences in behavior. One of the great things about the fifth edition of D&D is that not only the ability scores but the skills and features of monsters are specified precisely and consistently. Those skills and features give us clues as to how these monsters ought to fight.

However, because a Dungeon Master has to make one decision after another in response to player behavior (and the better the players, the more unpredictable their behavior), it doesn't take long for decision fatigue to set in. It's easy for even an excellent DM, well acquainted with their monsters' stat blocks and lore, to allow combat to devolve into monsters running directly at the PCs and going, "Rrrrahhhh, stab stab stab."

The way to avoid this is to make as many of these tactical decisions as possible *before the session begins*, just as a trained soldier—or an accomplished athlete or musician—relies on reflexes developed from thousands of hours of training and practice, and just as an animal acts from evolved instinct. A lion doesn't wait until the moment after it first spots a herd of tasty wildebeests to reflect upon how it should go about nabbing one, soldiers don't whip out their field manuals for the

first time when they're already under fire, and a DM shouldn't be contemplating for the first time how bullywugs move and fight when the
PCs have just encountered twelve of them. Rather than try to make
those decisions on the fly, the DM needs heuristics to follow so that
combat can progress smoothly, sensibly, and satisfyingly. That's what
I set out to provide in this book.

This book is aimed at:

- Beginning DMs, especially younger DMs and adult DMs with
  little or no strategy gaming experience
- Intermediate DMs who are looking for ways to add more flavor
  and challenge for their players
- Advanced DMs who could figure all this out perfectly well on
  their own but are too busy to put the time into it
- And players. Yes, players! I don't see anything wrong with your
  scoping this book for intel. If your DM is using these tips, it's
  going to make your characters' lives a little tougher, and I don't
  want them to get slaughtered. If your PCs know something
  about the creatures they're up against, they can begin to plan
  for it, and that's part of the fun of D&D.

WHY THESE TACTICS?

To analyze the stat blocks of the creatures in the *Monster Manual* and other books, I proceed from a certain set of assumptions:

- With only a small number of exceptions (mostly constructs and undead), every creature wants, first and foremost, to survive. Seriously wounded creatures will try to flee, unless they're fanatics or intelligent beings who believe they'll be hunted down and killed if they do flee. Some creatures will flee even sooner.
- Ability scores, particularly physical ability scores, influence fighting styles. In this book, I use the phrase "ability contour" to refer to the pattern of high and low scores in a creature's stat block and how it defines that creature's overall approach to combat.

  Two key elements in a creature's ability contour are its primary defensive ability and primary offensive ability. The primary defensive ability is either Constitution or Dexterity, and it determines whether a creature relies on its toughness to absorb incoming damage or on its nimbleness and mobility to avoid it. The primary offensive ability may be Strength, Dexterity, or a mental ability, and it determines whether a creature prefers to do damage via brute-force melee attacks, finesse or ranged attacks, or magical powers.

  Small, low-Strength creatures try to compensate with numbers, and when their numbers are reduced enough, they scatter. Low-Constitution creatures prefer to attack from range, from hiding, or both. Low-Dexterity creatures must choose their battles judiciously, because they're not likely to be able to get out of a fight once they're in it. High-Strength, high-Constitution creatures are brutes that welcome a close-quarters slugfest. High-Strength, high-Dexterity creatures are hard-hitting predators or shock attackers that count on finishing fights quickly; they'll often use Stealth and go for big-damage ambushes. High-Dexterity, high-Constitution creatures are scrappy skirmishers that deal steady, moderate damage and don't mind a battle of attrition. High-Dexterity creatures without high Strength or Constitution snipe at range with missile weapons or spells. If all three physical abilities are low, a creature seeks to avoid fighting altogether unless it has some sort of circumstantial advantage—or it simply flees without hesitation.

- A creature with Intelligence 7 or less operates wholly or almost wholly from instinct. This doesn't mean it uses its features *ineffectively*, only that it has one preferred modus operandi and can't adjust if it stops working. A creature with Intelligence 8 to 11 is unsophisticated in its tactics and largely lacking in strategy, but it can tell when things are going wrong and adjust to some degree. A creature with Intelligence 12 or higher can come up with a good plan and coordinate with others; it probably also has multiple ways of attacking and/or defending and knows which works better in which situation. A creature with Intelligence 14 or higher can not only plan but also accurately assess its enemies' weaknesses and target accordingly. (A creature with Intelligence greater than 18 can do this to a superhuman degree, detecting even hidden weaknesses.)

- A creature with Wisdom 7 or less has an underdeveloped survival instinct and may wait too long to flee. A creature with Wisdom 8 to 11 knows when to flee but is indiscriminate in choosing targets to attack. A creature with Wisdom 12 or higher selects targets carefully and may even refrain from combat in favor of parley if it recognizes that it's outmatched. A creature with Wisdom 14 or higher chooses its battles, fights only when it's sure it will win (or will be killed if it doesn't fight), and is always willing to bargain, bully, or bluff if this will further its interests with less resistance.

- Creatures that rely on numbers have an instinctive sense of how many of them are needed to take down a foe. Usually this is at least three to one. This sense isn't perfect, but it's accurate given certain base assumptions (which player characters may defy). The smarter a creature is, the more it accounts for such things as its target's armor, weaponry, and behavior; the stupider it is, the more it bases its estimate of the danger its enemy poses solely on physical size.

- A creature with a feature that gives it advantage on a roll (or gives its enemy disadvantage) will always prefer to use that feature. If it uses such a feature to initiate combat and the circumstances aren't right for it, it may never attack in the first place. On average, advantage or disadvantage is worth approximately ±4 on a d20 roll; with midrange target numbers, it can be worth as much as ±5. It can turn a fifty-fifty chance into three-to-one odds, or three-to-one odds into fifteen-to-one odds . . . or the reverse. By comparison, the rarest and most powerful magic weapons in fifth edition D&D are +3. Advantage and disadvantage are a big deal!

- A creature with a feature that requires a saving throw to avoid will often favor this feature over a simple attack, even if the average damage may be slightly less. This is because the presumption of an attack action is failure, and the burden is on the attacker to prove success; the presumption of a feature that requires a saving throw is success, and the burden is on the defender to prove failure. Moreover, attacks that miss do no damage at all, ever; features that require saving throws often have damaging effects even if the targets succeed on their saves.

- In fifth edition Dungeons & Dragons, unless otherwise specified, any creature gets one action and up to one bonus action in a combat round, plus movement and up to one reaction. Any creature that exists in the D&D game world will have evolved in accordance with this rule: It seeks to obtain the best possible result from whatever movement, actions, bonus actions, and reactions are available to it. If it can combine two of them for a superior outcome, it will. This principle is widely referred to as "action economy," and that's how I refer to it here.

- I make frequent reference to the Targets in Area of Effect table in chapter 8 of the *Dungeon Master's Guide*. It's intended primarily for resolution of area-effect spells and other abilities in "theater of the mind"–style play, but here I use it as a guide to the minimum number of targets against whom a limited-use area-effect spell or feature is worth using. For instance, if the table indicates four creatures in a spell's area of effect, I conclude that the caster is disinclined to waste it against three or fewer if it has any other reasonable choice of action.

- Good creatures tend to be friendly by default, neutral creatures indifferent, and evil creatures hostile. However, lawful creatures, even lawful good creatures, will be hostile toward chaotic creatures causing ruckus; chaotic creatures, even chaotic good creatures, will be hostile toward attempts by lawful creatures to constrain or interfere with them; and nearly all creatures, regardless of alignment, are territorial to some degree or another. Intelligent lawful monsters may try to capture and either imprison or enslave characters whom intelligent chaotic monsters would simply drive off or kill.

- I consider a creature that's lost 10 percent of its average hit point maximum to be lightly wounded, 30 percent moderately wounded, and 60 percent severely wounded. I use these thresholds to determine whether a creature will flee or otherwise alter its behavior or attitude toward its opponents. Except in rare and specific cases (such as trolls using the "Loathsome Limbs" variant rule), they don't affect what the creature *can* do.

CAVEAT ARBITER

Not all monsters' tactics are interesting.

Despite what I say about monsters knowing the best way to make use of their features and traits, the sad truth is that there are some monsters, including a few I've omitted from this book, whose features and traits don't lend themselves to anything *but* "Rrrraaaahhhh, stab stab stab." Most of these are brutes with only one means of attack, no special movement, and no feature synergy to give them any kind of advantage. Some could pose a special threat to particular opponents but don't, because they're too stupid to distinguish one opponent from another. Some are simplistic in a different way: They're too weak and fragile to do anything but run away when encountered.

The fact that the *monster* isn't interesting doesn't absolve you of the need to make the *encounter* interesting. Keep the following in mind when the situation that you're devising (or that appears in a published adventure) calls for a tactically dull monster:

- Sometimes monsters exist just to soften the PCs up, increasing the danger level of a subsequent encounter. When this is the case, make them weaker and more numerous. This way, the monsters' lack of sophistication is obscured by the challenge of having to fend off a horde of them. If there's no weaker version of the monster you're looking at, reduce its hit points to something at the lower end of its range (remember, you don't have to use the default average hit points *or* roll for them—you can assign any value within the random range).

- Sometimes a monster is narratively and/or thematically appropriate but otherwise not that interesting. Find other ways to enliven the encounter, such as unusual terrain that the PCs can exploit to outmaneuver a less mobile brute, environmental hazards, distracting developments taking place around the combatants, or an item that the PCs want and the monster has taken (or eaten).

- Sometimes a monster is less of an *enemy* and more of an *obstacle*. Offer your PCs two or three ways around it that they can discover if they're creative. A monster encounter doesn't always have to be a *combat* encounter.

- Sometimes monsters fight other monsters! Not every fight has to be two-sided. Introduce a more complex monster as a foil for the simpler one—*and* for your PCs. Your players will delight in the chaos of a three-way battle.

- If no other solution presents itself, let the battle end quickly, so that you and your players can move on to more interesting things.

WHAT MONSTERS WANT

Fifth edition Dungeons & Dragons organizes monsters into fourteen different types. In most cases, a monster's type is an excellent indicator of its basic goals and desires.

Beasts and **monstrosities** are easily grouped together, because their priorities are simple: They want food. Also, perhaps, territory, but territory is mainly a way to ensure uncontested access to food, along with individual survival. Monstrosities tend to have animal-level intelligence, although there are a handful of exceptions, notably krakens, sphinxes, nagas, lamias, and those yuan-ti that are considered monstrosities rather than humanoids. Even these exceptions will possess an animal-like instinct to establish and defend territory, despite coming up with more sophisticated rationalizations for this behavior. Combat with a beast or a monstrosity most often occurs for one of four reasons: It's trying to eat you; you're hunting it because it's been eating something or someone else; you've stumbled onto its turf, and it feels threatened; or another foe is employing it as a watchbeast.

Dragons are über-monstrosities with distinctive personalities. They want food and territory, but they also crave two more things: treasure and domination. The treasure thing is a compulsion, because it's not as though they're going shopping with all those hoarded coins and gems. They like beautiful, expensive things, and they want them—end of story. They also have a deep-seated desire to demonstrate their superiority over other beings. Although they generally don't have any interest in the practical aspects of ruling, they're quite fond of *being rulers*, and they think they're entitled to it. Thus, they may act like mafia bosses over a region, extorting wealth in exchange for "protection," by which they mainly mean protection from *them*. Even good-aligned dragons share this tendency, although their rule is benevolent rather than exploitative.

Other creatures in the dragon family lack either the power or the intelligence to dominate other beings in the way that true dragons do, but they still exhibit draconic avarice and wrath in the limited ways they're capable of. Pseudodragons gather shiny objects like magpies, wyverns exhibit dominance behaviors as they hunt and fight, and so forth.

Humanoid enemies (as opposed to humanoids just going about their business) are driven by the things you don't talk about at the dinner table: politics and religion. They're social creatures, and therefore their goals are typically social in nature, as are the units they form to bring these goals about. A humanoid boss enemy is a leader of like-minded humanoids who all want the same thing, and the sophistication and abstraction of the goal is proportional to the intelligence of the humanoid(s) pursuing it. Although they may still be fundamentally interested in territory, wealth, and domination, it's *shared* territory, wealth, and domination, and the superficial justifications for those pursuits take the form of ideologies built around tribal, clan, or national identity; moral or theological doctrine; sex or gender roles; caste roles; hierarchies of rulership and allegiance; or rules of trade. The psychologist Jonathan Haidt's moral foundations (fairness, kindness, loyalty, obedience, and sanctity) and their opposites (injustice, abuse, treachery, rebellion, and corruption) come into play: The "bad guys" may be committing one or more of the latter group of sins, or they may be going overboard in their attempts to root those sins out.

If dragons are über-monstrosities, then **giants** are über-humanoids. However, while dragons have broader interests than most monstrosities do, giants' interests tend to be narrower than those of most humanoids, and they're tightly dictated by their species and their place in the Ordning—the giants' status hierarchy. In terms of social ideology, giants are chiefly interested in their relationships with other giants, and this impinges upon humanoid society only to the extent that giants need to claim humanoids' territory, humanoids' wealth, humanoids' food supplies, or rulership over a humanoid group in order to establish their intragigantic status. In other words, giants' goals revolve around rivalries, and when this makes them the villains, it's usually because of the collateral damage they're causing around them.

Undead creatures are driven by compulsions generated by whatever spell, influence, or event caused them to rise from the dead. The simplest undead creatures are compelled by the orders of whoever or whatever controls them (or once controlled them). Ghosts are compelled by the need to resolve unfinished business. Other mid- and high-level undead are compelled by hunger, malice, and megalomania. Whatever the compulsion of an undead creature, *everything* it does revolves around that compulsion and serves it in some way. It supersedes everything else, sometimes including the creature's continued existence.

Celestials and **fiends** are two sides of the same coin. They're embodiments of good and evil, but they're not just quasi-humanoids that meander through everyday situations and always do the good or evil thing. They're concerned with cosmic order, and their goals revolve around purification and corruption. Celestials aren't just about doing good things—they're about purging evil influences. Fiends aren't just about doing bad things—they're about introducing evil influences, tempting people to do wicked things they might not otherwise do.

For these reasons, while celestial and fiend goals differ from humanoid goals, they make excellent complements to these goals. The involvement of a fiend might push a group of humanoids to take their ideological pursuits in an evil direction—or desperate humanoids might enlist the aid of a fiend in the pursuit of their goal, corrupting them and their goal in the process. Celestial involvement in humanoid affairs is a trickier needle to thread, and if you're going to make a celestial into a villain, it's almost by necessity going to have to be misinformed or overzealous—or corrupted and on the verge of a fall.

Aberrations, by definition, are beings whose ultimate goals make no sense to us, and for this reason, coming up with decent, plausible schemes for aberration villains can be challenging. Fall back on conventional schemes of domination, and you risk making your aberration into a funny-looking humanoid, for all intents and purposes. An aberration's behavior has to be *weird*. But also, for an aberration to be a villain rather than a mere curiosity, it has to pose some kind of threat. A good solution for aberrations with mind-control powers is to have them brainwashing ordinary people into participating in their weird schemes. No one wants to be a part of that. Aberrations' activities can have deleterious side effects on nearby habitations. Maybe they're causing nightmares, spooking livestock (the livestock are always first to know when bad juju is going down), disrupting the local economy with excessive demand for some random commodity, or using up a natural resource. Or maybe, like the stereotypical gray alien, they're abducting people, probing them with weird devices, then returning them to their homes. Aberrations' behavior doesn't have to make obvious sense—although, in at least some respects, it should make *internal* sense.

Fey creatures' goals, in terms of how much sense they make to an outside observer, aren't all that different from those of aberrations. However, while aberrations' goals are simply inscrutable, fey goals always have a clear emotional or aesthetic aspect, something that might not make logical sense but would seem perfectly sensible in a dream or to a child. Mischief is common; outright malice is unusual. The seven deadly sins are all well represented, however, as is every primary or secondary emotion, turned up to 11. A fey antagonist is an id without an ego to ground it. No matter how large or small the scale of a fey's goals, they're always *personal*, and the motivations behind them are explainable, if not excusable.

Constructs don't have goals, only instructions—specifically, the last instructions they were given. When the instructions no longer fit the circumstances, they sometimes go haywire trying to resolve unresolvable contradictions.

Oozes don't have goals either; they're sub-beasts that aren't even interested in territory, just food. Most **plants** are the same, although there are a small number of monsters categorized as plants that possess above-animal intelligence. Even an intelligent plant, however, is unlikely to possess any goal beyond survival, self-propagation, and protection of its environment; it simply develops more sophisticated means of pursuing these goals, ones that involve understanding other creatures, anticipating causation, and planning for the future. Cursed plants, like blights, have a wee dram of undead-ish compulsion in their mentalities.

That leaves **elementals**, which I find the hardest type to sum up. They're not full-on alien, like aberrations; simple, like beasts and monstrosities; mechanistic, like constructs; nor defined by their social structures, like humanoids. What they are, I think, is *temperamental*, in the sense that they're defined by temperaments associated with their elements. However, the classical humors, which you'd think might be a natural fit for this purpose, aren't. While it's easy to imagine elemental beings of fire as choleric (i.e., bad-tempered and irritable) and their goals as primarily involving destroying things out of anger, phlegmatic water elementals, melancholy earth elementals, and sanguine air elementals fit poorly in adventure narratives and feel off base, somehow. Traits drawn from Chinese astrology and traditional medicine fit better—elemental beings of fire being angry and volatile, those of water being aimless and impulsive, those of earth being stolid and hidebound—but they offer us no insight into air, which isn't one of the five *wǔ xíng* elements. It looks like we have to abandon ancient natural philosophy and rely on our imaginations.

In both literal and figurative senses, elementals are forces of nature, difficult for ordinary mortals to redirect once they get going. There has to be a sense of out-of-controlness about them, even—perhaps especially—the intelligent ones, like genies. We all share a pretty good sense that elemental beings of fire are about burning everything down, but what can we intuitively say about the rest? Elemental beings of earth want to solidify, to suffocate, to entomb—at least metaphorically, if not literally. Elemental beings of water are the flood, the tsunami—inexorable forces carrying away anything and anyone that's not tightly secured, whether it be a seaside village or people's common sense. Elemental beings of air are entropic—they want to scatter what's ordered, create disarray, rearrange everything, then rearrange it again, the opposite of their earthy complements, which seek to hold everything in place. In this respect, they're a bit like fey, except that fey can be reasoned with, if you know the rules of their antilogic, while elementals can't.

All the tactics I discuss in this book describe how to use a monster's features effectively, considering what it's capable of. The monster's type, as described here, tells us *why* the monster is doing what it's doing. Ultimately, a monster's choices, in or out of combat, are a function of this motivation, and when you're writing your own adventures, you should use this information not only to generate plot—to determine why your monster is a threat in the first place—but also to contemplate in advance how your monster is going to react when it realizes that the player characters aren't going to let it have what it wants.

THE MONSTERS

HUMANOIDS

Dungeons & Dragons is chock-full of low-challenge humanoid crea-tures, which inexperienced Dungeon Masters may not bother to distinguish from one another—an unhappy oversight, because their differences are key to making these encounters memorable. Goblins are sneaky and slippery. Kobolds are pathetic on their own but fierce in packs. Orcs are brutal zealots with an expansionist ideology. Lizardfolk are intensely territorial. Gnolls are driven by an ever-present gnawing hunger . . . and so on. Making full use of the features in their stat blocks will bring the personalities of these mooks, beastfolk, shapeshifters, underground dwellers, and astral nomads to the fore.

GOBLINOIDS

Here's what we know about **goblins** from the *Monster Manual*: First, from the flavor text, they live in dark, dismal settings; congregate in large numbers; and employ alarms and traps. They're low-Strength and high-Dexterity, with a very good Stealth modifier. Their Intelli-gence and Wisdom are in the average range. They possess darkvision and the Nimble Escape feature, which allows them to Disengage or Hide as a bonus action—very important to their action economy.

Because of their darkvision, goblins frequently attack under cover of darkness, when their targets may be effectively blinded (attack rolls against a blinded creature have advantage, while the blinded crea-ture's attack rolls have disadvantage). They'll also attack from hiding as much as possible, making use of their high Stealth modifier, and doing so in dim light decreases the likelihood that they'll be discovered, since many player characters will have disadvantage on Perception checks that rely on sight.

A picture of goblin combat is starting to coalesce, and at the center of it is a strategy of ambush.

A typical goblin combat turn goes Shortbow (action), move, Hide (bonus action). Because they attack from hiding, they roll with advantage. Regardless of whether they hit or miss, the attack gives their position away, so they *change it immediately*, because they can. (The sequence is important. Whenever possible, a goblin must end its turn hidden; otherwise, it's vulnerable. Move/Hide/Shortbow would achieve the same offensive result but leave the goblin exposed to retaliation between turns.)

Being a Small creature, a goblin has a good chance of Hiding successfully behind the trunk of a mature tree; even if it fails, it will still enjoy three-quarters cover (+5 AC). But since you can't hide while someone is looking directly at you, goblins have to use their movement to scramble out of the PCs' field of view, meaning they have to be close enough for their own 30-foot movement speed to describe a significant arc. At the same time, they don't want to be so close that a PC could close the gap between them and attack. So the optimal distance from the targets of their ambush is about 40 feet, no closer—and they don't want to move farther from the PCs than 80 feet, their bows' maximum range for normal shooting.

As long as they can stay out of the PCs' reach, they'll use this tactic over and over. Suppose, however, that a PC does manage to close with one of them. In that case, the goblin Disengages (bonus action) first. Then, depending on how great a threat the PC poses, it either Dashes (action) out of reach—forcing the PC to use a Dash action as well if they want to catch up—or, if it thinks it may be able to finish the PC off, moves its full distance to a place of cover, then Hides (action) again, preparing to attack with advantage on its next turn.

Incidentally, the goblins aren't trying to stay together as a group. They aren't looking out for their buddies—goblins don't do that sort of thing. They are, however, trying to goad the PCs into splitting up.

Goblins are squishy: They have only 7 hp. One good hit will seriously wound them—and also mean that their genius sniping strategy has failed. Therefore, a goblin reduced to just 1 or 2 hp flees the scene, end of story. But a moderately wounded goblin (3 or 4 hp) is thirsty and tries to regain the upper hand. It stalks the PC who wounded it, first retreating to a safe distance, then Hiding and moving with Stealth until it can get back to around 40 feet from its quarry, at which point it returns to its Shortbow/move/Hide sniping tactic. A captured goblin surrenders immediately and grovels for mercy, counting on its ability to escape as soon as its captor's attention wanders.

What if the PCs have the good sense to take cover themselves? Goblins aren't brilliant, but they aren't stupid either. They won't waste arrows on a target that's behind three-quarters cover, because that would completely negate the advantage they gain when shooting from hiding. Instead, a goblin stealthily repositions itself alongside or behind its target before shooting and giving its own position away.

A goblin that finishes off its target doesn't immediately go hunting after other targets. If another is already in view, it attacks that one. If not, the greedy goblin first ransacks the body of its victim for anything valuable. A clever and stealthy PC who's counter-stalking the goblins can exploit this weakness.

So far, the entire discussion has been about ranged attacks. Goblins carry scimitars as well, but they don't use these out in the open, because there's no advantage to it. The only time a goblin willingly engages in melee combat is when it has some other overwhelming advantage, such as a combination of numbers, darkness, and the ability to flank, which in fifth edition D&D means attacking from two *opposite* sides of a target creature. (Front-and-side isn't enough to gain advantage on attack rolls. See "Optional Rule: Flanking," *Dungeon Master's Guide*, chapter 8.)

A goblin's +4 attack modifier isn't quite good enough to give it two-to-one odds of hitting an armored enemy by itself, but when advantage is brought into play, a hit is almost guaranteed. If three goblins surround a PC in the dark, the chances are very good that they'll land three hits and not have to worry about retaliation. That being said, if those three hits don't finish the PC off, the goblins will realize that they've bitten off more than they can chew, and on their next turn, they'll Disengage (bonus action), go scampering off into the darkness (movement), and Hide (action) someplace where they may later be able to land a surprise hit on a wounded foe.

Also, goblins can tell the difference between a creature that's lost in the dark and one that has darkvision. They won't attack the latter close up if they can avoid it; instead, they'll prefer to shoot with their shortbows. However, in the narrow passages of a cave, establishing a good line of sight may not always be possible, and melee may be the only way to attack. If this happens, they'll use their knowledge of the terrain to tease the party into overextending itself: A lead goblin may use its Scimitar attack (action), Disengage (bonus action), then retreat down the passageway (movement) until it comes out into a more open cavern where it and several other goblins can all jump the first PC who emerges with Readied attack actions. Meanwhile, while the PCs are being drawn forward, other goblins may shoot or stab at them opportunistically from any side passages that exist along the way.

There is one other circumstance when goblins may engage in melee fighting: when commanded to do so by hobgoblins or bugbears, which goblins fear and defer to. They'll do it, but they won't like it. They know they're not good at it; they'd rather be sniping. If pressed into an infantry unit, they'll fight without coordination and desert at the first opportunity. However, that doesn't mean they won't keep attacking if they think there's something to be gained by doing it *their* way.

Goblins recognize the value of stealth and surprise, and they're not about to let anyone get the same advantage against them. They make extensive use of alarms and traps, but since they're not great inventors, by and large, most of these are crude: metal junk that makes a racket when disturbed, falling rocks, pits (with or without punji sticks), simple snares. Every once in a while, though, a lucky goblin may get its hands on a hunter's trap that both restrains its victim and does damage. These are prized possessions, and the goblins use them to protect their most important locations.

The **goblin boss** is distinguished from ordinary goblins by its Multiattack and Redirect Attack features and by the fact that it doesn't use a bow. Additionally, the Redirect Attack action is useful only in a context in which goblins are fighting side by side rather than in an ambush or skirmish. Based on this, I conclude that goblin bosses are found only in goblin *lairs*—caves, ruins, what have you—where large numbers of goblins can fight in close quarters.

By the way, have you read that Redirect Attack feature? The goblin boss uses its reaction to avoid a hit on itself and to cause it to land on one of its goblin minions instead. What a jerk! Here's a critter that's stronger, better at absorbing damage, and capable of landing more blows than most of its kind, and yet it possesses no notion of carrying the team. "Aw, sorry about that, Jixto! Send me a postcard from Hades!"

A creature like this, even if it fights in melee, is obnoxiously focused on self-preservation. Fighting in a group, it begins on the front line with everyone else, using its Multiattack action to attack twice with its scimitar (note that the goblin boss's Multiattack has disadvantage on the second swing). As soon as it's taken even one hit, however, it changes tactics: After its Multiattack action, it Disengages (bonus action) and moves 15 feet to a position behind the front line where melee opponents can't reach it and it has "meat cover" against ranged attacks. On subsequent rounds, it moves up to 15 feet into a nearby hole in the front line, Multiattacks (action), Disengages (bonus action), and moves back behind the front line again. (If there's no actual hole, remember that it can move through a square occupied by an ally as if it were difficult terrain. Thus, it has just enough movement speed to go *through* the front line, and back, if it has to.)

If the goblin boss's minions are wiped out, it's out of there, and ditto if it's seriously wounded (reduced to 8 hp or fewer).

Hobgoblins are very different from goblins—they're natural soldiers, tough and disciplined where goblins are squishy, lazy, and craven. They have no physical weakness, they're intelligent enough to make and use swords and bows and to conduct reconnaissance, and their Martial Advantage trait gives them bonus damage for fighting in close formation. On the other hand, they have no Stealth proficiency and no Nimble Escape.

Hobgoblins move and attack at night, when their darkvision gives them an advantage over PCs without it; if they don't have the advantage of darkness, they'll attack only with at least a two-to-one numerical advantage. In groups consisting only of hobgoblins, they move in tight teams of four to six. If there are multiple such teams, one consists of archers, positioned between 60 and 150 feet from the action. With goblin troops, they have to be careful: Hobgoblins don't lack the courage to fight on the front line, but they know that goblins do. Rather than set an example that the goblins won't follow, they give commands from behind the front line, where they can keep an eye on the goblins and shoot at opponents with their longbows. Martial Advantage helps them in this instance, even though they're not engaged in melee themselves, as long as they're choosing targets that the *goblins* are engaging in melee.

The more hobgoblin teams that are engaged in melee, the more sophisticated tactics they'll use. For instance, if there are three, one engages directly, one shoots from a distance, and one moves to whichever flank looks weaker before engaging. If there are four, one moves to *each* flank. Five or more try to encircle the PCs. These movements take place *before* the battle begins—hobgoblins are intelligent and disciplined enough to prepare. They also take place at a sufficient distance that their lack of Stealth won't be a hindrance.

Hobgoblins don't flee when they're losing; they execute an orderly retreat. When at least two hobgoblins in a team are seriously injured (reduced to 4 hp or fewer) or killed, the team begins to fall back, starting with the most injured hobgoblins. These Disengage and retreat at their full movement speed. On the next round, the two next-most injured Disengage and also retreat at their full movement speed, while the previous two fall back only 5 feet, so as to remain in contact with the hobgoblins that are now joining them. Meanwhile, in this round, the hobgoblin archer team, if there is one, notices the retreat and focuses its arrows on any potential pursuers, in order to cover the retreat. On the third round, any hobgoblins left in the team Disengage and retreat at full movement speed, joining up with those that have already retreated. They carry out this same maneuver repeatedly, until no enemy is engaging with them anymore.

Despite being the very model of discipline otherwise, according to the *Monster Manual*, hobgoblins flip their lids when they see an elf. They attack elves first, "even if doing so would be a tactical error." Does this mean they'll charge into combat prematurely, during daylight, with inadequate reconnaissance, just because they see an elf in the party's camp? That's the DM's call. You could play them this way, but given the extent to which they're built up as being militarily savvy, I'd say that before the action starts, their disciplined nature prevails— they simply construct their battle plans around taking out the elves first. Once the battle commences, though, maybe they allow a human warrior to score free hits on them while they concentrate their attacks on an elf warrior. Maybe the hobgoblin archers keep shooting at an elf mage when they should be covering their fellow hobgoblins' retreat. Maybe the sudden appearance of an elf rogue in its midst causes a hobgoblin melee group to forget what it was doing entirely and fixate on getting that elf. Or maybe they hold true to their disciplined nature, elf or no elf.

A **hobgoblin captain** is an extra-tough hobgoblin with Multiattack and Leadership. The Leadership feature is incredible: For 1 minute (that is, 10 rounds), as long as the hobgoblin captain isn't incapacitated, every allied creature within 30 feet of it gets a 1d4 buff on attack rolls and saving throws. It activates this feature just before melee combat begins, so as not to pass up its own attack action. In other respects, it fights as an ordinary hobgoblin. If there are multiple hobgoblin groups but only one hobgoblin captain, it's attached to the main melee group. Hobgoblin captains don't wield bows, but they do carry javelins. They'll hurl one of these at a fleeing opponent rather than break ranks to give chase.

A **hobgoblin warlord** is everything a hobgoblin captain is and more. It can Shield Bash to knock an opponent prone, and it can Parry a melee blow.

Parry adds +3 to AC as a reaction, so the decision of when to use it is easy: when a player rolls between 20 and 22 on an attack (assuming the hobgoblin warlord hasn't already used its reaction on something else, of course).

Shield Bash requires a little math to analyze. The hobgoblin warlord's Multiattack allows three consecutive melee swings in one action.

The Longsword attack does the most damage, so it's the default, but when is Shield Bash a reasonable alternative? Assuming a hit, Shield Bash does, on average, 2 hp less damage than a Longsword attack, so the crux is whether the chance to knock the opponent prone is worth these forfeited points. Attacks against a prone opponent have advantage, which raises the probability of a hit by an average of about 20 percentage points. If the hobgoblin warlord uses the Multiattack sequence Shield Bash/Longsword/Longsword, this means it will have advantage on two Longsword attacks after a successful bash. The longsword does an average of 8 damage on a hit,* 15 damage on two. Twenty percent of that is 3, so using Shield Bash before striking twice with a longsword increases the expected damage of those two hits by 3 hp—*if it works.*

The trouble is, the DC 14 for Strength saving throws against a Shield Bash isn't very high. Unmodified, the hobgoblin warlord has just shy of a two-thirds chance of knocking its opponent down. Modified by the opponent's Strength—and keep in mind that it's probably the party's toughest front-line fighters who'll confront the hobgoblin warlord—the chance of success recedes to the neighborhood of fifty-fifty, even less against PCs who get to add their proficiency modifiers to their Strength saves.

Hobgoblins aren't dumb; hobgoblin warlords even less so. They know from experience that a weak opponent (one with a negative Strength modifier) usually won't withstand a Shield Bash, but a stronger opponent often will. However, they also know that if one or more of their allies can land melee attacks on a prone target before they get up—if the advantage applies to their allies' attack rolls as well, not just to the hobgoblin warlord's two attacks—then the expected value of Shield Bash is much more likely to exceed its opportunity cost. Also, in most instances, if an ally of a hobgoblin warlord is near enough to take whacks at its target, it's near enough for the warlord's Martial

---

* In fifth edition D&D play, the general rule is to round fractions down. In this book, while analyzing damage probabilistically rather than applying it to a PC or monster, I round fractions to the nearest whole number, with one-half rounded to the nearest *even* whole number.

Advantage trait to kick in, which nearly triples the average damage of one of its Longsword attacks and roughly doubles the average total of the two together. Plus, if the ally is also a hobgoblin, its own Martial Advantage comes into play as well. Add it all together, and the Shield Bash tactic becomes effective enough to try even when it has as little as a one-in-three chance of success.

Bugbears are even stronger than hobgoblins, but they lack hobgoblins' intelligence and discipline. They do formidable melee damage, thanks to their Brute trait (which is like landing a crit with every hit), and their Surprise Attack ability allows them to nova on the first PC they engage. Bugbears are stealthy, too, so despite being brute fighters, they fit in well with the ambush strategy that goblins employ. The difference is, while goblins engage in hit-and-run sniper attacks, the bugbear lies hidden until its foe comes within reach (or creeps up on its foe unseen until it comes within reach), then springs out and smashes it to a pulp. It's indiscriminate in its target selection: It attacks whoever it can get at first. It doesn't distinguish between targets that look weaker and targets that look stronger. To the bugbear, they all look weak.

Bugbears carry two weapons: morning star and javelin. They don't fear in-your-face confrontation, and the morning star does more damage, so the only reason for them to use javelins is if for some reason they can't get close enough to whomever they want to attack.

Bugbears love mayhem and will chase down a fleeing opponent. Their survival instinct, however, is powerful. If one is seriously wounded (reduced to 10 hp or fewer), it will become confused and flee, using the Dash action and potentially exposing itself to one or more opportunity attacks. If by some miracle a group of PCs captures a bugbear alive, it will be humiliated, traumatized, and willing to do just about anything to preserve its own life.

A **bugbear chief** is an exceptional member of the species, with Multiattack and the Heart of Hruggek trait, which gives it advantage on saving throws against a variety of conditions. It also has Intimidation +2, so one might suppose that a group of bugbears led by a bugbear chief would initiate a "parley" (consisting mostly of taunts and threats) at the beginning of an encounter. However, bugbears' Stealth proficiency is one of their advantages, so why would they blow their cover simply to hurl taunts and threats? Bugbear chiefs have Intelligence 11 and Wisdom 12; that's not the sort of mistake they'd make. There can't be many circumstances in which a party of adventurers and a bugbear chief would have anything like a purposeful conversation, but I can think of a few: Maybe, somehow, the party has managed to surprise the bugbears rather than vice versa. Maybe one side is besieging the other, and they've reached a stalemate. Maybe the PCs are high-level enough that the bugbear chief realizes it will be hard to win a fight against them, yet they still have something the bugbears want. (Of course, the bugbear chief's idea of "negotiation" will still consist mainly of demands, threats, and insults.)

Kobolds

Kobolds differ from goblins in significant ways. Their Intelligence, Wisdom, and Constitution are all lower. They have Sunlight Sensitivity, which means that while goblins may prefer to dwell in the dark, kobolds *must*. Like goblins, kobolds set traps; unlike goblins, they're not nimble or stealthy.

What's most distinctive about kobolds is their Pack Tactics trait, which gives them advantage on attacks when ganging up on a target. That's the crux of how kobolds ought to fight. Kobold society has evolved to be highly cooperative. Unlike goblins, forever squabbling and looking out for themselves, kobolds instinctively work together, even without having to discuss what they're doing.

A kobold attack begins as an ambush: Hiding kobolds (which aren't exceptionally stealthy but may gain the element of surprise anyway, since they have decently high Dexterity and live in dark places) pop up and pelt the party with sling stones from 20 to 30 feet away in order to soften them up. This lasts until either the player characters close with the kobolds or the kobolds have lost any advantage they had, such as the PCs being restrained by a trap or blinded by darkness. At this point, the kobolds surge forward and engage in melee.

Kobold melee combat is all about swarming. No kobold will ever fight an enemy hand-to-hand by itself, not even one its own size. Any kobold that's the only one left fighting a single foe retreats, possibly regrouping with other kobolds fighting a different foe. However, a seriously wounded kobold (1 or 2 hp remaining) turns and runs. It's not smart enough to Disengage to avoid an opportunity attack; it Dashes instead. If at any point the attacking kobolds no longer outnumber the front-line PCs by at least three to one, they'll withdraw. They can't do much damage on their own—on average, just 4 hp per hit—so they have to make every attack count. But kobolds using Pack Tactics against a target wearing chain mail can still deal damage two times out of three.

That's basically it. Kobolds don't get bonus actions or reactions (other than opportunity attacks) that might increase the complexity of their behavior. They have Pack Tactics, so they attack in packs. When attacking as a pack no longer works, they cut their losses. They also know to stay out of bright sunlight. If their enemies retreat into a well-lit area, kobolds simply won't pursue. Kobolds that retreat don't bother switching to ranged attacks, because their slings don't have enough range to keep target PCs from closing with them again.

Winged kobolds are only slightly better. Because they can fly, they can sustain the ranged-ambush phase longer . . . unless they run out of rocks to throw. Their flying movement is enough to allow them to swoop down, grab a rock, swoop back up, and throw the rock, but if the PCs block their access to the rocks, so much for that. They also have two more hit points than regular kobolds, but that makes no difference with respect to when they'll flee.

If kobolds are lucky enough to defeat a whole party of adventurers, they'll haul them off as prisoners and taunt them for entertainment.

Orcs

Unlike goblins and kobolds, **orcs** are strong and tough. They're not very smart—their behavior is largely driven by instinct—but they possess average Wisdom and decent Dexterity. They have the Aggressive trait, which allows them to move their full speed toward a hostile creature as a bonus action, effectively allowing them to Dash forward, then attack. Curiously, they have proficiency in a social skill: Intimidation. Their standard melee weapon, the greataxe, deals damage that can be deadly to a level 1 character.

These are no hit-and-run skirmishers or snipers. Orcs are brutes. They charge, they fight hand-to-hand, and they retreat only with the greatest reluctance when seriously wounded. (Being fanatical valuers of physical courage, orcs—unlike most creatures—are willing to fight to the death.)

The Aggressive trait applies chiefly to one situation: when a group of orcs is between 30 and 60 feet away from the player characters. As a DM, you should therefore assume that first contact with a group of orcs always takes place at this distance, that the orcs will be initially hostile, and that they'll charge the second they decide talking is boring. However, the fact that orcs have any social skill at all—even if it's just Intimidation—suggests that there ought to be some opportunity to interact before combat begins.

Any parley with the orcs will be brief (no more than a handful of chances to cajole, bluff, or bully them) and somewhat one-sided, as the orcs will issue nothing but demands and threats. At this point, any hostile action on the PCs' part, including moving closer than 30 feet for any reason, ends the parley immediately and initiates combat.

However, a smooth talker may be able to stave off an attack by making a Charisma (Persuasion) check with disadvantage—against DC 15, say, or maybe DC 20 if the orcs are there for a specific purpose, such as guarding something or staking a territorial claim. If it succeeds, the orcs' attitude shifts from hostile to indifferent; if it fails, however, give the party only one more chance to successfully reach a détente.

The PCs may also try to bluff their way past the orcs by making a Charisma (Deception) check with disadvantage (no disadvantage if they've been talked into indifference), opposed by the orcs' Intelligence or Wisdom, depending on the nature of the bluff. If they succeed, the orcs believe their lie. If the lie fails, however, the orcs attack immediately.

Finally, a PC may try to threaten back! Have them make a DC 20 Charisma (Intimidation) check, opposed by a Wisdom check for the orcs. If the PC and the orcs both succeed, the orcs appraise the situation, attacking immediately if they're stronger than the party but retreating if they're weaker. (Before the encounter begins, use the XP Thresholds by Character Level table in chapter 3 of the *Dungeon Master's Guide* to determine which side is stronger. If the orcs' adjusted experience points would make them a Deadly encounter for the party, consider them stronger; otherwise, consider them weaker.) If the PC succeeds on their Intimidation check and the orcs fail their Wisdom check, the orcs are rattled, their attitude shifts to indifferent, and the PC gets advantage on their next social skill check with the orcs. If the PC fails, the orcs attack.

Orcs initiate combat by charging, using Aggressive (bonus action) plus their movement to close the distance between themselves and the party's front line, followed immediately by attacking with their greataxes (action). From this point on, it's a slugfest. As long as the orcs aren't seriously injured, they keep fighting, using their Greataxe action every round and moving on to the next PC back if they hew down one in the front line. If there's a PC between 30 and 60 feet past the one the orc has just felled, it has a chance to use Aggressive again—so why not? This should create a moment of excitement in your session and put a healthy fear of orcs into your archers and spellslingers.

Despite their aggression and stupidity, even orcs know when they're overmatched. Depending on how you, the DM, believe that this particular group of orcs should act, a seriously injured orc (reduced to 6 hp or fewer) may be willing to fight to the death for honor's sake, or it may possess more of a will to survive, in which case it will Disengage and retreat its full movement distance. (My own inclination is to have orcs that see their fellows retreating successfully be more willing to retreat themselves, while orcs whose fellows have been slain will fight to the death themselves.) An orc that finds itself fighting two or more foes rather than just one tries to reposition itself so that it has to fight only one, if possible. Since this will always involve moving out of at least one opponent's reach, there are three possible ways: Dodge, then reposition; Disengage, then reposition; or reposition, risking an opportunity strike, then attack. The first two, frankly, strike me as un-orc-like, while the third strikes me as *very* orc-like. If there's no way for the orc to evade its extra attackers without their simply closing with it again, then Disengage/retreat seems like the most likely response—either that or, if its fellows have been slain, fiercely fighting to the death.

The fact that a group of orcs has retreated doesn't mean combat is over. The survivors long for payback. Orcs aren't stealthy, so they won't stalk the characters, but they'll certainly keep an eye out for the PCs as long as they're in that vicinity. If they re-encounter the PCs, and if the PCs seem to be weakened in any way, the orcs will seize the moment and attack—once again, using Aggressive to charge in and strike the first blows.

The *Monster Manual* lists several orc variants that may appear in encounters with intermediate-level PCs. The **orog** is a much stronger, tougher, and smarter variant with many more hit points and two swings per Multiattack action. Ordinary orcs aren't smart enough to strategize, but orogs are. A group of orcs that includes one or more orogs and that knows the PCs are in the area doesn't go after them right away but rather waits until nightfall, to take advantage of the orcs' darkvision: In darkness, PCs who lack darkvision are effectively blinded and make attack rolls with disadvantage, while the orcs have advantage on their own attack rolls. Orogs also have the sense to Disengage before repositioning in melee combat and may even order regular orcs to do the same. However, their Wisdom is no higher than that of a regular orc, so they're prone to the same "death before dishonor" attitude when they're low on hit points.

An **orc war chief** is a formidable opponent, even more so than an orog. It possesses the orog's Strength and Constitution, a high Charisma, less Intelligence than an orog but more than an average orc, Multiattack ability, and proficiency bonuses on several types of saving throws, plus two fearsome features: Gruumsh's Fury and Battle Cry.

Gruumsh's Fury is a passive trait that increases the orc war chief's weapon damage by 1d8 on every hit. This doesn't affect its tactics at all; it simply makes the orc war chief a wickedly effective damage dealer. The real game-changer is Battle Cry, a once-per-day power that gives the orc war chief's warriors advantage on attack rolls for the next turn. The effectiveness of Battle Cry is maximized when it can buff the greatest number of orcs. Therefore, there's no reason at all for the orc war chief to wait to use it, save one: The war chief has to forgo its own attack to use it, because Battle Cry is an action. The cost/benefit analysis hinges on which is expected to do more damage: a horde of orcs with advantage or a single orc war chief swinging its greataxe.

By itself, an orc war chief, with +6 to hit, has a 70 percent chance to hit an AC 13 opponent. It does an average of 15 damage with every hit, and it gets two swings per Multiattack action. Therefore, its expected damage per round is 21. A regular orc, with +5 to hit, has a 65 percent chance to hit an AC 13 opponent; it does an average of 10 damage with every hit, and it gets only one chance per round. Ordinarily, therefore, its expected damage per round is 6. If the orc attacks with advantage, however, its chance to hit increases from 65 percent to 88 percent, so its expected damage increases to 8. In short, giving a single orc advantage on its attack roll increases its expected damage by about 2 (2.1, to be exact). From this, we can determine that the orc war chief will prefer to use Battle Cry rather than charge with its troops and Multiattack when it commands a force of no fewer than ten ordinary orcs.

Would an orc war chief have any way to calculate this? No. But it would know intuitively, from its battlefield experience (which comes mostly from fighting other orcs, who have AC 13—that's why I chose that number), that issuing a Battle Cry before charging seems to make a difference in a group of ten or more orc warriors, while in a smaller group, it doesn't.

All that being said, the Battle Cry action also allows the orc war chief to make a single attack as a bonus action, meaning that if it's already next to an enemy, it's giving up only one of its two potential attacks. So if the war chief is fighting alongside five or more other orcs, but fewer than ten, it still uses Battle Cry—*after* it's already charged with the rest of its band.

Last, there's the **orc Eye of Gruumsh**, a battlefield cleric. Smarter and wiser than an ordinary orc but not any stronger or tougher, the Eye of Gruumsh is distinguished most by its spellcasting ability. (It also has Gruumsh's Fury, but again, this is a passive trait whose only function is to increase weapon damage—although this makes more of a difference for the Eye of Gruumsh than for the war chief, because the Eye of Gruumsh uses only a spear, not a greataxe.) The variety of spells at its disposal potentially makes the Eye of Gruumsh's combat strategy much more complex, so we need to take a look at the effects and effectiveness of each spell and how it fits into the Eye of Gruumsh's action economy.

One spell stands out: *spiritual weapon*. Unlike all the Eye of Gruumsh's other spells, this one is cast as a bonus action and, in addition, gives the caster a new bonus action to use every round. This completely changes the Eye of Gruumsh's action economy. The Eye of Gruumsh still charges with all the other orcs, because otherwise, its Aggressive trait would be wasted. But on its second combat round it casts *spiritual weapon* as a bonus action, and on every subsequent round (up to the spell's 1-minute duration) it continues to use its bonus action, again and again, to attack tougher or harder-to-reach opponents with the Floating Spear of Glowy Force.

The question now is, what does the Eye of Gruumsh do with its action? *Spiritual weapon* won't require concentration, so it can start the battle off with a spell that does: *bless*, *guidance*, or *resistance*, of which *bless* is clearly the strongest. (Which of its companions would the Eye of Gruumsh bless? Orcs aren't exactly altruistic. I'd say it would first take a blessing for itself, then give one to the orc war chief, if there is one, then to any other individual that stands out in the group.)

How about once combat is underway? *Augury* takes a full minute to cast and has no purpose in combat. *Thaumaturgy* is interesting, but one has to consider its primary application to be during the parley phase, when the orcs are trying to maximize their fearsomeness. That leaves *command*.

Command can have a tide-of-battle-swinging effect. One possible beneficial outcome of *command* is that a PC may be forced into a position that gives opponents advantage on melee attacks. Another is that a PC, ordered to flee, may be subjected to one or more opportunity attacks.

Let's look at what the Eye of Gruumsh gives up by doing this: its Spear action. Against AC 13 (what most orcs are used to, as mentioned above), with +5 to hit, the Eye of Gruumsh has a 65 percent chance of dealing an average of 11 damage, for an expected damage per round of 7. For the Eye of Gruumsh to forgo its Spear action in favor of casting *command*, the effect of the spell needs to inflict at least 8 expected damage.

As we saw previously, giving an ordinary orc advantage on an attack roll increases its expected damage by about 2. That's not enough for the Eye of Gruumsh to give up its own Spear action. What about an orog? Still not enough: The damage increase is about the same, although it is doubled because of the orog's Multiattack. An orc war chief? Now it starts to get interesting, because the war chief does so much damage with each hit. But the increase in expected damage from attacking with advantage turns out to be surprisingly small: only about 3 per attack, or 6 altogether. And, of course, the Eye of Gruumsh doesn't itself benefit from ordering a foe to grovel, because it gives up one attack action to gain advantage on the next, allowing it one hit at most, rather than two. In addition, we have to remember that the target of a *command* gets to make a saving throw, so all these gains are attenuated by the probability that the target will shrug it off.

However, what if the Eye of Gruumsh can provoke multiple opportunity attacks on an enemy by ordering them to flee? For starters, opportunity attacks are *reactions*, meaning we're adding a new element to the action economy. Also, this isn't about the difference between attacking with advantage and attacking without it—it's about the difference between getting an attack and not getting an attack. One orc's expected damage per attack is 6—not as much as the Eye of Gruumsh's expected damage per attack—but *two* orcs' expected damage is double that, and three orcs' expected damage is triple that, and so on. An orog's expected damage per attack is 7, and an orc war chief's is 10. *Command*'s chance of success is only fifty-fifty even against an average person, so we have to figure that there need to be several orcs on hand to make opportunity attacks for this stunt to be worth trying.

Here's our conclusion: An orc Eye of Gruumsh forgoes its own Spear action in order to cast *command* against a foe that's within reach of four or more ordinary orcs, or two or more plus a leader. It issues the command "Scram!" (equivalent to Flee) in order to provoke an opportunity attack from every orc that can reach the target.

GNOLLS

Gnolls are described in the *Monster Manual* as rapacious raiders, scavengers, and nomads with hyena-like heads. They have high Strength and low Intelligence; their behavior is driven by their violent and destructive instincts. Like many other humanoid D&D monsters, they have darkvision. They wield spears and longbows, according to the *Monster Manual*, and they have one distinguishing feature, Rampage, which allows them to move half their speed and make a bonus bite attack after reducing a foe to 0 hp in melee.

Honestly, I'd dispense with the longbow—it doesn't make sense in the context of what else the *Monster Manual* says about gnolls. Their Strength is high enough that they gain little advantage from using one. They aren't smart enough to craft one or social enough to barter for one. According to the flavor text, gnolls prefer to strike at easy targets; longbows are designed to puncture armor. And gnolls' single unique feature is melee-oriented.

So my vision of the gnoll is strictly a hand-to-hand fighter. As creatures with high Strength, high-average Dexterity, average Constitution, and a respectable five hit dice, gnolls are shock troops. When they spot a vulnerable target, most likely during a nighttime patrol (darkvision provides advantage on attack rolls against PCs who don't have it), they strike at once. They're fearless and aggressive, using their full movement speed to approach their targets, then attacking with spears; if one such attack reduces an enemy to 0 hp, the gnoll Rampages toward another enemy within 15 feet and bites it (bonus action).

As vicious as they are, however, gnolls are creatures of instinct without ideology, and they place their own survival over such concepts as valor or honor. If one is seriously wounded (reduced to 8 hp or fewer), it turns tail and flees, using the Dash action to get away as fast as possible and potentially exposing itself to one or more opportunity attacks in the process.

A pack of gnolls may be led by a **gnoll pack lord**, which is a more able specimen in every respect, including getting two swings per Multiattack action and having the Incite Rampage feature. (It also wields a glaive, which I have to imagine—given that even the gnoll pack lord's Intelligence is only 8—consists of a pillaged sword lashed to the end of a spear. By gnoll standards, this surely qualifies as technological genius.)

Incite Rampage is part of the gnoll pack lord's Multiattack combo, so the gnoll pack lord doesn't have to forgo attacking to use it. Effectively, what Incite Rampage does is grant another gnoll in the pack (a technicality in the wording of Incite Rampage restricts its application to other gnolls, plus giant hyenas, since these are the only creatures with Rampage) the equivalent of an immediate opportunity attack against its opponent. This happens during the gnoll pack lord's action. Incite Rampage consumes that gnoll's reaction, so if its opponent moves out of its reach, it can't make an *actual* opportunity attack.

Aside from this feature, the only other distinctive thing about the gnoll pack lord is the fact that its "glaive" (snicker) gives it 10 feet of reach rather than 5 feet. None of this makes the gnoll pack lord's tactics any more elaborate than a regular gnoll's.

At first blush, the **gnoll Fang of Yeenoghu** also appears to be little more than an exceptionally able gnoll, with a Claw/Claw/Bite Multiattack in lieu of weapons. But the Fang of Yeenoghu has some actual intelligence, so it maneuvers around the battlefield and targets vulnerable PCs, particularly those who dish out a lot of damage but can't take it. Gnolls sense weakness and zero in on it, so assume that the Fang of Yeenoghu can "read" a PC's hit points and Armor Class and strike accordingly. This also allows the Fang of Yeenoghu to maximize the value of its Rampage feature, because by targeting PCs with fewer hit points first, it increases its chances of getting to Rampage more than once. If you're a tenderhearted DM who wants to protect the fragile flowers in your players' party, don't throw a Fang of Yeenoghu at them, because that thing's gotta follow its nature.

One other detail about the gnoll Fang of Yeenoghu, which has nothing to do with its tactics but is still worth noting: Unlike gnolls and gnoll pack lords, the Fang of Yeenoghu isn't categorized as a humanoid. It's a fiend, and as such it's detectable by a paladin's Divine Sense or a ranger's Primeval Awareness, and a *protection from evil and good* spell offers defense against it.

LIZARDFOLK

Lizardfolk aren't sophisticated, but they are significantly tougher than goblins, kobolds, and orcs. According to the *Monster Manual* flavor text, their most salient behavioral trait is their territoriality, followed by their generally acting like South Seas cannibals in a movie from the 1940s. On the flip side, the text does acknowledge that lizardfolk may occasionally form alliances with outsiders, but we'll set that aside, since it's not going to influence their combat tactics.

Lizardfolk, like orcs, are brutes: average Dexterity, high Strength and Constitution. They're also proficient in Perception and Stealth, and they're more or less amphibious—they can't breathe underwater, but they can hold their breath for up to 15 minutes, and they can swim as fast as they can move on land.

Based on this information, the most likely lizardfolk encounter scenario is with a group of scouts patrolling the outskirts of their territory. They'll be alert to intruders—it's why they're out there. Once they notice intruders, they start stalking them (from cover to cover if on land, underwater if in a swamp), until they're close enough to attack. Then they strike first, with surprise if possible.

The lizardfolk's Multiattack action specifies, "The lizardfolk makes two melee attacks, each one with a different weapon." The choices available are Bite, Heavy Club, Javelin, and Spiked Shield. Honestly, the only combinations of these that don't strike me as silly are Heavy Club/Spiked Shield and Javelin/Spiked Shield. The lizardfolk's upright physiology makes the idea of their lunging to bite absurd, let alone lunging to bite in combination with swinging or thrusting a melee weapon. Of course, it's all cosmetic, since every one of the lizardfolk's attacks has the same attack modifier and deals the same damage; the only difference is whether the damage done is bludgeoning (the club) or piercing (everything else), and even that isn't a real difference unless a PC is covered by a magic item or spell that provides resistance to one type of damage and

not the other. Let's just say that a lizardfolk's Multiattack action consists
of one weapon strike and one shield bash and leave it at that.

Lizardfolk don't have any feature that grants them bonus actions or
unique reactions, and their Intelligence is low, so we can assume that
they fight like primitives: They pick an enemy, they bash that enemy,
and they keep going until the enemy is dead or they're seriously wounded
themselves (reduced to 8 hp or fewer). At that point, whether they keep
fighting depends entirely on whether or not they're within their own
territory. If they are, they keep fighting to the death. If they're not—if
they were scouting beyond their borders, or if they were on a raid—they
Dash back toward their own territory as fast as they can, potentially
incurring one or more opportunity attacks. Instinctively, they always
attack from the direction of their own territory and position themselves
with their backs toward it. They may ambush, but they don't flank.

Long-range weapon attacks confuse them, and magic awes and ter-
rifies them. A lizardfolk shot by an arrow or crossbow bolt instinctively
moves in the direction of its territory. (If it's already within its territory,
it moves toward the center of that territory.) Depending on the type
of spell, the damage it does, whether the lizardfolk can see the caster,
and whether they can get to them, they either try to rush the caster or
run for their lives. Rushing is more likely if they can see the caster, the
spell does no more than light damage (5 or less), and/or there's no other
PC in the way. Running is more likely if they can't tell where the spell
came from, the spell does serious damage (14 or more), and/or there are
too many enemies between themselves and the caster.

Lizardfolk never surrender voluntarily: They assume that they'll
be killed. However, lizardfolk who are subdued and captured are im-
passive about it and will talk to their captors, if any of them speaks
Draconic, without sullenness or bluster. That being said, they'll also
turn against their captors in a heartbeat if their chances of success
look good. An unarmed lizardfolk *will* bite, as well as grab the nearest
handy object to use as an improvised weapon.

A **lizardfolk shaman** is basically a reskinned druid. It's distinguished by its spellcasting and shape-changing abilities, the latter of
which is restricted to the form of a crocodile. That's pretty good, com-

pared with most of the spells the lizardfolk shaman can cast. But one of its spells is so effective that the crocodile form has to be considered a secondary self-defense measure.

That spell is *conjure animals*, which requires concentration and therefore prevents the lizardfolk shaman from casting its other most potentially effective spell, *entangle*. But by itself, *conjure animals* should give a party of PCs pause. It allows the shaman to summon one CR 2, two CR 1, four CR 1/2, or eight CR 1/4 reptiles. There's no CR 1 reptile in the *Monster Manual*, but check out the other options:

- one swarm of poisonous snakes
- four crocodiles
- eight constrictor snakes
- eight giant lizards
- eight giant poisonous snakes

You can consider the different abilities these creatures have (crocs and constrictor snakes can grapple, giant lizards are tanks, giant poisonous snakes deal heavy damage), but you can also feel free to base your decision entirely on the emotional reaction you want to elicit from your players: Do you want icky-creepy-get-it-away-from-me (one square full of writhing danger noodles), moderate freakout (four crocs), or full-scale panic attack (eight king cobras)?

From the caster's point of view, "more" usually trumps "better." More creatures mean more attacks, and summoning four or eight rather than just one will bump up the encounter multiplier by one or two levels, unless the lizardfolk group already substantially outnumbers the PCs (see the Encounter Multipliers table, *Dungeon Master's Guide*, chapter 3).

Therefore, unless you're specifically looking to elicit a different reaction, the first thing the lizardfolk shaman is going to do once an encounter commences is cast *conjure animals* to call up as much reptilian backup as possible. After that, the shaman doesn't enter melee combat—not that it couldn't, being just as strong and tough as any other lizardfolk, but unlike them, it's smart enough to know that if it took a solid hit, its concentration could be broken, and then there'd go the cobras. Instead, the shaman lobs *produce flame* cantrips (which do 2d8 fire damage rather than 1d8, because the shaman is a level 5 spell-caster) at any enemies within 30 feet. Its fellow lizardfolk, incidentally, aren't afraid of *this* magic—on the contrary, since the shaman is on *their* side, they're feeling extra bold and are much more likely to rush an enemy caster rather than run from them. They'll also become mighty salty if anyone dares to assault *their* shaman.

Speaking of enemy casters, if one makes the mistake of coming within 30 feet of the lizardfolk shaman, it casts *thorn whip* and yanks them forward, so that the other lizardfolk can pound them into jelly.

What if the shaman is targeted by a ranged attacker? It's still caught off guard, but its greater mental flexibility allows it to come up with a purposeful response. If its concentration isn't broken, it sends a couple of the king cobras (or whatever creatures it summoned) after the PC who shot it. If its concentration is broken, its main contribution to the battle has just been negated, and until it takes care of that marksman, there's not a lot more that it can do: Most of its spells don't have great range. But since its fellow lizardfolk are useless against ranged attackers, the shaman has to take care of the problem itself. In a swamp, it can Change Shape into crocodile form, submerge, and go after the shooter. In jungle, this won't work, because a crocodile has only 20 feet of movement speed over land, so a marksman can easily keep their distance. The shaman will be forced to conclude that the battle is going south and cast *fog cloud*, either to cover the lizardfolk's escape (if they're outside their territory) or to enshroud the PCs so that the lizardfolk can reposition themselves more advantageously.

In general, any time a battle outside their territory goes badly for the lizardfolk—say, at least half of them seriously wounded—the lizardfolk shaman casts *fog cloud* to help them get away. (Inside their territory, the shaman will have already cast *fog cloud* on the PCs *first*, to allow the lizardfolk warriors to sneak up on them quickly.) If the *fog cloud* is dispelled (by *gust of wind*, say) while the lizardfolk are retreating, the shaman will follow up with *plant growth* to slow their pursuers even further. (What about *entangle* and *spike growth*? Their utility diminishes significantly in a swamp or jungle, where the terrain is already difficult. And the fact that they also require concentration forces a choice between one of them and *conjure animals* or *fog cloud*, which are clearly superior.)

The **lizard king/queen** isn't complicated at all. Mostly, it's a bigger, badder lizardfolk. For its Multiattack, it can use Claws/Bite, Trident/Bite, or Trident/Trident. Let's get real: If you're leading a bunch of tribespeople carrying clubs and shields, are you going to go out there and *chew* on your enemies? No, you're going to go out there with an even more impressive weapon and show everyone how it's done. Your Trident attack does more damage than your Bite attack (assume that it's wielded two-handed, since the stat block makes no mention of a shield), and besides, your Skewer feature only works with the trident. Of course you're going to use the trident for both attacks!

There is one other detail to note about the lizard king/queen: its immunity to the frightened condition. We can infer from this that the lizard king/queen ain't afraid of *nothin'* . . . least of all Trawiodol the Uncanny's *dancing lights*. The Royal Reptile isn't going to run from a spellcaster, *ever*. No, it's going to single the caster out for special pointy attention, just to show all the other lizardfolk why it's the boss and they're not.

YUAN-TI

Yuan-ti are snake-human hybrids, created in the earliest days of civilization, whose culture fell from an advanced, enlightened state into fanaticism and cruelty. They live in a caste-bound society in which those who most closely resemble humans make up the lowest stratum, while the most snakelike constitute the highest and most powerful. One distinctive characteristic they all share is the innate ability to cast *suggestion*: Like Kaa in *The Jungle Book*, they try to win your trust before they mess you up. Another is that they all have magic resistance, so they have no reason to fear spellcasters more than anyone else.

The most common and least powerful caste are the **yuan-ti purebloods**. (Counterintuitively, "pure" is a pejorative to the yuan-ti; the more adulterated by reptilian essence they are, the more they're esteemed.) Their physical abilities are average-ish, with a slightly elevated

Dexterity; their Intelligence and, particularly, Charisma are higher, implying a species that approaches combat from a mental angle first. This implication is emphasized further by their proficiency in Deception and Stealth. They have darkvision, suggesting that they're most at home in dim places and/or most active at night. Along with *suggestion*, they can cast the cantrip *poison spray* three times per day at its base damage level of 1d12 (I like to imagine that they spit it from their mouths). They can also cast *animal friendship* on snakes, for whatever that's worth.

According to the *Monster Manual* flavor text, yuan-ti purebloods often put on cloaks and try to pass for human in order to "kidnap prisoners for interrogation and sacrifice," so let's start with that: The yuan-ti wants to kill you, but it doesn't want to kill you right here and now. Instead, it wants to get you someplace where it can kill you in a way that makes its gods happy.

Therefore, a yuan-ti pureblood encounter is going to begin with the yuan-ti cloaked and hooded, using Deception to hide what they are, and casting *suggestion* as soon as the player characters approach within 30 feet, saying something along the lines of "This is a dangerous place, and you look like you could use some extra help. Come with us." I'd say that their moderately high Intelligence combined with the fact that this is an innate ability lets them "read" the PCs to pick out which ones have the lowest Wisdom saving throws and therefore will be most susceptible. Remember that a single yuan-ti can target only a single PC at once with this ability; if you want to charm more PCs, you need more yuan-ti.

If the *suggestion* succeeds, they'll take the PCs back to their settlement, overwhelm the PCs with numbers and grappling attacks, and prep for their sacrificial ceremony. If it fails, the PCs will undoubtedly attack, and if they don't, the yuan-ti will.

Yuan-ti purebloods are competent, though unexceptional, at both melee and ranged combat. In melee, they have Multiattack, letting them attack twice per turn with their scimitars. At range, they have only one shot per action, but their arrows are poisoned, which makes ranged attacks marginally better, though not enough to make a meaningful difference. Thus, whether they opt for melee or ranged combat depends in large part on where they are when combat begins. If they're in the thick of things, they choose melee; if they're at a distance, they choose ranged; and they pretty much stay wherever they are unless they're forced to flee. *Poison spray* doesn't offer them any real advantage over either a scimitar or a shortbow, unless they're disarmed somehow.

Yuan-ti have had hundreds of generations to live and adapt on their own, so they'll have the same self-preservation instinct as any evolved species. If they're seriously injured (reduced to 16 hp or fewer), they'll run away, using the Dash action (yuan-ti purebloods don't have the training to Disengage).

Combat with yuan-ti purebloods by themselves isn't that interesting; it gets better, though, when you combine them with **yuan-ti malisons**. Malisons are mostly-humanoids with serpentine heads (type 1), arms (type 2), or lower bodies (type 3); the third type is my personal favorite, because I think it synergizes best with the yuan-ti pureblood. All three types have high Charisma and Intelligence and also high Strength and Dexterity, making them good commanders and shock troops. They can also Shapechange back and forth between their yuan-ti form and a Medium-size snake form; their equipment doesn't change with them, however.

As a snake, a yuan-ti malison gets one Bite attack per action, doing 1d4 + 3 piercing damage plus 2d6 poison damage. In contrast, a type 1 or type 3 yuan-ti malison can attack twice with its scimitar, doing 1d6 + 3 on each hit for about the same total damage, or twice with its longbow, doing 1d8 + 2 piercing damage plus 2d6 poison damage on each hit, for roughly *twice* the damage. I know which one *I'd* choose. Changing into snake form offers the yuan-ti malison no combat advantage at all, except—implicitly—immunity to the prone condition (the stat block doesn't say this explicitly, but think about it for a second), and it comes with the disadvantage of divesting it of its weapons. I'd say this is a dubiously useful ability at best, and I wouldn't have a yuan-ti malison Shapechange during combat, except maybe to escape through a tiny hole.

One of the things I like about the type 3 yuan-ti malison is that it has the extra attacking feature Constrict, which does 2d6 + 3 bludgeoning damage *and* grapples its target, restraining it as well. Moreover, since it's grappling with its lower body, its hands are still free. That means that on its next turn, it can take two scimitar swings with advantage. I love both the tactical elegance of this combination and the visual image of it. Type 1 and type 2 don't offer anything of the kind. Plus, the idea of a person with snakes for arms—each with its own head—strikes me as goofy rather than horrifying.

Say you've got a party of four PCs, encountering a group of five yuan-ti: three purebloods and two type 3 malisons. The malisons hide 120 feet away from the purebloods, while the purebloods use *suggestion* to charm the PCs. If a pureblood's *suggestion* fails or is broken, it draws its scimitar and attacks with it. On cue, the malisons begin sniping at the PCs, targeting elves, gnomes, barbarians, and paladins first. (Why on earth *these* categories? Because they have the best resistance against being charmed.) Once all the purebloods are moderately wounded or any one of them is seriously wounded, the malisons then Dash in to fight hand-to-hand. They begin with a Multiattack comprising an attempt to Constrict followed by a Scimitar attack. As long as their targets remain grappled, they'll keep Multiattacking with their scimitars; if a target breaks free, they'll try to Constrict again. Like purebloods, yuan-ti malisons retreat when seriously injured (reduced to 26 hp or fewer), but unlike purebloods, they have the discipline to Disengage before retreating.

Yuan-ti abominations are the top caste: giant serpents with humanoid arms. Like malisons, they have the ability to Shapechange into snake form, and like malisons, they suffer from the same disadvantage of not getting to hold on to their equipment. They have the same Constrict ability as the type 3 malison and can combine it with melee attacks in the same way. They have spectacular ability scores across the board, but their Strength of 19 stands out. A yuan-ti abomination is a great boss enemy for a party of intermediate-level PCs.

Yuan-ti abominations have mostly the same toolkit as malisons, with one cherry on top: the ability to cast *fear* once per day. Why would they cast that, though? They're havoc in battle: Once they grapple an enemy, they can take three scimitar swings with advantage *and*

+7 to hit. (That's an 88 percent chance to hit against AC 15.) Whether they're attacking at range with longbows or in melee with scimitars, they do nearly double the malison's damage.

There are only two reasons why a yuan-ti abomination would opt for *fear* over simply beating the tar out of its opponents: Either it's protecting some kind of sacred or otherwise important place, and keeping trespassers away is its foremost priority; or its opponents are tougher than it bargained for, and it's losing the fight.

In the former case—that is, when the yuan-ti abomination is more interested in driving the PCs away than in murdering them—it casts *fear* at the very beginning of the encounter, then fights those too stubborn to go away. In the latter case, it casts *fear* when it's moderately injured (reduced to 88 hp or fewer), in order to reduce the number of enemies that it and its allies have to deal with right away, and if it's seriously injured (reduced to 50 hp or fewer), it Disengages and attempts to retreat.

A yuan-ti abomination fighting to protect a place of importance does so fanatically. If it's seriously injured in that scenario, it won't retreat but rather will fight to the death. If it's accompanied by yuan-ti malisons and purebloods, and if they're in a settlement or other location where reinforcements may be available, one or more of the yuan-ti abomination's allies will break off when the abomination is moderately injured and run/slither to fetch more.

Yuan-ti abominations are very intelligent. They issue commands to their allies, telling them what locations to attack or defend and which enemies to prioritize. Because all yuan-ti are magic-resistant, they don't place the same emphasis on spellcasters that other intelligent enemies might. Instead, they focus on strong and tough PCs, double- or triple-teaming them, and on particularly effective ranged fighters. They may single out PC clerics and paladins as well, simply out of sectarian loathing. Also, they direct their allies to make use of choke points, high ground, and other strategically useful terrain.

Finally, yuan-ti abominations monologue as they fight, because what more could you want from a fanatically religious enemy boss with Charisma 18? Chew that scenery!

BULLYWUGS

Bullywugs are petty, bad-tempered humanoid frogs, native to swampy areas. The *Monster Manual* flavor text describes them as "struck with a deep inferiority complex . . . desperately crav[ing] the fear and respect of outsiders" and says they'll generally prefer to capture trespassers rather than kill them outright, hauling them back to win favor with their rulers first. One way they do this is by taming giant frogs and having them swallow victims whole; however, this works only on Small or Tiny targets, meaning that unless a party of PCs is made up entirely of halflings and gnomes, this isn't a strategy they can rely on in a typical encounter.

For creatures with only two hit dice, bullywugs aren't too shabby in combat. All their physical abilities are modestly above average, and they have proficiency in Stealth and the Swamp Camouflage trait, which grants them advantage on Dexterity (Stealth) checks in swampy terrain. It's fair to say, therefore, that bullywugs won't venture outside such areas—not when they have such a natural advantage on their home turf.

Moreover, their Standing Leap ability lets them move their full speed of 20 feet per turn as a long jump, when the jumping rule would normally allow them to leap only 6 feet. This allows them to cover distance in difficult marshy terrain without having to halve their movement speed. If you want to be nitpicky about it, you can require them to succeed on a DC 10 Dexterity (Acrobatics) check when they land, per "Special Types of Movement: Jumping" in chapter 8 of the *Player's Handbook*, but personally, I'd say that bullywugs, whose natural habitat is the swamp, shouldn't have to make that check when landing. And for the sake of flavor, I like the idea of having bullywugs bouncing around like a bunch of ornery little Superballs during combat rather than trudging around in 2-D as we landbound humanoids must. (Mind you, this *doesn't* exempt them from opportunity attacks when they jump out of PCs' reach.)

Okay, so far we've established that bullywug encounters will occur in swamps. Let's also stipulate, based on the aforementioned features, that their favored strategy is ambush (their physical abilities don't indicate a preference for one form of combat over another, but their features do). Now let's add, based on their 40-foot swimming speed, that they prefer combat to take place near open water: This is their favored method of escape. From the bullywugs' point of view, the ideal ambush location is on ground solid enough to fight on but also near water deep enough to swim in. They're Medium creatures, so this depth will be at least 3 feet.

Wanting, ideally, to capture rather than kill, bullywugs attack in numbers large enough to surround and overwhelm a party of adventurers—let's say three to one. But here's a question: If you can get a free attack by popping out of hiding and surprising your enemies, will you really forgo that attack and demand their surrender when it costs you the benefit of surprise if they decide to fight back? Bullywugs aren't bright, but I think even they can grasp what the whole point of an ambush is. They'll take that surprise attack, thank you, and with any luck, the damage they do in the first round will serve as further incentive to stand down. If that damage should happen, by some fluke, to knock a target out, they'll make it nonlethal.

So here's what round 1 looks like: The bullywugs lie in wait, hidden, at a range of 15 to 20 feet from where they expect the PCs to pass. At the right moment, they spring out of hiding, land next to the PCs, and kick off melee combat with surprise, spearing and biting. In round 2, they keep attacking while demanding the PCs' surrender—in Bullywug, because they're too dumb to realize that the PCs don't speak Bullywug. In round 3, they also keep attacking and demanding the PCs' surrender, still in Bullywug but louder and more slowly. If any PC gets the message and drops their weapon, the nearest bullywug will grab and grapple that PC and pull them away from the fight, rifling through their pockets and pouches for anything valuable.

Bullywugs are cowards. If one is moderately wounded (reduced to 7 hp or fewer), it will leap away, but it won't flee just yet—it will look for an opportunity to get back in the fight alongside a couple of less wounded allies, and in the meantime, it Hides and repositions. However, a seriously injured bullywug (reduced to 4 hp or fewer) will indeed flee, using the Dash action to double its movement speed, leaping into the nearest water deep enough to swim in (and possibly incurring one or more opportunity attacks), then swimming away. If no water of sufficient depth is near enough, it simply leaps twice, 20 feet each time. Bullywugs also flee when their numbers are reduced to fewer than one-and-a-half the number of PCs, then attempt to regroup with other bullywugs in the area, stalk the PCs, and attack again when the opportunity presents itself.

KUO-TOA

Old-school D&D players will recall that the kuo-toa made their debut in the venerated, if somewhat incoherent, D series of adventure modules, which also introduced the drow. In the world of Greyhawk, AD&D's original setting, they and the drow were fierce enemies. In fifth edition, however, the kuo-toa have been retconned into broken ex-subjects of an empire of mind flayers, their rivalry with the drow now mentioned only in passing.

"Many weapons of the kuo-toa are designed to capture rather than kill," the *Monster Manual* flavor text informs us, but it leaves open the question of what they want to capture anyone for. Religious sacrifice, maybe? Interrogation? Enslavement? Found-art pieces? Regardless, I'm going to examine their tactics with the assumption that they are, in fact, trying to kill the PCs, or at least knock them out.

The basic **kuo-toa** stat block has high Strength but average Dexterity and Constitution, and it lacks proficiency in Stealth. This is tricky to interpret. Ambush isn't a realistic possibility, but neither is protracted toe-to-toe fighting. Kuo-toa need to be selective about their encounters and maneuver their foes into situations where they're restrained and helpless.

They do this primarily by using nets. A Net attack restrains an opponent, giving the kuo-toa advantage on attack rolls and giving the opponent disadvantage. However, because of their extremely short range, solo Net attacks always have disadvantage. Also, the net is effortless to escape from, so there need to be a second, third, and fourth kuo-toa on hand to throw more nets, ensuring a reasonable chance that a target will be trapped under at least two. Since a target can escape from only one net at a time, this guarantees that they'll remain restrained.

What this tells us is that kuo-toa don't attack without a four-to-one numerical advantage or better, throwing nets until a target is covered by two, then attacking with advantage using the Spear action. If you're using the optional Flanking rule (*Dungeon Master's Guide*, chapter 8), you can get away with a two-to-one advantage: Once the target is under a single net, the battle buddies quickly get on either side of them in order to maintain their advantage in case the captive wriggles free, then begin stabbing.

Kuo-toa can breathe underwater, from which we can infer another possible tactic: hauling enemies into the water and trying to drown them. Assuming that the kuo-toa double-team their foes, one grappling and the other taking the Help action to confer advantage on the check, the grapple-and-drown tactic is reasonable against opponents whose Strength (Athletics) and Dexterity (Acrobatics) modifiers are both +4 or lower; to have any real confidence of success, they both need to be +1 or lower. If there are more kuo-toa on hand, they can throw nets before grappling; this doesn't impose disadvantage on rolls to escape a grapple, but it overwhelms the target, giving them too many things they have to escape from. Once a target is both restrained and grappled, any remaining kuo-toa stab.

Kuo-toa can't read PCs' stats. They can only know from experience whether a tactic generally works or generally doesn't, and what experience tells them is that it's possible for two of them to drown one average or punier-than-average humanoid, but against a big or brawny one, it doesn't usually work.

The Sticky Shield reaction gives the kuo-toa a chance to disable an opponent's weapon. It's only usable in melee. Therefore, kuo-toa prefer melee over ranged combat and close to melee range as soon as they've thrown their nets. (The *Monster Manual* indicates that monsters with throwable weapons can be assumed to carry 2d4 of them, but nets are big and bulky. I wouldn't give a single kuo-toa more than one.)

If nets and grappling clearly aren't getting the desired result but the kuo-toa still outnumber their opponents at least three to one, they'll switch to attacking with Spear alone, to maximize damage. This is the full extent of their ability to adapt. If they no longer have the numbers, they Dash away (through water, if possible). They also have a normal self-preservation instinct and Dash away when seriously injured (7 hp or fewer).

The **kuo-toa whip** is actually a clerical spellcaster, not (as one might reasonably think) a kuo-toa with a whip. It has above-average Constitution and Wisdom; the former makes the kuo-toa whip a more durable melee fighter. Its pincer staff grapples opponents on a melee hit, not on a skill contest, and its escape DC makes it comparable to two regular kuo-toa working together, making it possible to execute the grapple-and-drown tactic with fewer attackers. The execution of this tactic depends on which has higher initiative, the whip or its kuo-toa allies. If the kuo-toa allies go first, they throw their nets, and then the kuo-toa whip Multiattacks, gaining advantage on its staff attack rolls if any nets landed. If the whip goes first, it Readies a Pincer Staff attack, the triggering condition being when a kuo-toa ally makes a Net attack; in this case, it doesn't get to Multiattack, because its attack is now a reaction.

Shield of faith is a bonus action but also a concentration-required spell with just one target. *Bane* requires concentration as well, affecting up to three creatures but also costing a full action. The kuo-toa whip is more likely to use *bane* if its allies need help netting their opponents, *shield of faith* if it's being attacked. The cantrip *sacred flame*, which costs an action, does 1d8 radiant damage to one target on a failed Dexterity saving throw. It's good to use against enemy spellcasters, especially close-range supporters; not so good against ranged weapon attackers, who are likely to have high Dex. Once combat has begun, *thaumaturgy* serves no purpose.

Kuo-toa in general aren't super disciplined, and the kuo-toa whip is no exception: It Dashes away when seriously injured (reduced to 26 hp or fewer). It doesn't stick around to help its allies disengage.

The **kuo-toa archpriest** stands outside the net-and-stab and grapple-and-drown tactics of regular kuo-toa and kuo-toa whips. With very high Strength and Constitution and decently high Dexterity as well—not to mention a magic scepter that does lightning damage—it's well-equipped for melee combat, but its repertoire of spells is impressive too:

- *Mass cure wounds* can be a tide-turner, good when half a dozen of its allies are moderately wounded or worse (kuo-toa reduced to 12 hp or fewer; kuo-toa whips reduced to 45 hp or fewer).
- *Scrying* is a 10-minute ritual, not suitable for combat.
- *Control water* is super if the kuo-toa are trying to drown their enemies. They can breathe underwater; the PCs, in all likelihood, can't. Therefore, it's a near guarantee that a kuo-toa archpriest will cast this during any encounter. The Flood option can fill a space that has any standing water in it at all to a depth of up to 20 feet, making this an automatic win if the ceiling is no higher than that. If players have already been pulled into a body of water, the Whirlpool option can keep them there and bludgeon them in the process. (One archpriest can't use the two effects in conjunction with each other . . . but two can.)
- *Divination* is a spell for social interaction, not combat.
- *Spirit guardians* is great—usually—but in this case, it's got to take a backseat to *control water*, since both require concentration. A kuo-toa archpriest casts this spell only when there's no water around to control, and really, why would a kuo-toa archpriest be anyplace where there *wasn't* water at hand? It seems to me that kuo-toa habitations should exist on a continuum from Venice to Atlantis.
- *Tongues* is the only way the kuo-toa can communicate with surface-dwelling creatures, since Undercommon isn't Common. But again, this is for social interaction, not combat, unless someone is signaling a desire to parley in the middle of a combat encounter.
- *Hold person* is always useful—as long as you're not trying to sustain either *control water* or *spirit guardians*.
- *Spiritual weapon* is always useful, period. It's a bonus action that creates a floating energy weapon (in this case, in the shape of a kuo-toa whip's pincer staff), doesn't require concentration

to sustain, and confers a bonus attack action on every subsequent round, for up to 10 rounds. Casting this spell is the first thing the kuo-toa archpriest does in any combat encounter.

- *Detect magic* is a spell for another occasion.
- *Sanctuary* is an interesting and useful spell but one that I have a hard time imagining a kuo-toa archpriest using, unless it were guarding some fishy-head VIP. I don't think it would cast this spell on any of its allies in combat. It might cast it on itself while Dashing away.
- *Shield of faith* is a bonus action and a self-defense measure. If a PC has eluded nets and drowning and is coming at the archpriest, it may be worth it to forgo a *spiritual weapon* attack for one turn in order to get this spell up and running. But it requires, yep, concentration, so the archpriest probably won't cast this spell unless and until things are going *really* awry.
- *Guidance* is a cantrip that requires concentration. Why bother?
- *Sacred flame* is useful for smiting a slow opponent at a distance, and that's about it.
- *Thaumaturgy* no.

Out of all these spells, only three leap out as unconditionally useful: *spiritual weapon*, *control water*, and *mass cure wounds*, in that order. Two more are situationally useful: *spirit guardians* and *hold person*. These should cover the entirety of a combat encounter. If the fighting drags on, a kuo-toa archpriest will probably just start smacking opponents left and right with its electric scepter rather than cast spells.

Like the regular kuo-toa and the kuo-toa whip, the kuo-toa archpriest flees when seriously wounded (reduced to 38 hp or fewer), underwater if possible. Unlike some boss monsters, the kuo-toa archpriest won't stand its ground over treasure or a holy site. It's gonna save its skin.

MERFOLK

Merfolk may occasionally enjoy sunning themselves on rocks, to be spied by passing sailors, but they pass the vast majority of their time under the sea. This is where their habitations are and where they're most likely to be encountered. With a 40-foot swimming speed and only a 10-foot land speed, getting into a scrap on dry land is a very bad proposition for merfolk. Underwater, their swimming speed is a huge advantage against any creature not native to the depths.

Although their ability scores all fall into a typical humanoid range, they do have above-average Dexterity and Constitution, and these, combined with their swimming speed, bias them toward a skirmish style of combat. Since the spears they carry can be thrown underwater at normal range without disadvantage, part of a group of merfolk can engage in melee while others throw their spears; some may even do both.

It's worth a closer examination to see just how big an advantage their swimming speed is for them. For a character who isn't innately aquatic or buffed by a magic item, every foot swum costs an extra foot of movement, effectively halving movement speed in most cases. This means that Silvio the Swordsman is slowed to 15 feet per round underwater, whereas his merfolk opponent can swim 40 feet per round.

How do they use this to gain an even greater advantage? Mainly, by goading opponents into splitting up. Rather than coalesce around a melee front line, merfolk initiate combat by throwing spears from a distance of exactly 20 feet—no more, no less—from all sides of their foes, if possible. If they're on defense and can attack from only one side, they form a line, from which the ones on the ends spread out while the ones in the center fall back, eventually forming a semicircle around their opponents. (Because underwater combat takes place in three dimensions, some can also go up or down.)

As they encircle (or en-semicircle, or en-hemisphere) their enemies, they fall back as those enemies advance, maintaining that 20-foot distance. If an enemy does manage to close the distance with a merfolk, it stops throwing spears and starts stabbing with one instead; ditto if the merfolk have managed to lure their foes into spreading out 30 feet or more from one another, or if the withdrawing merfolk is down to its last spear. It's only practical to carry so many spears—three or four is probably the limit—and a merfolk never throws its last one. A seriously wounded merfolk (reduced to 4 hp or fewer), or one forcibly disarmed of its last spear, Disengages and retreats. If reinforcements are available, it then Dashes off to fetch them.

Against a party of low-level adventurers, as many as five merfolk to one PC constitute a winnable fight (although two to one is fairer for novice adventurers just starting out),* so there should always be plenty of merfolk on hand to allow some to fight hand-to-hand, some to throw spears, and some to retreat.

Merfolk are neutral, not evil, which means their initial disposition toward strangers is indifference rather than hostility. They are cautious, however, and order any strangers who approach to between 20 and 60 feet to halt and state their business. If they're not satisfied by the reply they receive (they don't take "Blurrrbbblllpp!" for an answer), they cock their spears as a warning. But they don't attack unless and until their visitors take action that could be reasonably interpreted as hostile, and they won't chase down fleeing foes.

SAHUAGIN

Sahuagin are fierce amphibious fish-people who live underwater but emerge periodically to raid coastal settlements. Although the *Monster Manual* says they "dwell in the deepest trenches of the ocean," that's a bit far even for a creature with a 40-foot swimming speed. Those ocean trenches are as far from the coasts as the highest mountains are, and you don't often hear about the yetis of the Himalayas spending an afternoon staging a raid on Kolkata, or the Tatzelwürmer of the Alps popping down to Genoa for some late-night ravaging. These are distances of hundreds of miles we're talking about. So chances are, any sahuagin that PCs encounter are going to be denizens of shallower depths. Maybe they're the border reivers of the ocean kingdom.

---

* According to "Creating a Combat Encounter" in chapter 3 of the *Dungeon Master's Guide*, these merfolk-to-PC ratios constitute Deadly encounters. However, according to the alternative guidelines under "Encounter Building" in chapter 2 of *Xanathar's Guide to Everything*, they produce a balanced encounter. I ran a test scenario comprising ten merfolk against five level 1 PCs with *water breathing* cast upon them, which ended in the merfolk's being routed with only two PCs wounded. I conclude that *Xanathar's* is right.

When they come ashore to raid, they do so at night, as implied by their 120 feet of darkvision (which also helps them see deep underwater). They can't come far inland, since their Limited Amphibiousness gives them only four hours of air breathing before they have to return to the water. Unlike, say, merrows, sahuagin can move about on land as easily as any other humanoid.

In this environment, they're basic brutes. Their Multiattack gives them one Spear or Claw attack and one Bite attack. Since their Armor Class doesn't include a shield, we can presume that they wield their spears two-handed for the greater damage.

Because their Blood Frenzy trait gives them advantage on attacks against any opponent who's taken damage already, they'll press this advantage, continuing to attack any enemy they've bloodied rather than switch targets, even for opportunistic reasons.

However, sahuagin are not dumb. In fact, their Intelligence and Wisdom are higher than those of the average humanoid. They attack with discipline, in cohesive units, perhaps even splitting up to flank or encircle a group of enemies. They'll realize quickly when they're outmatched, retreating if all the members of their fighting group are moderately wounded (reduced to 15 hp or fewer) and their enemies aren't hurt even worse. When they come ashore, they're looking for an easy fight. A hard one isn't worth the effort. Retreating sahuagin are sophisticated enough to use the Disengage action.

In the water, they don't fight significantly differently, but they do have a couple of advantages they don't have on land.

First, they're usually accompanied by sharks. Thanks to the Shark Telepathy trait, any sharks fighting alongside sahuagin will show the same intelligence and discipline that the sahuagin possess.

Second, being naturally aquatic, they can easily recognize when other creatures *aren't* naturally aquatic. They're smart enough to know that a halfling isn't a sea creature, and therefore, if it's *breathing underwater* and swimming as if born to it, there's some kind of magic giving it that ability. Once they see a player character cast a spell, they'll draw the logical (though not necessarily correct) conclusion that that same PC is the one enabling their allies to breathe, and they'll focus their attacks on that PC. If they subsequently see a different PC cast a spell, some of them will break off to attack them as well. (They may or may not be aware that *water breathing* isn't a spell that requires concentration. If they are aware of this, they'll fixate less on hunting spellcasters, since they'll know that killing the caster won't break the spell.)

Sahuagin in the water are also more tenacious than sahuagin on land. When fighting underwater, they'll hang in there until a majority of them are seriously wounded (reduced to 8 hp or fewer). After that, they'll Disengage and retreat if they're on their own, but they'll fight to the death at the command of a sahuagin baron or priestess—usually in order to defend a location or object.

The **sahuagin baron** doesn't differ significantly from an ordinary sahuagin. It's stronger, tougher, and a little smarter; its Multiattack gives it one more poke with a melee weapon; and it gets proficiency on all the most important saving throws, so it has less reason to fear spellcasters—not that sahuagin *fear* them to begin with. When any group of sahuagin led by a baron launches a coordinated attack on a PC spellcaster, the baron takes part in that attack, rather than just hang back and give orders. Sahuagin raids on land don't usually include a sahuagin baron—not unless they're launching an all-out attack of conquest.

The **sahuagin priestess** is primarily a support caster that carries no weapon, although she still has a Claw/Bite Multiattack. She always casts *spiritual weapon* (bonus action) on the first turn of combat, but lacking any useful cantrip to cast along with it, she uses her initial action to Dodge.

On subsequent turns, the priestess's choice of spell depends on what else is going on. If the priestess's allies are focusing attacks on a spellcaster, the priestess casts *guiding bolt* at that caster to do some radiant damage and also give advantage to the next attacker. If it's clear that the players' ability to breathe water doesn't come from a sustained spell, the priestess casts *hold person* on the most dangerous-looking opponent who has the Extra Attack feature. If there are two, and the priestess can't choose between them, she spends a 3rd-level slot to boost the *hold person* spell and nab them both. However, that being said, sahuagin priestesses understand the connection between clerical spellcasting and the brandishing of holy symbols, and they also know that spells like *hold person* don't work as well on the devout, so paladins get a free pass from this.

The presence of a priestess also keeps a moderately wounded group of sahuagin in the fight longer: Anytime all the sahuagin in the group are reduced to 15 hp or fewer, the priestess casts *mass healing word* to top them back up, then uses either the Help action or the Dodge action, as in round 1, until all her 3rd-level spell slots are gone.

Finally, in any group of sahuagin with both a baron and a priestess, it's the *priestess*, not the baron, that's the de facto leader (whether or not the baron cares to admit it). If a PC tries to start a parley, the priestess will call a halt to combat and cast *tongues* to allow the two groups to communicate. It's unlikely that the sahuagin will ever initiate a parley on their own, however, unless they know they're outmatched and aren't guarding anything super important—and unless they have a priestess with them, because they know most land creatures don't speak their language.

Sahuagin priestesses call a general retreat when they're moderately wounded (reduced to 23 hp or fewer), unless they're guarding an important location or object, in which case they defend until they're seriously wounded (reduced to 13 hp or fewer). Sahuagin barons will always fight until they're seriously wounded (reduced to 30 hp or fewer), then call a general retreat.

AARAKOCRA

Aarakocra are raptor-humanoid hybrids, guardians of the boundaries between the material world and the Elemental Plane of Air. Being neutral good, they're generally friendly to any group of non-evil PCs. Unless there's been some kind of misunderstanding, an encounter featuring aarakocra will usually have one or more of them fighting alongside the party rather than against it.

Their digitigrade legs make their walking gait awkward and slow, but their flying speed is a swift 50 feet per round. Their ability scores are unremarkable overall, except for their high Dexterity, which serves as both their primary offensive and primary defensive ability. Since their ranged attacking ability is limited to throwing javelins and their Dive Attack trait works only with melee attacks, aarakocra are primarily shock attackers that strike from above. With their expertise in Perception, they make great scouts, and when fighting alongside PCs, they'll volunteer to act as scouts and strike at enemies who are attempting to hide.

Aarakocra strategy revolves around two things: getting the best use out of their Dive Attack and staying out of reach until they're ready to strike. Thus, if they observe that their enemies have missile or throwable weapons, they keep to an altitude just out of those weapons' normal range until they're close enough to dive; they also use tree canopies as cover, where available, since it's the only cover they're likely to be able to take advantage of. While scouting, they use the Search action if their passive Perception isn't high enough to spot a target, then switch to Dodge once they've found one and are closing in. Against enemies without ranged attack capability, they maintain a cruising altitude of 30 feet while Searching and Dodging; against other fliers, it's a dance in which the Dodging aarakocra try to goad their foes into approaching to a distance of 30 to 50 feet.

That range is the sweet spot for a Dive Attack, against either a ground-bound or an aerial enemy. (Reduce the upper bound a bit for aarakocra diving through a tree canopy, which must constitute difficult terrain for a flying creature.) As soon as an aarakocra can reach an enemy in a single round's flying movement, it dives and strikes, gaining an extra damage die thanks to Dive Attack. The Javelin action is preferred over the Talon action, just because the average damage is slightly better.

What happens next depends on the kind of society your aarakocra belong to. If it's larger and more organized than a simple band or tribe, at least the size and complexity of a chiefdom (see "Tribal Warriors and Berserkers," page 110), they may belong to a trained warrior class, in which case they'll know how to Disengage. If so, then after striking once with Dive Attack, their next action will be to Disengage and fly back up into the air, setting up for another Dive Attack on the following turn. If they're not trained warriors, then once they've closed with an enemy, they won't have much choice but to try to finish the fight in melee. Without Flyby or an equivalent trait, trying to get airborne again for another Dive Attack would invite an opportunity strike, and their Armor Class and hit points aren't good enough for them to risk that.

Aarakocra attacking foes that lack ranged attacks, or that wield only throwable weapons, slings, hand crossbows, or other missiles with very short range, may spend one or more rounds flying down to a height of 30 feet, throwing a javelin, then flying back up out of reach again until their foes are seriously wounded (reduced to 40 percent or less of their hit point maximum). At this point they finally use their Dive Attack to try to finish their enemies off. Both trained and untrained aarakocra may employ this tactic, which deals slightly more damage, on average, than making Dive Attacks on alternate turns—although it's limited by the number of javelins the aarakocra carry. An aarakocra never throws its last javelin unless it's retreating.

In short, against enemies with good ranged attacks, aarakocra emphasize melee fighting, and against enemies without good ranged attacks, aarakocra emphasize ranged attacks of their own. They Dive Attack to avoid incoming missiles, against seriously injured enemies, or when they're down to their last javelin. Otherwise, they do their best to stay out of reach.

Untrained aarakocra retreat from melee, using just their normal flying movement, when they're moderately wounded (reduced to 9 hp or fewer), but they'll continue throwing javelins, if it makes sense to do so, until they're seriously wounded (reduced to 5 hp or fewer). Trained aarakocra continue fighting until they're seriously wounded, then fly off to a safe distance as fast as they can. If they're engaged in melee, they Disengage; otherwise, they Dash.

Aarakocra fighting alongside PCs coordinate their attacks with whatever the PCs are doing, in a limited fashion. They're not master strategists, but they know good opportunities when they see them.

KENKU

Kenku, loosely based on the *tengu* of Japanese myth, are feathered bipeds with avian heads and feet; humanoid torsos, legs, and arms;

and a marked lack of wings, which their ancestors lost as punishment for their duplicity and avarice. Not only do they lack wings, they also lack speech: They can communicate only by repeating back sounds and phrases they've heard.

A kenku's only salient ability is its high Dexterity; all its other abilities are average. In combination with its proficiency in Perception and Stealth and its Ambusher trait, this gives it some melee shock attack potential, but in most cases it's better off as a sniper. Notably, kenku *don't* have darkvision, as many ambush attackers do. They set up ambushes, but they do so during the daytime, not at night.

A lone kenku may try to pick off an isolated individual, but kenku preying on groups need the force of numbers—at a minimum, two kenku per victim. Using Stealth, they either lie hidden or stalk their victims; when the moment is right, they let loose with a surprise volley of Shortbow attacks.

After the initial volley of arrows, one-half to one-third of a flock of kenku will rush forth to engage softer targets in melee with their shortswords, while their bow-wielding allies loose volley after volley at more formidable fighters. Kenku archers always try to maintain at least a 35-foot distance from their targets; if possible, they shoot from 65 to 80 feet away. When an enemy charges, they retreat the same distance, as other allies continue to shoot. If they have the room, kenku archers space themselves out so that an enemy charging one can't easily reach others. A kenku swordfighter Disengages and backs off if a capable melee fighter starts heading its way. Kenku communicate constantly, through a code of seemingly random sound effects, informing one another of the state of play and calling for help when they need it.

Kenku don't have much appetite for a knock-down, drag-out fight. A kenku will alert its allies when it's moderately wounded (reduced to 9 hp or fewer); if it's engaged in melee, it Disengages and retreats. An entire flock of kenku will withdraw and disperse if combat isn't over by their fourth turn—sooner if at least half of them are seriously wounded (reduced to 5 hp or fewer).

Kenku are greedy, but being chaotic neutral, they aren't necessarily malevolent. What they want is precious shiny stuff; killing people is just one way to get it. They understand Common speech and can be bought off for the price of, say, five gold pieces each, or an equivalent amount in gems. Double that price, and you may have bought yourself a favor; quintuple it, and you may have bought yourself a friend, or possibly a retainer. If the PCs happen to notice a flock of skulking kenku before they have a chance to attack, bribery is a good way to stop a fight before it starts.

THRI-KREEN

Being chaotic neutral, **thri-kreen**—mantis-like humanoids, not at all eusocial, as one might suppose them to be—largely want to be left to their own business. The *Monster Manual* flavor text does say they "consider all other living creatures as potential nourishment," and, in a silly twist, "they love the taste of elf flesh in particular." (I suppose that elves must taste like truffles or something.) This seems to me to verge on evil, so I'd say that thri-kreen don't attack other humanoids *just* to eat them unless they're experiencing some kind of shortage of other foods. That said, having already killed a humanoid for some other reason, they probably wouldn't have any scruples about consuming the corpse.

Thri-kreen have high Dexterity and above-average Strength and Constitution, and they're also fast-moving (speed: 40 feet per round), biasing them toward hard-and-fast shock attacks. They also have proficiency in Perception and Stealth, plus Chameleon Carapace, which gives them advantage when trying to Hide. All these factors point to ambush as their favored strategy.

Their Standing Leap trait is useful for surmounting obstacles, moving vertically between ledges and the ground, and crossing rivers or crevasses, but it doesn't do anything to enhance their speed over level ground—unless the terrain is difficult. Then it gives the thri-kreen a pronounced advantage over opponents who must move on foot, since their movement will usually be cut in half. And the thick, tall grass of the savanna, and the sharp rocks or shifting sands of the desert—the favored habitats of the thri-kreen—usually constitute difficult terrain.

Thri-kreen have AC 15, which isn't quite high enough to make opportunity attacks something they don't need to worry about. Since they can't engage and disengage with impunity, they need to make every attack count.

The biggest thing they have going for them is the poison in their bite. A poisoned opponent makes attack rolls with disadvantage, which gives the thri-kreen a better chance to elude a counterattack. However, the DC of the thri-kreen's poisonous Bite is pretty easy to beat, especially for an opponent with a high Constitution. Thri-kreen are simple-minded, but they're good at choosing targets, so rank-and-file thri-kreen will steer clear of tougher-looking opponents at first. They'll leave those foes to their armed allies.

From a place of hiding, thri-kreen initiate combat when foes come within 30 feet of them, springing out and attacking with the element of surprise, distributing their Bite attacks across all opponents who don't appear to have above-average Constitution, and continuing to fight hand-to-hand until either the opponent is down for the count or they themselves are moderately wounded (reduced to 23 hp or fewer). At that point, they'll chitter for help, and other thri-kreen who've managed to poison their opponents will leap over to assist, while they themselves leap away to go fight someone easier.

Thri-kreen communicate constantly during combat, in their impenetrable language, but mostly they just tell each other things like "I'm hurt," "This one is tough," "This one is fragile but dangerous," or "This one is poisoned." They exchange information, but they don't really *coordinate*. If one accidentally engages an opponent that's tougher than it thought, one or two other thri-kreen may come to help, attacking from behind for the flanking bonus ("Optional Rule: Flanking," *Dungeon Master's Guide*, chapter 8). When half of a group of thri-kreen are seriously wounded (reduced to 13 hp or fewer), or when all of them are at least moderately wounded, they'll call a retreat, favoring the Dash action if they're outnumbered and the Dodge action otherwise (non-variant thri-kreen aren't quite smart enough to know how to Disengage).

Variant thri-kreen that wield weapons may be considered to be better trained than ordinary thri-kreen, and with this training comes a discipline that does allow them to Disengage. However, these thri-kreen will stay in the fight long enough to cover their allies' escape before Disengaging. They're also the ones who will engage the toughest opponents, if they're present. First, they approach to a distance of 30 feet and throw two "chatkchas" in a single Multiattack action. After that, they close to melee range and fight with their double-bladed polearms, called "gythkas," also combining two attacks in one Multiattack action. When one of these "soldier thri-kreen" is engaged with a melee opponent, a regular thri-kreen will often come up behind it for a flank attack, in the hope of poisoning the foe with its bite. (In any thri-kreen encounter, it's good to have the thri-kreen slightly outnumber their opponents in order to allow a few to dart from opponent to opponent.)

Because *magic weapon* is no good without a weapon to enchant, psionic thri-kreen will usually also be weapon-wielding thri-kreen themselves or accompanied by weapon-wielding thri-kreen; otherwise, they'll never get to use their ability to cast *magic weapon*, which seems like a waste. Psionic thri-kreen engaged with the toughest of their opponents use *invisibility* to vanish and relocate when they take a particularly serious hit (one dealing 10 damage or more). Once they've used this once-per-day ability, they cast *blur* upon re-manifesting, giving their opponents the same penalty against them as if they were invisible. Thri-kreen cast *magic weapon* on their polearms, not on their chatkchas, which are single-use.

LYCANTHROPES

Werebeasts, aka lycanthropes, are wonderful enemies. A werebeast encounter can be awesome action or tragic drama. Werebeasts lend themselves perfectly to horror-mystery adventures, in which the players have no idea which of the villagers is the true villain. They threaten to transmit their lycanthropic curse to any character who fights them hand-to-hand—monsters who can make the player characters into monsters themselves. Practically by definition, werebeast encounters take place at night, when everything is scarier. And if the werewolf ever seems too clichéd an enemy, werebeasts come in four other varieties.

All werebeasts have proficiency in Perception and immunity to physical damage from nonmagical, nonsilvered weapons. They also have human forms, beast forms, and hybrid forms; their human forms are their "true" forms. My sense as a DM is that they take their beast forms to run around and hunt in the wild, but among people, they take their hybrid forms when their curse is upon them—at any rate, the hybrid form makes for more interesting and challenging combat encounters than the beast form, because it allows them to use their Multiattack action. (The exception to this pattern is the werebear, which has Multiattack in all its forms.) However, if you want to conceal the fact that the PCs are fighting a lycanthrope and not simply a big, ferocious beast, you may opt for the beast form after all, trading a reduction in damage for the increase in likelihood that the PCs will carelessly let themselves fall afoul of the lycanthropic curse.

Although the Shapechanger trait, common to all werebeasts, states that they can use an action to polymorph from one form to another, I'd disregard this, for two reasons. First, there's generally no advantage to it: Any equipment they're carrying isn't transformed, so, for example, a humanoid wearing armor and carrying a sword turns into a beast standing in a pile of armor and staring at a sword on the ground; or a hybrid with natural armor turns into a naked, unarmored, unarmed humanoid. Meanwhile, it's just spent a whole combat round transforming when it could have been, I don't know, attacking or running away? Second, isn't the whole point of lycanthropy that the afflicted individual has little or no control over their transformations? High opportunity cost, no obvious benefit, contradicts werebeast lore: There's only one logical situation in which to use this action, and that's at nightfall or daybreak, when the lycanthrope changes involuntarily.

Werewolves in their hybrid form lack any ranged attack, so they're strictly melee fighters. They possess proficiency in Stealth, so they strongly prefer attacking from hiding, with surprise. They have Keen Hearing and Smell, which gives them advantage on Wisdom (Perception) checks using these senses, but this *doesn't* negate disadvantage from attacking in darkness, since they lack darkvision. (Stat blocks aren't written in stone, though. If you want *your* werewolves to have darkvision, give them darkvision. Wolves are nocturnal, for pity's sake.)

Their immunity to normal weapons makes them unafraid of opportunity attacks, generally speaking, and as predators, they prefer easy prey to hard prey. Consequently, they attack the weakest first (in a village, that means commoners, not seasoned adventurers), and if struck by a ranged weapon attack or spell attack that does no damage or insignificant damage (5 or less), they immediately Dash out of sight, thereafter to Hide again and resume stalking prey. However, if a PC aims a melee attack at a werewolf and either misses or does no damage or insignificant damage, the werewolf counterattacks against that PC, clawing and biting. A werewolf struck for 6 or more damage by a spell attack or a magic or silvered weapon, either melee or ranged, flees using the Dash action.

Werewolves in their hybrid form can speak and understand speech, but they generally don't have much to say. When slain, they return to human form, and I like to use this moment to deliver the players an extra punch in the feels—for instance, by having a group of three slain werewolves revert to the forms of two young women and a teenage boy, who all bear a strong family resemblance to one another.

Werewolves are most likely to be found in country villages; **wererats** are urban creatures. Since wererats' Strength is lower than their Dexterity and Constitution, and since rats are naturally social animals, wererats congregate in gangs and favor skirmish fighting over crude brawling. They'll attack victims whom they outnumber at least two to one, sniping with their hand crossbows from hiding, from behind cover, and from multiple directions. Their overall strategy is to wear down, then close in when all their victims are seriously wounded (reduced to 40 percent of their hit point maximum or less—calculate this threshold for your PCs before the session). If a wererat's target charges and engages it in melee, it fights back fearlessly with its shortsword and its teeth, unless and until it's struck by a magic or silvered weapon or a spell attack. In that case, it Dashes into the shadows. Once other wererats realize that their fellows are being driven off by magical attacks or silver weapons, they too break off attack and withdraw.

That's not necessarily the end of it, though. The PCs may decide to give chase—at night, through the streets and alleys and shadows, which means that while fortune may have turned momentarily against the wererats, they still have the home field advantage. They'll scatter, but they won't go far, and once one finds an advantageous hiding place, it Readies a Hand Crossbow attack, shooting a bolt at any PC who passes before it—if there are multiple targets, favoring one carrying a magic or silvered weapon or casting injurious spells. On its next turn, it slips out of sight and Hides again. This continues until the PCs kill all the wererats or give up pursuit. And woe to the PCs if they split up: The wererats will quickly figure out which group is the smallest and weakest and converge on it.

Slain wererats often revert to the form of piteous street urchins. The feels! Right in the feels!

Boars are also social animals, so **wereboars** attack in gangs, but like werewolves, they range primarily in the country rather than the city. They're brute attackers with no skill at stealth; they initiate combat with a Charge, followed by a Tusk/Maul Multiattack. The Tusk attack comes first, because it may knock the target prone, giving the wereboar advantage on the subsequent Maul attack roll. If a wereboar's opponent tries to retreat, it presses, Charging if the opponent is at least 15 feet away; if it knocks an opponent unconscious, it Charges the next one.

Wereboars are tough and stubborn—their Relentless trait keeps them going even when they're reduced to 0 hp—but that doesn't mean they *like* being struck by magic or silvered weapons. They'll retreat after being moderately injured (reduced to 54 hp or fewer) by either of these types of weapon or seriously injured (reduced to 31 hp or fewer) by spells. Their version of retreating, however, isn't to Dodge, Dash, or Disengage but rather to deliver a parting Multiattack action before backing off at full movement speed, without concern for any opportunity attack this may incur.

Tigers are "solitary but social" animals: They hunt separately, but a group of female tigers may lair together. (Male tigers both hunt and lair alone.) Therefore, an encounter with a **weretiger** generally involves a single individual, unless the party has stumbled upon a lair belonging to a group of females or a female with offspring. Even so, this group won't be large.

Weretigers keep to remote areas and generally don't hunt humanoids; a weretiger that does is an exception to the rule, and this may be why the PCs are fighting it in the first place. It would also be a reasonable justification for having the weretiger fight in hybrid form, since according to the *Monster Manual* flavor text, weretigers generally prefer to keep to human form; using the hybrid form will highlight its deviant nature.

Weretigers have darkvision in all their forms and proficiency in Stealth, so these are nocturnal ambush hunters. Their Pounce feature is similar to a Charge but with the addition of a bonus Bite attack. They can wield longbows, but I think this is something that ordinary weretigers would use to defend their territory; a rogue weretiger would favor the potent melee combo offered by the Pounce feature.

Therefore the rogue weretiger (not to be confused with a weretiger rogue) stalks its prey from hiding, then Pounces with surprise. What does it consider prey? Probably not a whole party of well-armed adventurers—but then again, weretigers have only average Intelligence, so one may underestimate a group of PCs who aren't flaunting their accomplishments. Still, while a weretiger won't hesitate to attack a single PC and probably wouldn't balk at two, a group of three, four, or five is another matter: They'd have to be weak, or at least weakened, or the weretiger would have to possess some sort of situational advantage, beyond mere darkness. It won't touch a group of six or more, period.

Using the Pounce action in its surprise round, the weretiger gets 15 to 30 feet of movement, a Multiattack action comprising two Claw attacks, and a Bite attack as a bonus action. After that, is there any reason for the weretiger to bother drawing a scimitar and slashing away? Nah. As long as it's engaged in melee, it continues to use its Claw/Claw Multiattack.

Like other werebeasts, a weretiger knows that magic and silvered weapons can hurt or kill it, as can spells, and it will withdraw quickly when moderately injured (reduced to 84 or fewer hp), because anything that can deal a moderate wound to a weretiger can probably do worse as well. It Dashes away, then Hides as soon as the PCs lose sight of it. But as with wererats, the encounter probably won't end there, because the PCs will have been hunting the weretiger in the first place. As much as it can, it will use Stealth to avoid them and will fight back only against a single PC if the party splits up.

But suppose it's not a rogue weretiger we're talking about—suppose it's a regular, I-just-wanna-be-left-alone weretiger that the PCs are hunting? According to the *Monster Manual* flavor text, this kind of weretiger will prefer to keep to its humanoid form whenever it can, and in that form, it will prefer to hide and not be found. It won't even counterattack from hiding with its bow, because that would give away its position. It simply Hides and stays hidden until the PCs go away. If the PCs get too close—say, within bowshot range—this is the rare instance in which it makes sense for the weretiger to Shapechange from humanoid to tiger form, because in this form, it has a movement speed of 40 feet and thus can more easily run away. Only when defending its lair does it stand and fight, with its scimitar; and in this instance, it fights to the death, because it knows that if it doesn't prevail, it will most likely be killed.

Werebears are good creatures and solitary, and they *really* want to be left alone. If the PCs have a violent encounter with a werebear, it's either because they're trespassing in its home and refusing to leave or because they're evil characters who are hunting the werebear. Either way, it's a ferocious melee fighter, making two mighty Greataxe attacks per turn in its daytime humanoid form and two even mightier Claw attacks per turn in its nighttime hybrid or beast form. With 135 hp *and* immunity to damage from normal, nonsilvered weapons, the werebear takes no guff. Even if you can hurt it, while it might flee when injured in the wild (say, upon being reduced to 94 hp or fewer), it fights to the death when defending its lair. *"Leave! Me! Alone!"*

One thing the werebear generally won't do is bite. This is partly because, according to the *Monster Manual* flavor text, werebears prefer not to transmit their lycanthropy to others, but it's also because the werebear's Multiattack doesn't include a Bite attack. A single Bite is simply less effective overall than Claw/Claw.

JACKALWERES

As the name implies, **jackalweres**—not "werejackals"—aren't your ordinary lycanthrope. Rather than humanoids tainted with a bestial curse, they're jackals tainted with a human curse. Like lycanthropes, however, they typically adopt a hybrid form during combat.

Jackalweres have an unusual ability contour: high Dexterity but merely average Strength and Constitution, combined with above-average Intelligence. This is a contour usually associated with a sniper or a spellcaster, but jackalweres' attacks are largely melee-based. This suggests three things. First, jackalweres are shock attackers, not well suited to drawn-out combat, and will abandon a fight quickly if they don't immediately get the upper hand. Second, they rely heavily on guile. And third, the successful use of their Sleep Gaze feature—the closest thing they have to spellcasting—figures prominently in their strategy.

Jackalweres are proficient in Deception and Stealth—here's the guile, as well as a potential way to strike with surprise. They're immune to physical damage from nonmagical, non-silvered weapons, giving them a little more staying power than they'd have otherwise. Since they have only 18 hp to begin with, though, that's not saying a lot. They have the Pack Tactics trait, which suggests that another key part of their strategy is not starting fights at all unless they outnumber their victims substantially. (The *Monster Manual* flavor text notes that they often have ordinary jackals fighting alongside them, but these pose little or no threat to intermediate- or higher-level adventurers.)

Sleep Gaze is weak, as monster features go. All it takes to resist is a DC 10 Wisdom saving throw. The average adventurer has a 60 percent chance of succeeding on that roll; the average cleric, druid, paladin, warlock, or wizard, as well as any gnome, a 75 percent or better chance; and Fey Ancestry makes elves entirely immune to it. But that assumes one jackalwere and one target. Two jackalweres against one target . . . well, that's like giving the target disadvantage on the roll, reducing their chances of success to 36 or 56 percent (elves remain immune). How about three against one? Chances reduced to 22 and 42 percent. Four against one, 13 and 32 percent. (Note, as usual, the careful and highly literal phrasing of the feature: "A creature that successfully saves against the effect is immune to *this* jackalwere's gaze for the next 24 hours"—emphasis mine. Not *any* jackalwere's gaze, just *this* jackalwere's.)

Unlike a lot of monsters, jackalweres are intelligent—crafty, even. They may not be able to judge how experienced a PC is, but they *can* tell whether one is carrying a holy symbol or a staff, and they know that means they'll probably be a harder target. They also know that gnomes are resistant to their special ability and that elves are immune to it.

Their goal is to end the fight in the first round if they can. Thus, for jackalweres to initiate an encounter, their numbers must total the following: three per elf (to kill them), four per gnome or non-elf who displays a holy symbol or wields a staff (to overwhelm their resistance to Sleep Gaze), and two per other non-gnome/non-elf (ditto).

As an example, let's look at a six-character party I ran a campaign for. It consisted of a human barbarian, a halfling ranger/rogue, a dwarf ranger, a human paladin, an elf sorcerer, and a dwarf druid. A pack of jackalweres would have to number at least seventeen to be willing to attack this party. Two of them would use Sleep Gaze against the barbarian, two against the halfling, two against the dwarf ranger, four against the paladin, and four against the druid; the remaining three would draw scimitars and attack the elf sorcerer directly, using Pack Tactics to gain advantage on their attack rolls.

That's in the first round of combat. In the second, Sleep Gaze won't work anymore, because any foe who's still awake will have saved successfully against each of their assailants. On the other hand, any victims of the jackalweres who haven't been put to sleep will be greatly outnumbered, and all the attacking jackalweres will gain advantage from Pack Tactics. If a third round of combat isn't enough for them to subdue all their foes, they'll all Disengage and run away in the fourth round.

"Jackalweres kidnap humanoids for their lamia masters," the flavor text informs us. "A jackalwere's magical gaze renders a foe unconscious, allowing the monster to bind a creature or drag it away." What if a pack of jackalweres aren't working for a lamia? They're gonna eat you, son. They're chaotic evil. Once a target is unconscious, jackalweres lower their blades and switch to Bite attacks—which do critical damage against unconscious targets.

Because jackalweres won't fight without an overwhelming numerical advantage, think very carefully about pitting low-level PCs against them if they're hunting independently (as opposed to seeking captives for a boss lamia). Up to about level 4, any number of jackalweres willing to tangle with your PCs will be too many for them to handle. The sweet spot at which they'll be an appropriate challenge for your PCs is level 5. At level 6 or 7, they'll be a serious threat only as minions fighting alongside a lamia. At level 8 or above, you can safely play them for comedy.

An individual jackalwere that's seriously injured (reduced to 7 hp or fewer) will first Disengage, then Dash away. If at least half of a jackalwere pack has fled or been slain, the rest Dash away without bothering to Disengage. If a party of adventurers initiates combat against them—most likely, by catching them off guard—and they lack the numbers they'd need to start a fight themselves, they don't stand their ground. Instead, they immediately Dash and flee.

DROW

The basic **drow** in the *Monster Manual* is stronger, across the board, than a non-player character commoner with drow racial traits applied. So let's say that this drow is something more akin to a drow guard—a trained, regular fighter or scout.

Dexterity is the drow's highest stat, followed by Charisma. Its Strength and Constitution are average, its Intelligence and Wisdom only marginally higher (not enough even to get a plus to their modifiers). This is the profile of a sniper. Drow are armed with both shortswords (thrusting weapons akin to an ancient Greek *xiphos*) and hand crossbows, but their lower Constitution relative to their Dexterity strongly suggests a preference for the ranged weapon over the melee weapon. They have proficiency in Stealth, marking them as ambush fighters.

They also have the innate ability to cast *dancing lights* at will and *darkness* and *faerie fire* once per day each. The combination of double-range darkvision and Sunlight Sensitivity implies a creature that not only gets around well in darkness but is averse to light, so why would a drow want to cast *dancing lights* or *faerie fire*?

The answer is that the ideal illumination for a creature with darkvision isn't total darkness but rather dim light (if it really preferred total darkness, it would have blindsight). *Dancing lights* and *faerie fire* shed dim light, not bright light, which is perfect.

Meanwhile, *darkness* fills a 15-foot-radius sphere (engulfing three creatures on average, again per the Targets in Area of Effect table) with magical darkness that blinds even creatures with darkvision. Only magical light can penetrate it, but it has to be magical light shed by a spell of 3rd level or higher. The drow's *dancing lights* and *faerie fire* aren't enough: The *darkness* will swallow them up. This spell seems to be useful only as a way of temporarily debilitating enemies, particularly spellcasters who need to be able to see their targets.

Drow never fight aboveground in daylight. Only in the rarest instances—and out of necessity—do they venture aboveground in daylight at all.

All drow stat blocks include some form of poison. In the basic drow stat block, this poison requires a DC 13 Constitution save and imposes the poisoned condition, along with the unconscious condition if the target fails their saving throw by 5 or more. Referring to "Poisons" in chapter 8 of the *Dungeon Master's Guide*, this is "drow poison," which the drow manufacture themselves, so it stands to reason that they'd use it routinely. The drow's hand crossbow bolts are poisoned, but the shortsword isn't—yet another reason to assume they prefer sniping over melee.

Incidentally, since dwarves are resistant to poison (and also happen to be their number one competitors for the best underground real estate), it stands to reason that drow would find dwarves' presence particularly irritating, possibly enough to focus their attacks on them.

So here's our profile of drow combat: They patrol their caverns in darkness, using Stealth. They can detect enemies up to 120 feet away. When enemies come near, they fan out and Hide. When the player characters wander into their midst, one drow in the patrol (or two, if one isn't enough) casts *faerie fire* to illuminate the interlopers, whereupon the rest attack with surprise, using their poisoned hand crossbows, and paying special attention to any dwarf in the party. Between the subterranean darkness and the drow poison, once the PCs get their chance to act in the subsequent round, many of them will have disadvantage on their attack rolls, while the drow will have advantage—an advantage they'll retain even if the PCs fire up torches, lanterns, or *light* spells, thanks to *faerie fire*.

Being accustomed to underground combat, the drow will notice when one of their targets is trying to hide, and if that target isn't already lit up with *faerie fire*, the nearest drow will cast *dancing lights* to "chase" that PC with dim light, so that the drow don't suffer disadvantage on their Perception checks to contest the character's Stealth. Because the spell creates four independently movable lights, the pursuit doesn't have to be exact, and the drow can illuminate a wide swath around wherever the PC is likely to be hiding. On the flip side, if a spellcaster is causing persistent problems for the drow, and it's far enough away from the non-spellcasting PCs, the nearest one will drop a *darkness* sphere on it.

Drow may or may not take prisoners, but they are absolutely unwilling to *be taken* prisoner. Most will fight to the death, some will Dash away if seriously wounded (reduced to 6 hp or fewer), but none will ever surrender.

The **drow elite warrior** differs from the regular drow in four respects. First, its stats (except for Intelligence and Charisma) are higher, with above-average Strength, Constitution, and Wisdom and exceptional Dexterity. Second, it can cast *levitate* on itself once per day. Third, it's a more proficient melee fighter, with Multiattack (not usable with its crossbow because of the weapon's reload time) and Parry; also, its shortsword does poison damage on top of its piercing damage, for a painful total of 4d6 + 4 damage on every hit. Fourth, it has bonuses on *all* of the "big three" saving throws—Dexterity, Constitution, and Wisdom—suggesting that it laughs in the face of magic-wielding foes.

When a drow patrol ambushes a party of trespassers, it will undoubtedly become apparent to the drow that one or more of those trespassers are going to pose a particular problem; dealing with this problem is the drow elite warrior's job. For this reason, while the regular drow launch their surprise attack, the drow elite warrior positions itself between the crossbowmen and any PC who might charge them, so that the PC will incur an opportunity attack if they keep going. The drow elite warrior then engages this PC in melee, Parrying an attack roll of 18 to 20. If another PC joins the melee against the drow elite warrior, it Dodges while its regular drow allies focus their attacks on whichever of the drow elite warrior's melee opponents seems like the greatest threat, at least until it's moderately wounded (reduced to 49 hp or fewer) or all its opponents are poisoned or blinded. At that point, it stops playing games and starts attacking again.

A unit consisting entirely of drow elite warriors will stage an ambush in the same fashion as regular drow, except that they'll all attack with their crossbows in the surprise round (minus the one who casts *faerie fire*, of course). Then, in the following rounds, any warrior that's succeeded in poisoning its target (or is attacking a dwarf, since they're going to be too hard to poison) rushes in and Multiattacks with its shortsword to finish them off. One or more warriors may also use *levitate* to stage their ambush from above, although the one that casts *faerie fire* can't do this, because both spells require concentration.

Drow elite warriors are disciplined fighters that will serve as a rearguard to allow regular drow to escape and won't stop fighting as long as they have regular drow allies fighting alongside them. If they have no regular drow allies and are seriously wounded (reduced to 28 hp or fewer), they'll Disengage and retreat, except for the last, who'll always fight to the death.

Analyzing the tactics of the **drow mage** requires looking at all the different spells it can cast, but before I do that, I want to examine two other aspects of the drow mage stat block: Its Staff attack and its Summon Demon ability.

The staff is poisoned, of course, but it's evidently a different kind of poison from the one used on the basic drow's and drow elite warrior's crossbow bolts. This one doesn't impose any debilitating condition or require a saving throw; it just does a bit of damage of the poison type, like the poison on the drow elite warrior's shortsword, only less of it. Probably, this is to compensate for the fact that the drow mage has Strength 9 (and therefore a –1 modifier to its damage) and shouldn't be hitting people with a staff to begin with. Any drow mage that's engaging in melee combat is either desperate or delusional.

With the Summon Demon feature, the drow mage has either a 100 percent chance to summon a quasit (CR 1) or a 50 percent chance to summon a shadow demon (CR 4). This may seem like a bizarre choice to have to make: whether or not to use an action (which the drow mage only gets to take once) that has a fifty-fifty chance of failing entirely. But in fact, we make this kind of choice all the time when we cast a spell that requires a saving throw to resist its effects, such as *hold person*. In this case, the effect is that the drow mage gets to have a shadow demon hanging around for 10 minutes. Alternatively, the drow mage can go for the sure thing with the quasit, but how badly does a CR 7 drow mage need the assistance of a CR 1 fiend?

The quasit can attack once per turn, doing 1d4 + 3 piercing damage, plus a possible 2d4 poison damage if the target fails a DC 10 Constitution saving throw. DC 10 isn't very high, so let's say the target has a 70 percent chance of making that saving throw, for an expected 4 poison damage on a hit. That plus the piercing damage adds up to 9, and if the quasit has a 50 percent chance of hitting, we're looking at an expected 4 damage per turn. (There are also chances of imposing the poisoned and frightened conditions, but right now, we'll just look at how much damage the little stinker can do.)

The shadow demon can also attack once per turn; plus, it can Hide as a bonus action. Let's assume that the average PC has passive Perception 13. The shadow demon's Stealth is +7; this means it has a 75 percent chance to Hide successfully. The shadow demon does different damage depending on whether or not it attacks with advantage, and a hidden attacker has advantage on its attack roll. If the quasit, with +4 to hit, has a 50 percent chance of hitting, then an unhidden shadow demon, with +5 to hit, has a 55 percent chance; with advantage, this chance increases to 80 percent. Therefore we have two cases: a 75 percent chance that the shadow demon Hides successfully and Attacks with an 80 percent chance to hit for 4d6 + 3 psychic damage; and a 25 percent chance that it fails to Hide and Attacks with a 55 percent chance to hit for 2d6 + 3 psychic damage. Altogether, the expected damage per round is 12.

A guaranteed 4 damage per round, or a 50 percent chance of 12 damage per round? According to math, we should choose the latter. Shadow demon it is!

Whew. Okay. Now on to the spells:

- *Cloudkill* continues the poison theme that recurs whenever we talk about drow. It's a sustained, area-effect spell that hits the PCs' back line the hardest, doing 5d8 poison damage on a failed Constitution saving throw and half that on a successful one every turn the PCs are in it—an expected 17 damage per round each PC spends in the cloud, assuming a fifty-fifty chance of making the save. If you figure that the cloud engulfs four PCs (based on the Targets in Area of Effect table) and that one will spend one round in the cloud, one will spend two, one will spend three, and one will spend four, this is an expected 42 damage per PC altogether—assuming that the cloud fills the room, so that they can't get out of it. If the room is larger than the cloud, you have to assume that all the PCs will get out of the cloud as fast as they can, so most will take only one round's worth of damage.

- *Evard's black tentacles* grabs PCs who flunk their Dex saves and whomps them for 3d6 bludgeoning damage each turn. With a 50 percent chance of making the initial saving throw and of breaking free each subsequent turn, this works out to a total expected 10 damage per target in the area of effect. Plus, there's the nice bonus of restraining the PCs so that they can't fight back. On the downside, it's not boostable.

- *Greater invisibility* is the Get out of Danger Free card. The drow mage always keeps one 4th-level spell slot in reserve for this spell, if it doesn't cast it right away.
- *Fly* is less useful underground than it is aboveground, but in a large cavern, it might allow the drow mage to engage in aerial assault, provided it isn't concentrating on another sustained spell, such as *cloudkill*. Also, when transitioning from *fly* to *greater invisibility*, make sure you have a solid surface supporting the mage before dropping the former spell, or there may be complications.
- *Lightning bolt* does 8d6 raw damage on a failed Dexterity saving throw, half that on a success, or an expected 21 per target. If cast using a 4th-level spell slot, it does 9d6, for an expected 24 per target; using a 5th-level spell slot, it does 10d6, for an expected 26 per target.
- *Alter self*'s Natural Weapons option doesn't give the drow mage anything it doesn't already get from its staff, except a 5 percentage point greater chance to hit. Thus, the drow mage uses this spell only *before* combat begins, as a form of disguise (consistent with its proficiency in Deception), and it drops it as soon as combat begins so as to be able to cast other sustained spells.
- *Misty step* is the only spell that grants the drow mage a bonus action. It can use this spell in combination with a damaging cantrip (see below).
- *Web* does no damage but can restrain several PCs, giving the drow mage and its allies a leg up on them while they struggle to get free (which will probably take only one round, maybe two).
- *Mage armor* is probably the second thing the drow mage puts on when it gets out of bed, if not the first thing. Assume that it's always up and running and, accordingly, that the drow mage is down one 1st-level spell slot at the start of combat.
- *Magic missile* does 1d4 + 1 force damage with every dart and always hits. At base level, it hurls three darts, and it hurls an additional dart for each extra spell level. Thus, it does expected

damage of 10 when cast at 1st level, 14 at 2nd level, 18 at 3rd level, 21 at 4th level, and 24 at 5th level.

- *Shield* is cast as a reaction. The drow mage pops it whenever an attacker rolls between 15 and 19 to hit or targets it with *magic missile*.
- *Witch bolt* requires a ranged spell attack, and the drow mage has a good attack modifier for that (+6); it's probably more likely to hit with this spell than with *lightning bolt*. However, it does only 1d12 lightning damage per round, and that's assuming that it hits. To be assured of exceeding the damage of a single *lightning bolt*, the drow mage would have to sustain *witch bolt* for six rounds, taking no other action all the while. Of course, that's if it casts *witch bolt* at 1st level. Using a 2nd-level spell slot, the drow mage can do 2d12 lightning damage per round, for expected damage of 8 per round; using a 3rd-level slot, 3d12 damage, or 12 per round; using a 4th-level slot, 16 per round; and using a 5th-level slot, 20 per round. While it doesn't do as much damage as *magic missile* (and *magic missile* doesn't do a lot to begin with), it does have the advantage of being a damage hose that costs only a single spell slot to turn on. However, it also has the disadvantage of reaching only 30 feet, and there are better things to do with higher-level spell slots than use them to boost a 1st-level spell.
- *Poison spray* does 2d12 poison damage on a failed Constitution saving throw—a less-than-generous 6 expected damage—with a range of only 10 feet. But hey, it's just a cantrip.
- *Ray of frost* does 2d8 cold damage on a successful ranged spell attack, for 6 expected damage—*and* a reduction of 10 feet of movement speed. As a cantrip to pair with *misty step*, *ray of frost* beats *poison spray*, even if *poison spray* is more thematically appropriate for drow.

Compared with the various spells the drow mage can cast, Summon Demon seems below-average, but its value lies in what it adds to the drow mage's action economy: an independent damage-dealing agent that doesn't consume any of the drow mage's actions. Therefore, attempting to summon a shadow demon is always the first thing the drow mage will do. (Besides, if the summoning's going to fail, that's something you want to find out sooner rather than later.)

Once either the demon is summoned or the summoning has fizzled, the drow mage must decide whether to cast *cloudkill* or *greater invisibility*, its two best concentration-required spells. This call depends on two things: whether the room is small enough that it can trap the PCs within the poison cloud; and whether the PCs look like they can do a lot of damage, or there are more than six of them. One thing to note is that the drow mage doesn't have *counterspell*, so taking out enemy spellcasters quickly is crucial. Since they're most likely to be in the back line, which *cloudkill* will hit the hardest, the drow mage casts this spell if all three of the following conditions apply:

- There are at least two identifiable spellcasters in the party who aren't dwarves.
- The room is small enough to trap the PCs within the cloud, or at least the PCs are close enough together for the cloud to engulf at least the two non-dwarf spellcasters.
- The drow mage has an escape route that doesn't involve moving through the cloud.

Otherwise, it casts *greater invisibility*.

If it does cast *cloudkill*, the drow mage sustains it for up to three more rounds. As long as there's still a non-dwarf PC in the cloud, the drow mage keeps the *cloudkill* spell going. The drow mage always casts *cloudkill* at a point 20 feet away from itself—just far enough that the cloud doesn't reach it.

Once either *cloudkill* or *greater invisibility* is in effect, the drow mage starts targeting other enemies. Since it has *shield* but not *counterspell*, it's more concerned with eliminating enemy spellcasters than melee fighters or archers. If the drow mage is invisible, it maneuvers to a position where it can line up a shot at two or more PCs, at least one of whom is a spellcaster, and fire a *lightning bolt* at them, using the highest available spell slot. (If the drow mage cast *cloudkill*, it still keeps a 4th-level slot in reserve in case it needs to cast *greater invisibility* later; if it cast *greater invisibility*, it doesn't need to reserve the slot anymore.) Once it's out of slots for *lightning bolt*, it switches to *magic missile*.

If the drow mage isn't invisible or maintaining *cloudkill*, it casts *Evard's black tentacles* where it can trap the party's melee fighters, then completes its move to get as far from the party's melee fighters as it can. If a melee opponent has managed to close with the drow mage, it casts *misty step* (bonus action) to slip out of reach, then plinks the opponent with *ray of frost* (action). (It uses *ray of frost* second, rather than first, to avoid the disadvantage that comes with making a ranged attack at point-blank distance.) If all melee fighters have escaped from *Evard's black tentacles*, it tries to restrain them again with *web*.

Incidentally, while all this is going on, the shadow demon—which is immune to poison—is drifting through the back line, doing insensitive things to the enemy spellcasters. Once the spellcasters are down, it moves on to ranged fighters, then melee fighters.

The drow mage is fond of its skin. If it takes just moderate damage (reduced to 31 hp or fewer), it will already be thinking about retreating; if it's seriously wounded (reduced to 18 hp or fewer), it doesn't waste any more time thinking about it. Whether a moderately wounded drow mage skedaddles or not depends on whether it thinks its opponents can deal it another moderate wound (14 hp damage or more) in the upcoming round. If it thinks they can't, it keeps fighting for at least one more round, dropping *darkness* on any enemy spellcaster still standing as long as there's no melee attacker that it needs to *misty step* away from. If it thinks they can, it retreats, leaving the shadow demon behind (if one is present) as a rearguard.

The variations on the drow are capped off by a high-challenge spellcasting variant, the **drow priestess of Lolth**. The priestess's physical ability scores are unexceptional, although her Constitution is slightly higher than that of a regular drow, making her less exclusively a sniper and more willing and able to get scrappy. However, her mental ability scores are all high, especially Wisdom and Charisma. She's distinguished first by her spellcasting ability, second by her Summon

Demon ability (which, oddly, is less reliable than that of the drow mage), and third by her use of a melee weapon, a poisoned scourge.

The drow priestess's Summon Demon ability doesn't offer the choice between a consistent, lower-power version and a chancier, higher-power version. It offers only one version, which summons a CR 10 yochlol, has only a 30 percent chance of success, and deals 1d10 of psychic damage to the priestess if it fails. The drow mage's summonable demons were low- and medium-challenge fiends, but the yochlol is powerful—*more* powerful, in fact, than the priestess trying to summon it. The question is whether this gamble is worth spending an entire combat action on. The drow priestess has 71 hp, no more than the drow elite warrior. Her chief strength lies in her spellcasting, and spellcasting takes time.

Here are three possible reasons why the drow priestess might choose to try to summon a yochlol anyway: First, assuming that a +6 attack modifier gives a roughly 60 percent chance to hit, it does an expected 16 damage per round without costing the priestess a single action. Second, it can cast *dominate person* once per day and *web* at will. Third, it has 136 hp, allowing it to act as a rearguard to cover the priestess's escape.

Given that the chance of a successful summoning is only 30 percent, we have to calculate that it will take four or more rounds of combat *after* the summoning for it to pay off in full. Does the priestess have enough resources at her disposal to last that long before retreating? Not if the PCs can do 15 or more damage to her each round.

Let's see what spells she has at her disposal to keep that from happening:

- *Insect plague* fills a 20-foot-radius sphere with biting insects that do 4d10 damage on a failed Constitution saving throw and half that on a success (an expected 11 damage per target per round). This can put a real hurt on a party with a lot of squishy characters in it, but it requires concentration.
- *Mass cure wounds* lets her restore 3d8 + 3 hp each (16 hp on average) to up to six creatures in a 30-foot-radius sphere, including herself. That'll keep a fight going.

- *Divination* is irrelevant in combat.
- *Freedom of movement* is defensively useful but also highly situational—too much so for her to cast it prophylactically, especially since it lasts only an hour.
- *Conjure animals* brings two CR 1 giant spiders into the fray—more independent damage-dealing allies for the priestess, each of which deals an expected 8 damage per round and can trap the PCs in webs. This may be just as good as trying to summon the yochlol, and it certainly presents itself as plan B if the summoning fails. However, it also requires concentration.
- *Dispel magic* is handy for removing buffs and nerfs, but it does no damage on its own, so it's really useful only if the priestess has allies fighting alongside her.
- *Lesser restoration* lets her shake off blindness, deafness, paralysis, or poison. Frankly, these seem like conditions she's more likely to be inflicting than suffering.
- *Protection from poison*: Ditto.
- *Web* is good for restraining several PCs, then subjecting them to melee and ranged attacks and spells that require Dexterity saving throws to resist. The yochlol's melee attacks are great, but how many Dex-save spells have we seen so far?
- *Animal friendship*—seriously? Aside from negotiating an under-the-table truce with a ranger's beast companion, this spell offers nothing.
- *Cure wounds* is a last-ditch time buyer that in all likelihood will undo no more than a single round's worth of damage.
- *Detect poison and disease*—"Oh, look, I have those right here in my pocket."
- *Ray of sickness*—finally, another spell that makes sense! A solid chance of dealing 2d8 poison damage (approximate expected damage: 5) and imposing the poisoned condition, giving the enemy disadvantage on both its attack rolls and its ability checks to escape a web. Also boostable, doing approximately 3 more expected damage for each level it's boosted by: At 4th level, its expected damage is 14. Against a restrained foe, the

expected damage is increased by 40 percent, thanks to having advantage on the attack roll.

- *Guidance* and *resistance* require concentration and don't compare favorably to the priestess's other spells that require concentration.
- *Poison spray* does 2d12 poison damage on a failed Constitution saving throw, nothing on a success. It's a cantrip and therefore no worse than a melee weapon attack, which can miss. But the drow priestess's actual melee weapon attack is more impressive, thanks to its poison damage, and she gets two attacks with it per round. The only advantage poison spray has over the scourge is that it can be thrown from 10 feet away.
- *Spare the dying* sounds exactly like something a drow would do. Or not.
- *Thaumaturgy*: Smoke and mirrors; useful before the battle, not during.

On top of these, she has the same innate spellcasting abilities as other drow: *dancing lights*, *darkness*, *faerie fire*, and *levitate*. Unfortunately, she doesn't really have the time or the concentration available to use them.

You know what's missing here? Bonus actions. Many other clerical spellcasters can bolster their action economy with *spiritual weapon*; not the drow priestess of Lolth. She has to get by with a little help from her friends, and by "friends," I mean shapeshifting demons and giant spiders.

Before I get into nuts-and-bolts tactics, I want to call attention to her skills, specifically two: Insight and Stealth. Let's stipulate that ambuscade is a way of life among the drow. Whenever any kind of drow, from the lowliest commoner to the highest priestess, perceives the presence of an unknown creature, its instinctual reflex is to hide, observe, and if the creature turns out to be a trespasser, attack with surprise. The difference with the drow priestess of Lolth is that if her observation tells her that the trespasser poses a substantial threat—or, alternatively, *no* threat at all—she'll parley.

This is important because she's as strong in social interaction as she is in combat, if not stronger. Her Insight proficiency gives her an understanding of what the PCs want and are motivated by, which in turn gives her bargaining power. Her high Wisdom makes her hard to deceive; her high Charisma makes her a savvy negotiator. Note well: Even without proficiency in Persuasion, Intimidation, or Deception, her modifier in those skills is +4, just because of her Charisma. Any and all interaction with a drow priestess of Lolth should be slippery and treacherous; players should always have the feeling that they're being outmaneuvered. On a successful Insight contest, she'll zero right in on the PCs' psychological Achilles' heels—pity, ego, insecurity, curiosity, greed, grandiosity, complaisance, scruples—and present credible-sounding reasons why they should forget about what they came there for and do things that serve her interests instead.

As soon as the PCs balk, she calls that demon. If that doesn't work, then it's either *insect plague* or *conjure animals*, depending on whether there are at least four non-fighter (non-barbarian, non-paladin, non-ranger) PCs within 40 feet of one another. If so, *insect plague* on those PCs, which she sustains for as long as there are at least two PCs in the swarm; if not, *conjure animals*. If she does succeed in summoning the yochlol demon, she casts one or the other of these spells the following round. Also, if she casts *insect plague*, then drops it, she immediately casts *conjure animals* next.

Once she's got a sustained spell up and running, the next goal is to restrain as many enemies as she can. If she has giant spider allies, this means they spin webs, which they keep doing as long as there are enemies who aren't webbed (and as long as this ability is available to them, since it requires recharge). Then the priestess aims *ray of sickness* at those trapped, prioritizing those who are most likely to break free, and boosting it to 4th level because her 4th-level spells are largely useless. Once she's out of 4th-level spell slots, she switches to melee weapon attacks against webbed opponents, resorting to 1st-level *ray of sickness* against unwebbed opponents who are out of melee range but are headed her way.

Meanwhile, if the yochlol is on the scene, it picks out the PC with the highest Strength-to-Wisdom ratio and busts out *dominate person* on it, giving the drow priestess her final ally in the fight (or not, if the PC succeeds on their saving throw). If that fails, it casts *web* on any unrestrained PC—favoring melee fighters first—then goes to town on them with melee attacks. It changes into Mist Form only if the PCs flee into an enclosed area and close the door behind them or something like that.

The drow priestess of Lolth has high Wisdom and a respectable career, which argues for a strong self-preservation impulse—but she's also a fanatic, which argues for fighting to the death. Like advantage and disadvantage, these cancel each other out, and her flight reflex kicks in when she's seriously injured (reduced to 28 hp or fewer). She Disengages and retreats if she has allies to run interference for her; otherwise, she Dashes, potentially incurring one or more opportunity attacks.

Incidentally, all this assumes that the drow priestess is encountered on her own. It's more likely, though, that she'll be accompanied by a drow elite warrior bodyguard, at the very least, and possibly a full honor guard of four to six. When this is the case, she'll place more emphasis on casting control spells so that the elite warriors can do the melee fighting against restrained opponents and less on engaging in melee herself.

DUERGAR

Duergar's ability scores follow an unambiguous brute profile, their Duergar Resilience and Sunlight Sensitivity traits are passive, and they're armed with ordinary melee and ranged weapons. Generally speaking, their "tactics" are going to consist of charging, bashing, and stabbing. The only questions are when to use Enlarge and when to use Invisibility.

Enlarge increases the duergar's size, Strength (not numerically, but in the form of advantage on ability checks and saving throws only, not attack rolls), and damage, at the cost of one round's action. Except in the case of grappling, damage is the only one of these benefits that really counts. Since time is so valuable in fifth edition D&D, we have to calculate whether this benefit is worth the cost.

Let's start with raw damage numbers—assuming hits for the sake of simplicity, because the probability of a successful attack is the same regardless of what weapon the duergar is using or what its current size is. Let's also assume that the duergar is using its higher-damage weapon, the war pick. (You can do the math with the javelin; the conclusion will be the same.)

A hit with a normal-size duergar's war pick does 1d8 + 2 damage, or 6.5 damage on average, which I'm not rounding in this instance, because the half-points are going to accumulate over time. An Enlarged duergar hits for 2d8 + 2 damage, or 11 damage on average.

Here's how it breaks down over the length of a typical combat encounter (rounding accumulated damage half-to-even):

Rds	Normal	Enlarged
1	6	—
2	13	11
3	20	22
4	26	33
5	32	44

Fifth edition D&D assumes that the average combat encounter lasts three rounds, with two to five being typical. Here we see that three rounds is the approximate break-even point, at which Enlarge offers only a slim benefit. If a battle is going to drag on more than three rounds, the benefit of Enlarge is substantial. If it's going to be over quickly, Enlarge works to the duergar's detriment.

How do we know how long a battle is going to last? We don't—and neither does the duergar. We can only make educated guesses based on what we know about encounter building, and the duergar can only use intuition shaped by experience.

Let's consider the possibilities:

- An Easy encounter will be over quickly and decisively in the PCs' favor.

- A Medium encounter will last two to four rounds, with only light to moderate damage to the PCs.
- A Hard encounter will last three to five rounds, and the PCs may take moderate to serious damage.
- A Deadly encounter may last three to five rounds, with some PCs taking serious to fatal damage—or the PCs may get clobbered quickly. We're going to have to distinguish between "Deadly" and "Super-Deadly."

In an Easy encounter for the PCs, the duergar gets no benefit from Enlarging—and also has no hope of winning. This is where the duergar falls back on Invisibility. A duergar has only average Wisdom, but that's enough to know when it's badly outmatched and ought to flee.

A Medium encounter is harder to judge, but there's still only about a fifty-fifty chance that Enlarging will be of any significant help to the duergar. In this instance, it may recognize its predicament immediately, use Invisibility, and flee; otherwise, it will use Enlarge, *then* realize its mistake, use Invisibility, and flee.

A Hard or Deadly (not Super-Deadly) encounter is likely to drag on, and in this case, the benefit of Enlarge is indisputable. The duergar uses this feature in the first round of this encounter—earlier, if it can, but don't cheat and throw an already Enlarged duergar at your PCs if the duergar would have no reason to expect a fight. A duergar only turns invisible and flees if and when it's seriously wounded (reduced to 10 hp or fewer).

A Super-Deadly encounter is likely to be over relatively quickly, *and* the duergar is favored to win it. In this instance, it doesn't need to flee, and it doesn't need any greater advantage than it's already got. So it will fight at its normal size.

I've been referring to singular duergar here, but the same rules apply if they're attacking (or defending) in the plural. Use the "Encounter Building" rules in chapter 3 of the *Dungeon Master's Guide* to determine each encounter's difficulty and the reaction of your duergar to it, which may differ from encounter to encounter.

But wait, you may be asking, doesn't the difficulty of fighting a duergar differ depending on whether it's fighting normal-size or Enlarged? Won't that affect the challenge rating, and therefore the difficulty of the encounter?

Not really. The reason is, the duergar only fights at normal size when it's got an overwhelming advantage. Otherwise, if it's going to stick around and fight, it does so while Enlarged, and its CR assumes Enlarged damage.

Anyway, the long and the short of it is, you don't have to think about duergar tactics on the fly. All you have to do is figure out the difficulty of each duergar encounter beforehand, so that you know how the duergar will react to the PCs: vanish and run, Enlarge and charge, or simply charge.

QUAGGOTHS

The **quaggoth** is a creature of contradictions. Its *Monster Manual* illustration suggests a malevolent cunning belied by the low Intelligence score in its stat block; its brutality is curiously juxtaposed with chaotic neutral alignment; its history since its debut in the AD&D *Fiend Folio* is that of a servitor species, the only such species among the humanoid monsters of fifth edition.

So what's the deal with these guys, and why are they associated with the mostly neutral evil drow? According to current lore, they used to live aboveground as forest dwellers but were driven underground by surface elves; the subterranean drow harnessed their abiding resentment to make minions of them. Being chaotic neutral, they surely can't be the most reliable help. Ferocious they may be, even obedient after a fashion, but submissive they most certainly aren't. They fight when their territory is under threat, they fight when they're hungry, and if they're being commanded by drow, they fight when they feel like it. They may not always feel like it, though.

Quaggoths have very high Strength and Constitution and no other peak in their ability contour—the usual brute profile. Their Intelligence is on par with that of an ape, but their Wisdom is above average. This makes them instinct-driven and tactically inflexible but shrewd at picking their targets; if they know they're outmatched, and someone in the PCs' party speaks Undercommon, it may be possible to strike some sort of bargain with them. (Their primary interest is in territorial expansion, which the PCs can serve by striking at the quaggoths' nearby rivals.) Their long-range darkvision indicates a primarily subterranean lifestyle, with forays to the surface world taking place only at night. Their climbing movement indicates an affinity for caverns with lots of vertical space and many different levels.

It would be enough for them, as brute melee fighters, simply to launch themselves at a likely-looking target—judging entirely by size and strength, since they lack the Intelligence for more sophisticated assessment of strengths and weaknesses—and rip away with their double-Claw Multiattack. But there are two more oddities in the quaggoth's stat block that require attention.

One is their Wounded Fury trait, which doesn't kick in until they're down to 10 hp or fewer. This is well past the threshold beyond which a typically aggressive monster would retreat to save its own skin (by the reckoning I use throughout this book, 18 hp or fewer). The other is their proficiency in Athletics, which doesn't synergize naturally with any of their other features. How can we make effective use of it?

Well, for starters, Wounded Fury isn't so good that it's worth it for the quaggoth to take hits just to get down to 10 hp. But it does suggest something about *how* quaggoths might retreat when they do retreat. First off, like lizardfolk, they always place themselves between their foes and their territory (unless they're in their territory to begin with). Unlike lizardfolk, however, they don't Dash away home when seriously wounded, nor do they Dodge or Disengage, the other two most common actions to take while retreating. Rather, they remain aggressive even as they're backing off: Still facing their foes, they back up using their full movement and Ready a Claw attack against any enemy that comes within reach. If and when they take enough punishment, Wounded Fury will kick in, giving them advantage on their attack rolls and two more dice of damage on a hit—and, ideally, deterring their pursuers from further pursuit.

As for Athletics, this comes in handy when grappling or shoving. Grappling doesn't offer any real benefit to a quaggoth, but shoving can knock an opponent prone. How many allies have to get attacks against the prone target for this to be worth giving up a quaggoth's own Multiattack? Against a target with AC 15, a quaggoth's Multiattack deals 7 expected damage. With advantage, this increases to 10. Three quaggoths Multiattacking would deal 21 damage plus a fraction, while one shoving and the other two Multiattacking would deal 21 damage minus a fraction. For there to be any real benefit to this maneuver, a group of quaggoths has to outnumber its foes by at least four to one (or be accompanied by other creatures with stronger melee attacks). Ultimately, we have to write off this proficiency as something that helps quaggoths only in a defensive capacity—that is, if an opponent tries to grapple or shove one of them rather than vice versa.

The **quaggoth thonot** is identical to the ordinary quaggoth in every respect but one: It has psionics. These allow it to cast *feather fall* and *mage hand* at will and to cast *cure wounds*, *enlarge/reduce*, *heat metal*, and *mirror image* once per day each.

Of these, the one that immediately leaps out is *enlarge/reduce*, but unlike the duergar's Enlarge ability, the *enlarge/reduce* spell grants only an additional 1d4 to the quaggoth's melee damage. The opportunity cost is simply too high: Combat will have to last at least four rounds for the psionically enlarged quaggoth's attacks to outdamage a quaggoth that Multiattacks in its first round as well as in subsequent rounds, and at least five rounds for it to do so significantly. It's a nice scare tactic, but it doesn't help the quaggoth thonot kill things. As for the *reduce* side of *enlarge/reduce*, because it requires a failed Constitution saving throw, the only foes worth using it on are the ones best equipped to resist it.

Cure wounds returns only 1d8 + 1 hp; by the time they're fighting quaggoths, most PCs reliably deal more damage than that in a round. It also makes it less likely that the quaggoth thonot will take enough damage for Wounded Fury to activate. The latter is also true of *mirror image*, a strangely defensive spell for such an aggressive creature.

The sleeper hit of the quaggoth thonot's psionic repertoire is *heat metal*. First, it deals 2d8 fire damage automatically, which beats the expected damage of Multiattack against any opponent with AC 13 or greater (to a quaggoth, this translates to "wearing armor that looks like armor"). Second, it adds to the quaggoth thonot's action economy by allowing it to deal additional damage as a bonus action. Third, as long as the enemy doesn't doff or drop whatever metal item the thonot is heating, it imposes disadvantage on that enemy's attack rolls and ability checks.

Mage hand has no meaningful combat application; *feather fall* can be situationally useful in the kinds of places where quaggoths like to hang out.

Heat metal, then, is absolutely the quaggoth thonot's first-choice psionic trick. It doesn't even consider *mirror image* unless and until it's moderately wounded (reduced to 31 hp or fewer), it saves *enlarge/reduce* for use as a scare tactic when it's ready to retreat, and it doesn't bother with *cure wounds* until it's already retreated to a safe distance. That being said, however, if *cure wounds* brings it back above 18 hp and it still has allies in the fight, it may well go charging back in.

GITHYANKI

Old-school Advanced Dungeons & Dragons players will remember the githyanki as the poster monster of the *Fiend Folio*, the first supplement to the original *Monster Manual*. (They'll also remember the *Fiend Folio* as the book that gave us the flumph, but let's speak no more of that.) Githyanki aren't native to the world the player characters inhabit but rather travel there from their original home on some other plane of existence, to raid and conquer. They share a common origin with the githzerai.

Githyanki warriors are shock troops, with high Strength and Dexterity. Their Intelligence and Wisdom are also above average. They have innate psionic ability (treated in fifth edition as a form of spellcasting) that grants them at-will telekinesis in the form of the *mage hand* spell along with limited uses of *jump*, *misty step*, and *nondetection*. They have proficiency bonuses to Constitution, Intelligence, and Wisdom saving throws and a melee Multiattack.

What makes githyanki combat interesting is the intersection of their high damage-dealing capacity, low Constitution relative to their Strength and Dexterity (though it's still above human average) and mobility spells. Githyanki should move fast, strike hard, then be somewhere else. The fact that *misty step* is a bonus action rather than a normal action is the key ingredient in this recipe, enabling combinations like the following:

- Move toward an opponent, Multiattack (action), *misty step* (bonus action) past the opponent.
- *Misty step* (bonus action) toward an opponent, Multiattack (action) to finish the opponent off, move.
- Multiattack (action), *misty step* (bonus action), move out of sight.

Jump isn't a bonus action, but it doesn't have to be sustained, either. The effect of one *jump* spell, tripling a subject's jumping distance, lasts a full minute. Jumping isn't one of the best-understood rules, so let's go over what this means:

- A running long jump with a 10-foot head start carries a character their Strength in feet; a standing long jump covers half that distance. A jumping character can also clear an obstacle up to one-fourth the length of the jump in height. Thus, a githyanki warrior with Strength 15 can normally cover 15 feet in a running long jump or 7 feet in a standing long jump. With *jump* in effect, these become 45 feet and 22 feet, with the ability to clear heights of 11 feet and 5 feet respectively. However, within a single combat round, a creature is still constrained by its movement speed, meaning that even under the influence of *jump*, a creature with 30 feet of movement speed can jump no farther than 30 feet during the round without using the Dash action to gain additional movement. If it jumps farther, the movement carries into the next round; in between rounds, it's temporarily airborne.

- A running high jump with a 10-foot head start carries a character their Strength modifier plus 3 feet up in the air; a standing jump reaches half that height. Thus, a githyanki warrior with Strength 15 (modifier +2) can normally jump 5 feet in the air with a running start or 2 feet without one. With *jump* in effect, these become 15 feet and 7 feet, respectively.

When might a githyanki want to use *jump*? In close-quarters fighting, *misty step* offers far more utility. Even in areas with lots of horizontal and vertical space, *misty step* still costs only a bonus action, while *jump* initially consumes a full action, although it doesn't require concentration.

The githyanki's action will normally be a Multiattack, so logically, the time to use *jump* is when the githyanki isn't attacking. This could mean that the githyanki is about to launch an ambush, that the opponents have run away, that the githyanki has just defeated an opponent and is looking for another, or that the githyanki itself is fleeing. Since the effect of *jump* is bounded by a creature's movement speed, it requires a Dash action to gain any tactical advantage over an opponent—for instance, by leaping over and past a fleeing enemy to cut off its escape. The payoff comes on the githyanki's subsequent turn, when it can take an action again.

Githyanki warriors are intelligent and disciplined, and they Disengage when retreating. The least wounded warrior covers others who are retreating and will fight to the death in order to do so. Other githyanki warriors retreat when seriously wounded (reduced to 19 hp or fewer).

Githyanki knights have a more brutelike ability contour, with a Constitution that's higher than their Dexterity. In addition, they have access to one use of *plane shift* and one of *telekinesis*, a more sophisticated form of the ability than *mage hand* offers. With *telekinesis*, a githyanki knight can push or pull a PC up to 30 feet in any direction or even hold them suspended in the air. With *plane shift*, a PC can be transported permanently to another plane of existence, or the githyanki knight and its allies can abscond that way themselves.

In a group consisting of both githyanki knights and githyanki warriors, the knights engage the most formidable melee opponents and keep them occupied; they'll use *misty step* only to intervene if an opponent somewhere else is proving problematic to another githyanki, or after defeating one opponent to close swiftly with another. They also serve as the rearguard to allow their retreating allies to escape, making their own exit with *plane shift* when all their allies have gotten a safe distance away. They use *telekinesis* to hoist a pesky skirmisher up in the air, to shove an enemy off a ledge or into a hazard, to pull an enemy into an ally's melee reach, or to drag a fleeing enemy back to the fight—choosing conservatively, since they get to use this power only once each. They can make a good educated guess about which PCs have Strength or Charisma low enough for *telekinesis* or *plane shift* to work against them, though they can be fooled by appearances.

Githyanki knights don't retreat as long as githyanki warriors are present. When alone or accompanied only by other knights, they *plane shift* away when seriously wounded (reduced to 36 hp or fewer), unless they're duty-bound to guard a location.

Finally, unlike githyanki warriors, githyanki knights have the innate ability to cast *tongues*, meaning if anyone's able to parley with the PCs, it's the knights. They'll do so if given a chance, but they're lawful evil, so their idea of "parley" is going to consist mostly of telling the PCs how it's going to be; they don't care about the PCs' interests and will only indulge negotiation offers that meaningfully further their own.

GITHZERAI

Like their cousins the githyanki, the githzerai are a rigidly disciplined people from another plane of existence. Unlike the warlike githyanki, the githzerai apply their discipline to asceticism and self-defense. Essentially, they're psychic supermonks, bulwarks against chaos.

The **githzerai monk** has modestly above-average Strength and Constitution and high Dexterity, usually the physical ability contour of a sniper; a melee combatant with this profile generally has to use movement, surprise, and bonuses to damage to compensate for its reduced ability to take a hit. Thus, the githzerai monk is a shock attacker, with abilities tailored to taking out enemies with swift melee strikes.

The githzerai monk's Psychic Defense trait lets it add its Wisdom modifier to its Armor Class while unarmored, giving it AC 14. Its Unarmed Strike does 1d8 + 2 bludgeoning damage plus 2d8 psychic damage, and its Multiattack lets it make two such strikes per turn. One blow from the hand of a githzerai monk is like being smacked by a warhammer *and* subjected to a mini–Mind Blast. It's almost as though the sole point of the githzerai monk's powers were to punish foolish players who underestimate them.

Meanwhile, the githzerai monk can cast *shield* three times a day, boosting its AC from 14 to 19 as a reaction each time. Its hit points aren't astronomical, but it can survive awhile simply by not letting itself get hit. Key to this strategy, however, is not letting itself be double-teamed: The more attackers that are aiming blows at it, the more likely one of those blows will get through.

The innate *jump* spell has the same drawback for the githzerai monk as it has for the githyanki warrior: It costs an action, meaning it can't be combined with an attack. *Feather fall*, when you're designing encounters, provides a strong incentive to create vertical spaces in which the monk's opponents are at risk of falling, while the monk needn't worry.

If a githzerai monk is fighting you at all, it's probably got a good enough reason to want to finish the job if it can, but it will Dash away in the fourth round of combat or if it's seriously wounded (reduced to 15 hp or fewer), whichever comes first.

The **githzerai zerth** is a more advanced version of the monk, with higher Constitution (and thus a more skirmishy profile, although it's bereft of skills and features that would allow it to fight as such), even more Unarmed Strike damage, and the spells *phantasmal killer* and *plane shift*, which it can use once per day each.

Phantasmal killer is a surprisingly ineffective ability: At the time of casting, it demands a Wisdom saving throw to avoid the frightened condition, then grants another save, against psychic damage, at the end of the target's turn. Any successful save ends the spell. The spell save DC is 14; figuring an average +3 saving throw modifier, and thus a 50 percent chance of making the save, you can expect a PC to shake this spell off before ever taking any damage. Between its Intelligence 16 and the fact that this is an innate ability, we'll be kind to the zerth and assume it can make shrewd guesses about which of its enemies have Wisdom save modifiers low enough to make the attempt worthwhile—but honestly, I put "worthwhile" at −3, which is what it takes to give the zerth about a two-thirds chance of inflicting a single round's worth of damage.

Plane shift, on the other hand, only has to work once for a githzerai zerth to more or less permanently dispense with an enemy it really wants to see gone, and all it needs to feel good about its chances of success is a Charisma modifier of 0 or less. Alternatively—and more likely, if it's the only zerth in its group—it keeps *plane shift* in reserve for its own escape, with its allies in tow, if things go awry.

Like the githzerai monk, the zerth is most effective in melee against a single opponent. (Its AC is high enough that it *might* be able to handle two attackers at once, but definitely not three.) When it's seriously injured (reduced to 33 hp or fewer), it gives an audible signal and Readies the *plane shift* spell, triggered by its final ally's joining hands with it. If it has allies who are fleeing, it fights as a rearguard to cover their escape, making sure they're free and clear before using *plane shift* to save itself.

NPCs

Many of the humanoids whom player characters will encounter aren't "monsters" at all, just *people*—mundane villagers, townsfolk, warriors, criminals, nomads, vagabonds, and hermits, or arcane specialists with power and influence. With monsters, combat is often an overwhelming likelihood, but NPC encounters offer far more opportunities to address each side's interests through social interaction. The combat tactics described here are for when such talks break down.

Commoners and Nobles

In the fifth edition *Monster Manual*, the basic template for an NPC is the **commoner**. The commoner has all-average attributes, no special skills or features, and no weapon attack except a club, which is interchangeable with any improvised weapon.

The German psychologist Karen Horney (rhymes with "horsefly," not "corny") observed three tendencies in people's behavior: moving toward others, moving against others, and moving away from others. She later called these tendencies compliance, aggression, and withdrawal. In any given personality, one of these will probably be stronger than the other two. So a commoner thrown into a conflict situation might react one of three ways:

- **Fight.** This character reflexively attacks a perceived enemy. The attack won't be sophisticated. The NPC grabs the nearest weapon (improvised, if necessary), moves toward their opponent, and attacks until either the enemy is defeated or the NPC is seriously wounded (reduced to 1 hp) or knocked out. A rare commoner—for instance, a hunter—may know how to use a simple ranged weapon, in which case they attack without moving toward the opponent, but will give limited pursuit to an opponent who tries to escape.

- **Flee.** This character turns and runs. Lacking the training to know to Disengage, they instead Dodge while within an opponent's reach, Dash otherwise, and in either case move at full speed toward the nearest place of perceived safety.
- **Freeze.** In real life, this reaction to danger is surprisingly common. The character neither fights nor flees but stands rooted, paralyzed with fear. If the NPC can gather their wits (say, by succeeding on a DC 15 Wisdom check), they'll form the words necessary to surrender.

Why are you attacking commoners anyway, you naughty PCs? Well, a Dungeon Master may have good reasons for including commoners in an encounter. Maybe the commoners are being attacked by a monster and must be rescued. Maybe they've been charmed by a more powerful foe. Maybe the PCs have been charmed or magically disguised to appear as a threat. Maybe the commoners are xenophobic, and the PCs are foreigners to them. Maybe they're embroiled in a feud with some other commoners.

Nonhuman NPCs may be nudged toward one particular type of behavior based on their ability score modifiers and other racial traits. For instance, a mountain dwarf commoner would have two extra points of Constitution and two extra points of Strength. This nudges them toward the brute category and makes them more likely to fight toe-to-toe; additionally, their slow speed suggests that they'll be less likely to flee. Their Dwarven Combat Training suggests that even untrained mountain dwarf commoners will at least wield handaxes (their simple melee weapon of choice) rather than clubs. Here are tendencies for other races and subraces:

- **Hill dwarves:** Con 12, Wis 11. They take a defensive approach and are somewhat more likely to avoid fighting unless they have the advantage. They wield handaxes—as melee weapons, not as throwing weapons. Like mountain dwarves, hill dwarves are slow and therefore less likely to flee once fighting has begun.

- **High elves:** Dex 12, Int 11, plus cantrips. They snipe at range, using not just shortbows but also damaging cantrips such as *fire bolt* and *ray of frost*.
- **Wood elves:** Dex 12, Wis 11, plus Mask of the Wild. They attack from hiding, hoping to gain advantage and surprise through camouflage, and snipe at range, using shortbows. Being Fleet of Foot, they're more likely to flee if the tide of combat turns against them even a little bit. With luck, they'll have more chances to hide and snipe.
- **Dark elves (drow):** Dex 12, Cha 11, plus Sunlight Sensitivity and Superior Darkvision. They snipe at range, using hand crossbows; are nocturnal and/or subterranean; and will often try to parley—or bluff—their way out of a fight.
- **Lightfoot halflings:** Dex 12, Cha 11, plus Brave. They snipe at range using simple ranged weapons, defend themselves with daggers (the only simple melee weapon with the Finesse property), and will parley (or bluff) if they think it will help. But they're also plucky, more likely to fight than freeze, and unlikely to flee because of their slow speed.
- **Stout halflings:** Dex 12, Con 11, plus Brave. They snipe at range using simple ranged weapons and defend themselves with daggers. They're also more likely to fight and less likely to flee, and they're scrappy fighters if they're engaged in melee and have the numbers to put up a fight.
- **Dragonborn:** Str 12, Cha 11, plus a breath weapon. They choose their battles carefully, avoiding fighting unless they have the advantage, and attack from hiding, leading with their breath weapon and following up with melee attacks using clubs or other improvised weapons. Despite their ancestry and size, they're actually more likely to flee than to fight or freeze.
- **Forest gnomes:** Int 12, Dex 11, plus *minor illusion*. They seek to avoid fighting altogether and use Speak with Small Beasts

to employ forest critters as sentries. Forest gnomes who flee use illusions to cover their escape; forest gnomes who freeze reflexively use illusions to try to disguise themselves as rocks, bushes, tree stumps, or some such thing.

- **Rock gnomes:** Int 12, Con 11, plus Tinker. They seek to avoid fighting and use traps and alarms to warn them of intrusions and to repel or disable the intruder(s).
- **Half-elves:** Cha 12, two other ability scores 11. Aside from being more likely to parley or bluff, half-elves have no specific tendency and are equally likely to fight, flee, or freeze, as humans are.
- **Half-orcs:** Str 12, Con 11, plus Relentless Endurance and Savage Attacks. They almost always fight, hardly ever fleeing or freezing. They favor melee combat, with clubs or improvised weapons.
- **Tieflings:** Cha 12, Int 11, plus Infernal Legacy. Lacking both Strength and numbers, they flee from danger and use *thaumaturgy* to try to frighten off creatures that pose a threat.

The **noble** stat block reflects that even the most useless aristocrat nevertheless has a leg up on a typical commoner by virtue of education, not to mention access to better nutrition. It suggests a measure of swordsmanship training as well as courtly refinement and access to books of philosophy and lore. All three physical statistics are higher than those of a commoner, although not particularly high in the grand scheme of things; this suggests that a noble will be *selectively* brave. That is, a noble will have no fear of a commoner and may consider it their right to give the wretch a thrashing, but faced with, say, an owlbear, they'll promptly remember that discretion is the better part of valor.

Before a noble fights, flees, or freezes in the face of a sentient opponent, they'll try to negotiate—and they'll have a decent sense of whether they're doing so from a position of weakness or strength. Nobles wield rapiers and are proficient with them, but they can also tell when they're outclassed, and they know when and how to Disengage and retreat. The noble's sense of self-preservation is *very* strong, and it only takes being moderately wounded (reduced to 6 or fewer hp) for them to retreat or surrender. They then keep fighting only if given no quarter and no opportunity to escape. The role of honor in the life-or-death decisions of a noble is highly overstated.

GUARDS, THUGS, VETERANS, AND KNIGHTS

Take a commoner who's more physically fit than average, put a spear in their hand, give them some combat training, and you have a **guard**, the first line of defense against player characters who might otherwise run amok through the picturesque towns of your campaign setting.

With their above-average (though not exceptional) physical ability scores, guards are well suited for the simple, direct combat role of "Go ye forth and poke it, then poke it again." That said, they're essentially nothing more than well-trained commoners. Braver than average they are, and more motivated by duty, but this presumes that they're not facing any foe more challenging than another commoner. Throw a monster at them, and they're as likely to flee or freeze as they are to stand and fight.

They know how to use their weapons, but that's not the same as understanding strategy and tactics; their sophistication extends only as far as knowing that a surrounded foe is less likely to get away. If they outnumber their opponents, they'll flank, and if they don't, they'll form a line, circle up with their backs to one another, or send one of their number to run and get more guards. When they're in serious danger—reduced to 4 hp or fewer, or next to another guard who is—their discipline dissolves. They won't run without Disengaging first, however, unless they themselves are the ones seriously wounded. (The difference between their physical abilities and those of a commoner is significant enough that guards will take the direct approach to combat even if commoners of the same race wouldn't.)

Note that guards don't even have proficiency in the Intimidation skill. They can yell "Halt!" but it's more like a suggestion.

A **thug** has Multiattack, Pack Tactics, and a high-Strength, high-Constitution, melee-tailored brute profile. Thugs' standard combat style is to fight as a gang, getting as close as possible to their targets in order to give one another advantage on their attack rolls. Although they carry crossbows, they're not especially cut out for ranged combat (for one thing, their Multiattack won't allow them to reload a crossbow any faster, whereas it does allow them to strike twice per turn with a mace), and being shot at from afar is one of the few things that will make them think twice about a fight. If they can spare the numbers for at least two of them to break off and go after a ranged opponent, they will; but one alone won't, because then that thug would be giving up the Pack Tactics advantage, and they like their fights easy.

A seriously wounded thug (reduced to 12 hp or fewer) will Disengage and retreat, and in the following round that thug's allies will retreat as well, even if they themselves aren't seriously wounded. This in no way means that they consider the fight over. Thugs are available in seemingly infinite supply, and they may show up again looking for a rematch, at any time, in greater numbers than before. (Whatever difficulty the last encounter was, based on the XP Thresholds by Character Level table in chapter 3 of the *Dungeon Master's Guide*, make the next encounter one level more difficult, for as long as it suits your story to keep sending vindictive thugs against your PCs.)

Despite their respectable physical prowess and enthusiasm for fighting, thugs are lazy and would rather get what they want by Intimidation, and this is what they'll try first. After all, if a victim caves now, they're likely to cave again later, and again, and again . . .

A **veteran** is a trained, experienced fighter—a soldier of rank, a captain of the guard, a longtime mercenary, or the like. Schooled in warfare, they do know strategy and tactics and fight accordingly. They fortify their positions; take advantage of terrain, elevation, and choke points; recognize and counter their enemies' plans; seize opportunities to punish their enemies' mistakes; attack weaker fighters and Dodge and Disengage against stronger ones; and parley when their chances of victory look poor, whether or not fighting has begun. A veteran is hardly ever a fanatic; they have no interest in fighting to the death. A serious injury (being reduced to 23 hp or fewer) is enough to convince a veteran that surrender or retreat is the wisest course of action.

Most veterans fight hand-to-hand, either dual-wielding longsword and shortsword or wielding a longsword alone, one-handed with a shield (not mentioned in the *Monster Manual*—with a shield, the veteran's Armor Class is 19, not 17) or two-handed without. However, in any given group of veterans—or a group of guards and/or thugs led by a veteran—up to half may wield crossbows and use these either to attack ranged opponents or to cover the melee fighters as they move. The latter is accomplished using the Ready action, with the trigger condition being an enemy exposing themself to attack a moving melee fighter.

A veteran with a ranged weapon, or a ranged fighter under the command of a veteran, will make maximum use of any available cover; they won't shoot from a position out in the open. Wherever they may be, they're aware of what positions afford maximum combat advantage, place themselves on these positions beforehand, and stay on them for as long as they can hold out. They can't be fooled into leaving such a position to chase an opponent. They remain conscious of their purpose and won't be distracted from it. Also, guards being covered by ranged fighters know better than to move beyond the normal range of those ranged weapons.

One other thing that distinguishes veterans from guards and thugs is their Athletics skill. This has various applications, but the one that stands out to me is its use in grappling: Veterans are good at nonlethally subduing an opponent as well as escaping being grappled themselves. Guards, peculiarly, are not especially well-equipped to seize and restrain someone, but veterans are. Also, veterans may flee in the face of an overwhelming threat, but they never freeze, as a commoner might.

A **knight** is a fighter on par with a veteran, equally skilled at melee fighting, slightly less so with ranged weapons, with the Parry reaction and the Leadership action. The Leadership action is similar to the Battle Cry action of the orc war chief, only instead of granting advantage on attack rolls for 1 turn, it grants an additional 1d4—equivalent to a *bless* spell—on the attack rolls and saving throws of each of its allies within 30 feet for a full minute. Another key difference from

Battle Cry is that Leadership *doesn't* allow the knight to make an attack on the same turn.

To get the most use out of it, the knight uses the Leadership action as soon as combat either is imminent or has already begun; after that, they use the Multiattack action exclusively. The knight has no good reason to forgo the use of Leadership, even at the cost of their own Multiattack action for one round, because its effects are proportional to the duration of combat and the number of troops they command.

As for the Parry reaction, a knight uses it against whichever of their melee opponents (if it has more than one) does the greatest average damage per hit. The knight is familiar enough with a variety of both weaponry and enemies to be able to judge this accurately. For instance, if a knight is being attacked by a paladin with Strength 16 and a longsword (1d8 + 3, average 8 damage per hit) and a barbarian with Strength 18 and a greataxe (1d12 + 4, average 10 damage per hit), they know to let the paladin's blows land and parry the barbarian's. This is a function of experience, not Intelligence.

A knight may be mounted on a warhorse, which in addition to a melee attack with its hooves also has the Trampling Charge feature. A mounted knight always uses this feature, if possible, when first engaging with an enemy.* Since the warhorse has a base movement speed

---

* Technically, under D&D's mounted combat rules, a warhorse may be considered either a controlled mount or an independent mount ("Mounted Combat," *Player's Handbook*, chapter 9), and only an independent mount can attack, which it does on its own turn, not on the rider's. But I see two potential loopholes in this rule.

First, whether the mount is controlled or independent is the rider's choice. A warhorse is a beast trained for combat and knows what it ought to do in a combat situation, and it will defy its rider only if it's badly injured or frightened. Therefore, while acting independently, it can be assumed in most situations to do what its rider would most want it to do.

Second, it stands to reason that because a warhorse is specifically trained for war, and so is the knight, the knight should be able to use a controlled warhorse *as a weapon*. In this circumstance, the warhorse may only Dash, but the rider can make their own attack using the horse's Hooves and Trampling Charge, which is a more damaging attack than the rider's hand weapon.

Whichever way you decide to go, make sure you understand which rule you're applying and how—and remember that the most important rule in the *Dungeon Master's Guide* is in the introduction, in the final paragraph of "The Dungeon Master."

of 60 feet, and the charge only requires a 20-foot head start, a knight already in the thick of combat who defeats an opponent will circle away to get at least 20 feet from their next target, using the Disengage action if necessary, then go back in with Trampling Charge. They then attack the same turn if Disengaging wasn't required or on the next turn if it was.

Bandits and Assassins

The **bandit** stat block isn't the ideal template for your typical back-alley burglar or pickpocket—oddly, the fifth edition *Monster Manual* omits that archetype altogether. At the end of this section, I'll provide a homebrew stat block you can use for that type of NPC. Rather, the *Monster Manual* bandit is more like a highwayman (on land) or a pirate (at sea), and their primary motivation is loot.

The bandit's physical abilities are all modestly above average, with Dexterity and Constitution in the lead: Bandits are scrappy fighters who rely on their numbers. They wield "scimitars," for reasons I can only guess at—maybe this is the closest thing D&D has to a cutlass? Maybe because it treats shortswords as primarily stabbing weapons and thinks bandits ought to carry slashing weapons instead? I don't know. The weapon properties are the same, and the damage is the same except for the type, and if there's any kind of armor or enchantment that resists slashing damage but not piercing damage or vice versa, I haven't found it yet. In any event, you can let the flavor of the setting determine whether your bandits are carrying scimitars, cutlasses, arming swords, baselards, dirks, gladii, or whatever—they all deal 1d6 + 1 damage.

Bandits initiate combat by surrounding their targets in numbers large enough to encourage prompt surrender—three to one, at a bare minimum—and they count on their targets' surrendering readily. Thus, any encounter with a group of bandits *must* be at least a Medium-difficulty encounter and really should be at least Hard (see "Creating a Combat Encounter" in chapter 3 of the *Dungeon Master's Guide*); otherwise the bandits would have moved on in search of easier prey already. They surround their targets at a range of 40 to 80 feet, light crossbows at the ready, and issue their demands. (They have neither Intimidation nor Persuasion skill—they rely on their weapons and their numbers to do the convincing for them.) If the PCs refuse, they hold their positions, attacking at range, until the PCs come to them, at which point they switch to their blades.

A bandit who takes any wound at all will Dodge (not Disengage) and relocate to the side of the nearest fellow bandit, in the hope that two might be able to beat an enemy whom one alone can't. It takes only a moderate wound (reducing the bandit to 7 hp or fewer) to give a bandit the idea that these folks aren't the pushovers they're supposed to be; if half or more of a group of bandits are moderately wounded, they'll Disengage and retreat. Any single bandit who's seriously wounded (reduced to 4 hp or fewer) runs away using the Dash action, potentially incurring one or more opportunity attacks. On the flip side, if combat goes poorly for the PCs and they surrender, the bandits will happily rob them of all their valuables and bid them adieu . . . although if there's a PC of noble background in the party, they may take that PC captive and hold them for ransom!

The **bandit captain** is distinguished from an ordinary bandit by higher physical abilities (this time, Dexterity and Strength take the lead over Constitution), high Intelligence and Charisma, proficiency in Athletics and Deception, a Multiattack action, and a Parry reaction. A bandit captain will go beyond issuing a simple "stand and deliver" demand—they'll engage in actual negotiation. For instance, if it looks like it would be a challenge to make the PCs give up *all* their valuables, the bandit captain may suggest that for the modest price of 10 gold pieces per PC, neither side has to go to the trouble of seeing who really is tougher. Of course, bandit captains also have no compunction about lying through their teeth.

The bandit captain lacks proficiency in Insight and thus has no particular talent for reading PCs' motivations, but they can make some educated guesses based on appearances and fabricate a story accordingly. If the PCs are predominantly folk heroes and outlanders, the bandit captain may claim that their band of brigands are righteous rebels resisting a tyrannical aristocracy. If the PCs are softhearted acolytes or gullible nobles, the bandit captain may say that poverty has driven them to banditry out of necessity. If the PCs are mostly charlatans, criminals, or urchins, the bandit captain may drop all pretense and say it's all in the game, yo—or even recruit the PCs to join their outlaw band! These stories may be true, false, or some of both, but it doesn't matter one way or the other: All the bandit captain is interested in is getting loot out of the PCs by the easiest means possible. And if the PCs balk? "Well, then, I guess we're going to have to do this the hard way."

The bandit captain as described in the *Monster Manual* carries no ranged weapon except for throwable daggers. Since they can dual-wield a dagger alongside a scimitar (cutlass, arming sword, baselard, dirk, gladius, etc.), they'll generally prefer to do this rather than stand back and throw them, especially when surrounded by bandits with light crossbows that do more damage. Plus, the bandit captain's leading abilities are Dexterity and Strength, so they're going to go for swift strikes and big damage, which means the Multiattack action with two Scimitar attacks and one Dagger attack. Finally, the bandit captain can Parry one melee attack per turn, and like the knight, they can judge which of multiple melee opponents poses the greatest danger and therefore most needs to be parried.

The bandit captain has a generous number of hit points (ten hit dice, compared with an ordinary bandit's two) and doesn't mind being the focus of more than one PC's attacks: If double- or triple-teamed, they'll Dodge (action) and Parry (reaction) and let their bandit crossbowmen take potshots at the PCs from afar. The bandit captain isn't particularly afraid of magic, either, having proficiency bonuses on Dexterity and Wisdom saving throws—two of the "big three." However, if given an opportunity to attack with advantage, the bandit captain will seize it, even if they'd otherwise be Dodging. For instance, if the bandit captain is being attacked by both a fighter and a barbarian and the barbarian uses Reckless Attack, the bandit captain will take the opening and attack the barbarian.

Like bandits, bandit captains value their lives highly. If moderately wounded (reduced to 45 hp or fewer), they'll keep fighting but also reopen negotiations *during combat*: "Surely *[stab]* we can come to some *[stab]* mutually satisfactory arrangement?" If seriously wounded (reduced to 26 hp or fewer), they'll drop their weapons, surrender on the spot, and agree to whatever terms keep them breathing.

Assassins, in the fifth edition *Monster Manual*, are spectacularly dangerous, primarily for one reason: the poison damage they inflict with their weapon attacks. Based on the damage and effects, the assassin appears to use wyvern poison (see "Poisons," *Dungeon Master's Guide*, chapter 8). At 1,200 gp per dose, this is pricey stuff. It stands to reason, therefore, that assassins don't use this poison *all the time*— only when they're on a mission to murder a particular target. If you eliminate the poison damage from the assassin's weapon attacks, they become a CR 4 enemy, rather than CR 8.

Assassins are tactically fascinating but slightly complicated opponents. Their ultra-high Stealth skill, along with their Assassinate and Sneak Attack features, make them ambush attackers. Their high Dexterity and Constitution but average Strength suggest a scrappy skirmish style—yet a battle of attrition goes against their best interests. Assassins typically work alone, or at least in very small groups, so while they could stick around and fight, they don't want to. Consequently, that first strike is everything.

Here's how it all comes together:

- **Assassinate:** "During its first turn, the assassin has advantage on attack rolls against any creature that hasn't taken a turn. Any hit the assassin scores against a surprised creature is a critical hit." Therefore, assassins *won't attack at all* if they can't do so with surprise. If they're discovered before they attack—unlikely, given their +9 Stealth modifier, but possible—assassins beat feet.
- **Sneak Attack:** "The assassin deals an extra 13 (4d6) damage when it hits a target with a weapon attack and has advantage on the attack roll." The Assassinate feature confers said advantage.
- **Multiattack:** "The assassin makes two shortsword attacks." Since these attacks both occur during the assassin's first turn,

the assassin gets advantage on *both* of them, and they're both crits if they hit. However, Sneak Attack can be used only once per turn, so it applies only to the first successful weapon attack.

Suppose an assassin is hiding in the rafters, waiting to kill Lord Milan of Lombard. Lord Milan passes beneath the assassin. His passive Perception (10) isn't enough for him to beat the assassin's Stealth roll (19). The assassin drops to the floor (Acrobatics proficiency!) and uses the Multiattack action, with surprise, thus rolling with advantage both times. The first attack roll is a hit—and therefore a crit, because of Assassinate—and also a Sneak Attack, for 2d6 + 3 weapon damage, plus 8d6 Sneak Attack damage, plus 7d6 poison damage* (halved if Lord Milan makes his saving throw). The second attack roll is also a critical hit but not a Sneak Attack, and it does 2d6 + 3 weapon damage plus another 7d6 poison damage (again, halved on a successful save). Altogether, this adds up to 26d6 + 6 of potential damage, or 97 damage *on average*. Criminy.

That should be enough to remove a target from play. If it's not, the assassin skedaddles, using the rest of their move that turn to get as far away as possible. Note that while the fifth edition *Player's Handbook* specifies that climbing uses 2 feet of movement speed for every 1 foot scaled, *no* movement is consumed by *dropping*. So after a maneuver like the one described above, or one in which the assassin is hiding in the shadows or behind a drapery and waits for the target to move within reach of their weapon, the assassin may still have *all* of their movement available! If the assassin uses an Acrobatic maneuver to escape, such as climbing out a window, or a Stealth maneuver, such as vanishing into a crowd, the chances of escape are improved further, since would-be pursuers might not have the skill to give chase.

I can't stress this enough: *The assassin does not stick around and keep fighting.* If that initial strike isn't enough to finish off the target, too

---

* The poison damage dice aren't doubled by Sneak Attack, because they have a different delivery mechanism: The damage is resisted by the target's saving throw, not dealt by the assassin's attack roll.

bad. The assassin will try again later, when the right conditions present themselves. Not now.

The assassin also carries a light crossbow, so there's an alternative scenario to the initial attack, which is that the assassin shoots from a place of hiding. Multiattack doesn't apply to crossbows because of their reloading time, so in this instance, that first attack is everything. The assassin makes the attack roll with advantage, gets a crit on a successful roll, and applies the Sneak Attack bonus and the poison damage, for a potential total of 2d8 + 15d6 + 3 damage, or an average of 64. If at all possible, the assassin makes this attack from the maximum normal range of the light crossbow, which is 80 feet. This gives the assassin just enough distance to be able to take a second shot if needed, although it will no longer include the bonuses from Assassinate, which applies only to the assassin's first turn, or Sneak Attack, since the first shot will have given the assassin's position away. But there's still that poison damage, so the assassin can do another 1d8 + 7d6 + 3 damage, 32 on average, before hightailing it. That makes this method of assassination approximately as effective as the melee-based method described above.

Any encounter with an assassin is likely to be followed immediately by a chase, so get familiar with the "Chases" section of the *Dungeon Master's Guide* (chapter 8). It's worth it!

Cutpurse

Medium humanoid (any race),
any non-lawful, non-good alignment

Armor Class 13 (leather armor)
Hit Points 13 (3d8)
Speed 30 ft

Str 10 (0) **Dex** 14 (+2) **Con** 10 (0) **Int** 10 (0) **Wis** 12 (+1) **Cha** 10 (0)

Skills Acrobatics +4, Deception +2, Perception +3, Sleight of Hand +6, Thieves' Tools +6
Senses passive Perception 14
Languages any one language (usually Common), Thieves' Cant
Challenge 1/4 (50 XP)

Cunning Action. As a bonus action, the cutpurse can Dash, Disengage, Hide, or Use an Object; make a Dexterity (Sleight of Hand) check; or disarm a trap or open a lock using thieves' tools.

Second-Story Work. The cutpurse can climb at a normal movement rate and can make a running long jump of up to 12 feet.

Actions

Dagger. Melee or Ranged Weapon Attack: +4 to hit, reach 5 ft or range 20/60 ft, one creature. *Hit:* 4 (1d4 + 2) piercing damage.

TRIBAL WARRIORS AND BERSERKERS

I have a bone to pick with the fifth edition *Monster Manual*'s description of the **tribal warrior**, as well as the *Sword Coast Adventurer's Guide*'s description of the Reghed and Uthgardt barbarians. In brief, the repeated insistence that these people defer to a chief ("the greatest or oldest warrior of the tribe or a tribe member blessed by the gods") disregards the difference between bands and tribes on the one hand and chiefdoms on the other, as well as the egalitarian nature of traditional societies.

Every Dungeon Master who aspires to any degree of coherent world-building needs to be a Jared Diamond aficionado. His best-known book, *Guns, Germs, and Steel: The Fates of Human Societies*, examines the factors that cause certain societies to advance technologically and socially faster than others (spoiler: Abundant access to high-protein staple grains, easily domesticated animals, and long east-west trade routes give a people a major leg up). His book *Collapse: How Societies Choose to Fail or Succeed* examines the factors that cause societies to stagnate or go extinct: environmental degradation, changing climate, hostile neighbors, lack of friendly trading partners, and overly rigid ideology. And his most recent book, *The World until Yesterday: What Can We Learn from Traditional Societies?*, examines the features of such societies that set them apart from modern ones.

In the prologue of *The World until Yesterday*, Diamond explains the differences among bands, tribes, and chiefdoms. Bands are the smallest and simplest human societies, comprising just a few dozen nomadic hunter-gatherers or small-plot farmers belonging to no more than a handful of families. Everyone in a band knows everyone else, and they all share resources and make decisions together. There's no economic specialization and no official political leadership.

Tribes consist of hundreds of people from dozens of families, all of whom still know one another personally. Tribes usually need to farm or herd to feed themselves, although hunting and gathering can still work in very resource-rich environments. They either stay put, wherever their source of food is, or follow the seasonal grazing patterns of their livestock. Economically and politically, however, they work the same way as smaller bands do. "Some tribes may have a 'big man' who functions as a weak leader," Diamond notes, "but he leads only by his powers of persuasion and personality rather than by recognized authority."

Chiefdoms appear when populations grow to include thousands, requiring even greater food productivity. Economic specialization develops as the need to keep track of food emerges alongside the need to produce it. Political leadership develops as decisions can no longer be made by consensus and people have to resolve disputes with others whom they may or may not know personally. Chiefdoms have to deal with two problems that bands and tribes don't, Diamond explains:

> First, strangers in a chiefdom must be able to meet each other, to recognize each other as fellow but individually unfamiliar members of the same chiefdom, and to avoid bristling at territorial trespass and getting into a fight. Hence chiefdoms develop shared ideologies and political and religious identities often derived from the supposedly divine status of the chief. Second, there is now a recognized leader, the chief, who makes decisions, possesses recognized authority, claims a monopoly on the right to use force against his society's members if necessary, and thereby ensures that strangers within the same chiefdom don't fight each other. (14–16)

It should be obvious from this that any "tribal warrior" who follows a chief doesn't belong to a tribe at all but to a *chiefdom*, and that chiefdom is a settled, agrarian society; whereas any who lives in a nomadic hunter-gatherer or herding society of no more than a few hundred people belongs to a band or a tribe with no chief or other recognized authority figure. By analogy to a work of literature we all know, a case can be made that the dwarves, hobbits, and Rohirrim of Middle-Earth lived in chiefdoms; for examples of "tribal" peoples, you have to look to the Dunlendings and the Wood-Woses of Drúadan Forest. (Even in this case, J.R.R. Tolkien makes the mistake of naming Ghân-buri-Ghân the "chief" of the Woses.) Thus, when the *Monster Manual* says tribal warriors "live beyond civilization, most often subsisting on fish-ing and hunting" yet act "in accordance with the wishes of [their] chief," it's contradicting itself.

Why am I belaboring this in a book about D&D tactics? *Because "tribal warriors" belonging to chiefdoms will fight differently from "tribal warriors" from actual tribes.* The former are specialists—perhaps even belonging to a discrete warrior caste—who assume the burden of fighting on behalf of the entire society and are typically led by a war chief. The latter comprise every able-bodied man in the tribe, and sometimes women as well; possess no special knowledge or training; and make no distinction of rank. Therefore, to know how a "tribal warrior" will fight, you have to know what kind of society they belong to—a primitive band or tribe, or a more advanced chiefdom—because the combat behavior of a warrior from a chiefdom will more closely resemble that of a guard or veteran.

Referencing Diamond again, tribal warriors engage in pitched battles, raids, and ambushes, just like warriors from more advanced societies, but they also employ treacherous ruses such as inviting neighbors to a feast, then massacring them while they're eating. The self-sacrifice exalted as noble by soldiers in state societies doesn't exist in tribal societies: Outnumbered warriors will run away and leave their wounded or captured companions behind without hesitation. There's no coordination of movement or missile fire; even a battle that begins on cue devolves into chaos almost immediately.

Tribal societies engage in total war. They don't take enemy warriors prisoner, because without economic specialization, they have no use for prisoners. And they don't surrender, knowing that they'd kill any enemy they captured and expecting the same to be done to them. (For more details, read chapter 4 of *The World until Yesterday*.)

Let's look at the stats of the tribal warrior. Strength and Constitution are above average, suggesting a "brute" melee fighter, which is consistent with the pitched-battle style of traditional warfare. The warrior is armed with a spear, which is a logical weapon; a club, shortbow, or sling would also make sense. And the warrior has the Pack Tactics trait, granting advantage if an ally is up and about within 5 feet of the enemy.

One thing is conspicuously missing from this profile: the Stealth skill. Not only does a great deal of traditional warfare revolve around raids and ambushes, hunter-gatherers *hunt*. They have to be stealthy in order to be successful hunters! For pity's sake, give your tribal warriors Stealth +2 so they at least have a *chance* of sneaking up on an enemy. (This won't affect their CR.)

When you get down to actual combat, there aren't many decisions to make. In a pitched battle, tribal warriors engage in the "Rrrrahhhh, stab stab stab" style of combat, Dashing away when seriously wounded (reduced to 4 hp or fewer) or when outnumbered by more than, say, 50 percent (that is, when their numbers are two-thirds or less of their enemies' numbers). They don't surrender; they kill anyone who surrenders to them. They don't engage in flanking maneuvers or any other clever tactics. They fight in a close knot, to take advantage of proximity to their allies. That's about it.

In our own world, people of traditional societies are awed and frightened by those they believe have magical powers, and there's no reason why it should be any different in D&D. When they see a spellcaster cast a spell, they'll either try to rush the caster or run for their lives, depending on the type of spell, the damage it does, whether the warriors can see the caster, and whether they can get to them. Rushing is more likely if they can see the caster, the spell does no actual damage, and/or there's no other enemy in the way. Running is more likely if they can't tell where the spell came from, the spell does serious damage (7 hp or more in total), and/or there are too many enemies between themselves and the caster. It's extremely rare that a band or tribe has a spellcaster of its own (such talents usually only arise within the specialization allowed by a chiefdom), but if it does, its members' attitude toward magic is totally different: With a caster on their side, they're extra-bold and much more likely to rush an enemy caster than to run from them. They also become enraged if anyone attacks *their* caster.

Tribal warriors on a raid approach with Stealth and wait patiently (they can wait a *long* time) for an opportunity to kill defenseless enemies and/or to steal food, livestock, or weapons. Once they've got the loot they came for, or their targets pick up weapons and come after them, they flee. Ambushes work the same way, except the goal is strictly to kill. Ambushes are used to defend territory, deter trespassers, and settle scores. (People in traditional societies hold grudges like you wouldn't believe.)

Even though the Reghed and Uthgardt barbarians of the Forgotten Realms setting are culturally modeled on Vikings, their way of life isn't consistent with Viking life. The Vikings lived in chiefdoms and were mostly agrarian and sedentary; the Viking raids of lore were more often than not impulsive addenda to trading expeditions, undertaken by a small subset of the population. The Reghedmen and Uthgardt are portrayed as nomadic hunter-gatherers, traveling in groups of between a dozen and a hundred members and all taking part in their raiding activities together. This is entirely consistent with a tribal organization of society. They shouldn't have chiefs, at least not ones with any formal authority to compel obedience or deference.

But let's posit the existence of a slightly larger, more organized society, one that's begun to engage in agriculture and economic specialization. Let's say this society contains individuals who hew more closely to their former way of life, who aren't down with the whole farming agenda and just wanna raid like they used to in the good ol' days. Such a society might produce **berserkers**.

Berserkers are tough brutes with the Reckless trait, which is identical to the barbarian class's Reckless Attack. It grants advantage on incoming as well as outgoing attack rolls, but berserkers are like, yeah, whatever; look at this humongous axe I'm carrying, and look at all these hit points that I've got and you don't. There's no reason for them to have this feature and not use it *all the time*. They're not geniuses who can calculate whether the odds favor a more cautious approach. They're *berserkers*.

The only question is, do berserkers fight to the death? That's an interesting one, because chiefdoms are a transitional stage between traditional band or tribal societies, whose warriors care about saving their own skin, and modern state societies, whose warriors care about duty and honor. While you might presume that a berserker would be a violent fanatic, it depends a lot on whether they owe more to the traditional organization of society or to the modern one. If we think of them as primarily specialists, a modern concept, then yes, they may well fight to the death. If we think of them as primarily throwbacks to a more chaotic way of life, we have to conclude that berserkers do in fact care about their own survival and will Dash away when seriously wounded (reduced to 26 hp or fewer).

CULTISTS, ACOLYTES, PRIESTS, AND DRUIDS

A cynic might say that the only difference between an "acolyte" and a "cultist" is one's point of view, but the *Monster Manual* would disagree. Piety takes different forms depending on whether an NPC is an extra or an antagonist.

The fifth edition *Monster Manual* doesn't even do **cultists** the courtesy of giving them spells to cast. For the most part, they're just shifty commoners with exotic swords. They're not strong, they're not tough, and they're not even stealthy. They have proficiency in Deception, the only function of which as far as I can tell is either to try to convince you that they're not cultists at all ("Just ordinary villagers going about our ordinary business!") or for recruitment purposes ("How'd you like to come to our self-actualization workshop?"). Dark Devotion is an interesting trait but not one that suggests any distinctive combat tactic.

Normally, a creature whose only above-average ability is Dexterity is some sort of ranged sniper, but cultists don't even carry ranged weapons. And why on earth would a demon worshiper need to have slightly above-average Dexterity? What is their actual deal?

It seems to me that the only useful way to think of cultists is as commoners with unusually intense personalities. What does this mean? Well, for starters, their first and foremost priority is not to be discovered *as* cultists. If the player characters encounter them socially, they'll do all they can to conceal their loyalties. Only if their cover is blown will they either fight or flee—the former if they outnumber the player characters, the latter if they're the ones outnumbered. They'll also fight to the death, knowing that they could be executed for their heresies, but also believing that infidels such as the PCs deserve to die themselves. Aside from that, they fight with as little sophistication as any other commoner.

Cult fanatics, on the other hand, are no joke, mainly because of their spellcasting kit, which includes *spiritual weapon* and *inflict wounds*. *Spiritual weapon* is cast as a bonus action and continues to provide additional bonus actions over the next nine rounds, making it an indispensable component of the cult fanatic's action economy. *Inflict wounds* is a potent melee spell attack that does necrotic damage on a hit (my players have nicknamed it "the Bad Touch"). Compare it with the cult fanatic's melee Multiattack, which comprises two Dagger strikes for a potential total of 2d4 + 4 piercing damage (9, on average): Cast using a 1st-level spell slot, *inflict wounds* deals 3d10 necrotic damage (16, on average), and boosted to 2nd level, it deals 4d10 damage (22). That's serious.

Other spells the cult fanatic can cast include *hold person* (Wisdom save, causes paralysis, requires concentration), *command* (can provoke opportunity attacks by causing melee opponents to flee), *shield of faith* (bonus action, requires concentration), and *sacred flame* (does 1d8 radiant damage from a distance). All in all, a potent kit for a level 4 spellcaster.

As NPCs with high Dexterity and slightly above-average Constitution, the cult fanatic has two plausible modes of combat: ranged sniping and scrappy melee skirmishing. In either case, having numbers—either other cult fanatics or rank-and-file cultists who can divide the PCs' attention—is very important. If accompanied by rank-and-file cultists, cult fanatics will leave the toe-to-toe fighting to them for the most part, instead using *sacred flame* and *spiritual weapon* to do damage from a distance (at the cost of only one 2nd-level spell slot—what a bargain!). However, before casting *spiritual weapon*, they'll cast *shield of faith*, another spell that requires a bonus action, but only when it's first cast. After that first turn, they can keep *shield of faith* going and also use their bonus actions to cast and direct *spiritual weapon*.

There are other tactical combinations cult fanatics can use on PCs who require special attention. For instance, they can cast *command* to order a troublesome opponent to "Approach!," then follow up on their next turn with *inflict wounds*. They can drop *shield of faith* to cast *hold person* and paralyze a PC, then rain critical hits on them with *spiritual weapon* (even better if that PC is already engaged in melee with one or more rank-and-file cultists) and enjoy automatic saving throw failures against *sacred flame*. They can *command* a PC who's engaged with multiple melee opponents to "Scram!," thereby granting every one of those opponents an opportunity attack.

Cult fanatics, as their name suggests, will fight to the death.

Acolytes aren't really equipped for combat at all, except as backup. Their physical abilities are all average. They're armed with clubs, representing improvised weapons (in a temple or shrine, a nice, heavy candlestick is a good go-to). Effectively, they're commoners with above-average Wisdom and the ability to cast spells.

The key spells in their arsenal are *bless*, *cure wounds*, *sanctuary*, and *sacred flame*. They'll use *bless* if accompanied by allies who are engaging in real fighting, *cure wounds* on any ally who takes a moderate wound (30 percent of hit point maximum) or worse, *sanctuary* on a key ally who requires protection or on any ally who's seriously injured, and *sacred flame* in any other situation that would call for them to attack. Like commoners, they're as likely to freeze or flee as they are to fight; it depends entirely on the odds and on whom they're with. If the PCs threaten their superiors, their worshipers, or anyone under their protection, they're more likely to fight than they would be otherwise.

Priests are also not well suited for combat and generally fight only in self-defense, but they do have some tricks up their vestments. Notable among these is *spirit guardians*, a potent area-effect defense spell that requires concentration. If combat ensues, this is the first spell a priest will cast, forgoing their bonus action (which could otherwise have been used to cast *spiritual weapon*) in order to gain this powerful field of divine protection. On their second turn, the priest casts *spiritual weapon* as a bonus action and, if need be, the *sacred flame* cantrip, which deals 2d8 damage rather than 1d8 because of the priest's spellcaster level. If an enemy does close with the priest, most likely because the enemy's Wisdom is high enough to resist the effects of *spirit guardians*, they'll use Divine Eminence as a bonus action, then attack with their magically enhanced weapon. In most cases, however, the priest is looking to drive attackers away rather than kill them. A seriously wounded priest (reduced to 10 hp or fewer) will surrender or flee—unless the PCs are of an alignment directly opposed to the priest's or worship a deity inimical to the one the priest worships, in which case the priest may see a glorious death battling infidels as their ticket to sweet treatment in the afterlife.

In the presence of allies, the priest has a couple of other options. After casting *spiritual weapon*, a priest may choose to cast *guiding bolt* instead of *sacred flame* at an enemy whom one of their allies is engaging: A hit deals 4d6 radiant damage and gives the priest's ally advantage on the next attack roll against that enemy. Also, like the acolyte, a priest can cast *cure wounds* on an ally who's taken a moderate wound or worse, or *sanctuary* on an ally who needs an emergency bailout. (Remember that leveled spells cast as bonus actions, such as *sanctuary* and *spiritual weapon*, may be paired in the same turn only with cantrips, such as *sacred flame*—not with other leveled spells that are cast as actions, such as *guiding bolt*.)

Druids are scrappier than your average clergyperson, with slightly above-average Dexterity and Constitution and the delightful *shillelagh* cantrip, which boosts their attack modifiers with staves from +2 to +4 and their damage from 1d6 to 1d8 + 2 and costs only a bonus action. The big gun in their arcane arsenal, though, is *entangle*, an area-effect spell that has the potential to restrain enemies, granting them disadvantage on attack rolls and advantage on attack rolls against them—plus giving them disadvantage against damaging spells that require Dex saves. (Unfortunately, druids don't pack any of those.)

Druids keep to themselves, so any encounter with one will most likely be on their own home turf, and their goal in the event of a conflict will be to make the PCs go away (if they're weaker) or to get away from the PCs (if they're stronger). We're looking primarily at two tactical combinations here. One is to restrain the PCs with *entangle* on one turn, then lob fire at them with *produce flame* on the next, gaining advantage on the attack roll against the restrained targets. The other is *shillelagh* (bonus action) plus a melee weapon attack (action), with *thunderwave* as a backup for when the druid is confronted by three or more melee opponents and needs to take the heat off. Either may be effective for standing one's ground, depending on circumstances, terrain, and the opposition.

If a hasty departure is required, the druid casts *longstrider*, increasing their speed to 40 feet per round; then, on the next round, Dashing off into the wilderness. (*Barkskin* isn't worth the time it takes to cast; if the druid casts this spell at all, it will be before combat begins, and the druid will be down one 2nd-level spell slot.)

MAGES

Figuring out tactics for spellcasters is always complicated by the need to assess the relative merits of their spells, which requires application of game-theory math along with examination of their action economy.

The **mage** NPC is basically a level 9 wizard. Strength is below average, Dexterity above average: A mage is a ranged attacker by design. Intelligence is very high: A mage knows which enemies to target with which spells. Wisdom is above average: A mage prioritizes self-preservation. In fact, given the amount of training and education a wizard has to undergo in order to do what they do, and also given how squishy magic-users typically are, I'd say the mage has an *above-average* interest in self-preservation and will commence escape protocols after taking only moderate damage (reduced to 28 hp or fewer).

There's no reason for mages to employ weapons except in the direst of circumstances. They've got +5 to hit with a finesse weapon attack (that includes the dagger that the NPC mage is armed with) vs. +6 to hit with a spell attack, and even the *fire bolt* cantrip does 2d10 damage (11 on average) vs. the dagger's paltry 1d4 + 2 (4 on average).

Mages have only one spell that can be cast with a bonus action: *misty step*. That simplifies their action economy but also limits what they're able to do in a single turn. Since a spellcaster can cast no more than one leveled spell in a combat turn, *misty step* is likely to be combined with the *fire bolt* cantrip as a matter of course. *Shield* and *counterspell* are cast as reactions, enabling mages to buy time but also imposing a need to conserve their spell slots for these spells.

Mages have a lot of spell slots—fourteen altogether—but this is deceptive. *Shield* or *counterspell* can suck away one of those slots each round, not to mention the slot a mage uses on their own action. *A mage has to finish a fight fast.* And with a 17 Intelligence, they know it. Consequently, the mage's strategy looks something like this:

- **Always have a way to escape.**
  - Position yourself where you can get to an exit, using *misty step* to maneuver if needed.
  - If the room you're in has only one exit, draw your attackers away from that exit so that you can use it yourself.
  - If the room you're in has a window, keep it open so that you can use *fly* to get away.
  - Decamp *before* you run out of spell slots.
- **Avoid taking damage.**
  - Suppress opponents' actions.
  - Stay more than 30 feet away from opponents, using *misty step* to maneuver if needed.
  - Use *shield* and *counterspell* to thwart incoming attacks.
  - If possible, cast *mage armor* before combat begins.
- **Do the greatest damage to the most enemies with each spell.**
  - Cast area-effect spells and multiple-target spells before single-target spells.
  - Cast spells that impose debilitating effects on top of damage before damage-only spells.

Greater invisibility is a beaut: It takes care of both escape and damage avoidance. In fact, it can potentially obviate the need to do any damage at all. But a mage who *wants* to fight—out of either enmity toward the player characters, the need to defend a location or item, or a generally antisocial personality—may keep this spell in pocket, focusing first on dealing damage.

Mage armor, conveniently, lasts 8 hours with each casting. A particularly paranoid mage, or one who lives a life of danger and knows it, might keep *mage armor* up all the time. This means always being down one 1st-level spell slot, possibly two, further increasing the need to finish fights as quickly as possible. A less paranoid mage might toss *mage armor* up only when they hear a suspicious noise, an alarm is triggered, or a messenger runs in with a warning. *Mage armor* is an indispensable spell, but inconveniently, it's also one that may not be worth the action it takes to cast once combat is already underway. A mage who's caught off guard will need to prioritize damaging and disabling their opponents over adding those three points to their AC, which will only reduce the chances of taking damage, not negate them.

Intuitively, we believe that higher-level spell slots should always be worth more than lower-level ones, but this isn't true in every case. Another way to look at it, which I believe is more accurate, is that (a) a *scarcer* spell slot is worth more than a *less scarce* one, and (b) a higher-level spell slot can be used to cast certain spells that a lower-level one can't. So unless the higher-level spell slot is also scarcer, whether it's worthwhile to spend a higher-level spell slot on a lower-level spell, boosted, depends on which is more useful: a higher-level spell or the boosted lower-level spell.

The mage's 5th-level spell slot is extra-special, because there's only one of it. The mage uses this slot *only* to cast *cone of cold*; they'll never waste it on boosting a lower-level spell. The mage's 2nd- through 4th-level spell slots, however, are effectively interchangeable, except to the extent that higher-level spells require higher-level slots to cast.

With that in mind, let's look at what each damaging spell can do:

- *Cone of cold* deals 8d8 cold damage on a failed Constitution save, half on a success, affecting creatures in a 60-foot cone, or approximately six creatures (see the Targets in Area of Effect table in chapter 8 of the *Dungeon Master's Guide*). If we assume a fifty-fifty chance of making this saving throw (which I will throughout this analysis), this does an expected 27 damage per creature to six creatures, for a total expected damage of 162.

- *Ice storm* deals 2d8 bludgeoning damage plus 4d6 cold damage on a failed Dexterity save, half on a success, affecting creatures in a 20-foot-radius cylinder, or approximately four creatures. Thus, it does an expected 17 damage per creature, a total expected damage of 69. It also turns the storm's area of effect into difficult terrain, slowing enemies from approaching or pursuing the mage.

- *Fireball*, everyone's favorite, deals 8d6 fire damage on a failed Dexterity save, half on a success, affecting creatures in a 20-foot-radius sphere, or approximately four creatures. Thus, it does an expected 21 damage per creature, a total expected damage of 84. Cast using a 4th-level spell slot, it deals 9d6 fire damage, 23 expected damage per creature, total expected damage 95.

- *Magic missile* deals 1d4 + 1 force damage with every dart and always hits. At base level, it hurls three darts, and it hurls an additional dart for each extra spell level. Thus it deals an expected 10 damage when cast at 1st level, 14 at 2nd level, 17 at 3rd level, and 21 at 4th level.

- *Fire bolt* deals 2d10 damage to a single target and requires a successful ranged spell attack roll to hit. Assuming about a 70 percent chance to hit, it deals an expected 7 damage. Stop the presses! (Then again, it's a cantrip—a bit of free damage you get to deal when you cast *misty step*. To complain is churlish.)

Sorted preferentially by damage done (and nothing else), we have *cone of cold*, *fireball* (4th level), *fireball* (3rd level), *ice storm*, then a big drop-off in damage when we get to *magic missile* cast at any level. In fact, *magic missile*'s damage when cast using a 3rd- or 4th-level spell slot is so poor compared with *fireball* and *ice storm*, we have to conclude that the mage never casts *magic missile* at these levels, ever, and probably doesn't bother with the spell at all unless they're facing fewer than four opponents and are merely trying to finish them off—or are entirely out of 3rd-, 4th- and 5th-level spell slots, at which point it's long past time to skedaddle.

We're starting to get a picture of the mage's spell priorities, but we're not fully there yet, because there's a logjam at 4th level. This is the slot the mage needs in order to cast *greater invisibility*, but it's also the slot needed for *ice storm*, and we've already seen that a 4th-level *fireball* does even more damage than *ice storm*, although *ice storm* impedes movement in a way that *fireball* doesn't. I'd say that because of its utility in both escaping and avoiding damage, the mage always reserves one 4th-level spell slot for *greater invisibility* even if they don't cast it first thing. *Fireball* at 4th level is the mage's first go-to for damage, but they don't use that last 4th-level spell slot until it's apparent whether they'll need to cast *ice storm* to impede the PCs' movement—for instance, if they show a propensity toward charging at the mage. If it's clearly unnecessary, that last 4th-level slot can be spent on another boosted *fireball*; if the necessity becomes clear, *ice storm*. In the meantime, the mage can cast *fireball* using a 3rd-level spell slot instead, which still does more damage than *ice storm*.

But wait—there's also a logjam at 3rd level! This is the slot the mage needs in order to cast *counterspell* or *fly*. The former is indispensable. The latter is indispensable if and only if the mage has a window to fly out of. If there's no path of airborne escape available, that frees up a 3rd-level spell slot for another *counterspell* or *fireball*. Are you starting to see why it's so essential that the mage end this fight as quickly as possible? Three rounds, *maybe* four, then bail out: That's the most the mage will allow.

Round by round, then, here's the mage's combat heuristic:

ROUND 1

- **Do the PCs look like they can do a lot of damage, or are there more than six of them?** Cast *greater invisibility* right off the bat. Otherwise, cast *cone of cold*.
- **Has an attacker just rolled a 12 through 16 on an attack roll (15 through 19 with *mage armor* up)?** Cast *shield* (reaction) to repel it. (This applies on every subsequent round as well.)

- Has an attacker just cast a spell of 3rd level or lower that can damage you or keep you from getting away? Cast *counterspell* (reaction) to negate it. (This applies on every subsequent round as well.)

ROUND 2

- Did you cast *greater invisibility* in round 1? Cast *cone of cold* now.
- Are you visible, did any enemy close to melee distance, and can you see a place where you'll be more than 30 feet from any enemy? Cast *misty step* (bonus action) to get there, then *fire bolt* (action) against any attacker who's damaged you so far. (This applies on every subsequent round as well.)
- Are you visible, did any enemy close to melee distance, and can you see no place where you'll be more than 30 feet from any enemy? Cast *greater invisibility* now.
- Are you visible, and do you have no enemy within melee distance? Cast *fireball* now, using a 4th-level spell slot.

ROUND 3

- Are you visible and moderately wounded or worse? Cast *greater invisibility* and get out of there. (This applies on every subsequent round as well.)
- Are you visible, do you have no enemy within melee distance, and do you have a reason to keep fighting? Cast *ice storm* if the PCs have been trying to get within melee distance; otherwise, cast *fireball* using a 3rd-level spell slot, unless you need to keep one open for *fly*, in which case go ahead and cast *ice storm* after all.
- Are you invisible, and do you have a reason to keep fighting? Cast the best damaging spell you have available to you, and keep moving around to maintain a decent distance from any enemies.

ROUND 4

- Do you have only one or two opponents left, and will they be easy to pick off? *Magic missile*, 2nd-level spell slot.

- **Are your remaining opponents clustered?** Cast *fireball* using a 3rd-level spell slot, unless you need to keep one open for *fly*; in that case, cast *ice storm*.
- **Look, this is already starting to go on too long.** Cast *greater invisibility* if you're still visible, or cast *fly* if you have an open window; grab the nearest thing of value (free interaction); and get out of there.

ROUND 5
- **What are you waiting for?** *Get out of there.*

ARCHMAGES

The mage was complicated; the **archmage**, even more so. Strap in.

As with the mage, the archmage's ability scores imply an aversion to melee combat, a strong self-preservation impulse, and a strategically and tactically savvy view of the battlefield. We can also determine, by reading between the lines, that the archmage is a wizard of the abjuration school, because Magic Resistance is a feature that abjuration wizards obtain at level 14. Mechanically, that doesn't mean much, since Magic Resistance is the only abjuration feature the *Monster Manual* gives the archmage; still, this inference adds a dash of flavor to our archmage's personality. Abjuration is the magic of prevention. All other things being equal, the archmage's primary impulse is to shut you down.

The mage's spells topped out at 5th level, but the archmage's go all the way up to 9th, with only one slot at each of the top four levels. I assume this was to simplify an already extremely complicated and powerful enemy. What it means for us is that those four slots are reserved exclusively for the archmage's four highest-level spells: *time stop*, *mind blank*, *teleport*, and *globe of invulnerability*. And *mind blank*, according to the *Monster Manual*, is pre-cast before combat begins—along with *mage armor* and *stoneskin*—so that slot isn't even available. (How does the archmage know that combat is about to begin? Dude, *Intelligence 20*. "Nekrosius the Esoteric, *supra-genius!*")

Funny thing about that *stoneskin* spell, by the way: It requires concentration. That means that the archmage has to drop it in order to cast *globe of invulnerability, wall of force, banishment,* or *fly.* That means that the archmage can *lose* their resistance to physical damage from nonmagical weapons in the midst of combat. If that's not an oversight on the part of the designers, it means that the archmage has to consider *very* carefully whether dropping *stoneskin* to cast another spell that requires concentration makes sense in any given situation. Meanwhile, the archmage's action economy doesn't leave room for tactical combinations more elaborate than *misty step* plus *fire bolt.*

Speaking of action economy, what about spells cast as reactions? The archmage has only one: *counterspell.* (No *shield!*) Everything except this and *misty step* requires a full action to cast. Therefore, the archmage can't exploit clever combinations to optimize their efficacy. They have to cast the right spell at the right time, every time.

So let's take a look at these spells:

- *Time stop* is a doozy, allowing the archmage to take 1d4 + 1 turns in a row, uninterrupted—but only if none of those actions affects anyone else! As a way of supercharging the archmage's damage, it's a dud, but as a way of giving them time to set up various defenses, it has promise. We'll come back to that. It also has the obvious application of enabling a high-speed getaway, but . . .
- *Teleport* is even better for that. In fact, since it can only transport willing subjects and/or inanimate objects, escape is the *only* combat application for this spell that doesn't waste its power.
- *Globe of invulnerability* blocks any spell of 5th level or below, with the cost of having to drop *stoneskin.* This requires the archmage to calculate who's capable of inflicting greater damage: spellcasters slinging low- to mid-level combat spells or ranged and melee foes wielding nonmagical weapons. And the archmage can't really make this calculation until they see what their opponents can dish out. A sound conclusion is that the archmage makes the switch as soon as they're dealt more damage over the course of a single round by low- to mid-level spells than by nonmagical weapon hits—which means you as the DM need to keep track of both, separately.

- *Cone of cold* is a good way to whack around half a dozen enemies with 8d8 cold damage in a single shot. The archmage has to cast this one early, because of the spell's conical area of effect: It's easier to catch a whole bunch of enemies in a roughly 60-degree arc when they're far from you and generally all in the same direction than when they're closing in and surrounding you. This spell is boostable, but the archmage's higher-level spell slots are reserved for their higher-level spells.

- *Scrying* is a 10-minute ritual, mostly unsuitable for combat but with one amusing application: If the archmage knows 15 to 20 minutes in advance that enemies are approaching, they can cast *scrying* to observe them, then bombard them with *magic missile* from around one or more corners. It's a silly use of both spells, but sometimes silly can be fun.

- *Wall of force* is a marvelous way to keep an entire party of PCs at bay. It also requires concentration, which means it requires the archmage to drop *stoneskin* and precludes *globe of invulnerability*. It repels all physical objects, including missiles, but it's invisible, so it doesn't stop opponents from casting point-targeted spells into the space behind it (as opposed to effects that must go *through* it, which are stopped). A logical reason to cast this spell is if the archmage is taking more damage from magic ranged weapons than from spell and melee attacks combined. It may be useful cast as a defensive measure, before any of the PCs is able to get within 10 feet of the archmage. It does prevent the archmage from targeting foes on the other side of the wall with *cone of cold*, *lightning bolt*, or *magic missile*.

- *Banishment* targets, at most, two opponents (since the archmage's 6th- through 9th-level spell slots are off limits), and it also requires concentration. The time to use this spell is when one or two opponents are doing more damage than *all other opponents combined*.

- *Fire shield* is a pleasantly uncomplicated defensive spell that doesn't require concentration to sustain and does some freebie damage to melee attackers. Unfortunately, the archmage doesn't know whether to use it to resist fire damage and deal cold damage or vice versa until an enemy casts a spell that does one of these, so it's not a spell the archmage necessarily wants to cast right away.

- *Counterspell* is a no-brainer, and the archmage should feel free to cast it at up to 5th level (if only once) to keep incoming damage at bay long enough to choose the best defensive measure.

- *Fly* is a useful getaway spell . . . if you don't have *teleport*. If you have *teleport*, why would you bother with *fly*? Being a spell that requires concentration, it requires the archmage to drop whatever other defensive spell they're concentrating on. It looks cool, but considering its opportunity cost, I can't see what tactical application it might have.

- *Lightning bolt*—what more need be said? Zots enemies for 8d6 lightning damage apiece; position yourself right, or catch 'em while they're clustered, and you can nail several PCs with it at once. Casting it at 4th or 5th level is probably too greedy, since those slots may be required for *fire shield, cone of cold, wall of force*, or a clutch *counterspell*.

- *Detect thoughts* is useful for social interaction only, and it's super rude.

- *Mirror image* is a no-brainer, buying time against attacks from all non-spellcasters. I can't think of a reason why this wouldn't be the first spell the archmage casts.

- *Misty step* is good for tactical repositioning and, because it's a bonus action, can be paired with the *fire bolt* cantrip. (Or *shocking grasp*, but only if the archmage is already within melee reach of the target—they're not going to *misty step* toward a target and then cast *shocking grasp*, because if the spell attack misses, they'll be subject to an opportunity attack when they try to move away again.)

- *Detect magic* . . . *[shakes head sadly]*

- *Identify*—the only identifying the archmage needs to be doing right now is which PC to take out first.

- *Magic missile*—at level 18, an archmage casting *magic missile*, even boosted as high as 5th level, is like an electrical engineer building devices out of a Radio Shack 150-in-1 Electronic Project Kit. It's time to put away childish things.
- *Fire bolt*, when cast by a level 18 wizard, deals 4d10 fire damage, equaling or surpassing *magic missile* cast at 4th level or below without costing a single spell slot—although it requires a ranged spell attack to hit.
- *Shocking grasp*, similarly, deals 4d8 lightning damage on a hit, and the recipient of the jolt is deprived of their reaction for a round. It also requires the archmage to be next to the target, however, and that's probably not where they want to be, especially if the attack misses.

Although it's not spelled out explicitly, the archmage has Spell Mastery over *disguise self* and *invisibility*, which means the archmage can cast them at will. However, the archmage does still have to expend *time*, in the form of an action.

Since the archmage's choices depend so heavily on what their enemies choose to do, they have only one unambiguously sensible choice in the first round of combat, and that's *mirror image*. Additionally, the archmage will use *counterspell* to squelch one incoming damaging spell. (They won't waste *counterspell* on negating a spell that an opponent is using to buff their allies.)

Once the archmage has had a chance to see what the opposition can do, it's time for a reassessment of defensive measures. Is the majority of damage coming from spells of 5th level or lower? Then the archmage should switch from *stoneskin* to *globe of invulnerability*. From ranged weapon attacks? *Wall of force*, either between the archmage and all their foes or between the enemy's front and back lines. From one or two specific foes who aren't obviously bards, paladins, sorcerers, or warlocks? *Banishment*. (By the way, an archmage can tell a sorcerer or warlock from a wizard just by their *style*.)

For a fast switch-up combo, the archmage casts *time stop*. This gives the archmage a minimum of two extra turns. They bank one to finish with *cone of cold* or *lightning bolt*, if either is still available. They use one to switch from *stoneskin* to a different defensive spell requiring concentration, if need be. (If the archmage chooses *wall of force*, they have to place it mindfully, since it obstructs their damage-dealing spells.) If the opposition dealt or tried to deal fire or cold damage, the archmage's next priority is to cast *fire shield* to resist that type of damage. (If they dealt or tried to deal both types, the archmage will resist whichever type accounted for the greater portion.) If the archmage still has any action(s) left over, they'll Dash to the best location on the battlefield from which to cast *cone of cold* or *lightning bolt*. This spot will most likely be away from the melee fighters and behind the opposition's back line, unless the archmage cast *wall of force*. Still one left? Dodge.

If the archmage doesn't need to switch off *stoneskin* or to cast *fire shield*, the archmage won't bother casting *time stop* right now. They simply cast *cone of cold* or *lightning bolt* instead—or *misty step* plus *fire bolt* if there's an urgent need to be somewhere else, such as if the archmage is surrounded by melee foes and their *mirror image* doubles are already dispelled. (*Invisibility* works just as well if the archmage doesn't need to move farther than their maximum movement speed, and it doesn't cost a spell slot. But *invisibility* takes a full action and therefore can't be combined with *fire bolt*. All it does is buy time.)

There will quickly come a point at which the archmage is out of slots that can be used to cast damaging spells. (If the archmage has determined that *globe of invulnerability* is neither necessary nor useful in this combat scenario, the 6th-level spell slot can be considered available for a lower-level spell.) If victory doesn't seem close at hand, and if the archmage doesn't have some pressing reason to keep fighting—such as defending a location or item, or because they simply hate their opponents' guts—they'll *teleport* out of there. The same goes if the archmage has taken moderate or greater damage (reduced to 69 hp or fewer). If the archmage is seriously wounded (reduced to 39 hp or fewer), they'll abandon ship even with a good reason to keep fighting.

Surrendering generally isn't something even most good- or lawful-aligned archmages are inclined to do: They're withdrawn by nature, rather than aggressive or compliant, and many of them are suspicious of anyone who might hold power over them. Because of this tendency to distrust others, they'd rather make a clean getaway than plead for mercy. Stuffing the archmage's *teleport* spell with a *counterspell* may change their mind about that—or may cause them to freak out and fight to the death instead.

If the archmage does calculate that they can achieve victory despite being out of 3rd- through 6th-level spell slots, they continue to fight using *fire bolt*, *shocking grasp*, and/or *magic missile* to finish their enemies off.

MONSTROSITIES

The game is called "Dungeons & Dragons," so of course dragons are the stars of the show. But monstrosities make up the bulk of the supporting cast, lurking in forests and swamps, diving at prey from above, burrowing through the earth, prowling subterranean caverns, cloaking themselves in camouflage, turning victims to stone with their gaze, or simply terrorizing land, sea, and sky with their awesome size and might. Whether beasts of myth and legend, cursed beings, or oddities produced by magical practitioners with more skill than scruples, monstrosities have one thing in common: They're creatures of instinct, and their instincts make them dangerous.

ETTERCAPS

Ettercaps are arachnid-humanoid hybrids, and not the adorable, crime-fighting type. They live in forests, herd giant spiders, and generally lend an air of gloom and despair to wherever they dwell. Anytime a party of adventurers encounters an ettercap, it will be accompanied by at least a few giant spiders.

Ettercaps are robust in all their physical abilities, with Dexterity leading by a nose. They're not afraid of a toe-to-toe confrontation, but considering their high Dexterity, combined with their Stealth and Survival skills, it's likely to begin with an ambush, perhaps with the ettercaps hiding in trees (thanks to their Spider Climb skill). They also have darkvision, Web Sense, and Web Walker, making it advantageous for them to blanket dimly lit parts of thick forests with webs and wait for hapless travelers to get stuck in them. Alternatively, if there's a road or trail that passes through their forest, they may lay webs across the path; travelers who notice them and aren't caught in them will still be stopped, giving the ettercaps an opportunity to attack. An adventuring party that makes camp in the woods may wake in the morning to find its campsite entirely encircled by webs.

Ettercaps initiate combat from hiding whenever possible, and they try to gain the element of surprise. If an opponent is restrained within one of their webs, they attack that opponent first; if one of their spiders is moderately injured (reduced to 18 hp or fewer), the nearest ettercap focuses on whichever foe did the damage. Otherwise, they choose their targets indiscriminately.

Against a restrained target, an ettercap uses its Multiattack action to claw, then bite. Against an unrestrained target, it uses Web to try to restrain them. Web has a recharge, so if this action isn't available, an ettercap without a restrained target Multiattacks any opponent who's engaged it in melee, or an opponent who's poisoned by an ettercap or spider bite (it can tell). If it has no obvious target, or it's being attacked from range or by more than one opponent, it may choose the Dodge action instead, marking time until it can use its Web again and thereby gain an advantage. That being said, since ettercaps invariably have giant spiders fighting alongside them, and the spiders also have the ability to ensnare their targets in webs and poison them, there should be no shortage of debilitated targets to choose from.

Ettercaps aren't that smart, but neither are they lacking in survival instinct. If they're seriously injured (reduced to 17 hp or fewer), they'll back off (using the Dodge action, then their full movement speed, then Dashing when they're out of melee reach), and they'll take their spiders with them.

PHASE SPIDERS

Phase spiders differ from giant spiders in a variety of minor respects and two significant ones. First, while they have the Web Walker trait, *they don't spin webs.* Second, they have the Ethereal Jaunt feature, which lets them phase back and forth between the material plane and the ethereal plane. We'll take a quick look at its other traits and then come back to these, because I think the phase spider is in need of some flavor text that explains what it's all about.

Phase spiders are shock attackers, with high Strength and Dexterity and above-average Constitution. With Intelligence 6, they're also cleverer than you'd expect a spider to be. Although they're not clever enough to act beyond their instincts, those instincts can take them a long way: Intelligence 6 is equivalent to that of a chimp. It's not unthinkable that a phase spider might even use tools. The combination of Stealth proficiency and darkvision makes phase spiders nighttime or underground ambush predators.

So we have an ambush predator that can navigate webs but doesn't create them. Why the former ability and not the latter? And why the ability to phase back and forth between planes?

Here's my theory: Phase spiders didn't evolve independently. Rather, they're the result of a magical hiccup in the evolutionary process. Something created them *out of* regular giant spiders, and they continue to live side by side with their mundane sisters. In fact, that lovely cornflower blue illustration notwithstanding, I imagine that a phase spider is indistinguishable from other giant spiders until it begins blinking.

But wait a second. Spiders, by and large, are solitary creatures. In our world, there are tens of thousands of known spider species, yet fewer than two dozen of these are social. On the other hand, as a practical matter of gameplay, giant spiders cease to be solo boss monsters when our player characters hit level 2. We send groups of giant spiders at our players all the time. So I guess we have to say that in D&D, giant spiders just happen to be one of those social species, or at least subsocial. And phase spiders, occasionally, live among them.

Fighting on their own, giant spiders first seek to ensnare their prey in a web, if the prey isn't caught already. Then, once the prey is restrained, they bite (with advantage) to paralyze. When the prey stops moving, they wrap up their treat to enjoy later.

Phase spiders act in conjunction with this behavior, but since they don't make webs of their own, they aid their sister spiders by taking out moving targets, gaining advantage as unseen attackers by using

Ethereal Jaunt to appear suddenly behind their prey. Phase spider poison is no stronger than regular giant spider poison (we can infer this from the DC of the saving throw, which is the same), but the phase spider delivers a lot more of it (we can infer this from the greater damage it does, 4d8 vs. 2d8). Thus, contrary to predators' usual habit of primarily targeting the old, the young, the weak, the isolated, and the oblivious, a phase spider may attack the *larger* of its opponents, knowing on some dim level that it has a better chance of taking them out than other giant spiders do.

Phase spiders follow different action patterns based on whether they're "blinking in" (ethereal to material) or "blinking out" (material to ethereal). When blinking in to ambush, a phase spider first uses its Ethereal Jaunt bonus action, then its Bite action. To be fair to your PCs, the phase spider should make a Dexterity (Stealth) check, opposed by its target's passive Wisdom (Perception), to determine whether it can appear out of the target's field of view without making a sound before it Bites;* if it fails, the target turns and sees it, and it loses its advantage on the attack. When blinking out to escape a foe who's hurting it, it delivers a Bite out of spite, then uses the Ethereal Jaunt bonus action to vanish.

What if a phase spider blinking in to attack successfully paralyzes its prey on its first strike? Then it uses its movement to bring itself closer—within melee reach, if possible—to another opponent who *does* fit the usual prey profile. Bigger opponents are for engaging only with stealth strikes.

---

* Fifth edition D&D is agnostic on the matter of facing. Nowhere do the core rules specify that a creature ever faces a certain direction. On the flip side, nowhere do they say it doesn't. Attacks can target anyone within reach unless you're using the optional Facing rule in chapter 8 of the *Dungeon Master's Guide*, and line of sight extends in all directions, but the rules don't get any more specific than this. However, just as general rules apply unless a specific rule overrides them, I consider real-world laws of nature to apply unless a D&D rule—general or specific—overrides them. Usually this is just for the sake of flavor and has no impact on what a character or creature can or can't do. However, when a phase spider uses Ethereal Jaunt to appear immediately behind someone and attack, a DM may thereby justify allowing it a chance to stay hidden and gain advantage on its attack roll before it's seen, as specified in "Hiding," *Player's Handbook*, chapter 7.

Once it's engaged with a target, a phase spider remains engaged with that target until the target is paralyzed or the spider takes moderate damage (10 or more in a single round). If a phase spider takes that much damage in a round, it Bites once more (action), then blinks out (bonus action). When a phase spider is seriously injured (reduced to 12 hp or fewer), it blinks out and doesn't return.

DISPLACER BEASTS

An old-school monster dating all the way back to the 1974 *Greyhawk* supplement, the **displacer beast** is a pantherlike creature that walks on six legs but attacks with a pair of long, sinuous tentacles emerging from its shoulders. Its name comes from its power to make itself appear to be several feet from where it actually is.

Aside from this passive trait, there's not much in the displacer beast's stat block to make it anything but a straightforward brute. Its primary physical abilities are Strength and Constitution, its 40-foot movement speed makes charging a snap, and it has no feature that allows or encourages a unique method of attack.

So to find a displacer beast fighting style that differs at all from that of other "Rrrrahhhh, bash bash bash" brutes, we have to look to three things: its reach, its Armor Class, and the *Monster Manual* flavor text.

The fact that the melee reach of its tentacles is 10 feet, not 5 feet, means it doesn't have to get right next to its target to hit them. An attacking displacer beast gets only as close to its targets as it needs to, so that it doesn't have to concern itself with opportunity attacks unless and until its opponents subsequently close with it. (Displacement skews the beast's position only by "several feet," not enough to make it appear to be in an entirely different square or hex, so don't turn this combat into a game of Battleship.)

For a brute, the displacer beast's AC 13 is fairly low. What makes it hard to hit is its Displacement trait, which imposes disadvantage on attack rolls against it, giving it an *effective* AC of 17 or 18. However, by the time player characters reach intermediate levels, which is when they'll start running into foes like the CR 3 displacer beast, hitting

AC 17 or 18 is no longer all that difficult—a mid-level PC ought to be able to make that roll at least half the time, especially if they're playing smart. Since a successful hit disrupts Displacement, that means just one hit—even a lucky one—makes the displacer beast vulnerable to the next few.

Also, consider that any opponent of the displacer beast who attacks with advantage—for any reason, and even if there's some other disadvantage in play—thereby nullifies Displacement. Unseen attacker? Nullified. DM gave you inspiration last week? Nullified. A fellow PC using the Help action? Nullified. Flank attack, if your DM is using that optional rule? Nullified. *Faerie fire*? Nullified. The barbarian is using Reckless Attack? Nullified.

So the displacer beast's instinctive behavior set (its ape-level Intelligence 6 isn't enough to allow it to develop new strategies on the fly) should include reactions to taking a hit, right? Like, maybe after a successful attack on a displacer beast, the creature backs off, using its full movement speed (which will usually exceed that of any of its opponents), and waits for Displacement to kick in again?

Well, that's what I thought at first. But a hit on the displacer beast only disrupts Displacement until the end of its next turn. Let's look at the timing of this: Alfonso, Bethrynna, Creega, and Dabbledob are fighting a displacer beast. The beast is first in the initiative order, then the PCs attack in alphabetical order. Alfonso, on his own turn, lands a hit, disrupting Displacement. Then Bethrynna, Creega, and Dabbledob all get to make straight attack rolls against the beast's base Armor Class.

Now it's the beast's turn again. It could retreat—but why? Sure, it has AC 13 for the duration of its turn, but who's going to attack it *during* its turn? Nobody—unless it provokes opportunity attacks by retreating! So here we've got this weird situation in which what makes intuitive sense ("They found me! They hurt me! I'd better get away!") makes the exact opposite of tactical sense ("They found me, they hurt me, but this isn't going to make them any more likely to hurt me *again*, so I should just stay here and keep whapping them with my spiky tentacle pads").

Here we have to maintain intellectual discipline and remind our-
selves that instinct develops from what's evolutionarily successful. We
also have to look at the three possible methods of retreat: Dodge,
Dash, and Disengage. Dodge is a poor choice for the displacer beast,
especially if it's engaged by multiple melee attackers, because of its
low Armor Class. Dash is the most plausible, although it's not so good
when being attacked by multiple opponents who'll all get opportunity
attacks. The displacer beast's Intelligence isn't high enough to justify
Disengage, but I do occasionally sleaze this one for creatures that
have a knack for slipping away from opponents, making it a function
of instinct rather than a function of training and discipline. Plus,
Disengage is well-suited for situations in which one is engaged with
multiple melee opponents (likely, in the case of the displacer beast)
and/or faster than those opponents (also likely in the case of the displacer beast).

If a displacer beast has taken only one hit and the attacker had no
advantage on the attack that would counter Displacement, it stays
where it is and keeps fighting. If it's taken more than one hit or it's
getting ganged up on by melee opponents, it needs to reposition. Also,
if any of its attackers has an advantage that counters Displacement,
it needs to find a way to nullify that advantage if it can. In this case,
it uses the Disengage action and its movement to get out of melee
attackers' reach and take cover from any ranged attacker who has advantage. Since Disengage consumes its action, it's unable to attack this
turn, but it will return to the fight on its next turn.

The displacer beast's ability to analyze and respond appropriately
to the reasons why its opponents have advantage on attacks against
it is limited. An intelligent animal can grasp the danger of being
attacked from two directions, of being struck by an attacker it can't
see, or of facing a particularly ferocious foe. However, certain other
sources of advantage, such as being limned by a *faerie fire* spell, will
confound it. Not knowing how to respond, it will react in ways
that reflect its confusion. It won't know, for example, that it ought
to consider attacking whoever cast *faerie fire* to break their concentration.

If it's seriously wounded (reduced to 34 hp or fewer), it Dashes or Disengages, depending on how many melee opponents are engaged with it, and flees the scene.

The *Monster Manual* flavor text portrays displacer beasts as predators that hunt for sport as well as food and that toy with their prey before going in for the kill. We can look at this as a factor that influences target selection. Displacer beasts aren't smart, but they're savvy enough to choose their targets well. Like all predators, their preferred targets are the young, the old, the weak, the isolated, and the oblivious.

Despite the flavor text's assertion that displacer beasts "demonstrate skill at setting ambushes," they lack proficiency in Stealth. If this feels wrong to you, you can arbitrarily give them that proficiency (another +2, per "Creating Quick Monster Stats," *Dungeon Master's Guide*, chapter 9, for a total Stealth +4) without making them unfairly powerful for their CR.

When you run a displacer beast encounter, you should choose whether food or sport is the governing motivation and have your beast(s) behave accordingly. A displacer beast hunting for sport attacks and Disengages, attacks and Disengages, unless and until its opponents' reactions force it to respond in other ways. A displacer beast hunting for food, however, doesn't mess around: It attacks until its quarry is unconscious. Moreover, once it's reduced a target to unconsciousness, it picks that target up in its jaws (weight limit: 540 pounds) and Dashes away, having no further need to stick around.

OWLBEARS

A D&D classic, the **owlbear** is a creature of grizzly bear–like size, shape, and temperament with an owl-like head. Its high Constitution, extremely high Strength, and relatively low (though still above-average) Dexterity place it in the brute category, which means its preferred fighting style will be direct assault. Owlbears are dumb (Intelligence 3) and won't prioritize one target over another. They're not stealthy, but they're also hard to fool *with* stealth, having proficiency in Perception and advantage on Wisdom (Perception) checks based on sight or smell. They're fast as well, able to outrun most player characters. Finally, they have standard darkvision, so we can assume that they're active primarily at night and/or underground. An owlbear encountered in its lair during daytime hours will be sleeping, or at least resting, though the presence of other creatures may wake it up.

Owlbear tactics aren't sophisticated. An owlbear that senses prey Dashes after it if it's more than 80 feet away (the noise of which will prevent it from surprising its quarry). Between 40 and 80 feet away, it moves 40 feet toward its target, then Readies the Claws action against the first creature that comes within its reach. At less than 40 feet away, it charges in and Multiattacks. Each Multiattack consists of a Claws attack followed by a Beak attack.

The owlbear single-mindedly attacks the first target it senses unless and until it's struck by a melee attack, in which case it switches its focus to the last opponent who's dealt melee damage to it. (It doesn't understand ranged weaponry.) A trained owlbear—such things apparently exist—can be commanded to keep attacking a specific target, but I'd apply a check similar to that for maintaining concentration on a spell: a Wisdom check with a DC of 10 or half the damage inflicted by a different melee opponent, whichever is greater. On a failure, it reverts to instinct and attacks the foe who just wounded it rather than the one it was commanded to attack. (If it fails by 5 or more, it turns against its handler.)

In open wilderness, an owlbear flees when it's seriously wounded (reduced to 23 hp or fewer). If it's cornered in an enclosed space, however, it keeps fighting to the death.

If an owlbear in the wilderness reduces one of its opponents to 0 hp and no one hits it with a melee attack before the start of its next turn, it seizes the unconscious foe in its beak and Dashes back to its lair with them. It doesn't do this in an enclosed space or if it's in its lair already.

NAGAS

There are three different types of nagas, each of them distinguished primarily by the spells they can cast, and the lists are long. Plus, at least one of the types of naga is lawful good, so player characters won't often encounter it as an enemy.

Let's start by looking at what they all have in common:

- They're shock attackers. Their highest physical stats are Strength and Dexterity, with Constitution significantly lower in each case. They're melee fighters, but they try to strike fast and do as much damage as they can on their first attack, because they don't have as much staying power as a skirmisher or brute.
- Their main weapon is their Bite, which does only a modest amount of piercing damage but a lot of poison damage, and this is their default action in combat. They themselves are immune to poison, as well as to being charmed.
- Their mental abilities are strong across the board, indicating good combat sense and willingness to parley, within reason. Once combat starts, they focus their attacks on their most belligerent enemies, counting on their other opponents' losing the will to fight once the most thirsty are taken down.
- They have darkvision, indicating a preference for nighttime and/or subterranean activity. They won't be encountered outdoors during the day, at least not randomly.
- Nothing we can usually say about evolved creatures applies to them. Per the *Monster Manual*, "A naga doesn't require air, food, drink, or sleep." On top of that, living nagas (the spirit and guardian varieties) can't be slain without casting a *wish* spell: If you "kill" one, it returns to life, with full hit points, in just a few days. Thus, among other things, they never have any reason to flee.
- Living nagas also have no reason to fear spellcasters, since on top of their already high ability scores, they have proficiency in all the big three saving throws, plus Charisma (guardian nagas have proficiency on Intelligence saving throws as well).

The two types of living nagas are the evil **spirit naga** and the good **guardian naga**. The guardian naga is the stronger of the two, with slightly greater spellcasting ability and significantly greater hit points and poison damage. Unfortunately, their spell lists are completely different, with one exception: They both have *hold person*. (I like to imagine that they cast this while swaying back and forth and singing "Trust in Me.")

In lieu of a spell-by-spell breakdown, I'm going to make an observation about what's conspicuously missing from nagas' spell lists: spells that enhance their action economy (spirit nagas have none; guardian nagas have only one, *shield of faith*, which requires concentration to sustain, reducing its value) and spells that would enhance their first strike. *Hold person*, in fact, is the only spell either type of naga has that would give it advantage on an attack roll.

Well, that's not entirely true: The spirit naga also has *sleep*. Attackers have advantage against unconscious targets, and every up-close hit is an automatic critical. This seems ideal for setting up a combination.

The problem is how hard it is to put a PC to sleep with *sleep*. It doesn't work on elves at all, and the base 1st-level spell can only drop 5d8 hp of enemies. Figure that no creature is going to rely on an ability that doesn't have at least a two-thirds chance of success. For a 1st-level *sleep* spell to have a two-thirds chance of knocking a PC out, that PC would have to have 16 hp or fewer. How many mid-level adventurers have that few hit points? A 2nd-level *sleep* must be targeted at an opponent with 23 hp or fewer; 3rd-level, 30 hp or fewer; 4th-level, 36 hp or fewer; and 5th-level, 43 hp or fewer. To *sleep* a PC opponent with more hit points than this is a matter of dumb luck. So *sleep* followed by a Bite attack—a combo that requires two turns— seems unpromising.

Hold person, however, is only slightly better. It requires a Wisdom save, putting the onus on the opponent, but the spirit naga's save DC is only 14, so any opponent with a Wisdom saving throw modifier better than –1 is going to be a hard target; if it's +4 or better, it's not even worth trying. For the guardian naga, the odds are a little better, but not a lot: It has a good chance of success with *hold person* against a target with a Wisdom saving throw modifier of +1 or lower, and it can take a reasonable gamble on opponents with Wisdom save modifiers below +6.

So I'd have to characterize *hold person* plus Bite as "okay but not great"—and unless the naga has allies present, it takes two turns to pull off. On the upside, however, a naga can boost that spell to 3rd or 4th level and try to get two or three opponents with it at once. The chance of paralyzing a single, specific target is iffy, but the chance of paralyzing *one or more* of two or three targets is much better. I'd say, therefore, that this is a tactic that a naga might go ahead and try against a party of four opponents, in which case success would mean disabling half of them or more; but against five or more opponents, it probably wouldn't bother.

Spirit and guardian nagas are faster than most PCs (40 feet of base movement), and their bite is a potent attack, especially against low-Constitution enemies. But what about enemies beyond that range, or ones with higher Constitution?

The spirit naga has *lightning bolt* for direct ranged damage, and it requires a Dexterity save. If three of its enemies are unfortunate enough to have positioned themselves in a straight line, it will go for it. It's also got *blight*, but the range of *blight* is only 30 feet. For an enemy within 70 feet of the naga's original position, it can make this work by moving as far as it needs to in order to get within range of the opponent. *Blight*'s raw damage is greater than *lightning bolt*'s (8d8 vs. 8d6), but *lightning bolt* has the potential to affect multiple enemies, while *blight* targets only one. Unless its enemies are resistant or immune to lightning damage, the spirit naga is better off boosting *lightning bolt* to 4th level instead of casting *blight*.

The guardian naga's go-to spell for direct damage is *flame strike*, which does a maximum 4d6 fire damage, plus 4d6 radiant damage in a 10-foot-radius column 40 feet high, with a range of 60 feet. The spell is worth casting if the guardian naga can strike at least two enemies within the area of effect. Its only other damaging spell is *sacred flame*, which does only 3d8 radiant damage (the guardian naga is a level 11 spellcaster) on a failed save and none at all on a success.

As a general rule, I consider the value of a spell slot to depend on its scarcity more than its level. Thus, for a spirit naga, boosting *lightning bolt* (a 3rd-level spell) by spending a 4th-level spell slot to cast it is as good as using that slot to cast *blight*, because it has as many 4th-level spell slots as it does 3rd-level slots. But it has fewer 5th-level spell slots, so it saves those slots for its 5th-level spell (*dominate person*). Similarly, since a guardian naga has two 5th-level slots but only one 6th-level slot, it won't boost *flame strike* by spending its 6th-level slot to cast it—even though it has little reason to cast its 6th-level spell, *true seeing*, in combat. (Little reason, but not *no* reason—maybe a hostile PC has cast *greater invisibility*.) Either type of naga, if it casts *hold person*, will boost it as high as 4th level, targeting up to three opponents—but not to 5th.

To quickly go over the nagas' other spells:

Spirit nagas' repertoire is capped by *dominate person*, which is a powerful spell, but any damage dealt to the target gives them a chance to snap out of it. Therefore, this is a spell the naga would cast *before* a fight breaks out, for purposes of strife and misdirection—or, in combat, when a single action by the dominated target can have devastating consequences before they can be brought to their senses. *Dimension door* is a common escape hatch for creatures that value their lives, but a spirit naga doesn't care; it casts this spell only if its enemies tip their hand and cast their "No coming back from the dead!" *wish* spell before they've killed it. *Water breathing* makes a spirit naga effectively amphibious; if yours is near water, assume it's cast this spell in advance and subtract a 3rd-level spell slot. *Detect thoughts*, *detect magic*, and *charm person* are useful in social interaction but largely a waste of time in combat, although a spirit naga may cast a boosted *charm person* in order to neutralize its enemies before it attacks.

Guardian nagas can cast *geas*, which takes a full minute to cast, so forget about doing that in combat. *Banishment*, inconveniently, requires concentration to sustain (so no casting *hold person* at the same time), and the targeted opponent comes right back after no more than a minute anyway. An opponent can be taken out of the fight for the same amount of time with a lower-level spell slot by casting *hold person*, unless the target is very high in Wisdom and low in Charisma. *Freedom of movement* is useful if the guardian naga needs to escape from being restrained. *Bestow curse* affects only one target, ever, and it requires concentration; it doesn't stand up as a combat spell next to *hold person*. *Calm emotions* is another concentration spell, only situationally useful. *Command* has its uses, the most apt among them for a lawful good creature being "Begone!" (The guardian naga may be a capable fighter, but that doesn't mean it *wants* to fight. Unless your PCs are unabashedly evil, it will try to get them to leave peacefully rather than initiate combat itself.) *Cure wounds* is more likely to be cast as a boon to supplicant PCs than on the naga itself as a defense measure. *Shield of faith*'s +2 to Armor Class isn't worth the action the spell costs.

Incidentally, in all this talk of spells, I've glossed over the guardian naga's other combat action: Spit Poison. Bluntly, the guardian naga is a lawful good creature; it uses Spit Poison *only* against an evil attacker who won't relent. And only against one who's out of melee range, because the damage is the same as the poison damage from its Bite but without the accompanying piercing damage.

Both spirit and guardian nagas are good at identifying which enemies are likely to be weak to which of their abilities, and they'll both avoid battles that don't favor them, to the extent that their duty allows. Spirit nagas do so by deceiving or charming enemies into leaving them alone; guardian nagas use negotiation, persuasion, and if necessary, intimidation.

Bone nagas are undead, which brings the element of compulsion into play: Whatever purpose the bone naga was created for (probably by yuan-ti—those guys ruin everything), it's obsessive about serving. This may cause it to make what appear to be less rational decisions in combat, including fighting until it's destroyed even though bone nagas *don't* come back to life afterward. The conditions bone nagas are immune to are more extensive, including exhaustion and paralysis, but this doesn't affect their combat behavior. They *are* more vulnerable to spellcasters than living nagas are, however, and make these targets a higher priority.

Bone nagas don't do as much poison damage with their Bite, relative to their piercing damage, as living nagas do, but this is still their default action. Against smaller parties, bone nagas will still try the *hold person*/Bite combination, but it's not as likely to work, because of their much lower spell save DC. The fact that they try it anyway is part of their compulsion to behave as they did when they were still living.

Former spirit nagas use *lightning bolt* the same way and for the same reasons that living spirit nagas do. But a former guardian naga lacks *flame strike*, and what would an undead creature be doing casting *sacred flame*? To be frank, a guardian naga turned into a bone naga is a sad, defeated wreck of a thing that probably won't bother to cast spells at all, even those it still remembers, other than *hold person*. (Maybe, for creepy flavor, you could have it cast *command*, then issue commands that make no sense.)

Since bone nagas have a lower challenge rating, your PCs may encounter them at lower levels than they'd have to be at for an encounter with a living naga to be appropriate. Therefore, *sleep* has a higher chance of being effective. But if the bone naga behaves more or less the way it did in life, it may still believe *sleep* to be ineffective and forgo it! Conversely, it may believe it has a better chance to successfully cast *charm person* than it actually does, trying (and probably failing) to employ it the same way a living spirit naga would.

BEHIRS

The **behir** is an apex predator. A Huge monstrosity, in the neighborhood of 15 feet long, it's tough, strong, and able to run as fast as a lion and to climb faster than most humanoids can run. Its Intelligence is at the upper end of animal range, and it's a good judge of prey. It's also surprisingly stealthy, able to strike from ambush and do spectacular damage to its victims.

All this power comes at a cost: Behirs get sleepy as they digest their prey. Because of this, once a behir strikes and swallows its prey, it immediately breaks off and retreats to its lair or some other hiding place so that it can absorb its meal in peace.

As phrased in the *Monster Manual*, the behir's Multiattack is defined as "two attacks: one with its bite and one to constrict," but this is just alphabetical order. Unless a Multiattack clearly specifies a sequence of actions, it's DM's choice, and Constricting first, then Biting, makes much more sense. A successful Constrict action gives the behir advantage on its follow-up Bite. A successful Bite, on the other hand, does nothing to improve its chance of succeeding at a subsequent Constrict.

Normally, a creature with a recharge ability prefers it over any other method of attack, but in the case of behirs, Lightning Breath is an oddly limited-use feature. Its range is only 20 feet, meaning that in most cases, it's likely to strike only a single target (see the Targets in Area of Effect table, *Dungeon Master's Guide*, chapter 8), and while the damage it does is substantial—you can expect it to deal about 50—it doesn't help the behir *eat* anything.

In contrast, the behir's Multiattack comprises a Constrict action, which deals an average of 34 damage *and* restrains its target on a hit, and a Bite action, which does an average of another 22 damage, with advantage on the attack roll if the target is restrained. That's 56 damage right there, and the behir's chance to hit is extremely high, compared with its chance of doing full damage with its Lightning Breath. Finally, on its next turn, it can Swallow the creature it's restraining, which is what it came for.

Because of this, I see the behir's Lightning Breath as more of a self-defense feature than an attack option, which probably won't come into play unless and until it's moderately wounded (reduced to 117 hp or fewer). If a behir uses this action, it will certainly reposition itself first in order to strike *two* targets (or more, if possible) in its area of effect, if it can. This requires the targets to be within 20 feet of one another and the farthest target to be no more than 20 feet from the behir.

This entry is one of the few in the *Monster Manual* in which the flavor text genuinely enhances the reader's understanding of the stat block. I'm referring specifically to the paragraphs headed "Cavern Predators":

Behirs lair in places inaccessible to other creatures, favoring locations where would-be intruders must make a harrowing climb to reach them. Deep pits, high caves in cliff walls, and caverns reached only by narrow, twisting tunnels are prime sites for a behir ambush. A behir's dozen legs allow it to scramble through its lair site with ease. . . . Behirs swallow their prey whole, after which they enter a period of dormancy while they digest.

We can imagine a behir lying in wait, concealed in the darkness of a subterranean cavern or among rocks on a cliffside (twilight is ideal, because of its darkvision), for potential prey to pass by. When it does, the behir pounces, lunging forth from its hiding place (rolling with advantage from unseen attack), using its Constrict ability to grapple and restrain the target creature, then following up with a Bite (rolling with advantage, if the Constrict attack succeeded).

On its following turn, if the behir's target hasn't escaped the grapple, it uses the Swallow action (rolling with advantage, because the target is still restrained) to try to gulp down its target. If it succeeds, it immediately uses its full movement to scramble away, preferably in a direction where its victim's allies can't follow.

Note that a behir can Constrict a Large or smaller creature, but it can only Swallow a *Medium* or smaller creature. Quick-thinking spellcasters can preserve a Medium-size ally (or themselves) from being swallowed by snapping off an *enlarge* spell. Funny thing about being restrained: It *doesn't* interfere with the gestures and movements necessary to cast a spell with a somatic requirement!

A behir without a Medium or smaller grappled target simply tries its Constrict/Bite Multiattack again—it's not smart enough to change it up. Only when it's taken enough damage to realize it needs to defend itself (see above) does it introduce Lightning Breath into the mix, using this action whenever it's not on cooldown and Multiattacking whenever it is.

Once a behir is seriously injured (reduced to 67 hp or fewer), it says, "Fine, forget this," and retreats. A behir's Armor Class is high enough, and its hit points numerous enough, that it never concerns itself with opportunity attacks from a single melee attacker, simply Dashing away. If it's within reach of more than one, it Dodges until it's out of range, *then* Dashes. This applies whether it's running away because of its injuries or because it's already had its dinner.

HARPIES

The **harpy** is a foul-tempered predator with an alluring voice. It has a balanced physical ability profile, with slightly but not significantly higher Dexterity than Strength or Constitution, and it has no ranged attack. Instead, it uses the long-range ability Luring Song to bring prey into melee attack range.

Its Intelligence of 7 indicates that the harpy is instinct-driven, and its Wisdom of 10 indicates that it's indiscriminate in target selection but knows when to flee. This is consistent with one part of the *Monster Manual* flavor text: "If a fight turns against a harpy, it lacks the cunning to adapt and will flee and go hungry." It's less consistent with this part: "A harpy takes its time dismembering a helpless foe and can spend days torturing a victim." If this were instinctive to the harpy, it would be disadvantageous to its chances of survival. Granted, Intelligence 7 is the upper bound of instinct-driven behavior; I suppose it's *possible* that a harpy might toy with its prey or lure it into natural hazards before attacking it, but these behaviors feel too sophisticated to me.

This part, however, makes a lot of sense: "Harpies have no interest in a fair fight, and they never attack unless they have a clear advantage." All predators have an innate sense of which creatures are vulnerable enough for them to prey on and which creatures aren't. Since the harpy's physical ability contour doesn't suggest any one characteristic fighting style, it makes sense that it would have to find some other edge, something neither dependent on its own strengths nor compensatory for its weaknesses.

Here's the compromise I've settled on: Harpies congregate around natural hazards that other creatures frequently fall into, because these provide them the best hunting grounds. Luring other creatures into these hazards isn't something they do intentionally—it's just something that happens a lot, the natural consequence of their own abilities combined with the terrain. Harpies that roost near hazards simply survive better, having more opportunities to feed.

Now let's figure out what kind of creature is suitable prey for a harpy, one vs. one. The harpy is a CR 1 monster. Against a single PC, its encounter multiplier would be 1.5 (per the Encounter Multipliers table, *Dungeon Master's Guide*, chapter 3), for a total of 300 adjusted XP. That would make a single harpy a deadly encounter against a level

1 or 2 PC, hard for level 3. In other words, one humanoid is definitely suitable prey for one harpy. Since harpies aren't smart enough to make judgments like, "Oh, dear, that person is walking with confidence and carrying a very fine weapon; she may be too skilled a fighter for me to handle," a harpy might fearlessly attack humanoids even in groups of four or five. (Probably not more than five.) After all, against AC 10, a harpy has a 70 percent chance to hit with each of its attacks and can be expected to do 7 damage in one turn—more than enough to kill a commoner—and this is without the victim's being debilitated in any way. For the sake of encounter building, however, you'll want to calibrate the number of harpies to the number of PCs in your group and how difficult you want the encounter to be.

Finally, let's look at the Luring Song feature, because the way it's written makes it seem more complicated than it is, and it buries its implications. First, it has a range of 300 feet: A victim hears the song long before they ever see the harpy. An immediate Wisdom saving throw is called for, on which elves have advantage (owing to Fey Ancestry). If the saving throw succeeds, the creature is immune to the effect. If it fails, the victim is charmed (can't attack the harpy or harm it with magic or any other ability) and incapacitated (can't take actions or reactions) and must move toward the harpy by the most direct route. The victim gets to repeat the saving throw at the end of each of their own turns, with any success conferring immunity to the effect for 24 hours.

The DC for this saving throw is only 11—not very high. A PC with a +1 Wisdom saving throw modifier (i.e., this is an average ability score for the character, and not one they have class proficiency in) has a 55 percent chance of success each time they roll; with a +4 Wisdom saving throw modifier (i.e., this is a prime requisite ability and one they do have class proficiency in), they have a 70 percent chance of success. With the advantage conferred by Fey Ancestry, these probabilities rise to 80 percent and 91 percent. In other words, unless Wisdom is a PC's dump stat, it's unlikely they'll fail this save twice, and three failures would be a dismal run of bad luck. So anytime the harpy might use Luring Song, it has to cash in on its effect immediately. Even one more round is too long to wait.

Here's how I see all this fitting together: The harpy waits hidden, 20 feet above a natural hazard. When its prospective prey wanders within 25 feet of that hazard, it uses Luring Song to entice the victim into the hazard. At the edge of the hazard, just before stepping in, the victim gets another saving throw (if the hazard will cause actual damage and not just a debilitating condition), on which they'll probably succeed.

At this point, as the DM, you need to decide how smart your harpy is. If you want it to be more animalistic, just have it fly down and Multiattack immediately, then fly back up out of reach, regardless of whether or not the victim makes their saving throw. If you want the harpy to have a smidgen of cunning, it can attack immediately if the victim fails their save and steps into the hazard. If the intended victim succeeds on their save, on the other hand, then the harpy can attempt to *shove* its opponent into the hazard ("Melee Attacks," *Player's Handbook*, chapter 9) in lieu of its Multiattack, then use the rest of its movement to fly back up out of reach.

One Multiattack is normally enough to finish off a humanoid commoner. On the harpy's second turn, it flies down and Multiattacks one more time, against the same target, with its club and claws. If this isn't enough to bring its opponent down, the harpy has just barely enough wits to recognize that this isn't going to be easy prey after all, and it flies away. It never prolongs the fight beyond two rounds. On its third turn, it Dashes, fleeing at double its normal flying movement speed.

PERYTONS

The **peryton** is a monstrosity with the body of an enormous bird of prey and the head of a stag, albeit a carnivorous stag with nasty incisors. Perytons roost in mountains and rocky hills near settled areas where they can find prey. According to the *Monster Manual*, they favor humanoids in general and humans and elves in particular, and they'll often try to rip out their prey's heart and carry it off. "When attacking a humanoid," the *Monster Manual* says, "a peryton is single-minded and relentless, fighting until it or its prey dies." This lack of self-preservation instinct (which is contraindicated by the peryton's above-average Wisdom, so you may choose to disregard it) distinguishes it from an ordinary evolved predator.

All of a peryton's physical abilities are above average, but its Strength is especially high, so it's going to go for big-damage attacks, primarily by dive-bombing its prey. Its features include Dive Attack and Flyby: The former is an aerial charge that deals additional damage, while the latter exempts it from opportunity attacks when it flies out of an enemy's reach. The peryton has a flying speed of 60 feet, and its Dive Attack requires it to fly 30 feet to gain the extra damage.

This combination makes the peryton's preferred attack tactic obvious: Its first attack is always a Dive Attack, from a distance of exactly 30 feet if possible. It uses 30 feet of its move to conduct this attack; Multiattacks with Talons and Gore, gaining Dive Attack damage on the first of these; then, if its target is still alive and kicking, uses the other 30 feet of its move to fly away again. As long as its prey lives, it repeats this combination.

What will make a peryton deviate from this pattern? Well, if it succeeds in rendering its target unconscious, and it's not taking damage from a magic weapon (more on this in a moment), it may keep attacking its target until they're not merely unconscious but dead. (Remember that close-up melee strikes against an unconscious target are automatic critical hits, and each crit results in two death save failures.) At that point, it's torn out its prey's heart, and it proceeds to fly off with it. Alternatively, if the target is of Small size, it may simply pick the entire unconscious target up in its talons and carry them away to its nest.

Perytons have resistance to physical damage from nonmagical weapons, so when they're struck by magic weapons, they take notice. If a peryton has already rendered a target unconscious, but it's taking damage from a magic weapon, it doesn't remain on the ground with its prey. Instead, it continues its pattern of flying up out of reach in between attacks, and it refocuses its attacks on whoever's wielding that weapon. Perytons aren't super bright, but if someone's shooting one with a ranged weapon, it can figure out where that attack is coming from. If it happens to be a *magic* ranged weapon, that just might be enough to drive the peryton off . . . if it's alone. However, perytons often hunt in mated pairs, and not only will a *pair* of perytons not be scared off by Owena's magic bow, they'll ferociously focus their attacks on her.

When they're not focusing their attacks on a single antagonist in this way, perytons don't fight cooperatively. Instead, each peryton in a group (I'd have them appear only alone, in pairs or—on rare occasions, when necessary for encounter balance—in a group of four consisting of two mated pairs) picks out a separate target to focus on, because each is after its own meal.

When it's got its sights on a humanoid victim, the only thing that will drive a peryton away is being seriously injured (reduced to 13 hp or fewer), with magic weapons contributing at least 10 damage to the total it's taken. Even then, it will continue to reconnoiter its victim (and the possessor of the magic weapon), and it will return and attack again the next day, when it's feeling better. However, a peryton that gets what it came for—either a humanoid heart or an entire Small humanoid that it can fly away with—takes its prize and leaves, even if it's not wounded at all. If one of a mated pair succeeds in tearing out its victim's heart, its mate departs along with it when it leaves.

Note that perytons have keen senses and a high Perception skill— they're hard to hide from—but they don't have darkvision. Perytons are daytime hunters, making them good candidates for a random encounter on the road.

GRIFFONS AND HIPPOGRIFFS

The **griffon** and the **hippogriff** are closely related creatures, both originating in classical myth and living on in medieval and renaissance heraldry. They both have the heads, wings, and forelegs of eagles; the back half of the hippogriff is equine, while the griffon's is leonine. As you might surmise from that, the griffon is the more powerful of the two. Both, according to the *Monster Manual*, can be trained as flying mounts.

Neither is all that complicated a critter. Both can fly, although the hippogriff is the swifter of the two on land, the griffon in the air.

Both have exceptional Strength and above-average Wisdom; the griffon's Dexterity and Constitution are very high, while the hippogriff's are merely above average. Both have double proficiency in Perception plus Keen Sight, which gives them advantage on such ability checks as well.

Beyond these traits, both the griffon and the hippogriff have but a single melee Multiattack comprising one Beak attack and one Claws attack. They possess no other feature that enhances their action economy or gives them a tactical advantage.

The hippogriff, having the lower Dexterity and Constitution, is a hit-and-run predator. It uses its Perception and Keen Sight to spot prey—singling out the young, the old, the weak, the isolated, and/or the oblivious—and flies down for one good, hard Multiattack strike, which is enough to take down any ordinary prey animal. If that doesn't do the trick, the hippogriff cuts and runs, flying away using the Dash action (and potentially provoking an opportunity attack in the process).

The griffon is much more durable and therefore better suited to a prolonged scrap, so it will actually put up with an opportunity attack or two in order to fly in, Multiattack, and fly back into the air, out of melee reach. But it doesn't have much appetite for prey that fights back: Once it's moderately wounded (reduced to 41 hp or fewer), it too Dashes away through the air.

ANKHEGS

The **ankheg**, a large burrowing arthropod, is a mechanistic brute with Intelligence 1, and therefore no tactical sophistication and no ability to adapt to a situation that's not exactly what it expected.

Ankhegs tunnel just below the surface of the earth and wait for prey to pass overhead. They can't tunnel too deeply, because with only 10 feet of burrowing movement, they have to be able to burst out of the earth directly beneath their intended prey and attack in the same turn.

Does an ankheg lead with its Bite action or its Acid Spray? Generally, an ability that has to recharge is stronger than one that doesn't, but when it recharges only on a 6, it's something that a creature has to use judiciously, because in all likelihood, it will get to use it only once in a combat encounter. Moreover, by attacking just as it bursts from the earth, an ankheg can gain unseen-attacker advantage on its Bite, which requires an attack roll; it can't gain advantage on Acid Spray, against which a target has to make a saving throw. On the other hand, an ankheg can't use Acid Spray if it has a target grappled in its jaws, so shouldn't it use this ability first?

Well, which attack does more damage? A successful Bite deals 14 damage total, on average, and automatically grapples. An Armor Class of 13 is fairly typical for a low-level adventurer. With +5 to hit, an ankheg's Bite hits this AC 65 percent of the time, so expected damage is about 9—and over two turns, because a successful Bite on the first hit means advantage on the second roll, the per-round expected damage increases to about 10. Acid Spray deals 10 acid damage on a failed saving throw, 5 on a success, for an expected 8 damage against each target it hits (assuming a fifty-fifty save probability). According to the Targets in Area of Effect table in chapter 8 of the *Dungeon Master's Guide*, a 30-foot linear area of effect should only be expected to hit one target. Granted, any two targets make a line, provided they're close enough together, but ankhegs are subsentient; their brains can't handle the problem of lining up the shot. If they ever hit two or more targets with Acid Spray, it's a lucky accident.

So the ankheg initiates combat with a Bite. If it hits, it seizes the target in its jaws and continues to Bite that target again and again until they're dead (not just unconscious—*dead*). Plus, if it takes even one hit from another enemy, it starts burrowing again, trying to get away with its meal. Thus, a victim might successfully escape from an ankheg's jaws only to find themself trapped in a tunnel between the ankheg and a dead end. Its darkvision keeps it from suffering disadvantage while attacking its prey while underground.

Acid Spray comes into play only when the ankheg is aboveground without a target in its jaws. It sprays its digestive bile essentially at random, and any creature it happens to hit is the top-priority target for its next Bite.

Predatory creatures have little liking for prey that fights back. An ankheg retreats when only moderately wounded (reduced to 27 hp or fewer). A fleeing ankheg can only Dash, and its instinct compels it to do so by burrowing, even though this is much slower than running away over land. Woe to the ankheg whose foes thirst for vengeance.

BULETTES

Nicknamed "land sharks" because of an armored plate that resembles a dorsal fin and their propensity for breaching out of the earth while attacking, **bulettes** (emphasis on the second syllable) are brutes tailor-made to give your players jump scares. They're big, very tough (with extraordinary Strength and Constitution), surprisingly fast, and dumb as rocks. They have exactly one trick, and they use it again and again. But it's a good one.

An ambush predator, a bulette waits underground for prey to pass overhead, detecting it with tremorsense. The range on this sense is 60 feet, but the bulette conceals itself just 10 or 15 feet below the surface. When it detects prey, it uses its full movement—burrowing *and* regular, along with its Standing Leap trait—to launch itself out of the earth, through the air, and onto the poor, unfortunate souls who disturbed the ground. It concludes this maneuver with the Deadly Leap action, pouncing on up to four foes at once, depending on how closely they're clustered and whether you're using a square or hex grid. (If you're playing "theater of the mind," the Targets in Area of Effect table in chapter 8 of the *Dungeon Master's Guide* would suggest that the bulette should land on only one enemy, but it seems wasteful not to have it land on two, at the very least.)

Deadly Leap, in addition to the damage it does, has the potential to knock enemies prone, making it harder for them to get away—even by Dashing—by eating up their movement. When it's wounded an opponent, and that opponent stands up and tries to get away, the bulette makes an opportunity attack against it with Bite. Then, if its fleeing prey is still within 40 feet of it, it chases them down and Bites, then makes another opportunity attack if they try to run again. If its opponent does manage to get beyond its 40-foot movement range, it makes another Deadly Leap, against one or more other targets (two or more, if possible) 15 to 40 feet away. If none is within reach, it burrows into the ground, waiting beneath the earth to feel their vibrations. When it does, it starts the whole cycle again.

Technically, thanks to Standing Leap, the bulette can even use Deadly Leap to launch itself straight up in the air and come down on an enemy closer than 15 feet. It may subject itself to one or more opportunity attacks by doing this, but its Armor Class is 17, it has lots of hit points, and also, as I mentioned, it's very, very stupid.

The *Monster Manual* flavor text states that bulettes love the taste of halflings and dislike elf and dwarf meat. If that doesn't strike you as ludicrous, then have your bulette prioritize halfling opponents when selecting targets after its initial launch, and have it attack dwarves and elves only when they're prone and not pursue them when they're wounded.

Despite its minimal Intelligence, the bulette does have a normal survival instinct and will Dash away when severely injured (reduced to 37 hp or fewer). When it flees, it does so through the ground if at all possible, leaving a tunnel behind it. You can decide how stable this tunnel is and whether or not your PCs can safely pursue the bulette without the tunnel collapsing: Soft, sandy soil will collapse as quickly as the bulette burrows through it, while clay will hold up much longer. Unlike some burrowing monsters, bulettes can't tunnel through solid rock.

UMBER HULKS

Based on its ability contour, the **umber hulk** is a straightforward brute: extraordinary Strength, very high Constitution, comparatively lower (though still above-average) Dexterity; its mental abilities are unremarkable.

It has nothing in the way of special skills, such as Stealth, but it has 120 feet of darkvision and 60 feet of tremorsense—the ability to detect vibrations through earth—and it can burrow at a speed of 20 feet per round. Even solid rock is merely difficult terrain as far as the umber hulk is concerned, thanks to its Tunneler trait. So a burrowing umber hulk can lie beneath the ground, unseen, waiting for prey to pass overhead, then make its first strike with advantage as an unseen attacker. Most likely, though, that first attack is the only one it will get from hiding.

It has a fierce melee Multiattack: two attacks with its claws and one with its jaws. There's no decision to be made there, though. The only thing that makes the umber hulk unique from a combat perspective is its Confusing Gaze.

Confusing Gaze isn't an action, merely a side effect of fighting an umber hulk. Anyone within 30 feet of an umber hulk at the start of their turn, as long as it's not incapacitated and they can see it, has to quickly avert their eyes or make a DC 15 Charisma saving throw against being boggled. The effect of a failed save is similar to that of a *confusion* spell: Half the time the umber hulk's opponent just stands and stares, a quarter of the time they walk off in a random direction, and a quarter of the time they attack someone at random.

Again, there's no *decision* to be made here. A DM can run an umber hulk entirely on autopilot. However, there is one interesting implication buried in the interaction of these features.

Darkvision and tremorsense imply a subterranean creature—one accustomed to fighting in total darkness. Remember, against a blinded opponent—that is, any player character without either darkvision or a light source—it gains advantage on its attack rolls, while the blinded foe has disadvantage on attack rolls against it. However, anyone who does have darkvision, or who introduces a light source, is susceptible to the umber hulk's Confusing Gaze. Damned if you do, damned if you don't.

Thus, there are only two ways to fight an umber hulk without being handicapped: Either have a very high Charisma *and* proficiency in that saving throw, or keep your distance and attack it from range. Naturally, the umber hulk ain't having none of that. Its opponent retreats; it advances. It always looks to close to melee range with whatever enemy is nearest, without discriminating among them.

An umber hulk breaks off when seriously wounded (reduced to 37 hp or fewer). It burrows through loose earth to get away if it can, so that the earth collapses behind it (if it burrowed through rock, it would move too slowly to escape, and it would leave an easy-to-follow tunnel behind it). If that's not available, it Dodges while retreating for a couple of rounds. It moves backward, facing its enemies, counting on the likelihood that its Confusing Gaze will disorient its pursuers long enough for it to get away. Whether that works or not, after a couple of rounds of Dodging, it switches to the Dash action.

REMORHAZES

The **remorhaz** (pronounced *rem*-o-raz) has a simple brute profile: high Strength, high Constitution, low-to-middling everything else, without much in the way of tactics that might modify this. Let's see what there is in its stat block that might liven it up:

- Burrowing movement. Remorhazes aren't stealthy, but it doesn't take proficiency in Stealth to sit in a hole in the ground and wait for prey to stroll by. (I love how the *Monster Manual* handwaves the combination of the remorhaz's arctic habitat and its Heated Body trait by declaring, "While hidden under the ice and snow, it can lower its body temperature so that it doesn't melt its cover." Isn't that convenient!)
- Sixty feet of tremorsense. This I like, because it works the same way as the sandworms in *Dune*. It doesn't have to see you walking overhead: It can *feel* you.
- Heated Body. Touch a remorhaz, or hit it with a non-reach melee attack, and you take fire damage.
- The Swallow action. This is where the remorhaz gets interesting.

We can take it as given that a hunting remorhaz will lurk beneath the ice, waiting for prey; I can't buy the flavor text's assertion that it can lower its body heat at will, though. I'd give any PC with a passive Perception of, let's say, 16 or better a tip that *something* isn't right—they feel a strange warmth from below the ice, or the snow seems to have settled strangely over a certain spot—and allow that character to act during the "O HAI IT ME REMORHAZ" surprise round.

Remorhaz combat is going to revolve around the Bite/Swallow combination, which takes place over two or more rounds, since remorhazes get only one attack per round. A successful Bite attack imposes both the grappled condition and the restrained condition on its target. A successful Swallow attack, which can only target an already grappled opponent (implicitly, by a Bite attack), does an additional attack's worth of Bite damage and sends the target on an all-expenses-paid vacation through the remorhaz's digestive tract.

The limitations on these actions are crucial. After a successful Bite, a remorhaz holds its target in its jaws and therefore can't bite anyone else; it can only swallow the target. After an *unsuccessful* Bite—a missed attack—there's no grappled opponent to swallow. So the flowchart here is super simple: Anything in its mouth? If not, Bite. If so, Swallow.

What if a remorhaz's Swallow attack fails? Then the target is still in its jaws, taking no damage (albeit getting thoroughly coated in remorhaz slobber); the remorhaz can try to Swallow the target again on its next turn. If, as a DM, you use the optional Disarm rule from "Action Options" in chapter 9 of the *Dungeon Master's Guide*, you might allow your PCs to try to bash the remorhaz upside the head in order to make it drop an ally that it holds in its jaws; it's not likely that they'll succeed, given the remorhaz's extraordinary Strength, but at least the rule can be reasonably interpreted to cover the attempt. If you don't use optional actions, an allied PC can use the Help action to give the grappled PC advantage on their roll to escape, but the grappled PC had better take their turn before the remorhaz does.

A swallowed opponent is blinded and restrained, two conditions that impose disadvantage on attack rolls, which is relevant to any attempt that character makes to fight their way out. To make a remorhaz puke them back up, a swallowed opponent must inflict 30 damage in a single *turn*—not a single *round*. Generally speaking, therefore, the damage has to be done by one swallowed opponent. (But here's a loophole: If a second foe is swallowed, one can Ready an Attack action to take place right after the other's. In that case, both opponents' attacks, if successful, do damage on the same turn. Cute, huh?)

Here's the real bad news for anyone who gets swallowed by a remorhaz: This is an evolved creature with a fully functional survival instinct. When it's seriously wounded (reduced to 78 hp or fewer), it's going to skedaddle, throwing a wrench in any ongoing rescue attempt. Since it has the ability to burrow, it will.

Don't imagine that it leaves a convenient tunnel behind it, either; it's a monster, not a mining engineer. Any snow or ice it burrows through is quite likely to collapse behind it. Even if it doesn't, the remorhaz is like a biological Zamboni: Its body heat, melting the ice, is going to leave its path smooth and slick. Pursuers will find themselves moving over difficult terrain, no question.

CARRION CRAWLERS

The **carrion crawler** is a scavenger, drawn to the smell of death. It nourishes itself on the remains of the already dead, so when it's fighting, it's not hunting for food—it's defending the food it's already found. Its enemies aren't prey but rivals.

Carrion crawlers have climbing movement and the Spider Climb trait, so underground they'll happily travel along walls and ceilings and make use of vertical passages. Their very high Constitution makes them tough, relentless fighters, whether engaging in stationary melee or mobile skirmishing. The combination of darkvision and Keen Smell suggests that when they do venture aboveground, they do so only after nightfall.

They have two basic attack actions, Tentacles and Bite. Bite does simple piercing damage. Tentacles does poison damage and has a chance of imposing the poisoned and paralyzed conditions. Being poisoned is inconvenient, imposing disadvantage on attack rolls and ability checks, but being paralyzed is devastating. Tentacles also has a 10-foot reach, vs. 5 feet for Bite.

A carrion crawler's Multiattack consists of one use of Tentacles and one of Bite. It uses Tentacles first, because if the target fails their saving throw, the follow-up Bite attack will have advantage and deal critical damage. Note that the latter depends on the carrion crawler's being within 5 feet of the target. If not already engaged in melee, a carrion crawler attacks with Tentacles when it's still 10 feet away from its target, *then* closes in the rest of the way before using Bite.

A curiosity in the carrion crawler's stat block is that while Bite has only +4 to hit, Tentacles has +8. Against AC 15, these afford a 50 percent chance and a 70 percent chance to hit, respectively. This makes the expected damage from a Tentacles attack (3) almost as good as the expected damage from a Bite attack (4); plus, it comes with the benefit of the saving throw rider. Since the paralyzed condition is so strong, the carrion crawler has an incentive to let opponents leave its 5-foot reach radius without making an opportunity Bite attack—saving its reaction for an opportunity Tentacles attack if and when those opponents leave its *10*-foot reach radius.

Because carrion crawlers aren't predators but territorial scavengers, they fight more aggressively, refusing to back down until they're seriously wounded (reduced to 20 hp or fewer). They retreat using the Dash action.

RUST MONSTERS

Back when God's grandma was a little girl, D&D's focus was emphatically on the dungeons—and by "dungeons," it meant not just dank, subterranean lockups but vast underground complexes containing entire societies and ecosystems. PCs spent a lot of time exploring these networks of caverns, and there was little or no opportunity to pop back up to the nearest village and replenish supplies.

So when your front-line fighter got cocky and armored themself up like a Panzer IV, the *Monster Manual* provided a way to cut them down to size: the **rust monster**, whose sole raison d'être was the annihilation of plate armor when it was neither cheap nor convenient to replace.

This cheese beast lives on in fifth edition D&D, and despite the absurdity of a creature nourishing itself on a pre-oxidized, chemically stable substance, we have to look at this unaligned monstrosity as an evolved creature, because any other explanation of its existence is just too meta.

Rust monsters are chitinous cave dwellers (darkvision lets them see without sunlight), robust but not exceptional in all physical abilities, above average in Wisdom and with no Intelligence to speak of. The composite portrait is of a bold, instinct-driven critter that goes after what it wants without fear—or subtlety—but has enough of a sense of self-preservation to skedaddle when threatened.

Rust monsters want to eat, not fight, so they won't use their Bite action unless cornered. Instead, they'll primarily use their Antennae action, which "corrodes a nonmagical ferrous metal object it can see within 5 feet of it." This means they have to close to melee engagement range; it also means they have to know the metal is there.

Thus, until a group of PCs approaches within 60 feet of it, a rust monster moves around aimlessly. Once it detects movement, it ventures in that direction. When it comes within 30 feet of an iron or steel tool, weapon, shield, or armor—at which point its Iron Scent trait kicks in—it goes, "Aha! Lunch!" and moves directly toward whoever's carrying or wearing it, then uses its Antennae action if it can get within 5 feet.

The rust monster is most strongly attracted to the largest concentration of iron. It might start moving toward a PC wearing ring mail and carrying a shortsword but then come within sniffing distance of one wearing plate armor and carrying a longsword; in this case, it changes course toward the latter PC.

Before the session in which this encounter occurs, total up each PC's "iron points" to determine whom the rust monster will find most alluring: Medium or heavy armor has FeP equal to its Armor Class minus 12, an all-metal weapon has 2 FeP, a wood-hafted weapon or tool has 1 FeP, a shield has 1 FeP regardless of size (shields larger than a buckler are typically made of wood with metal fittings, not entirely of metal), and a quiver of 10 or more arrows or crossbow bolts has 1 FeP.

(Note the wording of the Iron Scent trait: "The rust monster can pinpoint, *by scent*, the location of ferrous metal within 30 feet of it"— emphasis mine. It can *smell* iron on an invisible creature, but it can't use its Antennae action on it, because it can't *see* it. Thus, the presence of an invisible plate armor–wearing PC boggles a rust monster profoundly. It wants the noms, but it can't have them. It just sits there, confused, waving its antennae in the air.)

Old-school D&D players will instantly recognize a rust monster—and the risk it poses—but if you're a DM sending them against players who've never encountered them before, don't describe their behavior as aggressive or hostile, because they're *not* aggressive or hostile. They don't "attack"—they "move toward," waggling their feelers. For all the PCs know, they may just be curious, even friendly! That is, until they wrap those corrosive antennae around the paladin's 1,500 gp plate armor and start rubbing them vigorously against it, leaving big patches of rust beneath.

Unless the PCs interfere, the rust monster won't attack them, only their iron belongings. If they attack it, it has to choose between feeding and fleeing. It bases this decision on how large a meal it has in front of it. Once a rust monster has taken damage equal to or greater than the FeP of the PC it's trying to feed off, it scuttles away, using the Dash action (it's not nimble enough to Dodge nor smart enough to Disengage). As mentioned above, a rust monster uses its Bite action *only* when cornered—that is, when it wants to flee but all paths of escape are blocked.

Rust monsters have a challenge rating of only 1/2, so one alone will pose a negligible challenge even to a party of level 1 PCs. More probably, therefore, a rust monster encounter will involve the PCs' stumbling across a *nest* of rust monsters. (The *Monster Manual* disagrees, saying, "Rust monsters are rarely found in large numbers, preferring to hunt alone or in small groups," but in that case, why bother? That being said, once your PCs are level 5 or higher, you can probably consider them to have outgrown rust monsters—at that point, they'll have to be outnumbered four to one to consider rust monsters anything but vermin.) Alternatively, like remoras schooling around a shark or an Egyptian plover picking the teeth of a crocodile, rust monsters may hang around the lairs of more fearsome creatures, scavenging iron from their victims.

Regardless of how many the PCs encounter, the rust monsters' behavior won't differ. In fact, they'll all be most drawn to the same PC—the one toting the most iron—and will crowd around them, eager to nosh. Only if a single PC is surrounded by *six* of them (regardless of whether you're using a square map, a hex map, or theater of the mind) will any additional rust monster(s) settle for second-best, and it will take the same amount of damage to fend off each of them as it would to fend off one alone. (A rust monster settling for the second-largest concentration of iron will be driven off by damage equal to or greater than that PC's FeP.)

The *Monster Manual* flavor text notes that PCs "can distract the creature by dropping ferrous objects behind them," which makes me wonder whether the authors have any experience at all with raccoons. Dropping food for rust monsters is an excellent way of *getting them to follow you*. To satiate them enough for them to lose interest in your mouthwatering weapons and armor is going to take a *lot* of discarded iron—say, 10 FeP worth altogether.

GRICKS

The **grick** is a grayish subterranean snake-worm monstrosity 5 to 8 feet in length, with a sharp, beaked mouth ringed by four clawed, suckered tentacles—in short, the stuff of nightmares. Normally a cavern-dweller, it occasionally ventures aboveground if food is scarce, ensconcing itself in rocky crevices where prey is likely to pass by.

Its Strength and Dexterity are high, in contrast with its average Constitution, so its preferred method of attack is an ambush strike. It's also primarily nocturnal, on the basis of its darkvision, though not exclusively: It may, for instance, hide in a dark crevice aboveground, yet attack creatures that are outside in the light. Although it has no Stealth skill per se, it has the Stone Camouflage trait, which gives it advantage on Dexterity (Stealth) checks in rocky terrain. Consequently, it will stick to this kind of area and remain hidden until a target creature draws near, then attack from hiding, with advantage.

The grick has Multiattack, but it's a limited Multiattack: It gets to make its Beak attack only after a successful Tentacle attack. In other words, it's gotta grab you before it can bite you. The larger and much tougher **grick alpha** has a more complex Multiattack: In addition to its Tentacle attack, it can also lash out with its tail. It, too, has to hit with its tentacles in order to attack with its beak, however.

Both the grick and the grick alpha, inexplicably, have resistance to physical damage from nonmagical weapons. Nothing in the *Monster Manual* flavor text suggests why this should be so; it just is. The conclusion I draw is that the grick is a persistent predator that won't be deterred by fighting back with ordinary weapons. Only elemental damage or a magic weapon will impel it to back off. However, thanks to its high Wisdom score, which implies a strong self-preservation impulse, it doesn't take much magical or elemental damage to make it back off, just enough to moderately wound it (9 or more magical or elemental damage for a grick, 23 or more for a grick alpha).

A grick has a normal movement speed of 30 feet and a climbing speed of 30 feet. The normal movement speed isn't enough to allow it to hide again once it's revealed its position by attacking. The climbing speed might be, if it can reach a crevice it can slither into, but there's a problem with using this tactically, which is that its opponent, upon seeing it slither into that crevice, can simply back well away from it and keep their distance, so that the grick has no way of successfully ambushing them again. I'd say, then, that it won't even try. Once it's blown its cover, it's committed to melee combat until it prevails or is forced to retreat.

Finally, a grick that renders its opponent unconscious will normally try to carry them back to its lair to devour, by wrapping its tentacles around them and dragging them off. Aboveground, however, that "lair" will often be a crevice that the victim doesn't fit into. In such a case, the grick has a lot farther to go: It will head for a cave, perhaps, or a burrow, or simply an out-of-the-way spot in the woods where it can find some measure of camouflage. It won't stick around and keep fighting just for the sake of fighting, however. It kills to eat, so when it's got something it can eat, it wants to go off and eat it in peace.

DRIDERS

The **drider** is a centaurlike monstrosity with the head and torso of a drow and the thorax and abdomen of a giant spider. (In both centaurs and driders, the torso of the humanoid replaces the head of the beast, creating a creature with, presumably, two whole cardiopulmonary systems. We're probably better off not thinking about this too much.)

Driders, according to the *Monster Manual* flavor text, are debased creations of the goddess Lolth, presumably produced with some frequency as pious drow fail the challenges of the Demonweb Pits. The text says nothing about whether driders reproduce to create new generations of driders; I'm going to assume they don't, meaning they're *not* evolved creatures. Because of the means of their creation, they may or may not have a strong self-preservation impulse—some of them may even have a death wish.

Driders are fighting machines. They have high Strength, high Dexterity, and exceptional Constitution, suiting them for any sort of combat—ranged or melee, ambush or assault, swift or prolonged. They have a triple Multiattack with either longsword or longbow and can replace one of either of those attacks with a poisonous bite. However, based on their proficiency in Stealth, let's say they prefer to start combat with a surprise attack.

Their Spider Climb ability allows them to maneuver along walls and ceilings, and their Web Walker ability lets them ignore movement penalties from the webs of giant spiders. (They don't have the ability to create webs themselves, however.) They're strictly nocturnal and/or subterranean, having both 120-foot darkvision and Sunlight Sensitivity.

The flavor text implies that they're solitary with respect to drow and other driders, but it also says they sometimes lead packs of giant spiders. Let's say, then, that a drider encounter is going to take one of these two forms: either one drider by itself, or a drider plus at least four giant spiders (as many as you need to achieve the desired encounter difficulty).

A drider by itself waits in hiding and observes its foes, sizing them up by how much armor they're wearing. When it's ready to attack, if at least two of those foes are wearing medium or heavy armor, it uses its surprise round to cast *faerie fire*. Why would it do that rather than attack with advantage? Because while attacking from hiding would give it advantage on *one* attack, *faerie fire* gives it advantage on *every* subsequent attack, and the more armored up its opponents are, the more of a difference it makes.

Ranged or melee combat? Ranged, to start with, for the simple reason that it's likely to be outnumbered, and if you keep your distance, you can attack anyone, while not everyone can attack you; whereas if you're engaged in melee, everyone can attack you, while your attacks are limited to your melee opponent(s). Plus, the bow does more damage.

The drider attacks when its targets are between 30 and 150 feet away (30 and 60 feet, if it's casting *faerie fire*), and it tries to maintain its distance, because maintaining its distance means maintaining that advantageous arrangement. It runs along walls and ceilings in order to stay out of melee attackers' reach. The primary targets of its attacks are the primary targets of its hate: first dwarves and rock gnomes, then elves, then clerics and paladins of deities other than Lolth, then everyone else. If a player character does manage to close with it and engage it in melee, it readily switches from bow to sword, substituting a Bite for one of its Longsword attacks.

If the drider is accompanied by giant spiders, it always casts *faerie fire*, while the spiders blanket the whole area with webs to catch their foes in. The drider follows the same targeting priorities as above, with one exception: It will always attack an unrestrained opponent before a restrained opponent, because the spiders instinctively attack the restrained ones; they aren't smart enough for it to train them to attack the unrestrained ones instead.

The spellcasting variant of the drider doesn't seem to offer much more, combat-wise, than the regular drider. It can cast *freedom of movement* to free itself or one of its spiders from a restraining or paralyzing effect, or *dispel magic* to terminate an inconvenient spell. It can cast *silence* or *darkness* to thwart spellcasters (webs help keep those casters from simply walking out of the area of effect) or *hold person* to paralyze a target who keeps breaking out of their web, though these require it to drop *faerie fire*. Its only damaging spell is the cantrip *poison spray*, and its longbow is better.

Driders will often fight to the death, but maybe one in three values its continued sad existence enough to run away when seriously injured (reduced to 49 hp or fewer). A drider with a "vow or vendetta" to fulfill will generally flee. A fleeing drider Dodges while retreating at full movement speed and runs along walls and ceilings.

HOOK HORRORS

If you're spelunking your way through the Underdark and you hear random clicking and clacking noises echoing through the caverns, what you're hearing may be **hook horrors** signaling to one another. Dating back to the AD&D *Fiend Folio*, hook horrors are territorial subterranean denizens just smart enough to cooperate. They communicate by rhythmically tapping their bony, hook-shaped arms against stone.

Hook horrors are brute melee fighters with exceptional Strength and high Constitution. Ability-wise, they don't have a lot else going for them. They have proficiency in Perception, can climb, and have 60 feet of blindsight in addition to their 120 feet of darkvision (some earlier editions misprinted this as 10 feet of darkvision, which would have been superfluous). All these suit them nicely to subterranean living. Their Keen Hearing gives them advantage on hearing-based Wisdom (Perception) checks, so it's hard for trespassers to slip by them.

In terms of fighting abilities, hook horrors have nothing but a Multiattack comprising two Hook attacks. They're Large creatures, so this does pretty solid damage, but that's it. Hook horror tactics boil down entirely to two things: their ability to climb and their exploitation of darkness.

Hook horrors' caverns have a lot of vertical space and multiple levels, so they can hide out on ledges and leap down to attack their prey (they can't hang from ceilings, lacking Spider Climb or an equivalent feature). Unlike most predators, hook horrors don't automatically zero in on the old, the young, the weak, the isolated, or the oblivious. Instead, they go for whoever's carrying the light source and try to extinguish it. You can use the "Action Options" rule in chapter 9 of the *Dungeon Master's Guide* to have a hook horror Disarm an opponent carrying a torch, lantern, or other illuminating device, a roll it has advantage on because of its size. Then it can use a free interaction to stamp it out, or one of its allies can as it moves in to attack. Dealing with magical light sources is trickier, because hook horrors aren't smart enough to understand magic. The first one tries to grab the light, which may or may not be successful, depending on whether the light is coming from an object (à la *light*) or just hovering intangibly (à la *dancing lights*); the others simply attack whoever's closest to the light.

During combat, hook horrors clack their hooks to tell one another when an opponent is giving them trouble, and they'll double- or even triple-team their toughest foes. They recognize physical force and size, but not other forms of might: They won't know to attack a highly skilled archer or powerful spellcaster.

Despite this, they recognize quickly when a battle isn't going their way. When all of a group of hook horrors are moderately wounded (reduced to 52 hp or fewer) and their opponents aren't, or when half of a group are seriously wounded (reduced to 30 hp or fewer), they call a general retreat. They Dash up the walls to reach higher ledges and escape passages, potentially provoking opportunity attacks as they leave their opponents' reach.

If any of their opponents can communicate with them—for instance, by use of a *tongues* spell—hook horrors may actually stop and chat. (This is more likely if they can tell they're outmatched.) Hook horrors are neutral: Despite being predators, they aren't malevolent by nature. If their foes are clearly too stalwart to be prey, they may be persuaded to allow safe passage in exchange for food.

ROPERS AND PIERCERS

Another monster classic, the **roper** is a dungeon predator/scavenger that nabs its prey by camouflaging itself as a stalagmite or stalactite. The latter is rarer, probably because in every illustration I can recall, the roper has always been depicted pointy side up; perhaps DMs don't consciously consider that ropers can also adhere to cave *ceilings*, thanks to Spider Climb.

Ropers have enormous toothy maws and sticky tentacles that lash out and seize their prey. Although their exceptional Strength and Constitution and below-average Dexterity suggest a brute fighter, ropers are ambush attackers, using their fast and flexible tendrils to compensate for their lack of mobility (their speed is only 10 feet per round, whether crawling or climbing).

Despite their low Dexterity, ropers have expertise in Stealth, along with the False Appearance trait, which allows them to blend in perfectly with their surroundings. I understand this to mean that passive Wisdom (Perception)—and even Searching—will never reveal a roper for what it is as long as it holds still. Its Stealth skill comes into play only if it's moving. Thus, a stationary roper takes its opponents by surprise, as long as its eye is closed and its tendrils retracted until it strikes.

The listing of actions in a Multiattack isn't necessarily an indication of what order a monster must take them in, but the roper's is phrased in an unusually specific way: "The roper makes four attacks with its tendrils, uses Reel, and makes one attack with its bite," which is neither alphabetical order nor the order in which these actions appear in the stat block. The roper's Tendril attack doesn't do any damage, whereas its Bite does, so normally I'd suggest that a creature like the roper would keep making Tendril attacks until one hit, then Reel in that target, then Bite it, then finally use any Tendril attacks it had left, keeping those targets it hit restrained at a distance (so as not to pull melee fighters into melee range). But based on the phrasing of the roper's Multiattack, I think it's likely that the designers intended *all* the Tendril attacks to be made first and all restrained targets to be Reeled in. The only variable is who gets attacked.

Answering this question requires looking at the roper's Wisdom—which is surprisingly high, actually. Although its Intelligence 7 indicates upper-bestial cognition and instinct-driven behavior, its Wisdom 16 suggests that it may be quite savvy when it comes to picking its battles—and its targets. On what basis would it judge? A roper has no way to know that the adventurers traipsing through its cavern have capabilities that ordinary folks don't. But it does know the difference between metal and flesh, and which is harder to bite through. Thus, PCs wearing heavy armor may get a free pass at first.

A roper has six tendrils (unless one or more have been cut off). Given its challenge rating of 5, a roper ordinarily would have no reason to fear six humanoids of any kind. With its four Tendril attacks, it starts with the least armored opponent (not counting Dexterity modifiers) within reach (50 feet!) and works its way up. If one of these attacks misses, it moves on to the next target, *unless* it has to choose between an opponent that it's attacked and missed and an opponent wearing a heavier type of armor, in which case it tries again on a less armored opponent. After Reeling its victims in, it uses its Bite attack on the first opponent it grabbed.

Note, however, that the Reel action pulls grappled creatures only 25 feet. If the roper grabs its intended prey from 50 feet away, it won't be able to bring them to its mouth in the same turn. So the roper doesn't attack as soon as a group of foes comes within 50 feet. Instead, it waits for four of them (or all of them, if there are fewer than four) to come closer: within 20 to 25 feet.

If the ceiling is less than 50 feet high, it makes no sense for a roper to hang out on the floor, because hanging from the ceiling instead gives it an array of benefits: It's farther away from anyone or anything that might threaten it, it can get away more easily if it's badly injured, and anyone that it picks up risks taking damage from a fall if they break free.

Any opponent who escapes the roper's clutches and tries to run away receives a rude surprise when they get 50 feet away, because as they leave the roper's reach, the thing gets an opportunity attack with one of its tendrils. Oops!

If an encounter goes south for a roper, it's much too slow to get away by Dashing or after Disengaging, even if it's up on the ceiling. For this reason, it's willing to abandon a fight relatively quickly—after being only moderately wounded (reduced to 65 hp or fewer).

However, it uses a tricky maneuver to do this, unique to itself: Since all its grappled opponents are also restrained and have disadvantage on attack rolls and Strength checks (including Strength checks to escape its grapple), and since it has a very high Armor Class of 20, it can avoid being hit by opportunity attacks relatively easily. Therefore, while holding its grappled enemies in place—being grappled, they have a speed of 0—it takes either the Dash action or the Dodge action, depending on whether all its enemies are grappled (Dash) or one or more are free (Dodge), and moves away as quickly as it can, allowing its tendrils to play out. If it began on the floor and can climb up a wall while retreating, it does. Once it's 50 feet away from a grappled enemy, it lets go of that enemy and withdraws its tendril, until it's released every one of them. This is its way of saying "Okay, fine, I'll let you go, but I don't want you coming after me."

The immature form of the roper is the **piercer**, which lacks tentacles but shares the roper's ability to disguise itself as a stalactite (piercers don't disguise themselves as stalagmites, for reasons that will be immediately obvious). A piercer's tail is surrounded by a hard, sharply pointed shell; it clings to cavern ceilings with a set of toothlike claws, and when prey passes beneath, it drops, shell downward, impaling its victim.

The piercer has only one method of attack: fall. Once it's fallen, it's not going anywhere else anytime soon, having a movement speed of only 5 feet. Even though piercers cluster in great numbers, as Medium creatures taking up an entire square (or hex), only one can attack any given target, since its Drop action targets "one creature directly underneath the piercer." It doesn't even have the standard 5-foot reach. Several piercers could Drop on a Large creature at once, but PCs are either Medium or Small. One piercer, one piercee.

This puts the lie to the flavor text in the *Monster Manual*, which says piercers "drop simultaneously to increase the odds of striking prey." On the contrary, this *reduces* the odds. It makes more sense for one piercer to Drop, causing its target to dodge into a neighboring space, whereupon the piercer above *that* space Drops, and so forth. In fact, as a DM, you may as well assume that piercers that haven't already Dropped have Readied their Drop action at all times, waiting for anything living to pass beneath them. This will certainly get more entertaining reactions out of your players than having the piercers Drop only on their own turns.

Piercers have double proficiency in Stealth, plus False Appearance, so they've got a good chance of making that first attack count: Even without the benefit of darkness, being indistinguishable from the surrounding terrain has to be construed as conferring unseen-attacker advantage. The greater the distance they fall, the more damage they do, topping out at a distance of 60 feet.

But hang on a moment. Piercers have 60 feet of darkvision and 30 feet of blindsight. The blindsight suggests that these cavern-dwellers are adapted to conditions of total darkness, so that's where they'll be encountered. Even in darkness, a creature with darkvision can still see as if it were in dim light. However, under that lighting condition, it makes Wisdom (Perception) checks at −5—and the piercer has passive Perception of only 8 to begin with. Consequently, one would have to be a real lummox, crashing through the Underdark like a rhino, or advertising one's presence with a bright light source, for a piercer even 35 feet up to realize it was time to take the plunge.

If a bunch of piercers are clustered within reach of their parent roper, it can reach out with one of its 50-foot-long tentacles and tap to signal a piercer when to Drop. But practically, what the roper is more likely to do is use its tentacles to grab and pull victims underneath the piercers. And neither ropers nor piercers have language, anyway; anything the roper does to feed its young is wholly instinctive.

So it seems that, in practice, the ideal cavern for the roper-piercer family to set up in is one with a ceiling between 30 and 35 feet high; this way, the piercers can perceive prey passing underneath without any penalty beyond their own lousy Wisdom modifier. (If you want to be more generous to these beasties, you can say that it's not the sight of prey moving beneath them that induces them to Drop but the *sound*. This is a bit of a reach, since there's nothing to suggest that they have a downward-aiming hearing organ in their tail shell, but if you do go this route, you can safely place them as high as 60 feet up.)

Piercers flee as soon as they take a hit that does any damage at all, but their "fleeing" consists of Dashing away at a blistering 10 feet per turn. If the parent roper is around, attacking a piercer draws its ire.

DARKMANTLES

Darkmantles are squidlike cave dwellers just large enough to wrap themselves around your head and suffocate you to death, which is exactly what they aim to do. With high Strength and Constitution slightly higher than their Dexterity, they qualify (barely) as brutes. What they really are, above all else, is ambush predators, as emphasized by their proficiency in Stealth, their False Appearance trait, and their Darkness Aura feature.

Hunting darkmantles cling to cavern ceilings, waiting for prey to pass by. The largest caverns aren't the best hunting grounds for a darkmantle, because of the 15-foot limit on their Darkness Aura; caverns and passages where the distance from ceiling to floor is 10 to 15 feet are ideal. When a likely victim comes within 15 feet of a lurking darkmantle (remember to reckon vertical as well as horizontal distance, accounting for the target's height), it releases its Darkness Aura, blinding every creature within the radius with its magical murk. Thanks to its False Appearance, it will nearly always gain surprise by doing this, but this is all it can do with its surprise round, because it consumes a full action. It has no reason to move until it's ready to attack.

Which is exactly what it does on its subsequent turn: Using its flying movement, it launches itself at its chosen target and uses its Crush action (with advantage on the attack roll, thanks to its blindsight) to envelop their head. If successful, this action suffocates the target, which has a number of rounds equal to their Constitution modifier, though no fewer than one, to struggle free (see "Suffocating," *Player's Handbook*, chapter 8).

Once the darkmantle has begun suffocating its victim, it's disinclined to let go. However, like most predators, it doesn't care for prey that fights back. Any injury more serious than a 1- or 2-damage scratch induces it to abandon its current prey and instead launch itself at whichever other creature is farthest away yet still within the 30-foot range of its flying movement (and not enveloped by another darkmantle). Moderately wounding it (reducing it to 8 hp or fewer) drives it off, as does any hit that manages to break its concentration on its Darkness Aura. Deafening a darkmantle scrambles its wits and causes it to flee as well. When it retreats, it does so using flying movement and the Dash action; as soon as it gets more than 60 feet from its foes, it Hides, disguising itself as a stalactite again and waiting for its enemies to move on.

The darkmantle counts on its Darkness Aura to keep other creatures blinded, so that it can finish suffocating its prey and start snacking on it. If it does manage to reduce a victim to 0 hp, it doesn't stop attacking, not until the victim is fully dead; each subsequent attack should be construed as the darkmantle eating the target's face.

DOPPELGÄNGERS

Invasion of the body snatchers! **Doppelgängers** are shapeshifting monstrosities that take on the appearance of humanoid beings for fiendish purposes.

They have high Constitution and extremely high Dexterity, making them scrappy attrition fighters. Their self-preservation instinct is strong, and they have high Charisma, along with proficiency in Deception and Insight. They can't be charmed, they can Read Thoughts, and they have the Ambusher and Surprise Attack features in addition to their Shapechanger power. All these abilities synergize to make the doppelgänger a sucker-puncher par excellence.

It begins with the disguise: A doppelgänger has to take on the semblance of someone who's beyond suspicion, or at any rate one whom the PCs are likely to underestimate. Read Thoughts is an unopposed ability that lets the doppelgänger lock onto anyone within 60 feet and scan its "surface thoughts" (i.e., whatever it's consciously thinking at the moment), granting it advantage on Deception, Intimidation, Persuasion, and Insight checks against that target. Being proficient in Deception, it favors this approach in particular, though it won't eschew Persuasion or Intimidation if the situation calls for one of them. To put it in more transactional terms, it's more inclined to bluff or seduce its way toward its desired goal than to rely on negotiation, pleading, demands, or threats. It may also exploit its Insight to shame someone into behaving a certain way or to insult that person in order to gain favor with others present.

But the key is this: The doppelgänger doesn't want to fight if it can help it. As long as it can advance its interests without fighting, relying solely on misdirection, that's what it will do. If it does have to fight, it certainly doesn't want its opponent to be the one who starts the fight. It attacks when the opponent has no reason at all to expect it.

The doppelgänger, you might say, has more EQ than IQ. It chooses its target not according to who poses the greatest tactical threat but who poses the greatest *social* threat—the one most resistant to its deceptions, who will generally be a character with a high Wisdom or one who's shown suspicion of the doppelgänger from the start. In fact, a blunt "I don't believe you" or "Who are you really?" may be the spark that sets the doppelgänger off.

Ambusher gives the doppelgänger advantage on attack rolls when its target is surprised; Surprise Attack gives it an extra 3d6 damage on a first-round surprise attack. It gains these attack and damage bonuses for the entire first round of combat, meaning it can apply them to both attacks in its Multiattack. Two attacks each dealing 4d6 + 4 bludgeoning damage—an average of 18 points per hit, 36 if both land—can take out one or even two low-level PCs before anyone has a chance to react.

Unfortunately for the doppelgänger, that first-round nova attack is its only trump card. After that, it has no way to regain the upper hand in combat, although it does still enjoy two attack rolls per action and a large reservoir of hit points. (This is much less advantageous once PCs have reached level 5 and gained Extra Attacks of their own.)

Once its enemies are no longer surprised, it's torn between the desire to finish them off and the desire to get away and hide in a new form. If it seems to be winning the fight, it won't flee until it's seriously injured (reduced to 20 hp or fewer), but if it's obviously going to lose, it commences evasive maneuvers when only moderately injured (reduced to 36 hp or fewer). In a more ambiguous situation, it makes the decision somewhere in between.

One thing it absolutely doesn't want is to let itself be surrounded. If engaged by three or more melee attackers, or if flanked by two, it Disengages and repositions itself so that (a) it can face all its enemies at once and (b) it's closer to the exit.

Otherwise, it attacks whoever's engaging it, then uses its movement to reposition itself—without leaving its opponent's reach—so that it can flee if it needs to. When fleeing, doppelgängers Disengage to avoid opportunity attacks, unless they're engaged in melee with only a single opponent, in which case they chance it and Dash, risking a single opportunity attack for the greater chance of escape.

There's a good chance that combat with a doppelgänger will be followed by a chase (see "Chases," *Dungeon Master's Guide*, chapter 8), because no one wants to let a doppelgänger get away and disguise itself again. Of course, this is exactly what the doppelgänger wants most. Ideally, it wants to vanish into a crowd, but reaching a less populated location where it can transform itself into someone who seems to belong there—a farmer in a field, say, or an angler by a lake or stream—is the next best thing, as long as it can make its transformation out of its pursuers' view. It takes one action for the doppelgänger to transform, so it needs to have enough of a lead to go unseen for a full turn.

MIMICS

Since the days of Advanced Dungeons & Dragons, the **mimic** has been one of the dirtiest tricks a Dungeon Master can pull on incautious players: a "door" or (more often) "treasure chest" that turns out to be a carnivorous monster. How on earth could such a thing evolve? At some point in prehistory, the mimic's ancestors must have disguised themselves as natural objects, using octopus-like camouflage, only later adopting the forms of manmade objects after exposure to humanoid beings. This suggests a unique, specialized intelligence, akin to the ability of parrots and certain other birds to mimic human speech . . . but one that's used to lure and capture prey.

With strong physical ability scores across the board but especially high Strength and Constitution, the mimic is a brute adapted to close-range fighting. Yet it also has high proficiency in Stealth, along with darkvision: This is an ambush predator as much at home underground as aboveground. It has a sticky surface with which to ensnare its prey and advantage on attack rolls against any creature it's caught this way.

The mimic's particular combination of features is so calculated, there's really only one way for it to behave:

- The mimic chooses a disguise (Shapechanger) and lies in wait for prey to approach (False Appearance).

- The mimic attacks with surprise, using Pseudopod to grapple its target, who has disadvantage on their escape checks because of the mimic's Adhesive surface.
- Against a grappled victim, the mimic switches to its Bite attack, on which it has advantage (Grappler) and which does more damage than Pseudopod.
- This is my own extrapolation: Once its victim is reduced to 0 hp, the mimic starts eating it, continuing to inflict Bite wounds on the victim each turn until—and after—they're dead.

What if another opponent attacks the mimic while it's trying to consume its prey? My take is that it simply moves away at the greatest speed it can while dragging its victim along (half speed, or 7 feet per turn, for conscious Small or Medium-size victims; full speed for unconscious victims weighing less than 255 pounds; 5 feet per turn for unconscious victims weighing more), while continuing to Bite its grappled prey, doing critical damage each time if the victim is unconscious. It will probably incur opportunity attacks this way, but the mimic's Intelligence is only 5; the "zone of control" concept is far beyond its comprehension.

Mimics are evolved creatures and do have a self-preservation instinct. However, they're also slow, so outrunning an enemy isn't a realistic proposition. A mimic that's seriously injured (reduced to 23 hp or fewer) lets go of its prey, reverts to its amorphous form, and backs away. Effectively, this is a Disengage action: Although the mimic isn't intelligent enough to know what disengaging is, the way it backs off is the same as a deliberate Disengage action for all intents and purposes. It no longer has the Adhesive property, and on its next turn, it Bites the next creature that comes within its reach; if no creature pursues it, it Dashes away in reverse, always keeping its mouth turned toward those who drove it off.

Let's take a step back for a moment and read the description of the Adhesive trait carefully: "The mimic adheres to *anything that touches it*" (emphasis mine). Not "any *creature*"—*anything*. To me, that means that if you strike the mimic with a melee weapon, *the weapon sticks to it.* The rest of the description is less helpful: "A Huge or smaller creature adhered to the mimic is also grappled by it (escape DC 13). Ability checks made to escape this grapple have disadvantage." It doesn't say anything about how to free an *object* stuck to the mimic.

It seems reasonable to me that a player character who wants to free their weapon from the mimic's gluey surface should have to make the same "escape" check as a PC who's grappled by it. Thus, you can hit the mimic with your sword on round 1, but you have to spend round 2 pulling it loose (DC 13 Strength check, disadvantage) before attacking again on round 3. That should add interest to a fight that otherwise has little to offer in the way of tactics or maneuvering. It will also give ranged fighters and spellcasters a leg up on the melee fighters.

COCKATRICES

The **cockatrice**, aka Hell's Chicken, is a weak but scrappy monster originating in medieval English folklore. Stupid and aggressive, cockatrices have a sense of what kind of prey is small and weak enough for them to strike at and what isn't, but they also suffer from a somewhat defective survival instinct: When startled, they fly into a violent frenzy, which they snap out of only when whoever or whatever startled them is turned to stone by their bite.

Cockatrices are nocturnal browsers, which we can deduce from their darkvision. They fly twice as fast as they walk, giving them the ability to strike from the air. Beyond these, they have no distinctive trait other than their petrifying Bite.

Bite is a simple melee attack, but one with a rider: On a hit, the target must make a Constitution saving throw or begin to turn to stone. After the first failure, the target is restrained, which makes them easier to hit and eggs the cockatrice on. No matter what else happens, if a cockatrice manages to restrain a target with Bite, it always attacks that same target again on its next turn.

The funny thing about petrifaction in fifth edition D&D is that it's much more of an inconvenience than a mortal danger. Petrified creatures take *less* damage from incoming attacks, even though they're easier to hit. Also, the cockatrice's petrifaction wears off after just a day, so against any creature with more than 7 hp or so, this isn't even a potentially deadly attack. Rather, it's a defense mechanism that gives the cockatrice a chance to escape from larger creatures that might pose a threat to it.

Once we understand this, we realize that a cockatrice isn't fighting to kill at all. All it wants to do is petrify whatever's scared it, and as soon as it's done so, it will fly away at top speed, using the Dash action. Unfortunately, because it's so dumb, it doesn't know when to quit, and any friends of its target may end up killing it before its self-defense strategy has time to take effect. It also doesn't know what to do when a target makes its saving throw against this ability. It gets confused and angry, but it only flies away if no one else has hurt it. If someone has, it transfers its aggression to that other foe.

A cockatrice's Armor Class is very low, and it doesn't have Flyby or any similar trait that might allow it to avoid opportunity attacks. So while it flies in to engage a foe, flying back into the air between strikes to avoid melee attacks isn't a feasible tactic for it. It will, however, fly from a petrified enemy to attack another who's also alarmed it.

CHIMERAS

The **chimera** is a Large, mid-level monstrosity whose conglomerate nature is reflected by behavior that thumbs its nose at evolutionary imperatives. According to the *Monster Manual* flavor text, it has "a vicious, stubborn streak that compels it to fight to the death"; it "often toys with its prey, breaking off an attack prematurely and leaving a creature wounded and terrified before returning to finish it off"; and yet, despite being unable to speak itself and understanding only Draconic, "if offered food and treasure, a chimera might spare a traveler." Want a monster that puts the "chaotic" in "chaotic evil"? Here you go!

With exceptionally high Strength and Constitution yet merely average Dexterity, the chimera is an out-and-out brute that closes to melee range as quickly as it can; this is reinforced by its Fire Breath feature, which has a range of only 15 feet. Stealth isn't in its repertoire, but don't try to sneak up on it: It has double proficiency in Perception.

It also has darkvision, so it typically attacks at dusk or at night; it may dwell underground as well.

Chimeras are stupid (Intelligence 3) as well as brutal. They aren't the slightest bit choosy about their targets, nor do they recognize whether one foe seems to pose a greater threat than another. They attack whatever happens to be in front of them. That being said, when they first enter combat—with a flying speed of 60 feet—they position themselves, if possible, to catch as many targets as they can within the 15-foot cone of their Fire Breath. If they can't get at least two, it's hardly worth using, since it has to recharge afterward.

The chimera's Multiattack allows it to combine its Fire Breath with two melee attacks. While its Fire Breath is recharging, it gets three melee attacks rather than two. For the sake of flavor, I'd go by the portrait in the *Monster Manual* and say that if the chimera is fighting multiple opponents, its goat head attacks left, left-forward, or forward; its dragon head right, right-forward, or forward; and its lion head forward, left-forward, or right-forward.* (Alternatively, maybe your chimera is "left-handed," with the dragon and goat heads switched.) Horns is the goat-head attack action, Fire Breath is the dragon-head attack, Bite is either a dragon-head attack or a lion-head attack, and Claws has the same attack arc as the lion head.

The feature allows the chimera to substitute Fire Breath for either its Bite attack or its Horns attack, but I'd substitute it only for Bite unless its positioning is such that it has no opponent in goat-head range but does have an opponent in lion-head range.

The chimera uses its Fire Breath every time it recharges, as soon as it recharges, and repositions itself, if necessary, to catch the greatest possible number of targets within that 15-foot cone. If possible, it simply circles one of its current melee opponents to achieve this posi-

---

* As mentioned previously, fifth edition D&D has no universal rule governing facing, and a DM may consider real-world laws of nature to apply, in the absence of a rule that contradicts them, for the sake of descriptive flavor. Determining that a monster is pointed a certain way doesn't influence what target(s) it *can* attack—the rules specify that it can attack any creature within its reach—but it may influence what target(s) the monster *does* attack.

tioning, but if it has to move, it does so, regardless of whether this may provoke one or more opportunity attacks.

The chimera has Wisdom 14, which I'd interpret as having a strong self-preservation instinct and a good sense of when to retreat, but the flavor text specifically says chimeras fight to the death. Personally, I'd at least give that self-preservation instinct a chance to kick in when the chimera is seriously injured (reduced to 45 hp or fewer). Maybe it has to make an Intelligence check akin to maintaining spell concentration (DC 10 or half excess damage, whichever is greater) to have the sense to take flight and Dash away.

Similarly, if you want to go by the flavor text and have the chimera toy with its prey, keep track of your PCs' hit points, and have the chimera break off when every PC is reduced to 40 percent or less of their hit point maximum, then come back no more than half an hour later, before the PCs have a chance to complete a short rest.

Finally, since the chimera's flying speed is greater than its land speed, it maneuvers during combat by leaping, and it isn't hindered by difficult terrain. In fact, it may even prefer to live and hunt in difficult terrain, where its prey is likely to be slowed.

BASILISKS

The **basilisk** originates in continental European mythology and, interestingly, seems to have inspired the myth of the cockatrice, which may be why both these creatures share the ability to turn foes to stone. Unlike the half-reptilian, half-avian cockatrice, however, the basilisk is all lizard; it's also significantly bigger and tougher.

With high Strength and Constitution and not much else going for it, the basilisk is a melee-oriented brute. With a movement speed of only 20 feet, however, it's not going to have much luck closing to melee range with an enemy that doesn't want it to. This is where its Petrifying Gaze comes into play.

Petrifying Gaze allows the basilisk, at the start of a nearby enemy's turn, to force that enemy to make a Constitution saving throw. If the enemy fails, they begin to petrify. This imposes the restrained condition, which reduces the enemy's speed to 0 and grants the basilisk advantage on attack rolls. At the end of their next turn, the enemy must make another save, the result of which either sets them free or completes the petrifaction process.

Thus, when a basilisk sees potential prey, it immediately (and unsubtly—basilisks have no aptitude for stealth) Dashes forward, hoping to get close enough that its Petrifying Gaze can begin to take effect. With a Wisdom of only 8, it's completely indiscriminate, going straight for whoever's nearest.

Here's the one and only aspect in which the basilisk shows any glimmer of wit: Even though it could, it doesn't use its Petrifying Gaze when it's only 25 or 30 feet away, but rather waits until it's closed the distance to 20 feet. Why? Because petrifaction confers damage resistance on the target.

Suppose a basilisk uses its Petrifying Gaze when it's just 30 feet from Lissevië Ambariel and she fails her saving throw. On its turn, it can move only 20 feet closer to her without also using its action, and thus it can't get near enough to Bite. When her turn comes around again, she fails her second saving throw and turns entirely to stone. Now the basilisk can finally close the distance, but now that she's petrified, its Bite deals only half damage to her.

Suppose instead that it's only 20 feet away when it uses Petrifying Gaze. Then, on its turn, it can close the entire distance with its movement *and* use its action to Bite Lissevië while she's only restrained, not yet petrified. Now it has advantage on the attack roll, does full damage, and will get to do so again on its next turn if she makes her saving throw and the effect wears off.

That being said, if the basilisk has more than one enemy within 30 feet, it uses Petrifying Gaze on everyone within range as long as *one* enemy is no more than 20 feet from it: All it cares about is taking down one tasty morsel. Everyone else is as good turned to stone as not—better, in fact, since they can no longer interfere with the basilisk's meal.

When a basilisk has reduced its opponent to 0 hp, it doesn't stop attacking but rather continues to Bite for as long as its unrestrained foes will let it. Once its target is dead—that is, eaten—it strolls away, sated.

Basilisks have just barely enough sense to turn tail when they're moderately wounded (reduced to 36 hp or fewer)—like most predators, they don't like it when the prey fights back. They Dodge as they retreat, and they *back* away, hissing, keeping their eyes toward their pursuers and using Petrifying Gaze on every enemy within range. Once they're more than 60 feet from their opponents, they switch from Dodging to Dashing and run away in earnest.

MEDUSAS

Medusa, in Greek myth, is the snake-haired horror with the petrifying gaze, quarry of Perseus. In the fifth edition *Monster Manual*, this unnatural being is explained as one who made an infernal bargain for immortality and beauty, then paid the price when the latter wore off but the former didn't. There's no satisfactory natural explanation for the medusa, so in this case, evolutionary imperatives don't necessarily apply; the medusa seems more like a being driven by compulsion, as undead creatures are.

Medusas have high Dexterity and Constitution, typical of a skirmisher. They have enough Intelligence to plan and lay traps, enough Wisdom to choose targets carefully and avoid battles they won't win, and more than enough Charisma to parley when it's advantageous. These abilities are paired with proficiency in Deception and Insight, along with Stealth. Thus, a medusa stays hidden from threats and uses its wiles to lure trespassers to their doom. (The flavor text describes a medusa's lair as "shadowy ruins . . . riddled with obstructions and hiding places," meaning it contains lots of places of concealment to take advantage of.)

The medusa has two distinctive features, Petrifying Gaze and Snake Hair. The latter is a simple melee attack that does some poison as well as piercing damage. Petrifying Gaze is more complicated and demands closer examination.

First, the range of Petrifying Gaze is 30 feet. That means that the medusa has to draw its opponents close enough to use this feature. Although the medusa has a ranged weapon attack (Longbow), it's not in the monster's interest to start a sniper battle, because then its opponents will remain at too great a distance. Instead, the medusa should wait until its opponents are within range.

Second, the petrifying process isn't necessarily instant. The Difficulty Class of the Constitution saving throw to resist petrifaction is 14. An average PC without class proficiency in this saving throw has a 40 percent chance of making this saving throw; a PC of intermediate level (therefore assuming a +3 proficiency modifier, rather than +2) with Constitution as their primary defensive ability, proficient in this saving throw, has a 65 percent chance. Failing the saving throw by a difference of 5 or more results in immediate petrifaction; the chances of this are 40 percent and 10 percent.

If petrifaction isn't immediate, the target of the Petrifying Gaze has to fail a second saving throw to be petrified; a success on this second throw frees the target. So we have four cases to look at here: success; failure, then success; failure, then failure; and critical initial failure. The latter two result in petrifaction, and the former two result in escape. For the average PC, the chance of two successive failures is 12 percent; for the high-Constitution, proficient PC, 9 percent. Putting these probabilities together, the total chance that a medusa will petrify an average PC (in either one round or two) is 52 percent; a high-Constitution, proficient PC, 19 percent.

These aren't inspiring probabilities, which brings us to our third item: A creature halfway through the petrifaction process is restrained. Attacks against a restrained creature have advantage, and the creature's own attacks have disadvantage. This tells us that a medusa wants to promptly follow up its use of this feature with melee attacks, to exploit this momentary edge. And it is momentary—logically, it can't last more than 1 round, because after that, the target either turns to stone or shakes off the effect entirely.

Fourth, "a creature can avert its eyes to avoid the saving throw at the start of its turn"—*unless* it's surprised. Therefore, making that first appearance with surprise is essential for the medusa.

Fifth, a creature has to be able to see the medusa for its Petrifying Gaze to have an effect. This means that, despite its darkvision, the medusa is ill-served by hiding in darkness. It needs at least dim light to be sure that trespassers will be susceptible to its gaze. On the other hand, bright light leaves the medusa vulnerable to catching its own gaze in a reflective surface and turning *itself* to stone. The medusa can't risk that. Dim light is the happy medium.

Finally, although the feature is easily misread as affecting only one creature at a time, it can in fact affect every creature within its range. Note the wording: "When a creature that can see the medusa's eyes starts its turn within 30 feet of the medusa, the medusa can force it to make a DC 14 Constitution saving throw . . ." Not "*one* creature that can see the medusa's eyes"—*any and every* creature.

On the other hand, seeing the back of the medusa's head doesn't hurt anyone. So we can think of this feature as having an approximately semicircular area of effect with a 30-foot radius. (Or we could think of it as a cone; going by the Targets in Area of Effect table in chapter 8 of the *Dungeon Master's Guide*, the number of targets is the same either way.) This tells us that if the medusa can't catch at least three opponents in its gaze when it first unveils it, it's not worth revealing itself to try.

Putting it all together: When a medusa detects trespassers in its lair, it hides—someplace where it will be able to pop out and catch by surprise at least three opponents (ideally, *all* its opponents, but three is the minimum) in its field of view. Because the medusa would rather not have to try to get away from multiple melee opponents, it makes its appearance within 30 feet of its would-be victims, but outside their melee attack reach. That way, it won't have to fight both unrestrained opponents and opponents restrained by a single, non-critically failed saving throw at the same time. Only those not affected at all by Petrifying Gaze will be able to attack the medusa after its first turn. Starting on its second turn, the medusa focuses its attacks first and foremost on its restrained opponents.

Unlike some features (e.g., Frightful Presence), Petrifying Gaze doesn't confer immunity on a successful saving throw. This means that the medusa benefits from prolonging combat, because it will get one opportunity after another to petrify its opponents. It will fight a single opponent toe-to-toe, but anytime it's attacked by two or more, it Dodges and moves to a place of concealment. If its opponents don't chase it down, it uses its next turn's action to Hide, then moves stealthily to a new position where it can pop out and catch its opponents in its Petrifying Gaze once more. An opponent who averts their gaze to avoid being turned to stone is just begging for a stab in the back: As an unseen attacker, the medusa has advantage on attack rolls against opponents who are intentionally looking the other way. Once an opponent is turned to stone, of course, the medusa moves on to other, still-moving targets.

A medusa is torn between the desire for release from its curse and the fear of death that drove it to seek immortality in the first place. When it's seriously injured (reduced to 50 hp or fewer), it starts looking for a way out of its situation, Dodging as it backs away in the hope that its opponents may carelessly expose themselves to its gaze.

CENTAURS

Centaurs are the half-horse, half-human hybrids of Greek myth for which, it has been observed, no one has yet come up with a definitive way to design trousers. Which to me clearly indicates that they don't wear any. Don't come to me with your hang-ups, man.

In the Harry Potter series, centaurs are standoffish, territorial, and even a bit malicious, but in D&D, as far back as I can remember, they've been labeled good creatures—although I'm pretty sure they were originally chaotic good rather than neutral good, which makes more sense to me. The upshot is, centaurs are unlikely to attack unprovoked and may prefer to try to subdue and capture their enemies rather than kill them. Doesn't mean they can't give you a good hoof clout, though.

With a single-peak ability contour—exceptional Strength, but merely above-average Dexterity and Constitution—centaurs are also another sort of hybrid, between brutes and shock attackers. As I use the terms, shock attackers hit fast and hard, then get out, because they're not cut out for prolonged melee engagement; brutes engage and tank it out until their enemies are dead. With centaurs, we're maybe looking at something in between: a creature that engages for just two or three rounds, then disengages.

The Charge feature gives centaurs a good boost on that initial shock attack, adding 3d6 piercing damage when they move 30 feet in a straight line toward their targets just before attacking with pikes. Note also that the centaurs' pikes give them 10 feet of reach, which gives them the ability to strafe and maybe sidestep that whole "Brute or shock attacker?" question by not coming within their opponents' melee reach in the first place.

However, the centaur's movement speed is only 50 feet. At least 30 feet of the centaur's movement will be consumed by the initial charge, leaving it no more than 20 to move away. That means that on its next turn, it has to use at least 10 feet of its movement to move away before turning around and Charging again. After that second Charge, it's in melee and staying put.

Plus, the centaur's Hooves attack is a couple of points better than its Pike attack, its reach is only 5 feet, and the centaur's melee Multiattack comprises one Pike attack and one Hooves attack, never two Pike attacks. So even though the centaur can strafe without provoking an opportunity attack, it probably won't. Instead, its initial attack will be to charge from a distance of 35 to 50 feet, strike with Pike for the extra Charge damage, then follow up with Hooves for maximum first-round damage and remain engaged in melee for a round or two.

The next question is at what point the centaur withdraws from melee. Let's say that as long as the centaur is unhurt or only lightly wounded, it keeps fighting toe-to-toe. Once its enemy has managed to moderately wound it (reduce it to 31 hp or fewer), it makes one final Multiattack, then moves away at its full speed. This risks provoking an opportunity attack, but the centaur's nowhere near death's door yet, and it's willing to eat that one attack knowing that it can easily outpace nearly any humanoid opponent.

Centaurs making Longbow attacks do so from a distance of 45 to 50 feet, and they actively try to outflank and encircle their enemies. However, the centaur's Longbow attack is objectively inferior to its melee attacks, in terms of both hit probability and damage. Plus, you can't attack to subdue with a ranged weapon, only with a melee weapon. So we have to think about *why* the centaur is fighting. If it's defending its territory against an aggressive invader, it's not going to be overly concerned with whether it kills the invader or not. And it's rare that PCs will be fighting against centaurs unless either (a) the PCs are evil-aligned and *are* aggressive invaders; (b) the PCs are trespassing on the centaurs' territory, but without aggressive intent; or (c) it's all just a crazy misunderstanding.

In cases (b) and (c), the centaurs are better off not using their bows at all, because of the risk of accidental murder. But also, if the PCs really are nonhostile, somebody should pipe up and offer parley before the centaurs are wounded badly enough to make them back off, and also before any PC is knocked unconscious. In case (a), on the other hand, figure that one out of every four centaurs is an archer that provides long-range fire support for its melee-engaged comrades, and that if one of those comrades has to retreat due to injury, the archer centaur charges in to relieve it, while the injured centaur assumes the former archer's role.

When a majority of a group of centaurs are seriously injured (reduced to 18 hp or fewer), they'll call a retreat. Any uninjured or only lightly injured (still at 32 hp or more) centaurs will act as a rearguard for a round while the more injured ones Disengage and run away. Then they'll Dash off to join them.

MERROWS

Not to be confused with ordinary merfolk, **merrows** are larger-than-humanoid monstrosities, the descendants of merfolk warped by demonic influence in the ancient past. Since they've bred and survived since then, we can consider them evolved creatures despite their supernatural origin.

Merrows are water-dwelling creatures, drawn to coastal areas with a lot of marine traffic, where they prey on anyone and anything weaker than themselves. While they can breathe both air and water, they flounder about at a pitiable 10 feet per turn on land, whereas in water, they swim at a brisk 40. Their exceptional Strength and very high Constitution place them in the brute category, eager to get up close and personal with their prospective victims. They're not that bright, but they can tell when they're getting beaten. They also have darkvision, so the hours from twilight to dawn are particularly dangerous times to be messing about in boats where merrows roam.

Most humanoids are strongest on land and weak in the water; merrows are strongest in the water and weak on land. It's a given, therefore, that when merrows attack, their first and foremost goal is to pull their opponents into the water.

Their Harpoon attack gives them the means to do this. When a merrow lands a harpoon hit against any Huge or smaller creature, the two must make opposing Strength checks—and the merrow, with its exceptional Strength, has a good chance of coming out on top. If the merrow wins, it yanks its opponent up to 20 feet toward itself. (The harpoon's melee reach is only 5 feet, but the merrow can throw it up to 20 feet without disadvantage on the roll, up to 60 feet with.) Since the merrow is in the water and the target presumably isn't, that means . . . well, now the target *is* in the water.

Aquatic combat is a mess for anyone without the innate or magically endowed ability to swim. First, any such combatant has disadvantage on melee attack rolls unless they're wielding a thrusting weapon: a dagger, shortsword, javelin, spear, or trident. Most ranged weapon attack rolls at normal range are made with disadvantage, and ranged weapon attacks at long range automatically miss. A character with a Constitution of 9 or lower can hold their breath for only 30 seconds—five combat rounds. (Characters with higher Constitutions are good for the duration of virtually any combat encounter—if they get the chance to take a deep breath before going under.)

And let's talk about grappling. It's a contest between the grappler's Strength (or Athletics skill) and the grapplee's Strength (Athletics) or Dexterity (Acrobatics), which, again, is probably in the merrow's favor. A grappled creature's speed, including its swimming speed, becomes 0. Even if they can wriggle free, a creature without a specific swimming speed can move through water at only half normal speed, and in rough water (such as merrows surely like to inhabit), they need to make a Strength (Athletics) check to do even that. So once a merrow has an opponent in the water, that opponent's likely to remain there awhile.

And let's talk about visibility! On a bright, sunny day, you can see a ways down through clear, rippling water. However, it's hard to see through any depth of choppy water in the best of conditions, let alone in dim light or darkness. Thus, while merrows lack proficiency in Stealth, they can often remain unseen simply by staying underwater. As a DM, I'd rule that choppy water is always one level more obscured than the open air above it, so a merrow underwater during daylight hours is lightly obscured to an observer looking down into the water from the surface, and it's heavily obscured at any other time. A heavily obscured creature is unseen by definition; a passive Wisdom (Perception) check to spot a lightly obscured creature comes with a −5 penalty.

So the merrow's strategy begins to take shape. It stalks a boat, harpoon in hand,* making a token Dexterity check for stealth purposes, just to give it a shot at a surprise round (multiple merrows attack from multiple directions, with the intent of pulling their targets apart from one another). When it closes to a distance of 15 or 20 feet, the merrow pops up out of the water, hopefully unnoticed, and hurls the harpoon with advantage on the attack roll for being an unseen attacker if the target's passive Wisdom (Perception) doesn't beat its Dex check. If it hits, it tries to haul its target into the water alongside it, and if it succeeds at that, it follows up with a Bite.

What the merrow does next depends on its target, and also on whether it missed with its initial Harpoon attack. If it did miss, rather than retrieve or reel in its harpoon, it swims up alongside the vessel and switches to Claws/Bite. If it hit, however, and if the target hasn't gotten away between turns, it takes its harpoon by the shaft and continues to stab its target while also Biting.

A weak swimmer probably won't be able to make it back to the relative safety of their vessel, and the merrow will continue to use its Multi-

---

* Although the *Monster Manual* says to assume that monsters with throwable weapons have 2d4 of them, sometimes you have to step back and ask how much sense this makes. It's one thing to hold half a dozen javelins in your hand, but for a harpoon to function as a harpoon, it needs a line. Along with half a dozen harpoons, is a merrow going to carry half a dozen coils of rope as well? One reusable harpoon per merrow is a much simpler and more plausible assumption.

attack. A stronger swimmer may be able to cover some distance, and if so—let's say they manage to swim 15 feet or more away from the merrow—then the merrow forgoes its Multiattack in favor of a grapple attack. If it succeeds, it hauls its target 20 feet back in the other direction (40 feet if its target is Small). On its next turn, while holding its foe grappled (assuming they haven't gotten away), it resumes Multiattacking.

Also, it goes without saying that the merrow uses its reaction to make an opportunity attack against an opponent who manages to swim out of its melee reach, using whichever available attack does the most damage, i.e., Harpoon if it has it in hand, Claws otherwise.

A seriously injured merrow (reduced to 18 hp or fewer) will think better of the encounter and retreat, using the Disengage action (reflecting instinct and the advantage of living in the water, not training or discipline) to submerge and swim away, and releasing any grappled opponent. Any merrow whose opponents somehow manage to drag it *out* of the water, regardless of how much damage it may have taken, Dashes back toward it—it's not about to fight on solid ground, however strong it may be.

YETIS

Scourges of the arctic peaks, **yetis** are reclusive apex predators renowned for their bloodlust. Being impervious to the cold and having a keen sense of smell, they may be encountered wandering the foggy terrain around a white dragon lair or venturing out to hunt in a swirling blizzard.

With exceptional Strength and Constitution and merely above-average Dexterity, yetis are brute melee fighters, but they do have a couple of features that they gain an edge from. One is their proficiency in Stealth, which combined with their Keen Smell and Snow Camouflage traits gives them tremendous incentive to ambush prey in low-visibility conditions, such as the darkness of night or the whiteout of a snowstorm. The other is Chilling Gaze, which is part of its Multiattack.

Chilling Gaze requires the yeti to be within 30 feet of its target, so it has to exercise patience, staying hidden until its prey is close enough for it to strike—but that doesn't mean it leaves this to chance. Yetis have Wisdom 12, high enough for them to exercise care in choosing their targets, and like other predators hunting for a meal, they favor the young, the old, the weak, the isolated, and the oblivious. They'll actively maneuver to bring themselves within striking range of such a target, counting on the combination of their Stealth proficiency, their Snow Camouflage, and vision-obscuring conditions to keep themselves from being seen until they attack.

Once its range to target is 30 feet or less, the yeti moves in and strikes. Barring a good enough passive Wisdom (Perception) on the part of its victim, it gains unseen-attacker advantage on its first Claw attack, which can't help but draw its victim's attention. Then it makes eye contact, bringing Chilling Gaze into play. DC 13 isn't an especially high bar to clear—the average adventurer will make this Constitution saving throw roughly half the time. But the consequences of a failure are catastrophic, comprising not only cold damage but paralysis, the demon king of all the debilitating conditions.

Regardless of the outcome of Chilling Gaze, the yeti makes a second Claw attack, because you can't change the terms of a Multiattack in mid-action. However, if Chilling Gaze does work, the yeti gains advantage on this attack roll, and it's an automatic crit on a hit. Just to lay it out: With an unsuccessful Chilling Gaze, a yeti that lands two Claw hits will inflict an average 22 damage altogether. With a successful Chilling Gaze, one regular Claw hit, one critical Claw hit, and the damage of the gaze itself add up to an average 40 damage.

On its next turn, the yeti's action depends on whether or not it's managed to incapacitate its intended prey. If not, it most likely Multiattacks again. But if it has incapacitated its target, it scoops them up in its arms and Dashes away! Seriously, why would a predator stick around and keep fighting when there's a meal there for the taking? Besides, the yeti is faster than most of its foes, and it can easily elude them if vision is obscured. It will leave obvious tracks, but if it can put a few hundred feet between itself and its pursuers, it will have time to finish its meal before they catch up.

So what does it take for a yeti's opponents to drive it away from a potential meal? Well, the yeti is an evolved creature with a will to live, so if it's seriously wounded (reduced to 20 hp or fewer), it will Dash away (potentially provoking one or more opportunity attacks), with or without its prey. Yetis also aren't accustomed to encountering resistance, so if at least two other opponents engage it in melee while it's trying to finish off its intended victim, it experiences internal conflict. If they can do more than light damage to it—15 or more in a single turn—its survival instinct wins out, and it Dashes off. (Yetis are indifferent to ranged attacks, unless and until they're seriously wounded.)

And then there's fire. The Fear of Fire trait imposes disadvantage on attack rolls and ability checks anytime the yeti takes fire damage, but you may as well roleplay its fear as well. Strike a yeti with an open flame, and it nopes out.

On the other hand, what if none of these conditions applies? What if, for example, just one opponent engages the yeti in melee, while someone else drags its intended victim away to safety? This will enrage the yeti, and it will turn its Multiattack on its melee opponent.

The **abominable yeti** is a Huge superyeti with extraordinary Strength and Constitution, more than twice as many hit points, and the additional Cold Breath feature. This feature has a 30-foot conical area of effect, so the abominable yeti will seek to use it against at least three opponents (see the Targets in Area of Effect table, *Dungeon Master's Guide*, chapter 8). Rather than use it against its intended prey, however, it uses it against any other opponents who try to interfere with its predation. Its method of hunting is otherwise the same as the regular yeti's: a Claw attack from hiding, a Chilling Gaze, and a follow-up Claw attack, then running off with its prey at the first reasonable opportunity.

Neither the regular yeti nor the abominable yeti makes grappling attacks, even though they're both more than equipped to do so. This is largely a matter of timing. As long as their prey isn't incapacitated, they're better off making additional Multiattacks than spending an entire action on a grappling attempt. Once their prey is incapacitated, they don't need to make a grapple attack to pick them up and run— the victim is dead weight.

That being said, if a victim paralyzed by Chilling Gaze manages to make their saving throw on a repeat attempt, they can try to escape the yeti's clutches, using the normal rule for breaking a grapple

(*Player's Handbook*, chapter 9, "Melee Attacks"). Again, however, if its prey wriggles free, the yeti won't try to grapple them—it will simply attack with its claws until they stop moving, and will pursue relentlessly if they flee.

MINOTAURS

Everyone who took sixth-grade social studies has heard the story of the **minotaur**—literally, the Bull of King Minos, which inhabited the labyrinth into which the tyrant threw his prisoners. In the myth, the minotaur (there was only one) was the cursed offspring of a bull and Minos's wife, Pasiphae (ew), and the labyrinth was built by Daidalos to contain it so that it didn't rampage through the populace, devouring the king's subjects. In D&D, minotaurs (plural) are a humanoid species with bovine heads and hooves.

So . . . evolved creature or not? The *Monster Manual* flavor text seems to want to have it both ways, stating on the one hand that minotaurs are "humanoids transformed by the rituals of cults" and on the other that they "can breed true with one another, giving rise to an independent race."

If the *Monster Manual* can't commit to one explanation or the other, maybe we can't either. Maybe we have to accept that some minotaurs are evolved beings, and some aren't. Maybe the logical extension of this premise is that some minotaurs behave as an evolved creature would, while others don't, depending on whether they're born as minotaurs or transformed by a curse. In other words, if your adventure includes a minotaur, in order to know how it behaves, you need to give it a backstory.

A minotaur is a high-Strength, high-Constitution brute, and a stupid one at that. If it's a transformed minotaur we're talking about, it might be interesting to consider its low Intelligence as a possible source of resentment—surely it wasn't that stupid *before* it was transformed, and maybe it has memories of what it used to be like to know and understand things.

In contrast to its Intelligence, its Wisdom is very high. The designers probably gave it this ability simply to make it hard to sneak up on (it has proficiency in Perception as well, with a +7 skill modifier), but we have to consider what else this score implies, especially in combination with its pitiable Intelligence.

A creature with Intelligence 7 or less operates purely from instinct. That doesn't mean it uses its features *ineffectively*, only that it has one preferred modus operandi and isn't going to be able to adjust if it stops working. On the other hand, an evolved creature with Wisdom 14 or higher chooses its battles carefully and fights only when it's sure it will win (or will be killed if it doesn't fight). So not only does a minotaur perceive the world around it keenly, it's also good at basic threat assessment, though not to the extent of being able to identify its enemies' particular weaknesses. Will it parley if it recognizes that it's outmatched? Probably not: Judging by its below-average Charisma and its lack of proficiency in any social skill, talking isn't really its style. But it will keep its distance, glaring menacingly.

That being said, a transformed minotaur probably doesn't have the same self-preservation drive that a natural-born minotaur does. It may sense that it's outmatched yet attack an enemy or group of enemies anyway, simply out of hatefulness, hoping to cause its foes as much pain as possible before they release it from its miserable existence. Natural-born minotaurs, on the other hand, know no other existence and are keen to keep their lives going as long as possible.

Minotaurs have darkvision, so they're subterranean and/or nocturnal—you won't find them roaming around outside in broad daylight. They also have Labyrinthine Recall, a nod to the Minos myth, which doesn't have any impact on their combat tactics. The real meat of their tactics is in their other two features, Charge and Reckless.

Reckless is the same as the barbarian class feature Reckless Attack: It gives the minotaur advantage on all attack rolls while giving its opponents advantage on their own attacks against it. The wording of the feature makes it clear that it's strictly optional.

I think a transformed minotaur is more likely to be Reckless—it has nothing to lose. A natural-born minotaur, on the other hand, has more respect for its own skin. Consider that, having darkvision, minotaurs prefer to fight in the dark. Against blinded enemies, they make attack rolls with advantage already, so adding Reckless onto the pile doesn't help them. Meanwhile, those blinded enemies make their attack rolls with disadvantage, which adding Reckless would negate, actually hurting the minotaurs. So while they possess barely a flicker of cognitive activity, they do at least have the horse sense (bull sense?) not to use Reckless against opponents who are already blinded by darkness. Instead, natural-born minotaurs attack Recklessly only when they have no other advantage against their opponents, especially if their opponents already have advantage on attacks against them anyway.

Minotaurs use Charge to initiate combat. Although their base movement speed is 40 feet, their Charge requires them to move only 10 feet before attacking, and it can push their targets up to 10 feet away, setting up Charge after Charge. This is the core of the minotaur's attack sequence, which isn't complicated. On its first round, it attacks a target with Charge, most likely the nearest one. Charge nearly doubles the damage of a Gore attack and requires the target to make a Strength save or be thrown up to 10 feet back and knocked prone. If the target doesn't get back up, or if it gets up but then moves away, the minotaur repeats its Charge until the target is obliterated. If, on the other hand, the target gets up and moves *toward* the minotaur, or another enemy engages it in melee, it switches to simple melee attacks with its greataxe.

With their bestial Intelligence, minotaurs have no heuristic for target selection. Whatever's closest, they headbutt or chop at, and they keep headbutting and chopping until their enemies don't get back up or they themselves don't. Transformed minotaurs, in all likelihood, will fight to the death. Natural-born minotaurs may decide, upon being seriously injured (reduced to 30 hp or fewer), that they'd rather live to fight another day. Not being smart or disciplined enough to Disengage or deft enough to Dodge, they Dash away when they flee.

MANTICORES

The **manticore** is one of the few creatures whose tactics are already laid out in the *Monster Manual* flavor text, exactly as I'd envision them: "A manticore begins its attack with a volley of tail spikes, then lands and uses its claws and bite. When outdoors and outnumbered, it uses its wings to stay aloft, attacking from a distance until its spikes are depleted."

Given the manticore's stat and feature profile, these tactics make sense. Tail Spike is a strong attack with good damage and a generous range, and the manticore can hurl three in a single Multiattack action. Its Strength, Dexterity, and Constitution are all very high, suiting it equally for ranged and close-in combat. It stands to reason that it would use its strongest, safest attack first, then close in to finish off injured enemies. (The part where it talks smack to its targets, offers them quick deaths if they grovel, and trades mercy for food or treasure makes a lot less sense, although this is a monstrosity we're talking about, after all, so some of its behaviors are going to be weird.)

The manticore's Intelligence is 7; its Wisdom, however, is 12. I don't think it would be possible to trick a manticore into accepting a bad deal. In fact, I think it would have very little imagination with respect to what might constitute a *good* deal. The only thing that would be more appealing to a creature like this than food would be *more food*, perhaps a steady and easily obtained supply of it. A greater challenge, though still possible, would be offering to eliminate a known territorial rival (the *Monster Manual* lists chimeras, griffons, perytons, and wyverns as being among these). I think a manticore is simply too dumb to recognize the value of anything beyond food and territory.

As for target selection, a manticore is indiscriminate. As a Large creature with formidable physical ability scores and low Intelligence, it sees all PCs as equally weak and doesn't distinguish between ranged fighters and melee fighters or spellcasters and non-spellcasters. A PC who can deal it 20 hp or more of damage in a single turn will certainly get its attention, but that's as likely to enrage it as it is to make it hesitate.

The manticore has darkvision, so it has an advantage over many PCs when attacking at night or twilight. It has a land speed of 30 feet but a flying speed of 50 feet, so it isn't hindered by difficult terrain; furthermore, it probably lives and hunts in difficult terrain, where its prey is slowed. It flees when seriously injured (reduced to 27 or fewer hp) by Dashing away through the air—it's not smart enough to Disengage, and it's tough enough that it normally wouldn't have to anyway. And finally, the *Monster Manual* flavor text notes that manticores often hunt in packs, so despite having a challenge rating of only 3, they may still make good opponents for intermediate-level PCs.

LAMIAS

Another monster incorporated into D&D straight from classical mythology, the **lamia** was originally a queen who dallied with Zeus and was cursed by Hera to devour first her own children and then the children of others. Later, it was described as a monster with the torso of a woman and the lower body of a serpent. In the depiction of Edward Topsell, a 17th-century clergyman who fancied himself a naturalist, it became a creature with a woman's head on a lion-like body covered with serpentine scales, finished off with human breasts and an equine tail. Recurring themes in lamia myths include seduction, gluttony, filth, and bloodlust.

D&D's lamias have their roots in Topsell's interpretation. In AD&D, the lamia was drawn as having leonine paws in front and cloven hooves in back, and was vaguely described as having the lower body of "a beast." After several evolutions (including a mystifying fourth edition departure in which it became a corpse animated by devoured souls transformed into insects), the fifth edition lamia has returned to something near the original concept, with the nonspecific "beast" body now specifically the body of a lion, sans horse tail. These lamias, rather than slovenly and gluttonous, are smooth seducers, corrupters of virtue, and admirers of beauty and power.

Although its high Strength and Constitution, compared with its merely above-average Dexterity, suggest a brute, the lamia has high mental abilities as well; in fact, its ability contour strikes me as possibly one of the least spiky of all, aside from the humanoid commoner's. The fact that its two highest ability scores are in Strength and Charisma should make us consider that the lamia, behaviorally, is in a class by itself.

Lamias have proficiency in Insight and Stealth and expertise in Deception. This, together with their Charisma, implies that lamias are inclined to employ guile as much as brute force. Given that it's easier to punch someone after fooling them has failed than it is to fool someone after punching them has failed, manipulation is plan A, and melee combat is plan B.

With that in mind, let's take a look at the lamia's unique feature, Intoxicating Touch. For one hour, a creature struck by this attack has disadvantage on Wisdom saving throws and all ability checks. The obvious application of this effect is to increase the target's susceptibility to the lamia's Deception and Insight skills and to *charm person*, *suggestion*, and *geas*. (It reduces resistance to *disguise self*, too, but I'll talk about the hitch in that in a moment.)

The funny thing is, the lamia's Multiattack allows it to attack once with Claws and once with either Dagger or Intoxicating Touch. It seems to me that if a lamia is clawing at someone, it's probably too late for it to get much mileage out of Intoxicating Touch. Much more likely is that it will use Intoxicating Touch by itself, well in advance of any outbreak of violence. Once combat has already ensued, what use can Intoxicating Touch have? It can impose disadvantage on grappling rolls or on a rogue's attempts to Hide. If the lamia has an ally with the *command* spell, it can make the target more susceptible to that. But really, if the lamia is already in melee combat with someone, the goal is no longer to bend them to its will. The goal at this point is to slash and stab.

Back to the lamia's spellcasting—which is Innate Spellcasting, so there's no boosting *charm person* to affect more than one target. Similarly, *suggestion* and *geas* affect only one target apiece. And you can't really get away with casting any of these spells on someone when their friends are around. The upshot is, a lamia has to carefully control access to its presence.

The flavor text tells us, "These decadent monsters take what has been forgotten and make it the seat of their hedonistic rule, surrounding themselves with sycophants." This means they'll often be in a position to decide who gets to see them and who doesn't. We can therefore conclude that a lamia will grant an audience to only one PC at a time. It uses *disguise self* to hide its monstrous nature, Deception to make the fact that it's walking up to the PC and caressing their face seem perfectly plausible, Intoxicating Touch to lower the PC's resistance, Insight to glean their intentions, and finally *charm person* or *geas* to bend the PC to its will. Once the PC is securely under the lamia's control, it may then invite another PC in to receive the same treatment.

Disguise self allows the lamia to appear in a humanoid form, although the illusion is strictly visual. Normally, this spell can change a creature's apparent height by no more than a foot, and lamias are Large creatures. If we adhere to this rigidly, a lamia using *disguise self* to appear as short as possible will still be around 7 feet tall, and that's going to stand out. On the other hand, another way to interpret "any humanoid form" is that the lamia appears as a humanoid of typical size as well as typical shape. Again, this doesn't change the lamia's *actual* size and shape, so whether or not they see through the illusion, the architecture and furnishings of its abode may clue them in that this reclusive potentate is something out of the ordinary.

They'd better make their DC 13 Intelligence (Investigation) check to figure out whether there isn't something else funny about the situation *before* the lamia puts the whammy on them, though. Once its Intoxicating Touch takes effect, they'll have to make that check with disadvantage.

A lamia resorts to violence only when its cover is irreparably blown, and even then, it has the Wisdom to try bargaining first if it sees that it's outmatched. Its first action in combat is to cast *mirror image*, just because it can—if you can reduce incoming damage by 75 percent, surely that's worth the cost of one turn's worth of attacks. When the third duplicate is destroyed, the lamia casts *mirror image* again, and when the third of *those* duplicates is destroyed, it casts *mirror image* for the third and final time.

On every other of its turns, it makes a straightforward Claws/Dagger Multiattack (there's no longer any point to using Intoxicating Touch). Lamias have enough Intelligence to assess opponents' strengths and weaknesses accurately. Their own Armor Class is unexceptional, so opponents with Extra Attack are high priorities. Glass-cannon spellcasters are also attractive targets if they can be reached, since lamias deal an average 20 damage in a turn if both their hits land. Lamias will also want to destroy high-Wisdom opponents out of spite, but their Intelligence and Wisdom are high enough not to let this urge overcome their battlefield judgment.

Lamias are often accompanied by minions (canonically including—though not limited to—jackalweres), and as the battle unfolds, they'll direct these minions wherever the need is greatest, i.e., at whichever opponents are attacking most effectively.

A lamia that's seriously wounded (reduced to 38 hp or fewer) attempts to surrender and bargain for its life. At this point, it's worth considering what a lamia values most: beauty and power. Beautiful creatures and objects are easy to come by, but power isn't. A lamia will give up a great deal of treasure in order to keep its influential position. It's more than willing to trade favors—scrying services, for example, or manpower from among its minions. But it absolutely won't agree to even the smallest degree of public abasement, and it will yield control of territory only with the greatest reluctance. It also won't readily release a slave or thrall, and it will offer all kinds of generous alternative proposals to avoid doing so. Also remember, at bottom, lamias are covetous, unprincipled, and scheming. If a lamia can avoid fulfilling its end of the bargain—or if it has *any* opening in which to turn the tables on the PCs—it will.

Finally, don't assume that a lamia has to be feminine in appearance. Masculine lamias exist—and can be good fakeouts, if the PCs or their players don't know they exist.

Gorgons

The **gorgon** is an underutilized monster, a good enemy for intermediate-level parties. Thematically, it fits in well alongside golems and other constructs. Yet it's categorized as a monstrosity, and reading between the lines of the *Monster Manual* flavor text, it's evidently meant to be an evolved creature, so it has the same survival instinct as any other monstrous beast.

Gorgons are high-Strength, high-Constitution brutes, and their Intelligence is animal-level low, so they're *indiscriminate* brutes. Their senses are keen, though (Perception +4), so it's hard to slip past one unnoticed. They feed by petrifying their prey, then smashing it into gravelly Grape-Nuts that they can consume. They're not evil per se, but they are apex predators, and once they've locked on to potential prey, it takes a lot of damage to get them to reconsider their plan.

The gorgon attacks when the distance between itself and its target closes to between 30 and 40 feet. At that moment, it charges forth and makes a Gore attack, using the Trampling Charge feature to try to knock its target prone. If it succeeds, it gets to strike again with Hooves as a bonus action.

Although its Petrifying Breath feature is powerful, the Trampling Charge feature is better for initiating combat; the gorgon uses its breath weapon primarily to keep its prey from getting away. Read as written, the Trampling Charge trait seems to allow the gorgon to continue to gore and trample a victim as long as it remains prone, so that's what it does; only if the target gets back up, or if three or more foes come at it at once, does it use its Petrifying Breath against them. If it uses its breath weapon against multiple creatures and some are petrified while others aren't, it prioritizes a target who's still moving over those who are immobile during its next attack.

Incidentally, the minimum distance for a Trampling Charge is 20 feet. The gorgon's movement is 40 feet. That means that in a single turn, a gorgon can run 20 feet away from its prey, then turn around and charge it again. In doing so, it may subject itself to one or more opportunity attacks, but a tough, stupid brute like a gorgon won't care. Plus, a restrained target has disadvantage on its attack rolls. So when the gorgon has knocked an opponent prone, and that opponent gets back up, it first uses its Petrifying Breath against it, then runs 20 feet away; on its next turn, it turns around and charges back, in order to try to knock it prone again. (The target doesn't have disadvantage on the Strength saving throw—the restrained condition only affects Dexterity saves.) It also performs this maneuver if it's just tried and failed to knock a target prone in the first place.

A gorgon retreats when it's seriously injured (reduced to 45 hp or fewer). It uses its Petrifying Breath, if available, one last time before retreating, then backs away at its full movement speed, irrespective of opportunity attacks against it, and on subsequent turns Readies a Gore action against any creature that comes within range.

HYDRAS

A straightforward brute with extraordinary Strength and Constitution, the **hydra** is extremely stupid and indiscriminate when it comes to target selection. It also has only one method of attack: one Bite for each of its multiple heads, of which it initially has five. Running a hydra encounter is primarily a matter of accounting: tracking how much damage has been done to it; whether any of that was fire damage; and how many heads it has at the moment, since (a) destroying one head without cauterizing it causes two to sprout in its place, and (b) it gets an additional opportunity attack for every extra head.

The only question you have to answer, round by round, is where the hydra is going to position itself. The answer is, wherever it can attack as many targets as possible, up to the number of heads it has. In other words, if possible, a five-headed hydra will try to position itself where it can reach five targets; a seven-headed hydra will go where it can attack as many as possible, up to seven; and so on. It doesn't have to be immediately adjacent to these targets, since its heads have a reach of 10 feet: A target is still within reach if there's a single square or hex between the target and the hydra, even if there's another creature in that square or hex. (Because of the hydra's height, an interposed Medium-size ally doesn't give a humanoid creature any cover.)

It's not smart enough to avoid opportunity attacks, so a hydra begins its turn by moving to the optimal attacking location within 30 feet, then attacks with every head. It attacks every opponent within reach with one head, and if it has one or more heads left over, it attacks its biggest opponent one more time, then its second-biggest opponent, and so on. Exception: Anytime an enemy does enough damage to cut off one of its heads, if two grow in its place, both of those heads attack *that* enemy.

Hydras have advantage on saving throws against a variety of conditions, and as repeatedly noted, they're morons, so they don't know a spellcaster from any other walking Slim Jim, nor can they tell a magic weapon from any other kind of weapon except by how much it hurts.

A hydra is seriously wounded when it's reduced to 68 hp or fewer, at which point it doesn't flee, exactly, but it does retreat. It uses the Disengage action—not as a thoughtful tactic but as an instinct, snapping and feinting at its enemies with its jaws—and backs away to the nearest body of water. Upon reaching water, it dives and swims away.

SPHINXES

Sphinxes are bosses. Probably somewhat underutilized bosses, since you can only employ the solve-the-riddle, access-the-vault trope so many times before it gets tiresome (and that number of times is generally one, if not zero), so the first challenge you have to overcome as a DM, before dealing with its tactics, is figuring out a way to make a sphinx encounter feel fresh.

AD&D had four varieties of sphinx; the number peaked in third edition, v.3.5—the "More is always better" edition—at nine. But the fifth edition *Monster Manual* includes only two: the masculine **androsphinx** and the feminine **gynosphinx**. The androsphinx remains the more powerful of the two, because patriarchy. (The gynosphinx, strangely, seems to have a mane, although on closer inspection, it may just be a wig.)

Androsphinxes and gynosphinxes have many features in common. Physically, they're brute fighters; mentally, they're champs across the board, although androsphinxes have less Intelligence and more Charisma. (If you think this makes them sound like the types who typically get promoted to management, you're not alone.) They have double proficiency in Perception and 120 feet of truesight; they can't be charmed or frightened, and they're immune to psychic damage.

At a minimum, they're resistant to physical damage from nonmagical weapons (androsphinxes are fully immune). They can fly at a speed greater than their normal movement. Their Claw attacks are magical, and they get two per Multiattack action. They have three legendary actions, which they take on other creatures' turns: a single claw attack, teleportation, and casting one spell. (Since this last costs three actions, they use it only in case of dire emergency.) They have the Inscrutable trait, an ability primarily applicable to social interaction, which shields them from mind-reading. And they have a repertoire of spells they can cast at high levels.

Since they're brutes, their default fighting mode is toe-to-toe melee, and they don't have any compelling reason to vary it. If for some reason they decide they need to attack someone who's not right next to them and not within flying distance, they'll teleport at the end of that foe's turn, when running away is no longer an option. If they get another legendary action in between, they'll spend it on a Claw attack against that foe.

Any variety in their combat is going to emerge from the spells they cast—and the androsphinx and gynosphinx have very different lists of spells (*banishment* and *dispel magic* being the only spells that both can cast). Most of the spells in both lists, however, are spells that a sphinx might cast as a favor or a service to a supplicant, such as *legend lore*, *remove curse*, and *greater restoration*; only a few of the sphinxes' spells have combat applications.

Since *banishment* and *dispel magic* appear in both lists, we can conclude that they're important to both androsphinxes and gynosphinxes:

- A 4th-level spell, *banishment* lets the caster pack a target off to another plane for up to a minute or (if the target is native to another plane) permanently. Cast using a higher-level slot, it can shoo away another target for each level higher. The gynosphinx is a level 9 spellcaster and thus can boost *banishment* to 5th level, removing two targets, if it knows it's not going to be casting *legend lore* today; but the androsphinx is a level 12 spellcaster and can boost it as high as 6th level, removing three. Their spell save DCs are 16 and 18 respectively, and the gynosphinx's Intelligence is high enough that it can "read" target creatures' stats and know whether their Charisma is high enough for them to resist the spell (the spell is a safe bet for a gynosphinx if the target's Charisma saving throw modifier is +1 or lower, for an androsphinx if it's +3 or lower). An androsphinx, with its slightly lower Intelligence, can make very good guesses about the Charisma of a potential target but may be fooled by appearances. It knows better than to try *banishment* on a bard, paladin, sorcerer, or warlock, but if it hasn't had a chance to interact with a fighter, ranger, or back-alley rogue—classes not known for their magnetic personalities—or if such a character has failed a social skill check to a mortifying degree, it may infer a lower Charisma than the PC actually has. In any event, the purposes of *banishment* are twofold: to punish the impertinent and to remove a threat, which is to say, anyone wielding a magic weapon or casting high-powered damaging spells.

- *Dispel magic* takes care of an irksome nerf or buff. Use only if said nerf or buff is giving the sphinx actual trouble. Worth boosting with a 4th-level spell slot if needed, but not a 5th- or 6th-level slot—those are too scarce.

The gynosphinx has the following other combat-applicable spells:

- *Greater invisibility* can't be used at the same time as *banishment*, since both require concentration, and being a brute fighter, a gynosphinx will probably opt for the latter over the former. Only if there's no good target for *banishment* does a gynosphinx opt for *greater invisibility* instead, and only if it seems necessary somehow—for instance, if it's taken moderate damage (40 hp or more) from ranged weapon or spell attackers.
- *Darkness* is highly advantageous to the gynosphinx, which has truesight, but since it requires concentration, it's not sustainable

at the same time as *banishment* or *greater invisibility*, both of which are preferable.

- *Suggestion* is so underpowered compared with the gynosphinx's other abilities, I think it would only cast this spell to mess with opponents who are already failing to do any meaningful damage to it, such as telling a ranged attacker, "I think the tension of your bow is off. You really should restring it before you try to use it again, shouldn't you?"
- *Shield* is an automatic reaction in those instances when an attacker with a magic weapon rolls between 17 and 21 to hit.

The androsphinx has these combat spells:

- *Flame strike* is serious business, but it's worth casting only if the androsphinx can strike at least two enemies with it at once. Good against airborne opponents. Boosting this spell increases its damage, not its area, and the sphinx would probably rather keep its 6th-level spell slot free for boosting *banishment*, so it sticks with casting this spell at 5th level. It also won't cast this spell right out of the gate unless at least half of its opponents are clustered within its area of effect. It will have an even better moment to use this spell later on, after it uses its Second Roar.
- *Freedom of movement* is good only for freeing the androsphinx from magical restraint. (Paralysis would keep it from casting the spell at all, since it includes incapacitation.)
- *Command* is only useful if the sphinx has allies or minions at its disposal. With everything else the androsphinx can do, it just doesn't seem worth its action cost.
- *Sacred flame*, because the androsphinx is a 12th-level spellcaster, does 3d8 radiant damage. Could do worse.

The androsphinx also has one last feature up its sleeve: its Roar. It gets three of these per day, and it doesn't get to choose which effect to use. They happen in a specific order.

The First Roar frightens every non-deafened creature within 500 feet who fails their Wisdom saving throw, giving them disadvantage on all their attack rolls and ability checks as long as the androsphinx is within sight. It also keeps them from moving any closer to the sphinx, meaning that if it flies, leaps, or teleports away from a frightened melee opponent, that opponent can't chase it down. It takes a +4 Wisdom save modifier or better to have even a one-in-three chance of resisting this effect. It's a no-brainer: The androsphinx's first action on its first turn, when it can get the most out of this feature, is always to Roar.

The Second Roar frightens, deafens, *and* paralyzes. This last condition is devastating: A paralyzed creature can't take actions or reactions, can't move, can't speak, and automatically fails Strength and Dexterity saves (right after this Roar is the perfect moment to cast *flame strike*), and the sphinx gets advantage on all attack rolls against the creature, with automatic critical hits against melee opponents. The time to use this action is when half or more of the androsphinx's active opponents are no longer frightened from the First Roar.

The Third Roar does massive thunder damage and knocks opponents prone if they fail a Constitution save. The time to use this action is after the androsphinx has either followed up its Second Roar with a *flame strike* or decided not to.

Being divinely summoned spirits, sphinxes aren't evolved creatures, so their principal motivation is duty, not self-preservation. No matter how severely injured a sphinx may be, it won't flee, but rather will fight to the death in service to its mission.

ROCS

There aren't too many Gargantuan creatures in the *Monster Manual*. Ancient dragons grow to Gargantuan size; aside from that, you've got the dragon turtle, the kraken, the purple worm, the tarrasque, and the **roc**, a monstrous avian whose name, curiously, shares an etymology with "rook," the chess piece (from Persian رخ *rukh*, by way of Arabic), but *not* with "rook," the corvid bird (from Old English, an imitation of its croaking call).

This terror with a 200-foot wingspan—roughly the size of a Boeing 747—hunts big, slow-moving game, snatching up an elk, a buffalo, or even a giant as easily as a hawk or owl would seize a squirrel. It's unaligned and has only bestial Intelligence. Its Strength and Constitution are extraordinary; its Dexterity, as ordinary as you can get.

Rocs are fearless. Aside from their enormous pool of hit points, they have proficiency in all of the "big three" saving throws (Dexterity, Constitution, Wisdom), plus Charisma. Magic doesn't scare them, and it takes massive damage to even deter them: From their average maximum of 248 hp, they'll need to be reduced to 99 hp or fewer to be driven off.

Probably, the common folk's fear of rocs is far greater than the threat they truly pose, because the average humanoid isn't large enough to make much of a meal. If you see one diving toward your trade caravan, chances are it's planning to carry off one of your horses, not you. A roc would have to be starving to bother to carry off an adventurer.

A roc has only one method of attack: its Talons/Beak Multiattack. A successful Talons attack grapples and restrains its target, giving it advantage on a follow-up bite. Real-life birds of prey generally don't try to carry their game off alive and kicking—they strike hard to stun it, or they grab it and tear open an artery so that it bleeds to death. So while it's entertaining to think of a roc flying off with a moaning buffalo in its talons, the truth of the matter is, it's going to try to finish off the buffalo first, then fly it back to its nest while it's still fresh, or maybe even eat it on the spot. A roc does an average of 50 damage in a single round if both its attacks hit. That's enough to do in a giant elk, or seriously injure an elephant.

As long as a roc holds a living creature in its talons, it continues to attack that creature, and only that creature—unless it's attacked itself. Then it pecks back at its attacker with its beak, while still digging its talons into its prey. Once the prey is itself seriously injured (reduced to 40 percent or less of its hit point maximum), the roc simply flies away with it, without regard for opportunity attacks. It has a *base* flying speed of 120 feet, so there's no way any other creature is likely to catch up with it if it Dashes, short of casting *wind walk*.

PURPLE WORMS

Gigantic, opportunistic predators of the Underdark, **purple worms** pierce their way through earth and rock as easily as beetle grubs chew through the pages of a book, leaving twisting tunnels behind them. When they feel the vibrations of moving creatures, they burst forth and gnash at them with astonishing speed.

There's nothing subtle about a purple worm's attacks: Although its Strength and Constitution are extraordinary, all its other abilities are unimpressive. In particular, its rock-bottom Intelligence indicates a bare flicker of awareness. It zeroes straight in, first on whatever prey it senses first (larger wins ties), then on anything that manages to deal it more than a light wound (25 damage or greater) with a melee attack. Purple worms are too stupid to understand magic, and their blind-sight isn't precise enough to be able to tell where a ranged weapon attack came from.

A purple worm's Multiattack comprises a Bite attack, with a chance of swallowing its target whole, and a Tail Stinger attack. Although a target swallowed by a purple worm's Bite is restrained, it's because they're now inside the purple worm, so they're no longer a suitable target for the worm's stinger. Therefore, unfortunately for the worm, there's no particular order of operations here that offers any advantage on either attack roll. However, Tail Stinger plus Bite against a single target maximizes the damage against them before swallowing them, making it less likely that they'll fight their way out.

As a general rule, then, we can say that the purple worm's default is to sting and bite its intended prey, and if it takes the aforementioned light wound, it changes its "prey" designation to whoever dealt it that wound. But what if more than one melee opponent each manages to deal 25 damage or more to it? Then it divides its attention, biting whichever one is nearer to its mouth and stinging whichever is nearer to its tail. Also, whenever an opponent leaves its reach, it makes its opportunity attack with whichever end is closer.

As stupid and aggressive as they are, purple worms do understand one thing: pain. It takes a *lot* of pain to drive off a purple worm, though: It won't retreat until it's seriously wounded (reduced to 98 hp or fewer). Instinctively, it retreats by burrowing, even though it could move faster through an already existing tunnel, and even though its tunnels are stable and a determined pursuer can easily keep up with it. Too stupid to Disengage, too stupid even to Dodge (even though its high Armor Class would make this a practical choice), a seriously wounded purple worm Dashes away through the earth, lashing out behind it with its tail stinger if an enemy catches up with it. It hasn't evolved a better way to save itself, because there are few things in nature that can threaten the life of a purple worm.

KRAKENS

A high-level boss monster that player characters won't encounter until they're masters of the realm, if not masters of the world (if you, as their DM, have a shred of decency in you), the **kraken** isn't so much a creature as it is a natural disaster.

Running a kraken, like running a dragon, requires keeping track of legendary actions and lair actions as well as regular and bonus actions and reactions. One consolation is that, of all boss monsters, the kraken is probably the most likely to be encountered *outside* its lair, unless the PCs are on a mission to slay it. On the other hand, if the kraken is encountered within 6 miles of said lair, its regional effects mean that PCs will have to run a gauntlet of hostile crocodiles; swarming schools of quippers; giant crabs, frogs, and seahorses; sharks of all kinds; and water elementals. They'll also have to contend with torrential rain and storm-strength winds, imposing disadvantage on navigation checks, Wisdom (Perception) checks that rely on sight or hearing, and ranged weapon attack rolls. In colder climes, they'll have to make DC 10 Constitution checks against exhaustion every hour—and saving throws every *minute* if they fall into the frigid waters—unless they have natural or magical protection.

In its lair or out of it, the kraken is a juggernaut, with only average Dexterity but godlike Strength, Constitution, *and mental abilities*.

No, it's not just a mindless engine of devastation. It's smarter than anyone in your adventuring party and most likely wiser as well, and its massiveness and majesty are mesmerizing. Its decisions in combat should convey a sense of calculated malice and cruelty. It knows *everyone's* weaknesses, and it doesn't miss an opportunity to exploit them. If it chooses to communicate (via telepathy), it's only to taunt, belittle, and humiliate its victims; there's nothing a kraken wants that the PCs can tempt it with.

A kraken has proficiency on *every* kind of saving throw except Charisma, so spellcasters don't impress it—unless they try to cast *banishment*, *plane shift*, or *divine word*. The first two of those spells will get its attention, and not in a good way, if it makes its saving throw against them. As for *divine word*, for it to have a meaningful effect, the target has to have 40 hp or fewer. The average kraken starts with 472.

A kraken is immune to lightning damage and to being frightened, paralyzed, or magically restrained. It's immune to physical damage from nonmagical weapons. It has an Armor Class of 18. It's fearless, and opportunity attacks concern it not at all. Its Siege Monster trait doubles the damage it does to inanimate objects and structures. If you show up in a ship, it's not going to attack you—it's going to attack the *ship*, then deal with you when you're floating in the water, making saving throws against hypothermia.

On its own turn, the kraken has three choices of attack action: a triple Multiattack comprising three Tentacle or Fling attacks; a single Bite attack; or a single Lightning Storm.

- Tentacle is a bludgeoning attack with a 30-foot reach that automatically grapples on a hit. A grappled target is restrained, giving it disadvantage on attack rolls and giving the kraken advantage on attack rolls against it.
- Fling can be used only on an enemy who's already grappled. The *Monster Manual* says the enemy is thrown "in a random direction," but I'd overrule this. The kraken has Intelligence 22. It's not going to fling anyone or anything in a *random* direction. It's going to *aim*. If there's another enemy within

60 feet who's annoying the kraken, it flings its victim *at that enemy*, potentially doing bludgeoning damage to that enemy and knocking them prone as well (and remember, the kraken has advantage on attack rolls against a prone enemy it's within 5 feet of). If there's no one the kraken particularly wants to throw its victim at, it Flings the victim as far as it can at a solid surface—and as any diver will tell you, *water* is a solid surface if you don't enter it properly. I'd suggest requiring an opponent flung into the water to make a DC 18 Dexterity (Acrobatics) check to pull into a dive and enter the water without taking damage. Also, there's nothing that says the kraken *has* to Fling an opponent it's holding grappled. It can keep making Tentacle attacks against that opponent, squeezing it or smacking it against things, and it rolls with advantage because the opponent is restrained. Whether a kraken Flings an opponent or keeps it grappled depends on the likelihood that the opponent will struggle free. An opponent with an Acrobatics or Athletics skill modifier of +3 or lower is fairly unlikely to escape, so the kraken may as well hold on. It's got ten tentacles; it's not likely to run out of them.

- Bite can be used on a grappled or ungrappled opponent. Against an ungrappled opponent, it simply does damage. But a grappled opponent, on a hit, is *swallowed*. A swallowed opponent is blinded, has no movement, and has disadvantage on attacks against the kraken from inside. They're also subjected to acid damage from the kraken's digestive juices every round. This is a good way to take a troublesome opponent out of play, especially one likely to break the kraken's grapple.

- Lightning Storm can strike up to three targets at once—or a single target three times! The Dexterity saving throw DC is huge, and the attack deals damage even if the target succeeds. This is the kraken's nuclear option for dealing with a low–hit point, high-damage enemy such as a wizard or sorcerer, but it's also a highly effective way of striking enemies it can't reach with its tentacles.

As a DM whose players have risen to level 11 or higher, you should have a good idea who in the party is most dangerous, who's most durable and who's most fragile, and the loss of whom is most likely to demoralize the party. *The kraken knows everything you know.* It can "read" the PCs' abilities as if it had their character sheets in front of it, and it can calculate their threat level as if it were referring to "Creating a Combat Encounter" in the *Dungeon Master's Guide*. It can also sense immediately whether any of them has a weapon capable of harming it. It uses this information to choose its actions:

- If, as previously mentioned, the PCs are on a ship, or some other floating whatsit that's keeping them dry, the kraken attacks it first, attempting to destroy or at least capsize it. Contrary to what you might expect, it does this with Lightning Storm, not with tentacle attacks, because it does more damage (both mean and maximum) and because inanimate objects can't make Dexterity saving throws, so the hits are automatic. However, if the PCs' vessels are Large or smaller—say, if they're in rowboats or kayaks—the kraken *will* strike them with its tentacles, and if they're not destroyed outright, it will seize them and Fling them. A PC who's "knocked prone" owing to their boat's being Flung should be considered to have fallen overboard.

- If the PCs are unsupported by some other structure, either in the water or on land, the kraken's threat assessment comes into play. At first, when it's undamaged or only lightly wounded (having 331 hp or more) and if the encounter is rated Deadly for the PCs, it contemptuously attacks the weakest and most vulnerable targets first. If the three most vulnerable are *all* more than 30 feet away, and its movement won't allow it to close the distance in order to reach them, it strikes them with Lightning Storm. Otherwise, it strikes with its tentacles. Its number one target is the PC most likely to make your players go "*Nooooooooo!*"

    Note that a kraken doesn't have to attack three *different* targets, nor does it have to wait until its second turn to Fling, squeeze, or bludgeon a grappled target. It can seize one target with a tentacle as its first attack, Fling that target as its second, and grab another target as its third. Or it can seize two, then Fling one. (What it can't do, though, is grab an opponent and swallow them in the same turn.) Its goal is to do as much damage as it can to each one; if it grabs one who's got a good chance of struggling free (Acrobatics or Athletics modifier +4 or higher), it either tries immediately to bash them unconscious (if they have 52 hp or fewer) or grabs, bashes, then Flings them at another opponent between 30 and 60 feet away.

- Once the kraken is moderately wounded (reduced to 330 hp or fewer), or if the encounter is rated Easy, Medium, or Hard for the PCs, it takes its opposition more seriously, and it focuses its attacks not on the most vulnerable but on the most dangerous. Again, it uses Lightning Storm if its biggest threats are out of tentacle reach; otherwise, it attacks with its tentacles. It doesn't Fling an opponent it considers especially dangerous unless that opponent has a good chance of struggling free (Acrobatics or Athletics modifier +4 or higher), but it also doesn't try to swallow any opponent who might be able to do 50 hp or more damage in a single turn from inside it. Any such opponent, it simply holds on to with its tentacle and keeps squeezing or bashing until it no longer needs to.

- At some point, it's possible that the kraken will have grappled *every* opponent within reach whom it considers a major threat. If this has proved effective—if it's neutralized their ability to do any meaningful harm to it—it keeps grabbing up its other opponents, until it runs out of either opponents or tentacles. (The former is more likely.) It then moves to get the ones who've been out of reach so far. If it can't get at them with its tentacles, it strikes at them with Lightning Storm.

The kraken also has legendary actions, taken at the end of other creatures' turns. These comprise a single Tentacle or Fling attack, a Lightning Storm attack (which costs two legendary actions), and Ink

Cloud (which costs three). Ink Cloud can be used only underwater; the kraken uses it as a defensive measure as soon as it's moderately wounded (reduced to 330 hp or fewer), anytime *all* its opponents are within a 60-foot radius around it, and once more when it's seriously wounded (reduced to 188 hp or fewer) and about to retreat. At the end of the turn of any opponent who tries to attack it in melee, it makes a legendary Tentacle attack against that opponent. If it hasn't yet had a chance to Fling an opponent it probably won't be able to hold on to, it does so at the end of the turn just before that opponent's. If enough PCs' turns have gone by that it's obviously not going to need to make more Tentacle or Fling attacks before its own turn, and it still has two or more legendary actions left, it uses Lightning Storm. Otherwise, it uses any legendary action left over on a gratuitous Tentacle attack before its own turn starts.

If a kraken encountered outside its lair is seriously injured (reduced to 188 hp or fewer), it flees back to its underwater lair, forcing its foes to fight it on its own turf if they want to finish it off. In its lair, the kraken has a choice of three lair actions, always taken on initiative count 20:

- A strong current pushes opponents away from the kraken.
- Lightning damage is doubled against creatures within 60 feet for one round.
- The water itself does lightning damage to creatures within 120 feet.

Per the wording of the lair action descriptions in the *Monster Manual*, the effects of the second and third lair actions can't be stacked: *Either* lightning damage is doubled, *or* the water does lightning damage, but never both. Also note that, unlike chromatic dragons or mummy lords, the kraken isn't restricted from using the same lair action two turns in a row. Thus, lair action No. 3 is the default. Anytime the kraken doesn't plan specifically to use lair action No. 1 or No. 2, it uses No. 3.

Lair action No. 1 pushes creatures out of the kraken's reach—but most of the time, the kraken *wants* its opponents within reach so that it can grab them. This lair action is appropriate only under specific, limited circumstances: Either the kraken is seriously wounded; or it's got hold of a dangerous opponent whom it doesn't want to let go of, while another opponent within 30 feet, who'll be hard for the kraken to grab or keep hold of, is trying to help them get free.

The kraken's Lightning Storm ability reaches out to 120 feet, but its second lair action doubles lightning damage only within 60 feet. Since the kraken generally prefers to attack enemies within reach with its tentacles rather than Lightning Storm (grappling them restrains them and confers advantage on attack rolls, along with the option to devour), lair action No. 2 is appropriate when the kraken plans to use Lightning Storm against opponents who are between 30 and 60 feet away from it.

A kraken out of its lair is playing offense; a kraken in its lair is playing defense. If the PCs have enough chutzpah to confront a kraken in its own lair, it has to take them seriously from the get-go, and it doesn't mess around abusing vulnerable opponents for the fun of it. It goes straight for the most powerful of its enemies and does its level best to disable or debilitate them. Its primary goal is to neutralize; killing, as an end in itself, is secondary. Thus, it uses Tentacle attacks exclusively until all its opponents are restrained, then switches to Bite; it no longer bothers with Fling, and uses Lightning Storm only in conjunction with its second lair action.

A kraken staring death in the face in its own lair is in a terrible bind: It wants to flee to save itself, but it's also stronger inside its lair than outside it. It *really* doesn't want to leave its lair, nor does it want to die. Thus, it has to consider what means of defending itself will be most effective against its attackers. If they're more agile than they are tough, an Ink Cloud does poison damage to every enemy in a 60-foot radius, gives them disadvantage on all their attack rolls by heavily obscuring the area, and makes the kraken harder to target with spells. If they're tougher than they are agile, Lightning Storm does guaranteed damage, albeit to only three enemies at a time—but lair action No. 2 can double that damage. If it doesn't have confidence in either of these recourses, it uses lair action No. 3 (if its enemies are all badly injured) or lair action No. 1 (if not) one last time before either Disengaging (if it's within reach of a melee attacker) or Dashing (if not) and swimming away at full speed, using its Ink Cloud legendary action once each round to hinder its pursuers.

TARRASQUES

There's only one creature in the fifth edition *Monster Manual* with a higher challenge rating than an ancient red or gold dragon: the **tarrasque**.

The tarrasque is basically a *kaiju*. It's 50 feet tall and 70 feet long, quadrupedal but walking on its hind legs and using its tail for balance (the *Monster Manual* compares this to a bird of prey, but a better comparison is to a dinosaur or—let's be honest—some kind of hellish kangaroo). With Intelligence 3, it's overwhelmingly a creature of instinct, with no more ability to learn, adapt, or strategize than a cat or dog. Its Strength and Constitution peg the meter, but its Dexterity is a merely average 11—unsurprising, given how much mass it has to move. Its Wisdom and Charisma are similarly average, so it's the tarrasque's brute Strength and Constitution and very low Intelligence that define its behavior.

Tarrasques are immune to fire and poison damage as well as physical damage from normal weapons. They have proficiency on only two of the big three saving throws: Constitution and Wisdom. This means that Dex saves are the closest thing the tarrasque has to an Achilles' heel—but it also has Legendary Resistance, giving it automatic successes on up to three saving throws. Those are always going to be the first three failures, unless a player character lobs something at it that's not even worth dodging, such as a *fireball* spell. The tarrasque also has Magic Resistance, giving it advantage on saving throws against spells and other magical effects, *and* Reflective Carapace, which causes ranged spell attacks, *magic missiles*, and spells with a linear area of effect, such as *lightning bolt*, to bounce off it—occasionally, back in the direction of the caster.

So let's pause here and enumerate what kinds of damage *can* get through the hide of a tarrasque:

- Physical damage from magic weapons. That, at least, you can depend on.
- Acid. Mundane, undiluted acid flung in its face. (Whether you can obtain enough of it to make a difference is another matter.)
- Direct acid, cold, lightning, thunder, radiant, necrotic, force, or psychic damage from a magic weapon. These are reliable because they require only weapon attack hits to convey, not saving throws to resist.
- Radiant damage from sources like the paladin's Divine Smite feature. Again, it's direct damage, no saving throw required.
- Certain kinds of magical damage requiring a Dex save *if you can suck up its Legendary Resistance first*. Also, if possible, you'll want to restrain, paralyze, or stun the tarrasque to negate its advantage on the roll. Of course, this will generally require it to have failed a Constitution or Wisdom save first, so I wouldn't pin your hopes on it.
- The breath weapon of a dragon, which is a *biological* effect, not a magical one. Acid (black, copper), cold (white, silver), or lightning (blue, bronze) will work; fire (red, gold, brass) and poison (green) won't. Also, the breath weapon of a dragonborn, although that character will normally get to use it only once, and it will do only about 18 damage on average, and even that assumes no more Legendary Resistance.

Based on this list, dealing with a tarrasque isn't going to be easy by any stretch of the imagination, although it will be *easier* for sturdy PCs equipped with the finest in magic weaponry—or for ones who have good working relationships with the right kinds of dragons. Also, they'll have to do their research first or suffer through some painful trial and error as they try to figure out what works and what doesn't.

How painful? Let's turn to what the tarrasque can do to its opponents.

With +19 to hit, all its melee attacks are virtually guaranteed to land. Its Bite does an average 36 damage per hit, grapples, and restrains; its Claw does an average 28 damage; its Horns do an average

32 damage; and its Tail does an average 24 damage and has a good chance of knocking its target down. Its Multiattack incorporates *five* attacks: two Claw attacks and one each with Bite, Horns, and Tail. That's an *average* of 148 damage per turn—plus the effects of the tarrasque's Frightful Presence.

As part of its Multiattack, the tarrasque can substitute Swallow for its Bite if it holds an opponent in its jaws. This action inflicts an additional Bite attack (with advantage, since the target is restrained, although the tarrasque's attack modifier is so great, this will hardly make a difference) and transports the opponent to its gut, where said opponent will be rapidly digested if they can't inflict 60 damage in a single turn while blinded and restrained.

It also has legendary actions—actions that let it act on other creatures' turns. It can make a single attack with its claws (target in front of it) or its tail (target behind it), it can put on a burst of speed, or it can make a single Bite or Swallow attack at the cost of two of its legendary actions. So add another *average* 84 damage to the amount it can potentially dish out on its turn.

If all this damage were directed at a single character, that character would have to be a level 20 barbarian with Constitution 20 to have a *chance* of surviving. In fact, a party of six level 20 PCs will have an extraordinarily difficult time taking down a tarrasque. To do so will require them to dish out 676 damage in, well, six rounds or fewer, basically, with each round diminishing the amount of damage they can deal. About 200 of that damage will have to be dealt in the first round.

There are silver linings, though. First, a tarrasque isn't going to direct *all* its attacks at a single target, ever. It uses Bite, Horns, and Claw against opponents in an arc in front of it, but its Tail attacks are directed at targets behind it. (Tarrasques have 120 feet of blindsight, so don't count on their not seeing you creeping up on them.)

Second, tarrasques choose their targets indiscriminately. They're so massive that their hunting instincts don't have to be fine-tuned, which means they're not singling out weak or isolated targets. In fact, they're more reactive than anything else. Whoever does the most damage to them in a given round is likely to be their main target in the next one—provided that they know where the damage came from.

Third, they want to liiiiive! That means you don't have to kill a tarrasque to drive it off. If you can get it down to 270 hp or fewer, Godzilla will return to the ocean.

Fourth, a tarrasque is less likely to attack creatures who are fleeing its Frightful Presence—that is, unless one of those creatures is directly in front of it. Then, like a dog, it instinctively chases that target.

And fifth, if it's being fought from a fortified position, the tarrasque is as likely to direct its own attacks (specifically, Claw and Horns attacks) at the fortification itself as at the opponents inside.

The tarrasque's Multiattack sequence generally follows the order Claw/Claw/Horns/Bite, with any Tail attack (if applicable) occurring at a random point in that sequence, but if it has a grappled victim in its teeth, it Swallows first, then uses its move, then finishes its Multiattack with Claw/Claw/Horn. Claw and Bite attacks will be directed against the same target, but the Horns attack *may* be directed elsewhere, depending on who's in front of the tarrasque and how much they're bothering it.

It uses its Chomp legendary action anytime it has a victim in its jaws on another creature's turn. This is reflexive behavior, not necessarily optimal behavior—and since Chomp consumes two legendary actions, this may also be construed as a silver lining for everyone other than the living snack. If the tarrasque has no grappled opponent in its jaws, but there's an opponent within reach directly in front of it, it uses its Attack legendary action to Claw; if there's no one within reach in front but there is someone within reach behind, it makes a Tail attack. If there's no one within reach in front *or* behind, it uses its Move legendary action to get closer to whomever it's chasing, or to the nearest potential target.

The tarrasque's behavior is *very* random, and cynically, the best place for PCs to encounter one is in, say, a crowded city, where there are lots of innocent bystanders for the tarrasque to attack while the PCs get their first licks in against it. If they confront it in the wilderness, in contrast, its full attention will be on them and them alone. However easily distracted it may be at first, once a tarrasque is lightly wounded (reduced to 608 hp or fewer), it stops attacking bystanders and focuses its attention on whoever's hurting it. When it's moderately wounded (reduced to 473 hp or fewer), it becomes very aggressive and focuses all its forward-facing attacks on whichever single opponent has done the most damage to it. When it's seriously wounded (reduced to 270 hp or fewer), it lumbers away, using the Dash action on its own turn unless there's a pursuer within reach of its tail, in which case it makes a Tail attack. It also uses its Attack legendary action to take tail swipes whenever a pursuer gets too close.

DRAGONS

The folklorist Sandra Martina Schwab calls dragons "the emblem of fantasy," and she hits the nail on the head. Why else would the most popular fantasy roleplaying game ever invented include them in its name? If you're going to include one of these awe-inspiring beasts in your adventures, make sure it lives up to the examples of majesty and menace set by Fáfnir, Zmey Gorynych, Smaug, Yevaud, and the countless unnamed, marauding drakes, wyrms, *sárkányok*, and *lóng* of myth. The best dragons' personalities are as big as their wingspans. Even their cousins, from the Tiny pseudodragon to the Gargantuan dragon turtle, use their tactics not only to win battles but to show off their dispositions as well.

CHROMATIC DRAGONS

The *Monster Manual*'s section on dragons is one of the longest in the book and, at first glance, one of the most complicated. But unlike, say, demons, which are all over the place in terms of what they can do, dragons are easy to work with, because they all follow the same pattern.

First, there are certain things that all dragons have in common. They all fly, at twice their land movement speed, and all have one additional movement ability, depending on their color. They have high Strength and Constitution. They have bonuses on the "big three" saving throws (Dexterity, Constitution, and Wisdom), plus Charisma; proficiency in Perception and Stealth; and blindsight and darkvision, suiting their subterranean dwelling preferences. They begin as uncomplicated "wyrmlings," then gain abilities and features as they age and grow. And they all have breath weapons.

This last feature is dragons' defining characteristic. Every dragon, even a wyrmling, has a breath weapon, with effects depending on the dragon's color. The breath weapon does powerful damage over a cone-shaped area of effect (except blue and bronze dragons' Lightning Breath, which is linear). Because of its power, it has to recharge: At the start of each of its turns, roll a d6 for the dragon. If you roll a 5 or a 6, it has access to its breath weapon again. *On average*, this means the dragon will get to use its breath weapon once every three turns. But dice are fickle. My players once fought a dragon that got to use its breath weapon three rounds in a row because the dice happened to fall that way. (They beat it anyway, very cleverly, I'm happy to report.)

Taking high Strength and Constitution as indicative of a "brute" profile, a tough creature with a strong preference for toe-to-toe fighting, most dragons are brutes, even at the wyrmling stage. Of the chromatic dragons, only black and green wyrmlings lack the Constitution to take on any comer in melee. Despite their Strength, these may prefer simply to use their Stealth to avoid combat unless they're attacked. Dragons of every other color and age won't hesitate to get directly up in your grille.

Wyrmlings are the youngest and least complicated dragons. They prefer to rest during the day; aboveground, they move about in twilight or at night. Before combat begins, they always use their Stealth ability, either to stalk prey (if outside their lairs) or to conceal themselves (if within them). Their alternative movement ability indicates their method of ambush: Black and green wyrmlings, which can swim, may come up out of the water to attack, like a crocodile. Blue and white wyrmlings, which can burrow, may come up out of the earth. Red wyrmlings, which can climb, may drop from a branch or rocky overhang. Any type may also choose simply to fly in, on owl-silent wings.

When prey is within striking distance, wyrmlings attack with their breath weapons first; on subsequent turns, if their breath weapons haven't recharged, they Bite. They don't like engaging in melee with more than one opponent, though. If a wyrmling is ganged up on and it has its breath weapon available, it uses that breath weapon, backing up (and potentially provoking one or more opportunity attacks) far enough to catch all its melee attackers, then using the remainder of its movement to fly, burrow, swim, climb, or crawl to a more favorable position, one where it can fight just a single melee opponent at once. If its breath weapon isn't available, it Dodges, then repositions. If reduced to 40 percent of its hit point maximum or less, a wyrmling will Dodge and fly away.

Young dragons add a Multiattack to their repertoire: Their single Bite turns into a Claw/Claw/Bite. Aside from this, and the fact that young black and green dragons are more likely to stand and fight than black and green wyrmlings are, there isn't really any significant difference between a young dragon and a wyrmling. All the same tactics and behaviors apply, with one difference: A young dragon is willing to engage two melee attackers at once, although not three. Attacked by three melee opponents, a young dragon backs off as a wyrmling does.

Young dragons also show adolescent variations on their adult personalities. Young black dragons are snarling bullies; young blue dragons, preening narcissists; young green dragons, cocky hustlers; young red dragons, arrogant punks; and young white dragons, barely articulate predators.

Adult dragons are where things get most interesting, because they're considered legendary creatures. This means they get legendary actions and lair actions, which have game-changing effects on their action economy.

Chromatic dragons' lair actions fall into three rough categories:

- **Movement restrictors.** These include the black dragon's grasping tide, which can knock PCs prone; the blue dragon's ceiling collapse, which can bury them under rubble; the green dragon's grasping roots, which can restrain them; the red dragon's tremor, which can also knock them prone; and the white dragon's wall of ice, which can block their way.
- **Direct damage.** These include the black dragon's swarming insects, the blue dragon's arc lightning, the green dragon's thorny

brush, the red dragon's magma eruption, and the white dragon's ice shards.
- **Debilitators.** These include the black dragon's darkness sphere, the blue dragon's cloud of sand, the green dragon's enchanting fog, the red dragon's volcanic gas, and the white dragon's freezing fog.

The general rule of lair actions is that you can never use the same one two turns in a row, and any lasting effect (as opposed to an instantaneous effect, like the damage from the white dragon's ice shards) remains until the legendary creature uses that same lair action again someplace else, or dies.

Which lair action a dragon chooses to use depends on a few factors. One is area of effect. Many lair actions affect a sphere with a 20-foot radius, while others affect an area with some other shape, like the blue dragon's arc lightning, which occurs along a straight line. Another factor is how closely clustered its opponents are, and whether it can catch enough of them—ideally, at least four—within a single area of damaging effect. Another is whether the dragon is trying to keep the PCs from coming closer—or trying to keep them from getting away. A healthy dragon likes to pin its targets down so that it can nail them with its breath weapon or a Wing Attack. A seriously wounded one might want to restrain them in order to keep them from pursuing it as it flees.

To get more specific:

- A black dragon's lair actions can knock its enemies prone or blind them. Knocking enemies prone is good against melee opponents. Blindness is good against everybody, since dragons have blindsight. It's particularly good for shutting down spellcasters, though, especially if there are at least three within 30 feet of one another, because so many spells require the caster to see the target.
- A blue dragon's ceiling collapse affects only one creature and offers both a Dexterity saving throw and a Strength check to

overcome it, so obviously, it's best aimed at someone with not much of either. Its cloud of sand imposes blindness across a 20-foot radius, and that's good against everybody, especially spellcasters.

- A green dragon's lair actions can charm one creature (ideally, a non-elf with low Wisdom) or restrain several, which is good against melee opponents.
- A red dragon's lair actions can knock enemies prone across a huge radius or poison and incapacitate them. Knocking enemies prone is good against melee opponents; poison is good against all opponents making melee or ranged attacks, and incapacitation shuts a PC down completely—but if you really want to get the best effect out of it, aim it at the PCs with the richest action economy, especially those with access to bonus actions and/or Extra Attack.
- A white dragon's freezing fog can heavily obscure an area, effectively blinding those within it as well as dealing cold damage. It's useful for shutting down spellcasters and blocking the view of ranged attackers.
- All mobility-restricting lair actions are good for cutting off the escape of PCs who may attempt to run away.
- All damaging lair actions are good against, well, anybody within range. They're good go-tos for softening the PCs up when no other lair action seems more useful.

All dragons—chromatic and metallic alike—have the same set of legendary actions available. Two of them are attacks: Tail Attack and Wing Attack. Tail Attack has sufficient reach to hit any one PC up to 15 feet away. Wing Attack affects all PCs within 10 feet; it also costs two legendary actions.

Because of this cost, and the fact that a Wing Attack does slightly less damage than a Tail Attack (though it also has a very high probability of knocking targets prone), it's generally not worth using against just one PC, and two are a borderline case. As soon as a third PC approaches within 10 feet of an adult dragon, though, it's Wing Attack time! After attacking, it uses the bonus flying movement to resituate itself so that it's no longer flanked (see "Optional Rule: Flanking" in chapter 8 of the *Dungeon Master's Guide*).

A dragon also uses Wing Attack after a melee attack has seriously injured it (reduced it to 40 percent of its hit point maximum or less), in order to knock its attackers prone (so that they have disadvantage on attacks, including opportunity attacks) and use the bonus flying movement it receives to initiate its escape.

The Tail Attack is a freebie the dragon can use against a PC impertinent enough to try to get up on it from behind. It won't do this twice in a round, unless there's no chance of its being surrounded by three melee attackers and needing to make a Wing Attack before its own turn.

There's also a third legendary action the dragon can take: Detect, which is just a free Wisdom (Perception) check. This is good anytime there's no PC within range of a Tail Attack or Wing Attack; any attempted stealthy movement of the PCs within the dragon's line of sight should trigger a Detect action. Dragons are *very* hard to sneak up on!

As adults, dragons gain the Legendary Resistance trait, which they can use three times per day, each time turning a failed saving throw into a success. Dragons' saving throw modifiers are so good to begin with that they'll use this feature every time they fail a save, without worrying about running out.

As with younger dragons, an adult dragon's preferred attack on its own turn is its breath weapon, as long as it's available. Before using its breath weapon, a dragon always repositions to catch as many opponents in the blast as possible. This may provoke one or more opportunity attacks; the dragon doesn't care about your puny opportunity attacks, not when it's about to hit you with a breath weapon that a third of your party won't get up from. If its breath weapon isn't available, a dragon has a spectacular Multiattack: one use of Frightful Presence, which affects *every* PC aware of the dragon within 120 feet, followed by a Claw/Claw/Bite combo. (Note that only the first use of Frightful Presence really matters, unless it misses somebody. Either it gets you, and you're frightened until you make your Wisdom save, or it doesn't, and you're immune for twenty-four hours. If it doesn't work on you the first time, it won't work on you the second time, and if it works on you once, it won't work on you twice.)

When it's seriously wounded (reduced to 40 percent of its hit point maximum or less), a dragon hightails it. Its life is too valuable to risk on foes capable of doing so much harm to it. However, between being moderately wounded (reduced to 70 percent of its hit point maximum) and being seriously wounded, different types of dragons react differently to the situation.

White dragons are dense and truculent; they'll simply keep fighting. Red dragons are wrathful and arrogant; they'll keep fighting too.

Blue dragons, however, are patient and pragmatic. When they see a battle isn't going their way, they'll Disengage, fly to a safe distance, and take potshots with their Lightning Breath, making sure to catch at least two PCs, and preferably three or more, in each blast. If the party has ranged attackers or spellcasters who continue to do damage to a blue dragon, it will fly out of sight . . . for the time being. But it will be back, again and again and again, until either it or the PCs are dead. Its pride demands it.

Black dragons are cruel and brutal, and they target their weakest enemies first, so if a black dragon's opponents have managed to inflict real damage on it, something's gone horribly wrong, and it will skedaddle. It might accept a sufficiently attractive bargain offered by the PCs, but it will never surrender to them or agree to any limit on its independence.

Green dragons are the craftiest and most manipulative of the chromatic dragons; as soon as one is moderately wounded, it will stop fighting and parley, making full use of its proficiency in Deception, Insight, and Persuasion (skills no other type of chromatic dragon is proficient in) to keep itself alive. It will even surrender, albeit on terms favorable to itself, and always with an eye toward any opportunity to turn against its new "masters."

On its 801st birthday, an adult dragon becomes an **ancient dragon**. It doesn't gain any new features; it simply grows larger and gets better at the features it already has. Its save DCs increase, the ranges of its attacks are extended, and that's basically it. In all other respects, it fights the same way as an adult of the same type.

METALLIC DRAGONS

Metallic dragons are the good complements to the evil chromatic dragons. Looking just at their statistics, they're identical in most ways: Their physical abilities follow the high-Strength, high-Constitution "brute" profile. They have proficiency bonuses on all of the "big three" saving throws, plus Charisma. They have blindsight, darkvision, flying movement, and one alternative movement mode (burrowing, swimming, or climbing)—although I have to put an asterisk by this last one, because the *Monster Manual* seems to have either neglected or declined to give silver dragons an alternative movement mode. Adult and ancient metallic dragons have the same legendary actions as chromatic dragons of those ages, and they share the chromatic dragons' Legendary Resistance and Frightful Presence features. In addition, young, adult, and ancient metallic dragons have the same Claw/Claw/Bite Multiattack. And, of course, they all have breath weapons.

Metallic dragons differ from chromatic dragons in four ways:

- Young, adult, and ancient metallic dragons all have social skill proficiencies in addition to Perception and Stealth.
- Ancient brass and copper dragons, and adult and ancient bronze, gold, and silver dragons, can Change Shape.
- Adult and ancient metallic dragons have only two lair actions available to them, rather than three.
- Each metallic dragon has *two* types of breath weapon, one of which is nonlethal and can be used to subdue without injury.

Given that these are good creatures, an encounter with a metallic dragon is going to play out very differently from an encounter with a chromatic dragon. Rarely will it begin with the dragon attacking the player characters—or, for that matter, with the PCs attacking the dragon.

Metallic **wyrmlings** will generally be friendly and gentle, if aloof. A brass, copper, or silver wyrmling may even walk right up to a party of adventurers and try talking to them in Draconic; a bronze or gold wyrmling will hide itself and observe them watchfully but not flee if approached, unless they seem belligerent. If a fight breaks out, a wyrmling's first action will be to use its nonlethal breath weapon once in an effort to repel its attackers, then fly, burrow, or swim away at maximum speed. Only if attacked and damaged will it fight back with its damaging breath, and only if cornered will it engage in melee and Bite.

Young dragons of the metallic varieties also show adolescent versions of their adult personalities: Young brass dragons are prattling blabbermouths, young bronze dragons are shy observers, young copper dragons are clowns and comedians, young gold dragons are aloof and a bit stuck-up, and young silver dragons are sweethearts. Young brass, copper, and silver dragons will initiate social interaction; young bronze and gold dragons generally won't, but may engage in conversation if approached with clearly nonhostile intentions.

The type of social interaction young dragons engage in is indicated by their social skill proficiencies. Young brass dragons enjoy conversation, exchanges of compliments, and bargaining; so do young gold dragons, although they'll be quicker to pick up on insincerity and mixed motives in the PCs. Young bronze dragons are more guarded, trying to get a read on what the PCs want before engaging on a deeper level. Young copper dragons like to bluff and brag, to see who can put the more outrageous story over on the other. Silver dragons are interested in exchanging knowledge.

If it looks like an encounter is about to turn hostile, young bronze and gold dragons won't waste time—they'll fly away immediately. Young copper dragons will use Deception to try to misdirect the PCs or trick them into dropping their guard, then hit them with Slowing Breath before flying away. Young brass dragons will try to talk their way out of the situation before resorting to their Sleep Breath and fleeing, and good-natured young Silver Dragons may not even realize they're in danger unless and until combat actually breaks out, whereupon they'll use their Paralyzing Breath, then fly away. Like wyrmlings, young dragons use their nonlethal breath weapons as a harmless but effective sucker punch before retreating, use their damaging breath weapons only if they're already hurt themselves, and use their melee Multiattacks only when cornered.

Like chromatic dragons, metallic dragons past the wyrmling stage reposition themselves before using their breath weapons, potentially incurring one or more opportunity attacks, in order to catch as many targets as possible in the area of effect. This holds whether they're using their nonlethal breath weapons or their damaging ones.

Metallic **adult dragons** and **ancient dragons** have access to their lair actions, which don't follow as consistent a pattern as chromatic adult dragons' lair actions do. Roughly speaking, they can be divided into nonlethal "cloud actions" and more aggressive "push actions." Cloud actions include the brass dragon's Cloud of Sand, the bronze and silver dragons' Fog Cloud, and the copper dragon's Mud (which stretches the definition of the category). Push actions include the brass dragon's Strong Wind, the bronze dragon's Thunderclap, the copper dragon's Spike Growth, and the silver dragon's Cold Wind; all but the first do damage, and all but the last inhibit movement.

The gold dragon's lair actions, however, don't fit this pattern at all. Its two lair actions are Glimpse of the Future, which gives it advantage on attack rolls, ability checks, and saving throws for the entire round; and Banishment, which works like the spell of the same name, though only for one round. It will rely on Glimpse of the Future as long as no blood has been drawn; afterward, it uses Banishment to suspend its most threatening opponent's fighting privileges whenever it can.

Adult and ancient metallic dragons, like young metallic dragons, would rather talk than fight, although their personalities are more mature and fully developed. Unlike young metallic dragons, they *will* start a fight themselves if they get the sense that the PCs they're dealing with have evil intent. However, they'll still do so by nonlethal means—their "cloud" lair action and nondamaging breath weapon—as long as this appears workable. Unlike chromatic dragons, they use their melee Multiattacks *before* their damaging breath weapons, because their Multiattacks include Frightful Presence, which may be effective at keeping opponents at bay. Their damaging breath weapons are a last-ditch trump card to play when it's obvious that the PCs are evil and not to be deterred otherwise.

Unless they're defending their lairs, adult and ancient metallic dragons won't fight past the point of being moderately wounded (reduced to 70 percent of their hit point maximum or less): Any creatures that can harm them that badly can probably do worse as well, and are therefore to be evaded. A retreating metallic dragon Disengages, then flies away at maximum speed—or burrows, swims, or climbs away if and only if its attackers can't follow it that way.

Like their chromatic counterparts, adult and ancient metallic dragons use their Legendary Resistance whenever they fail a saving throw.

Finally, any adult or ancient metallic dragon with the Change Shape feature prefers to go about in disguise when it's outside its lair, especially when venturing into civilized lands. They blend in with their surroundings, taking human form among humans, elven form among elves, beast or bird form in the wilderness, possibly even a genie form in the desert. If threatened in its disguised form, a dragon will do its level best to talk its way out of any situation, even surrendering if necessary to avoid a fight, in order to avoid revealing its true nature. As soon as eyes are off it, however, it will either revert to dragon form or assume a different form that allows it to escape.

SHADOW DRAGONS AND DRACOLICHES

The fifth edition *Monster Manual* includes listings for two "dragons" that aren't individual creatures per se but rather templates that can be overlaid on any chromatic or metallic dragon stat block. Shadow dragons are dragons that have made lairs in the Shadowfell—a parallel plane of existence full of negative energy, dreary and desolate—and suffered the sorts of effects you'd expect from living for decades or centuries in such a place. Dracoliches are dragons that, like humanoid liches, have turned themselves into undead horrors in the misguided pursuit of immortality.

Shadow dragons and dracoliches are created by applying certain modifications to the stat block of an adult or ancient dragon of another type, either chromatic or metallic. (Yes, it seems that even metallic dragons can become shadow dragons or dracoliches, supposing that they were subjected to some sort of sufficiently powerful corrupting influence or curse.) What effects might these modifications have on their combat tactics?

Shadow dragons have increased proficiency bonuses in the Stealth skill, along with the Shadow Stealth and Sunlight Sensitivity traits. Shadow Stealth grants the ability to Hide as a bonus action; Sunlight Sensitivity imposes disadvantage on attack rolls and Wisdom (Perception) checks in daylight. So here's our first difference: Shadow dragons won't come out during the daytime. They're strictly nocturnal and subterranean.

Despite their having the same brute melee fighter profile as other dragons, Shadow Stealth gives them an incentive to fight in a more skirmishy style: attack, retreat, Hide, repeat. Their high Constitution, Armor Class, and hit points make them unconcerned about the opportunity attacks they might provoke by retreating. However, I don't think it would be very much in character even for a corrupted dragon to fight this way every round. Maybe have it switch from slugfest to skirmish if it's having trouble landing melee blows, or if its foes are landing too many or are surrounding it too easily.

The other alteration that might affect a shadow dragon's tactics is Shadow Breath, which turns all damaging breath weapons into waves of necrotic energy with the potential to turn enemies into undead thralls. This gives the shadow dragon an incentive to focus its attacks on its less durable foes. Identifying these foes requires a certain measure of Intelligence, however, one that former blue, green, red, and metallic dragons are likely to possess; former white dragons, not so much.

The *Monster Manual* gives the Dungeon Master the choice of whether or not to allow a shadow dragon to use the lair actions of its former type. In general, I find that the debilitating lair actions of chromatic dragons fit neatly with the shadow dragon concept; movement-restricting lair actions reasonably well, with modifications to their flavor; and direct-damage lair actions less consistently well. The black dragon's stinging insects have an echo in the mummy lord's *insect plague* spell, and a green shadow dragon could generate black, gnarled, thorny roots, but I think a blue or red shadow dragon would lose its ability to generate lightning or raise magma. Metallic dragons' lair actions all fit adequately enough with the shadow dragon template.

Aside from these alterations, shadow dragons have no compelling reason to fight differently from adult or ancient dragons of their original types.

The **dracolich** template, to my disappointment, offers even fewer interesting modifications to dragon behavior—which is to say, *none*, really. Like the shadow dragon template, the dracolich template can be applied only to an adult or ancient dragon. And what does it offer? Resistance to necrotic damage. Immunity to poison damage and to being charmed, frightened, paralyzed, or poisoned. Immunity to exhaustion. Resistance to magic. That's it. Nothing that enhances what it can do, only features that take away from what you can do to it. Boooo-ring.

So, obviously, a dracolich is going to fight the same way it did when it was a living dragon, even to the point of fleeing when it's seriously injured. It didn't go through all the trouble of becoming immortal just to be wasted by a group of punk "adventurers." If they're capable of dishing out that much damage, it would rather be someplace else. Yeah, if its physical form is destroyed, its phylactery gives its soul a place of refuge until it finds a new body to inhabit, but that's a pain, and in the meantime, someone might find the phylactery and destroy it. Not a chance worth taking.

PSEUDODRAGONS

Less capricious than their cousins the faerie dragons, **pseudodragons** are good-natured but reclusive creatures more inclined to hide from passersby than to tease them. They rarely have any reason or inclination to fight, and they'll only ever approach larger beings out of curiosity, usually about something shiny left out in the open. Even then, they try to stay hidden.

A pseudodragon involved in a combat encounter is either defending itself from some obnoxious jerk or fighting alongside a wizard as their companion. Either way, it's not strong in combat and has to be careful around more powerful entities.

Pseudodragons have very low Strength but high Dexterity and above-average Constitution; since they have no ranged attack, this makes them skirmishers. Like most predators, they have proficiency in Perception and Stealth, but they use their ambush capability only when hunting tiny creatures for food; with respect to larger creatures, they use these skills to hide and observe instead.

With both darkvision and blindsight, pseudodragons are mostly nocturnal, occasionally subterranean. If they approach the PCs, it will be under cover of darkness. (A pseudodragon companion maintains its circadian rhythm, dozing on a wizard's shoulder or inside their clothing during the day unless woken up, alert and frolicsome at night. This makes it handy to have around during an overnight watch shift, when it can Help on Perception checks.)

Should a fight break out, a pseudodragon's first impulse is to fly up into the air, out of reach—ideally, about 30 feet up. If it's attacked and has no ally present, it Dashes away. If, instead, it has one or more allies engaged in a fight, it Dodges and observes.

Pseudodragons are wise enough to stay out of the fight unless and until they can provide useful assistance, which generally means attacking an opponent that's already engaged in melee with one of their allies. If an enemy attacks a pseudodragon's wizard, it rallies to their defense. If its wizard tells it to help an ally—or merely feels great concern for an ally, an emotion that the pseudodragon's Limited Telepathy can pick up on—it attacks whatever's engaged in melee with that ally. If you're using the optional Flanking rule (*Dungeon Master's Guide*, chapter 8), the pseudodragon flanks the enemy it's attacking to gain advantage on the attack roll.

Bite or Sting? There's not much call for Bite, since Sting has the same reach and the same to-hit bonus and deals the same amount of damage but additionally forces a saving throw against being poisoned. Granted, the save DC is so low, even the weakest enemy has a fifty-fifty chance of making it. But a slight net benefit is still a net benefit.

Pseudodragons don't engage in melee unless their targets' attentions are already occupied. If an enemy turns against a pseudodragon, the pseudodragon switches from Sting to Dodge—even when it hits, the damage it deals is so modest that it's better off just distracting the enemy while its ally delivers the meaningful hits. However, if the opponent has Multiattack, continuing to hang around for even one more turn isn't in the pseudodragon's best interest; in this case, it Disengages and flies away to a safe altitude and distance. (On their own, pseudodragons aren't smart and disciplined enough to be capable of Disengaging, but you can sleaze this by assuming a strong bond of friendship with its wizard that makes a pseudodragon capable of things it couldn't do on its own. If you want to be stricter about it, you can have a pseudodragon Dodge, then fly away—drawing the opportunity attack, but *only* the opportunity attack, and imposing disadvantage on the roll.)

A pseudodragon that's moderately or seriously wounded (reduced to 4 hp or fewer), once it's out of melee, beelines to a place of refuge and Hides there until the threat has passed. A pseudodragon companion doesn't return to the fight, even if its wizard demands that it do so; ordering a wounded pseudodragon companion to dive back into the fray is a sure way to hurt its feelings and possibly lose its loyalty forever.

If it's unwounded but also not actively engaged in a fight, and it spots something shiny on an enemy combatant, a pseudodragon may fly down, snatch it away, and fly off with it. Pseudodragons *are* dragons, after all, and they like to keep their own little hoards.

FAERIE DRAGONS

There's not much reason for PCs to get in a fight with a **faerie dragon**, unless they're just bad people. Faerie dragons are cute, good-natured, and mostly harmless, teasing passersby with mischievous illusions—

nothing spiteful, mind you. PCs who take their pranks in good fun have nothing more to fear from them. React aggressively, though, and they'll respond in kind.

Faerie dragons are Tiny and very weak, but their Dexterity is extraordinary, their Constitution above average. They're also clever and very charismatic. They have nothing in the way of ranged attacks, so any fighting they do has to be the hit-and-run kind.

This is facilitated by their high flying speed—60 feet per round—and their Superior Invisibility, which lets them turn invisible at will for as long as they concentrate on staying that way. This means they can freely move, attack, use objects, or even cast spells without becoming visible, although they can't cast a spell that also requires concentration.

They can communicate telepathically with other faerie dragons nearby. If you find yourself fighting more than one, you're in for a world of misery, because they're going to call in all their friends for backup. By the third round of a fight with two faerie dragons, you'll be fighting five. A couple of rounds later, you'll be fighting a dozen. Then three dozen. Does this seem like dirty pool? I don't care, man. You attack a good creature, you reap what you sow.

The main weapon in the faerie dragon's arsenal is Euphoria Breath, a short-range effect that works a little like a limited *confusion* spell: If the target blows its saving throw (which isn't super likely, given that the save DC is only 11), it either runs around randomly or just zones out for a round. This ability recharges, making it available roughly once every three rounds.

It's not much of a threat—*from one faerie dragon*. But from three dozen, well, figure that a dozen of them have their Euphoria Breath charged up in any given round, and divide that by the number of PCs attacking them. One DC 11 Wisdom save is easy to make. Two to six in a row, less so.

As mentioned, faerie dragons can do this while remaining invisible. But why would they do that when they can taunt you by turning visible (no action cost), using their Euphoria Breath on you (action), then immediately turning invisible again (bonus action) before you can react? "All right, that's it—I Ready an Attack action against the first one I see appear within reach!" Nice try, friendo, but faerie dragons are smart. If they see you in the Ready stance, they simply won't attack *you*—or they'll go ahead and use their Euphoria Breath but remain invisible as they do.

The faerie dragon's Bite action is paltry, doing only 1 point of damage on a hit. It doesn't use this action unless its Euphoria Breath is on cooldown. Otherwise, it uses it the same way it uses Euphoria Breath: turns visible, Bites, then immediately turns invisible again; or doesn't turn visible at all, just Bites, if the enemy is ready and waiting for it to appear.

The combination of their rapid flying speed and their Superior Invisibility means that even a small number of faerie dragons, by zooming from target to target, can make themselves seem like a larger number of faerie dragons, and this is in fact a staple strategy of theirs. They're not trying to kill their enemies, just harass them, maybe scare them a little, and ultimately drive them off.

They also have the ability to cast a variety of illusion spells, gaining more spells the older they get. Every faerie dragon can cast *dancing lights*, *mage hand*, and *minor illusion*. These aren't going to have much application in combat. *Color spray* can blind an enemy or two for a round, although this is usually unnecessary, since faerie dragons can turn invisible at will. *Mirror image* is yet another way of making a few faerie dragons seem like many. *Suggestion* isn't going to get much traction once combat breaks out. *Major image* is a serious multisensory illusion that can appear as anything from a charging rhino to a howling vortex to a shrieking wraith to a pillar of flame—but it requires concentration, so a faerie dragon can't turn invisible while casting it. (Hopefully, the illusion will serve as enough of a distraction to keep any heat off the faerie dragon that's producing it.) *Hallucinatory terrain* doesn't require concentration and can make the ground appear to be falling away, buckling, or flooding. And *polymorph*, which also requires concentration, can turn an opponent into a toad, a badger, or a slug. (Keep in mind, though, that any spell that the faerie dragon has already used before combat for its own amusement is no longer available once combat breaks out.)

Faerie dragons aren't really into fighting for fighting's sake, and they like being alive, so it doesn't take much damage to drive them off: Being moderately wounded (reduced to 9 hp or fewer) is enough to do the trick. But that's just to drive off *one* faerie dragon, not the whole flight, which will keep gassing, nipping, and deluding their assailants until their allies and their territory are safe and secure.

WYVERNS

The **wyvern**, a none-too-bright, beast-grade member of the dragon family, is in most respects a basic brute. But there's a subtlety in its constellation of features that's easy to overlook.

Wyverns have a basic "walking" speed of 20 feet per turn but a flying speed of 80 feet. With that kind of gap, there's no reason for it to hold still and engage in stationary melee, as other high-Strength, high-Constitution brutes are happy to do. Wyverns are melee fighters, but they're *strafing* melee fighters that never touch the ground if they can help it, nor do they remain within reach (and therefore engagement range) of their enemies.

In addition to their teeth and claws, wyverns have scorpioid venomous stingers in their tails, which can do massive poison damage on top of their typical-for-a-Large-creature piercing damage. That's a no-brainer: A wyvern will always try to get at least one Stinger attack in. But the wyvern's Multiattack action offers the option of substituting a Claws attack for either element of the basic Bite/Stinger combo.

At first glance, it seems like a good deal: The wyvern's Claws attack does slightly more damage than its Bite (d8s rather than d6s). But look at the reach on those attacks. Claws has a 5-foot reach, so the wyvern has to get right up to its enemy to use it. Bite, on the other hand, has a 10-foot reach, as does Stinger. What this means is that a wyvern can do a flyby Bite/Stinger attack (despite not having the Flyby trait) without ever coming closer than 10 feet to its opponent, which means without coming within their reach, which means not *leaving* their reach, which means *not provoking an opportunity attack*. Thus, even though the wyvern doesn't have Flyby, it can accomplish exactly the same effect, thanks to the 10-foot reach on its attacks. (Except in the unlucky instance in which its chosen prey is wielding a polearm. Unfortunately, wyverns aren't clever enough to alter their tactics to fit new, unexpected facts. This modus operandi is the only one they've got.)

Does this mean the wyvern never has any reason to attack with Claws? Not at all. If it's grounded somehow (knocked prone, grappled, or restrained) and its foes have closed with it, once it gets its movement back it makes a Claws/Stinger Multiattack instead of its usual Bite/Stinger Multiattack, for that extra couple of points of expected damage, in the process of launching itself into the air again— heedless of opportunity attacks because, at worst, it can only take one hit per opponent while it's taking off. If it stays on the ground, it risks taking a lot more than that if its opponents have Extra Attack, and if they're fighting a CR 6 monster, they probably do. If it can't get airborne, it can only use the Bite/Stinger option. Finally, the wyvern also uses Claws/Stinger if it's engaged in melee in the air by a flying opponent.

Like other predators, the wyvern is primarily interested in a meal, which means going after the weakest-looking individual in a group— ideally, one who's isolated or oblivious. Once it's chosen its prey, it singles that individual out for the full measure of its aggression. When the prey is rendered unconscious, the wyvern forgoes its Multiattack, snatches them up, and flies off back to wherever it nests. As long as the prey weighs a total of 570 pounds or less, the wyvern can fly away at full speed.

Wyverns are fierce and bad-tempered, but they still want to live. Seriously wound one (reduce it to 44 hp or fewer), and it will Dash off in search of easier prey.

DRAGON TURTLES

Not all dragons dwell on land. The **dragon turtle** is a draconic creature that inhabits the ocean, sometimes sinking ships for their treasures, sometimes—following the chess dictum that the threat is stronger than the execution—extorting tribute along heavily traveled shipping lanes. It grows to Gargantuan size, and its dorsal spines grow into a thick shell along its back, from whence it gets its name.

Unable to fly, the dragon turtle has an energetic 40-foot swimming speed; it can move only 20 feet per round on land, so it sticks to the water unless enraged. Its extraordinary Strength and Constitution stand out against its other ability scores, which are all quite ordinary; it also has proficiency in all of the "big three" saving throws and resistance to fire damage. It's a fearless juggernaut of a brute.

Steam Breath is a recharge ability, and whenever it's available, a dragon turtle tries to position itself to get at least six enemies (or all its enemies, if they number fewer than six) in its conical area of effect. If it can't, it keeps this action in reserve for a round; the second round it has Steam Breath, it uses it if it can position itself to get at least four enemies; the third, if it can get at least two. (Keep in mind that underwater, the dragon turtle can move vertically as well as horizontally.) Since its Multiattack does an average total of 58 damage if all three attacks hit, it's never worth passing it up to use Steam Breath against only one target.

When Steam Breath is unavailable, the dragon turtle falls back on its Claw/Claw/Bite Multiattack. The Claw/Tail combination has value only on land, since the comparative advantage of Tail over a Claw and a Bite lies in its knocking enemies prone. (There's nothing in the rules that says one can't be prone underwater, but trying this on a PC is an invitation to an argument, and I personally would take the player's side in this dispute.)

All this assumes that the dragon turtle is fighting its enemies directly. If it's attacking a seagoing vessel, it breaches only to use its Steam Breath and only uses that feature when it can do so to maximum effect. When Steam Breath is unavailable, it submerges and attacks the vessel from underneath, attempting to sink it. Here also, there's no reason for it to use its Tail attack: A boat isn't a creature, nor can it be knocked prone, so a Tail attack would do nothing but bludgeoning damage.

Dragon turtles have humanoid-average Intelligence and slightly above-average Wisdom. Their features don't lend themselves to tactical flexibility, but their Wisdom does grant them some savvy in target selection, as well as a sense of when to cut their losses. Any party that can inflict moderate injury on a dragon turtle, which has a massive reservoir of hit points, is not to be trifled with. Dragon turtles aren't malevolent, just greedy. Reduce one to 238 hp or fewer, and it will stand down and seek to strike a bargain that lets it live and keep (most of) its treasure. If its enemies refuse to relent, it fights until it's seriously wounded (reduced to 136 hp or fewer), at which point it swims away at full speed, Dodging as it retreats.

GIANTS

The main thing to remember about giants is that they care about "small folk" about as much as humans care about squirrels, pigeons, or ants. At best, they're patronizing to smaller beings, or simply indifferent to them; at worst, they take brutal pleasure in abusing them. Most often—especially among lesser giant-kin, such as ettins and trolls—they see smaller folk simply as food. Even so, there's a lot of variety in giant behavior and personality. With greater power comes—usually—greater sophistication.

TRUE GIANTS

Going solely by their extraordinary Strength and Constitution, it would be easy to lump all true giants together as brute fighters. If we want encounters with giants to be more than boring bash-fests, we have to look for clues not just in their stat blocks but also in the *Monster Manual* flavor text.

Take the matter of rock throwing. Every race of giants has this ranged attack alongside its melee attack, and on average, it does more damage. Yet every race of giants also has a Strength much, much higher than its Dexterity, so based on the assumptions I've been using all along, they should consistently prefer engaging in melee to attacking from a distance. Also, giants' Multiattacks apply only to their melee attacks, not to throwing rocks. So why include a ranged attack at all?

Well, let's start with **hill giants**. They're stupid, mean, undisciplined, and aggressive. Barely sentient, they're driven by instinct and impulse. Of course they're going to charge and bash. But with a speed of 40 feet and a reach of 10 feet, they're unable to reach an enemy who's more than 50 feet away.

If you're a hill giant, and you see a target 100 feet away from you, which would you rather do: Dash toward them so that you can bash next round, or pick up a rock and throw it as you approach?

Hill giants don't have the patience to wait until they're within melee reach to start fighting. They start walking toward their prey immediately, then pick up a rock (assuming one's available—if the party is in the hill giant's own territory, one will be) and throw it.* Range is irrelevant: If its target is more than 60 feet away, a hill giant will still throw a rock, even though it rolls with disadvantage, because it's just that bad-tempered. Once the hill giant starts its turn within 50 feet of its target, though, it closes the distance and switches to bashing.

Stone giants, on the other hand, *love* throwing rocks. They make an art of it. They're also much more introverted and less belligerent than other kinds of giants; they'd rather drive trespassers off than tangle with them. So a stone giant won't move any closer to its target, even if it's at long range and attacking with disadvantage, because its attack is meant mainly as a deterrent. A shot across the bow can be as good as one directly into the hull.

Stone giants also have Stone Camouflage, which gives them advantage on Stealth checks to hide in the rocky terrain where they live. A stone giant that spots trespassers first will Hide until they come within range, then throw its first rock from hiding. This gives it advantage on the attack roll, which will either enhance a normal-range attack or cancel out the disadvantage of attacking at long range.

Note that when other giants throw rocks, they just do damage, but when stone giants throw rocks, they can knock their targets prone. A prone target is easier to hit with a melee attack but harder to hit with

---

* Although the *Monster Manual* says you can assume that monsters with throwable weapons carry 2d4 of them, I can't imagine a hill giant being resourceful enough to make itself a bag to keep rocks in—it's not even as smart as a chimp. A better assumption is that wherever a hill giant would normally find rocks to throw, there are 2d4 good, throwable ones lying around.

a ranged attack. So when a stone giant knocks targets down, it considers itself finished with them—point scored, message delivered—and it moves on to the next. It also has enough Intelligence and Wisdom to recognize when something is out of the ordinary—for instance, if there's a powerful spellcaster or some other exceptional threat among its opponents—and to respond accordingly, either by targeting that threat or by shouting for reinforcements, if any are available.

There's one thing about the stone giant stat block that surprises me, so much that I checked the *Monster Manual* errata to make sure it wasn't a mistake, and that's that the stone giant's rock attack has the same to-hit modifier as its melee attack. Based on the usual methods of attack modifier calculation (given in "Creating a Monster Stat Block," chapter 9 of the *Dungeon Master's Guide*, if you're feeling wonkish), this is exactly what you'd expect. But the flavor text says of stone giants:

> Despite their great size and musculature, stone giants are lithe and graceful. Skilled rock throwers are granted positions of high rank in the giants' ordning, testing and demonstrating their ability to hurl and catch enormous boulders. . . . A stone giant hurling a rock performs not just a feat of brute strength but also one of stunning athleticism and poise.

Given that, shouldn't a stone giant be not just as good, but *better*, at throwing rocks than at hitting things with a club? And look at that Athletics skill that the stone giant has! Shouldn't that skill be useful for something? Based on these premises, as Dungeon Master and therefore god-emperor of my game world, I'd have stone giants make Rock attacks using their +12 Athletics skill rather than their normal +9 attack modifier. (If you do this, bump their challenge rating up from 7 to 8.)

Frost giants are the orcs of giantkind: aggressive brutes not just by nature but also by ideology. They'll fight more like hill giants, throwing rocks only until they come within 50 feet of their targets, then charging into melee. Like stone giants, they can adapt somewhat if something out of the ordinary happens. Unlike stone giants, they're indiscriminate in their choice of targets. The one exception to this is that they may specifically target their physically strongest opponent as a dominance gesture, just to prove that they're even stronger.

If frost giants are like orcs, **fire giants** are like hobgoblins, militaristic and disciplined. Although they could throw rocks from as far as 240 feet away, they'll first close the distance (using the Dodge action if necessary to avoid ranged weapon or spell attacks) until they can attack without disadvantage. At 60 feet away, they initiate combat by hurling a rock; on their next turn, they advance another 20 feet and hurl another. On their third turn, they charge in, using their full movement, and commence melee fighting with a greatsword Multiattack.

Fire giants are savvy in their target selection. If there's a "glass cannon" (high damage output, low durability) among their opponents, fire giants zero in on them. They can adapt to unexpected situations, and they use terrain to enhance their advantages.

Cloud giants aren't as stupid as hill giants, as reclusive as stone giants, as aggressive as frost giants, nor as disciplined as fire giants. What they are is shrewd. Before they engage in combat, they ascertain whether those they encounter are really a threat. They're willing to parley, maybe even curious as to trespassers' motives. Their Insight proficiency gives them a window into what their interlocutors are after. But they also won't hesitate to initiate combat if they conclude that someone is out to get them—or their treasures.

Consequently, cloud giants won't often have occasion to throw rocks. By the time combat breaks out, they'll generally be within melee range already, or at least close enough (50 feet or less) to close and engage. With them, the question isn't when they choose to throw a rock but rather when they choose to cast a spell. They can cast *control weather* and *gaseous form* once per day; *feather fall*, *fly*, *misty step*, and *telekinesis* three times per day; and *detect magic*, *fog cloud*, and *light* at will. From these spells, *misty step* is the one that leaps out, for two reasons: First, because it's cast as a bonus action and therefore enhances the cloud giant's action economy, and second, because it's consistent with the cloud giant's trickster nature. Glass cannons beware: A cloud giant won't hesitate to *misty step* behind you and give you two good clouts with its morning star. Cloud giants also use *misty step* to escape being surrounded by enemies or to get up in an archer's face—ranged attacks have disadvantage at a distance of 5 feet or less. You can try to back up to 10 feet away, which is still within the storm giant's melee reach, so it won't provoke an opportunity attack. But that'll be hard if the cloud giant uses its action—and its +8 Strength modifier—to grapple you first.

The rest of the cloud giant's spell repertoire is underwhelming. *Feather fall* will most likely come into play only if a cloud giant and the player characters are on the same side, fighting against other giants. *Fly* consumes an action and doesn't offer a lot in return, since a cloud giant rarely has any reason to fear on-the-ground melee engagement. That said, its Armor Class is a little on the low side, so maybe it might like to hover 10 feet up in the air, where it can reach its opponents with melee strikes but its opponents can't reach it. *Fly* also improves the cloud giant's speed from 40 feet to 60 feet, which may make a difference if the fight is out in the open and the giant's opponents are widely spread out. *Telekinesis* is iffy for moving other creatures, since it's just a contest between their Strength and the cloud giant's Charisma; as for objects, since the spell's range is only 60 feet, and the cloud giant has 40 feet of movement, it may as well just Dash over and pick the things up. *Gaseous form* is an escape hatch, *control weather* has a 10-minute casting time, *fog cloud* impedes the cloud giant as much as it does its opponents (the fog may only reach up to its neck, but it still has disadvantage on attack rolls against foes obscured by the cloud), and *detect magic* and *light* are fluff.

Storm giants are generally good guys, and they won't fight unless they have no other choice. When they do, their go-to is Lightning Strike, a highly damaging area-effect attack with a 10-foot radius.

Because of the radius, they greatly prefer to hurl it where they can strike two or more enemies with it at once, but they won't pass it up if they can't, because even against just one target it still does more damage than two Greatsword hits. Like most other giants, they prefer melee attacks over throwing rocks, and they only do the latter when there's no reachable melee target and Lightning Strike is still recharging.

Their spell repertoire is entirely cosmetic, except for *control weather*—as mentioned above, not usable in combat because of its 10-minute casting time. However, we can posit that storm giants (and cloud giants as well) cast and sustain *control weather* in order to set up the conditions in which combatants will find themselves. Most likely, they'll choose torrential rain and either a strong wind, a gale, or a storm. This combination imposes disadvantage on all ranged attack rolls and on Wisdom (Perception) checks that rely on sight or hearing, douses open flames such as torches, and inhibits flying, requiring airborne creatures to touch down at the end of each turn or fall out of the sky ("Wilderness Survival: Weather," *Dungeon Master's Guide*, chapter 5). If they aren't anticipating a fight but simply want to confuse trespassers, they may instead prefer to blanket the entire area in heavy fog, effectively blinding everyone in it.

Do giants ever run away? Depends on the giant:

- Hill giants, which are basically animals, Dash away when severely injured (reduced to 42 hp or fewer).
- Stone giants tactically withdraw when only moderately injured (reduced to 88 hp or fewer), continuing to throw rocks as they do so, and flee when seriously injured (reduced to 50 hp or fewer), Dodging any additional incoming attacks.
- Frost giants view retreat as cowardice and fight to the death.
- Fire giants have the discipline to Disengage when seriously injured (reduced to 64 hp or fewer) in melee combat; if they're seriously injured and out of melee range, they Dodge while retreating.

- Depending on what spells they're sustaining or still have available, cloud giants *fly* off, go into *gaseous form*, or enshroud their enemies in a blinding *fog cloud* and walk away.
- A storm giant who's seriously injured (reduced to 92 hp or fewer), believe it or not, surrenders and seeks to negotiate terms. If it has any reason at all to believe that its foes will negotiate in good faith, this is far preferable to the risk of being finished off as it flees. Storm giants didn't get to the top of the Ordning by being rash.

ETTINS

Ettins are fundamentally a "Rrrraaaahhhh, bash bash bash" monster without any sophistication or subtlety. Clumsy brutes with extraordinary strength, exceptional Constitution, and not much Dexterity or Intelligence, they rely on tanklike durability and crushing force to confront enemies head-on.

The one thing that makes an ettin interesting as an enemy is that it's difficult to surprise. Thanks to its Wakeful trait, you can never catch an ettin napping: While one of its heads sleeps, the other remains alert. Plus, ettins have expertise in Perception *and* advantage on Perception checks, along with 60 feet of darkvision. Even in the dead of night, an ettin's got a good shot at spotting you. For this reason, orcs and other cleverer beings may employ ettins as sentries.

Once an ettin spots one or more foes, it goes straight into aggro mode. Perceiving the biggest enemy as its greatest threat, it charges right up and Multiattacks with the battleaxe it holds in one hand and the morning star it holds in the other. It uses both of these weapons unless it's engaged in melee by a second enemy. In that instance, it turns each of its heads to face a different melee opponent and divides its attacks between them. The illustration in the *Monster Manual* shows an ettin with its morning star in its right hand and its axe in its left hand. Sure, go with that.

Ettins are very stupid, though not so stupid that they can't figure out what's going on if archers or spellcasters are plinking them

Ogres and Cyclopes

Ogres and cyclopes are dumb, simple brutes. They have no tactics.

There are only two details worth noting in the **ogre's** stat block. First, ogres have 60 feet of darkvision. This means that an ogre prefers to fight in dim light or darkness. It doesn't mean that an ogre won't fight in daylight, or even that it won't *start* a fight in daylight. But it only goes *hunting* at night. If an ogre encounter happens at night, it's probably because the ogre found the PCs. If it happens outside during the day, it's because the PCs found the ogre.

Second, ogres do have both a melee attack and a ranged attack. But with extraordinary Strength, very high Constitution, and subpar Dexterity, ogres are melee fighters by both nature and inclination. Plus, their greatclub does more damage than their javelin. Therefore, an ogre will use a javelin only when it has enough movement to get between 10 and 30 feet from an opponent, but no closer.

Despite being categorized as giants, ogres are essentially predatory beasts in a vaguely humanoid shape. If they have the chance to choose a target—all other things being approximately equal, that is—they'll try to pick off the smallest and weakest first, or one who's isolated from their companions. Otherwise, they're indiscriminate.

With a Wisdom of only 7, an ogre doesn't have the good sense to run away when it's seriously wounded. Once it starts fighting, it keeps fighting until it's dead.

Cyclopes don't even have darkvision, and their Poor Depth Perception would make them even worse at ranged attacks if the normal range of their Rock attack didn't top out at 30 feet anyway. Their Intelligence is higher than ogres', though still below humanoid average; their Wisdom, even lower. They close, they bash, and they don't have the sense to withdraw until it's too late.

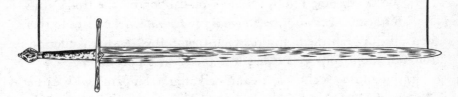

from a distance. Their primary attack mode, though, is in-your-face melee, and as long as there are still enemies engaging it in that mode, it's not going to think to break off and go after a ranged attacker. Only once it's dispatched its melee foes does it chase down enemies farther away.

Unlike an ogre or cyclops, an ettin has a normal, healthy survival instinct. Once it's seriously wounded (reduced to 34 hp or fewer), it Dashes away, each of its heads berating the other for fighting badly. (It's not nimble enough to Dodge, nor intelligent enough to Disengage.)

TROLLS

The vanilla **troll** isn't all that interesting. It's a straightforward brute, with exceptionally high Strength, extraordinarily high Constitution, and low-to-middling mental abilities. It's got darkvision, so it prefers to operate at night or underground. It operates more by smell than by sight, regenerates damage unless it's been struck by fire or acid, and has a Claw/Claw/Bite Multiattack.

Such a monster would be an uncomplicated opponent: It would close to melee range immediately, slash and chomp away, and retreat only if seriously injured or attacked with fire or acid.

But if you use the Loathsome Limbs variant, trolls become a lot more fun. I love this variant because it creates trolls that hark back to my favorite troll combat scene ever, from *Three Hearts and Three Lions* by Poul Anderson; and because I once ran a solo adventure for a friend in which he and a couple of NPCs had to fight one such troll without ever being told what it was. The suspense was heightened by the fact that they didn't know what it could do, and they had to discover its weakness by trial and error.

In the Loathsome Limbs variant, you can lop off the troll's arms, legs, and head—*and they keep fighting independently!* Not only that, the troll can grab them and reattach them! This is what Anderson's troll did, and it adds tons of flavor to the combat encounter.

Fifth edition D&D is a streamlined affair, compared with earlier editions of D&D (and other roleplaying systems such as Pathfinder and GURPS), with little in the way of directed attacks or limb-specific injuries, so when you hit an opponent, you deal *x* damage. What does "*x* damage" mean? It means you've come a certain amount closer to defeating your opponent. It doesn't mean you've crippled its arm, opened a gushing wound, or given it a concussion. In fact, unlike in some game systems, having taken serious damage doesn't even reduce a character's or monster's efficacy in combat. So the specificity of being able to cut off a troll's arm is deliciously enlivening. And the fact that the arm keeps grabbing at you afterward is both horrific and hilarious.

To sever the limb or head of a troll, you have to inflict 15 or more slashing damage. Even then, half the time, nothing special happens. But the other half of the time, you have a 40 percent chance of cutting off a leg, a 40 percent chance of cutting off an arm, and a 20 percent chance of cutting off its head. Each arm is responsible for one of the troll's Claw attacks, and the head is responsible for its Bite, so if you cut off an arm, for instance, you end up with a troll with a Claw/Bite Multiattack and an arm that can only Claw.

A severed leg can move but can't attack, a severed head can attack but can't move, and a severed arm can do both. Every part regenerates independently, so if you cut a troll apart, it actually recovers *faster*. But a troll would still rather remain intact, so it doesn't take advantage of this fact.

Most of the time, trolls are indiscriminate in choosing targets: They attack whoever or whatever is closest. Their vulnerability to fire and acid, however, means that such attacks draw their attention. If they're lightly wounded or less (59 hp or more), these attacks provoke them, and they focus on whoever struck the blow, if they can figure it out easily enough. If they're moderately wounded (reduced to between 34 and 58 hp), however, they recoil, using their movement to reposition themselves farther away from the source. And if they're seriously wounded (reduced to 33 hp or fewer), they flee from it, using the Dash action to move away at top speed.

Since a severed leg can't attack, it uses its 5 feet of movement to move back toward the troll. A severed arm attacks with disadvantage if the troll can't see both the arm and its target, so in that case, it also uses its 5 feet of movement to drag itself back. If the troll *can* see both the arm and its target, however, the arm can attack without penalty, and it keeps fighting independently until it's destroyed. A severed head can't move, so the troll moves toward it instead.

Neither the Loathsome Limbs feature nor the troll's stat block says anything about the troll's being able to reattach its limbs, but it does get a mention in the flavor text: "A troll can even reattach severed body parts, untroubled by its momentary disability." As a DM, I allow a troll to pick up and reattach one severed body part as a bonus action; to do so, it has to be in the same square or hex.

The limbs' movement "decisions" may become scrambled if *they're* attacked with fire or acid. Each independent limb, as well as the troll's body, reacts the same way to fire or acid as an intact troll would—except a severed head, which can do nothing but sit there and yowl. That is, a severed arm that has 8 hp or more after taking fire or acid damage slashes back angrily, one that has 5 to 7 hp moves away from the source at its full movement speed of 5 feet, and one with 4 hp or fewer Dashes away at 10 feet per turn—even if this means it's not moving back toward its body. But the body, if *it* hasn't been burned by fire or acid, doesn't react at all to the burning of its severed arm, doesn't chase after it, doesn't target the source of the fire or acid. If its severed head is being burned, the body stops moving toward it. However, if the body is struck with fire or acid, any severed leg or arm that's trying to make its way back to the body keeps doing so.

PCs, once they see a troll reattaching its severed limbs, will surely try to carry off any subsequent limbs they sever. The limbs fight this! Treat any limb that a PC has picked up as grappled. (With respect to its effect on the grappling PC's movement speed, a troll arm or leg is Medium-size, and a head is Small.) A leg tries to resist the grapple—using Athletics, rather than Acrobatics, because its Strength is so much higher than its Dexterity. An arm keeps clawing at whoever's holding it if it would normally attack and tries to struggle free if it would normally be working its way back to its body. A head tries to bite whoever's holding it.

This fairly simple heuristic creates battles that are far more complex and entertaining than they have any right to be.

ONI

Oni are cousins to ogres, more intelligent, with innate spellcasting ability, and capable of regeneration. Unlike, say, trolls, which can be prevented from regenerating by burning them with fire or acid, oni regenerate regardless of what kind of damage they take or how much, short of killing them.

Physically, oni have the typical brute ability contour of very high Strength and Constitution relative to their Dexterity, which is merely average. The fact that they excel at toe-to-toe melee fighting, however, doesn't necessarily mean that it's always their first choice. They also have high Intelligence and Charisma, and even their Wisdom is above average. This means that they can plan, assess their opponents' weaknesses accurately, use this information to select the targets of their various abilities, and employ deceit as well as raw strength in order to achieve victory. Oni also have proficiency on all of the "big three" saving throws—Dexerity, Constitution, and Wisdom—improving their resistance to magic, despite their not having the Magic Resistance trait per se. And they can fly!

The timing of their abilities may be an issue, though, because despite their various advantages, one thing they lack is any feature that enhances their action economy. Just the opposite, in fact: Their Change Shape feature costs a turn's action. On the other hand, being able to cast *invisibility* at will gives them a way to avoid damage while setting up for other things. Oni's Regeneration makes them masters of attrition fighting: The longer they can drag a battle out, the better. Their opponents have to hit hard and end the battle as fast as possible, or the oni will wear them down.

In addition to *invisibility*, oni can cast *darkness* at will. They also have a handful of once-per-day spells. In order of power and effectiveness, from greatest to least, these are *cone of cold*, *gaseous form*, *sleep*, and *charm person*.

- *Cone of cold* is the big gun, an area-effect combat spell that deals cold damage to every creature in a 60-foot cone, even ones who make their Constitution saving throws. The Targets in Area of Effect table in chapter 8 of the *Dungeon Master's Guide* indicates that six is a good number of opponents to nail with this spell. Given that the oni gets only one chance per day to cast it, however, I don't think it will use *cone of cold* right out of the gate, even if its potential targets are properly aligned. First, it's got to have some indication that its opponents aren't pushovers, and thus that it may need a spell like *cone of cold* to deal with them. A good sign of this is if the oni's foes can deal it moderate damage (reduce it to 77 hp or fewer).

- *Gaseous form* is primarily a time-killer, a way of avoiding serious damage long enough to regenerate if *darkness* and *invisibility* aren't working for some reason. It's also a way to pursue victims who mistakenly think they can escape by locking a door behind them. One thing it's not is a particularly effective method of escape, because it reduces the oni's movement speed to 10 feet, and its enemies can still damage it, just not as much or as fast. It requires concentration, and it prevents the oni from casting any other spell while it's in effect.

- *Sleep* ceases to be useful once the squishiest of the oni's enemies has more than 16 hp—that's how few an opponent has to have for the oni to have a two-thirds chance or better of dropping them. Basically, we're talking about a wizard or sorcerer of level 3 or below. Not many of these are going to be facing an oni. (Yes, *sleep* could also take out a seriously wounded opponent, but if the oni has already managed to wound them that badly, why would it bother to put them to sleep?)

- *Charm person* is useful against a low-Wisdom target before combat begins, in order to soften the target up for Deception or keep them out of the impending fight. After combat begins, it's a waste of an action.

As for *darkness*, since oni have darkvision but not blindsight or truesight, this spell impedes the oni as much as it does its opponents. Therefore, rather than black out the entire area, an oni prefers to use it to blind its enemies only—in particular, troublesome enemy spell-casters. *Darkness* requires concentration, so an oni who's sustaining it can't cast *invisibility* without dropping it. Since *invisibility* is so useful, *darkness* has to take a backseat unless *invisibility* isn't doing the job for some reason (such as a *see invisible* spell) or those enemy spellcasters are *really* troublesome.

There's some odd wording in the oni's other distinguishing feature, Change Shape. "The oni can polymorph into a Small or Medium humanoid, into a Large giant, *or* back into its true form" (emphasis mine), but in its true form, it *is* a Large giant. I think this has to be interpreted to mean that the oni can polymorph into the form of *any other* Large giant, which would include ogres, half-ogres, ettins, and trolls. (It can't polymorph into giants of any other size, nor into Large creatures of any other kind.)

Change Shape doesn't offer any obvious combat advantage except when changing from a Small or Medium form into a Large form so as to increase the damage of the oni's glaive. But does it offer any *non*-obvious advantage? No, because the oni's Change Shape doesn't alter its stats in any way or grant it a reservoir of hit points as the *poly-morph* spell does; the only things that change are its size and appearance, plus the damage of the glaive, if the weapon was shrunk along with the oni. It doesn't pick up new features, increase (or decrease) its ability scores, or gain alternative attack actions.

So I conclude that the oni uses Change Shape mainly to pass unnoticed among other people, and that it reverts to its true form only when it's time to throw down. This will be the first action it takes in combat, but it won't have much of a chance to catch its opponents by surprise—not if it wants to use its glaive, because if it's not holding that thing when it transforms, the glaive won't transform with it. I think that if the PCs start a fight with an oni (or vice versa) while the oni is passing as a member in good standing of humanoid society, that oni's got to simply Hulk out there on the spot and fight with just its claws, or with its glaive if and only if the humanoid form it's using has a decent reason to be carrying one.

Oni can fly, and thanks to the 10-foot reach of their glaives, the hover-in-the-air, fly-down-to-attack, fly-back-up tactic that many other monsters use is feasible, because they can attack without entering their enemies' reach and thereby avoid opening themselves up to opportunity attacks. On the other hand, being a brute rather than a skirmisher, an oni may be content simply to fight toe-to-toe. You can play it either way.

How does an oni choose whom to attack? It depends on how badly its opponents are able to hurt it. If they're all (or mostly) doing comparable damage, it will want to reduce their numbers, and it will focus on taking weaker opponents out of the fight right away. But if one or two opponents are doing far more damage than everyone else, then it's not going to worry about the weaker opponents; it's going to focus on the strongest. And, obviously, it's not going to attack anyone who's under the sway of its own *charm person* spell.

Oni won't willingly initiate combat during the daytime. If an oni chooses to attack, it does so at night, when it has the advantage of darkvision. In most cases, though, oni aren't interested in starting a fight at all, at least not one with opponents who could give them any trouble. What they want is to be able to kidnap people and eat them in peace. A fight with a group of experienced adventurers puts that whole state of affairs in jeopardy. On the other hand, sometimes oni join forces with other evil creatures, and in these instances, they may fight on those other creatures' behalf; this is when PCs are most likely to get into a drawn-out battle with one or more oni.

If an oni has no interest in standing its ground, it casts *invisibility* as soon as it's moderately wounded, Hides, and never shows itself again. An oni that's serious about defeating its foes, on the other hand, fights the aforementioned battle of attrition, taking advantage of its Regeneration ability to outlast its foes. After any round in which an oni's opponents deal it more than, say, 30 damage (enough to bring it down in five or six combat rounds, taking its Regeneration into consideration), the oni casts *invisibility* and Hides the following round, lying low an additional round for every 10 damage its opponents did above and beyond that threshold. Then it positions itself behind its chosen target and attacks with advantage on the roll, becoming visible again as it does. (The advantage comes from attacking while invisible, not from attacking from behind, so why do it that way? It's just cooler. If you could turn invisible and sneak up on your enemies to attack them, why *wouldn't* you do it from behind?)

Alternatively, upon being moderately wounded (reduced to 77 hp or fewer, after Regenerating), if it can position itself to catch all of its opponents—or six of them, if there are more than that—in a *cone of cold*, it casts that spell rather than take its Multiattack action. If its opponents include a non-elf spellcaster with 16 hp or fewer, it drops a *sleep* spell where it can catch that opponent and as many others as possible, although if it knocks anyone out aside from that one target, that's merely icing on the cake. It uses *gaseous form* only to pursue its enemies or to gain time if they're penetrating its *invisibility* with magic. (Remember that, while the oni can cast *invisibility* at will, it can cast *gaseous form* only once.)

Even an oni that wants to win a fight recognizes when it's seriously wounded (reduced to 44 hp or fewer, even after Regenerating) that it's not going to end well, unless its last opponent is just barely holding on. In that instance, it may cast and sustain *invisibility* and Hide just long enough to Regenerate back above 44 hp, then try to deal the coup de grâce to its opponent. Otherwise, it uses *invisibility* and its flying movement to flee the scene. If an opponent is able to penetrate its *invisibility*, it will use the Dodge action as it flees—and if it manages to Regenerate back up above 77 hp, it may decide to turn around and start fighting again!

FOMORIANS

Fomorians are a manifestation of the "evil equals ugly" trope, which I wish would go away. Once a noble and beautiful strain of giantkind, they were cursed with a warped and hideous appearance for their hubristic crimes against the Feywild. Not only was their pulchritude taken from them, they lost their intellectual brilliance as well: The average fomorian has Intelligence of only 9.

Extremely strong and tough brutes, with a hefty reservoir of hit points, fomorians barrel directly into the fray. Their Evil Eye feature works out to a range of 60 feet, but they use it from the midst of melee. Long-range darkvision suggests that they dwell in darkness—either underground, where they're most commonly found, or in the densest and gloomiest of forests—and don't attack when there's a bright light source present.

Fomorians' situational awareness is a mixed bag: They're pretty good at assessing whether or not a fight is winnable, and they refrain from engaging when it's not, but they lack tactical breadth and target selection savvy. Once they've committed to a fight, their behavior is relatively simple, their decisions arbitrary.

Thanks to their expertise in Perception and proficiency in Stealth, they're capable ambush attackers, and they may trail a group of characters for a while before deciding whether or not to attack. Once they choose to do so, they try to make that first attack while still unseen, to gain both advantage and surprise. Based on their lore, they might strike first at elves and other races with Fey Ancestry if possible, just out of spite, although there's nothing in their stat block that compels them to.

Once they've engaged in melee, they strike at whoever's nearby and striking at them. Their Greatclub attack deals an average of 20 damage per hit; their Evil Eye deals 27 on a failed save and 14 on a success, for 20 expected damage, give or take. These seem equivalent until you consider that a melee hit isn't assured: The expected damage of a melee attack is less than the average damage on a hit, owing to hit probability. Even with +9 to hit, a fomorian still has only, say, a 60 percent chance of damaging an enemy wearing chain mail and carrying a shield, reducing its expected melee damage to 12. Evil Eye is definitely stronger.

However, based on their low Intelligence, I suggest that fomorians have tunnel vision: Having chosen a target to whomp, they keep whomping that target unless and until they take damage from another source. Only then do they start using the Multiattack option of splitting their attacks between Greatclub and Evil Eye. Moreover, because of their brutish melee bias, they use Evil Eye only against targets who are beyond the 15-foot reach of their clubs. If they're taking both melee and either ranged or area-effect damage, they always use Evil Eye against an attacker who dealt one of the latter.

Curse of the Evil Eye is a one-use-per-combat feature, and it also consumes a full action, which might otherwise be used to Multiattack. Thus, despite being the fomorian's most powerful attack, it's also one that it has to use judiciously—and fomorians aren't mentally equipped for judiciousness in the midst of battle. We need a simple criterion that will trigger the use of the fomorian "nuclear option."

How about this: If and when an opponent manages to singlehandedly do moderate damage—at least 45 points—to a fomorian, that's when it gets enraged enough to use Curse of the Evil Eye, and it uses it against that opponent. If this curse doesn't succeed, the fomorian is prudent enough to realize that the tide of battle is turning against it, and it begins to retreat, continuing to attack while moving away from its foes.

If the fomorian is never driven to use Curse of the Evil Eye but is seriously injured (reduced to 59 hp or fewer), it also recognizes that it's time to leave; in this instance, however, it simply Dashes away rather than continue to swing its club as it retreats. If it's pursued by only a single enemy, it may slow down to use Evil Eye against that enemy as it continues to move away.

UNDEAD

A fundamental premise of this book is that evolved creatures know how to use the abilities they were born with. But undead creatures *aren't* evolved—at least, not anymore. The transformation to undeath doesn't entirely erase what a ghost or zombie was in its previous life, nor does it necessarily come with a set of survival rules that every undead creature will adopt. Undeath is a curse, and as such, it creates what I think of as *compulsions*. That is, whatever spell, influence, or event caused a creature to rise from the dead—the magic of a necromancer, the trauma of a violent death, the transmission of a curse, the vain pursuit of immortality, the lingering aura of an ancient battlefield, the punishment for betraying a sacred oath—also drives that creature to behave in ways that have nothing to do with its own self-preservation. In fact, since the creature has already experienced death, the concept of "survival" is essentially meaningless to that creature. Consequently, an undead creature's tactics have less to do with how to effectively guarantee its continued existence and more to do with the particular compulsion that drives it.

SKELETONS AND ZOMBIES

Two types of undead that player characters will encounter often at low levels are **skeletons** and **zombies**. Both are (usually) former humanoids, raised from death through necromancy to act as minions without free will or personality. Their compulsion is obedience to the orders of their controller, which usually involves killing interlopers. When idle, a skeleton reverts to habitual behaviors from its former life (the *Monster Manual* offers, as an example, the skeleton of a former miner miming digging with a pick), while a zombie just stands around. Both are literal in their interpretations of instructions and lack independent problem-solving ability, although skeletons have an easier time circumventing obvious obstacles. Both will fight until they're destroyed, regardless of the amount or kind of damage they've taken or the strength of the opposition.

How a skeleton fights depends on how it would have fought in its previous life. A former archer, for instance, instinctively knows to maintain a certain range from its targets (40 to 80 feet, if possible). A former duelist occasionally uses the Dodge action to avoid incoming blows from multiple targets or the Disengage action to relocate to more favorable ground. Most of the time, though, skeletons are former guards or other shlubs and take a simple, direct approach to melee fighting: engage, swing sword, repeat. That being said, a skeleton ordered to guard a room, for instance, will break off combat with any opponent who leaves that room. It won't pursue, and it may even forgo an opportunity attack against an opponent who's obviously leaving the scene, because it's accomplished what it was commanded to do. Skeletons are vulnerable to bludgeoning damage, but they're not reflective enough to avoid a PC with a mace. Skeletons will retrieve dropped weapons, open doors, avoid hazards, and approach their targets by the *easiest* path.

Zombies retain no vestige of their former selves. They approach their targets by the *most direct* path, even if this means marching straight through an environmental hazard. They won't pick up a dropped weapon (and if they're not carrying one in the first place, they never will, unless their controller orders them to). They may break through a closed door, but they won't ever think to unlatch it. They'll pursue their targets until either those targets are dead or their controller orders them to break off.

Dungeons & Dragons zombies aren't like television zombies: They don't eat their victims, and they don't turn their victims into new zombies. But you don't need to tell your players that! Their one unique feature, Undead Fortitude, makes them frighteningly relentless (one way to emphasize it is to have them fall prone when damage would otherwise reduce them to 0 hp, then immediately get back up).

Beyond that, whatever the players believe about zombies—whether they're right or wrong—will make the experience of fighting them that much more thrilling. Because, honestly, any thrill that comes from fighting zombies won't come from their dazzling tactical skill.

Zombie encounters are as likely to result in comedy as excitement. For example, a rogue with Expertise in Acrobatics might entice a zombie into pursuing them out a third-story window. As a Dungeon Master, you absolutely should reward your players when they come up with ways to exploit zombies' fundamental flaws.

SHADOWS

An interesting low-level undead creature that's not used nearly as often as it deserves is the **shadow**. Great for horror campaigns, subterranean dungeons, and other creepy settings, the shadow's compulsion is to siphon the vitality from living beings, especially ones who are pure of heart. Shadows avoid light, particularly direct sunlight (it gives them disadvantage on every type of roll); running into open sun is the only sure way to escape from a shadow. Its other features are Amorphous (it can pass through the crack under a door) and Shadow Stealth (Hide as a bonus action in dim light or darkness), and it has not only a high Stealth proficiency but resistance to all sorts of damage, including physical damage from normal weapons, and outright immunity to most debilitating conditions. Its sole weakness is radiant damage, so not only is your good cleric or paladin its juiciest victim, they're also the one who's best equipped to defeat it. That's fair.

Its Stealth proficiency and Shadow Stealth trait together define the shadow's tactics. First, it lies in wait for a victim. When one appears, it uses its bonus action and its movement to Hide, then approach with stealth to within reach of the target. If it's not spotted, it attacks the same round, rolling with advantage, using Strength Drain (action). If the target notices it, it keeps moving, to try again next round. The beauty of this tactic is that, even if a PC spots the shadow, the DM can say, "You saw a shadow move past you," and the fact that the shadow *is a creature* may not even occur to the players at first. All they'll know for sure is that *something* is there.

Once the shadow attacks successfully, it no longer has the ability to Hide until it moves out of view again (unless the PCs are foolish enough to be stumbling around in total darkness without darkvision), and this is where its compulsion comes into play: Once it latches on to a PC, it keeps draining their Strength, even though slipping away for another surprise attack might be more effective.

What has the power to make a shadow think twice about what it's doing? Probably nothing but radiant damage, being struck by a magic weapon, or a cleric or paladin's Turn Undead feature. If one of these is used against it, it Disengages (action), moves out of view, Hides (bonus action), and waits for its victim to come within striking distance again.

Strength Drain can be nasty, not so much because of the average 9 necrotic damage it does with each hit but because it reduces its target's Strength by 1d4 *each time it hits*. The ability points are gone, potentially affecting the PC's attack and damage rolls and ability to use certain types of heavy armor, until the player completes a short or long rest—and if the PC's Strength is reduced to 0, they die on the spot. They don't simply fall unconscious. *They die.* Skeletons and zombies have long since lost any ability they may have had to frighten players, but an encounter with a shadow should terrify them. Don't overlook this monster.

GHOULS AND GHASTS

Ghouls and **ghasts** are a classic pair of flesh-devouring undead creatures, ghasts being the more dangerous of the two. Unlike skeletons and zombies, which are created by necromancers casting *animate dead*, ghouls and ghasts are purported to have demonic origins (although there exists a spell usable by player characters, *create undead*, which produces them as well—here the lore and the rules contradict each other).

Both ghouls and ghasts are immune to poison and to being charmed or exhausted, and both have darkvision. They have high Dexterity and Strength, in that order, and can attack with either Claws or Bite. The Bite attack does more direct damage, but the Claws attack has a greater chance to hit as well as a chance of paralyzing its target, rendering it incapable of action, movement, or speech; granting advantage to all attack rolls against it; and turning hits on it into crits. (Ghouls' Claws attack doesn't have this effect on elves, but ghasts' Claws attack does.) Although its chances of success are low, its potential effect is so powerful that it has to be considered the attack of first resort, except against elves. Finally, ghasts have the Turning Defiance trait, which grants advantage on saving throws against turning not just to themselves but to any ghoul within 30 feet of them. (They have resistance to necrotic damage, too, but that's probably not going to be your players' first choice against them.)

Ghouls and ghasts share a compulsion: hunger for the flesh of the living. This, combined with their average-level Wisdom, suggests that they possess a stronger self-preservation instinct than mindlessly obedient skeletons and zombies, since the whole point of eating is to fuel one's continued existence. It also suggests that their goal is to obtain living flesh to eat, and that once they've achieved this goal, they have no immediate reason to keep fighting.

Since ghouls have no Stealth skill to speak of, they move in as soon as they sense the presence of potential prey. ("Potential prey" excludes elves, since they're immune to ghouls' paralysis. Ghouls prey on elves only when desperate and deprived of other options.) Driven by instinct and compulsion, they're not daunted by being outnumbered. They approach their chosen prey (whichever non-elf PC is closest) directly and attack with Claws. Each ghoul repeats this attack until it finally succeeds in paralyzing its prey. Once this happens, it starts snacking, switching from Claws to Bite and attacking with advantage, with every hit a critical. That's 4d6 + 2 damage per bite! This is a good moment for the overly committed DM to indulge in graphic, cringe-inducing descriptions of ravenous ghouls tearing chunks out of the PCs.

A ghoul's victim gets to repeat its saving throw against paralysis every turn, so the ghoul wants to finish its meal as fast as it can. If a PC recovers midfeast, the ghoul goes back to Claws, hoping to paralyze them again.

What if another PC comes up and begins attacking the ghoul in the middle of its dinner? Rather than fight back, it will try to drag its meal away (weight limit: 390 pounds). Here, however, the ghoul faces the "eat-or-run" dilemma. Its chances of escape are best if it uses its action to Dash—and it can still lug the paralyzed PC with it while doing so. But every round spent running away is a round in which dinner might wake up, and a ghoul is always hungry. Once it has a paralyzed victim, it can't resist the compulsion to keep eating. So the ghoul retreats from its attacker, using its full movement (and potentially provoking an opportunity attack), but then stops for another Bite against its victim. In all likelihood, the PC pursuer will catch up with the ghoul and attack it. It will react the same way again: move, then Bite.

This cycle repeats until one of three things happens: (a) the ghoul is reduced to 8 hp or fewer, in which case it drops its dinner and Dashes away; (b) the ghoul is destroyed; or (c) the victim is reduced to 0 hp, in which case the ever-ravenous ghoul turns against its erstwhile pursuer and tries to make a meal of them as well. As before, it starts with Claws, switching to Bite if and when the PC is paralyzed.

If a ghoul is shot from range while in the middle of a meal, rather than attacked hand-to-hand, it simply ignores the attack and keeps eating, until it's reduced to 8 hp or fewer. Then it runs away.

The more intelligent ghast is only slightly more sophisticated. It doesn't exempt elves from its definition of "prey," and if it's accompanied by a pack of ghouls, it identifies stronger PCs and directs the ghouls to gang up on them, two or three on one, depending on the relative numbers of ghasts and ghouls vs. PCs. The ghast, meanwhile, goes after a delicious elf. If the ghasts and ghouls are outnumbered by the PCs, a ghast instead goes after the strongest PC itself (being best equipped to do so, not just because of its Strength and Armor Class but because of its Stench trait) while the ghouls go after the *weaker* PCs—less resistance, same nutritional value. The ghouls always remain within 30 feet of the ghast, in order to benefit from its Turning Defiance, except when one is trying to abscond with a paralyzed victim.

Despite their greater intelligence, ghasts do have the same carnivorous compulsion as ghouls and consequently follow the same approach to escaping with a paralyzed victim when attacked hand-to-hand. Their noxious Stench offers them some slight protection from opportunity attacks, since a PC in melee range may be poisoned by it and therefore attacks with disadvantage. Also, if a ghast is hit more than once by ranged attacks or spells while consuming a victim, yet not enough to seriously wound it (reduce it to 14 hp or fewer), it will get annoyed enough to get up and go after the ranged attacker, Dashing until it can close the gap with its normal movement, then attacking with Claws.

SPECTERS, WIGHTS, AND WRAITHS

Ghouls and ghasts are flesh eaters; specters, wights, and wraiths are life drainers. Driven by malice, envy, and despair, they compulsively consume the vitality they themselves can never again possess. They all have darkvision and shun the sunlight, so they're encountered only at night; in some shuttered, haunted locale; or underground.

Specters are incorporeal: They have no material existence and can pass through solid objects and other creatures, although they can be harmed by stopping inside one. They have a very fast flying movement speed of 50 feet per turn. Their only exceptional ability scores are Dexterity 14 and Strength 1. They're immune to most debilitating conditions, although they can be blinded, deafened, frightened, incapacitated, or stunned. They're immune to necrotic and poison damage and resistant to other forms of damage, except for radiant damage and physical damage from magic weapons. Being of normal humanoid Intelligence and Wisdom, they have the sense to back off from an opponent that starts inflicting these types of damage upon it.

A specter might be expected to identify and zero in on weaker victims, and if it were an evolved creature, it might act that way. But specters are driven by their compulsion, not by adaptive survival instincts. When they sense the presence of a living victim, they don't evaluate how easy or hard it will be to devitalize. They just wanna kill everybody, and it doesn't matter who's first.

Theirs is a scrappy fighting style: They move around a lot but also attack relentlessly. Once they've identified a target, they go straight for it and Life Drain until (a) the target is dead; (b) the target flees into sunlight, where they won't follow; (c) they take any radiant damage, or physical damage from a magic weapon; or (d) they take moderate or greater damage (7 points or more from one opponent in a single round) of any other type(s). In the latter two cases, the specter doesn't break off combat—it wheels around and attacks a different victim instead, avoiding the source of the damage until other targets are dispensed with. In case (c), it Disengages and moves to a place of safety 50 feet away, then swoops in and attacks its new target in the next round. In case (d), it flies to its new target and attacks immediately, without seeking to avoid an opportunity attack, since most opportunity attacks can't hurt it much. Alternatively, if it was hit by a ranged attack, it dive-bombs the ranged attacker and engages them in melee. Once a specter has found victims to drain, nothing will make it stop attacking—even Turn Undead will deter it for only 1 minute at most. As soon as the effect wears off, it attacks again.

The **poltergeist** variant of the specter doesn't Drain Life—it hurls objects and people around instead. Its target selection is mostly random, varying from round to round, but its choice of action depends on its choice of target. It uses Telekinetic Thrust to pick up and hurl a player character with Strength 10 or less, or to hurl a Small or Medium-size object, such as a piece of furniture, at any PC; against other targets, or if it's just hurled an object, it uses Forceful Slam. Unlike the ordinary specter, which shies away from PCs that do radiant damage or carry magic weapons, the poltergeist is even further enraged by these things and *targets* those characters—albeit from a distance, if possible, by hurling objects until there are no more objects to hurl. It also doesn't stop attacking until it's destroyed, or until the PCs leave whatever area it haunts.

Wights are corporeal and tough. They possess Stealth proficiency and are capable fighters both in melee and at range. They aren't immune to as many debilitating conditions as specters (only exhaustion and poison) and are resistant only to necrotic damage and physical damage from nonmagical, nonsilvered weapons, but their high physical ability scores, moderately high hit points, and Multiattack action make them even harder to kill. Moreover, they have above-average Wisdom and Charisma as well, so it's difficult to bring them down with spells and magic items that require saving throws to resist.

Wights relentlessly attack anyone who invades the dark and desolate burial places where they dwell. First, they move with Stealth to the nearest distance they can reach without being seen, then they attack with surprise. If they're beyond melee range, they make two Longbow attacks; within melee range, they make two Longsword attacks. With each round, they advance, moving at the start of their turn (if applicable) and attacking at the end. When a wight's target is reduced to 18 hp or fewer, it uses Life Drain as its second melee attack; when its target is reduced to 6 hp or fewer, it uses Life Drain as its *first* melee attack, rather than its second. It would like to use Life Drain to finish off its target in order to raise the target as a zombie under its control, but its Intelligence isn't *quite* high enough for it to hold back in order to be sure it doesn't accidentally kill the target with a weapon strike instead. These guidelines are as close as it can get.

Wights, according to the *Monster Manual*, "pursue [a] malevolent agenda . . . relentlessly and without distraction . . . relying on their hunger for destruction to overwhelm any creature that stands before them." Therefore, they're undeterred by elemental damage, by foes with magic or silvered weapons, or by unusually tough or talented opponents. Unlike specters, which put off engaging with foes who can harm them more easily, and poltergeists, which focus their attacks on those foes, wights don't care one way or the other. Taking damage would only make them angrier, if they could be any angrier than they already are. How much more angry can they be? The answer is, none. None more angry. The only thing that will get them off their chosen victims—aside from those victims' successfully fleeing into the sunlight—is Turn Undead, and once that wears off, they come right back.

Wraiths are like extra-powerful specters, possessing the same resistances and immunities, the same incorporeal nature, and the same Life Drain ability. All their ability scores are higher, making them above-average in everything except Strength, but most notably in Dexterity, Constitution, and Wisdom—the "big three" of saving throws. These traits, plus a sizable wodge of hit points and a wicked-fast 60-foot flying speed, make them terrifying foes.

Just like specters, wraiths want to murder everyone and everything, so they're not super-concerned with who dies first. However, wraiths have just enough Intelligence and Wisdom to choose their targets, and they choose on the basis of . . . goodness. Wraiths' compulsion is malice, and the purer the heart, the more they want to see it stop beating. They fly in, lock on to the greatest paragon of goodness in the party, and start Life Draining. Multiple wraiths will probably all be drawn to the same target, but be mindful that even one wraith is a Deadly encounter for a party of four level 3 characters or a single level 9 character (see "Creating a Combat Encounter," *Dungeon Master's Guide*, chapter 3). While normally I advocate having a monster follow its nature, come what may, Life Drain's potential to kill a character outright is serious business. If you're even a little bit of a softy, you should generally avoid having more than one wraith attack a single PC at once unless they're a "master of the world," level 17 or higher.

That said, wraiths, like specters, recoil from radiant damage and silvered or magic weapons—and unlike specters, even as they switch their attacks to less dangerous opponents, they don't forget who's got the shiny, burny weapons that hurt them, nor do they forgive. If at any time one or more wraiths are looking for a new target, their attention will immediately turn back to Burny McRighteousface. But even Burny, who's asking for it, shouldn't have to fend off more than one wraith at a time up to level 10, more than two wraiths at level 11–16, or more than three at level 17 or higher. Burny's comrades-in-arms need to have at least a chance of staging a rescue.

One feature wraiths have that sets them apart from specters is Create Specter: They can take a humanoid who's died violently within the last minute (this includes dying as a result of Life Drain) and raise a specter from their corpse. Naturally, they'll be particularly keen to do this to the victims they lusted most to kill. But turning a PC into a specter is a cold thing to do. This is beyond *remove curse*, beyond *greater restoration*, beyond *raise dead*—it requires, at a minimum, *resurrection* (some DMs might argue that it requires *true resurrection* or even *wish*). *Revivify* can save the victim if applied expeditiously enough, but the window of opportunity slams shut quickly.

Use Create Specter judiciously. Don't do it to a PC without some-how letting your players know that it can be undone, even though the undoing may be an ordeal, and allow the player whose PC has been enspecterated a role to play while their character is waiting to be brought back to life. Or just don't do it to a PC at all—but feel free to tell them, "You recall having been told once that wraiths have the power to drain people's life forces and turn them into spectral thralls," just to make them shriek.

While Strength points lost to the shadow's Strength Drain are restored by any rest, short or long, hit point maximums reduced by the Life Drain feature of a specter, wight, or wraith are restored only by a long rest. (On the other hand, Strength Drain losses are automatic; Life Drain reduces hit point maximum only upon a failed Constitution saving throw.) This makes these enemies a particularly rough threat at the beginning of the adventuring day; on the other hand, placing them at the end of the adventuring day nerfs their life-draining effects to the point of insignificance. The middle of an ad-venturing day consisting of multiple encounters seems about the right time to have your PCs run into them.

GHOSTS AND MUMMIES

Aside from being horror-film staples, ghosts and mummies don't have a lot in common with each other, except for one thing: Each is bound to a specific location. A ghost has "unfinished business" and haunts an area closely related to whatever trauma it needs to resolve; it's com-pelled by the urge to resolve this trauma. A mummy is the guardian of a tomb or other burial place, compelled to punish transgressors against either the tomb itself or, sometimes, the person buried there. (In the latter case, the mummy may leave the tomb to hunt down the transgressor. In the former, it always stays put.)

Ghosts may be malicious, but they don't *have* to be. (A malicious ghost that for some reason is permanently prevented from resolv-ing the trauma connected with its death may end up as a poltergeist instead—see "Specters, Wights, and Wraiths," page 275.) They may want to punish people who wronged them in their previous lives, but they may also be sorrowful, lonely, lost, or even deceiving themselves that they're still alive. Revenge against those who wronged them might satisfy them, but so might making amends to those whom *they* wronged. You really can't have a decent ghost without a backstory.

Ghosts are immune to the same debilitating conditions as specters and wraiths and mostly resist the same types of damage (the exceptions are silvered weapons, which don't bother them, and cold damage, to which they're entirely immune). They also possess darkvision and Incorporeal Movement. This is where the similarities end, however. Ghosts don't Drain Life, nor do they have Sunlight Sensitivity (they prefer the dark, but they aren't harmed by the light), nor are they driven to kill every living being they encounter. They have a different toolkit and a much different sort of compulsion: the resolution of their death traumas.

Possession allows a ghost to take control of a target humanoid. A ghost will possess a PC to perform physical actions that it can't perform in its incorporeal state (such as opening a door or a container or retrieving an object), to talk to people to whom it doesn't want to reveal itself as a ghost, to move outside the place it haunts, and so forth. A lawful good or neutral good ghost will even ask a PC for their permission before possessing them. A chaotic evil ghost, on the other hand, not only will possess a PC against their will but may even relish making them do degrading things. Regardless, the ghost always possesses people specifically to bring about the resolution of its trauma, although the connection between the trauma and the possession may not be direct or obvious. While a ghost could possess a PC and force them to attack other party members, it generally won't bother to do so, because more often than not, it can do more damage on its own with Withering Touch.

Withering Touch does an unpleasant amount of direct necrotic damage, and that's it. In general, even if an encounter with a ghost goes south, the ghost won't attack *everybody* in the party—only the PC(s) who attack it or who actively interfere(s) with the resolution of its trauma. A ghost uses Withering Touch primarily for deterrence and self-defense, not with intent to kill (unless that's part of the resolution of its trauma). If one or more PCs fight back with magic weapons or do radiant damage to a ghost, it will back off right quick, Disengaging and retreating at full movement speed in a straight line away from the party, through any creatures, objects, or physical barriers in the way. A ghost can't resolve its trauma if it lets itself be destroyed, so its self-preservation instinct is much stronger than those of most undead creatures. Similarly, if a ghost is repelled by Turn Undead, unlike most undead, it keeps its distance from the PC who turned it. Anyone who isn't going to help a ghost resolve its trauma is no longer relevant to its interests.

Horrifying Visage causes targets to be frightened and, if they fail their saving throws by 5 points or more, to age 1d4 × 10 years on the spot. Again, whether and when a ghost uses this feature depends first and foremost on the nature of its trauma and what's necessary to resolve it. A compulsion to keep people away from a certain place is one reason why a ghost might use it. To haunt a person who wronged the ghost in its previous life is another. Ghosts will also use Horrifying Visage against those who offend or upset them, and they don't have complete control over their use of it, so even good ghosts that lose their cool may bust out with a Horrifying Visage, although they'll be remorseful and apologetic about it afterward. (Evil ones won't feel a lick of regret.) A ghost won't use this feature round after round, because there's no good reason to do so: Characters affected by it will have run away, and unaffected characters will be immune to it for the next 24 hours anyway. But if the ghost is upset or offended again, it may do so regardless, involuntarily, even though it won't have any further effect.

In short, ghosts aren't interested in combat unless it involves killing someone they're compelled to take revenge against. They'll fight back with Withering Touch to defend themselves, but as soon as it's no longer necessary—or they're hit with damage that truly hurts them, or they're turned—they're done. (Incidentally, as a DM, I wouldn't award experience points for "defeating" a ghost that the PCs merely drive away. I would, however, award full XP to PCs who resolve a ghost's trauma and thereby release it without destroying it.)

Mummies are compelled by obedience to the will of their (nearly always evil) creators. They're brutes, with high Strength and Constitution but low Dexterity. They also receive a bonus on Wisdom saving throws, which makes them strong against two of the "big three" saving throw abilities. They're resistant to physical damage from nonmagical weapons and immune to necrotic and poison damage, but vulnerable to fire. They have darkvision (important, if your full-time job is guarding a tomb) and are immune to several debilitating conditions.

Rarely, a mummy may be sent out into the world to pursue the targets of a curse laid by its creator, but most of the time, they stand guard inside a tomb to punish would-be robbers or desecraters. Once a PC enters a part of the tomb that's off limits, or opens a coffer or coffin that they oughtn't, the mummy arises and attacks. Unless it's attacked back by someone else, it targets only the transgressing PC. Its movement is slow (20 feet) but relentless. On its turn, it advances toward its target, then attacks if it can. Beyond melee range, this attack consists of a Dreadful Glare; since success means the target flees and failure means the glare has failed to elicit suitable dread, it uses this feature only once per transgressor. Within melee range, the attack consists of a Dreadful Glare if the mummy hasn't already used this feature on the target, followed by a Rotting Fist. (The latter may be an opportunity attack if Dreadful Glare caused the target to flee; otherwise, it's used alone, or it's just the second part of the mummy's Multiattack.) Once the mummy has closed with its target, it pummels them with Rotting Fist until they fall unconscious or the mummy is destroyed . . . or . . .

Fire! Mummies are driven by compulsion, but they do have a sense of self-preservation, albeit a weak one. Fire pits the one against the other. If attacked with fire in melee, they'll Disengage and retreat 20 feet, but they won't flee, because they still have the same compulsion to defend their burial place against transgressors. Instead, they remain in a standoff, waiting for the source of fire to go away so that they can attack again. If attacked with fire at range (e.g., a thrown Molotov cocktail or fire-based spell), they'll direct a Dreadful Glare at the source of the damage. If the attack fails, they'll retreat 20 feet; if it succeeds, however, they'll go right back to what they were doing before. If a full round goes by without their taking any more fire damage, they'll also go back to what they were doing before. Mummies are extremely mechanical in their behavior: You might expect an area-effect fire spell such as *burning hands* or *fireball* to scramble their circuits, but aside from avoiding the source of the damage and trying to make it go away, they never deviate from their orders. Using Turn Undead against a mummy doesn't deter it in the slightest: As soon as it wears off, the mummy returns to the slow-motion chase.

MUMMY LORDS

Mummy lords are in a totally different league of monster from your rank-and-file mummy—and the power difference between a mummy and a mummy lord is much wider than that between an orc and an orc war chief, a hobgoblin and a hobgoblin warlord, or a gnoll and a gnoll Fang of Yeenoghu. Mummy lords are bosses on par with adult dragons and tougher than giants. Only experienced adventurers need apply.

Their array of powers makes them complicated to run, so this is going to be a long and thorough breakdown:

- **Abilities**: Average Dexterity and Intelligence; very high Strength, Constitution, Wisdom, and Charisma. They're brutes, but they're not fools. And they have personality—conceited, toxic personality, but personality nonetheless.
- **Damage and Condition Immunities**: Same as regular mummies but with an added immunity to physical damage from nonmagical weapons. They're not afraid of your pigsticker unless it's got a plus in front of it.
- **Damage Vulnerability**: Fire, same as regular mummies.
- **Saving Throws**: Hefty bonuses on Constitution, Intelligence, Wisdom, and Charisma saves. That's two of the big three and two of the little three, and with Strength 18, it doesn't need to worry about that one either. The only gap in this fortification is Dexterity. However . . .
- **Magic Resistance**: Even its lower Dexterity (only in relative terms) isn't too much of a hindrance, because it rolls *all* its saving throws against magic with advantage.
- **Rejuvenation**: *You can't even kill it* unless you jump through the extra hoop of destroying its heart. (For this purpose, I recommend fire.)

- **Spellcasting**: More on this in a moment.
- **Legendary Actions**: Every turn, it can perform up to three legendary actions on other characters' turns. These include an out-of-turn attack, an area-effect blind, an area-effect stun, suppression of healing, and turning momentarily incorporeal.
- **Lair Actions and Regional Effects**: All the preceding applies if you happen to encounter a mummy lord on its way to the bodega to get milk. A mummy lord in its lair is even more powerful, granting advantage on saving throws to other undead creatures in the lair, providing them with the equivalent of radar, and giving anyone else who tries to cast a spell a punishing necrotic jolt.

Like I said, a boss. With the attitude of a boss to boot. The mummy lord's rational and justifiable assumption is that you ain't jack.

What does it take to show a mummy lord that you are, indeed, jack? Magic weapons, especially ones imbued with fire damage. Non-spellcasting abilities (such as Divine Strike/Divine Smite, Sacred Weapon, Wrath of the Storm, and Elemental Wild Shape) that do direct, nonphysical damage with no saving throw to resist. Managing to inflict 30 damage of any kind in a single round. A mummy lord will be taken aback by these things, and its vanity and arrogance will compel it to vanquish whichever attacker(s) produce the aforementioned damage, which is bad for them but good for the littler fish in the party. (Forget about Turn Undead. The mummy lord gets +9 and advantage on that saving throw.)

Now let's look at its spells. I'm going to group these according to their casting time, because this highlights the roles they play in the mummy lord's action economy.

ACTIONS (instant or self-sustaining)

- *Harm* is the mummy lord's nuclear option. It gets to cast this spell only once, so it's going to choose its target and its moment carefully. If a PC with Extra Attack smacks the mummy lord twice with a +1 *flame tongue* sword while calling down a Divine Smite each time, that PC's *harm* request is expedited and approved immediately.

- *Contagion* is the mummy lord's way of showing its contempt. If it suspects a PC may actually be dangerous and hard to kill, the mummy lord inflicts Slimy Doom, hoping to weaken their resistance to Rotting Fist and *harm*. Otherwise, it inflicts Blinding Sickness, because this disease has the most devastating effect overall, thanks to its imposing the blinded condition. (Filth Fever and Seizure affect melee and ranged attackers specifically, but Blinding Sickness nails them both—and also shuts down spellcasters, who generally need to be able to see their targets.) This is a touch attack, and the mummy lord can use it no more than twice, so it reserves *contagion* for PCs who offend it or pose a threat. And it casts it early, because it takes three to five rounds to kick in fully; in the interim, the target is merely poisoned.

- *Divination* is useless in combat. It applies only in the extremely rare event that your PCs are petitioning the mummy lord for the use of its oracular services.

- *Guardian of faith* does up to 60 damage against characters who dare to approach the mummy lord, consuming only a 4th-level spell slot and the action taken to cast it. This is a spell to lead with—normally. That being said, is a mummy lord really going to think it needs this level of protection against a bunch of pathetic mortals? I think it will hold off on casting this spell in combat until it feels threatened.

- *Animate dead* requires the presence of actual corpses. In a tomb, there are bound to be a few of those lying around; the question is how conveniently located they are, since the spell has a range of only 10 feet. After casting the spell, the mummy lord can control its servant(s) with a bonus action, so this is a desirable spell to cast if and only if the basic conditions are met. Otherwise, *spiritual weapon* accomplishes the same thing without humanoid remains, and it can be cast without consuming an action.

- *Dispel magic* is familiar and uncomplicated.
- *Command* is usually best used to provoke opportunity attacks from allied creatures, but thanks to the mummy lord's legendary actions, it can benefit from commanding a PC with whom it's engaged in melee to "Grovel!" as long as someone else gets a turn before the PC does. The flip side is, a *command* must be issued in a language that the target understands, and it's not only possible but probable that a mummy lord speaks only ancient, dead languages, so this may be one to skip.
- *Guiding bolt* is a cheap damage-dealer (4d6 is good for a 1st-level spell, and the damage increases when using higher-level spell slots) that also grants advantage on a future attack. However, the mummy lord's Rotting Fist attack is even more powerful, so *guiding bolt* only compares favorably if something is imposing disadvantage on the mummy lord's attack rolls, such as if it's blinded or restrained. On the other hand, this disadvantage also affects whether *guiding bolt* works in the first place. It's a bit of a Catch-22. Maybe use it only against a PC whom the mummy lord can't reach just yet but will be able to reach on its next turn—or whom one of its minions can reach, if it has minions.
- *Sacred flame* does 2d8 radiant damage on a failed Dexterity saving throw and no damage on a successful one. Weaksauce. There's only one situation when this is worth using: when no one in range is susceptible to Dreadful Glare, no one is within reach of a Rotting Fist attack, and there's no other spell worth casting.
- *Thaumaturgy*? Only for amplifying its voice while monologuing.

ACTIONS (continuous, require concentration)
- *Insect plague* fills a 20-foot-radius sphere with biting insects that do 4d10 damage on a failed Constitution saving throw and half that on a success. This can put a real hurt on a party with a lot of squishy characters in it.

- *Hold person* is familiar and uncomplicated.
- *Silence* is good for shutting down several troublesome spell-casters, especially bards, if they all happen to be within 40 feet of one another. Attempt to nab four, at least.

BONUS ACTIONS (instant or self-sustaining)
- *Spiritual weapon* is extra damage, round after round, for the cost of the mummy lord's bonus action. Why not?

BONUS ACTIONS (continuous, require concentration)
- *Shield of faith* is carrying coals to Newcastle, since the mummy lord's AC is already 17. It may be worth casting anyway if the mummy lord doesn't have a different continuous spell that it would rather sustain, but if combat has already begun, it would probably rather spend its bonus action hitting somebody with a *spiritual weapon*. It seems to me that a mummy lord should cast *shield of faith* only when it's taking more hits than it's dishing out, which isn't going to happen often, or when it needs to buff a key minion more than it needs to take a whack with its *spiritual weapon*.

Now that we've looked at the benefits of each of these spells, let's consider the costs: spell slots. Intuitively, we believe that higher-level spell slots should be worth more than lower-level ones, but this isn't true in every case. Another way to look at it, which I believe is more accurate, is that a scarcer spell slot is worth more than a less scarce one and that a higher-level spell slot can be used to cast certain spells that a lower-level one can't. So unless the higher-level spell slot is also scarcer, whether it's worthwhile to spend a higher-level spell slot on a lower-level spell, boosted, depends entirely on whether the lower-level spell is more useful boosted than the higher-level spell is unboosted.

- 6th level: The mummy lord has only one 6th-level slot. It's going to reserve it for *harm*.

- 5th level: The mummy lord has two 5th-level slots and two valuable 5th-level spells, *contagion* and *insect plague*. It saves these slots for these spells.

- 4th level: *Divination* has no purpose here, and *guardian of faith* is the kind of spell you only bother casting once. The other two 4th-level slots, therefore, are available for boosting lower-level spells.

- 3rd level: *Dispel magic* is one to keep in your pocket at all times, so these slots will be retained for it. (*Animate dead* is so situational that we can safely disregard it.)

- 2nd level: *Spiritual weapon* is an auto-cast, and *hold person* and *silence* are good to keep in reserve. *Hold person* can be cast at higher levels to affect more targets; *silence* can't. *Spiritual weapon* can be cast at higher levels to do more damage, but the cost is two levels per damage die, and it's not worth that.

- 1st level: The least scarce spell level—and also the least useful, given the mummy lord's spell set. *Command* and *shield of faith* can't be boosted by casting them at a higher level; *guiding bolt* can, but it's already compromised by the fact that you mostly want to cast it when its chances of succeeding are poorer. Why would you risk a higher-level spell slot on a spell you'll probably be casting with disadvantage on the attack roll, even if you do have +9 to hit? You'd only do it when you *weren't* rolling with disadvantage—that is, when you were using it to set up an attack on a target whom you couldn't reach yet but would be able to reach on your next turn. Even so, is a 4th-level *guiding bolt* better than a 4th-level *hold person*? Nope. Save the slots.

The conclusion I draw here is that two of the mummy lord's three 4th-level spell slots are flex slots, which it's most likely to spend either to boost *hold person* or to cast *dispel magic* after running out of 3rd-level slots. Otherwise, it casts spells at their base levels.

With all that analysis finally out of our way, let's get down to specific tactics.

When combat is inevitable, the mummy lord doesn't wait until its own turn to begin using its legendary actions to shut its foes down; it uses them as soon as they take hostile action.

- If more than one opponent engages the mummy lord in melee, it uses Blinding Dust to raise a swirling, blinding cloud around itself.
- If at least four opponents are within 10 feet of the mummy lord, it uses Blasphemous Word to stun them.
- If it's reduced to 38 hp or fewer and it has two or three legendary actions left, it uses Whirlwind of Sand to retreat 40 to 60 feet from any PC(s) engaged in melee with it. If it has only one legendary action left, or none, it uses Whirlwind of Sand at the next available opportunity.
- If none of the above situations applies, it uses Attack, directing its Dreadful Glare at the foe who's just taken a turn.

Using these legendary actions is crucial, because for all its offensive might, the mummy lord has a glass jaw: 97 hp is scanty for a CR 15 creature. If it neglects to use its legendary actions, a strong and/or lucky party with good initiative rolls can take it out before it can lift a bony finger.

When its own turn arrives, if it's only lightly wounded (still at 68 hp or more), it follows its default attack pattern: using its movement to approach the PC whom it considers the number one aggressor or transgressor; its action to use Dreadful Glare against that PC, along with Rotting Fist if the PC is within reach; and its bonus action to cast *spiritual weapon*, which takes the form of a spear or flail. It does the same on subsequent turns, except that if the first PC hasn't fled, it directs its Dreadful Glare at a secondary target while continuing to attack the primary target with Rotting Fist (action) and *spiritual weapon* (bonus action). If they have fled, it uses all these abilities against the secondary target.

However, it abandons this default attack pattern under certain conditions:

- If it's not yet (or no longer) engaged in melee, and there are at least four non-fighter (non-barbarian, non-paladin, non-ranger) PCs all within 40 feet of one another, it drops an *insect plague* on them.
- If an opponent manages to attack it with a magic weapon, inflict direct fire damage, *and* do 30 damage to it in a single round—or if they do any *two* of these things—the mummy lord casts *harm* on that foe. If two or three foes each manage to do any one of those things, it casts *hold person* at 4th level on them. If just one foe does any one of them, and it's still the first or second round of combat, the mummy lord casts *contagion*, afflicting that foe with Slimy Doom. If the mummy lord no longer has a 5th-level spell slot available to cast *contagion*, or if two rounds of combat have already gone by, it casts *hold person* at 2nd level instead, paralyzing just that one opponent.
- If an opponent who is otherwise a capable damage dealer successfully hits the mummy lord with a weapon attack or spell but does insignificant damage to it (9 hp or fewer) or tries to inflict a condition to which the mummy lord is immune, and it's still the first or second round of combat, it casts *contagion*, afflicting that enemy with Blinding Sickness.
- If four or more spellcasters are all within 40 feet of one another, and the mummy lord isn't already sustaining *insect swarm* or *hold person*, it drops a sphere of *silence* on them. (It lets *silence* go if it needs to cast *hold person* at 4th level, but not at 2nd level.)
- If an opponent casts a continuous spell or creates some other continuous magical effect that significantly benefits the party or impedes the mummy lord (or any of its minions), it casts *dispel magic* to get rid of the effect.
- If it's chosen a target whom it can't yet reach with a melee attack but will be able to reach on its next turn, and it's already tried Dreadful Glare against that target, it casts *guiding bolt*.
- If it's reduced to 38 hp or fewer and has retreated using Whirlwind of Sand (see below), it casts *guardian of faith* at a point in

between itself and its enemies where anyone trying to charge it will have to pass within 10 feet of the spectral guardian.

Whichever of these spells it casts, it continues to strike at its foes with its *spiritual weapon* as a bonus action, if this spell is already in effect.

After the first round of combat, the mummy lord has one more legendary action open to it:

- When at least two-thirds of the party are injured, or any one player starts complaining about how low their character's hit points are, it uses Channel Negative Energy to prevent healing (unless it's already used Blasphemous Word).

It may also use its legendary Attack action to strike a melee opponent with Rotting Fist rather than use Dreadful Glare.

Finally, a mummy lord in its lair uses its lair action on initiative count 20 to inflict wracking pain on enemy spellcasters for the first round during which they have a chance to cast spells and on alternating rounds thereafter. On rounds when it can't use this lair action, it uses whichever of the other two is more applicable to the situation; if neither applies, it forgoes its lair action for the round.

The mummy lord's compulsion is vainglory. At first, it doesn't believe the PCs are *capable* of hurting it, and it devotes its energy to shutting them down and punishing them for their insolence unless and until they prove to be a significant threat. Only then does it make a wholehearted effort to destroy them.

VAMPIRES

Before I examine the vampire, which is another boss-level undead creature only slightly less powerful than the mummy lord, let's look at the less powerful **vampire spawn**, the minion of a full-fledged vampire.

Vampire spawn have exceptional physical abilities, plus above-average Charisma. They receive bonuses to Dexterity and Wisdom saving throws, which, combined with their high Constitution, means they're hard targets for any spell resisted by one of the "big three" saving throws, but especially Dexterity. They're resistant to physical damage from normal weapons, plus necrotic damage, and they regenerate hit points each turn if they aren't in sunlight or running water. They can't enter someone's home without an invitation. They have a high Stealth skill, along with Multiattack in two possible combinations: Claws/Claws or Claws/Bite.

Since Bite is limited to one of the two actions, you can assume that it's preferred and that the vampire spawn will use it whenever it can; however, a precondition of the Bite attack is that the victim be grappled, incapacitated, restrained . . . or willing. The vampire spawn doesn't have any feature that imposes the incapacitated condition or the restrained condition, nor does it have the power to charm. But grappling happens to be built into its Claws attack.

With high hit points and high physical ability scores across the board, vampire spawn have no reason to think they can't overpower most opponents. But their high Stealth score suggests that they'll stalk or ambush their victims rather than charge them headlong.

There's also the vampire spawn's compulsion, which is to feed. Vampires, including vampire spawn, are apex predators. When a predator's prey are social animals, rather than attack one in a group—who are likely to fight back—it picks off the young, the old, the weak, the isolated, and the oblivious. Vampire spawn do the same. They sometimes live and hunt in groups, too; they're willing to take on any group whose numbers are less than or equal to their own, but not greater.

Of course, because of their Sunlight Hypersensitivity, they have to hunt at night. Sunlight Hypersensitivity is a step beyond Sunlight Sensitivity; unlike kobolds, say, which strongly prefer the dark but may be active during daytime hours, vampire spawn are strictly nocturnal. (Since predators require abundant prey to survive, vampires and vampire spawn are more likely to be found near medium-size towns and large cities, rather than near small villages or in the wilderness.)

Therefore, a vampire spawn encounter begins with one or more vampire spawn stalking one or more PCs or waiting to ambush them. They attack with surprise, and their first Multiattack action begins with a Claws attack with intent to grapple rather than deal damage. The second part of their Multiattack depends on what happens in the first part. If its target is grappled, a vampire spawn follows up its Claws attack with a Bite. If the target escapes despite not having Athletics or Acrobatics proficiency, the vampire spawn recognizes this weakness and tries again to grapple. If the target escapes and *does* have Athletics or Acrobatics proficiency, the vampire spawn realizes it's probably not going to get a meal out of this one, and it gets angry and tries to kill the PC out of spite. It completes its Multiattack with a Claws attack for damage, and from that point on, it uses Claws/Claws—unless, somehow, it gains an advantage, such as flanking ("Optional Rule: Flanking," *Dungeon Master's Guide*, chapter 8). If it's got advantage, it will try grappling one more time, just to see whether it can pull it off. Success? Munch! Failure? Eh, forget it; go back to Claws/Claws.

A vampire spawn with a grappled victim will also try to drag it away to a place of hiding, especially if there's anyone else nearby. It can move 15 feet per turn while dragging its struggling prey.

What if a vampire spawn is attacked by another PC while it's feeding? While continuing to hold on to its victim, the vampire spawn uses Claws on the attacker for damage—but then its compulsion to feed kicks in again, and it inflicts another Bite upon its grappled victim. It still uses its movement to try to drag its prey away, and if possible, it uses its Spider Climb trait to take itself and its victim where the attacker can't follow. (Unlike the *spider climb* spell, this trait doesn't give the vampire spawn a climbing speed, so it can travel only 7 feet up a wall in one turn while carrying a grappled victim, or 15 feet by itself.)

Be aware that the vampire spawn's Bite doesn't just subtract hit points from the victim—it *restores hit points to the vampire spawn*, equal to the amount of necrotic damage its Bite inflicts (but not the piercing damage, so always roll the two separately).

Once a vampire spawn reduces its victim to unconsciousness, it's satiated for the time being and returns to its resting place, using a Disengage action if necessary to avoid opportunity attacks—unless it's under orders from a vampire to kill whomever it encounters, in which case it moves on to the next PC.

All vampires, including vampire spawn, have a much more powerful survival instinct than most undead, because their compulsion is to feed—and by extension, to continue their own existence. Reduce a vampire spawn to 32 hp or fewer, and it will flee back to its resting place by the most direct route—which, thanks to its Spider Climb trait, may be straight up the wall of a building and across rooftops. However, if a vampire spawn is under the command of a vampire, whatever commands it's been given supersede its inclination to save itself.

Vampires possess all the attributes of vampire spawn, plus the Shapechanger, Legendary Resistance, Misty Escape, Charm, and Children of the Night features, along with three legendary actions that allow them to move, grapple, and Bite on other creatures' turns. In addition, *all* their ability scores are exceptional, they receive a bonus on Charisma saving throws as well as Dexterity and Wisdom, and they enjoy 120 feet of darkvision. Finally, their Bite has the power not just to drain a target dry but to turn it into a vampire spawn.

Vampires are physically powerful; they're also shrewd. A vampire never, ever attacks recklessly. It chooses its targets with utmost care and values its continued existence over all else, despite its compulsion to feed. It chooses victims it knows are unlikely to be missed—or, if they're missed, whose disappearances are unlikely to be investigated. It conceals its nocturnal nature by hiring (or charming) go-betweens to conduct its affairs during normal daytime hours. A lonely or bored vampire may even charm a living mortal into serving as its companion, although eventually, proximity and intimacy will make the temptation to turn this companion into a vampire spawn too great for the vampire to resist.

A vampire that can't feed by having its agents bring victims to its lair hunts by going out at night, either alone or in the company of one or more of its agents. Vampires with access to wealth go out in closed carriages and offer rides to their prospective victims, mostly late-night revelers. Nonwealthy vampires stick to sketchier parts of town and prey on beggars, burglars, and the occasional hapless watchman.

But vampires are careful about this. Unless PCs have been stalking a vampire themselves, they're unlikely to encounter one on the street:

It will avoid a group of their party's size. To get in a scrap with a vampire, at least as a group, your PCs will probably have to invade its lair. And it will have layers of security: mortal human guards, vampire spawn, and other lesser undead. If it's expecting the unwelcome visitors, it will also have the aforementioned Children of the Night—swarms of bats or rats or, outdoors, a pack of wolves.

Let's take a look at that feature for a moment. It's usable only once per day. It takes 1d4 rounds for the beasts to show up, and they stick around for one hour. Obviously, it would be silly for a vampire to use this ability if it didn't know its lair were being invaded. On the other hand, this is a slow ability to invoke—and spend an action on—once combat is already underway. If the PCs are high-level and prepared, the vampire may be destroyed already by the time the bats arrive. So whatever kind of early-warning system the vampire has, at some point, it triggers the vampire's invocation of Children of the Night. Figure that the vampire has at least one or two rings of security which are sufficient to keep out run-of-the-mill intruders: burglars, nosy neighbors, Xander Harris. If an intruder gets past these rings—say, physical security such as a castle wall, plus some mortal guards—the vampire goes on yellow alert and summons the Children of the Night to run extra interference. After the beasts come the vampire spawn, then finally the vampire itself.

The feature summons 2d4 swarms of bats or rats (an average of five, a ceiling of eight) or 3d6 wolves (an average of ten, a ceiling of eighteen). A wolf is a CR 1/4 creature, as is a swarm of bats or rats, so these really are nothing to a serious party of vampire-hunting PCs *except* interference. They buy the vampire time to make other preparations, or maybe lead a party on a chase in the wrong direction, or stand by to assist if the vampire gets into a realio-trulio fight.

A vampire doesn't want to fight an entire party of PCs unless *they're* an easy encounter for *it*. Vampires are smart: It will take one just a single round of combat for it to evaluate whether a party constitutes a deadly threat. It can easily handle three level 7 or 8 PCs, four level 6 PCs, five level 5 PCs, or six or seven PCs of level 4 or lower all by itself; add a couple of levels if the PCs are already good and cut up from previous encounters in the lair, and add several if the vampire is encountered not alone but accompanied by one or more vampire spawn and Children of the Night. If the PCs are this overmatched, the vampire goes for the kill—and takes villainous satisfaction in turning the PCs into obedient vampire spawn. If the PCs are strong enough for the vampire (along with any accompanying allies) to constitute no more than a Hard encounter (see "Encounter Building," *Dungeon Master's Guide*, chapter 3), and they're *not* badly wounded, it abandons its lair and flees to another resting place. (No self-respecting vampire has just one resting place. It always establishes several. The act of trying to establish a new one might be the hook that allows the PCs to track a vampire down.)

The in-between cases are interesting. The vampire won't want to fight toe-to-toe, but it won't be ready to abandon its lair yet either. It will stalk the PCs, looking for opportunities to divide the party and pick off an isolated PC or two.

But I'm getting ahead of myself. When the PCs finally encounter a vampire for the first time, it will be at the moment and place of the vampire's choosing, and it will . . . *greet* them.

Before the vampire gets into any kind of scuffle at all, it wants to size its opponents up, find out what they want, and determine whether they can be bought off somehow. It's compelled to feed, but it also has the Wisdom to delay gratification (avoiding combat now may mean *decades* of undisturbed feeding) and the Intelligence to recognize meaningful tells in the PCs' behavior. It will be courteous, if maybe a bit conceited, and it will try to keep its guests talking for as long as possible. It will even suggest compromises and collaborations that serve both their interests and its own. But it will also keep its eyes and ears open for any sneaky rogue who thinks they can outflank the vampire during the parley and make a Sneak Attack.

Its top priority during this parley is to identify the most weak-willed PC—the one with the lowest Wisdom saving throw, padding elves' modifiers by +4 to account for their racial advantage against being charmed—and use Charm on them *during the conversation*.

At some point during the conversation, when the vampire has had a chance to observe all the PCs and when it seems like it would make sense to have everyone make a Persuasion or Insight check or some such thing, roll a d20 for the vampire and have every player roll one as well. The vampire is making a Stealth check to determine whether it can charm its target without being caught. The target is making a Wisdom saving throw against being charmed. Everyone else is making a Wisdom (Perception) check against the vampire's Dexterity (Stealth) roll to determine whether they spotted the Charm. (You need to know each PC's relevant modifier, so that you don't have to ask. Make this part of your session prep.) If the Charm is successful, the vampire will shortly thereafter slip a quip into the conversation that, taken ironically, sounds like wit, but taken *literally* is a command to the charmed PC to serve and protect the vampire (e.g., "Naturally, I expect all my guests to return my hospitality with absolute, undying loyalty, ha ha!").

Around this time, you'll need to secretly inform the player of the charmed character that they've been charmed. You'll also need to secretly inform any player whose character caught the vampire in the act, "You're pretty sure that vampire put the whammy on Erwan."

If the Charm is successful, and no one else spots it, the vampire may try to charm another PC, then another. It will charm the whole party if it has a decent shot of getting away with it. Then, one by one, it decides whether each PC seems most promising as an agent, a vampire spawn thrall, or a juice box.

The parley can end in any number of ways: The PCs and the vampire may reach an agreement! Or the vampire may manage to charm the whole party. Or, more likely, a PC will get tired of talking and attack; or all the PCs will get tired of talking and attack; or the PCs will insult the vampire, or accuse it outright of trying to charm their companion(s), and the vampire will attack; or the vampire will gain all the information it needs, decide the party is too strong to fight head-on, and vanish into a cloud of mist.

If combat ensues and the vampire goes first, it doesn't attack immediately; instead, it takes the Dodge action, allowing the PCs to come to it so that it has a chance to assess their combat skill. When one PC comes within melee reach and attacks, it uses its Unarmed

Strike legendary action against that PC at the end of their turn. When a second PC comes within melee reach and attacks, it does the same thing. If a *third* PC comes within melee reach and attacks, however, the vampire uses its third legendary action to Move away from its attackers without provoking an opportunity attack—climbing a wall if there's not enough space to simply retreat. After the first round of combat, the vampire renders its judgment about the strength of the PCs and either flees its lair, retreats temporarily, or goes for the kill.

If it decides to go for the kill, it does so in the manner of the vampire spawn, using its Multiattack to grapple, then Bite, and reacting in the same manner to a failed grapple. But it specifically chooses the PC with the lowest Athletics or Acrobatics skill (whichever of the two is higher) within reach of its movement, not counting the charmed PC, because this is the quickest way to remove enemies from the equation. A vampire that has judged itself capable of defeating an entire party without difficulty will feed on them without compunction, but if attacked while grappling a victim, it will strike its attacker for damage twice—as opposed to striking, then feeding, as a vampire spawn would. It will also use its legendary actions to drain its grappled victim faster and to land one additional Unarmed Strike on anyone who attacks it. It doesn't try to drag its victim away from the fight—it tries to *finish* the fight.

If it decides to flee, it Shapechanges into mist and exits the scene, leaving any charmed PCs behind to run interference.

If it decides to retreat but not flee, it Shapechanges into a bat and flies out of the room. This is misdirection: As soon as it's out of sight, it changes out of bat form and into mist form, then circles back around and stealthily follows the party. When convenient, it rematerializes in a place of concealment where it will be able to whisper commands to a charmed PC. When it can do so, it tells the charmed PC to sneak off from the party, find a hiding place, and wait for further instructions. Then it turns into mist again and reassesses its odds. If it can reduce the party in this way to a number of foes that it can handle more easily, it goes in for the kill.

A vampire uses its Legendary Resistance anytime it fails a saving throw. Its saving throw modifiers are so good to begin with that failures will be rare, so it's not going to worry about conserving its three daily uses of this feature.

Whatever else it's up to, a vampire doesn't like being hit with radiant damage or holy water at all (because these suppress its Regeneration), and it will use its legendary action Move to get away from a PC who's inflicting these discomforts on it. If it can't get away from that PC, it grapples them instead and tries to eliminate the problem by eating it.

To vanquish a vampire that's sized up its odds and decided to fight, the PCs will have to reduce it to 57 hp or fewer and do so, at least in part, with radiant damage or holy water. At that point, the seriously wounded vampire takes stock. Do the PCs seem to know that it's necessary to stake a vampire in order to destroy it in its resting place? Do they already know where its resting place is? Can it survive another round of damage at the rate they're dealing it? Are any of the PCs close to elimination? If the answers to these questions are on balance unfavorable to the vampire, it gives up and flees its lair. If they're favorable, it keeps on fighting, relying on Misty Escape to ward off absolute defeat—but the more PCs who are successfully inflicting damage on the vampire, the more likely it is to choose Dodge as its action, rather than attack, and to use only its legendary actions to inflict damage on the PCs.

The **warrior vampire** differs from an ordinary vampire (as if any vampire were ordinary) in that it wears plate armor, wields a greatsword, and has the additional Multiattack option of making two melee attacks with that sword. What does this change?

Well, certainly, there's no reason for a vampire to become stupidly reckless simply because it's wearing a tin can and waving a poker. Nor is it going to deviate from its basic desire: to maintain its ability to feed without interference.

The fact that its increased Armor Class and its greater weapon damage output place it in a higher challenge rating bracket (CR 15 rather than CR 13) does mean it can take on a stronger group of enemies than other vampires can, and this factors into its decision whether to fight, flee, or parley. But the biggest difference lies in how the warrior vampire approaches melee combat itself.

The standard vampire attack, once the vampire's decided it's no longer playing around, is a two-parter: first, an unarmed strike with intent to grapple; second, a bite that does both piercing and necrotic damage, the latter of which restores hit points to the vampire. The first does no damage; the second does an average of 18 damage, while giving the vampire an average of 10 hp back.

A dual Greatsword attack, by comparison, does an average of 22 damage, assuming both hits land, and restores no hit points. (We don't have to worry about hit probabilities, because the attack modifier is the same +9 no matter what method of attack the vampire is using.) On top of this, a vampire that's holding a big sword in both hands is in no position to grapple anybody—not without dropping that sword on the ground, or at least giving up its ability to attack with it. So a vampire that's chosen to wield a sword is committing to a particular endgame: It's trying to *kill* its enemies, *not* feed on them or spawnify them. A living victim is full of juicy potential; a chopped-up corpse is of no use or interest anymore.

How does the vampire decide which path to follow? Once again, think like a predator. Predators, hunting social animals, attack the weak, not the strong. A warrior vampire defending itself against stronger opponents is *fighting*, not *hunting*: It uses the sword. By doing so, it forfeits the opportunity to restore its own hit points by feeding. But it has no real choice but to make this trade-off. It has to hope that its extra two points of AC are enough to prevent the damage it would otherwise restore.

On the other hand, a warrior vampire confident that it's more powerful than its foes and looking forward to making a meal of them is better off not drawing its sword, instead using the standard vampire grapple/Bite combo. If at some point it realizes it's underestimated the opposition, it may then choose to draw its sword after all and fight that way instead. Once it's made that choice, it sticks with it to the end.

At this point, you may be asking yourself whether the warrior vampire is all that much of an improvement over the vanilla vampire. I think the answer is: not really. It's a variant; it's not an *elite* variant. Use it if and when you want a vampire to wear plate armor and wield a sword.

The **spellcaster vampire** is a different matter. This one's spell repertoire gives it a variety of extra tricks it can use to take its enemies down. From most to least powerful:

- *Dominate person* is big, and it's the only thing the spellcaster vampire uses its 5th-level spell slot for. It has twice the range of the vampire's innate Charm ability, removes the target's free will, and gives the vampire "total and precise control" over the target if it wishes. The downside is that the saving throw is slightly easier to make, and if combat is already underway, the target will probably get to make that roll with advantage. In this situation, it's better for stopping an opponent in their tracks than it is for getting that opponent to *do* things on the vampire's behalf. But if the vampire can cast this spell before fighting breaks out—or later on, during a lull in the action—it can be potent. It doesn't explicitly make the target a willing target for a Bite attack, but I'd say that a command along the lines of "Let me bite you" would suffice.

- *Blight* is a powerful single-target attack that's especially good at taking out glass-cannon enemies around the periphery of the battle, who typically rely on Dexterity rather than Constitution as their primary defensive ability. It does a whopping 36 average damage on a failed save, half on a success; this means you can reasonably expect to do around 27 damage and can potentially deal up to 64. Also, it's necrotic, which is thematically appropriate.

- *Greater invisibility* is an even better evasive maneuver than the vanilla vampire's Shapechanger ability.

- *Animate dead* is one of those spells that, perversely, is more useful for PCs than for NPC villains: An NPC reduced to 0 hp is dead by default, but a PC reduced to 0 hp is merely dying. On the other hand, the kind of vampire that studies wizardry is probably also the kind that has a corpse storage room in its house. Unless it's in this room, it probably won't have the opportunity to cast this spell—but if it *does* get the opportunity, it will do so without hesitation, and if it has the opportunity to cast it on *three* dead targets, it will use a 4th-level slot to cast it.

- *Bestow curse* is expensive, in terms of action economy, for what it gives the caster, but there's one situation in which it becomes particularly useful for a vampire: The target of the spell is grappled (and therefore already being touched), any incoming attacks are largely ineffectual, and the vampire *really* wants to spawnify the target it's grappling. In this instance (and only in this instance, really), it's worth it to spend one action to cast *bestow curse*, choosing the bonus necrotic damage die option. This option speeds up the rate at which the vampire's Bite drains the target's hit points, which also has the effect of fortifying the vampire. This spell is actually most effective outside combat, if and when the vampire can lure a charmed victim to a place of privacy.

- *Nondetection* is how a fleeing vampire keeps its pursuers from tracking it.

- *Detect thoughts* might be superficially useful during parley, except that anyone can tell that the vampire is casting a spell, so the element of surprise is blown. If the vampire can get a charmed person alone, however, it can use *detect thoughts* to read its mind without undesirable repercussions.

- *Gust of wind* can be used to blow out all the torches in the room just before the vampire flees. Or it could just cast *greater invisibility*.

- *Mirror image* is the first thing a spellcaster vampire does when combat breaks out. It's all upside, no downside.

- *Comprehend languages* is a ritual for a situation that probably won't even come up.

- *Fog cloud* can slow a fleeing vampire's pursuers. Additionally, a *very* sneaky vampire can cast *fog cloud*, then change shape into mist form (it has to cast the spell first, since it can't take actions in mist form) and float through the cloud, indistinguishable from it, before re-manifesting and doing something nasty to whoever's next to it. There's no point in using a higher-level spell slot to boost it.

- *Sleep* is not going to be of any use against PCs of a high enough level to go vampire hunting.
- *Mage hand*, *prestidigitation*, and *ray of frost* are pretty inconsequential, although *ray of frost* can do 2d8 cold damage (an average of 9) to an opponent out of the vampire's reach.

Nothing in this repertoire alters the vampire's fundamental strategy of preying on the weak, fleeing from the strong, and trying to strike bargains with its equals. Except for *dominate person* and *blight*, these spells are mostly damage-control measures, but some of them (*greater invisibility*, *mirror image*, *fog cloud*, and to a lesser extent, *nondetection*) are quite good damage-control measures. In particular, *mirror image* is a good substitute for the turn in which the vampire would otherwise make temporizing Unarmed Strikes in order to get a sense of its opponents' capabilities.

LICHES

The **lich** (rhymes with "itch," not "ick" or German *ich*) stands out not only as the alpha undead creature going all the way back to AD&D but also as the only type of undead creature that's undead because it *wanted* to be. It's what you get when a wizard decides they want to be immortal, reads the fine print on the contract, and says, "Yeah, I'm down with that." To become a lich to begin with, a wizard must necessarily be monomaniacal, as well as malicious, sadistic, and/or vengeful, and the transformation of undeath intensifies these traits. A wizard who becomes a lich must also necessarily be a genius and a world-class spellcaster, and the lich retains these traits as well.

Although it has only the Strength of an average humanoid, all of a lich's other ability scores are exceptional, most of all its Intelligence. It gets sizable bonuses to Constitution, Intelligence, and Wisdom saving throws (notice that two of the "big three" are in that bunch); resists cold, lightning, and necrotic damage; and is immune to poison damage and to physical damage from nonmagical weapons. It can't be charmed, frightened, paralyzed, or poisoned, and it never suffers

MIX IT UP!

Years ago, I read a book titled (I swear I'm not making this up) *Sherlock Holmes vs. Dracula, or The Adventures of the Sanguinary Count*. It was written by Loren Estleman in the style of Arthur Conan Doyle, and as I recall, it was less cheesy and far more entertaining than you might assume . . . although I don't think I've read it since I was in college, so take that with a grain of salt.

Anyway, there's one bit of that novel that sticks in my mind as being particularly cool: At one point, Dracula walks right into Holmes's room, in the middle of the day, and Holmes expresses surprise that Dracula can go out in broad daylight. Oh, sure I can, Dracula says; it's just that I don't have any of my supernatural powers when I do.

I thought that was an interesting spin on vampire abilities. One of the crucial elements of horror is exploiting the fear of the unknown: We're most afraid of a monster when we're not sure what it is, what it can do, or how far it can pursue us. One of the best ways to spice up a D&D game is to take familiar monsters and give them unfamiliar powers, or have the familiar powers manifest in unfamiliar ways. Trolls, for example, are great for this: Use the variant that allows severed limbs to keep moving and even fighting independently, have the troll periodically pick up its limbs and stick them back onto itself, and watch your players wig out. (As I mention on page 258, this version of the troll originated with a scene in *Three Hearts and Three Lions* by Poul Anderson.)

It's so taken for granted in our popular culture that vampires are burned by sunlight, the thought of a vampire who's merely weakened by it, not hurt—let alone destroyed—would never occur to most of us. The vampire in the *Monster Manual* is the conventional burned-by-sunlight variety, but what if you removed that weakness and substituted one that merely disabled the vampire's special traits in daylight?

Try this sort of variation out—if not with a vampire, then with some other monster whose powers players assume they already know.

from exhaustion. It has truesight—the ability to see in darkness, into the ether, and through illusions, transmutations, and invisibility—out to a range of 120 feet, along with a passive Perception of 19. And it's proficient in both Perception and Insight, so not only does it notice you're there, it knows what you want.

A lich receives additional powerful lair actions when it's encountered in its lair. Why, then, would it ever leave? It won't, if it can help it. No lich ever leaves its lair unless it must, in order to do something that it can't get an agent to do for it.

Follow-up question: Who on earth would sign up to be an agent of a lich? Well, who on earth would sign up to be an agent of Adolf Hitler? The answer is, someone of like mind—in the case of a lich, another evil wizard hoping to gain access to its voluminous reservoir of arcane knowledge. Or someone who considers the lich's long-term goals to be aligned with their own. Or someone who fears the lich's power and hopes that they can earn privileged treatment by showing sufficient loyalty and obedience. (Spoiler: not likely.) Or, barring all that, someone whom the lich has magically dominated. Agents of a lich must be powerful enough for it to consider them useful, and they'll generally be ambitious enough for service to a lich to seem like a reasonable arrangement.

Aside from its spells, what powerful features does a lich possess?

- Legendary Resistance, which lets it reroll a failed saving throw. Like a vampire, a lich fails saving throws so rarely that it invokes Legendary Resistance anytime this happens, without worrying about conserving its three daily uses.
- Turn Resistance, which gives it advantage on its Wisdom saving throws against the Turn Undead feature . . . which it has +9 on to begin with. " 'Begone, unholy abomination'? Oh, that's so cute."
- Rejuvenation, which means that "destroying" it is only a temporary setback unless its phylactery (read: horcrux) is also destroyed.
- Legendary actions that include Frightening Gaze, Disrupt Life, an additional use of its basic Paralyzing Touch attack, and lobbing a cantrip (probably *ray of frost*, since its other two cantrips lack direct combat applications).
- Lair actions that include summoning a spirit to inflict a whopping 15d6 of necrotic damage; "grounding" itself to a PC, so that the PC takes half the damage that the lich would have taken; and regenerating a spell slot.

What we have here is a picture of a creature that has no reason to fear anyone or anything. No reason that it knows of, anyway.

Does a lich think you may become a threat someday? Then it will destroy you before you get that strong.

Does a lich have a use for you? Then it will use you, up until you're no longer useful. Also, you may be more useful dead. Or undead.

Does a lich have no use for you? Then it will kill you without a second thought, if killing you advances its goals in some way. Otherwise, you're not relevant to its interests.

Does a lich like you? No. A lich doesn't like anybody.

For such a powerful spellcaster, the lich has an odd dearth of spell slots at 6th level and above—just one of each level between 6th and 9th. It won't be using any of these slots to boost lower-level spells. It needs to reserve them for spells of those levels.

- *Power word kill* is the lich's nuclear option. It gets to cast it only once. How does it choose a target? Fun fact: This spell automatically affects any target with 100 hp or fewer—and automatically fails otherwise. At the levels where PCs will feel confident taking on a lich, who's still going to have 100 hp or fewer? Squishy spellcasters, that's who, at least until the battle has been going on for a while. And whom will a lich see as its most credible rivals? Other spellcasters, especially other wizards. So the top priority target for this spell is the highest-level wizard in the party, followed by the highest-level warlock or draconic sorcerer, then either the highest-level cleric or druid or the second-highest-level wizard or warlock, whichever seems at that point to pose the greatest threat while still having 100 hp or fewer.

    Why not a Wild Magic sorcerer? Because to a lich, a Wild Magic sorcerer isn't a "real" mage, just a punk! It has nothing but disdain for Wild Magic sorcerers and refuses to consider them worthy of killing with a single word. Only if it's wiped out the "real" spellcasters in the party already, or there weren't any to start with, will a lich consider casting *power word kill* on a PC who's a non-spellcaster, a half-caster, or a Wild Magic sorcerer.

- *Dominate monster* affects any visible *creature* within range, not just any "monster." Since there's unlikely to be any monster in a lich's lair that it doesn't already control, it will cast this spell on a PC that it considers—well, let's not put too fine a point on it, a "nobody." But a strong nobody, with average or below-average Wisdom, so that they're more susceptible to domination, as well as capable enough to be useful to the lich. Rival wizards are for killing; attacking fighters are for dominating and turning against their own companions. (Liches are intelligent enough to know that a raging berserker barbarian can't be charmed; they won't make the mistake of trying.)

- *Power word stun* is a temporary measure that affects any target with 150 hp or fewer and automatically fails otherwise. It requires a Constitution saving throw to resist, so it's not going to be much good against a high-level melee fighter. If there's a glass cannon in the PCs' party, they're the prime target of this spell.

- *Finger of death* is another potential glass cannon smasher, but it's also useful against tougher targets that have taken a lot of damage, because it inflicts an average 30 damage even on a successful Constitution save. (Against a failed save, it does an average 61 damage.) Plus, if a character is killed outright by this spell—meaning the overspill damage, beyond what's necessary to reduce a character to 0 hp, must equal or exceed that character's hit point maximum—their corpse is raised as a zombie, adding insult to catastrophic injury. Probably, then, the lich will wait to use this spell until it can finish someone off with it.

- *Plane shift* is an unnecessary escape hatch, since the lich also has the lower-level *dimension door* and more 4th-level spell slots than 7th-level. More likely, if a lich uses this spell, it will be to banish an enemy to another plane. It requires a Charisma saving throw, and we all know how often Charisma is chosen as a dump stat.

- *Disintegrate* delivers an average 75 direct damage on a failed Dexterity saving throw—but nothing on a successful save. Consequently, a lich doesn't waste this spell on a PC who's likely to make their Dex save. Instead, it reserves this spell for obviously clumsy targets or inanimate obstacles, or to knock down magically generated force fields.

- *Globe of invulnerability* is the lich's way of showing weaker spellcasters how pathetic they are. It requires concentration to sustain, making it incompatible with *cloudkill*. Consequently, it uses this spell situationally, not as a default defense.

- *Cloudkill* is a sustained spell, requiring concentration, that lobs a rolling cloud of poisonous gas, 40 feet in diameter, that does an average of 22 poison damage to creatures that fail their Constitution saving throws and half that to those that succeed. It can cast it up to three times, but it's also incompatible with *globe of invulnerability*.
- *Scrying* is a 10-minute ritual, not combat-relevant.
- *Blight* does an average 36 direct necrotic damage to creatures that fail their Con saves, half that on a success. But it's strictly short-range, good only within 30 feet of the caster. Is it better than the lich's Paralyzing Touch attack, which gets +12 to hit, does an average 10 cold damage on a hit, and has a strong chance of paralyzing the target for one or more rounds? I think it is, considering that paralysis is also subject to a Con save.
- *Dimension door* is the lich's escape hatch, in case *invisibility* doesn't do the trick. It will always keep one 4th-level spell slot in reserve for this spell. Sure, it can survive being reduced to 0 hp, but it's such an inconvenience.
- *Animate dead* is only good if you're standing right over a corpse. Meh. Of course, if you've just *created* one . . .
- *Counterspell* is one of three spells competing hard for the use of the lich's three 3rd-level spell slots. If the lich is sustaining a *globe of invulnerability*, *counterspell* is redundant—low-level spells can't get through the *globe*. But if not, *counterspell* is necessary to slap them away.
- *Dispel magic* is another competitor for those 3rd-level slots. If the PCs are buffed by a continuous spell of 3rd level or lower, shut it down. Even with a +5 Intelligence modifier, the lich's chances of dispelling a 4th-level or higher spell aren't that great—around fifty-fifty—and the lich will hesitate to spend a slot plus an action on a spell without at least a two-thirds

chance of success. But the higher-level spell slots to boost this spell just aren't plentiful enough.

- *Fireball*—there's the Dex-save direct damage we were waiting for! Combine a few PCs incapacitated by Paralyzing Touch with a *power word stun*, then drop a *fireball* on the lot, and presto—adventurer barbecue. The lich has no better attack combo than this. Is it worth it to boost the *fireball* by spending a 4th- or 5th-level spell slot to cast it? In my opinion, not really: Each extra spell level adds only 2 or 3 expected damage per target caught in the blast, and each higher-level spell slot spent is one fewer chance to cast *cloudkill* or *blight*. But it depends on the party makeup. *Fireball* works better against a high-Con, low-Dex party. Against a low-Con, high-Dex party, *cloudkill* and *blight* are more effective. If the party is balanced, the lich errs toward taking out the "real" threats: the spellcasters.
- *Detect thoughts* has no combat application.
- *Invisibility* is the kind of spell the lich needs to cast only when things have already gone unfathomably wrong. It considers casting this spell only when it's seriously wounded (reduced to 54 hp or fewer) and isn't ready to give up the fight entirely yet. (If it thinks it really does need to bug out—most likely because the PCs are able to detect invisible beings—it casts *dimension door*.) Nevertheless, it keeps a 2nd-level spell slot reserved for it, just in case.
- *Melf's acid arrow* is a lame spell, and it's out of character for the lich to have it prepared.
- *Mirror image*, as far as the lich is concerned, is a cheap parlor trick. But if the party manages to inflict at least moderate damage (41 or more) on it in a single round, it will get over its prejudice right quick.
- *Detect magic*—not applicable.
- *Magic missile*—If a lich is reduced to casting *magic missile*, this battle has already gone on as ludicrously long as the brawl be-

tween "Rowdy" Roddy Piper and Keith David in *They Live*. No reason at all to cast it at a higher level.

- *Shield*, on the other hand, is as automatic for a wizard as yanking your foot back when you drop a pair of scissors. It casts this as a reaction whenever an attacker rolls between 17 and 21 to hit or casts *magic missile*.
- *Thunderwave* I can imagine casting at some absurdly high level—say, 4th or 5th—to deter melee attackers from getting close. But let's get real: It requires a Constitution saving throw to resist. Obviously, melee attackers are going to have high Cons. Even at 4th or 5th level, *thunderwave* isn't going to impress anybody—not with expected damage of 14 to 18. Compare this to the lich's Disrupt Life legendary action, which does about the same amount of necrotic damage to *everyone within 20 feet*, and it's comical that this spell was included in the lich's list at all.
- *Mage hand* and *prestidigitation*—only if the lich is so utterly unimpressed by the PCs that it wants to waste an action on tapping their shoulders to say, "Hey, look behind you!"
- *Ray of frost*, on the other hand, is a realio-trulio combat spell when slung by an 18th-level spellcaster, doing 4d8 cold damage and reducing the target's movement speed by 10 feet. For a cantrip that doesn't expend a single spell slot, that's a heck of a deal.

Notice something missing here? Bonus actions. A lich gets legendary actions, and it can cast *shield* or *counterspell* as a reaction, but on its *own* turn, it only ever gets to do one thing, and that one thing can be Paralyzing Touch, or it can be casting a spell. If it wants to do both, it has to cast the spell on its turn, then spend two legendary actions on the Paralyzing Touch. If a lich has any weakness, here it is: It's slow, and it has almost too many options, considering how few opportunities it gets to act.

Actually, a lich has one other weakness, and that's its arrogance. When the PCs first encounter it, unless things have already happened along the way to prove to the lich that they're a force to be reckoned with, it won't believe at first that they pose any threat to it, so it won't break out immediately with its 6th- through 9th-level spells (each of which, remember, it gets only one use of).

So what's the first thing a lich does when combat breaks out? That depends on how many PCs it's facing and where they are, but a likely opening play is to cast *cloudkill*. The cloud of gas is 40 feet in diameter, and the lich itself is immune to poison damage, so it casts this spell at ground zero, thereby maximizing the amount of time the PCs—in particular, any PCs who might try to engage the lich in melee—have to spend in it. How the PCs react to this spell will tell the lich certain things about what they're capable of. Are certain PCs obviously less affected by the spell than others? They're probably ones not to target with future Con-based spells. Is there a spellcaster who counters *cloudkill* with *counterspell*, *dispel magic*, or *gust of wind*? That one's clever and should be eliminated quickly.

This assumes that the lich gets to act before any of the PCs does. If a PC goes first, the lich answers a ranged weapon attack from 60 feet away or closer with a *ray of frost* cantrip (one legendary action) and a melee attack with a Frightening Gaze (two legendary actions), since anyone attacking a lich in melee is likely to have more Constitution than Wisdom. A second melee attack will leave the lich without enough legendary actions to use Frightening Gaze again, so it waits until its turn to strike back by casting *blight*. A *third* melee attack means stronger measures than *blight* are called for, so the lich casts *cloudkill* on its turn, followed by the Disrupt Life legendary action at the end of the next PC's turn if it still has three or more melee attackers surrounding it, or four or more of any kind of foe within 20 feet.

Its actions on subsequent rounds depend in part on the opposition it faces. Specifically, how does it decide which spell to spend its 6th-, 7th-, or 8th-level slot on?

- Who's causing the lich more trouble: a high-Wisdom, low-Constitution spellcaster; or a low-Wisdom, high-Constitution frontline fighter? If the former, take it out with *power word stun*. If the latter, take control of it with *dominate monster*. (When in doubt, lean toward *dominate monster*—then send the front-liner after the spellcaster.)

- Who's causing the lich more trouble: a high–hit point, low-Charisma fighter, barbarian, or ranger; or a low-Constitution, high-damage character who's already taken a hit or two? If the former, use *plane shift* to banish them to Thanatos (or, if the lich has a wicked sense of humor, to whatever plane represents the polar opposite of the PC's alignment—see "The Outer Planes" in chapter 2 of the *Dungeon Master's Guide*). If the latter, *finger of death* should erase that problem. (When in doubt, lean toward *finger of death*. The best answer to a glass cannon is to smash it.)

- Which is causing the lich more trouble: a group of persistent casters plinking it with low-level spells; a barrier of magical force; or a slow, ungainly brute? If the first, and *cloudkill* has already run its course, toss up a *globe of invulnerability*. If one of the latter two, zot that nuisance with *disintegrate*. (When in doubt, lean toward *globe of invulnerability*, since its effect can be sustained.)

If none of these things poses a particular problem to the lich at the moment, it uses its action to cast a suitable lower-level spell. *Fireball* is the go-to if two or more of the lich's opponents are already paralyzed, especially if it can catch at least four in the blast; *blight* against a high-priority target that's less than 30 feet away but not within melee reach; *dispel magic* to remove low-level buffs from the PCs; *mirror image* if the PCs hit for at least moderate damage (41 or more) in any given round.

And if none of these situations applies? Then the lich goes after the target it considers the biggest threat—that is, the PC with the highest Intelligence, adjusted by –2 for half-casters and –4 for non-spellcasters (and Wild Magic sorcerers). If it's already engaged in melee with this target PC, it attacks with Paralyzing Touch. If it's not engaged in melee with its priority target but is engaged in melee with other PCs, it Disengages and moves up to its full movement speed toward its priority target, closing to melee reach if it can. If it's not engaged in melee at all, it moves up to its full movement speed toward that target, then attacks with Paralyzing Touch if it can reach its target; if it can't, but it's within 30 feet, it casts *blight*; and if it's between 30 and 60 feet away, it casts *ray of frost*. If it doesn't have to Disengage, and the target is more than 30 feet away, it uses its action to Dash. The lich is willing to forgo attacking on its own turn because its legendary actions allow it to attack on others' turns.

As for the legendary actions, as previously mentioned, it uses the Disrupt Life legendary action at the first opportunity if it has three or more melee attackers surrounding it, or four or more of any kind of foe within 20 feet. If not, but a low-Wisdom PC ends their turn within 10 feet of the lich, it uses Frightening Gaze against them (if it hasn't already failed against that PC previously). If neither of those things happens, but a PC ends their turn within melee reach of the lich, it uses Paralyzing Touch against them. And if none of those things happens, and the number of PCs with turns left is equal to or less than the number of legendary actions the lich can still take, it casts the *ray of frost* cantrip at a target of opportunity.

Finally, there are its lair actions. Each round, it gets to choose one to use on initiative count 20, never using the same one two rounds in a row. It uses the "roll a d8, regain a spell slot" lair action after each spell of 6th, 7th, or 8th level it casts. Otherwise, it alternates between the other two actions, using them against whichever enemy it considers its top priority, favoring the "grounding tether" lair action if it's within melee reach of any PC and the "necrotic apparitions" lair action if it's not.

The lich always keeps one 2nd-level spell slot and one 4th-level spell slot in reserve: the former for *invisibility*, if it's reduced to 54 hp or fewer and considering retreat, and the latter for *dimension door*, in case *invisibility* isn't enough to give its foes the slip.

Every encounter with a lich on its own terms should be frustrating and unsatisfying and end with the lich's escape. You want to destroy a lich? Forget about fighting it and go after its phylactery instead. When the PCs get near it, the lich will show up and unleash every power it has in order to defend it. Then, if the PCs are equal to the task, they'll have it over a barrel: It can't flee, knowing that if it does, there will be nothing to stop them from destroying its phylactery. It will have to fight until it's destroyed, and with the destruction of the phylactery, it will finally be no more.

DEMILICHES

Demiliches have the same compulsion—the will to power and immortality—as liches, but unless they've shed their bodies willingly, there's an additional element to their character: frustration. They've forgotten to feed their phylacteries, or they've been prevented some-how from doing so. As a result, the immortality they worked so hard to attain has cheapened. They've lost their sense of purpose and their ability to cast spells. They may even have forgotten that they can regain their physicality by feeding new souls to their phylacteries. If reminded of this fact, they'll forget every other concern and fixate on restoring themselves to lichdom. (Strangely, neither the demilich's stat block nor its flavor text explains how a soul is fed to its phylactery. Seems like kind of an important omission.) As long as this memory is lost to them, however, they'll act with malice, tinged with the occa-sional random miscalculation that stress produces.

Aside from the lack of spellcasting, a demilich differs from a lich in the following ways:

- Lacking a body, it has no Strength and reduced Constitution. Weirdly, its Wisdom and Charisma are *higher*. I guess the ex-perience of failure does teach us things, and there is something mesmerizing about a floating skull that one still attached to a withered body lacks.
- It has proficiency in Charisma saving throws, making it harder to banish.
- Although it possesses the normal susceptibility to cold and lightning damage, it's now immune to necrotic and psy-

chic damage, and it resists physical damage even from *magic* weapons.

- In addition to the lich's condition immunities, it can't be deafened, petrified, knocked prone, or stunned.
- It no longer has proficiency in any skills, and its passive Perception is correspondingly lower.
- Its Turn Resistance is dialed up to Turn Immunity, and the Avoidance trait lets it dodge some or all damage from effects that require saving throws.
- Since it can't touch anything any longer, its Paralyzing Touch is replaced by a terrifying, potentially heart-stopping Howl and a hit point–Hoovering Life Drain. Like Paralyzing Touch, both of these features target Constitution.
- Its legendary and lair actions are completely different.

Although it's missing from the stat block, a demilich does possess the lich's Rejuvenation trait, except that its skull re-forms minus a body (this is specified in the flavor text, in the paragraph titled "Enduring Existence").

The upshot of these changes, behaviorally? Well, the main takeaway is that demiliches are *even more fearless* than liches. Although their raw damage output may be lower thanks to their lack of spellcasting, they're so impervious to so many ways in which one might try to harm them that any attempt to do so is nothing more than a nuisance. But a demilich, which has a hard enough time just unliving with itself, rids itself of nuisances by annihilating them. The name of the game is *overreaction*. No matter what the provocation, a demilich reacts with the most extreme and violent means available to it.

Legendary Resistance is the "Get Out of Failed Saving Throw Free" card. But since the demilich is proficient in four out of six saving throws, and two out of the big three, it uses this specifically to undo failed Dexterity saves—every time. (It could use them to undo Strength saves, but why bother? Failed Strength saves rarely do anything other than move you from one place to another.)

Howl is on recharge, so we can conclude that this action is always the demilich's first choice. Since it affects targets within a 30-foot radius, it always precedes this action by moving to a point where as many of its foes as possible, ideally six or more, fall within this circle. If it has to choose between two or more points, the tiebreaker is whichever point includes the opponent(s) who can bypass its resistances and immunities—i.e., those that can deal acid, cold, force, lightning, radiant, and/or thunder damage. Usually, this means spellcasters. Remember, despite its madness, the demilich is still a supra-genius. Its primary consideration is identifying the worst things its opponents can do to it, then preempting them.

Life Drain is what the demilich does when it can't Howl. First, it uses its movement to bring itself within 10 feet of three enemies if possible, two if it can't reach three, and one if it can't reach two, using the same target selection criteria as it does for Howl. Then it lets loose with the life-leeching.

After the first Life Drain attempt, if the demilich has realized it should be trying to get its phylactery back online, at least one of its targets will always be someone that it's successfully Life Drained already—but if it didn't successfully Life Drain anyone on its first attempt, it will move on to an entirely new set of targets, hoping for better results. Once an opponent is reduced to 0 hp by Life Drain, let's say that using Life Drain on it one more time absorbs the opponent's soul, and from there the demilich speeds off in the direction of its phylactery to make a deposit. (If the demilich *doesn't* recall that feeding its phylactery can restore its corporeal form, it continues with the default target selection criteria.)

Legendary actions take place on other creatures' turns, and the demilich gets three between each of its turns. The demilich uses Flight either to get out of range of an enemy who does one or more of the damage types listed above or to speed its departure toward its phylactery. Cloud of Dust blinds all creatures within a 10-foot radius; there's no reason ever to use this on just a single target. Energy Drain costs two actions and has a 30-foot radius, so as with Howl, the demilich wants to be in range of as many opponents as possible—at least six, or if it's facing fewer than six opponents, all of them. Otherwise, the cost isn't worth it.

Vile Curse is a tricky one, because the curse imposes disadvantage on attack rolls and saving throws. This means it's of little use against opponents who attack using spells or other effects that require saving throws, i.e., most spellcasters. It costs *three* actions, which is huge, so the demilich has to be absolutely positive that it's choosing the right target. It uses Vile Curse *only* to shut down an enemy who (a) relies mostly or exclusively on weapon or spell attacks that (b) do acid, cold, force, lightning, radiant, or thunder damage, and who (c) is the *only* one of the demilich's enemies who poses any real threat to it.

Then again, the demilich is insane with anger and frustration, so maybe, just maybe, it uses Vile Curse as a reflex action against an enemy who hits it with a weapon or spell attack that does one of those types of damage, wasting its other legendary actions on an act of reckless, irrational fury. We can't rule these things out.

Demiliches are unusual among legendary monsters in that they get to use their lair actions only half the time, on average. They're subject to the common restraint of being unable to use the same lair action two rounds in a row. The *antimagic field* is the most broadly useful of the three, completely shutting down a key enemy spellcaster for a full round. The healing suppression option is a good second choice if the demilich's opponents include a cleric, druid, paladin, or bard. The trembling ground is only good for messing up front-line melee fighters and skirmishers who rely on direct engagement.

At this point in its unlife, a demilich is beyond fleeing. If you don't destroy its phylactery, it's just going to come back anyway. And if you do have the power to destroy both its phylactery and its floating bony head, it may as well let you try, because what's left? You're still going to have to work for it, though.

WILL-O'-WISPS

In building effective encounters around **will-o'-wisps**, the "devil lights" of swamps, marshes, and desolate battlefields, it's necessary to bear in mind the prime directive of horror: fear of the unknown. To create suspense, it's best never to name the enemy that the heroes are facing, and to keep them in the dark about what it can do for as long as possible. The number one way to spoil a will-o'-wisp encounter is to tell the players they see will-o'-wisps.

Will-o'-wisps are like fantasy UFOs: They can bob and hover in one place or move up to a zippy 50 feet per round. They're immune to exhaustion, grappling, paralysis, poison, falling prone, restraint, unconsciousness, and lightning damage, and they're resistant to physical damage from nonmagical weapons along with several types of elemental damage. They have darkvision out to a range of 120 feet but shed their own light out to a range of between 10 and 40 feet, although they can also wink in and out of visibility.

Will-o'-wisps have no physical attack. Their Shock attack is a melee spell attack (Wisdom-based, by mathematical inference), and against unconscious opponents, they can follow it up with the nasty Consume Life feature, which has the potential to kill a PC outright. However, between their many resistances and immunities and their preternatural Dexterity of 28, which gives them an Armor Class of 19, they have nothing to fear from a melee opponent.

The first trick for them is to lure victims into coming into contact with them. This is better accomplished when the area is highly obscured by fog, mist, or darkness, and best of all when the PCs are in unfamiliar territory and unsure which way to go. The will-o'-wisp's modus operandi is to move like a person out walking with a lantern or torch, in order to attract the PCs' attention and get them to investigate.

When characters get close enough that they might be able to identify the will-o'-wisp as nothing more than a ball of insubstantial light—figure about 60 feet, unless the area is blanketed by fog, since this is the standard range of PC darkvision—it uses the Invisibility action, which you can assume is always Readied so that it can be used as a reaction, and vanishes. Alternatively, it may drift away from the investigating PCs, luring them toward quicksand or some other

CRAWLING CLAWS

Like Thing from the Addams Family movies (but not the original television series, in which Thing wasn't a disembodied hand but rather a character who remained hidden because all of him *except* his hand was too horrible to look at), the **crawling claw** skitters around independently, performing acts of malice. According to the *Monster Manual* flavor text, it once belonged to a murderer and was reanimated so that it could kill again—and again, and again. Despite being undead, crawling claws behave more like constructs, following the instructions of their creators; their only compulsion, when left to their own devices, is to act out their own past homicides.

Crawling claws are fragile and slow, but their Strength and Dexterity are above average. Their ability contour is that of a shock attacker, which eschews prolonged combat in favor of doing as much damage as possible up front. But their only attack is the Claw action, whose damage is meager. Is there any means of improving it?

Well, for starters, the crawling claw has blindsight. This means it's not hindered by total darkness. Since it isn't, while other creatures are, there's zero reason for it to move around where there's any degree of illumination. In fact, whatever necromancer created the crawling claw should probably cast *darkness* to help it along, because otherwise, its chances of accomplishing much aren't great.

Next, it can climb. If it can climb, it can drop. And if it can drop from someplace unseen, 5 feet or less above its target, it can gain not only a surprise round but also unseen-attacker advantage on its initial attack roll, even against targets with darkvision.

Finally, it has good Dexterity, so even though it lacks proficiency in Stealth, it can still make Dexterity (Stealth) checks with a positive modifier to the roll. And since it moves around only in total darkness, every other creature who might try to spot it using darkvision must do so with disadvantage on their rolls.

This is all the optimization we can squeeze out of this CR 0 creature. It's good for a jump scare, but that's about it.

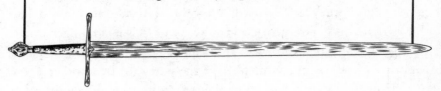

hazard.* When a PC is restrained, prone, incapacitated, blinded by darkness, or under attack by another enemy, the will-o'-wisp moves in swiftly and attacks. It attacks the same target again and again unless and until it's driven off (see below) or the target is dead.

A PC attacking a will-o'-wisp isn't blinded by darkness, because the will-o'-wisp sheds its own light, so they won't have disadvantage on attack rolls unless it's the result of some other debilitating condition, such as being restrained. However, its Armor Class makes it difficult to land an attack. When a PC does score a hit, whether with a weapon or with a spell, the will-o'-wisp goes invisible, then moves away, choosing a different, more immediately vulnerable target on its next turn.

When a PC is rendered unconscious—either by a will-o'-wisp or by another attacker—the will-o'-wisp uses its Consume Life bonus

---

* Relevant fact: In real life, as opposed to the movies, you can't really sink into quicksand and be suffocated. It's dense enough, and you're buoyant enough, that you'll stop sinking when you're about waist-deep. But you can get badly stuck in it. A character who steps into quicksand may be considered grappled immediately and restrained after a round of sinking deeper in, and the more they try aimlessly to get out—as opposed to relaxing, lying down, and patiently backstroking to safety—the harder it will be to pull them free.

action. Even if the PC makes their saving throw, you should still describe this in horrible terms ("Dazed, unable to move or speak or act, you struggle weakly against the will-o'-wisp as you feel it try to suck the life from your body . . ."), to drive home the urgency of rescuing that PC before they fail.

Will-o'-wisps' Wisdom is high enough that they ought to know when to retreat from a battle they're losing, but since undead creatures are cursed with compulsions that defy common-sense survival impulses, there's nothing wrong with choosing to have them keep fighting until they're destroyed. However, I think there are a few things that will make them decide a party of PCs is no longer worth the aggravation: being turned by a cleric; being struck by a magic weapon or spell by every member of the party (or by another party member wielding such every time they try to attack a more vulnerable PC); or being struck repeatedly by force, psychic, or radiant damage, the three types of damage to which they're neither immune nor resistant. When a will-o'-wisp decides to retreat, it simply goes invisible, moves away, and never shows itself to the PCs again.

FLAMESKULLS

Flameskulls weren't among the original undead creatures of D&D; they existed only in supplementary material until the fourth edition, when they first appeared in the *Monster Manual*. I can't help thinking of them as being comical and cartoony (It's a skull! That's on fire! And hovering! *And talking to you!*), but in fact they can be dangerous foes, especially to low-level characters.

Following the *Monster Manual* flavor text, their compulsion is obedience—specifically, to their duty of protecting a place, item, or person. Because they're bound to this duty, they have no self-preservation impulse; if they must fight, they fight till they're destroyed.

And as it happens, it's tough to destroy a flameskull: Its Rejuvenation trait causes it to re-form, fully healed, one hour after being reduced to 0 hp, unless its fragments are cleansed with holy water or a *dispel magic* or *remove curse* spell. So an unhappy party of adventurers may vanquish a flameskull in order to enter a forbidden area, only to find that they have to fight it again on their way out. (Of course, this raises the question of whether a flameskull that's sworn to keep them out of a place has any duty to keep them from *leaving* that place once they've already been in it. Play that one as it lies, Dungeon Master.)

Other features of the flameskull include resistance or immunity to various types of damage and debilitating conditions, magic resistance, spellcasting, and both darkvision and Illumination. This last combination is curious: It can shed light up to 30 feet away, but it can also see in the dark up to 60 feet away. Why would it need both? It doesn't. It's an undead creature, therefore non-evolved, so its abilities don't necessarily have to make sense. But to make what sense we can of it: Darkvision is what the flameskull relies on; Illumination is simply a spooky special effect. I'd say that the flameskull's base state is a dim glow, and that it escalates to a bright glow either to let trespassers know they've been spotted or when it gets its dander up. Either way, these features don't have much bearing on the flameskull's combat tactics, except that it *doesn't* use darkness to hide.

The flameskull's ability scores are almost irrelevant, because it has nothing but ranged magical attacks. The one that does have bearing on its behavior is its Intelligence of 16, because this means it can make smart targeting decisions. Being undead, it knows to prioritize targets who can drive it away from its task (clerics, paladins), along with those who can match it in magical ability (wizards, warlocks, sorcerers, druids).

Its base attack is Fire Ray, which it can use twice per Multiattack action. It has +5 to hit with this ability, doing 3d6 fire damage with each hit. Let's assume that the average low-level adventurer has an Armor Class of 13. That means that the flameskull has a 65 percent chance to hit, and therefore the total expected damage of its Fire Ray Multiattack is 14. (This is assuming, however, that the targets are more than 5 feet away. Fire Ray is a ranged attack, meaning the flameskull has disadvantage on its attack roll if it tries to use it at point-blank range. That reduces its chance to hit to 42 percent and its total expected damage to 9.)

Now let's look at its spells:

- *Fireball* does up to 8d6 instantaneous fire damage to every target in a 20-foot-radius sphere. Going by the area-effect estimates in chapter 8 of the *Dungeon Master's Guide*, we can expect this to catch four targets. Figure that the average low-level adventurer's Dexterity saving throw modifier is +2; this means that a player character has a 50 percent chance to dodge, and therefore the expected damage is 21 per target, or 84 altogether.

- *Flaming sphere* does 2d6 fire damage to creatures within 5 feet of it; however, it does this on the targets' turns, and most intelligent beings, feeling the toasty warmth of a 5-foot ball of fire, will feel the urge to move away from it. Happily, however, *flaming sphere* is a sustained spell that adds bonus actions to the flameskull's action economy—specifically, ramming it into enemies. This also requires a Dexterity save, so the expected damage is 5 per target per turn, over up to 10 turns. (Combat encounters almost never last that long, however—usually they're over within four or five rounds, sometimes in as few as two.)

- *Blur* is also a sustained spell, so it can't be cast at the same time as *flaming sphere*. What would make a flameskull want to cast *blur* instead? Perhaps it's been hit by a weapon or spell attack that dealt one of the types of damage it's neither immune nor resistant to: bludgeoning, slashing, acid, radiant, or thunder.

- *Magic missile* fires three darts of magical force that always hit and that do a total of 10 damage on average—less than a pair of Fire Ray attacks. Cast using a 2nd-level spell slot, it fires four darts for average total damage of 14, and there's a good chance that the flameskull will have a 2nd-level slot available, since it can't sustain both *blur* and *flaming sphere* at the same time.

- *Shield* is a reaction and the no-brainerest of no-brainers in the magical arsenal. Anytime an opponent rolls between 13 and 17 on an attack, the flameskull pops *shield*.

- *Mage hand* is just so that the flameskull can play solitaire when there are no adventurers to scare off.

Scenario: Adventurers show up. Flameskull says, "You! Shall not! Pass!" Adventurers say, "Oh, yeah, we *shall* pass. We're passing." DM says, "Roll for initiative."

First, do the PCs have more than 40 feet of room to move around in? If so, the flameskull knows that they may spread out beyond the range of its *fireball* spell, so it casts this spell before they have a chance to. But if not, the flameskull keeps this spell in reserve, at least for a round, just in case it's not needed.

If one or more PCs act first, and they deal bludgeoning, slashing, acid, radiant, or thunder damage that the flameskull can't block with *shield*, its first action is to cast *blur*. If they don't deal any of these types of damage, or if the flameskull is able to block it, it casts *flaming sphere* instead, and it rams that ball of fire into any PC displaying a holy symbol—clerics first, then paladins—or, barring that, into anyone who looks like a spellcaster. The flameskull also casts *flaming sphere* if it gets to act first, because of the bonus actions it will provide.

On subsequent rounds, when the flameskull has taken moderate damage (reduced to 28 hp or fewer), it decides playtime's over and drops *fireball* on the PCs. Alternatively, if it's cast *flaming sphere*, but it's also taken at least 12 bludgeoning, slashing, acid, radiant, or thunder damage, it rams the *flaming sphere* into a PC one last time (bonus action), then drops *flaming sphere* and casts *blur* (action). Otherwise, it aims two Fire Ray attacks (action) at any PCs not within melee range: clerics first, then paladins, then other spellcasters, then anyone else. If *all* its enemies are engaging it in melee, it casts *magic missile* at the highest available level, distributing the darts among clerics, paladins, and other spellcasters until they're all downed. Whatever action the flameskull takes, it rams its *flaming sphere* (if it's sustaining this spell) into a PC as a bonus action, and from the second round on, it prioritizes PCs who are engaging it in melee (clerics first, then paladins, then anyone else).

The flameskull doesn't retreat or flee, ever, and once it's run out of slots for a spell it would otherwise cast, it simply substitutes the Fire Ray Multiattack action. If it's ever turned, as soon as the turning wears off, it beelines right back to its post and resumes its duties, attacking anyone present if they deserve it.

BANSHEES

Banshees are curious creatures: accursed undead elves, without any clear explanation of who did the cursing. They're the "mean girls" of elvenkind, beautiful but cold, shallow, and manipulative, who instead of remaining eternally youthful become more and more debased and drained of vitality and end up wallowing in empty alienation forever.

Banshees have no physical form, so their only movement is flying, at a brisk 40 feet per round. They have above-average Dexterity and very high Charisma, but owing to their lack of substance, they have virtually no Strength. Thus, it's unlikely that they'll ever engage in prolonged toe-to-toe melee combat; instead, they'll use their ranged powers first, then make hit-and-run attacks. They're not worried about opportunity attacks, because they're resistant to physical damage from nonmagical weapons.

In addition to laughing at mundane iron and steel, banshees are also resistant to acid, fire, lightning, and thunder damage and outright immune to cold, necrotic, and poison damage, along with the vast majority of debilitating conditions. Thus, they have as little to fear from spellcasters as they do from loutish fighters. A magic weapon, on the other hand, puts them on red alert.

Banshees have darkvision, so they're more active at night or in dark places. Also, good luck getting the drop on them: They can sense the presence of living creatures up to 5 miles away. They won't run—their curse binds them to remain where the last flicker of life left them—but they'll know you're coming.

While a banshee may want to prolong its own existence, it's not only unwilling but unable to flee the place where it resides. It may also pick a fight out of rage, but if quick-thinking PCs preemptively appeal to its basic desire—to possess objects of great beauty—a banshee will refrain from attacking and may even be willing to barter for information.

The banshee has three combat actions: Horrifying Visage, Wail, and Corrupting Touch. The first two are effectively usable only once per combat encounter. Horrifying Visage has the greater range, but Wail has the stronger effect. While I like the idea of kicking off combat with Horrifying Visage—a sudden transformation from creepy, ethereal beauty to blood-chilling hideousness—I think Wail has to come first, because a frightened creature can't willingly move closer to the source of its fear. This means that a banshee could frighten an enemy outside the range of its Wail and thereby prevent it from coming within range.

So Wail comes first, and before using it, the banshee plonks itself down right in the midst of its opponents, so that as many of them as possible (ideally, all of them) are within a 30-foot radius of it. The saving throw DC isn't high, but it's not a gimme, either, and any opponent who flubs their save is down for the count, while the rest begin combat an average of 10 hp down. After using Wail, the banshee flies 10 or 15 feet up in the air, out of reach of melee attacks (so make sure its initial relocation doesn't consume more than 25 feet of movement).

Horrifying Visage comes the following round. If it works, it's good till the effect wears off. If it doesn't, it's not going to, so there's no benefit in using this power more than once. While using this ability, the banshee continues to hover in the air, out of melee reach.

Starting in the third combat round, the banshee starts strafing its enemies with Corrupting Touch, flying down to attack, then flying back up out of reach, heedless of opportunity attacks. This time, instead of positioning itself in the midst of its enemies, the tricksy banshee spends its time between turns on the *outside* of the fray, with its victim between it and its other opponents. Since a frightened creature can't move any closer to the source of its fear, a frightened enemy can't come any closer to aid their companion.

For the same reason, the banshee begins by targeting enemy spellslingers, marksmen, and skirmishers—those who are most likely to be positioned far from the center of the battle. Remember, a banshee has no fear of spellcasters, and, if there's any enemy it hates more than any other and needs to take down quickly, it's an archer wielding a magic bow. Other ranged attackers pose a threat, but not as much of one.

Beyond that, other things being equal, a banshee's vanity also generates a furious envy, and it will bear a particular hatred (combined with a weird sort of infatuation and craving) toward any exceptionally attractive person. While peaceful talks are going on, a banshee will listen to such a person more attentively, treat their proposals with greater consideration, and even try to entice them to remain in the banshee's company. As soon as things turn south, the banshee will badly want to destroy that person more than any other.

A banshee that's seriously wounded (reduced to 23 hp or fewer) won't flee its home, but it will begin acting more erratically and irrationally—attacking foes at random, grabbing objects and hurling them, using its movement to loop and careen around in a frenzy, trying to seize items of jewelry from its opponents. This happens especially if its only remaining foes are wielding magic melee weapons, which it's afraid to come within reach of.

Can a banshee be male? In legend, no. The word "banshee" comes from Irish *bean sí,* "fairy-mound woman"; there's no male equivalent. And the *Monster Manual* defines the banshee as "a spiteful creature formed from the spirit of a *female* elf" (emphasis mine). It's funny, though, that beyond that, the *Monster Manual* is silent on the subject. Two paragraphs later, it says, "Banshees are the undead remnants of elves who, blessed with great beauty, failed to use their gift to bring joy to the world." Not "female elves," as in the first paragraph—just "elves." So in principle, there doesn't seem to be any reason why a narcissistic male elf couldn't also go banshee. If you wanted to be etymologically finicky about it, however, you'd have to refer to that creature as a "farshee."

REVENANTS

Revenants are undead creatures bent on pursuing revenge against individuals who wronged them in their previous lives. As undead creatures, they have no survival instinct per se; instead, they're driven by the compulsion to avenge themselves.

Now you might argue, hey, you can't get revenge if your enemy (or someone else) destroys you. And revenants have high Wisdom, high enough to understand the truth of this—and above-average Intelligence, high enough to understand the fact of it. So you might think a seriously wounded revenant would break off fighting and retreat—that is, unless it was getting too close to its one-year deadline.

But you can't destroy a revenant. Its Regeneration trait restores 10 hp every round unless it's taken fire or radiant damage; only if the damage that finally reduces its body to 0 hp is fire or radiant damage will the body it inhabits be destroyed. And even when the body is destroyed, the soul returns 24 hours later in a different body.

The only way to keep this from happening is to banish the revenant's soul to its appropriate afterlife while it's disembodied, using a *wish* spell. Only the most powerful wizards and sorcerers—veritable masters of the world—will have access to that. What kind of favor do you think you'd have to do for one to get them to cast a *wish* spell on your behalf? (The *Monster Manual* doesn't mention this possibility, but I think you could probably also stop a revenant by bringing it back to life with a *true resurrection* spell. But this is also a 9th-level spell; instead of wheedling a favor out of Saruman, you've got to get it from the pope.)

Revenants have exceptional Strength and Constitution along with above-average Dexterity, giving them a brute combat profile. They resist necrotic and psychic damage. They have darkvision, so bet on them coming for their adversaries at night. They can't be charmed, exhausted, frightened, paralyzed, poisoned, or stunned, and they have proficiency on Strength, Constitution, Wisdom, and Charisma saving throws. The word "juggernaut" comes to mind. But note that they *don't* have resistance to physical damage from normal weapons, so even though they have a lot of hit points, most PCs will have little problem doing damage to them. The problem is simply that no amount of damage is enough to stop them entirely.

But on to tactics. Driven by compulsion, the revenant is interested in only one target: the one who wronged it. No matter what company its target is in, it always directs its attacks solely at that one individual. Using its Vengeful Tracker trait, it zeroes in on its foe until it can see them. Even if its foe is hiding, it knows where they are, but that's not quite enough—to use its Vengeful Glare, the revenant has to be able to *see* its target, and also be within 30 feet. As soon as these two conditions are met, the revenant uses this action to try to paralyze its enemy.

Next, the revenant uses its Multiattack, first to grapple its foe, then to pummel them. It makes these attack rolls with advantage as long as its foe is paralyzed. As long as it holds its foe grappled, it continues to pummel, so on its first round, its Multiattack may be grapple/pummel, but on the second, it may be pummel/pummel.

Note that the target remains paralyzed only until it takes damage. Grappling does no damage, so the revenant has advantage on both the grapple attack roll and the pummel attack roll that immediately follows it. Any subsequent Fist attack rolls are made normally. However, the target remains frightened once their paralysis wears off.

Here's a funny twist: To have disadvantage on attack rolls owing to being frightened, the revenant's foe has to be able to see it. But in total darkness, they won't be *able* to see the revenant (unless they have darkvision). In that case, however, they have disadvantage on attack rolls owing to being blinded! Either way, they lose.

What if Vengeful Glare doesn't work? The revenant tries a second time—but not a third time. Similarly, if it fails to grapple, it will try a second time but not a third time. Revenants are smart enough to adapt if a certain tactic isn't working. If these tactics *do* work and simply wear off, however, the revenant uses them again after a round of normal attacks.

Clever players may use magic to make the revenant's target invisible. This won't stop the revenant from pursuing and attacking its foe—thanks to Vengeful Tracker, it always knows its quarry's exact distance and direction. But it will stop the revenant from using its Vengeful Glare, and it also gives the revenant disadvantage on its attack rolls.

A revenant will fearlessly pursue a PC in a party of level 3 or 4 characters on its own. Above that level, however, it's going to enlist allies to keep its enemy's companions occupied while it concludes its own business. The revenant itself won't hesitate to take on its own quarry one-on-one unless they're level 17 or higher—one of the aforementioned masters of the world—but keeping the rest of the party tied up may require considerable manpower (and/or monsterpower). If the revenant's body is destroyed, its allies will typically scatter, using their usual manners of flight.

Suppose the revenant's target isn't a PC—suppose, for instance, that they're an NPC whom the PCs are charged with protecting. In this scenario, the revenant never attacks any of the PCs! It singlemindedly pursues its foe and only its foe, relying on allies to run interference and prevent the PCs from coming between it and its quarry.

What kind of allies does a revenant enlist? They have to be persuadable creatures—beings of more than animal intelligence. They have to be accepting of the revenant's mission and of the idea of partnering up with the undead. They also have to share a plane of existence with the revenant, which can perceive its quarry on another plane of existence but can't go there by itself (unless it was a spellcaster in its previous life and knew the appropriate spell), so devils and demons are unlikely, though not impossible. Religious or political fanatics, on the other hand, make fine candidates, as well as others of a race, nation, or faction that the revenant once belonged to who might also see its quarry as an enemy. Other intelligent undead creatures, such as ghasts, specters, and wights, are potential allies as well (and a ghast may come with a pack of subservient ghouls in tow).

DEATH KNIGHTS

When a corrupted paladin dies without making amends for their misdeeds, they may be raised as a **death knight**, an undead warrior that retains a tenuous connection to its former divine link.

What kind of compulsion might drive a former paladin, particularly one who strayed from the path of good? One leaps out at me as so obvious that it hardly seems worth considering any other: the desire to *punish*. Punish whom, for what? Does it matter?

The death knight is a brute, with extraordinary Strength and Constitution and a large reservoir of hit points, but not an unthinking brute: All its mental ability scores are above average, and its Charisma in particular is exceptional. It has proficiency on Dexterity and Wisdom saving throws, two of the big three, plus advantage on spell saves in general from Magic Resistance. It's immune to necrotic and poison damage and can't be poisoned, exhausted, or frightened. It doesn't possess any resistance or immunity to physical damage from normal weapons, however.

The death knight's formidability lies primarily in three things: its Longsword Multiattack, which deals substantial necrotic damage on top of the slashing damage from the blade itself; its spellcasting ability; and its Marshal Undead feature.

Let's look at that last one first. As features go, it's not unusually powerful: It extends protection against being turned to other undead creatures within 60 feet of it. The formidability of this feature lies less in the mechanic itself than in what it says about the death knight. This monster isn't just undead, it's a *leader* of undead.

If you look at the Targets in Area of Effect table in chapter 8 of the *Dungeon Master's Guide*, a circular effect with a 60-foot radius can reasonably be expected to affect a dozen creatures. Here, we have a feature that affects allies in a 60-foot radius. What I draw from this is that the typical death knight is accompanied by a dozen undead followers.

What kind of undead followers depends on the difficulty of the encounter you want to create, but I'd say that ghouls, ghasts, mummies, wights, and wraiths stand out as particularly suitable choices. Undead that are bosses in their own right, like vampires and liches, not so much; ditto undead that are too low-level to pose a meaningful threat to intermediate- and high-level adventurers, such as skeletons and zombies.

A death knight's power is going to vary according to the number of undead followers it has, up to a dozen (less so according to the strength of those followers, since the higher their challenge ratings, the more resistance to being turned they'll already have), and I'd go so far as to say that a death knight encountered alone, with *no* followers, is hardly a whole death knight, because it's not even using a valuable part of its kit. By the same token, although the *Monster Manual* flavor text says death knights are sometimes followed by fiends, Marshal Undead does nothing for them; it's the undead followers that really matter.

Especially at low level, paladins often struggle against a shortage of spell slots, but the death knight is a 19th-level spellcaster, so it doesn't suffer from this problem. Moreover, it possesses two *smite* spells, *staggering smite* and *searing smite*, both of which are bonus actions that enhance its action economy. Unfortunately, they're not the best two *smites* in the paladins' repertoire. However, the death knight also has *banishment* and *hold person*, which are outstanding, and its spell list is crowned with the epic *destructive wave*; it has *two* 5th-level spell slots for that, and nothing else to use them on.

In addition, there's Hellfire Orb, which I include among the death knight's spells because it's effectively a spell for which the death knight has exactly one "5th-and-a-half-level" slot that it can't use for anything else. It's a double-strength boosted *fireball* that does half fire damage and half necrotic damage. If it has any drawback at all, it's the 20-foot radius, which means (again referring to the Targets in Area of Effect table) that while it's not worth using on fewer than four creatures, it's not likely to affect more than that. If the death knight's enemies are clustered up enough that it can indeed strike more than four of them, that's just icing on the cake.

Since Hellfire Orb is technically not a spell, it can be used in the same turn as a *smite* spell. There wouldn't be much point in doing that, though, since a *smite* spell is wasted if the caster doesn't attack with a melee weapon in the same turn. (Yeah, you can sustain it and attack with your weapon on your next turn, but in the meantime, you're risking having your concentration disrupted. It's always better to cast a *smite* spell at the *beginning* of your turn, then attack.)

So what about the other spells in the death knight's repertoire?

- *Dispel magic* is important to keep on hand at least until the death knight can size up how great a threat any spellcaster among its enemies poses. "Threat," in this case, essentially means the ability to cast spells that require Constitution saves, can mow down one's undead minions, or offer defenses against the death knight's own spells. Spells other than these, the death knight can safely ignore.

- *Elemental weapon* is nice, but it requires concentration, which makes it incompatible with *banishment* and *hold person*, as well as the *smites*; and it's also an action, which means the death knight has to forgo its Multiattack. Together, these constraints make it almost too situational to bother with.

- *Magic weapon* is just an inferior *elemental weapon*—although it is a bonus action, so the death knight can use it opportunistically when it's not slinging any other magic. Even so, *hold person* is a better use of a 2nd-level spell slot.

- *Command* is most likely to be useful against targets being swarmed by the death knight's minions.

- *Compelled duel* is tactically sound, but let's be honest: The death knight is going to use this one primarily for *dramatic* purposes. Because chances are, there's one PC in the party who *has* to be the one to face the death knight one-on-one, right? In case it's not already obvious, the death knight will *make* it obvious. If it so happens that there's not one obvious designated adversary, then the death knight probably won't bother with this spell—unless there's one front-line PC who's threatening to make short work of its undead minions, in which case it may cast *compelled duel* to pull them off that job.

My rule of thumb for spellcasters is that spell slots are used according to their scarcity, which usually means that 1st-level spells are cast only with 1st-level spell slots, top-level slots are reserved for top-level spells, and the spell slots in between are fungible. In the case of the death knight, this means that it will cast *command*, *compelled duel*, or *searing smite* only with a 1st-level slot (*compelled duel* can't be boosted anyway), and it will use its 5th-level slots only for *destructive wave*, but it may use its 3rd- and 4th-level slots to boost lower-level spells. In particular, it will use those slots to cast *hold person* against a second or third target in order to paralyze any and all melee opponents who engage with it, unless one of them is the target of *compelled duel*.

Okay, so here's our overall strategy for the death knight: First of all, in all probability, there's one PC who's the target of the death knight, and this PC is the focus of its attacks. Or, alternatively, one or more party members, or the entire party, run afoul of the death knight by transgressing in some way that it feels compelled to punish. The death knight marches right up to any such transgressor(s) and gets right to punishing.

Being a brute, the death knight takes position on the front line of the battle. Depending on the makeup of the two sides, it may *be* the front line. Its undead minions fan out across the battlefield and engage any non-front-line PCs according to their usual modi operandi, the only difference being that the death knight's commands override their usual target selection heuristics. (But not completely: If the death knight's minions comprise different types of undead creatures which choose their targets differently, they'll divide the labor according to their normal preferences. As the DM, you'll want to figure this out before your session, because it may be confusing to figure out on the fly.)

For the most part, the death knight's top priority is to destroy those it feels compelled to punish. As long as they're obliging enough to engage in melee with it, it uses *hold person* to paralyze them, then hacks and slashes at them, one by one, with Multiattack, which deals an average of 150 damage per round if all its Longsword hits land on a paralyzed target. If they prove resistant to this, and if at least three of them are obligingly arrayed within a 30-foot semicircle in front of it, it will bowl them over with *destructive wave*.

Banishment is reserved for use against a single opponent other than the target(s) of the death knight's ire who insists on interfering with its agenda. As long as *banishment* is sustained, all the death knight's other concentration-required spells are off the table—but *destructive wave*, *dispel magic*, and *command* are still available, as is Hellfire Orb. The death knight is savvy enough not to try *banishment* against a bard or paladin, but it doesn't necessarily know enough about arcane magic to be able to tell the difference between a wizard (good target) and a sorcerer or warlock (bad target). However, it's most likely using its undead minions to deal with problematic spellslingers, anyway. A more likely target for *banishment* is a high-level cleric or a problematic skirmisher or shock attacker, such as a rogue or monk.

Dispel magic is an expensive use of a turn, since it does no damage— with its three-swing Multiattack, the death knight needs a compelling reason to use its action on anything else. So, as mentioned above, the death knight casts this spell only to negate a sustained spell that requires a Constitution save to avoid damage, does direct damage to undead, or offers protection from fire and/or necrotic damage, primarily the latter. The list of spells that fit these criteria is short: *enlarge/reduce, moonbeam, ray of enfeeblement, elemental bane, sickening radiance, dawn, insect plague, holy weapon, wall of light, flesh to stone, sunbeam, holy aura, storm of vengeance, protection from energy, dispel evil and good, globe of invulnerability, primordial ward,* and *invulnerability*. Moreover, the death knight's chances of dispelling any of these spells cast at 5th level or higher aren't very good—less than 50 percent—and it will bother to try only if it has a chance of either shutting down a spell that's affecting multiple targets or dispelling all magic on a creature that's affected by multiple spells.

The death knight casts *compelled duel* only when its chief antagonist insists on avoiding the single combat for which they're obviously destined. It casts *staggering smite* only when it's clearly not going to need to cast *banishment* or *hold person* at any time for the remainder of the encounter, in which case it's a why-not enhancement of its next successful melee attack. It casts *command* as a poor man's substitute for *compelled duel* when it's concentrating on another spell that's equally important, ordering its enemy to "Approach!" Otherwise, it uses *command* only when it has no need to make a melee attack and can use the spell to make an enemy more vulnerable to its minions' attacks, such as shouting "Grovel!" to make that enemy fall prone. It doesn't bother with *searing smite* or *magic weapon* unless it's used up every other trick in its bag, and it doesn't bother with *elemental weapon* at all.

As for Hellfire Orb, the death knight is judicious in its use of this action, since it really is extravagant overkill. For the death knight to use its Hellfire Orb, two conditions must apply: First, at least four enemies must be close enough to one another to fall within the 20-foot-radius area of effect. Second, at least two of those enemies must have infuriated it in some way—by casting one of the spells that makes a death knight consider using *dispel magic*, by singlehandedly inflicting 54 or more damage against it, by inflicting any amount of radiant damage, by calling it by its onetime name (death knights *hate* being reminded of their former lives as fallen paladins), or through simple cheeky defiance. Hellfire Orb is punishment *on top of* the punishment that the death knight's victims have already earned.

Finally, the death knight has the Parry reaction, which it uses when it's struck by a melee attack roll of 20 to 25. But it has to be judicious with this as well if it's facing multiple non-incapacitated melee opponents. If one of them has a weapon that does extra damage against undead, or with some kind of elemental effect other than necrotic or poison, it takes its licks from any other weapon and saves its reaction to Parry this one.

A death knight with a warhorse skeleton or nightmare mount follows the same strategy as a death knight on foot; there's no reason for it to fight any other way. And it probably goes without saying that a death knight *never* retreats. It may stand down once it's killed everyone it perceives as a transgressor (in which case, it's the lucky survivors who must retreat), but as long as one such reprobate remains alive, the death knight fights until it's destroyed.

ABERRATIONS

I n fifth edition Dungeons & Dragons, "aberrations" are monsters that come from somewhere other than the material world that the player characters inhabit—from other planes or even other universes. We can still presume that they've evolved, although the conditions they've evolved in may be very different from our own, and that they still behave in ways that further their own survival, no matter what alien thought processes they may possess. When running aberrations— be they weird entities that dreamed themselves into existence, psionic invaders from the Far Realm, monstrous abominations, helter-skelter creatures of chaos, or ancient entities of the unexplored depths—it's important to convey their alienness. Their more unusual features help with this, but even their ordinary attacks benefit from being depicted through a warped lens. Remember, your player characters aren't people to them; they're animals . . . or *objects*. Maybe aberrations aren't attacking out of what we understand as malice—maybe they're attacking for the same reason we'd smack a malfunctioning vending machine.

BEHOLDERS

The **beholder** is such an iconic D&D monster that the host of my weekly group, even though he knew hardly anything about the game before we began playing, told me near the beginning of our campaign, "All I want is to run into an 'eye of the beholder,' and I'll be happy."

The beholder is an aberration—a magically summoned creature of extraplanar origin—with a hateful, avaricious, and territorial temperament. It has little purpose in life beyond guarding its chosen turf. Though not high in Strength, it has powerful mental abilities along with a high Dexterity and very high Constitution, making it strong at all of the "big three" types of saving throws. As you'd expect from a floating blob with a giant central eye, its Perception skill is through the roof; it also has darkvision out to 120 feet. It has an innate ability to hover, so it can never be knocked prone and remains in the air even if its speed is reduced to 0.

At melee range, it has a Bite attack, but the beholder's trump card is its Eye Rays, which emanate from the many smaller eyes at the ends of stalks extending from its body. These rays have a range of 120 feet, enough to keep trespassers at a distance for two to five combat rounds. It can also project an Antimagic Cone from its central eye, but this ability is problematic, as we'll see in a moment.

Finally, a beholder in its lair has access to three lair actions: slippery slime on the floor, grasping appendages flailing from the walls, and random beholder eyes appearing on nearby surfaces. And a beholder encounter almost always happens in its lair.

The beholder is aggressive, malicious, and antisocial, so when trespassers appear, it's not going to indulge any attempt to negotiate passage—it's going to attack immediately.

At the start of its turn, it must decide whether to use its Antimagic Cone. Here's the problem: According to the *Monster Manual*, the cone "works against the beholder's own eye rays." Imagine that the beholder spends all its time with its gaze focused on the entrance to its lair, because that's exactly the sort of thing an aberration would do. A group of intruders appears in the doorway. Every instinct it has tells it to kill the intruders—and the only function its Antimagic Cone will have is to interfere with its killing the intruders.

As written, the Antimagic Cone seems at first to be a power of highly questionable usefulness. A beholder is going to position itself as you'd place a security camera: in a high-up corner where it can see everything and no one can maneuver behind it. Wherever it aims its Antimagic Cone, it's also going to catch creatures it wants to shoot its eye rays at.

But with a little geometry, we can see how the Antimagic Cone can be made to work effectively. In fifth edition D&D, a cone-shaped area of effect covers a distance of x feet, out to a width of x feet at that distance. Regardless of the cone's range, this means it covers an arc of about 53 degrees, or slightly less than one-sixth of a circle. The upshot is that, while enemies are at a distance, the Antimagic Cone is practically useless. But when they're *close*, and they're surrounding the beholder, it can isolate one or two opponents within the cone while projecting Eye Rays in other directions.

Okay, so the intruders have appeared, the beholder is attacking, it's choosing *not* to use its Antimagic Cone just yet—but what if the intruders see the mean expression on this thing's H. R. Giger–draws–Mike Wazowski face, roll higher initative, and act first? The beholder's got three Eye Ray legendary actions it can use between its turns, and it's going to use one against each PC who gets a turn before it does.

When its own turn comes, it projects three eye rays. These rays are chosen at random, based on three d10 rolls (with duplicates rerolled). How does the beholder choose its targets? Let's examine the saving throws needed to resist the various rays:

- **Strength:** Telekinetic Ray
- **Dexterity:** Slowing Ray, Petrifaction Ray, Disintegration Ray, Death Ray
- **Constitution:** Paralyzing Ray, Enervation Ray
- **Wisdom:** Charm Ray, Fear Ray, Sleep Ray

The beholder has Intelligence 17, so it knows better than to use its Telekinetic Ray against a hulking barbarian brute, its Disintegration Ray against a hyperactive halfling rogue, its Paralyzing Ray against a doughty dwarf, or its Charm Ray or Sleep Ray against an elf.

Let's say you roll that the beholder is using its Telekinetic Ray, its Paralyzing Ray, and its Sleep Ray. It aims the first at a weak-looking wizard, the second at a frail-ish rogue or warlock, and the third at a non-elf fighter or rogue. It may be right; it may be wrong. But its first guess is always going to be a *sensible* guess.

On subsequent rounds, the beholder refines its choices. If a ray didn't work against a particular player character, it won't use that ray—or any of its sibling rays—against that PC again. If it did work, it uses that ray's sibling rays against that PC as well.

After it's taken its turn, the beholder uses its legendary actions on the next three PCs' turns, but now with a twist: Instead of automatically attacking whichever PC has just taken their turn, it chooses targets according to what it knows about the PCs and their susceptibility to its various rays.

Also, on initiative count 20, the beholder uses a lair action. If one or more PCs is charging in to fight the beholder up close, it favors slippery slime. If one or more PCs is near a wall, it favors grabby appendages. If neither of the above situations applies or it's already used its only favored lair action on the previous turn, it chooses random wall eye.

As long as the PCs remain out of melee range, the beholder will use nothing but its Eye Rays against them; it also won't willingly move from its chosen location, which will be hovering at least 10 feet up if the space allows it, so as to remain out of characters' reach even if they run up to it. But there is one twist here: Beholders may be summoned as guards by other magic-using entities. Say a beholder is under a *geas* to guard a passageway out of a chamber. Even though it would *prefer* to hover high out of reach, if a PC approaches that passageway, the beholder will be compelled to descend in order to block them. Then the PCs may be able to reach it with melee attacks.

If enough of its attackers close with it, it then starts using its Antimagic Cone to shut down spellcasters, provided that it can do so and still target *non*-spellcasters with its Eye Rays. Maintaining its use of the Eye Rays is always the beholder's higher priority. It Bites only if (a) it's within melee range of a target *and* (b) all the PCs it can attack with its Eye Rays have already proved themselves resistant to two or more types of them. Or, alternatively, if a particular melee opponent has proved resistant to two or more types of Eye Ray, yet they're the only one whom the beholder still considers a genuine threat.

A beholder is so ultraterritorial, if it's encountered in its lair, it *always* fights to the death; ditto if it's been summoned as a sentinel. Only a beholder encountered outside its lair (it does have to feed from time to time) and under no obligation to stay put will flee from combat, and it does so after taking a relatively modest amount of damage (reduced to 126 hp or fewer). First it Disengages and ascends out of the PCs' reach, then it Dashes on a beeline back to its lair.

The **death tyrant** is a high-concept monster: an undead beholder. In most respects, it behaves exactly the same way as a normal beholder does. But there are a couple of exceptions.

First, its Negative Energy Cone doesn't interfere with its own Eye Rays the way the beholder's Antimagic Cone does, so the Negative Energy Cone is *always on* as long as intruders are present. It keeps this cone oriented in whichever direction catches the most opponents in it, including unconscious ones (who may die and be raised as zombies).

Second, the death tyrant is *never* found outside its lair unless it's been summoned as a magical sentinel. Either way, it doesn't flee, no matter how much damage it's taken. Its compulsion to guard supersedes everything else, including its own survival.

Finally, the Death Tyrant has Intelligence 19. As the DM, you can construe this as allowing it to "read" PCs' ability stats. In other words, it doesn't just chuck an Enervation Ray at Radwin because he looks frail—it chucks an Enervation Ray at Radwin *because he has a −1 Constitution modifier*. It aims each of its Eye Rays first at the PC who's least equipped to resist it, then works its way up.

On the other end of the danger spectrum, we have the **spectator**, a lesser cousin to the beholder that's not malicious, just dutiful. It has no territory of its own; it's summoned as a magical sentinel, and that's its one and only responsibility. It's willing to speak civilly (via telepathy) with PCs who encounter it, although it's liable to come off as offbeat, high-strung, and suspicious. And the PCs had best not mess with whatever it's guarding.

Spectators have only four types of Eye Rays: two (Confusion, Fear) that target Wisdom and two (Paralyzing, Wounding) that target Constitution. They also shoot only two per action, rather than three. They have no legendary or lair actions. In other respects, however, they fight similarly to beholders—in particular, they strongly favor their Eye Rays over their Bite attack, and they Bite only if there's an opponent within melee range *and* the Eye Rays aren't working. They also have the unique Spell Reflection ability, which upon a successful saving throw lets them redirect spells cast at them onto other targets. Unlike beholders, spectators don't possess genius-level Intelligence; they redirect spells not toward whoever's most vulnerable to them but toward whoever's causing them the most hassle. Finally, like others of their kind, they don't flee. They have a job to do, and by gum, they're going to do it or die trying.

INTELLECT DEVOURERS

It's a brain! With feet! What's not to love? Well, the fact that it feeds on your consciousness and takes over your body, for one thing.

Old-school players of Advanced Dungeons & Dragons will remember the **intellect devourer** as one of the two most memorable monsters with psionics—that strange, complicated supplementary rule set that allowed for telepathy, telekinesis, and psychic combat. Fifth edition D&D has dispensed with all that. Psionic power is now treated as either a special trait, a form of spellcasting, or both. In the fifth edition intellect devourer, this is encapsulated in its telepathy and its Detect Sentience, Devour Intellect, and Body Thief features.

According to the *Monster Manual* flavor text, intellect devourers are created to serve the interests of mind flayers. They're not independent creatures. You're not going to randomly run into one in the woods. Rather, any intellect devourer your PCs encounter will be on some kind of mission. That fact will affect whom it uses its powers on and when.

Intellect devourers have very low Strength alongside high Dexterity and Constitution, the profile of a skirmisher that relies on superior numbers. One doesn't get the impression, however, that intellect devourers are a numerous species, so they're not going to get many opportunities to overwhelm their opponents. They have slightly above-average Intelligence and average Wisdom and Charisma (by humanoid measure), so they're not just animals—they can plan and adapt. They have proficiency in Stealth, and although they have no eyes or ears, they have 60 feet of blindsight and 300 feet of Detect Sentience.

Their Multiattack includes one use of the Devour Intellect power, and Devour Intellect may inflict the stunned condition or knock an opponent unconscious. Both of these conditions include incapacitation, and Body Thief requires an incapacitated humanoid opponent, so there's how these features fit together: The intellect devourer uses Devour Intellect until it stuns an opponent, then uses Body Thief against it.

How long does it take for Devour Intellect to stun an opponent? That depends on the opponent's Intelligence. Let's look at three cases: an ordinary commoner, an average adventurer, and an adventurer whose prime requisite ability is Intelligence and who has proficiency in Intelligence saving throws:

- A commoner with Intelligence 10 has a 55 percent chance of failing their saving throw against Devour Intellect, whereupon the intellect devourer has about a 62 percent chance to stun. Chance of both happening: about 34 percent.
- An average adventurer with Intelligence 12 has a 50 percent chance of failing their saving throw, and the chance to stun is about 37 percent. Chance of both happening: about 19 percent.
- A low-level wizard with Intelligence 15 and a +2 proficiency modifier has a 35 percent chance of failing their save, and the chance to stun is only about 9 percent. Chance of both happening: about 3 percent.

Doesn't look like any adventurers are getting their brains eaten today, does it? It takes two rounds for the devourer to have a better than 50 percent chance of stunning a commoner, three rounds to have a better than two-thirds chance. In contrast, three rounds aren't enough to give the intellect devourer even a fifty-fifty chance of stunning the average adventurer, and the wizard can wait that brain-puppy out more than long enough for his associate Hrodvald Thunderfist to squash it.

This leads us to an interesting conclusion: When a party of PCs first encounters an intellect devourer, it probably won't be in the form of an intellect devourer. Instead, it will be puppeting the body of a commoner whose intellect it's already devoured. The only PC an intellect devourer is ever likely to attack with Devour Intellect is one who's chosen Intelligence as their dump stat.

Let's pause for a moment and note that stunning and unconsciousness aren't the only conditions that include incapacitation. A person who's paralyzed or petrified is also incapacitated, so a humanoid in the grasp of a *hold person* spell, for example, would also be vulnerable to a Body Thief attack, and *hypnotic pattern* and *Tasha's hideous laughter* are two low-level spells that can inflict incapacitation directly. An intellect devourer that had already taken over the body of a spellcaster who knew *hypnotic pattern* (an extraordinarily unlucky spellcaster, we'd have to conclude from the probabilities above) could easily use that spell to prepare host bodies for other intellect devourers without their having to Devour Intellect at all. (*Sleep* would work as well.) Note also that Body Thief doesn't give the target immunity if the intellect devourer doesn't succeed on its first try.

Okay, so what's an intellect devourer doing while it's puppeting a host body? Whatever it's been instructed to do, as unobtrusively as it can. The host body is only useful as long as the guise is maintained.

An intellect devourer ejected from its host* runs like a rat, fighting only if cornered. In that situation, it uses its Multiattack, attacking with Claws and using Devour Intellect on its opponent, but it may or may not use Body Thief on an incapacitated opponent—it depends on whether that would help it make its getaway. It's resistant to physical damage from nonmagical attacks, its Armor Class isn't especially high, and it has a high movement speed, so a fleeing intellect devourer

---

* There's an error in the stat block in some early printings of the *Monster Manual*. It's not enough to reduce the host body to 0 hp in order to drive the intellect devourer out: The body must actually die, or one of the other two listed methods must be used. This isn't an issue if you're treating the host as a monster that dies when reduced to 0 hp, but it is if the host is a PC, or if your PCs are deliberately inflicting nonlethal damage on the host, thinking this will help somehow.

will Dash rather than Dodge, with one exception: On its first turn trying to escape, if it's got two or more unsurprised melee attackers in adjacent squares or hexes, its first action is to Disengage.

And what about that instance in which the brain-puppy tries Devour Intellect on a dimmer PC? It's not going to do it out in the open, that's for sure. It will use Stealth to hide in ambush, until the PC comes within 10 feet of it. It will use only Devour Intellect, *not* its Claws/Devour Intellect Multiattack. This way, it doesn't give its position away if it fails, because Devour Intellect technically is not an attack—Hrodvald simply has an unexplained splitting headache all of a sudden. If the intellect devourer can't bring down its target in three rounds, it abandons the effort and scampers away. *That* gives its position away, but it should have little or no trouble escaping.

Mind Flayers

Mind flayers are like classic pulp supervillains: brilliant, twisted, scheming, always wanting to take over the world—but first, they have things they want to do to your brain. They even wear outfits straight out of *Flash Gordon*. And yet fifth edition mind flayers feel unsatisfying to me, maybe because, as written, they just aren't very efficient.

The *Monster Manual* flavor text characterizes them as "psionic commanders," declaring, "Mind flayers possess psionic powers that enable them to control the minds of creatures such as troglodytes, grimlocks, quaggoths, and ogres." And the feature they use to accomplish this is . . . *dominate monster*, which they can use once per day, and which affects one creature, requires concentration, and lasts for one hour?

This is paltry. It's unworthy of a supervillain. I'll talk about the tactics of the mind flayer as written, but then I'll discuss how to make a mind flayer capable of enthralling, and keeping enthralled, more than one minion at a time.

Mind flayers' physical abilities are nominally average to slightly above average, but they're no better than the average adventurer's and downright weak compared with those of most intermediate-level boss monsters. Mind flayers compensate with exceptionally high mental abilities across the board, especially in Intelligence, and with proficiency in all mental ability saving throws. They also have proficiency in Stealth, Perception, Insight, Persuasion, and Deception (also Arcana, but that's strictly for flavor). They're resistant to spells and other magical effects, and in addition to *dominate monster*, they can also cast *detect thoughts* and *levitate* at will and *plane shift* once per day on themselves.

Their primary method of self-defense is the Mind Blast action, which has a recharge and which affects every creature in a 60-foot cone, potentially stunning them. Secondarily, they can attack with their face-tentacles, which both grapple and potentially stun their target on a hit, and Extract Brain against an already incapacitated (by either stunning or some other means) and grappled opponent. But the mind flayer doesn't really want to use this secondary attack against a still-functioning opponent. Ideally, no opponent should ever get within melee range of a mind flayer under its own power. Instead, mind flayers would rather incapacitate their opponents at range, *then* move in to consume their brains. Even a cornered mind flayer prefers Mind Blast, if that action is available, over a melee attack with Tentacles.

To ensure that its enemies don't get close, a mind flayer uses minions to run interference. The creatures listed above (troglodytes, etc.) are good choices, as are enthralled humanoid commoners. Grells also make a good fit thematically, continuing the brain and tentacle themes of the mind flayer and its dogsbody, the intellect devourer. PCs attacking a mind flayer in its lair will have to fight their way through waves of minions before ever getting near it, and in the meantime, it's hanging back 60 feet behind the action, *levitating* about 10 feet in the air so that melee attackers can't reach it, and Mind Blasting anyone who breaks through the line.

Mind flayers value their survival highly, but like a pulp supervillain, they value their schemes as well. They don't want to give up their lairs if there's any chance at all that they can win a battle, so they'll hold out until they're seriously injured (reduced to 28 hp or fewer) before casting *plane shift* to make a hasty exit. But this presumes they have only one lair and one scheme going. If they're up to different things, and the lair the PCs are attacking isn't the most important one, they'll cut their losses earlier, after being only moderately injured (reduced to 49 hp or fewer), and let any remaining minions handle the job from there.

Now, how to make a mind flayer capable of taking over more than a tollbooth? I've thought of a few possibilities, though I'm sure there are others:

- Borrow the vampire's Charm feature. This affects only one creature at a time, but it lasts up to 24 hours and doesn't require concentration. Still, it doesn't do anything to address the real conundrum of *dominate monster*, which is how the mind flayer keeps its minions enthralled once the effect wears off. Also, its casting range is only 30 feet.

- Borrow the aboleth's Enslave feature. Again, this affects only one creature at a time (though the aboleth can do it three times per day, which is an improvement), but it lasts *indefinitely*, although the target can repeat its saving throw once per day if it can get a mile or more away (a risk easily mitigated by commanding the target never to venture more than a mile away). It also doesn't require concentration. Enslave also has only a 30-foot range.

- Change *dominate monster* to *geas*. Although it affects only one creature at a time, it lasts 30 days and allows no subsequent saving throw after the target fails the first one, not even if the target takes damage. It also leaves open the possibility that targets can resist the commands they're given—but gives them a nasty psychic shock if they do. The one drawback is that it takes a full minute to cast, rather than a single action, but if you like the idea of having a mind flayer take over a PC's mind in the middle of combat, you can handwave that, particularly considering that *geas* is a much lower-level spell than *dominate monster*.

For Charm or Enslave, I'd change the listed saving throw DC to 15, to match Mind Blast and Tentacles. Following the example of the aboleth's Enslave feature, you might also allow a mind flayer three uses of Charm or *geas* per day rather than just one—or, maybe, give it Enslave as written, plus a single daily use of *geas*. This will give an entrepreneurial mind flayer a chance to build up a decent-size posse around its new base of operations in a reasonable amount of time.

With any of these powers, a mind flayer can mind-control a PC into fighting against their allies. That's its second-choice tactic, after Mind Blast. Charm or a fast-cast *geas* is better for this than Enslave, however, since Enslave allows so many saving throws that the turned PC probably won't stay turned for more than a round, unless their allies scrupulously refrain from fighting back. As for *dominate monster*, the fact that it requires concentration means the mind flayer can't cast both it and *levitate* at the same time, and it also offers a new saving throw every time the target takes damage.

The obvious thought is to brainwash the biggest, baddest warrior in the party. It's obvious to us because we don't have Intelligence 19. The mind flayer, however, does. It can compel other monsters to form an offensive line, it can psychically debilitate anyone who tries to charge it, but it knows what its one real vulnerability is: archers. Mind flayers resist magic, but they don't resist arrows, and their longest-range attacks top out at 60 feet. Against the mind flayer's middling AC, a ranged weapon attacker—especially a Hunter ranger with Colossus Slayer, specializing in Archery—will make quick work of it. *That's* the one the mind flayer will want to mind-control. Plus, if you're using the Enslave alternative rather than the Charm or *geas* alternative, a ranged weapon attacker is likely to be positioned farther away from their allies, so they won't take damage so soon and therefore are likely to remain enthralled longer.

To pull this off, however, the mind flayer has to get within 30 or 60 feet of the archer, which the archer will strenuously avoid. To make this tactic feasible, it may be necessary for the mind flayer's other minions to herd this enemy in the mind flayer's direction. Alternatively, it may bait out a charge from a melee opponent, mind-control them, and send *them* to go take care of the archer.

GRELLS

Technically, a **grell**'s body only *looks* like a big brain, according to game lore, but it does originate from the Far Realm—also the home plane of the mind flayer and the intellect devourer. So if you need another aberration to round out an encounter with these psionic nemeses, the grell is a good fit.

Grells are above average in all their physical abilities, but the balance is tipped toward Strength, with Dexterity coming in second, suggesting a hit-and-run shock attacker. Their primary mode of movement is flying, with the ability to hover, and they have high proficiency in Stealth.

One thing they don't have, however, is much flexibility. Beyond an unexplained immunity to lightning damage and the ability to sense without eyes, the grell's features are limited to a simple Multiattack comprising one Beak attack and one Tentacles attack.

The tentacles are the grell's distinguishing feature. A successful Tentacles hit requires the grell's target to make a (not very difficult) Constitution saving throw to avoid paralyzing poison; it also grapples and restrains the target. The grappled/restrained condition is the more interesting of the two. Although the grell is only a Medium-size monster itself, it can grapple and carry any Medium or smaller target.

And so the grell's modus operandi takes shape: It hovers in the air, waiting patiently and still for a victim to pass by. It lashes out with Tentacles first, because a successful hit with Tentacles means advantage on the Bite attack. Once it's got hold of a victim, it doesn't hang around—it floats off to enjoy its feast in peace. Note that this halves the grell's speed, according to the rules of grappling, meaning that the grell's first movement will be *upward*, out of reach of any other enemy.

Grells are intelligent creatures—as intelligent as the average adventurer—so they don't operate solely by instinct. And they're evolved creatures, despite having evolved on another plane of existence, so their sense of self-preservation is intact. A grell can plan and strategize, and it can recognize a situation in which attacking would be detrimental, but it's also tough enough (against common humanoids, at least) that merely being outnumbered usually isn't enough to deter it from attacking. It may or may not make good choices when it comes to selecting targets—it may, for instance, go after a stouthearted halfling because they're small, not realizing that they're also tough. Among grells that live in subterranean colonies, it's common knowledge that dwarves make poor prey, owing to their resistance to poison, but a lone, feral grell or one that associates mainly with other aberrations may not be aware of this fact.

If a character can communicate with a grell (it does speak, in its own language), there may even be room for negotiation, although there's not a whole lot they want beyond easy access to food and uncontested territory to hunt in. Also, as the *Monster Manual* flavor text describes, they're not likely to see much value in negotiating with beings they classify as edible. If the party can somehow demonstrate that they're "great eaters" capable of hunting and killing a grell, the prospects for negotiation are much more favorable (though not, for obvious reasons, with any grell they've hunted and killed to prove it).

A grell retreats when seriously injured (reduced to 22 hp or fewer), and it has the savvy to Disengage from any melee opponent(s) before floating away. As it does, it may gabble out a petulant concession of defeat in its own language, offering player characters a clue that it's capable of speech and conversation.

GIBBERING MOUTHERS

The **gibbering mouther**, an oozing blob dotted with mouths full of teeth and horrifying noises, is a weird and repulsive denizen of places no one in their right mind would go, and where no one stays in their right mind for long. It has average Strength, very high Constitution, and low Dexterity, an atypical ability contour. It's not strong enough to be a brute, it's not fast enough to be scrappy, and it has no aptitude for stealth. Its low Dexterity suggests that, since its ability to avoid damage is poor, it needs some kind of compensatory advantage to make combat worthwhile, and simply being able to soak up damage isn't enough.

Its mental abilities are typical of an animal: average Wisdom (reflecting little except its perceptive ability), low Charisma, and very low Intelligence. Entirely instinct-bound, it makes no distinction of any kind among potential targets; one is as good as another. It may sometimes retreat when injured, but that's the extent of its ability to adapt to changed circumstances.

Aside from its darkvision (necessary for a subterranean dweller), it has no skills, vulnerabilities, resistances, immunities (except to being knocked prone, since it's amorphous), or unique senses. It can't speak or comprehend speech. Its most distinctive features are Aberrant Ground, Gibbering, and Blinding Spittle:

- Aberrant Ground handicaps melee attackers by causing the terrain around the gibbering mouther to soften and heave. Enemies who fail their Strength saving throws are unable to move; enemies who succeed are slowed by half, unless they have the ability to negotiate difficult terrain at full speed.
- Gibbering causes an effect similar to that of the *confusion* spell in enemies within 20 feet who fail their Wisdom saves.
- Blinding Spittle is a ranged, area-effect attack with a radius of only 5 feet, thus affecting only one target in most cases. On a failed Dexterity save, it causes the blinded condition, but it does no damage.

Remarkably, given these unique features, the gibbering mouther's real strength seems to lie in its Bite attack, which does a whopping 5d6 piercing damage and can also knock an enemy prone. There's that compensatory advantage we were looking for.

So how do these fit together? Of the gibbering mouther's four features, two—Bite and Blinding Spittle—can impose debilitating conditions. The blinded condition gives a target disadvantage on attack rolls and gives enemies advantage on attack rolls against them. Prone does the same, except that only attackers within 5 feet of the target have advantage on attack rolls against them; attackers from farther away roll with disadvantage. But the gibbering mouther's only direct attack is a melee attack, so that's not a problem for it. Ideally, therefore, the mouther wants to blind a victim or knock it down, *then* chomp on it. This means that when it Multiattacks, it uses its Blinding Spittle first (if it's available) and Bites afterward.

But what about the other two features? They don't offer the mouther any advantage on its attacks, their saving throw DCs are paltry, and the effect of Gibbering can't even be relied on.

Their impact is measured by their ability to keep allies of the mouther's victims from fighting back. Once the mouther has blinded a victim and is moving in to devour it, it wants to be able to do so without interference. Both Aberrant Ground and Gibbering discourage would-be melee attackers from getting too close; if one does approach and engage, Gibbering causes them to do something other than attack the mouther between 25 and 40 percent of the time, roughly.

The real mystery is why anyone would get within 15 feet of a gibbering mouther (the range of its Blinding Spittle) in the first place. It can sense potential prey up to 60 feet away, and there's nothing to suggest that it wouldn't reflexively start making horrific noises as soon as anyone came within range. It can move only 10 feet per round. It's not stealthy. It's not smart enough to lay traps. How can it hunt when the only reasonable reaction to it is to run the hell away?

Here's the best answer I can come up with: It swims. According to the *Monster Manual* flavor text, the gibbering mouther "swims through water, mud, and quicksand with ease." There's your element of surprise. A gibbering mouther can't conceal itself in plain sight, but it can hide unseen and unheard in mud, muck, quicksand, or dark water. When prey passes by, out it pops, discharging its Blinding Spittle at the easiest target it spots.

The gibbering mouther seemingly ought to flee when it's seriously injured (reduced to 26 hp or fewer), but none of the three basic flight actions—Dodge, Dash, or Disengage—works all that well for it. It's neither smart enough to Disengage nor fast enough to get good use out of it. Its Armor Class isn't high enough to make Dodge worthwhile, nor does it have any reason to prolong a losing battle. And its Dash distance is less than most PCs' base movement speed. I'd conclude, therefore, that it fights to the death simply because it has no good way of *not* fighting to the death, and its best (and, really, only) hope is to land lots of Bite attacks and hope that its other abilities keep the aggro off.

What's really going to ruin a gibbering mouther's day, even more than being seriously injured in melee combat, is any kind of ranged attack—weapon or spell. It has no way of countering such a thing; it may not even understand what's happening, especially if the attack comes from farther than 60 feet away. But it knows which side of its body hurts. If the mouther takes damage from one of these sources, doesn't already have an enemy blinded or knocked down, and isn't engaged in combat with a melee opponent, it Dashes in the direction opposite wherever the attack came from.

NOTHICS

Nothics are categorized as aberrations, although based on their *Monster Manual* flavor text, it seems like they belong more in the category of "monstrosity," which includes beings created by magic: Nothics are described as onetime wizards whose avarice for secret knowledge led to their being cursed by the lich Vecna. This "origin story" seems to make them cousins to the undead as well. In any event, since they clearly aren't evolved creatures, it's hard to say whether nothics should play by the usual rules of natural selection or not. I treat them as weird hybrids that follow those rules sometimes but are also subject to undead-esque compulsion.

Nothics have proficiency in Stealth and Perception, but also in Arcana and Insight. The latter two skills, along with their Weird Insight trait, suggest that nothics seek out social interaction as well as prey, and the flavor text corroborates this, sort of: "Most times, a nothic is content to watch, weighing and assessing the creatures it encounters." In other words, this "social interaction" is likely to be one-way unless the PCs make it otherwise. Nothics also have truesight to a distance of 120 feet.

Although the *Monster Manual* makes no mention of it—the only form of communication it attributes to the nothic is Undercommon—one published adventure declares, "The nothic communicates using telepathy." I'd suggest reading this as evidence that *some* nothics possess telepathy and others don't, and that it's up to you as the Dungeon Master to decide whether any given nothic does or doesn't communicate this way. If you want any interaction to take place between your PCs and the nothic, I suggest giving it telepathy, because the PCs aren't likely to be fluent in Undercommon, which is the only spoken language the nothic knows.

A nothic (there will only ever be one at a time—nothics are intensely solitary) will be aware of the PCs as soon as they approach within 120 feet of it. Rather than hostile, however, it will be curious at first (treat it as "indifferent" for the purposes of social interaction—see "Resolving Interactions," *Dungeon Master's Guide*, chapter 8), and it will be torn between the desire to stay hidden and the desire to learn whether the PCs know anything interesting. If a particular area of a dungeon (castle, cavern, etc.) is home to the nothic, and other areas are inhabited by other creatures, the nothic stays put, hoping eagerly that the PCs will wander its way; if it's the only sentient creature in the area, it stalks the PCs.

Once the PCs approach within 30 feet, it starts using its Weird Insight on them, learning a secret fact about each one, which you can extrapolate from their backgrounds and characteristics. If the nothic does communicate telepathically, it will share its disturbing observations telepathically out of a nihilistic compulsion to show them the "truth" about themselves. It puts its own sinister, overheated spin on each secret, as in these examples from a campaign I've run:

- *You think you survived because you were strong . . . you survived because you were nothing! Your people were nothing! And they will be forgotten, like everyone and everything else!*
- *An estate built on a crumbling foundation . . . a tainted pedigree . . . orc blood! It would ruin them if the secret got out! Do the others know?*

- *Dark, bloody thoughts . . . that's why she didn't want you! She knew, and she was horrified! Disgusted!*
- *Abnormal . . . freak . . . recluse . . . your clan meant everything to you, and they didn't want you!*
- *An empty hole where your home used to be . . . you have no place to go back to . . . the world has turned its back on you!*

If your players are like mine, their reactions will split roughly 80/20 between being thoroughly creeped out and saying matter-of-factly, "Yeah, that's about right," which I think is a good split.

All the while, the nothic uses its Stealth skill to remain hidden from view—its use of telepathy won't give away its position. It emerges from hiding only if a PC tries to engage it in conversation. Its behavior is eccentric and sinister, but it won't threaten the PCs, and it tries to keep a distance of 20 to 30 feet away. If it's cornered, or feels cornered, it becomes even more erratic and deranged and may at that point initiate combat itself, reflexively using its Rotting Gaze like a skunk uses its spray. But if engaged in conversation, it reveals its interest in secrets, especially magical secrets, and lets the PCs know that it may share what it knows in exchange for a gift of a magic item.

Once combat begins, if the nothic has first initiative, it Readies its Rotting Gaze to use against the first PC to come within 20 feet of it (or, if the PCs are already closer than that, the first PC to move toward it). Otherwise, it Dodges (it doesn't have the combat training to know how to Disengage) and moves away from the PCs attacking it to a place of maximum cover. Only if it has nowhere to run does it use its double Claw Multiattack against a melee attacker. If that attacker is reduced to 0 hp and other enemies are attacking it from range, it uses its Rotting Gaze against any of them within 30 feet of it, then tries to find a new escape route.

Unlike many monsters, the nothic doesn't wait until it's seriously wounded to try to run away. It doesn't want to fight at all. It attacks only in self-defense, and it always seeks to hide or escape if it can, rather than fight. But it will keep using Rotting Gaze against any PC who tries to pursue it, if they get too close.

PC FEARS

If you want to add an extra creep factor to the nothic, you can decide that if it makes its Weird Insight check by a certain margin (say, 5 or more), it gains an extra measure of awareness of what the PC fears and customizes its telepathic whispers accordingly. Unless a player has gone into a lot of depth in describing their character's personality, determining a PC's fears will involve some guesswork; it should have a meaningful connection to PCs' backgrounds and characteristics, but it doesn't have to be perfectly accurate. All the nothic's Weird Insights are distorted by its own insanity, so you can't expect it to be the perfect psychoanalyst.*

LAWFUL GOOD
- There's a defect in your character, a taint in your soul. Sooner or later, it will impair your judgment and lead you astray.
- You don't belong among these people; none of them will look out for you when the chips are down.
- No one cares about what you feel or need. If you complain, they'll hate you.

NEUTRAL GOOD
- You're useless and helpless; you don't contribute anything of value.

---

* For these sample fears, I'm indebted to *Personality Types: Using the Enneagram for Self-Discovery*, revised edition, by Don Richard Riso and Russ Hudson, a useful resource for both DMs and players looking for a quick way to give characters personalities that are plausible, coherent, and internally consistent.

- Nothing good can last. There's always trouble lurking around the corner.
- In the grand scheme of things, who you are isn't that important, is it?

CHAOTIC GOOD
- Freedom and happiness can't last forever. At some point, the well will run dry.
- You're nobody. The minute you let someone else overshadow you, no one will care about you anymore.
- You can't let yourself go soft, or they'll take away your freedom while you're weak.

LAWFUL NEUTRAL
- They know you haven't lived up to your own standards. They'll condemn you for it.
- You can never make everyone happy. Sooner or later, they'll all abandon you.
- The one you love loves somebody else more.

NEUTRAL
- You're not the expert you claim to be, and they know it. The world has no use for you.
- There are changes coming, whether you like it or not, and nothing will be the same. You're going to have to change too, and you're not ready, are you?
- Nobody appreciates you for who you are; no one cares what you feel. You're wasting your life on fantasies.

CHAOTIC NEUTRAL
- This life is boring and frustrating and not giving you enough of what you want. But what if there's nothing better?

- They can all see right through you. They know you're a fraud.
- You don't have a handle on things anymore. These people don't respect you, and they'll turn on you any minute.

LAWFUL EVIL
- You're out of control. You've been wrong about what was important all along, and there's no way to justify the mad things you've done.
- They hate you; they'll destroy what little security you have left. You have to destroy them first.
- Your selfishness is driving people away from you; at this point, they'll never want to come back.

NEUTRAL EVIL
- You can't defend yourself from the forces closing in on you. You can't run. You can't hide.
- You brought these troubles on yourself, you let it all happen, and there's no way to undo it now.
- Your situation is hopeless. Everything is pointless. You're on your own.

CHAOTIC EVIL
- You've ruined yourself and your life. You can never be happy—you're not even capable of it anymore.
- You're an empty phony. They're going to catch you and expose you, and when they do, you'll be ruined.
- How much longer can you hold out against those who want to get back at you, who want you to submit, to surrender? Not much longer.

OTYUGHS

The **otyugh** is an old-school monster, dating all the way back to AD&D—and in all that time, arguments have raged over how to pronounce its name. Countless gamers over the years have made their best guesses, usually settling on something like *oh*-tee-yug, while the Final Fantasy video game series has adopted the pronunciation oh-*tyoo* (second syllable stressed, to rhyme with "through"). But according to a 1985 *Dragon* magazine article, it's *ot*-yug; that's the one I'd go with.

The *Monster Manual* categorizes otyughs as aberrations, not monstrosities, though it doesn't explain why—maybe because of their Limited Telepathy trait or their odd morphology. They're not described as extraplanar, they're not evil, and they're not especially intelligent; in all respects other than their telepathy, they seem to behave like an evolved creature.

Otyughs are brutes, with high Strength and extraordinary Constitution. They have a well-developed survival instinct, including the ability to discriminate between easy and difficult prey. However, despite their ability to communicate verbally in their own language, their Intelligence is animal at best—about what you'd expect of a sign language–using gorilla. Theoretically, it may be possible to bargain with an otyugh, by appealing to its one and only interest: food.

They have long-range darkvision, suggesting a subterranean lifestyle, although you might find one aboveground in places that don't get much light, such as a thick swamp or jungle or the bottom of a cellar garbage pit. They're not penalized for moving around in daylight; they simply like the dark better. They can see fine in it, and their prey generally can't.

Normally, they're not even aggressive. All they really want is food, lots and lots of it, and their definition of "food" is much looser than other beings'. An aggressive otyugh is a famished otyugh, whose supply of refuse isn't hitting the spot. If an otyugh is attacking you, it's because it intends to eat you.

So what's an otyugh going to want to talk about with this Limited Telepathy it has? Most likely, there's only one thing it ever has to say:

"Hungry!" (The otyugh's telepathy is coherent enough that the PC will understand that some other, psychic creature is trying to tell them that *it's* hungry—the PC won't mistakenly start to feel that *they're* hungry.)

Wise PCs will chuck some food the otyugh's way and steer clear of it. Foolish PCs may ignore the warning or, worse, approach to investigate. A hungry otyugh attacks when they come within 10 feet of it. A *starving* otyugh attacks when they come within 40 feet.

The otyugh's Multiattack consists of a Bite attack and two Tentacle attacks, but the Tentacle attacks come first, because they can grapple and restrain. If the first tentacle strikes, grapples, and restrains its target, the second tentacle grabs for a second target if one is within reach; if not, it smacks the target held in the first tentacle a second time. The otyugh always directs its Bite attack at a grappled target, if it has one, because it makes this attack roll with advantage. If an otyugh starts its turn with a grappled victim in one or each of its tentacles, it uses its Tentacle Slam action instead, to try to bludgeon them into submission.

Since the goal of an otyugh is to consume its victims, it keeps Biting a grappled target even after reducing them to 0 hp, not moving on to another target until the unconscious victim is dead, i.e., eaten.

As a DM, though, I wouldn't throw an otyugh at a party if it had a significant chance of getting to eat one of them. It just isn't a compelling boss monster candidate; it functions better as a hazard than as a nemesis. An otyugh encounter shouldn't present greater than Medium difficulty to your players (see "Combat Encounter Difficulty," *Dungeon Master's Guide*, chapter 3).

An otyugh doesn't move around if it doesn't have to, and it doesn't usually have to. If it's hungry enough, though, and its potential meals back away from it, it will move toward them at normal speed. It gives up and retreats only when it's seriously wounded (reduced to 45 hp or fewer), and if it's starving, even that won't be enough to deter it.

CLOAKERS

The **cloaker's** first appearance in a core book was in the second edition *Monstrous Compendium*, in which it was described as "impossible to distinguish from a common black cloak." Fashion mimic! Wisely, later editions have depicted it in more evolutionarily plausible terms, although it's still categorized as an aberration rather than a monstrosity.

Cloakers have exceptionally high Strength and high Dexterity but merely above-average Constitution, an ability contour that I associate with shock attacks; combined with their proficiency in Stealth and their False Appearance trait, this contour indicates an ambush predator that seeks to take down its prey in a single strike, if possible. A fight that lasts more than a couple of rounds isn't to a cloaker's liking.

Cloakers' Intelligence and Wisdom are above average, but not unusually so, so while they're selective about their targets, their judgment may sometimes be off. (And then there's that strangely high Charisma. What's that for? Resistance to banishment? Fashion sense? I have no good explanation.) They have 60 feet of darkvision and Light Sensitivity and speak Deep Speech and Undercommon, so obviously, they're subterranean dwellers that have little or no reason to venture aboveground.

Attacking cloakers wrap themselves around the heads and upper bodies of their prey, and their Damage Transfer trait causes half of all incoming damage to go right through their thin bodies and into the unfortunate saps they're suffocating, but this added staying power doesn't necessarily make them any more inclined to stay around.

The cloaker's Multiattack is a Bite/Tail combination. The Tail attack has a long reach but otherwise is simple, straightforward damage. Bite employs the common fifth edition practice of adding a rider to a successful hit, but this time with an unusual qualifier: The initial attack roll must be made with advantage. Attacking while lurking in pitch darkness or hidden behind its False Appearance isn't just beneficial for the cloaker—it's practically mandatory.

When the cloaker Bites with advantage and hits, its prey is not only blinded but also unable to breathe. The side effect of being blinded is simple—disadvantage on the creature's own attack rolls, advantage on attack rolls against the creature—but the *Monster Manual* stat block doesn't elaborate on the effects of suffocation. For that, we have to refer to "Suffocating," in chapter 8 of the *Player's Handbook*, which states that a creature "can hold its breath for a number of minutes

equal to 1 + its Constitution modifier (minimum of 30 seconds)."
After that, "it can survive for a number of rounds equal to its Constitution modifier (minimum 1 round)," then "drops to 0 hp and starts
dying." In the case of the cloaker, we skip straight to the out-of-breath
condition, deeming that the target hasn't had a chance to prepare
with a deep inhalation—an interpretation supported by at least one of
D&D's designers. Without it, this feature is of questionable use; with
it, it's meaningfully threatening.

If you can't breathe, you can't speak, and if you can't speak, you
can't yell for help. Also, you can't cast a spell that requires a verbal component while you're suffocating. Under the core rules, that
reduces the number of spells you can cast with a cloaker wrapped
around your head to nine—two of which are rituals, and one of
which requires you to be able to see your target. But hey, at least you
can still cast *counterspell*, *friends*, *hypnotic pattern*, *minor illusion*, *mis-
lead*, or *true strike*.

The last two actions in the cloaker's arsenal are Moan and Phantasms. Phantasms is the cloaker's version of the *mirror image* spell, and
there's no good reason whatsoever for the cloaker not to use this action
as soon as it spots prey, before it makes its first attack: Being neither a
spell nor an attack, it doesn't give away the cloaker's position. It functions only in dim light or darkness; bright light dispels it.

Moan frightens most creatures within a 60-foot radius. What's the
effect of the frightened condition? It imposes disadvantage on attack
rolls against the source of fear, and it prevents one from moving any
closer to that source. This is a great way for the cloaker to make sure
that no one comes to rescue its prey. The timing is tricky, though. A
hidden creature is revealed when it makes a sound ("Hiding," *Player's
Handbook*, chapter 7), so it's unwise to use this feature before attacking unless the cloaker has some means of attacking with advantage
other than stealth. After it attacks, however, it wants to finish its prey
off, not spend a whole action trying to scare their friends away. Plus,
that saving throw DC isn't high, the effect doesn't last long, and once
another creature has engaged the cloaker in melee already, it loses a lot
of its usefulness.

How can we make this feature work? Here's what I've come up with:

First, the cloaker selects its prey. In the manner of other ambush predators, it chooses someone old, young, weak, wounded, isolated, or oblivious. (Looks can be deceiving, however, and the cloaker can be deceived. It doesn't know that an elderly halfling can also be a level 7 Way of Shadow monk, for instance.)

Second, while still in shadow, it uses the Hide action and begins to stealthily stalk its prey.

Third, it uses the Phantasms action and closes to a distance of 40 feet.

Fourth—the first chance its prey and its prey's allies have to realize what's going on, unless the cloaker has screwed something up in the first three steps—the cloaker glides up and strikes. It Bites first, because a successful Bite/envelop means it makes its follow-up Tail strike with advantage.

Fifth, on its next turn, if it hasn't been driven off (see below), it Multiattacks again, only this time it uses Tail against an ally of its prey if it needs to.

Finally, the moment of truth arrives. If the cloaker hasn't at least seriously injured its prey at this point, it's smart enough to realize it's not going to get a meal out of this, detaches itself, and withdraws. If it has, it makes one last Bite attack. Either way, when it decides it's time to leave, that's when it Moans, because this is its most effective way to keep anything from following it.

Why doesn't it try to carry its prey away with it? Normally, I'd say it would. But here's the problem: The cloaker's Bite attack doesn't grapple, as so many other predators' attacks do. Whoops. No taking its leftovers to go, unless the victim has fallen unconscious and weighs no more than 255 pounds (including all gear).

So what makes a cloaker decide discretion is the better part of survival?

- A moderate injury or worse (reduced to 54 hp or fewer). Opportunistic predators have little tolerance for armed resistance.

- Bright light shoved in its face. Nope nope nope nope nope nope.
- Melee engagement by three or more opponents other than its prey.

On the other hand . . . if, by some fluke, the allies of the cloaker's prey don't come to their rescue at all, it will happily stick around long enough to finish its meal, even if it takes three or more rounds.

SLAADI

Slaadi are beings of pure chaos, native to the outer plane of Limbo, vaguely resembling humanoid salamanders. There's no good reason for them to be hanging out on the prime material plane, but as beings of pure chaos, they don't need a good reason to be doing anything.

Slaadi come in a variety of colors, tied to their bizarre reproductive cycle. Red slaadi deposit eggs that hatch into slaad tadpoles (I think the writers missed a great opportunity by not calling them "slaad-poles"), which grow up into blue or green slaadi. Blue slaadi, in turn, infect victims with a bacteriophage that transforms them into red or green slaadi. Green slaadi are more powerful and intelligent than red and blue slaadi, and they eventually metamorphose into gray slaadi, which in turn can metamorphose into death slaadi by eating the corpses of other death slaadi.

Being aberrations, slaadi should behave—and fight—in ways that reflect their origin on the plane of chaos, a factor that has to be considered alongside their abilities and features. Slaadi are high-challenge monsters, so as tempting as it may be to ramp up the chaos they create by having the player characters encounter many of them at once, it can be deadly to throw more than one slaad at a party of low- or even intermediate-level PCs. Moreover, their ability to reproduce by turning humanoids into slaadi and slaad hosts can have exponential effects, so even one slaad is a threat that needs to be squelched pronto.

The **slaad tadpole** is tiny and weak but frisky: It has high Dexterity and proficiency in Stealth. It has few hit points, but it's resistant to acid, cold, fire, lightning, and thunder damage and has advantage on saving throws against magical effects. Thus, in a reversal of the more common monster paradigm, regular melee fighters should have no trouble harming it, but spellcasters will be frustrated.

A slaad tadpole's primary motivation is to grow up into a big slaad. Consequently, it has no desire to hang around and fight anybody. As soon as it emerges from its host, it flees to a place of hiding, using the Dash action (it's not bright enough to do anything else). It has no special movement such as swimming, climbing, or burrowing, so it darts under furniture, through cracks in the wall, and so forth. It may be helpful to imagine it doing exactly what a rat would do if you spotted one and started chasing it. It Bites only if grabbed.

If the PCs try to pursue it, use the "Chases" rules in chapter 8 of the *Dungeon Master's Guide*—and absolutely use the optional chase complications. I'd even go so far as to say that the slaadpole's chaotic nature *causes* complications to occur: If a chase participant rolls 11–20 on the first roll, have them roll a second time and use that result. (Having the chase participants roll d10s—or even d12s—rather than d20s is probably going too far.)

As soon as the slaadpole leaves the PCs' field of vision, assume that it Hides, and apply its Stealth modifier to its pursuers' attempts to spot it (skill contest, Stealth vs. Perception).

Red slaadi and **blue slaadi** are dumb brutes without Stealth but with the same damage resistances as the slaadpole. They're vicious toe-to-toe melee fighters, with lots of hit points and very high Strength and Constitution, and their goal is to deposit their eggs or bacteriophages in humanoid hosts, so they want to make as many Claw attacks as possible against as many targets as possible. They're indiscriminate in target selection, directing their attacks at the nearest humanoid enemy whom they haven't already hit with a Claw attack. (Once they've Clawed a target, they have no way of knowing whether they've managed to infect them; they just assume success and move on to the next target.) On each turn, they use their Multiattack to Claw/ Claw/Bite, attacking the same target again only if both Claw attacks miss. Once they've Clawed every humanoid in the immediate area, they Dash away in search of another group of humanoid targets. If the

PCs give chase, consider applying the same chaos-inducing second roll for chase complications rule as described above.

Green slaadi are sentient spellcasters whose primary goal is to discover the key to metamorphosis into gray slaadi, so they generally try to stay on the down-low. As long as they're in or near any inhabited area, they use their Shapechanger trait to assume inconspicuous humanoid forms, often those of their former hosts. However, their ability to assume a particular physical form isn't enough to fully conceal their true nature, so even if they look totally normal and respectable—possibly even attractive—their behavior will be glaringly, unmistakably weird. (For one thing, they no longer speak Common or whatever other language their hosts spoke, only Slaad.) Only if their slaad-nature is discovered and called out do they resort to fighting.

When a green slaad fights, its primary goal is not to kill its opponents but to escape. That being said, killing your pursuers is a reliable way of keeping them from pursuing you, and green slaadi, despite having Intelligence superior to that of other slaadi, still aren't overly endowed with Wisdom. Also, note their innate ability to cast *fireball* and their Hurl Flame feature. A panicking green slaad will set lots and lots and lots of stuff on fire.

Let's evaluate each of its abilities with an eye toward how it can help the green slaad make its getaway (noting, first and foremost, the fact that it *doesn't* have proficiency in Stealth):

- *Fireball* drops the bomb on a sphere 40 feet in diameter—large enough, on average, to char four enemies (per the Targets in Area of Effect table, *Dungeon Master's Guide*, chapter 8), not to mention igniting all flammable objects in the area.
- *Fear* affects up to three enemies, on average (again, per the Targets in Area of Effect table), causing them to drop whatever they're holding and run the other way if they fail their Wisdom saving throws. It requires concentration to sustain.
- *Invisibility* allows the green slaad to move unseen, though not to attack or cast spells while invisible. It also requires concentration.

- *Detect magic* has no bearing on the green slaad's ability to escape. Its application is in social interaction situations, in which the green slaad—always keen to learn anything that might help it metamorphose into a gray slaad—scans the PCs to O HAI I SEE YOU HAVE A MAGIC ITEM WITH MAGICAL PROPERTIES MAY I LOOK AT IT PRETTY PLEASE? Of course, social interaction with a green slaad is always going to be oddball at best, since unless a party member speaks Slaad, it will have to be conducted via either telepathy or gesticulation.

- *Detect thoughts* is a useful early-warning system that the green slaad uses constantly to ascertain whether it's been found out.

- *Mage hand*, normally, is useful for picking up the teakettle without burning yourself. However, cast by a slaad, it becomes a micro-poltergeist that can slam doors, use objects that are on fire to set other objects on fire, prod animals into stampeding in front of pursuers, yank guards' weapons out of their scabbards and keyrings off their belts, throw cabbages (not to deal any damage, but simply because throwing cabbages is hilarious), and engage in all sorts of other mischief that doesn't involve lifting or pushing more than 10 pounds of weight.

- The green slaad's Multiattack can consist of two uses of Hurl Flame, two Staff attacks (in humanoid form), two Staff attacks plus a Bite (in slaad form), or two Claw attacks plus a Bite (in slaad form). The melee attacks have a better chance of hitting than the Hurl Flame attack, although as DM you can rule that a Hurl Flame attack that misses its target hits something else and sets it on fire. To account for the difference in attack modifiers, we'll apply a 77 percent multiplier to Hurl Flame's damage for the sake of comparison (based on to-hit probabilities vs. target AC 15). Thus, two Hurl Flames = 16 damage, two Staff attacks = 22 damage, Staff/Staff/Bite = 33 damage, and Claw/Claw/Bite = 26 damage. This tells us that, when mayhem ensues, the green slaad would prefer to revert to its slaad form rather than stay in its humanoid disguise.

Fifth edition D&D bases its combat-balancing decisions on the assumption that combat encounters typically last three rounds, but to take down a green slaad that quickly, PCs will have to be capable of dealing a combined 49 damage per round (thanks to its Regeneration trait), more than that if they're relying on magic to deal the damage. Even so, spending one turn to revert to slaad form will cost the green slaad precious time, during which the PCs can deal it quite a bit of harm.

So it won't do it the simple way. And anyway, why would a slaad do anything the simple way?

The first thing a busted slaad does is turn invisible. The next thing it does is revert to slaad form, which it can do without becoming visible, because changing shape is neither an attack nor a spell. *Then* it attacks. Or maybe it doesn't even attack. Maybe it just runs away, still invisible. It can keep that spell going for a full hour, after all.

But maybe the PCs have means of detecting or tracking an invisible opponent. If the green slaad observes that it's being pursued despite being invisible, then it drops *fireball* and *fear* on its pursuers, the former while still invisible (thereby rendering it visible to all). It doesn't stop fleeing, although while it's using these actions to disrupt pursuit, it can't also Dash. If the environment contains enough loose and/or flammable objects that it can use to cause further mayhem, it may spend actions on *mage hand* or Hurl Flame, but most likely, once it's used *fireball* and *fear*, it will simply Dash until it escapes or is cornered. If cornered, it will fight with Staff and Bite, using *invisibility* a second time if an escape path presents itself. Given a choice between fleeing and fighting, it always prefers to flee.

Gray slaadi, on the other hand, have reached the pinnacle of their "natural" metamorphosis and relish fighting. In fact, they're usually on the prime material plane in the first place on some specific mission of mayhem. They can cast *invisibility* at will, but rather than use it to escape, they use it to approach enemies and get the jump on them. Although they natively speak only Slaad, they can use *tongues* to disguise their inability to speak the PCs' language(s). Their emergency exit, if somehow the PCs manage to seriously injure them (reduce them to

50 hp or fewer), is *plane shift*. But even gray slaadi have low Wisdom, and their choice of targets is more or less random, unless they're on a mission to attack one or more specific people.

Gray slaadi probably won't bother to use *fear* against enemies they mean to fight, only against bystanders who get in the way of whatever mission they may be on. They can cast *major image* at will, and this can be useful for creating distractions during chases or even entirely fake personae for them to interact with the PCs through. A gray slaad may disguise itself as a VIP and conjure up a *major image* of a bodyguard or adviser—or vice versa! For super-duper mayhem during combat, gray slaadi can cast *fly*, gaining a flying speed of 60 feet and allowing them to swoop in to attack twice with Greatsword and once with Bite, then soar back into the air, out of reach of melee attacks. (With AC 18, they're indifferent to opportunity attacks.) And, of course, they still have good ol' *fireball*, only unlike green slaadi, they can cast it *twice* per day.

In general, having higher Strength and Dexterity than Constitution (though all three are very high), they favor running around and dealing large amounts of damage in single-turn Multiattacks over staying in one place and fighting toe-to-toe. As long as they have their greatswords, they favor this attack action over Claws.

According to the *Monster Manual* flavor text, **death slaadi** lead invasion forces of red and blue slaadi to ravage other planes. Remember how I said that just one slaad was a potentially deadly encounter? A death slaad accompanied by many red and blue slaadi is a potentially deadly encounter even for top-tier adventurers. When you design death slaad encounters, make absolutely certain you're not burdening your players with an enemy they're not equipped to take on.

Death slaadi don't bother with skirmishing—they're brutes. When they cast *fly*, they do it to close quickly with an enemy they want to pound the stuffing out of. They also have a bizarrely high Charisma for being hideous, spiky salamander people from a chaos plane. I can only assume this is to help them blend in better while Shapechanged into humanoid form. They'll still be weird, but . . . I don't know . . . *intriguingly* weird, maybe? *Compellingly* weird?

In addition to all the powers of a gray slaad, death slaadi have one daily use of *cloudkill*. There's a difference between how they use *fireball* and how they use *cloudkill*: *Fireball* is for causing mayhem and, incidentally, doing damage to pesky PCs getting in the death slaad's way. *Cloudkill* is specifically for killing people the death slaad wants to kill.

Like gray slaadi, death slaadi prefer to use Greatsword rather than Claws in melee combat, and they prefer to fight in their slaad form rather than their humanoid form, in order to include Bite in their Multiattack. They retreat when seriously injured (reduced to 68 hp or fewer), using *plane shift* to escape back to Limbo.

Alone among slaadi, death slaadi are canny enough to be able to guess at PCs' alignments, and they'll zero in on lawful characters. After defeating one, they'll move on to another lawful character, who may not necessarily be the nearest. If and when all lawful opponents have been defeated, only then will they move on to other PCs, choosing targets largely at random.

CHUULS

Chuuls are, more or less, enormous semi-uplifted crayfish, servants of the mighty, ancient aboleths. They're amphibious, chosen for their role because of their ability to survive on land as well as in the water. They're larger than human-size and exceptionally strong and tough, predisposing them to be brute fighters. Although they're not exceptionally dexterous, their chitin gives them an Armor Class of 16. They can sense magic, and we can infer from the flavor text that they're drawn to it, obeying an ancient, instinctual command to gather powerful items for the aboleths that ruled them.

Chuuls have darkvision, suggesting that they move about on open land only at night and spend the rest of their time either underground or underwater. Judging from the flavor text, they don't seem to have a lot of motivation to go wandering around but rather stick close to locations that they feel some urge or duty to guard. They aren't conscious of any such duty, however: With Intelligence 5, they operate strictly by instinct.

As brute fighters, indiscriminate in target selection, they generally move to attack the first enemy they sense. The range of their senses, however, varies: Their darkvision allows them to see another creature out to a range of 60 feet, but their Sense Magic trait extends to 120 feet, so the presence of a spellcaster or the possession of magic items in an adventuring party will catch their attention. And they're proficient in Perception, so good luck sneaking by.

The chuul's basic attack action is a Multiattack comprising two Pincer attacks, plus one Tentacles attack if it has a creature grappled. The grappled condition comes from the Pincer attack: Any hit with a pincer is an automatic grapple, from which a target can try to escape on its own turn.

Despite being a brute fighter, and thus generally unconcerned about taking hits from a melee opponent, the chuul has a 10-foot reach, so it doesn't need to get any closer before it attacks. Consequently, when it moves to attack, it stops moving as soon as it's within its own reach of its target.

The Multiattack action doesn't specify the order of the chuul's attacks: They can go Pincer/Pincer, Pincer/Pincer/Tentacles, Pincer/Tentacles/Pincer, or (if it's the second round or later and the chuul has an enemy grappled already) Tentacles/Pincer/Pincer. The Tentacles attack does no damage but injects a paralyzing poison. This poison prevents a victim who fails their saving throw from taking actions or reactions, causes them to automatically fail Strength and Dexterity saving throws, grants advantage on attack rolls against them, and turns every hit into a critical hit as long as the attacker is within 5 feet. It lasts 1 minute but wears off sooner if the victim succeeds on a DC 13 Constitution saving throw—which they probably will at the end of their first turn after being poisoned, so the chuul doesn't have a lot of time to take advantage of this state.

Thus, a chuul's first action is a Multiattack, starting with Pincer. Every Pincer attack that misses is followed by another Pincer attack. Every Pincer attack that hits is followed by a Tentacles attack. Every Tentacles attack is followed by a Pincer attack—but not necessarily against the same opponent. If a chuul has an enemy grappled but is unsuccessful at poisoning them, it directs this next Pincer attack at someone else, aiming to grapple a second victim. On the other hand, if a chuul does have a poisoned victim in its pincer, it keeps Pincering that victim.

Let's say the chuul's first attack is against Berach the elf sorcerer. The first attack is always a Pincer attack, and it hits, grabbing the elf and pulling him closer. The second attack, since the first was successful, is a Tentacles attack. Berach, unfortunately, is a fragile flower—his player chose Constitution as his dump stat—and he fails his saving throw. He's poisoned, paralyzed, and incapacitated. The third attack is another Pincer attack against Berach, with advantage, and when it hits, it's an automatic crit. Owww. Poor Berach is down already.

In the next round, no one else smells like magic quite as much as Berach did, but the sword that Guthrún the barbarian is swinging sure does. The first attack is a Pincer attack; it hits, and Guthrún is grappled. The second attack, since the first was successful, is a Tentacles attack, but Guthrún has Constitution 18 and is unaffected. What now?

Often, in the fifth edition *Monster Manual*, when a monster has an attack that automatically grapples on a hit, the grappled target is also restrained, but that's not the case with the chuul. Since it has no advantage on attack rolls against an unpoisoned, unparalyzed, fully capacitated barbarian, rather than attack her again, it turns its attention to Amalric the paladin and aims a Pincer attack at him. Amalric is wearing chain mail, though, and the chuul's attack fails—it can't get a grip on him.

Between the second and third round, Guthrún breaks free of the chuul's pincer. When it tries to attack her again, it misses. Meanwhile, also between rounds, "Three-Cheeses" Jack, the stout halfling rogue, comes around and tries to hamstring it with a magic dagger. This draws the chuul's attention away from Amalric, and its next Pincer attack is aimed at Three-Cheeses. It gets him, and now the chuul can use its Tentacles attack on him. Three-Cheeses resists the poison as well, but he's not strong enough to break the grapple on his own turn.

Thus, at the start of the fourth round, while the chuul holds Three-Cheeses in its claw, it uses its Tentacles attack to try again to poison him, fails again, then aims its next Pincer attack not at Three-Cheeses but at Guthrún again. See the pattern? The chuul only Pincers a grappled target if that target is poisoned. The chuul can tell whether or not Three-Cheeses is poisoned, but it's not smart enough to figure out that if the poison didn't work on him the first time, it probably won't work on him the second or third time either. So it gets stuck in a loop, attacking other targets with its Pincer attacks yet trying again and again to poison Three-Cheeses with Tentacles. Meanwhile, Three-Cheeses, grappled but not restrained, can aim attacks of his own at the chuul and roll without disadvantage or any other penalty.

Chuuls do have a flight instinct that kicks in when they're seriously injured (reduced to 37 hp or fewer). Lacking the intelligence to Disengage, they Dodge as they retreat toward the nearest body of water, then switch to the Dash action as they swim away.

ABOLETHS

From their description, you'd think **aboleths** were among the bossest of all boss monsters, but in fact, they have a challenge rating of just 10—well within the power of a party of medium-high-level adventurers to take on, assuming they have some way to reach the creatures' underwater lairs.

The *Monster Manual* classes them as aberrations, but they don't originate from some other plane of existence, despite having a connection to the Elemental Plane of Water. Rather, they antedate all the gods and intelligent beings of the contemporary material world. They are the Old Ones. I like to think of them as the product of a different, much more ancient path of evolution, like holdovers from the world-sea of the Ordovician period in our own history, four hundred fifty million years ago, and their connection to the Elemental Plane of Water as a way they discovered of perpetuating their existence over the eons.

Aboleths have high Constitution and extraordinary Strength, but it's their exceptional mental abilities that define them. With their high

Wisdom and exceptional Intelligence and Charisma, they're schemers and manipulators par excellence, with superior situational awareness. Because they can't be permanently slain, according to the *Monster Manual* flavor text, their self-preservation impulse doesn't manifest the same way it would in an ordinary mortal creature.

As for their physical abilities, they fit the brute profile most closely, though not perfectly, their Constitution falling somewhat short of their Strength. They have no ranged attack and engage in melee without reluctance, but their preference is for a short and decisive battle, settled by their phenomenal Strength, over a drawn-out one.

Aboleths have proficiency in Constitution, Intelligence, and Wisdom saving throws, but not in Dexterity, leaving them vulnerable to damaging area-effect spells. This suggests that they have little concern for spellcasters in general, but an opponent who casts this particular type of spell will become a high-priority target.

Aboleths also have proficiency in History (not that they're generous about sharing their knowledge) and Perception, they have darkvision out to 120 feet, and they can make a Wisdom (Perception) check on another creature's turn as a legendary action, so it's hard to get close to one without its noticing. Unless a PC knows Deep Speech, aboleths communicate only by telepathy—and they're not interested in communicating with anyone they can't use to further their own interests. They come to this judgment through their Probing Telepathy ability, which grants them insight into a creature's desires if that creature answers their telepathic call, and once they deem a creature minion-worthy, they seal the deal with the Enslave feature. More on that later.

For now, let's talk about the aboleth's melee capabilities. Its tentacles and tail have 10 feet of reach, and it's surrounded by a 5-foot-thick Mucous Cloud that has the unsettling effect of infecting other creatures with a pathogen that prevents them from breathing air. Thus, it can easily reach and strike an opponent who can't easily reach it to strike back. Its tentacles transmit a similar pathogen, one that even more unsettlingly causes a target's skin to become slimy, translucent, and effectively allergic to open air, and its Multiattack comprises three Tentacle attacks in a single action. The aboleth's Tail attack, which does more raw damage than a Tentacle attack but has no pathogenic effect, isn't part of its Multiattack, but it is available as a legendary action.

Aboleths have a swimming speed of 40 feet; meanwhile, your PCs can swim at only half their base movement speeds, unless they're granted a swimming speed by a spell (such as *alter self*) or magic item (such as a *cloak of the manta ray*). Thus, it should be relatively easy for an aboleth to pursue and attack any target it chooses, although it may take a couple of rounds.

Finally, the aboleth has the Enslave ability. Yes, its targets get to repeat their Wisdom saves anytime they take damage. But remember, aboleths are crafty: All your party needs is one weak link, and they'll zero in on it. Are an aboleth's opponents able to roam and breathe underwater because of a spell cast by a single character? Fine—it will Enslave *that* character, then command it to dispel its own handiwork. Enslave is hardly worth using for purposes so prosaic as making party members fight among themselves, and besides, any damage they take can cause them to snap out of it. More likely, an aboleth will try to Enslave a character already poisoned by its tentacles, telling them that it's useless to resist: Their prior life is over, and their only future now is as a servitor of the aboleth.

So who are the aboleth's top-priority melee targets? Elves, who have advantage against being charmed. Spellcasters who throw area-effect spells that require Dex saves. Anyone in possession of a magic item that threatens the aboleth. Anyone capable of inflicting moderate damage (more than 40 hp) to the aboleth in a single turn. High-Wisdom characters, who are better equipped to resist Enslave—*unless* the aboleth is moderately injured (reduced to 94 hp or fewer), in which case it switches its focus to *low*-Wisdom characters, those with Wisdom save modifiers of 0 or less. Depending on how many such characters are within its reach, it may aim all its Tentacle attacks at one opponent or divide them up among several.

Aboleths are legendary creatures; I've already mentioned two of their legendary actions, Detect and Tail Swipe. It uses Tail Swipe to counterattack on a character's turn anytime that character tries to flank-attack it, Detect on the turn of any character who Hides and tries to sneak up on it. The third legendary action is Psychic Drain, which absorbs hit points from an Enslaved creature. An aboleth uses this legendary action on any turn in which (a) it's moderately or seriously injured, (b) it has a creature already Enslaved, and (c) it has the legendary actions to spare (since Psychic Drain costs two). Note that this damage gives the creature another saving throw to break free of Enslave, so the aboleth prefers to use Psychic Drain on *unimportant* Enslaved creatures—ones it Enslaved opportunistically, as opposed to, say, ones it Enslaved because they were buffing their companions.

An aboleth in its lair also has access to lair actions. One is a *phantasmal force* spell, whose only useful purpose is to distract a low-Intelligence opponent from fighting the aboleth itself, presumably while it focuses on more important enemies. One is a grasping tide that pulls creatures from land into a pool of water. This is useful in a situation like the Watcher in the Water scene in J.R.R. Tolkien's *The Fellowship of the Ring*, but it's not at all useful when a battle is taking place entirely underwater.

The third lair action is the only consistently useful one, requiring all underwater enemies within 90 feet to make a Wisdom save against psychic damage. Unfortunately, while an aboleth isn't restricted in general from using the same lair action two rounds in a row, it can't use *this one* a second time without using one of the others in between. The practical upshot is that an aboleth either uses the *phantasmal force* lair action as a reset button or forgoes the use of further lair actions altogether, because the grasping tide lair action is so wholly situational. Because it may never get a second chance to use it, an aboleth uses the rage water lair action only when *all* its opponents are within 90 feet of it.

Because its lair actions aren't nearly as overwhelmingly advantageous as other legendary creatures' lair actions are, an aboleth is more willing than they are to retreat from its lair in order to preserve its continued physical existence. Having to be reborn on the Elemental Plane of Water is better than dying outright, but it's still an inconvenience. An aboleth that's seriously injured (reduced to 54 hp or fewer) will retreat from the engagement, Disengaging if necessary but otherwise Dodging as it moves away, and continuing to use its legendary actions as appropriate.

All this, however, relates strictly to combat. Before combat ever ensues, there's an opportunity for social interaction with the aboleth, and this should be as weird and scary as you can make it. Remember, the aboleth has a memory going back 450 million years, and its intelligence is as different from a PC's as a squid's, a sea urchin's, or a lamprey's would be. Also, at best, it considers the PCs useful idiots, and their gods annoy it. It communicates with the PCs telepathically, knows exactly what they want most, probably finds this either drolly amusing or senseless and absurd, and considers it self-evident that they'd be better off as slimy, aquatic servant beasts.

FIENDS

The incarnations of evil fall into three groups: lawful devils and their servants, chaotic demons and related creatures, and neutral yugoloths. Each type of encounter has its own distinct flavor. Devils are tyrants, but they're tyrants who play by a set of rules—sadistic, arbitrary, and rigged rules, but rules nonetheless. Demons are unbound forces of devastation, killing anything that moves and destroying or desecrating anything that doesn't. And yugoloths, while sociopathic, are also opportunistic—and may be open to persuasion if you can make it worth their while.

LESSER DEVILS

The driving motivation of a devil is to dominate. In the hierarchy of the Nine Hells, authority is absolute, rules are binding, and obedience is imperative—but within those rules, every devil seeks to maximize its advantage, elevate its position, and increase its power over others. Every devil's bargain *looks* fair, but no devil will ever accept an agreement that *is* fair. Agreements between devils, or between a devil and another creature, always contain exploitable loopholes that a devil can use to ensnare the sap foolish enough to accept its terms.

Generally speaking, devils stick to the Nine Hells and their own infernal rat race. Devils encountered on the material plane where the player characters live their lives are there for one of two reasons: Either they've been summoned magically by some idiot who thinks they can benefit from dealing with them, or they're working to advance the interests of a higher-level devil.

Because of this, PCs probably won't encounter the lowest-level devil, the **lemure**, anywhere except in the Nine Hells. Simple, mindless brutes, lemures have no self-preservation instinct and no tactics beyond running up to their foes and pummeling them with their fists.

Imps are errand runners, information gatherers, and mischief makers. PCs will most likely encounter them while they're acting as intermediaries between a greater devil or archdevil in the Nine Hells and a mortal spellcaster or agent of an infernal cause. With low Strength, high Constitution, and very high Dexterity, they fight as skirmishers, using flight, invisibility, and stealth to zip in and out of combat. They can Shapechange into various beast forms, of which the most advantageous is the raven, which has the same base movement speed but a faster flying speed than the imp in its true form.

Imps have 120 feet of darkvision and Devil's Sight, suggesting a strong preference for going about their business at night and underground. They also have resistance to unsilvered normal weapons, cold damage, and magical effects, and are immune to fire damage and poison. Thus, despite their few hit points, they can afford to close with an enemy to deliver a poisonous sting or bite.

However, an imp dares not let itself be diverted from its assigned task. If combat with a group of PCs would prevent it from fulfilling its duty, it's going to prioritize escape over attack, and its most effective way of escaping is simply to turn invisible and fly off. Imps are suited for only the most menial guard duty, but a group of them might be ordered to watch a spot and dive-bomb anyone who trespasses there. In that case, they assume their diabolical raven form and perch 30 feet up in the air, concealing themselves with Stealth; when trespassers arrive, they fly down, attack their targets, and fly back up out of reach. This means possibly incurring one or more opportunity attacks with each strike, but because of their resistance to damage from normal weapons, they're not too worried about this—unless and until they're struck by a magic weapon, at which point they'll stay engaged in melee if duty compels them to and keep their distance if it doesn't. An imp ordered to guard a location won't flee.

Spined devils are also messengers and spies. With high Dexterity, average Strength, and only slightly above-average Constitution, they prefer sniping over melee engagement and therefore favor the use of their double Tail Spine Multiattack. So that they don't have disadvantage on their attack rolls, they maintain a range of 40 feet (preferably aerial), fly in to a distance of 20 feet, fling a pair of spines, then fly away again. If an opponent closes to melee distance, a spined devil retreats 20 feet, attacks with its tail spines again, then retreats another 20 feet.

Only when they've run out of tail spines (each one has twelve) do they use their Bite/Fork Multiattack, and they do this the same way that imps do: Fly down, attack, fly up. The difference is that spined devils have the Flyby trait, which lets them avoid any incoming opportunity attack as they swoop back up. But like the imp, a spined devil won't fight at all if that isn't part of what it was ordered to do; instead, it will fly away as fast as it can. Also like the imp, if it *was* ordered to fight, it won't retreat, no matter how badly wounded it is.

The **bearded devil** is a diabolical warrior. With high physical attributes across the board but no ability to fly, and wielding a polearm with a 10-foot reach, it closes to this distance and engages fearlessly. This devil is content to remain at a distance of 10 feet and attack with its glaive alone, which inflicts "infernal wounds" that cause a target to bleed hit points on subsequent rounds; at this distance, opponents with normal-reach weapons won't be able to fight back. If an opponent chooses to close to within 5 feet, then the bearded devil uses its Multiattack, striking with both its glaive and (LOL) its beard. Note that while a target is beard-poisoned, it can't regain hit points even by magical means, but magical healing can still cause an infernal wound to stop bleeding out. Bearded devils fight to the death and never retreat.

Barbed devils are soldiers and bodyguards. They have very high physical attributes across the board but can't fly, and their melee Multiattack (Claw/Claw/Tail) does slightly more damage than their ranged Multiattack (Hurl Flame × 2) and is also slightly likelier to hit. Therefore, they generally prefer melee engagement over ranged attacks, using the latter only against ranged attackers striking them with magic weapons or ammunition, or spellcasters casting combat spells that either require Dexterity saving throws to avoid or inflict elemental damage other than cold, fire, or poison (e.g., acid). They're not sophisticated fighters, but they do have the sense to determine who their most dangerous enemies are and focus those down, rather than waste time on opponents who can't do much (or anything) to hurt them.

Chain devils are jailers and torturers. They're brutes, with exceptionally high Strength and Constitution and no ability to fly, but their chains have a 10-foot reach, so rather than stroll right up to their opponents, they close only to within 10 feet before attacking.

Their Animate Chains feature is intriguing and requires careful reading to grasp. This feature doesn't animate the chains that a devil is holding and using as weapons. Rather, it imagines chains lying around wherever the devil happens to be (a prison or torture chamber, probably), which the devil then brings to life to fight as its allies. These chains do the same damage as the devil's chain weapon and can also hold enemies restrained, causing them damage and granting the devil advantage on attack rolls against them. There's no duration limit on this ability, and it adds so much to the chain devil's action economy that we have to assume it uses this ability right away at the start of combat, even though it can't take any other action that turn.

The chain devil can make reasonable guesses as to which opponents pose the greatest threat, and it focuses both its grappling attempts and melee attacks on these. Although the text doesn't make it entirely clear, the devil wields more than one chain, so it can continue to flog a target grappled with one chain using another chain; it simply can't use the chain in its left hand to grapple a second target when one is already grappled by the chain in its right. Animated chains, on the other hand, *can* grapple one additional target apiece. So figure that the chain devil itself uses the chain in one hand to strike and grapple what it believes to be its most powerful enemy, uses the chain in the other hand to continue beating it, and uses its animated chains to seize the enemies it believes to be next-most powerful.

As for its Unnerving Mask feature, this is a reaction, usable against only one opponent per round. I figure that devils probably have a pretty good sense for foolishness in mortals, so the chain devil can judge accurately which of its nearby enemies is most likely to flub a Wisdom saving throw.

It should go without saying at this point that chain devils don't retreat, even when seriously injured.

Bone devils are infernal middle management, overseers of lesser devils and damned souls. Their physical ability profile marks them as brutes, but their Dexterity isn't far behind their Strength and Constitution. They also have no ranged attack. However, they *can* fly. Based on these facts, I conclude that the bone devil fights hovering in the air, just because it can, at a range of 10 feet from its chosen target(s), so an opponent who can't reach a height of 10 to 15 feet with their weapon will be unable to fight back. Like barbed devils, bone devils can judge accurately who their most threatening enemies are and prefer to attack them. And like all the devils above, they never abandon their duty by retreating.

Is the polearm variant any better than the standard variant? Against AC 15, a +8 attack modifier means a 70 percent chance to hit. A Claw/Claw/Sting Multiattack can therefore be expected to do 33 damage per turn (setting aside the Constitution save against being poisoned, which is equal between variants). The polearm Multiattack grants only one use of the weapon, but the weapon also does *two* dice worth of damage, for the exact same amount of expected damage. The polearm grapples a target but doesn't restrain it, so there's no advantage on attack rolls against that target, nor does the target make attack rolls with disadvantage. The bone devil is also restricted, at that point, from using its polearm on any other target. On the other hand, the target can't get away. Overall, I'd say it's a wash, the polearm variant imposing a minor loss of flexibility on both sides, which favors the side with the greater numbers.

There's another variant rule under "Devils" in the *Monster Manual*, "Devil Summoning," which allows certain devils to summon assistance. Among the lesser devils, barbed, bearded, and bone devils have this ability. They have to give up one turn's action to do this, and there's no guarantee that they'll succeed.

In the case of barbed and bearded devils, this action summons another devil of the same kind, essentially doubling the power of the original devil. However, their chance of success is only 30 percent. Should they bother? It depends on how much they gain from the one round of attack actions they give up. Fifth edition D&D assumes that the average combat encounter lasts three rounds. Based on this, a devil that uses its first turn to summon an ally gives up one action and has a 30 percent chance of gaining it back, plus one more—a net expected loss of four-tenths of an action. On the other hand, in an encounter in which the devil isn't favored to win, doubling the number of devils should nearly double the length of the combat. Suppose bringing in a second devil turns a three-round encounter into a five-round encounter. Now the devil gives up one action and has a 30 percent chance of gaining it back, plus *three* more, a net expected *gain* of two-tenths of an action.

To me, this isn't worth the likelihood of failure. Instead, for these two types of devils, I think summoning an ally is the last-ditch tactic of a devil that suspects it's about to die. Consequently, they'll use this action when they're seriously injured (reduced to 44 hp or fewer for a barbed devil, 20 or fewer for a bearded devil), provided they're not able to finish off their opponents in a single attack themselves.

A bone devil, on the other hand, has a 40 percent chance of summoning 2d6 spined devils or another bone devil. A 40 percent chance, as opposed to 30 percent, makes the summoning of an equal-strength ally a better deal: Now going from three rounds of combat to five means giving up one action but gaining 1.6, a net expected gain of six-tenths of an action, which could actually amount to something. But never mind that, because a 40 percent chance of summoning, on average, *seven* flying devil porcupines is absolutely worth it. Each of them, flinging its tail spines, can deal an expected 8 damage per turn against AC 15. Seven of those equals 56 damage per turn, significantly better than a single bone devil can do. Now, instead of a 40 percent chance of gaining four actions for the cost of one, we're looking at a 40 percent chance of gaining 6.8 actions for the cost of one, a net expected gain of 1.7 actions. In other words, attempting to summon 2d6 spined devils is at least as good as getting an extra full round of bone devil actions, very likely two. That's a no-brainer. Do it in round 1.

GREATER DEVILS

Like the lesser devils, all the greater devils have certain traits in common. They have darkvision out to 120 feet and the Devil's Sight trait, indicating a preference for operating in darkness. They're immune to fire and poison and resistant to cold (except ice devils, which are immune to cold as well), magical effects, and physical damage from normal, unsilvered weapons. And they all tend toward a brute ability profile—high Strength and Constitution—indicating a preference for melee combat.

Finally, since it's in the nature of devils to obey those with power over them, a devil fighting in the course of carrying out an assigned duty will never flee from combat, no matter how badly injured it is.

Horned devils, aka malebranche (mah-leh-*brahn*-keh), are described in the *Monster Manual* as "reluctant to put themselves in harm's way," but there's no reason why they should be: They have extraordinary Strength and Constitution, a triple melee Multiattack, and a huge number of hit points, and they can also fly. This last trait gives them the ability to hover in the air, swoop down, attack a foe, then swoop back up out of reach. They don't even have to come within 5 feet of an opponent to attack, since both their Fork attack and their Tail attack have 10 feet of reach, allowing them to attack from beyond opportunity attack range of any foe except one wielding a whip or polearm.

When will they choose to Hurl Flame rather than make a melee attack? Their Multiattack allows them to substitute Hurl Flame for any melee attack. Against AC 15, Hurl Flame's +7 attack modifier gives them a 65 percent chance to hit, for a total expected 9 fire damage. In contrast, their +10 attack modifier on melee attacks gives them an 80 percent chance to hit, for 12 expected damage on a Fork attack and 8 on a Tail attack. However, the Tail attack additionally requires a saving throw against the inflicting of a bleeding "infernal wound." This adds an extra 5 expected damage (80 percent chance to hit, times 65 percent chance of failed save, assuming a +3 Constitution saving throw modifier), plus more later on. This is a nasty attack that the horned devil won't be quick to give up.

To elicit Hurl Flame from a horned devil, an opponent must be out of melee range (i.e., more than 70 feet away—really, more than 30 feet away, so that the devil has movement left to retreat), within range of the feature (i.e., 150 feet away or less), and conspicuously more threatening than any of the devil's likely melee opponents. This entails inflicting damage of a type that the horned devil doesn't resist, such as acid or radiant damage, and/or using a magic weapon. Simply casting spells—even spells that require Constitution saves—isn't enough, because of the devil's Magic Resistance. Horned devils are very good judges of which enemy or enemies pose the greatest threat to them.

Having only a 30 percent chance of success at summoning another horned devil under the Devil Summoning variant rule, they use this action only as a last-ditch measure when seriously injured (reduced to 71 hp or fewer).

Erinyes (eh-*ree*-nee-yees; singular "erinys," eh-*ree*-nis), aka furies, are warriors, enforcers, and agents of retribution. Winged and grand in appearance, they might be mistaken for celestials at first glance, but that misapprehension won't last long once combat ensues. Their Dexterity is closer to their Strength and Constitution than one usually sees in devils, so their ranged attacks compare more favorably to their melee attacks. Fundamentally, they're still brutes, but they have a good reason to initiate combat with ranged attacks and only then close in: Their Longbow attack has a chance of inflicting the poisoned condition, which imposes disadvantage on attack rolls and ability checks. Thus, they'll try to poison their enemies before casting their bows aside, closing in, and engaging them in melee, especially if they're not fighting in darkness.

Erinyes have 60 feet of flying movement, which they use to hover, swoop in, attack, and swoop back out of range. Unlike horned devils, they don't have extra-long reach with their weapons, but they do have the Parry reaction, which they can use if needed to bat away an opportunity attack that might inflict a meaningful amount of damage. (Parry is good only against melee attacks—they can't use it to knock away a missile fired from range.)

On top of Magic Resistance, erinyes have proficiency in all the "big three" saving throws: Dexterity, Constitution, and Wisdom. Charisma, too, so save your *dispel evil* and *banishment*. Combat with erinyes is where magic goes to die.

Under the Devil Summoning variant rule, an erinys has a 50 percent chance of successfully summoning allies, so it requires only two subsequent rounds of combat for one erinys to pay for its spent action by summoning another. How do its other options compare? Poorly, in the case of 1d6 bearded devils, but *very* favorably, in the case of 3d6 spined devils. Although they're relatively weak, even an average number of them can present a formidable challenge, and a greater number of them will be ferocious. Erinyes will absolutely attempt to summon spined devils as their first action.

Ice devils are, frankly, somewhat uninteresting brutes. Their one distinctive feature is Wall of Ice, which works similarly to the spell of the same name. With high Intelligence and Wisdom, they can make shrewd decisions about where to place these walls in order to shut enemies either out or in—or whether to simply drop them on top of opponents for big cold damage. Beyond that, though, all they have are melee attacks, albeit melee attacks with a 10-foot range. Thus, their goal in placing walls is to ensure that those who need to die, die.

The ice spear variant is more interesting, potentially reducing opponents' movement speed and shredding their action economy. The damage done is significantly less—47 per turn, on average, if all weapons hit, vs. 66 per turn for Bite/Claws/Tail—but the slowing effect keeps the ice devil in the fight longer, adds welcome variety, and will give a good scare to players who think their characters may be outmatched in the encounter. If the PCs are high-level enough for an ice devil encounter to be anything less than Hard, however, I'd stick with the vanilla attack and its optimized damage.

That being said, ice devils, unlike the devils described above, have a *60* percent chance of successfully summoning another ice devil. This means that they come out ahead if the battle lasts even two more rounds afterward, and fifth edition D&D assumes that the average combat encounter lasts three rounds. Therefore, this action is the very first one they'll take.

Pit fiends are the mightiest of the greater devils. These brutes have an average of 300 hp, a *fourfold* Multiattack, a Fear Aura that can impose disadvantage on attackers within 20 feet of them, and the ability to cast *fireball* at will. *At will.*

When initiating combat, a pit fiend identifies its most powerful enemy—with Intelligence 22, it can make this identification unerringly—

and goes straight for them. If this enemy is between 60 and 90 feet away, the pit fiend first casts *hold monster* to render them immobile.

If you're using the Devil Summoning variant, however, the pit fiend calls for backup first. It has a 100 percent chance of success, so there's no reason for it not to do this right away. Summoning 1d4 barbed devils offers the greatest average benefit, thanks to encounter difficulty multipliers: Bearded devils are numerous but not powerful enough, and a single erinys is powerful but not numerous enough.

Pit fiends have the ability to fly, but using the same swoop-in, attack, swoop-out tactic as other flying devils would undermine the effect of their Fear Aura. A pit fiend wants to be within 20 feet of the enemies it's fighting on *their* turns. Thus, it begins using the swooping tactic only when all its opponents have developed immunity to its Fear Aura with successful saving throws.

As a Large creature, the pit fiend takes up four 5-foot squares (or three 5-foot hexes). This means it can surround itself with a ring-shaped *wall of fire*, 20 feet in diameter, and force enemies trapped inside with it either to take damage from the flames or to remain within reach of the pit fiend's bite. If it can catch at least two enemies this way, that's exactly what it does. For extra savagery, it can then cast *fireball* on *itself,* exploiting its immunity to fire to subject every enemy inside the wall, and possibly a couple outside, to 8d6 fire damage (halved on a successful Dexterity save). And it can do that as many times as it likes, forcing panicking PCs to take 5d8 fire damage while running through the flaming wall to get out.

Looking at the pit fiend's melee Multiattack, we can calculate total expected damage per turn as 95 against AC 15—and that's not even counting the chance of becoming poisoned by the pit fiend's bite. By comparison, a *fireball* that catches four opponents who have a fifty-fifty chance of resisting the effects does only an expected 84 damage. Thus, after pulling its *wall of fire* stunt, a pit fiend favors its melee Multiattack anytime it's surrounded by four enemies or fewer. But it will make an exception if its melee opponents' attacks are ineffectual, while a ranged opponent is managing to damage it with damage types it doesn't resist (acid, radiant, etc.) and/or striking it with magical weapon attacks. Pit fiends also lack proficiency in Charisma saving throws, so even though their raw Charisma is quite high and they have advantage on saving throws against spell effects, trying to cast *dispel evil*, *banishment*, or *plane shift* on them will infuriate them.

In these instances, if a pit fiend can't reach the enemy nuisance in a single turn's movement, it flies to within 90 feet, then casts *hold monster* to keep its victim-to-be from running away or doing anything else. It sustains concentration on this spell until it can close to melee distance, then give the nuisance a thorough drubbing. It won't release its hold until the enemy is beaten unconscious.

Pit fiends will also use *fireball* against any group of four opponents clustered together within the spell's area of effect beyond their 60-foot flying distance, or against any group of five or more clustered opponents, period.

In short, a pit fiend encounter should strike fear into even the highest-level PCs. Don't hold back.

HELL HOUNDS

Doglike fiends native to the Lower Planes, **hell hounds**, like their mundane counterparts, may be found roaming in wild packs or faithfully serving fiendish masters. One hell hound will rarely be found alone, unless it's acting as a guard dog, so despite having a challenge rating of only 3, hell hounds are foes more suitable for medium- and high-level PCs.

Hell hounds are very fast—their base movement speed is 50 feet per round—and have exceptional Strength, along with high Constitution. Although not quite intelligent enough to act beyond their instincts, they're as smart as an ape, and they have above-average Wisdom, allowing them to choose targets wisely and even recognize when they're outmatched. They also have double proficiency in Perception, plus Keen Hearing and Smell, which gives them advantage on such checks. This makes them outstanding sentinels and trackers, the two roles in which trained hell hounds are encountered most often. To take advantage of their darkvision, hell hounds pursue their quarry by night.

Their Constitution isn't quite high enough to make them unambiguous brutes, but their Fire Breath is limited to a range of 15 feet, so they're melee fighters by necessity. Because of their Pack Tactics feature, hell hounds instinctively zero in on one or two vulnerable enemies—the oldest, youngest, weakest, and/or most isolated—and gang up on them.

When attacking a solitary target, hell hounds rely on their Bite action, but whenever there's a second target close to the first, they use their Fire Breath, provided it's available. Hell hounds aim their Fire Breath to engulf the greatest number of enemies, regardless of whether there's another hell hound in the area of effect—they're immune to fire damage, so they can't hurt each other this way.

Not only do hell hounds gain advantage from Pack Tactics by swarming their targets, they also gain multiple opportunity attacks if and when those targets try to run away, *and* they easily run those targets down again with their superior movement speed.

Hell hounds steer clear of enemies who are significantly stronger than they are. Their ability to assess this is limited, but as a simple rule of thumb, if an opponent has a Strength modifier of +3 or higher—that is, equal to or higher than theirs—they don't attack that opponent unless commanded to. However, if that opponent comes to the aid of a weaker ally that they're attacking, half of them (round down) will turn to face the stronger opponent, crouching and snarling, while the other half continue to maul the weaker foe.

Their fiendish savagery gives them a determination akin to what would be described as zealotry in a sentient creature. Consequently, damage alone isn't enough to drive one away; individually, hell hounds will fight to the death. However, a pack of unaccompanied hell hounds can be driven off once enough of its number are killed. Against PCs of level 6 or lower, a hell hound in a pack runs away only when it's the last one remaining (and thus can no longer take advantage of Pack Tactics). Against level 7 through 10, hell hounds run when they no longer equal or outnumber their foes. Against level 11 and above, they run when they no longer outnumber their foes by at least two to one. Trained hell hounds accompanying their masters never retreat unless their masters do.

When retreating, trained hell hounds use the Disengage action and match pace with their masters, if present, whereas feral hell hounds only know how to Dash and always use their full movement.

RAKSHASAS

Hands down, the **rakshasa** had the coolest illustration in the original AD&D *Monster Manual*; I can't help but think that the current illustration is in part a tribute to that original David A. Trampier drawing. Rakshasas were rarely encountered, but when they were, you knew the encounter would be memorable, because it had to live up to that illustration.

The fifth edition rakshasa is likely to be another rarity, because its challenge rating is a high 13—too difficult a boss for low- or mid-level player characters. Rakshasas aren't on the level of full-grown dragons, but they're as tough as a beholder or vampire, and tougher than genies, which should give you a sense of the kind of status they should have in a campaign.

The rakshasa's highest physical ability scores are Dexterity and Constitution, but these are exceeded by its Charisma. What we have here is a creature that, while built to survive a battle of attrition, would rather fight using magic—or words—than using its claws. But that doesn't mean it always gets its way.

The rakshasa is an expert in Deception and Insight—a born con artist. With its Limited Magic Immunity, it can nope out of spells cast against it unless those spells are 7th, 8th, or 9th level. And it has very powerful Innate Spellcasting, specializing in illusion and enchantment—although, as we'll see, its spell repertoire is optimized for social interaction, not combat.

The rakshasa is immune to physical damage from nonmagical weapons, but it's *vulnerable* to piercing from magic weapons "wielded by good creatures." This is an oddity for fifth edition D&D, which shuns the assumption of former editions that alignment rules us all. Instead, it offers us spells like *protection from evil and good*, which defends against celestials and fey as well as fiends and undead—not to mention elementals and aberrations, which have always stood outside the number one cosmic feud as neutrals and an opportunistic third faction, respectively. So a celestial with a spear can do double damage to a rakshasa, but an aberration or fiend with a spear can't? What about a good PC? What about a nominally good PC whose player plays their alignment poorly? Or a nominally neutral PC whose actions are consistently good, even if their motivations aren't?

Welcome to Judgment Call City. I see no clear path forward on this issue, but my own inclination would be to use alignment as written for monsters and non-player characters, and alignment *as acted* (not necessarily as declared) for PCs. A character's sudden discovery that they unexpectedly deal double damage—or unexpectedly *don't*—may make for an interesting character development inflection point.

Tangentially, this is one of a bare handful of instances I'm aware of in fifth edition D&D in which it matters what type of physical damage a weapon does. Magic spears, bows and arrows, daggers, shortswords, and rapiers are going to seize a rakshasa's attention in a way that other magic weapons don't.

The four spells that the rakshasa can cast at will (*detect thoughts, disguise self, mage hand, minor illusion*) have no direct combat application, although *disguise self* is useful in the circumstance of an urban chase, since a rakshasa can use it to vanish in a crowd.

Of the spells it can cast three times per day, *detect magic* has no combat application, *charm person* has the salient disadvantage of working poorly against combat opponents, and *suggestion* may get opponents to abandon a fight but isn't likely to win it. *Major image* may serve as a distraction, fooling opponents into thinking the rakshasa has conjured some other creature to fight alongside it, but as soon as they "land a hit" and discover nothing there, the illusion is dispelled. *Invisibility*, however, has obvious tactical benefit—especially since the rakshasa's Limited Magic Immunity means *see invisibility* and even *true seeing* won't work on it.

As for the spells it can cast once per day, *dominate person* has the same drawback as *charm person* (though it's a lot more useful and effective than *charm person* if the rakshasa can cast it on someone before combat begins, and it's also good for casting on innocent bystanders), *true seeing* is primarily defensive, and *fly* has a nasty drawback that I'll look at in a second. But *plane shift* is always useful as an escape hatch, which a rakshasa, having Wisdom 16, will unhesitatingly use as soon as it's moderately wounded (reduced to 77 hp or fewer). Anyone who can do 33 damage to a rakshasa is not to be tangled with.

The problem with *fly*, which otherwise is a great spell for getting out of reach of melee opponents, is that ranged weapons tend also to be piercing weapons. If none of the rakshasa's opponents has a magic ranged weapon, then the rakshasa can use *fly* to station itself in the air, out of melee reach, swoop down to attack, and then fly back up. (With a natural Armor Class of 16 and immunity to normal weapon damage, it's not going to worry too much about opportunity attacks.) But if there is an opponent with a magic ranged weapon, then not only does *fly* offer no protection, it guarantees that the rakshasa's opponents will rely on that very weapon to bring it down.

While a rakshasa's spell kit isn't so useful in combat, it's superb for allowing a rakshasa to carry out its predatory schemes, and that's what it counts on: keeping its presence and its nature concealed so that it can hunt and feed without having to fight openly. Just like vampires, rakshasas are predators, and predators don't attack hard targets—they pursue the young, the old, the weak, the isolated, and the oblivious. Unlike vampires, however, rakshasas are hustlers. If the PCs discover a rakshasa, the first thing it will do is use its wiles to try to make *them* out to be the villains, so that they're not just going up against the rakshasa—they're going up against the entire community. As it does so, though, it also begins laying the groundwork for its own escape, in case it becomes necessary. Rakshasas aren't geniuses, but they're prudent, and they try to anticipate what their opponents have the power to do to them and preempt these threats before their opponents can carry them out.

If a combat encounter ensues, it's because all the rakshasa's other schemes and precautions have failed, and it's cornered. In this case, the rakshasa can fall back on its dual-Claw Multiattack. (The magical curse of the claw takes effect once combat is over; it has no effect during the encounter itself.) With its relatively high AC, quick movement speed, and immunity to physical damage from normal weapons, the rakshasa is a natural skirmisher: It tries to keep 35 to 40 feet away from its opponents, waits for one of them to overextend, then rushes in and engages them in melee. But as soon as one of that opponent's allies runs up to help, or if that opponent has Extra Attack, it Disengages and retreats to a safe distance again. If it's being engaged in melee by more than one opponent and doesn't have room to retreat, it casts *invisibility*, then repositions itself near a weaker, isolated opponent before attacking again. It can execute this stunt only three times, so if it's out of uses, it must simply Dodge and use its movement to try to circle around to where it has more room to maneuver. Also, when it retreats, it tries to do so in a direction that puts it within 35 to 40 feet of a *different* opponent.

Although the rakshasa is hard to kill, it's not capable of doing a great deal of damage itself. Even if it lands both claw hits, the most it can do in one Multiattack is 28 damage, and around 18 is more likely. That won't faze a high-level, front-line attacking PC. Thus, as tough as they are, rakshasas strongly prefer to surround themselves with allies, either willing or charmed, who can keep their opponents occupied while they do their attack-and-retreat dance. It also inclines them to attack their most preylike opponents first, if possible (see criteria above).

Rakshasas can't be permanently killed except in the Nine Hells, but they still intensely dislike being "killed" on the material plane. Being immune to any hurt that an ordinary mortal can dish out, they have the sense to recognize that anyone who can wound them can also kill them. Also, when it comes to the kinds of magic weapons that they're vulnerable to, they're straight-up cowards—not necessarily afraid of the opponents wielding the weapons, but very afraid of the weapons themselves. Thus, as mentioned before, a rakshasa will seek to flee after taking only moderate damage, as well as upon being struck by a weapon that it's vulnerable to. Depending on the extent to which its duplicity is known, it may simply try to escape on foot: As soon as it gets out of sight, it can use *disguise self* to mask its identity, which is useful not only in crowds but also in castles, because who's more inconspicuous than a liveried servant? But if its opponents are too clever to fall for that, it uses *plane shift* to slip away to another dimension.

LESSER DEMONS

Unlike devils, which rarely stray onto the prime material plane except on a mission of malice, demons like to exploit holes in the cosmic fabric, popping through to ruin things for everyone on the other side. Thus, an adventuring party is much more likely to stumble upon a random demon than a random devil. There's also the possibility that a demon has been summoned as a servant or ally by an evil spellcaster but broken free of its bonds.

AD&D numbered demons by type, but by the second edition, descriptive names were already supplanting numbered types (second edition D&D didn't even use the word "demon," probably cowed by rampaging fundamentalists). Fifth edition D&D brings back the numbered types, but they take a backseat; each variety of demon is referred to primarily by name.

One trait that all demons have in common—which is described in the *Monster Manual* flavor text, *not* in their stat blocks—is that they can't be permanently killed on any plane except the Abyss. If the player characters destroy a demon anyplace else, such as on their own home plane, that demon isn't killed, merely dispelled, and it immediately re-forms in the Abyss in a nasty mood and with a new grudge.

The upshot of this, from a tactical perspective, is that demons don't fear death and have *no* self-preservation instinct that will induce them to back down from a fight, even after taking substantial damage. Only in the Abyss, or if its essence is contained in a demonic amulet that the PCs possess or might be able to get ahold of, will a demon exercise anything that might be described as caution.

Another feature common to all demons is that they're either resistant or immune to cold, fire, and lightning damage and immune to poison. They also have either darkvision or truesight, indicating a preference for operating in darkness, where characters without darkvision or a light source will be at a disadvantage.

Manes (*may*-neez, both singular and plural) are spirits of the evil deceased, demonic analogues to lemures. They're shapeless and weak, but unlike lemures, they're occasionally summoned to wreak havoc on the material plane. There's little to say about them, though: They're stupid and slow and neither unusually strong nor unusually agile, and their only combat ability is a melee attack with their claws. Point one in a certain direction, and it lurches forth and dully tries to shred whatever it runs into.

Type 1 demons represent a substantial leap upward from manes in threat level. This type includes shadow demons, barlguras, and vrocks, with challenge ratings of 4, 5, and 6; in contrast, manes are CR 1/8.

Shadow demons not only possess darkvision out to 120 feet but also have Light Sensitivity, which penalizes them in bright light, and Shadow Stealth, which lets them Hide as a bonus action in dim light or darkness. Other demons prefer darkness; for shadow demons, avoiding the light is an imperative. If a PC casts a spell that creates bright light, a shadow demon will shrink from it. Shadow demons are vulnerable to radiant damage as well, and if struck with it, they'll be simultaneously enraged and terrified, and they'll do whatever they can, short of fleeing, to avoid the enemy who inflicted it.

Shadow demons' physical ability profile is that of a skirmisher. Their Claw attack does two extra dice of damage if they have advantage on an attack roll—similar to a rogue's Sneak Attack. Combining this with Stealth proficiency and the ability to Hide as a bonus action, we have the elements of a tactical combination: The demon Hides in dim light or darkness, giving it advantage on its first attack from hiding and thereby boosting its damage. This attack gives away its position, however.

In order to Hide so that it can strike with advantage again, the shadow demon has to get out of the light. It can do this easily if the PCs' only light source is a torch, a lamp, or a hooded lantern and none of them have darkvision. But if any PC does have darkvision, it has to get at least 40 feet away from the nearest light source. In this instance, it can't move far enough in one turn to escape being seen without either some kind of cover present or using the Dash action. Although its resistance or immunity to every type of damage except radiant damage and physical damage from magic weapons gives it some defense against opportunity attacks, it simply isn't fast enough to attack or Disengage, get out of sight of every foe with darkvision, *and* Hide in a single turn. Even accounting for Incorporeal Movement, which lets the demon pass *through* the opponent it's just attacked and keep going, we have to assume that the opponent has the time to turn around in order to make the opportunity attack to which they're entitled and see where the shadow demon is headed.

On the other hand, it does enough damage with its Dexterity-based Claw attack that we may be able to treat it like a brute, despite its lack of Strength. Still, it probably behooves shadow demons to favor weaker targets over stronger ones. Thus, they choose the opponent with the fewest hit points (with Intelligence 14 and Wisdom 13, they're able to judge this accurately) and strike fast and hard, in the hope of finishing off the foe in a round or two.

If the first blow doesn't do at least severe damage (60 percent of the opponent's hit point maximum), or if the second doesn't finish the opponent, the shadow demon has to make a judgment call. If none of its opponent's allies have come to their aid, it can take a third round to try to deliver the coup de grâce. Otherwise, it uses its next turn to Dash (action) away, potentially subjecting itself to one or more opportunity attacks, then to Hide (bonus action) once it's out of the light. While hidden, it maneuvers around stealthily until it can creep up on its victim again. It's not fleeing when it Dashes away, only repositioning, and it may fly for part or all of its movement. It repeats this sequence until either it or all its opponents are defeated.

Barlguras are dumb brutes, but they're dumb brutes with some interesting capabilities. For one thing, they're actually proficient in Stealth, and this combined with their Running Leap trait gives them a potent surprise Multiattack, albeit not one from hiding (it's hard to miss a large red demon ape barreling through the air toward you) and therefore without advantage on the attack rolls. But wait, there's more! They also have Reckless, identical to the barbarian class feature Reckless Attack, which grants them advantage on all their attack rolls in exchange for advantage on attack rolls *against* them. Given their Intelligence of 7, I'm inclined to think they use this feature all the time, even when they don't need to. It's just part of their demonic nature.

How much would you pay? Don't answer yet! Barlguras have innate spellcasting ability, and one of their innate spells is *invisibility*. They can attack from hiding after all! Would they, though? Are they smart enough to? How would a basically stupid creature employ spells like *disguise self* and *phantasmal force*, which are most effective when used with creativity? What's a good way to make use of these spells that will work in most cases without any kind of variation, since they don't have the Intelligence to adjust their strategy from situation to situation?

Here's one idea: Barlguras use *phantasmal force* to create an illusion that will draw victims to it, such as a pile of treasure, a table piled with food, a cute baby animal. Then they lie in wait, hidden. When victims approach to examine the illusory bait, the barlguras cast *entangle* beneath them, restraining those who fail their Strength saving throws. Then they come barreling in and start attacking Recklessly. (If there are multiple barlguras in the encounter—the flavor text says they often roam in packs—just one of them casts *entangle*, while the others, invisible until the moment they strike, exploit the element of surprise. If there's only one, its attack won't be a surprise anymore the round after the PCs have found themselves suddenly entangled by magical vines.)

In an encounter like this, it's important to keep track of what advantages and disadvantages both the barlguras and the PCs possess, because any and all advantages cancel out any and all disadvantages, and vice versa. Barlguras may have advantage from attacking unseen, from Reckless, from attacking a restrained opponent, and/or from attacking a blinded opponent (one who can't see in darkness). PCs may have advantage from attacking a Reckless barlgura, and they may have disadvantage from being blinded and/or restrained.

A barlgura has a 30 percent chance of summoning one other barlgura. That's spending one action in the hope of gaining, say, two or three extra, equivalent to those of the summoner. Not worth it, especially since there are probably multiple barlguras on the scene already.

Vrocks are flying brutes with 60 feet of flying speed and resistance to physical damage from normal weapons. Therefore, they can hover in the air, fly into melee, attack, then fly back out of reach; they may incur one or more opportunity attacks in doing so, but they're not overly concerned about that.

The question with vrocks is which of their attacking actions they use on any given turn: their melee Multiattack, their Spores, or their Stunning Screech. The Stunning Screech can be used only once per day, so let's look at that first. It can stun creatures within a 20-foot radius, but for only one round. A stunned creature automatically fails Strength and Dexterity saving throws, attack rolls against a stunned creature have advantage, and a stunned creature can't move or take actions or reactions. The radius of Stunning Screech suggests that it should affect four enemies, on average (based on the Targets in Area of Effect table, *Dungeon Master's Guide*, chapter 8). Whatever is going to happen to the stunned victims has to happen within the next round, or the opportunity is wasted.

The *Monster Manual* doesn't say whether vrocks hunt in flocks; if they do, they stand a much better chance of getting some real benefit from a Stunning Screech. Vrocks may also be summoned by more powerful demons that can take advantage of their enemies being stunned. For a lone vrock, though, this feature hardly seems worth the bother.

Vrock Spores, on the other hand, poison enemy creatures and can potentially continue to do damage round after round, as well as impose disadvantage on the poisoned creatures' attack rolls and ability checks. This one's a no-brainer. Whenever vrocks have the Spores feature available and can position themselves to affect at least three enemy creatures, they'll use it.

A vrock has a 30 percent chance of summoning one other vrock or 2d4 dretches. The one-vrock option isn't worth it, for the same reason it's not worth it for one barlgura to summon another. As for the dretches, their Fetid Cloud is somewhat redundant to the vrock's Spores, and with their low challenge rating of 1/4, even five of them don't add up to a whole lot next to the vrock's CR 6, even if their numbers do increase the difficulty of the encounter; my suggestion to other Dungeon Masters who want dretches to be part of their vrock encounters is to just put them there in the first place.

The middle of the demonic hierarchy comprises the type 2 and type 3 demons: chasmes, hezrous, glabrezus, and yochlols.

A **chasme** (*kaz*-mee) is a four-legged demonic mosquito the size of a horse. Chasmes most often go forth to retrieve escaped demons and return them to their overlords, but they're not above attacking adventurers for the heck of it. As high-Strength, high-Dexterity creatures, they're built for high-damage strikes. With a flying speed of 60 feet, they maneuver into the midst of their foes, holding position in the air within 30 feet of as many of them as possible, so that they're affected by its sleep-inducing Drone. This is one of those features that affect an enemy either right away or not at all, so once they've had a chance to lull everyone in the PCs' party, they no longer have any need to stay in one particular spot.

They're indifferent in their selection of targets (except that they attack conscious targets before unconscious ones), but once they've chosen one, they focus their attacks on that target alone. Although they could fly in, stab the target with their probosces, and fly away again, this would incur at least one opportunity attack every time, and chasmes don't have resistance to damage from normal weapons, so getting hit by an opportunity attack would actually bother them some. Instead, they stay within reach and take their licks. It's not so bad—they themselves can do severe damage with just a single attack. They do have magic resistance and proficiency in Dexterity and Wisdom saving throws—two of the big three—so spellcasters don't impress them as uniquely dangerous.

A chasme has a 30 percent chance of summoning one other chasme. Not worth it.

A **hezrou** is a foul-smelling brute that can overwhelm nearby enemies with its stench. That's it. It's dumb and tough and limited to melee attacks. It's a "Rrrrahhhh, stab stab stab" (or, in this case, "Rrrrahhhh, claw claw bite") monster with operating instructions you could fit in a fortune cookie. A hezrou has a 30 percent chance of summoning one other hezrou or 2d6 dretches; see "vrocks," above.

The **glabrezu** is the first type of demon that's interesting from a noncombat perspective, because its goal, according to the *Monster*

Manual flavor text, is to tempt mortals to their own destruction. It's also one of the types of demon more likely to be summoned by a spell-caster looking for an ally or servant. Glabrezus make very bad allies and servants. Jeez, people, you're *summoning a demon*—what do you expect, your next employee of the month?

Anyway, based on this description, a glabrezu is more likely to initiate an encounter with parley than with fisticuffs. Glabrezus don't have proficiency in any social skill, but they do have Charisma 16, which gets them off to an adequate start. With 120 feet of truesight and telepathy, they can detect approaching creatures and open negotiations before those creatures even know what they're talking to.

In fluent doubletalk, a glabrezu makes grandiose, ambiguous promises of unparalleled power, riches, and experiences in exchange for the PCs' pledge to perform tasks for it—tasks calculated to bring them to ruin. For example, a character motivated by a need to prove himself may be sent to fight a creature he can't defeat, while the rest of the party is made to appear to betray him. A character may be sent undercover for a job and lose her true self—no one will remember who she is, recognize her, or remember her name. A character motivated by a search for knowledge may be sent off on a solo journey and driven mad. An experience-seeking character may be granted whatever she wants, in a way that will bring her pain and unhappiness, or destroy her capacity to enjoy or even feel life by turning her into a specter. A character seeking purpose and connection may be sent to heal refugees with a magic staff that will trap her soul, condemning her to solitary confinement.

If the characters express doubt (as opposed to outright refusal), the glabrezu raises the stakes ("What fool would take such promises without proof? Look well at what I offer!"), presenting beautiful magic items to tempt the PCs, each one tailored to a particular character. It doesn't give the PCs these items, however, unless they agree to do its bidding. If the glabrezu is slain, these items remain behind. Need I mention that *every* one of them is cursed? (I like to have the curse trigger after a delay, with players making a saving throw every ten days against a DC equal to the number of tendays they've owned the cursed item. When they fail a save, as they eventually will, the bomb goes off.)

If the PCs refuse to be tempted, then the glabrezu dismisses them irritably ("Weakling creatures—if you hunger for nothing, then be food for the worthy yourselves!") and attacks, beginning with the weakest character within reach. With Intelligence 19 and Wisdom 17, a glabrezu can "read" characters' stats to assess their relative power, along with their susceptibility to *confusion* (Wisdom save) and *power word stun* (Constitution save).

A glabrezu can cast *darkness* at will, obscuring a sphere with a 15-foot radius. *Darkness* overcomes darkvision, as well as any light-producing spell of 2nd level or less. In this magical darkness, every PC unassisted by magic will be blinded and therefore have disadvantage on attack rolls against the glabrezu, while the glabrezu will have advantage on every attack roll against a blinded opponent, thanks to its truesight. Clearly, then, this is the very first thing the glabrezu will do, and the PCs are hosed if they don't have *daylight* or a higher-level illumination spell.

The four-armed glabrezu has an unusual Multiattack: It can either make two Pincer attacks and two Fist attacks, or make two Pincer attacks and cast a single spell. It can seize and hold a single target creature with each of its two pincers, which have a 10-foot reach, and it has a speed of 40 feet. Thus, its first attack is to try to seize the weakest opponent it can get to; if it succeeds, it tries to seize a second. Then it pulls these opponents into adjacent squares or hexes (no movement required to do this, but a contested Strength check would be fair) or moves into an adjacent square or hex itself, and finally pummels them with its fists.

This is the glabrezu's default tactic, but it has others:

- Against two or more clustered, ungrappled opponents within 90 feet of it, it can cast *confusion*. This spell and *darkness* both require concentration, so they can't be sustained at the same time; the deciding factor is whether *darkness* alone is sufficient to shut those characters down or more drastic measures are required. *Confusion* is useful against strong melee fighters and especially useful against strong melee fighters with Extra Attack, because it has a 60 percent chance of denying their action entirely (brutal to the action economy of a character with Extra Attack or a bonus action) and a 20 percent chance of redirecting it at another opponent.

- Against a single irritating, ungrappled opponent within 60 feet, *power word stun* shuts them down temporarily, as long as they have 150 hp or fewer and fail a Con save. The glabrezu can tell whether an opponent has more than 150 hp or a Constitution saving throw modifier of more than +1 (it's reluctant to use this once-per-day power without at least a two-to-one chance of success, although it will do it anyway if necessary to clear the field).
- And finally, if any of its opponents are getting buffed by one or more sustained spells, it can cast *dispel magic* at will to put an end to that. Woe to the PC who casts *daylight* using only a 3rd-level spell slot.

A glabrezu has a 30 percent chance of summoning one other glabrezu, 1d2 hezrous, or 1d3 vrocks. Forget the other glabrezu: Not only is it not worth it tactically, they just aren't the collaborative type. What about the hezrous or vrocks? Now we do begin to see that the addition of even a couple of extra enemies can have a real effect, thanks to their moderate challenge ratings. Hezrous could be useful for distracting or shutting down ranged attackers that are giving the glabrezu problems, but I think vrocks would be even better for this, because of their Spores, their Stunning Screech, and their ability to fly. The low probability of succeeding in the summoning, however, means that this is not an ability that the glabrezu should wait until it's in real trouble to use. I think a glabrezu would try to summon vrocks as soon as it realized its opponents posed a meaningful threat to it, which is to say, if they managed to at least moderately injure it (reduce it to 109 hp or fewer) in the first turn of combat.

Even so, let's drill down to actual probabilities, because a glabrezu *is* capable of calculating these things. It has a 30 percent chance of summoning an average of two vrocks; let's say combat will continue for three more rounds if it succeeds. The vrocks' powers grant them and the glabrezu advantage on all attack rolls. Spores has a 50 percent chance of dealing 6 damage each to three opponents. On the two subsequent turns, each vrock has a 60 percent chance (against AC 15) of dealing 24 damage with its Multiattack. Putting it all together, the summoning attempt can be expected to do an additional 14 damage, plus the effects of advantage and disadvantage on whatever damage the glabrezu itself does. In contrast, the glabrezu, with a 75 percent chance to hit (94 percent with advantage), does an expected 37 damage per turn against the same AC, all by itself. In other words, the total damage inflicted by the vrocks over multiple rounds—even accounting for their effect on the glabrezu's own damage—doesn't equal what the glabrezu can do itself in one turn. Sure, it will also reduce the damage the PCs are able to do to the glabrezu, but when you get right down to it, the likelihood of failure is so much greater than the likelihood of success that the glabrezu is going to err on the side of DIY. Final verdict: no summoning.

Without question, despite being merely a type 3 demon, the glabrezu is a boss enemy. Build your adventure accordingly.

A **yochlol**, in contrast, is most likely to appear as part of an encounter with a drow priestess of Lolth who summons it (and thus can't summon other demons itself). In this scenario, the priestess is the boss; the yochlol appears in giant spider form and uses its abilities to synergize with the priestess's. This means first using its innate ability to cast *dominate person* on the PC with the highest Strength-to-Wisdom ratio. Once that PC makes a saving throw to shake this spell off, the yochlol then casts *web* on any unrestrained PCs, favoring melee fighters first. Any turn on which it's not casting a spell, it uses its two-Bite Multiattack action.

The yochlol's Mist Form feature is of somewhat limited usefulness, since it obviates the demon's ability to deal direct damage. It can potentially incapacitate a single character, but this is only useful if the yochlol has one or more allies that can follow up with an attack against the incapacitated character—or, conversely, if the yochlol needs to *rescue* its allies from attacks *by* the incapacitated character. The thing is, with only a DC 14 Con save needed to resist being poi-

soned and incapacitated, the target has to have a Con save modifier
of −1 or worse to give the yochlol 2-to-1 odds of success. Under most
circumstances, it simply isn't that effective.

GREATER DEMONS

The upper management of the demonic hierarchy comprises the type 4
nalfeshnee, the type 5 marilith, and the type 6 balor and goristro.

Nalfeshnees are often encountered in command of lesser demons,
rather than on their own. They follow a straightforward brute profile,
with extraordinarily high Strength and Constitution—but also extraordinarily high Intelligence, although their Wisdom is in the high-average
range. The latter indicates a monster that can plan and coordinate, adapt
on the fly, accurately assess its enemies' strengths and weaknesses, and
choose targets for itself and its minions accordingly. It may even refrain
from combat in favor of parley if it knows it's outmatched, but with demons, the embodiment of chaotic evil, that's a big maybe. As mentioned,
their drive is to destroy, and death is only an inconvenience to them.
It would probably take a chaotic evil character to negotiate any useful
cooperation out of a nalfeshnee. Or any kind of demon, for that matter.

The nalfeshnee's most distinctive feature is its Horror Nimbus, an
ability that requires a Recharge and is usable, on average, one turn out
of every three. Like a dragon's Frightful Presence, this is one of those features that a creature can hit each of its enemies with only once, because
if they're not affected on the first try, they're not going to be affected at
all in the same encounter. Also, the Horror Nimbus is part of the nalfeshnee's Multiattack. Consequently, it's most useful against whichever
opponent(s) the nalfeshnee is engaged in melee with at the moment. So
although the nalfeshnee could easily expect to hit three opponents at
once with it (based on the Targets in Area of Effect table, *Dungeon Master's Guide*, chapter 8), not only does it *not* try to position itself to affect
as many opponents as possible, it does just the opposite: tries to position
itself to affect *only its current opponent(s)*, or the opponent(s) whom it's
about to engage. It doesn't want the effect to wear off too soon.

Because of its flying ability, the nalfeshnee generally fights from
the air, flying down toward an opponent, using its Multiattack action,

then flying back up. With AC 18 and 184 hp, it has very little to fear from opportunity attacks.

Between its Magic Resistance and Teleport features, the nalfeshnee is good at taking out spellcasters who are giving its minions trouble. (If they try to flee when the nalfeshnee appears, it uses its Bite attack for its opportunity strike.) Aside from that, it focuses on the opponents who pose the greatest threats to itself and its minions. In most cases, any player character using a magic weapon (especially one that does extra damage against demons or evil creatures in general); inflicting acid, thunder, radiant, necrotic, or psychic damage; or casting spells that require Dexterity saving throws to avoid will fall into this category.

With the nalfeshnee, the chance of successful summoning of other demons increases from 30 percent to 50 percent; we're also looking at a demon that's likely to have many minions behind it already, so it isn't doing all the work itself. It can afford to take a turn to bring more allies into the fight. Therefore, rather than calculate to-hit probabilities and expected damage, I base this assessment on the effect on the total experience points of the encounter. Summoning 1d4 vrocks would bring an average of 5,750 XP of new demon blood into the encounter; 1d3 hezrous, 7,800; 1d2 glabrezus, 7,500; and one more nalfeshnee, 10,000. None of these summonings is likely to increase the encounter multiplier. But consider something else: Summoning one more nalfeshnee just brings a rival commander onto the field, so we can write that one off. Subtracting that option, the hezrous look like the preferred second choice.

Mariliths are demonic Cuisinarts, wielding six longswords and possessing a prehensile tail to boot. This tail can grab and restrain an enemy, giving a marilith advantage on every attack roll against them. In addition, the marilith's Reactive and Parry features together give it an effective AC 23 against one melee attack each turn—not each of *its* turns, but each of *anyone's*. Mariliths *love* melee combat. That being said, their physical abilities follow a skirmisher profile, and they have a 40-foot movement speed, so they're not just going to sit in one place and fight whoever comes to them.

Mariliths have exceptionally high Intelligence and very high Wisdom, so they're also good at planning, coordinating, adapting, and selecting targets. Like nalfeshnees, they're often commanders of other demonic troops, and they assess threats according to the same criteria that nalfeshnees use. They also share nalfeshnees' Teleport feature, and with their fell Multiattack, they can make enemy spellcasters' lives very, very short. If a spellcaster tries to run away, a marilith lashes out against them with its tail and puts a quick stop to that.

In melee combat, its first attack will always be a Tail attack; if this attack hits, grappling the target, all Longsword attacks for the remainder of the Multiattack will be against the restrained enemy. On subsequent turns, if an enemy is grappled by a marilith's tail already, it divides its attacks equally among that enemy and any other(s) engaging it in melee, aiming any remaining attack(s) at the grappled enemy.

A marilith doesn't want to summon another marilith—that's just asking for a power struggle. Summoning 1d6 vrocks would add an average of 8,050 XP, with a 50 percent chance of raising the encounter multiplier. Summoning 1d4 hezrous would add an expected 9,750 XP; 1d3 glabrezus, 10,000 XP; 1d2 nalfeshnees, 15,000 XP. Raising the encounter multiplier one level increases the AXP by half the total XP value of all monsters in the encounter; for the marilith alone, that's another 3,750 AXP. If the total XP of the marilith's existing minions are equal to or greater than those of the marilith, the vrocks take pole position. Otherwise, stick with the nalfeshnees.

Balors fight as generals at the head of demon armies. With their brute ability profile and their Fire Aura trait, which burns every creature in an adjacent square or hex, not only do they love toe-to-toe combat, they're happy to be surrounded by as many enemies as possible. And like nalfeshnees and mariliths, they're very good at assessing their enemies and targeting the biggest threats.

The balor's Multiattack consists of a Longsword strike and a Whip strike; it can use the Whip strike to snag an enemy as far as 30 feet away and yank them into its hot zone, then follow up with Longsword. On subsequent turns, it may continue to use this Whip/Longsword combo against the same opponent; finish off a seriously injured opponent with its sword, then use its whip to seize another; or continue to fight an opponent already within reach with its sword while using its whip to pull more enemies into its Fire Aura. Or, like the nalfeshnee and the marilith, it may Teleport to the position of an enemy spellcaster and make a Longsword opportunity attack if that enemy tries to get away. Although they can fly, balors generally fight on the ground, because their Fire Aura takes effect at the start of their turns, so they need to be adjacent to their enemies at that moment.

The *Monster Manual* isn't explicit about whether a balor's Death Throes applies to the destruction of its physical form on a plane other than the Abyss or only to its final destruction on its home plane, but it's been officially confirmed that this feature applies to its physical form on any plane. Because of this, a seriously injured balor (reduced to 104 hp or fewer) tries to place itself within 30 feet of as many enemy creatures as it can, in order to take them with it when it goes.

Summoning 1d8 vrocks adds an expected 10,350 XP and has a 68 percent chance of raising the encounter multiplier; 1d6 hezrous, 13,650 XP and a 50 percent chance of raising the multiplier; 1d4 glabrezus, 12,500 XP; 1d3 nalfeshnees, 20,000 XP; 1d2 mariliths, 22,500 XP; and one goristro, 18,000 XP. We can toss out the goristro right away—*unless* the balor's enemies are hiding inside or behind a structure that a goristro could demolish. As for vrocks and hezrous, unless the balor has a formidable army behind it, it's going to be hard for them to add enough AXP to the encounter to outweigh the effect of bringing one or two mariliths onto the field. I think the mariliths have it.*

Finally, the **goristro** is described by the *Monster Manual* flavor text

---

* At this point, I want to throw in a caution to other DMs. One thing I as a DM appreciate about fifth edition D&D is that it's given us tools for calculating encounter balance. The more uncertainty we introduce into an encounter, the more likely our players will experience either an unsatisfying cakewalk or a demoralizing team wipe.

In every single demon-summoning scenario, either a failed summoning or an unusually successful one (in which the boss demon summons the greatest possible number of minions) has the potential to tip an encounter way off balance. To be blunt, I think that unless your players are experienced and have good judgment about when to fight and when to run, you shouldn't use the "Demon Summoning" variant rule as written. Instead, decide beforehand whether you want minions to appear at a certain point (or from the outset), then declare it to be so. Random summoning works in some instances, but I've concluded that this isn't one of them.

as a "living siege engine." Like the other high-level demons above, its physical ability profile is that of a brute. Unlike them, it's stupid, operating purely and solely from instinct. It can recognize a threat the same way an animal can and choose targets accordingly, but it can't make detailed assessments about PCs' abilities or features, nor does it adapt to changing situations.

The goristro's most distinctive ability is its Charge, which requires it to move at least 15 feet straight toward a target, then gore it, potentially knocking it prone. A failed Strength saving throw also means the target is thrown 20 feet away, meaning the goristro can charge it and knock it down again the following turn! (This is a lot of fun for goristros. They call it "head golf.") The goristro's Charge does massive damage—14d10 + 7 piercing damage on a hit, or 84 damage on average. In contrast, its Fist/Fist/Hoof Multiattack, against a target less than 15 feet away, does only 3d10 + 6d8 + 21 bludgeoning damage, or 64 damage on average. Even if it's already engaged in melee, therefore, it would rather back up 20 feet (do you think a demon with AC 19 and 310 hp cares about opportunity attacks?) and then Charge again.

But let's say that, like a dog chasing a thrown ball, the Charge is an instinctual reflex reaction to seeing an opponent at a certain distance. What if a goristro charges an opponent and fails to knock it down? Does it back up for another charge, or does it Multiattack with its fists and hooves?

I think this all depends on its relative likelihood of landing a hit, something the goristro wouldn't be able to calculate but would have an instinctual sense of. A Charge attack is all-or-nothing: The goristro gets just one attack roll, and if it fails, no damage at all. Its Fist and Hoof attacks have the same probability to hit, but it does get three chances to land a hit (or miss). I'd say that if the goristro has a two-thirds or better chance of making its attack roll, it goes for the Charge, but if its chance to hit is lower than two-thirds, it hedges by making three attacks rather than one. With a to-hit modifier of +13, that means it must be attacking a target with AC 20 or greater (with disadvantage on the attack roll, AC 17 or greater; with advantage, AC 22 or greater) to prefer the Fist/Fist/Hoof Multiattack.

QUASITS

The **quasit** is a Tiny fiend with very low Strength, very high Dexterity, and average Constitution. This ability profile would normally suggest a sniper, but the quasit has no ranged attack. Therefore, this is a creature that has to be able to repeatedly strike, then slip away. Maybe it doesn't even initiate an attack itself—maybe it waits in hiding, using its Invisibility trait, until its master or an ally is already engaged in combat with an enemy, then pops out to deliver sneak attacks from behind ("Optional Rule: Flanking," *Dungeon Master's Guide*, chapter 8), or maybe it takes advantage of its high speed and Invisibility to ambush ranged attackers and spellcasters. Either of these would be consistent with its proficiency in the Stealth skill.

Quasits are none too bright: Their Intelligence score of 7 indicates that they operate primarily by instinct. However, they can assess, in a very broad sense, whether an opponent is "tough" or "not tough." Big targets, armored targets, and targets with large or heavy weapons are "tough." Small targets, unarmored targets, and targets using small or simple weapons are "not tough." Against a "tough" opponent, they lead with Scare, attempting to startle the opponent and throw it off before attacking with Claws or Bite. Against a "not tough" opponent, they skip Scare and go directly to melee attacks.

If an opponent does any damage at all against a quasit, its next action is to turn invisible. It doesn't attack again unless and until a potential opponent is otherwise engaged.

Quasits have the ability to assume the form of a bat, centipede, or toad; each of these forms enhances its movement in some way, none of which is quite enough to make the tactic of maintaining distance in order to dart in, attack, and dart back out workable. The risk of a successful opportunity attack is simply too great for a monster with Armor Class 13 and only 7 hp, even one with resistance to physical damage from normal weapons, and even if the enemy has disadvantage on attack rolls from being frightened or poisoned.

SUCCUBI/INCUBI

Originating as a mythological explanation for erotic dreams (and, possibly, sleep paralysis episodes as well), the **succubus** and its masculine counterpart, the **incubus**, were imagined as devils who tempted people in their dreams. What did they want? The same thing devils always want: to lay claim to your soul, in their case by getting you to corrupt it of your own free will by giving in to the deadly sin of lust.

Despite including some of the trappings, D&D doesn't share Christianity's religious cosmology, but the flavor text in the fifth edition *Monster Manual* assigns succubi and incubi essentially the same mission: "[W]hen a succubus or incubus has corrupted a creature completely . . . the victim's soul belongs to the fiend. . . . After successfully corrupting a victim, the succubus or incubus kills it, and the tainted soul descends into the Lower Planes."

Therefore, we have to take a bigger-picture view of succubus and incubus tactics. They're not about simply gaining an edge in a happenstance combat encounter. They don't have happenstance combat encounters. Rather, these tactics are steps toward the fiends' final goal.

Let's look at the features of the succubus and incubus and how they fit into this plan:

- The Etherealness trait facilitates "reconnaissance, spying on opponents, and moving around without being detected" (*Dungeon Master's Guide*, chapter 2, "Ethereal Plane").
- Proficiency in Deception, Insight, and Persuasion gives them the means to identify a target's basic fears and desires and play upon them with a calibrated, flattering mixture of truths, half-truths, and lies.
- Telepathy allows them the ability to communicate with any creature telepathically up to a range of 60 feet.
- The Charm feature lets them charm a single humanoid for a day. (The DC and the time limit are important to note, and we'll look at these in detail below.)

- Telepathic Bond gives them the ability to communicate at an unlimited distance with charmed targets, even between different planes of existence.
- The Shapechanger trait lets them assume an ordinary humanoid form of Small or Medium size—all the better to seduce you with, my dear.
- Proficiency in Stealth gives them the ability to approach their victims without being detected by others.
- The Draining Kiss feature lets them suck hit points from a charmed (or willing) target, killing the target if their hit points are reduced to 0 by this method alone. (If the target is taking damage from other sources, a succubus or incubus must use Draining Kiss to drain hit points equal to the target's maximum before killing the target in this way.)

I list the features in this order because this is the order in which they'll most likely be put to use.

One of the most helpful (and, occasionally, maddening) features of fifth edition D&D is how carefully all its rules are written for absolutely literal interpretation. If they don't mention something, that something doesn't apply. With this in mind, I note that nowhere in the rules is it written that a target must be *conscious* to be charmed! Both the *charm person* spell and the Charm feature of the succubus and incubus specify only that the target must be visible and within a certain range. (In contrast, the vampire's Charm feature specifies that the target must also be able to see the vampire, which necessitates being awake.)

The key restrictions on the succubus's or incubus's Charm feature are its DC, which isn't stupendously high, and the fact that its effect lasts only 24 hours. This means a couple of things: First, the succubus or incubus typically favors low-Wisdom targets, ideally those with a Wisdom saving throw modifier of 0 or less. (Between their Intelligence 15 and the fact that they do this for a living, we can presume they can "read" a player character's stats to determine this.) That being said, according to the flavor text, "The more virtuous the fiend's prey, the longer the corruption takes, but the more rewarding the downfall." So a particular succubus or incubus might intentionally target a higher-Wisdom PC, just for the pleasure of the challenge. Second, because the charmed condition wears off after 24 hours, the succubus or incubus has to visit its target repeatedly on successive nights to maintain it.

Here, then, is how I envision a succubus or incubus encounter—and remember, unlike most monster encounters, this isn't a single scene, it's a whole act, maybe even a subplot running throughout the whole play:

- The succubus or incubus chooses a target, spying on them from the Ethereal Plane.
- Having chosen a target, it comes up with a marketing plan based on the target's fears and desires. (You can infer these from a PC's Ideal, Bond, and Flaw.)
- Using Etherealness to travel to the target's location, then Stealth so that its presence won't be detected, it approaches the target while they're sleeping, then attempts to Charm the target. If it succeeds, mwahahaha! If it fails, it uses Etherealness again and slips away, to try again the next night.
- During the day, it may transmit telepathic suggestions to its charmed victim, compelling them to behave in sinful ways. (In case you're not familiar with the "Peg's Law" mnemonic, the traditional seven deadly sins are pride, envy, gluttony, sloth, lust, avarice, and wrath.) Or it may shapechange into a form alluring to the target, stroll right up to them, and use its feminine or masculine wiles to wheedle the target into acting against their better judgment. Or both.

Now, if a PC is suddenly smitten with a gorgeous stranger who shows up out of nowhere, and that stranger starts encouraging that normally straitlaced PC to, say, engage in public displays of affection, steal coins from blind beggars' bowls, etc., other PCs are going to figure out right quick that things ain't right. So a succubus or incubus visiting a PC in the flesh will probably avoid being seen by others and will absolutely discourage the PC from revealing their involvement to others ("What we have is so special . . . how about we keep it our little secret?").

But then again, a succubus or incubus may lead a public life, perhaps even as a prominent figure, so that no one would question a PC's involvement with it—or its desire to keep personal relationships discreet. Only behind closed doors does it give free rein to its fiendish identity.

- Once the succubus or incubus has wormed its way into a PC's affinity, and once that PC has debauched themself to its satisfaction, it makes one final nighttime visit, during which it goes in for the kill with its Draining Kiss. Note that, since this does harm to the PC, they get to make an additional Wisdom saving throw to resist its Charm with each use of Draining Kiss. For this reason, ideally, the succubus or incubus will have established a level of trust with the PC that will cause them to accept the kiss *willingly* at first, *without* being Charmed. In other words, the succubus or incubus uses Draining Kiss first, *then* attempts to Charm the target again, *then*—if it succeeds—uses Draining Kiss a second time. Depending on how committed your players are to roleplaying, a succubus or incubus who flubs the re-Charm might endeavor to simply *persuade* the PC that they're already so morally compromised, there's nothing more worth living for, and they should accept the final Draining Kiss as the inevitable consummation of their downfall.

- If the re-Charm fails, or if the second Draining Kiss isn't enough to finish off the PC, the succubus or incubus has failed in its mission, because it's not likely ever to get a second chance to execute this combo. It spends one action reverting to its true, fiendish form—which offers no tactical benefit, only cinematic effect—then, on its next action, makes its getaway via the Ethereal Plane.

There's always a chance that the succubus or incubus will get busted before it has a chance to carry out its nefarious plan. As a DM, how do you handle this situation? The Etherealness trait offers a mostly foolproof escape hatch, but you might decide, for the sake of showmanship, to have the succubus or incubus reveal its fiendish nature before skedaddling. If ethereal escape is somehow prevented, and the succubus or incubus is forced to fight rather than flee, it will revert to its fiend form to gain access to its Claw attack, since its humanoid form isn't built for fighting.

Will an unmasked succubus or incubus stick around and fight? Not if it has a choice, I'd say. It's a creature of subterfuge, not direct aggression, and even though it has resistance to physical damage from nonmagical weapons, it's not immune to them, nor does it have any protection from acid, force, necrotic, radiant, or thunder damage. It has no territory to guard, no family to say goodbye to—nothing it values more than its own life, and it's very attached to that. It escapes via the Ethereal Plane if it can, flies away if it must, and uses its Claw attack only if inescapably cornered.

YUGOLOTHS

In AD&D, the neutral evil analogues to lawful evil devils and chaotic evil demons were "daemons," but since midway through D&D second edition—perhaps to avoid conflation with demons, or perhaps to avoid confusing Philip Pullman fans—they've been called "**yugoloths**." Yugoloths are neither as obedient as devils nor as recalcitrant as demons: They have a mercenary mindset, and in fact are often used as mercenary warriors by archdevils and demon lords, according to the *Monster Manual* flavor text.

There's little reason for a yugoloth to be encountered in any other context, and therefore little likelihood that PCs will run into one on their home material plane. But I can imagine a scenario in which an evil ruler asks a court wizard or archpriest to summon a yugoloth for aid in battle against a rival, figuring that it might be easier to control than a demon and less likely to demand something unacceptable in return than a devil.

There are four types of yugoloth listed in the *Monster Manual*. From weakest to strongest, they're the mezzoloth, the nycaloth, the arcanaloth, and the ultroloth. However, even mezzoloths have a challenge rating of 5. These are not opponents for low-level adventurers.

All yugoloths are proficient in the Perception skill; are immune to acid and poison and resistant to cold, fire, lightning, and physical damage from normal weapons; have Magic Resistance; have blindsight or truesight, along with the ability to cast *darkness* innately; and can Teleport. The mezzoloth, nycaloth, and arcanaloth all have high Strength and Constitution and comparatively lower Dexterity, the ability profile of a brute fighter; ultroloths have a more balanced profile with a slight emphasis on Constitution, making them tankish. Finally, like demons and devils, yugoloths can be permanently killed only on the plane of Gehenna; anyplace else, their physical bodies are destroyed, but their essence returns to Gehenna and re-forms there. Thus, they have no reason to retreat or flee when seriously injured.

Mezzoloths have low Intelligence, indicating that they operate mainly on instinct. They can cast *darkness* twice per day, and they have blindsight, so it stands to reason that they'll take advantage of this ability as their very first action in combat. They can also cast *dispel magic* twice per day, so they'll use this ability if they happen to fail a saving throw against a spell or other magical effect that's causing them severe inconvenience (by "severe," I mean inconvenience they can't disregard and can't evade by merely moving or Teleporting someplace else).

Their third innate spell ability is *cloudkill*, which they can use once per day. The flavor text implies that they use this power when surrounded by enemies, but they have a more natural method of escape, Teleport, that's not use-limited. Instead, I see no reason why they wouldn't use *cloudkill* offensively, as it's designed. They're immune to poison themselves, so they can cast it anywhere they like, at any time. Moreover, the spell as written implies that it's cast in a particular direction, and even the flavor text says the mezzoloth "exhales" the cloud; it doesn't simply emanate outward from the mezzoloth in all directions, so it's not useful for dealing with flankers. Therefore, I'd expect mezzoloths to lob *cloudkill* in the direction where it's likely to catch the greatest number of enemies at once, preferably four or more, given the spell's 20-foot radius (see the Targets in Area of Effect table, *Dungeon Master's Guide*, chapter 8). After that, they scamper into the cloud of poison and start stabbing and slashing at their poisoned enemies.

There's a snag, though. Both *darkness* and *cloudkill* require concentration to sustain, which means a mezzoloth can't use both at once. This isn't an issue if there's more than one mezzoloth: One casts *darkness*, and another casts *cloudkill*. But if there's only one, it can cast *cloudkill* only if it doesn't need to sustain *darkness* to make it dark. That being said, even in less than total darkness, *cloudkill* beats *darkness*, hands down. *Cloudkill* heavily obscures an area, the same as *darkness*; darkvision doesn't penetrate it, nor does *daylight* dispel it; and it inflicts poison damage within its area of effect even on a successful saving throw. What's not to love?

Mezzoloths have no fear of magic per se, but the types of damage they're not immune to—radiant, necrotic, psychic, and thunder—are annoying to them, and they lash out immediately at any opponent who succeeds in inflicting one of those damage types on them. If they aren't adjacent to that opponent already, they'll Teleport to a square or hex behind them, then Multiattack the following turn, using Claws for any opportunity attack they get to make.

Nycaloths are not just brutes, not just flying brutes, not just stealthy flying brutes, but stealthy flying brutes that can cast *darkness* and *mirror image* at will. This is a crazy combination of features that can and should be used to freak players out. They have no ability that requires them to remain adjacent to their opponents, so they'll fight from the air, swooping down to attack, then swooping back up out of reach. With AC 18, 123 hp, and resistance to a wide variety of damage types, they needn't be concerned about opportunity attacks.

Darkness is the nycaloth's default first action, because its blindsight gives it advantage in that circumstance. If this fails, or if its enemies are somehow unaffected by it, it follows up with *mirror image*, so that those who can see it may end up fighting an illusory duplicate instead. It casts *dispel magic* under the same circumstances that a mezzoloth does.

The synergy between *invisibility* and Teleport is interesting, because while *invisibility* ends when the caster casts any other spell, in the case of the nycaloth, Teleport is an action, not a spell. Thus, it can cast *invisibility*, then Teleport on its next turn without making itself visible again. This allows it not just to Teleport to the location of another enemy, as a mezzoloth can, but to turn invisible, then Teleport, then attack with advantage when its foes don't expect it. This takes an extra round, but the nycaloth can make an educated guess about whether the benefits are worth the delay—for instance, depending on whether the opposition seems to include strong healers who can use that round to patch up their allies.

Arcanaloths, as their name suggests, are spellcasting specialists with a voluminous repertoire, but the first things I want to call attention to are their very high Charisma, their extraordinarily high Intelligence, and their proficiency in Deception and Insight. These are smooth customers who will parley *first* if given the chance. They're all about getting what they want the easy way rather than the hard way.

What do they want? More than anything, information. Magic items, too, but mainly ones that help them obtain information, either directly or by trading them away to someone else. Their avarice for information is boundless. The information provided had better be of significant value, though.

When determining the relative value of spell slots, level doesn't matter as much as scarcity. An arcanaloth has only one 6th-, one 7th-, and one 8th-level spell slot. As a rule, it's not going to use these slots to cast any spell other than the spells of these levels. That being said, *mind blank* is a spell that might be useful in a battle of wits, but when it comes to a battle of stabs, not so much. Does this mean that the arcanaloth's 8th-level spell slot is free to cast, say, a massively boosted *fireball*? Well, it could do that, but that's the only chance it will ever get to cast a spell at 8th level; surely this slot deserves to be used for something a little more special. And, indeed, *chain lightning* presents itself as a spell that can be boosted by casting it at 8th level. This is the better choice, allowing the arcanaloth to cast this very powerful spell twice rather than just once.

With that in mind, let's open the spellbook and take a look-see:

- *Mind blank*, as mentioned, is a social interaction spell, with limited combat application (although it's worth holding on to if the arcanaloth's foes start casting divination or enchantment spells). Our 8th-level spell slot is potentially open for repurposing.
- *Finger of death* is strong but can't be boosted. The arcanaloth will get only one chance to cast this spell, so it reserves it for an opponent with a Constitution saving throw modifier of +2 or lower.

- *Chain lightning* is strong and *can* be boosted. When the arcanaloth wants to do a lot of damage fast, it first casts *chain lightning* at 8th level, striking up to five targets. If and when it casts the spell again, it casts it at 6th level, striking up to three.
- *Contact other plane* is a ritual, not suitable for combat.
- *Hold monster* is an ironic and unfortunate inclusion in this spell repertoire, since the arcanaloth is designed as an enemy for PCs, not for other monsters. If the arcanaloth were able to cast *hold person*, it could use a 5th-level spell slot to paralyze four humanoid enemies, but because it can only cast *hold monster*, it has to spend that same slot to paralyze just one. What a waste. So does the arcanaloth use *hold monster* as an expensive, emergency-use-only *hold person*, or does it save a 5th-level slot to boost a 2nd-through 4th-level spell? Here's my call: It reserves the slot for *hold monster* if and only if it's facing one opponent who obviously poses a significantly greater threat than any other opponent and whose Wisdom saving throw modifier is +2 or lower, giving the spell a two-thirds or better chance of success. (Its Intelligence is high enough that it can effectively "read" PCs' stats just by observing them.) Alternatively, it can use this spell against any nonhumanoid ally that the PCs summon, such as an elemental.
- *Banishment* is a strong method of dealing with a troublesome opponent with a Charisma saving throw modifier of +2 or lower. If a 5th-level spell slot is available, it can banish two. Depending on the PCs' stats, this may be a preferable alternative to *hold monster*.
- *Dimension door* is a handy escape hatch. An arcanaloth doesn't fear death, but it might consider it inconvenient to have its present physical form destroyed.
- *Counterspell* is an automatic reaction against any spell attack (ranged or melee—as opposed to a spell that requires a saving throw) of 5th level or lower. Against a 4th- or 5th-level spell, the arcanaloth will go ahead and spend a slot of the necessary level to squelch it automatically (but it won't use its last 4th-level slot for this, in case it needs to cast *banishment*).

- *Fireball* is what the arcanaloth turns to for damage dealing when it's out of slots for *chain lightning*. It will use an available 4th- or 5th-level spell slot to boost this spell if possible (although, again, it won't use its last 4th-level slot to do so). There's some competition here with *counterspell* for the use of available 3rd-, 4th-, and 5th-level spell slots, but by the time the arcanaloth is casting these spells, it should be clear whether it's playing primarily offense (*fireball*) or defense (*counterspell*).

- *Fear* is a somewhat counterproductive spell for a monster that's pretty sure it can kill you if it needs to. It's also a concentration spell, so it can't be cast at the same time as, say, *banishment*. Here are the upsides: First, by causing melee opponents to Dash away, it can give the arcanaloth an opportunity attack against one of them. Second, by causing them to drop what they're holding, it can give the arcanaloth a way to disarm an opponent who's wielding a magic weapon, then either snatch the weapon up or kick it away. Again, if the key opponent doesn't have a Wisdom save modifier of +2 or lower, there's no point. Let's call this spell "situational."

- *Detect thoughts* is a social interaction spell whose only combat application is to detect invisible opponents. A whole turn's action is too high a cost.

- *Heat metal*, one of the arcanaloth's innate spells, is a nice jerk move against an opponent wearing metal armor or wielding a magic weapon. It requires concentration, though, and there are other sustained spells that have higher priority.

- *Mirror image* is a good spell, but it may be a bit beneath a fiend that can cast *chain lightning*, *fireball*, and *banishment* at its foes. Still, if it doesn't look like its opponents are going to be deterred by such things, *mirror image* remains a good way to confound melee and ranged attackers.

- *Phantasmal force* would be better for the arcanaloth if it didn't require concentration or if it were boostable. At 2nd level, all it can really do is dink damage—possibly useful if everyone's getting worn out, but otherwise, nah.

- *Suggestion* requires concentration and isn't boostable, and its effects aren't going to last long in a combat situation if there's any chance that the target will take damage. Best-case scenario, it takes someone out of the fight ("You know, that horse you've got tied up outside is totally exposed to the elements right now. Don't you think you should go check on it, maybe put a blanket over it in case it rains?") without a pricey spell slot expenditure. Again, Wisdom save mod +2 or less, or don't bother.
- *Detect magic* and *identify* are social interaction spells.
- *Magic missile* . . . nah. Not when you've got *chain lightning* and *fireball*.
- *Tenser's floating disk* cannot be used as a damaging Frisbee.
- *Shield* is what all those 1st-level spell slots are for. Keep in mind, though, that the arcanaloth gets only one reaction per round. A reaction that's used for *counterspell* can't be used for *shield*, nor vice versa. The arcanaloth can quickly and intelligently determine which one it needs more.
- *Firebolt*, because the arcanaloth is a 16th-level spellcaster, does 3d10 fire damage, or an average of 16 damage. By comparison, its Claw attack does an expected 8 slashing damage plus 8 poison damage.

Like all yugoloths, the arcanaloth is happier fighting in the dark (it's got 120 feet of truesight), so it drops *darkness* first thing unless there's nothing to be gained from it. It sustains that spell until it needs to cast some other sustained spell, most likely *banishment*. Its first combat spell is 8th-level *chain lightning*, followed by 6th-level *chain lightning*. It uses *hold monster* or *banishment* (not both) to remove one or two extremely troublesome enemies from the field, unless there's no opponent whose Wisdom or Charisma save modifier is low enough for the arcanaloth's comfort. Against a single highly threatening opponent with a low enough Constitution save modifier (especially one with 60 hp or fewer, for a shot at zombification), it casts *finger of death*. It repels incoming spell attacks with *counterspell* and weapon attacks with *shield*, depending on which poses the greater threat. It casts *fireball* against clusters of four or more opponents within the spell's radius once its uses of *chain lightning* are expended, first at 5th level, then 4th, then 3rd—but it never uses its last 3rd- or 4th-level slot on this spell.

If it can catch a melee opponent and at least two others in the cone of effect, and that melee opponent is using a magic weapon, it casts *fear* to try to cause the opponent to drop the weapon and to gain an opportunity attack when they Dash. Confronted by a highly skilled opponent attacking with a melee or ranged weapon, it casts *mirror image*. And it can fly, so as long as it doesn't have to engage with an opponent, it hovers out of reach, casting its spells from 15 feet up in the air, descending only when it has to.

Ultroloths aren't team players; only one will ever be encountered at a time. They're happy to wade—or rather, float, since they can fly—into the thick of battle, attacking once per turn with Hypnotic Gaze, then three times with Longsword (an enemy stunned by Hypnotic Gaze can't fight back, and attack rolls against that enemy have advantage). Between turns, they hover 30 feet in the air, swooping down on their turns to attack, then swooping back up; they don't care about opportunity attacks.

If capturing enemies rather than killing them is within an ultroloth's brief, it may try to accomplish this with a *mass suggestion*: "You cannot hope to win this battle. Lay your weapons down and surrender, and I may show you mercy." But then again, if it knows that this would be a waste of time—because the PCs are mostly elves and thus hard to charm, say, or if most of them have Wisdom save modifiers of +3 or better—it doesn't bother. Unlike arcanaloths, ultroloths aren't interested in negotiation, only victory.

Like other yugoloths, an ultroloth casts *darkness* first thing if this would be of any benefit to it (it has 120 feet of truesight). Once per day, an ultroloth can cast *fire storm*, which it does if it can catch all its enemies within the spell's area of effect. When surrounded by four or more enemies, it uses *wall of fire* to ring them in and force them to choose between getting scorched or coming within the ultroloth's melee reach. Then, just to be a jerk, it flies or Teleports out to attack any enemy remaining outside, leaving its other enemies trapped in the ring. It employs *fear* as described above, to get opponents to drop magic weapons and open themselves up to opportunity strikes, and *dimension door* to avoid the inconvenience of disincorporation. Otherwise, it sticks to its Multiattack, wielding its longsword with two hands, since it carries no shield.

NIGHTMARES

In AD&D, the **nightmare** was simply the equine equivalent of the hell hound—an infernal horse, ridden by devils. Apparently, the lore has changed. Have you *read* the fifth edition *Monster Manual*'s description of the nightmare? It's not just some devil horse anymore—now it's what you get when you rip the wings off a pegasus. Seriously. That's some sick stuff, man.

Whichever origin story you prefer, nightmares are clearly *not* evolved creatures, so they're not going to possess the same survival instincts as most other monsters. They're not undead, either, so there's not necessarily any compulsion driving them. They're categorized as fiends, so their primary motivation, underlying any other they may have, is malevolence. Their job is to transport devils and demons, and it suits them.

Aside from their average Intelligence, every one of a nightmare's abilities is above average. Its physical abilities, especially its Strength, are exceptionally high, but it also has a curiously high Charisma. It doesn't seem to *use* its Charisma for anything, so I think that's simply a representation of its being difficult to banish (*banishment* is one of the tiny handful of spells that require a Charisma saving throw). You might think of it as a brute fighter, given that its highest two ability scores are in Strength and Constitution, but its speed also suggests a shock attacker element to its combat. It tries to maximize the damage it does on its first strike, but it doesn't necessarily need to retreat after delivering that strike. Because nightmares' flying speed is greater than their normal speed, they move around the battlefield by flying leaps, unless something prevents them from flying.

Nightmares are immune to fire damage, and they Confer Fire Resistance upon their riders. This would probably be more tactically valuable if they had some kind of Flame Aura trait of their own, but they don't, so Confer Fire Resistance is more of an "oh, by the way" feature than a core capability. The same goes for Illumination, a primarily cosmetic trait with the side benefit of compensating for the nightmare's lack of darkvision.

Ethereal Stride seems more interesting—at first. As an action, a nightmare can transport itself and up to three willing creatures into or out of the Ethereal Plane. What advantages does this offer? Chiefly, beings in the Ethereal Plane are invisible to beings in the material plane, making it a great way to get the drop on one's enemies (unless they've got *see invisibility* or *true seeing*). Effectively having a surprise attack round at the outset of every combat encounter would be an outstanding trait for a shock attacker—except the nightmare, unlike a phase spider (see page 134), has to use its action to emerge from the Ethereal Plane, giving it no chance to attack! Arrrrgh.

Okay, but at least it can appear adjacent to an enemy, or appear within 90 feet and approach within reach of that enemy, so that if the enemy freaks out and tries to run, it gets an opportunity attack. Or—and I think this is the real utility of the feature—the nightmare appears adjacent to an enemy, and then its *rider* gets an immediate surprise attack. Moreover, the nightmare can carry its rider back into the Ethereal Plane after the rider's next attack, through judicious use of the Ready action. (That is, if the rider takes its turn first, it Readies an attack action to occur when the nightmare carries it onto the material plane; if the nightmare goes first, it Readies an Ethereal Stride action to occur immediately after its rider attacks.)

So basically what we have in the nightmare is a creature designed not as an attacker per se but as a delivery mechanism for other fiends, which just happens to have an attack of its own when it's not busy carrying them into and out of the Ethereal Plane. Also, note that Ethereal Stride doesn't just affect the nightmare's rider—it affects up to three willing creatures within 5 feet of it. So you can have a "knight" fiend mounted on the nightmare, plus up to two "squire" fiends on foot alongside it. They just have to make sure they're all grouped up when the nightmare blinks out again, so that they don't get left behind.

Devils and demons typically don't fear death on the material plane, because they can be truly killed only on their home planes, so a nightmare won't need to flee on their account. I also can't think of any reason why a nightmare should care enough about its own survival to flee when injured. After having its *wings ripped off* (sigh), it's probably contemplating the misery of its existence 24/7 and satisfied to spend every last moment of its life taking its resentment out on someone else.

Here, then, is the basic pattern of nightmare combat:

- A nightmare appears in the midst of a group of enemies using Ethereal Stride, bearing a rider (usually a mid- to high-CR devil, demon, or yugoloth) and up to two other, lesser fiends. Those fiends then either execute Readied attacks, if their turns came before the nightmare's, or attack on their own turns, if their turns come after.
- In intermediate rounds, the nightmare attacks on its own turn, and its allied fiends attack on theirs. A nightmare normally attacks whomever its rider is attacking; it doesn't pick its own targets independently of its rider. But an unmounted nightmare favors softer targets, i.e., those with a lower Armor Class. Or paladins, just because.
- At some point, the nightmare Readies an Ethereal Stride action, to occur when the last of its allied fiends has attacked—or, if it goes last in the initiative sequence, it simply uses this action. What's the criterion for blinking out? It depends in large part on what the nightmare rider's purpose is. Maybe the rider wants to get away from a group of enemies without incurring multiple opportunity attacks. Maybe it wants to launch a shock attack on an isolated enemy who's doing a lot of damage from a distance. Maybe it's pursuing an equally mobile target. Or maybe its work here is simply done.

CAMBIONS

The **cambion**'s particular combination of abilities and features is intriguing. This is not a *straightforward* monster. On the contrary, it offers more flexibility than most.

First, although its physical abilities are all very high, its two highest are Strength and Dexterity. The cambion is a shock attacker, optimized for moving fast and hitting hard, for quick and decisive battles rather than drawn-out slugfests. But it also has high Intelligence and even higher Charisma, meaning it has the option to talk its way out of a fight that's dragging on too long—and so do its opponents.

It has proficiency in several saving throws, but of them, only Constitution is one of the big three—the ones that most damaging or debilitating spells require. It's got a good enough Dexterity to compensate, maybe, but not Wisdom. So despite its other advantages, the cambion does have reason to be apprehensive around spellcasters, especially bards, sorcerers, and wizards with a lot of mind-controlling or restraining spells in their repertoires.

The cambion's social skill proficiencies include Deception and Intimidation but not Persuasion, so good-faith negotiation isn't its style—against weaker opponents, it bullies, and against equal or stronger ones, it tries to outfox them. It's also proficient in Stealth, which combined with its shock-troop ability profile indicates an aptitude for ambush.

Cambions are resistant to physical damage from normal weapons, along with cold, fire, lightning, and poison. These resistances, combined with its high Armor Class, suggest a lack of concern with being struck by opportunity attacks. Since cambions can fly—quite fast, in fact—the tactic of hovering in the air, flying down to strike, then flying back up out of reach is feasible.

The cambion's Multiattack comprises either two melee attacks (the only such attack listed in its stat box is Spear, which it uses two-handed, since it's not listed as carrying a shield) or two uses of Fire Ray. Spear's damage edges out Fire Ray's, but barely, so the cambion is happy to attack at any distance. If its chosen target is fighting with dull iron, it can strafe them with its spear; if its target carries a magic weapon, it can hurl fire from a safe distance instead.

The cambion can innately cast *alter self*, *command*, *detect magic*, and *plane shift* (self only). The last of these is its escape hatch, which it uses when it's seriously wounded (reduced to 32 hp or fewer). *Com-

mand can be used to force an opponent to provoke an opportunity attack by running out of reach (or to fall prone, but this is useful only if the cambion has allies that can follow up with their own attacks before the target gets back up). *Detect magic* is rarely useful in the midst of combat.

Alter self, at first glance, seems mainly to be how the cambion passes among humanoid society without being seen for what it is. (Horns, wings, tails, and crimson skin have a way of setting people on edge.) But if an enemy of the cambion, while engaging it in melee, manages somehow to both corner and disarm it, it can cast *alter self* to sprout claws à la Wolverine and keep brawling, since it would attack with disadvantage if it tried to use Fire Ray at melee range.

Interesting question: Should it do an additional 1d6 fire damage if fighting with a melee weapon other than its spear? I would say yes, and here's why: If you reverse-engineer the cambion's attack, spell save, and skill modifiers, you can determine that it has a +3 proficiency bonus. You can then determine that its spear isn't a magic weapon: It has no bonus to hit and no bonus to damage. The fire, therefore, comes from the cambion itself, not from the cambion's weapon, and so it should get that extra fire damage die even when it's attacking with a different weapon, including natural weapons sprouted courtesy of *alter self* (which, incidentally, *are* magic, with an extra +1 to hit and to damage).

Finally, the cambion has Fiendish Charm, a simple *charm person* analogue that differs in two ways: First, the charmed target obeys the cambion's commands, and second, a successful saving throw immunizes the target for 24 hours. Fiendish Charm is usable on only one target at a time, too slow for use in combat. But a cambion has only to see a target to charm them, and Fiendish Charm *isn't an attack*, so a cambion can use this ability from hiding and remain hidden even if it fails. The only hitch is, it risks breaking the enchantment if it attacks its target. (A less important consideration is that its Intelligence isn't high enough for it to "read" characters' stats—it can only make educated guesses. It knows better than to try to charm a cleric, druid, ranger, or monk, or an elf, hill dwarf, or gnome of any class. Non-elven, non–hill dwarf, and non-gnome bards, rogues, barbarians, fighters, sorcerers, warlocks, and wizards are better bets. Paladins are a crapshoot; a cambion may go ahead and try, just out of contempt and to test its luck.)

So the questions that you as the DM have to answer in advance are these: Why is the cambion there in the first place, what would it want from interlopers such as the PCs, and how badly does it want them dead? Whatever a cambion's interests are, it will look to further them the easy way. If it can get your PCs out of its hair—or even get them to do its own work for it—by charming a couple and fast-talking the rest, it will. If the PCs are likely to be violently uncooperative, so be it. A single cambion can take on a whole party of level 1 or 2 PCs by itself, maybe even level 3 if there aren't too many of them. Against intermediate-level PCs, it needs allies or minions.

A cambion that's serious about killing your PCs lays an ambush for them. While hidden, it uses Fiendish Charm against those within 30 feet whom it surmises to be promising targets and who may cause trouble if *not* charmed. When it's ready, it attacks from hiding with surprise, using Spear if an opponent is within reach, Fire Ray otherwise. Having already charmed one or more members of the party, it can command them, "Do not interfere!" without having to use an action. It can tell them to do other things as well as the fight goes on, as long as it doesn't involve their coming to harm and thereby getting more saving throws.

Priority targets include spellcasters, particularly fragile-looking ones; anyone wielding a magic weapon; and anyone within 60 feet who's isolated from their allies. The cambion fights from between 10 and 30 feet in the air, flying down to stab with its spear, then flying back up again, unless and until its target lands a couple of opportunity strikes; after that, it shoots Fire Rays from the air instead. If any of its opponents has a magic weapon, it may cast *command* (action) to order the opponent to drop the weapon, then fly down (movement) and snatch it up (free interaction). Of course, once it's picked up the opponent's weapon, it wields its own spear with one hand only. If it has allies or minions surrounding an opponent, it may cast *command* to order that opponent to flee, incurring a flurry of opportunity strikes. However, the cambion casts *command* only against opponents it considers "charmable"; against anyone else, it's likely to be a waste of an action, and the cambion does *not* want to waste time in combat. If it can't dispatch roughly one opponent per round, it's going to consider the whole fracas more trouble than it's worth.

After one round of combat has gone by for each uncharmed enemy, if the cambion hasn't defeated them yet, it starts losing patience and barking out orders to surrender (if they're weaker) or offers to let them live if they give it what it wants (if they're of comparable strength or stronger). It keeps fighting all the while, but it's talking as it fights, and it stops fighting only if the two sides manage to come to a deal midcombat. It starts talking even sooner if it's moderately wounded (reduced to 57 hp or fewer) or if all its opponents have shown they have ways to hurt it badly.

The cambion's fiendish parentage influences its alignment and determines how closely it keeps its word. The offspring of a devil adheres strictly to the letter of any agreement it comes to, although it's forever alert for loopholes that will let it subvert the spirit. The offspring of a demon breaks its word the second it's advantageous to do so. The offspring of a yugoloth keeps its word as long as it's getting something it wants out of the deal, and no longer. The offspring of a succubus or incubus keeps its word as long as doing so amuses it.

Cambions *can* be killed on the material plane, and their self-preservation instinct is strong. They'll bug out with *plane shift* when they're seriously injured, and they may even do so sooner if the fight is going badly for them and their opponents seem determined to fight to the death rather than make a deal.

CELESTIALS

The word "angel" comes from Greek *angelos* "messenger," and this is the sort of role that celestials usually play: emissaries, observers, givers of boons. Occasionally, if magically summoned, they fight on the player characters' side. Whether it's a powerful being from the outer planes or a terrestrial creature of immaculate virtue, there's not much occasion for a celestial to play the role of antagonist in an adventure, unless you have a party of evil-aligned PCs. But even though a celestial is an avatar of good, it can still develop a distorted perspective on worldly activities and adopt an overzealous approach in its pursuit of purification. At worst, it can become corrupted, doing great harm with what it believes to be the purest of intentions.

ANGELS

Who gets in a fight with an angel? "Evil characters" is the obvious answer, but it's not the only answer. Angels being lawful good, a dedicated group of chaotic player characters could find just as much reason to beef with them—and even PCs who are neutral on either the good-to-evil spectrum, the law-to-chaos spectrum, or both, and who find themselves gadding about on Mount Celestia (or the Seven Heavens, as we called them back in the day), might somehow run afoul of the ruling authority in a way that needs to be kiboshed.

Angels in the *Monster Manual* come in three levels: devas, planetars, and solars. These qualify as boss opponents for mid-level, high-level, and top-level adventurers, but realistically, players are rarely going to run across them before they acquire access to the 7th-level spell *plane shift*, and that doesn't happen until level 13. Lower-level

PCs might journey to the Outer Planes through the use of a magic item that allows them to cast *plane shift* or a portal created by the *gate* spell, or they might manage to summon an angel to serve them using *planar binding* or *planar ally*. Even so, we're still talking level 9 and up.

The upshot of this is that a **deva** is unlikely to play the role of boss enemy. Rather, devas are angelic minions, encountered either before or alongside a more powerful planetar or solar. The *Monster Manual* describes them as "messengers or agents." They follow orders; they don't issue them.

Before going into what distinguishes a deva from its more powerful cousins, let's look at what all angels have in common:

- Mind-blowing ability scores, across the board.
- Proficiency in Wisdom and Charisma saving throws. (Most important upshot: Angels are hard to control or banish.)
- Resistance to radiant damage, as well as physical damage from mundane weapons.
- Immunity to being charmed, exhausted, or frightened.
- Knowledge of all languages, plus the ability to communicate telepathically.
- Angelic Weapons, which are magic and deal bonus radiant damage.
- The innate ability to cast *detect evil and good*, *commune*, and *raise dead*.
- Advantage on saving throws against magic.
- Healing Touch, which not only restores hit points but also removes curses, neutralizes poison, and cures disease, blindness, and deafness.
- The ability to fly—*fast*.
- And one more thing, whose importance may not be immediately obvious: lawful good alignment.

Why is that last item so important? Because it means *angels don't want to hurt you*. They're consummately just, kind, and other-centered.

They'll kill fiends, all right, and they'll destroy undead creatures. But as far as other living beings are concerned, they have two overriding rules: Commit no harm, and prevent harm from coming to others. I don't agree entirely with the flavor text's assertion, "An angel slays evil creatures without remorse." I'd maintain instead that angels slay only *intrinsically* evil creatures without remorse.

Thus, except against fiends and undead, they always attack to subdue, not to kill (see "Knocking a Creature Out," *Player's Handbook*, chapter 9). This holds true even if their opponents are of evil alignment. It doesn't mean they'll hesitate to fight—it just means they'll do no more damage, and no damage more lethal, than is necessary to stop their non–lawful good opponents from doing whatever rotten things they're doing.

Other conclusions we can draw from those common traits: Angels fight while hovering in the air. They have no particular fear of spellcasters, although they'll treat any who cast spells requiring Dexterity saves with some caution. (Devas extend that same caution to casters of Constitution-save spells.) They're similarly cautious around magic weapons. If they have minions of their own nearby, they'll use Healing Touch to top them up when they're 20 hp down or seriously wounded, whichever happens first.

And you can't fool them. They know your weaknesses as if you were wearing them on a T-shirt. They'll talk before fighting if it seems likely to be fruitful, but with Insight +9, devas are likely to see right through you if you're lying, and with Divine Awareness, planetars and solars *always* will. They can fight in whatever fashion fits the situation best, but they'll generally come back to good old-fashioned toe-to-toe melee.

Okay, back to devas specifically. Their Multiattack—two swings with a mace—is straightforward. Change Shape, though, is a tricky one. A polymorphed deva takes on the Armor Class, movement, senses, Strength, and Dexterity of its humanoid or beast form; it also takes on that form's other capabilities and features, minus class features, legendary actions, and lair actions. (It retains its own Constitution, hit points, saving throws, resistances, and immunities.)

When is this a good trade? A deva's normal Armor Class is 17; no beast is going to beat that, nor is it going to have better than 120 feet of darkvision. A deva might go whale or dolphin for the ability to swim, but aside from that, any humanoid or beast form a deva could take would be trading down, no matter what special features it had.

So I conclude that Change Shape is something a deva uses only to pass among people in disguise. If a combat situation is likely to ensue, it immediately uses its action to revert to its true form—both to regain access to its superior stats and for its deterrent power ("Are you sure you're committed to this course of action, now that you know this badger is in fact a powerful heavenly being?").

Devas prioritize their targets by alignment: chaotic evil foes first, then chaotic neutrals and neutral evils, then lawful evils and neutrals (they cut the chaotic goods a bit of slack here, unless they're on their home plane and the CGs are causing a ruckus), then lawful neutrals and chaotic goods, then neutral goods, and finally lawful goods. The idea here is that if they remove the worst elements first, the others may be more amenable to correction.

Once a deva has selected a target, its manner of fighting depends on that target's own strengths and weaknesses. Against a front-line brute fighter, it will skirmish, hovering high up in the air, swooping down to make its two weapon attacks, then swooping back up, without concern for opportunity attacks. Against a skirmisher, ranged attacker, or spellslinger, on the other hand, it will close to melee range *and stay there*, making its own opportunity attack when its target tries to get away.

Unlike devils and demons, angels *do not* zop back to their home plane when their bodily forms are destroyed. If you destroy an angel, *you kill it*. So despite their commitment to duty, devas may or may not retreat when seriously injured (reduced to 54 hp or fewer); it depends on whether their duty *requires* them to fight to the death. Against fiends and undead, they're likely to fight to the bitter end, but in certain other circumstances, there may be more to gain from flying away and reporting back to their heavenly superiors.

A retreating deva Dodges as its first action against a melee opponent with only a single attack, Dashes if its opponent has Extra Attack or Multiattack, and Disengages if its melee opponents outnumber it. Once it's clear of melee opponents, it Dodges until it's out of range of missile fire and spell attacks, then finally switches to Dash.

Planetars are celestial elite troops. They have proficiency on Constitution saves in addition to Wisdom and Charisma saves, their weapons do an additional die of radiant damage, and their Healing Touch restores two additional dice. Thanks to Divine Awareness, you can't lie to them at all without being caught, and they have truesight, so don't bother with those illusion spells. They can cast *invisibility* on themselves at will, and they also have limited uses of *blade barrier*, *dispel evil and good*, *flame strike*, *control weather*, and *insect plague*.

In most respects, planetars fight the same way that devas do, but their spellcasting ability adds a wrinkle. Let's look at the merits of each spell:

- *Control weather*—eh, forget this one. It's just showing off, and it takes 10 minutes to cast.
- *Blade barrier*, aka "wall of razors," is a planetar's "Go to Jail" card, the primary use of which is to isolate one particular enemy who's significantly more chaotic and/or evil than all the rest. The planetar airdrops next to that enemy and casts this spell in a ring around itself, trapping the enemy inside with it and shutting everyone else out.
- *Dispel evil and good* has a couple of different uses. If the planetar's opponents include a single celestial, elemental, or fey creature, it may use the Dismissal option to eject that enemy from the game. If there are multiple such enemies on the field, or one or more fiends or undead creatures, it's more likely to maintain concentration on this spell to give them disadvantage on attack rolls against it. The Break Enchantment option is situational.
- *Flame strike* is a powerful, instantaneous damaging spell that requires a Dex save against fire and radiant damage in a 10-foot radius column. Referring to the good ol' Targets in Area of Effect

table in chapter 8 of the *Dungeon Master's Guide*, we can determine that a planetar wants to catch at least two enemies in this area of effect if it can. But here's the twist: It wants both those enemies to be *its top-priority targets*. If it can't cast this spell without also affecting someone further back in line, it will refrain.

- *Insect plague* is similar to *flame strike*, except that it requires concentration and affects a 20-foot-radius sphere, so a planetar wants to catch at least *four* enemies in this area of effect. The same no-queue-jumping rule applies: All four (or more) enemies must occupy the top of the planetar's hit list.

- *Invisibility*, so strong in so many other circumstances, seems oddly inapplicable to the planetar, which seems rarely to have any need for it. But I can imagine at least one use: to thwart attacks from enemies *it doesn't want to fight*. Suppose, for example, that the planetar is tussling with a group of PCs who are mostly chaotic neutral, but somehow they've fallen in with a lawful good paladin, who's fighting the planetar out of loyalty to his associates. When the pally engages in melee with the planetar, the planetar—who has no beef with the pally, and in fact is hoping that the pally will see reason once all his CN companions are subdued—simply vanishes from the pally's sight and relocates itself to a more tactically advantageous position, as far as possible from the pally, before reappearing.

This is a long list of possible circumstances, but these circumstances are also narrow and specific. If none of them is met, then the planetar defaults back to deva-like, melee-centered behavior. Its threshold for deciding whether to retreat is 80 hp.

At the top of the angelic hierarchy is the **solar**. Like the planetar, it possesses Divine Awareness and truesight. Also like the planetar, it can cast *blade barrier*, *dispel evil and good*, and *invisibility* (*control weather* too, but we know how useful that one is) and does so under the same circumstances and for the same reasons. However, it one-ups its junior angels: Instead of *raise dead*, it can cast the even better *resurrection*.

A solar has three legendary actions it can take. The costliest—requiring it to expend all three legendary actions it gets each turn—is Blinding Gaze. It targets only one creature, it imposes a serious but not disabling condition, and its save DC is an astonishingly low 15. Why on earth would a solar blow all its legendary actions on this one option? It would do this only if it had just one opponent it needed to defeat.

Much more consequential is Searing Burst, which requires a DC 23 Dex save (thank you, that's more like it) against a burst of fire and radiant damage, and which can be targeted selectively against any opponent(s) within 10 feet of the solar. Naturally, it uses this ability when it can strike at least two targets this way, and when those targets are at the top of its list. (If only its number one opponent is within range, it won't bother.)

But if you really want to drive your players crazy, the way to do it is with Teleport. The solar's Intelligence is 25: It can read out the battle like it's playing a bridge hand. Just before an opponent gets a chance to attack it, it teleports out of range or out of sight, always one step ahead of its foes. It gets to do this three times per turn, on its *opponents'* turns. (Of course, if an opponent doesn't even have the power to hurt it, it doesn't bother—it just takes the hit.)

The solar has two weapons, a greatsword and its Slaying Longbow. Let's compare the two:

- Greatsword: +15 to hit, average 49 damage on a hit, up to two attacks per turn.
- Slaying Longbow: +13 to hit, average 42 damage on a hit, only one attack per turn—but if the target has fewer than 100 hp and it blows a Con save, *it straight-up dies.*

Now, maybe I'm too literal-minded, but going by the *Monster Manual* illustration, it seems to me that the solar's wings would get in the way of any weapon it tried to stow on its back, so how's it supposed to bring *both* a sword and a bow into combat? Reading its features, I think there's only one way the solar can pull it off: using its Flying

Sword action to send the sword forth to do its own thing while the solar attacks with the bow. It's weird, but it works.

On the other hand, *it works, but it's weird*. And how much benefit does it bring, really—trading an average 7 damage per round for a low chance of killing an enemy outright, when an angel isn't necessarily trying to kill anyone anyway?

By my reckoning, it comes down to this: A solar brings its Slaying Longbow along only if it's going to be fighting fiends or undead, which need killin'. In any other situation, it sticks with the greatsword alone. It's not as if bringing only a sword instead of a sword and a bow impedes the solar's ability to deliver justice, since it can fly at 150 feet per turn (!), it can hover, it can Teleport on other creature's turns, it gets two sword attacks in its Multiattack action, and its base AC is a bigger number than you can roll on a d20.

A solar wielding only a greatsword fights the same way as a deva or planetar (including its application of *blade barrier*), with the exception of its Teleport trick and the occasional surgical Searing Burst. A solar wielding a sword *and* a Slaying Longbow, however, mostly stays in the air, loosing arrows hither and yon, and sends its sword down to do its dirty work below. With its sword, it may attack to kill (fiends and undead only, please) or to subdue (everyone else), but with the bow, it *always* attacks to kill, and it chooses its targets accordingly.

If some deity considers a situation important enough to send a solar to take care of, you'd best believe it's serious enough that the solar is going to stick around until the job is done. No retreat with this one. It keeps fighting until either the battle is finished or it is.

EMPYREANS

The fifth edition *Dungeon Master's Guide* describes four tiers of play, based on PC level. From level 1 to level 4, PCs are "local heroes," saving one village at a time. At levels 5 through 10, they're "heroes of the realm," regionally renowned. At levels 11 through 16, they're "masters of the realm," on whose deeds the fates of kingdoms turn. And at levels 17 through 20, they're "masters of the world," the ones you call to deal with your annoying Vecna infestation.

If your PCs are coming face-to-face with an **empyrean**, they'd better either be masters of the world already or have very good health insurance coverage. Empyreans are, essentially, demigods. Titans. Boss monsters on par with the most ancient dragons. Most of them are chaotic good, residing on the plane of Arvandor, Arboria, or Olympus, depending on how old-school you like your cosmology. But sometimes they go on a spring break bender in Tartarus or something (excuse me—Carceri), and they're not the same when they come back. These depraved empyreans end up exiled to the material plane, where they take over kingdoms as a hobby. If a 20-foot-tall god-child can't make Posleslavny great again, who can, am I right?

Every one of an empyrean's abilities is extraordinary, but with beyond-extraordinary Strength and Constitution 30, it's a brute to rule all brutes. A single hit from its maul can potentially kill a PC with up to 23 hp instantly. Its Armor Class, *unarmored*, is 22. It has more than 300 hp. It's immune to physical damage from nonmagical weapons, and its own weapon attacks are inherently magical. It also has advantage on saving throws against magic. It's not afraid to mix it up with you—even if it *should* be, you being a master of the world and all.

Generally, then, the empyrean favors the direct approach to dealing with its enemies: charge, bash, repeat. (With a 10-foot reach and the ability to fly, it can make its Maul attacks from the air, where most opponents' melee weapons can't touch it.) Its ranged Bolt attack, while potent, isn't as damaging as its melee attack, and it uses this attack—which has the ridiculous range of 600 feet—only to strike at a distance against opponents whom it can't yet engage in melee with. Thanks to its Intelligence of 21, it knows, automatically, exactly which type of damage will harm its targets the most.

Hypothetically, an empyrean might use Bolt to shut down a spellcaster who could cast spells that bypassed its immunities and resistances. The thing is, thanks to its spectacular saving throw modifiers, *there aren't any*—with the possible exception of *earthquake* or *meteor swarm*. Even against these, despite having a Dexterity saving throw modifier of only +5, it still has Legendary Resistance, allowing it to leap clear of the fissure or take only half damage from the meteors.

Like other monsters with Legendary Resistance, which grants three automatic successes per day on failed saving throws, the empyrean rarely, if ever, fails a saving throw; when it does, it's probably a Dex save. Consequently, it doesn't bank its uses of this feature. It uses it any and every time it fails a save, until its uses of the feature are exhausted.

Once per day, an empyrean can cast *fire storm*, which does 7d10 fire damage on a failed save, half that on a success, and ought to be able to engulf every one of the empyrean's opponents. It doesn't lead with this spell, nor does it wait until the last minute to cast it. Rather, it casts it when it realizes it has to take its opponents seriously, i.e., when they've managed to moderately wound it (reduce it to 219 hp or fewer).

Earthquake, on the other hand, it casts as soon as combat begins, because it can sustain this spell, probably for the entire duration of combat, and it offers the empyrean nothing but advantages: creating difficult terrain (which the empyrean can effortlessly fly over—in fact, it will probably spend the entire combat encounter floating several feet above the ground), distracting spellcasters who are trying to concentrate, knocking enemies prone, opening cracks in the ground that enemies may fall into.

Plane shift, as usual, is an escape hatch, which the empyrean uses when it's seriously wounded (reduced to 125 hp or fewer). Players, of course, will find this profoundly unsatisfying. At the highest adventuring levels, however, PCs may be able to boost a *counterspell* high enough to foil it, or they may have access to *plane shift* themselves and thus be able to pursue, if they can determine where the empyrean has gone.

The empyrean's other spells are largely irrelevant; it casts *dispel evil and good* only if a PC has summoned one or more celestials, fiends, or undead creatures that the empyrean can't dispatch with Bolt or by smacking with its maul, or simply ignore.

Empyreans can take up to three legendary actions per round, at the end of other creatures' turns. One, Attack, lets them make an additional Maul or Bolt attack. This is their default choice, because it makes up for their otherwise lackluster action economy (unlike most boss monsters, empyreans have no Multiattack).

Bolster only applies when an empyrean has allies fighting alongside it, and if that's the case, heaven help your PCs, because the empyrean is plenty deadly all by itself.

Trembling Strike is a crowd-control feature—actually something of a desperation measure, since it costs *two* legendary actions, and all it does is knock opponents prone. By inference, its purpose is to manage the number of enemies the empyrean has to fight at one time (especially relevant if you're using the optional Flanking rule—*Dungeon Master's Guide*, chapter 8). It fears nothing, but fighting half a dozen enemies simultaneously, as Fezzik would tell you, comes with its own complications. Trembling Strike has a radius of 60 feet, so it's overkill against most adventuring parties, and the empyrean will probably bother only if all its opponents are in the area of effect. Against a party that's brought an army of its own minions along, though, its standard differs: It wants to catch *either* all the PCs *or* at least a dozen enemies—it doesn't matter *which* dozen—in the area of effect. After they fall prone, it can retreat half their top speed, plus 10 feet, past where they can reengage easily.

As mentioned above, the empyrean would rather scram than die. Also as mentioned, PCs powerful enough to seriously wound an empyrean are powerful enough that they may be able to pursue it when it casts *plane shift*. An empyrean that's seriously wounded but has already blown its single daily use of *plane shift* could Dodge, Dash, or Disengage, and any of these might be feasible; in practice, though, I think it would favor Dodge or Disengage over Dash. This is because the empyrean already has a movement speed higher than almost any PC can match without magical enhancement (a barbarian with the Mobile feat could just barely keep up). What are the chances, if the PCs have magic that lets them travel at more than 50 feet per round, that the same magic won't also let them travel at more than 100 feet per round? The empyrean Dashes away *only* if it knows for a fact that its enemies can run it down if it moves away at its normal speed but not if it moves away at twice that. (And with Intelligence 21, if this is the case, the empyrean does know it.)

Whether the empyrean chooses Disengage or Dodge depends on the number of enemies engaged in melee with it. If there are only one or two, it Dodges as it retreats; three or more, it Disengages. Either way, retreating isn't the same as quitting. It uses Dodge or Disengage as its turn action, but with its *legendary* actions, it continues to lob attacks back at its pursuers (this is the other thing that its Bolt attack is good for), and if it's being chased by a dozen or more enemies at once, it uses Trembling Strike to stop them cold.

Unicorns

"Are there **unicorns** in these woods? I want to see a unicorn!" Venture into any idyllic forested setting, and you're sure to hear this request from one of your players.

Unicorns are elusive beasts—actually, not beasts, according to D&D's classification system, but celestials. They're gentle, exuding a spirit of tranquility that extends to the other creatures that dwell in their vicinities, but they're also alert defenders of their domains. A unicorn may choose to reveal itself to a good-hearted creature, but any character who takes ill advantage of a unicorn's good nature will be made to regret it.

In fifth edition D&D, unicorns are surprisingly, impressively formidable. As I mention in "Mix It Up!" on page 304, it's fun to take familiar monsters and give them unexpected powers, and when I first began thinking about unicorns, I thought it would be entertaining to suggest that they should summon hordes of angry woodland creatures, disappear by running behind a tree and reappear behind another one, fire trebuchets, and rear up on their hind legs and deliver stunning roundhouse kicks like Chuck Norris. It turns out, I don't need to! Unicorns are pretty tough already.

Normally I start at the top of a monster's stat block and work my way down, but in this case, I'm going to start at the bottom, with the unicorn's legendary actions. That's right—even as written, the unicorn is a legendary creature. The Hooves action allows the unicorn to make a single attack with its hooves on another creature's turn. Shimmering Shield, which costs two of the unicorn's three legendary actions, gives it (or another nearby creature) a +2 bonus to its Armor Class until the end of its next turn—given its very high Wisdom, it can easily foresee a situation in which this will be necessary, and it won't wait until an attacker lands a hit to use it. Finally, Heal Self, which costs all three legendary actions, restores an average 11 hp, roughly one-sixth of the unicorn's hit point maximum; it's a suitable measure to take when the unicorn is moderately wounded (reduced to 46 hp or fewer).

As for other features, I'd been amused by the notion of allowing unicorns to gore and trample like a triceratops—and what do you know, *they already can*. The Charge feature delivers extra piercing damage on a successful Horn hit, and it requires the target to make a Strength saving throw or be knocked down. If you combine this with the unicorn's Multiattack, which comprises a Horn attack and a Hoof attack, gore-and-trample is exactly what you get. Note that if the target is prone, the unicorn has advantage on the melee Hoof attack roll.

Unicorns also have Innate Spellcasting. The most combat-relevant of the spells they have available are *entangle* and *dispel evil and good*, each of which they can cast once per day.

Entangle is a concentration-required area-control spell that creates difficult terrain and requires targets to make a Strength save or be restrained. The *Monster Manual* doesn't indicate that the unicorn can move freely through this terrain, but it doesn't really matter, because its base movement speed is 50 feet per round, and it needs to move only 20 feet to take advantage of Charge, so it can still attack with advantage *and* gain bonus damage against any target it can reach. (You may want to allow the unicorn to move through it without impediment anyway, because *unicorn*.) The spell's 20-foot radius, combined with the fact that the unicorn gets to cast it only once, is a strong argument for not using it unless and until it can catch four or more opponents in the area of effect (see the Targets in Area of Effect table, *Dungeon Master's Guide*, chapter 8).

Dispel evil and good is also a concentration-required spell that can be sustained to impose disadvantage on attack rolls by other celestials, elementals, fey, fiends, or undead; or cast instantly to banish or break an enchantment cast by one of those types of creatures. Obviously, this isn't going to do anything to a PC, so this comes into play only if a PC has summoned one or more extraplanar allies. If one of said allies has charmed, frightened, or possessed an ally or ward of the unicorn, it will use the Break Enchantment option; if not, and there's only one such ally, it will use Dismissal to try to banish it; otherwise, it will sustain the spell for as long as said allies are on the field.

Calm emotions may also be relevant, but only if a PC or party-allied NPC is casting enchantment spells on wards or allies of a unicorn. Unicorns' at-will spells—*detect evil and good*, *druidcraft*, and *pass without trace*—are more applicable outside combat, and it lets them expire as soon as combat begins.

Aside from its Hoof and Horn attacks, the unicorn has two other actions that it uses primarily in defense of a creature that it's guarding: Healing Touch and Teleport. But it can also use Teleport as a method of escape if it's seriously wounded (reduced to 26 hp or fewer) or use Healing Touch against a moderately wounded ally if it's not guarding anyone, or outside combat as a boon.

Along with their exceptional Strength, unicorns have high Dexterity and Constitution. The former makes them shock attackers at the start of combat, while the latter seems like it ought to allow them to keep fighting in melee like a brute. But unicorns' AC isn't very high, so they're less durable than you might think, despite their nine hit dice. For this reason, a unicorn will Charge one turn, then Disengage (action) and run away the next, then Charge, then Disengage, and so on. Unicorns are *not* resistant to physical damage from normal weapons, and with their low AC, they can't risk incurring opportunity attacks. They'll also make extensive use of their Shimmering Shield legendary action, even though the cost might make you, the Dungeon Master, leery of doing so.

Unicorns' very high Wisdom means they're careful in choosing their targets, focusing on evil foes first, then chaotic ones, and taking out ranged and melee weapon attackers before spellcasters (they can afford to, because of their Magic Resistance). It also means they won't initiate a fight if they're overmatched: They'll use *pass without trace* to conceal themselves and their wards, and their natural speed to stay out of reach. If you're setting up a unicorn combat encounter—because, say, the PCs are after someone a unicorn is guarding, or they're just rotten people—you should always include enough other unicorns or fey or beast allies to make it a Deadly encounter for the party (see "Combat Encounter Difficulty," *Dungeon Master's Guide*, chapter 3). Unicorns never flee without first making sure that anyone they're guarding can also get away (the Teleport feature helps with this by including up to three other willing creatures).

So you've done all this, and it still looks like your PCs are going to kill a unicorn? *You must not allow that to happen.* Seriously, in this case, pull out all the stops. Have the unicorn rear up and whinny, and have three unicorns for every PC step out of the woods in a circle around the party, glowering angrily. Give them Pack Tactics and Evasion and Uncanny Dodge and Flurry of Blows and Stunning Strike. Let them innately cast *conjure animals* and *conjure woodland beings*. Have them fire bolts of radiant damage from their horns. And if you do all this and the PCs *still* manage to bag one of the noblest creatures in all the realm, give them only the normal 1,800 XP for defeating a CR 5 creature. Why? *Because you attacked a* unicorn, *you reprobates.*

PEGASI

If there's no opportunity for your PCs to meet a unicorn, that's okay; an encounter with a **pegasus**, the winged horse of Greek myth, will excite them almost as much. Of course, they probably won't be fighting the pegasus. Instead, most likely, it will play the part of an allied mount.

Mounted combat in fifth edition is a funny affair (see the rules in chapter 9 of the *Player's Handbook*). Normally, a mount may be either controlled (acting on the rider's turn and unable to take any action other than Dodge, Dash, or Disengage) or independent (acting on its own turn and doing whatever it darn well pleases). But an "intelligent" mount always acts independently, and with Intelligence 10, a pegasus counts as intelligent. Being a good creature, it does its best to act in ways that benefit both itself and its rider.

Pegasi are *fast*: Their normal movement speed on the ground is 60 feet per turn, and their flying speed is 90. Along with their exceptional

Strength, they have both very high Dexterity and very high Constitution, offering a stylistic choice between swift strikes and prolonged melee. But since they lack any kind of automatic disengagement or other defense against opportunity attacks, they're more or less stuck committing themselves to melee. That's probably okay, though, since their riders can help them out.

Pegasus tactics aren't sophisticated: They fly up to a foe and strike with Hooves as they land. (It makes no sense for them to stay in the air, because they can't fly away without provoking an opportunity strike, and if by some misfortune they should happen to get knocked prone while aloft, they'll take falling damage.)

But pegasi have an excellent sense of how dangerous an enemy is, and they can use this sense to help their riders make better target selection choices. A pegasus doesn't change the criteria by which a rider selects a target; it simply adopts those criteria and uses its superior judgment to choose. If a PC happens to be riding a pegasus and orders it to attack an overly powerful enemy, the pegasus will hesitate, shifting around uneasily, as if to say, "Are you sure you want to do this?" A pegasus is also reluctant to attack another good-aligned creature; on the flip side, it gets excited by the chance to attack a fiend.

An unmounted pegasus rarely fights at all, except to thrash a fiend; even in self-defense, it prefers simply to Disengage and skedaddle.

Unless ordered by its rider to stay in the fight, a pegasus Disengages and flies away to safety when seriously wounded (reduced to 23 hp or fewer).

COUATLS

The **couatl** is rarely encountered in D&D campaigns, partly because of its distinctly Mesoamerican flavor (most campaign settings remain stubbornly quasi-European) and partly because of its lawful good alignment (good monsters make bad enemies), but the winged, feathered serpent has been part of the game since the first AD&D *Monster Manual*. In fifth edition, it's categorized as a celestial.

Couatls have exceptional ability scores across the board, but their Dexterity and Wisdom are especially extraordinary. Their mental ability scores are higher on average than their physical ability scores, suggesting a preference for spellcasting over messy tooth-and-claw conflict (though their spell repertoire turns out not to support this preference especially well). Their 30-foot slithering speed is put to shame by their 90-foot flying speed; this, plus an awesome natural Armor Class of 19 and an immunity to physical damage from nonmagical weapons, implies that if they do engage in physical combat, they'll most often hover in the air, dive-bomb their targets, then fly back out of reach without concern for opportunity attacks.

In addition to being immune to normal weapon damage, couatls are also immune to psychic damage and resistant to radiant damage. They have proficiency in two of the "big three" saving throws, Constitution and Wisdom, as well as Charisma, and magical mind-reading and scrying don't work on them. They also have truesight with a range of 120 feet.

Strangely, even though Wisdom is their highest ability stat, Charisma is the ability they use for spellcasting—perhaps as a kindness to their opponents. Also, most of their spells are geared toward social interaction situations, not combat. This is especially true of their once-per-day spells, *dream, greater restoration*, and *scrying*, all of which are favors that player characters might petition a couatl for. Similarly, *detect evil and good, detect magic, detect thoughts, create food and water*, and *lesser restoration* are all spells without direct combat application.

From a tactical standpoint, the key spells to be aware of are *bless, cure wounds, sanctuary*, and *shield*. *Bless* is a powerful support spell that a couatl will cast on its allies, if any are present, and sustain for the duration of combat. It does this before it engages in any attack of its own, because lawful good, yo. *Sanctuary* is cast as a bonus action—important, since aside from this spell and *shield*, the couatl's action economy is limited to one action per turn—and wards its target against attack, so a couatl will cast this on the most vulnerable creature under its protection.

Shield, cast as a reaction, is a simple self-defense measure that the couatl can cast up to three times, once per turn, as soon as an enemy rolls between 19 and 24 on an attack roll. *Cure wounds* is weak for its action cost, consuming a full action to restore an average of only 8 hp. For this reason, a couatl probably won't use it except to save a seriously wounded ally from imminent death, and in that case, it follows up with a *sanctuary* spell on its next turn, then spends the remainder of combat closely defending that ally.

Even though it seems like a couatl should prefer spell attacks over melee attacks (couatls have no ranged attack), there's really nothing in its repertoire that allows it to fight this way. Instead, it has two melee attack actions, Bite and Constrict. Bite does nominal damage but also has the potential to put an opponent to sleep. Constrict is the real power attack, because not only does it do more damage, it also grapples *and* restrains on a hit. What does this mean? First, that the couatl gets advantage on attack rolls against a grappled target on a subsequent round. Second, the couatl can fly up into the air with its target and still do so with respectable speed, despite its movement's being halved (see "Moving a Grappled Target," *Player's Handbook*, chapter 9).

Like other lawful good creatures, a couatl is unlikely to pick a fight, except with intrinsically evil beings such as fiends and undead creatures. However, some couatls are charged with guarding individuals, sacred places, or holy relics, and if a fight is what it takes to do that, a fight is what you'll get.

An attacking couatl uses its first turn to cast *bless* on any allies present if it needs to, along with *sanctuary* if one ally requires special protection. Otherwise, a couatl's standard modus operandi is to hover in the air, out of reach of melee weapons; swoop down on the enemy who's most ideologically opposed to it (see "Angels," above); and attack to constrict. If it misses, it flies back up out of reach; if it hits, it flies back up with its grappled target wrapped up in its coils.

On its next turn, a couatl with a grappled target in its coils Bites it (with advantage, since the target is restrained), hoping to put it to sleep. If it succeeds, the next thing it does—if it can afford to leave its post—is to fly its opponent outside and dump them, like a celestial bouncer. Then it returns to see whether its remaining opponents are more open to reason.

This is a time-consuming tactic, though, so it's only suitable for use against small groups (say, three-ish) or against medium-size groups (say, five-ish) with only a couple of determinedly evil and/or chaotic members. A couatl that has to fight off more than two or three enemies to accomplish its purpose has to forgo the benefits of attacking a restrained target and deal with its foes with more dispatch. In that case, it relies on its Bite attack instead, prioritizing its enemies by chaoticness and evilness and, one by one, swooping down and Biting them until they pass out.

Couatls are creatures of duty, and they know when they'll die, though not how. A couatl with a person, place, or thing to protect will do so until death, but in the absence of such a duty, it retreats to save itself when seriously wounded (reduced to 38 hp or fewer), flying at full speed while taking the Dodge action to avoid incoming attacks.

FEY

The denizens of the Feywild—seelie and unseelie alike—are creatures of passion and impulse, equally quick to laugh and to take umbrage, living in an eternal present yet also harboring grudges for centuries. Their logic is child-logic, dream-logic, fever-logic. Their moods can turn on a dime, depending on the last thing to happen or the last word spoken. If treated with respect, they may grant a favor. If not, they can turn a combat encounter into a waking nightmare.

PIXIES, SPRITES, AND DRYADS

Pixies are simultaneously gregarious and shy, curious and aloof. They don't fight, period. If a combat situation emerges—and this will be 100 percent of the time because your players are choosing to be jerks—they flee.

The simplest way is to vanish using Superior Invisibility. But if that's not enough to make the player characters move along, they also have *confusion*, *dispel magic*, *entangle*, *phantasmal force*, *polymorph*, and *sleep* in their repertoire. These are all once-per-day powers, but pixies are never alone. (With Strength 2 and Constitution 8, why would they be? Tiny, fragile creatures seek safety in numbers.) Invariably, there will be enough of them around to unleash *all* those powers, round after round, plus *druidcraft* and *dancing lights* for extra disorientation. They'll use *sleep* against non-elven spellcasters; *dispel magic* against all spells the PCs attempt to cast; *confusion*, *phantasmal force*, and *polymorph* against fighters; and *entangle* against everyone else. Pixies should systematically thwart any attempt to hurt them; as a DM, don't go out of your way to be fair to players who are picking on pixies.

Sprites are the fighters of fairyland, but even they don't fight to kill. Their "longsword" does an epic 1 damage when it hits, but they only use this weapon when someone grabs them. Normally, they shoot opponents with their bows, which have a chance of delivering a dose of knockout poison. Like pixies, sprites congregate in overwhelming numbers, so even though each of them deals only 1 hp per hit, a swarm of angry sprites can turn a PC into a humanoid pincushion— an *unconscious* humanoid pincushion. Again, forget about being fair: Go right ahead and make your players make a dozen saving throws against that poison. They asked for it.

Sprites' ideal combat range is 40 feet: near enough for normal chances to hit with their bows, far enough that most PCs can't close the distance. If a hostile PC approaches closer than 40 feet, they use Invisibility to disappear, resituate themselves 40 feet from the PC in another direction, then shoot again the following round.

If a PC does manage to hit a sprite, it will probably die on the spot, so choosing whether to flee isn't a function of how much damage one takes but rather how many of them have already been killed. If, somehow, the PCs manage to kill 60 percent of a swarm of sprites, the rest fly away.

Dryads are less good-natured and much less social, but they're also unlikely to initiate combat, unless the PCs are engaging in wanton destruction in their woods. One possible exception, however, is if a dryad has taken a shine to a PC and charmed them, and the other PCs try to interfere.

They're not weak, but their mental abilities are superior to their physical abilities, so they rely on these and avoid combat if they can, especially melee combat. If a scuffle seems imminent, they Ready *barkskin* and cast it as a reaction when a PC initiates hostilities; if it comes as a surprise, casting this spell is their first full action. They use their clubs if angered (first casting *shillelagh* as a bonus action) or cornered, but it's nearly impossible to corner a dryad, especially in its native forest. Dryads never venture far from a living tree, and if PCs try to close in on them, they use Tree Stride—an innate trait, not an action!—to slip away (ideally, they'll use trees that are also within their attackers' reach, so as not to provoke opportunity attacks). From a safe distance of 60 feet, they then cast *entangle* at the unwelcome visitors' feet and make their escape. Even when angry, they withdraw from combat when seriously injured (reduced to 8 hp or fewer).

"Dryads work with other sylvan creatures to defend their forests," the *Monster Manual* flavor text informs us, but given their ability profile, it seems probable that they leave the actual fighting to others, for the most part, relying on enchantment (Fey Charm) to dissuade lone trespassers and deception (*druidcraft*) to befuddle small groups, and calling in the unicorn cavalry to deal with more numerous enemies.*

SATYRS

Satyrs, aka fauns (depending on whether you're feeling more Greek or Roman), are the party animals of fairyland. These creatures aren't inclined to start a fight, but if *you* start one, they have ways of finishing it.

Average to slightly above-average in Strength and Constitution but well above average in Dexterity, satyrs avoid melee fights in favor of ranged sniping. In a way, this is disappointing, because the most distinctive and delightful attack in their arsenal is Ram—but they have no good reason to use it. Being Strength- rather than Dex-based, it has a poorer chance to hit than a Shortsword or Shortbow attack; it does marginally less damage than either of those; and it doesn't even knock the target down. It would have been much better if the satyr's stat block had included a Charge feature, which would have given Ram some real punch. A satyr engaged in melee is better off using its action to Dodge.

When a fight breaks out, satyrs scatter. They take cover behind trees and Hide if they can, counting on their enemies to be unable to keep track of them all. Their ideal range from their enemies is 40 to 60 feet: well within normal bow range, close enough that their enemies can hear the tunes from their enchanted pipes, far enough away that those enemies can't close the distance in a single round.

---

* "Unicorn cavalry" is a metaphor here, although it does conjure up an awesome mental picture, doesn't it?

If the satyrs in an encounter number roughly the same as their opponents, they either use Shortbow (if within ideal range at the start of the turn); use Shortbow, then move away (if closer than 40 feet); or move closer, then use Shortbow (if farther than 80 feet). If you're using the Satyr Pipes variant, one satyr within 60 feet of all its opponents uses its Panpipes to play a Frightening Strain, which imposes disadvantage on the attack rolls of enemies who fail their saving throws and can't be ended prematurely, as Charming Melody and Gentle Lullaby can. (These latter tunes are more likely to be played for mischief than in self-defense.)

If the satyrs outnumber their opponents significantly, they adopt a deadlier tactic: While one satyr plays its pipes, *half* the rest shoot at their opponents with Shortbow, while the other half move to new positions, out of their last targets' field of view, and Hide. The following round, those who are hidden shoot with advantage, giving their positions away, while those who just shot Hide themselves again, taking advantage of their opponents' distraction. They do less damage per round this way, but they also *take* less damage per round, and their use of Stealth to dictate the pace of combat works to their advantage, as their chance to hit goes up from, say, 55 percent to nearly 80 percent against AC 15, while their careful use of tree cover boosts their own AC from 14 to 16 (half-cover) or 19 (three-fourths cover).

Satyrs' Intelligence is high enough for them to coordinate an attack in this way, but their merely average Wisdom means they're not particularly discriminating about target selection. Because they have Magic Resistance, they're not more apprehensive about spellcasters than they are about anyone else. On the contrary, if they're going to focus fire on anybody, it will be whoever's biggest—or whoever's managed to get within attacking reach of one of their brethren. Otherwise, they shoot at whoever's closest.

Satyrs do their best to stay out of melee range of their opponents; if someone does manage to close with one, they Dodge and retreat, using their full 40-foot movement distance. (Their Intelligence is high enough for them to understand what Disengaging is, and their speed would make it advantageous, but their Wisdom isn't high enough for them to possess the discipline to do it.)

A seriously wounded satyr (reduced to 12 hp or fewer) Dodges while retreating further into the woods. If at least 60 percent of a group of satyrs are all seriously wounded or slain, they stop Dodging and Dash away—wounded and unwounded alike.

HAGS

Evil fey creatures, hags rely on magic and deceit to befoul everything and destroy everyone around them. In many cases, by the time players realize that one or more hags are what their characters are up against, it's already too late to avoid the encounter.

All hags possess very high Strength and Constitution, and they can do fierce damage with their claws, suggesting that they won't shy away from toe-to-toe melee combat. When they come together in covens of three, they also gain access to a powerful repertoire of spells. To cast these spells, they must all be within 30 feet of one another, which limits their mobility somewhat. So that they're not forced to retreat out of range, we can suppose that they fight facing outward, their backs toward one another. Thus, if they're knocked back, for instance, they fall toward the others rather than away from them. This leaves them vulnerable to being surrounded, but it also offers some protection against flanking, since most PCs won't want to run right into the midst of the trio.

Hag covens can also create hag eyes, little surveillance cameras they can all see through. The *Monster Manual* flavor text says a hag eye "is usually entrusted to a minion for safekeeping and transport," but it can also be hung in an unobtrusive location that allows a hag coven to spot creatures approaching its lair. When they do this, however, they're careful to conceal it, because if it's destroyed, they'll not only suffer minor to moderate damage but also be temporarily blinded.

Let's look at the spells available to a hag coven:

- *Eyebite* is a sustained spell requiring concentration which can impose a debilitating condition (unconscious, frightened, or "sickened"—effectively poisoned) on a succession of targets who fail their Wisdom saving throws.

- *Contact other plane* and *scrying* apply less to combat than to social interaction scenarios in which the PCs might be petitioning the hags for otherworldly wisdom.
- *Phantasmal killer* is weaksauce, requiring not one but two failed Wisdom saving throws for a target to take any damage, and it requires concentration as well. Sea hags might use it anyway, however, because all they require to set up their Death Glare is that the target be frightened, and that requires only one failed save.
- *Polymorph* can turn a PC into a newt. They'll get better, but not for an hour, or until the spell is dropped or disrupted. In the meantime, the hag who casts it can't use any other sustained spell.
- *Bestow curse* is yet another spell requiring concentration— *unless it's cast using a 5th- or higher-level spell slot*, and it just so happens that our hags have *two* 5th-level spell slots that they're probably not going to use in combat! So when they use *bestow curse*, they do it with one of those slots, meaning they don't have to concentrate to sustain it, and the effect lasts 8 hours.

What kind of curse should they bestow? If a hag is likely to land more hits than its target, it should go for the necrotic damage boost option. If the target is likely to land more hits, it should go for the attack disadvantage option. (There's an easy way to predict who's likely to land more hits, the hag or the target: whichever one gets the lower result from subtracting their own attack modifier from the opponent's AC.) In either case, however, if the target has the Extra Attack class feature, the hag should go for the wasted action option, because this has a *much* greater effect on the action economy of an opponent who can attack more than once in a single action.

All this being said, the Wisdom save DC of 14 (13 for a sea hag) isn't that tough to beat for a PC with a decent Wisdom score or proficiency in that particular saving throw. A hag generally will try *bestow curse* only against an opponent with a zero or negative Wisdom saving throw modifier, and absolutely won't bother against an opponent with a modifier of more than +3.

- *Counterspell* is an automatic reflex against any incoming damaging spell. It uses a reaction, so the hag doesn't have to spend an action on it—but it does also cost a 3rd-level spell slot.
- *Lightning bolt* competes with *counterspell* for the use of that 3rd-level slot. If the hags in a coven spot an opportunity to nail three or more opponents in *lightning bolt*'s linear area of effect, have already gotten as many targets as they're going to with *bestow curse*, and still have a 5th-level spell slot left, they'll cast it at that level. But if there's no 5th-level spell slot available, or if they're going to want to cast *bestow curse* again, they'll cast *lightning bolt* using a 3rd-level slot only if all spellcasters in the PCs' party are already shut down. Otherwise, they want to keep that slot free for *counterspell*.
- *Hold person* requires concentration and, like every such spell we've looked at so far, a failed Wisdom saving throw. But it ain't half bad, and if it's cast using a 5th-level slot (see above), it can paralyze up to four opponents.
- *Locate object* and *identify* are divination spells, not appropriate for combat.
- *Ray of sickness* is the one ranged spell attack that all hags in the coven possess. It requires a roll to hit rather than a saving throw to resist, which makes it useful against low-AC, high-Wisdom opponents. It's also an instantaneous spell, no concentration required. If cast using a 5th-level spell slot, it deals 6d8 damage on a hit, which is about as good as a 3rd-level *lightning bolt*, and may poison the target as well. This can cripple a low- to mid-level wizard or sorceror, if not take them out of the game completely. Just be sure you don't need that 5th-level slot for *bestow curse*.

Note the preponderance of spells that call for Wisdom saving throws. A hag coven can wreck a low-Wisdom party, but against a high-Wisdom party, they'll have to rely on Claws, *ray of sickness*, and whatever other features their type possesses.

Now let's look at the three types of hag:

Sea hags are the weakest type, unable to disguise their hideousness; at best, they can appear as normal humanoids who happen to be very ugly. Nevertheless, they maintain this illusion unless and until they attack or are attacked, in the hope of luring their victims close enough to use Horrific Appearance.

When all the PCs are within 30 feet of one or more sea hags, they revert abruptly to their true, horrible appearance (bonus action), at which point the PCs must make a DC 11 Wisdom saving throw or be frightened, giving them disadvantage on all ability checks and attack rolls as long as the hags are within view. Each hag then directs a Death Glare (action) at a frightened opponent, starting with the one who seems like they ought to have the lowest Wisdom saving throw modifier. (Sea hags are smart enough to make good guesses about this, but not so intelligent that they can "read" PCs' stats infallibly.) If no one was frightened, they attack the nearest PCs with Claws; if they're in a coven, one casts *phantasmal killer* (not *eyebite*, because this would cause opponents to Dash out of Death Glare range) and tries again to frighten a PC who resisted the sea hags' Horrific Appearance.

The following round, the sea hags' actions depend on whether or not they're in a coven and whether or not they're close to a frightened opponent. A sea hag that isn't sustaining *phantasmal killer* and is close to a frightened opponent hits them with a Death Glare. One that isn't close to a frightened opponent but is near one who might botch a Wisdom save tries *eyebite* (to sicken), *bestow curse*, *polymorph*, or *hold person* (in that order, depending on what spell slots are available), prioritizing opponents who are engaging it in melee. One that isn't close to a frightened opponent but has no realistic chance of getting a spell past an opponent's Wisdom save attacks with Claws if an opponent is within easy melee reach and *ray of sickness* if not. If a hag isn't in a coven, it's a far simpler decision: Death Glare if there's a frightened opponent within 30 feet, Claws if not. (Unlike Horrific Appearance,

Death Glare can be repeated on a target who's already made a successful saving throw as long as that target is still frightened.)

In the third round of combat, the hags attempt other spells, such as *bestow curse*, *hold person*, and *lightning bolt*, although by this point they'll know better than to try the first two if all their other Wisdom-save spells have been fizzling.

A sea hag who's seriously wounded (reduced to 20 hp or fewer) flees, Dashing away (by water, if possible, so that it can use its superior swimming speed). If the seriously wounded hag happens to be a member of a coven, the coven is broken. At that point, if any of the three sea hags still has 37 hp or more while another on the field of battle is seriously wounded, it turns against the seriously wounded hag and tries to kill it. Once one member of the coven is killed, the other two cease to coordinate and fight as individuals.

Green hags are able to disguise themselves as normal, even attractive, humanoids, and they use this disguise to lure victims to them. Green hags don't have any features that lend themselves to tactical combinations, so they're almost always found in covens. They use *eyebite* to put tough melee fighters to sleep, sicken ranged attackers and skirmishers, and panic spellcasters. They don't bother with *phantasmal killer*, cutting straight to *bestow curse* instead, followed by *polymorph* and *hold person* if needed, though they too will give up on Wisdom-save spells if they're obviously not working and switch to Claws attacks and *ray of sickness*.

In a coven, green hags use Invisible Passage to try to knock off isolated enemies who are causing them trouble, converging on them and reappearing all at once to attack with Claws. They all take the action of turning invisible at the same time and move together, in order to stay within 30 feet of one another. One green hag in a coven won't use Invisible Passage alone—unless it's seriously wounded.

A green hag who's reduced to 32 hp or fewer will flee, using Invisible Passage to vanish and run—if possible, in the direction of the coven's hag eye, which the wounded hag will try to secure. Successful retrieval of the hag eye keeps the coven intact for the time being. But if it can't do this, for whatever reason, then just as with sea hags, a green hag with 58 hp or more will turn against a seriously wounded sister hag who's still within range, and once any one of the three is dead, the other two no longer coordinate.

Night hags are categorized not as fey but as fiends; like succubi and incubi, they delight in corrupting mortal humanoids and laying claim to their souls. Unlike sea hags and green hags, which can disguise their appearance visually but not to the touch, night hags Change Shape, physically transforming into humanoid guise. (This transformation takes an action to undo, so a night hag can't use it to gain surprise, as sea hags or green hags can.)

Night hag tactics revolve around the combination of Etherealness and Nightmare Haunting. Etherealness allows a night hag to travel to a victim's place of rest, while Nightmare Haunting causes the victim to have brutal dreams that disrupt their rest, not only denying the restoration of hit points that comes with resting but also reducing their hit point maximum. The night hag's goal is to bring that maximum to zero at a moment when the victim has been sufficiently corrupted by the commission of evil deeds; the night visions can themselves help bring about these deeds, such as by deceiving a decent character into suspecting innocent others of having committed foul crimes.

In other words, a night hag "encounter" is more like a long-running subplot, just as succubus and incubus encounters are. They share many of the same elements—possibly including the cultivation of a daytime relationship with the night hag in disguise, definitely including nightly stealth visits while the victim is asleep—and the only reason for a night hag to fight is if its cover is blown.

Night hags may or may not belong to covens; I'm inclined to believe that they're more likely to work alone, since they wouldn't be able to agree on who'd get to take the soul of a single target. If they did work together as a coven, they'd have to target three different victims, and those victims would have to be physically near each other as well, so that the coven members would be able to support one another with spellcasting if something went wrong.

This seems like a high bar to clear, and I'm not sure they'd consider it worth the trouble. But if they did, they'd prioritize their spells in much the same way that green hags do. Other than *plane shift*, the night hag's innate spells don't add much to the package and are useful only if it doesn't have access to coven spells:

- *Magic missile* offers a modicum of guaranteed-hit ranged damage but nothing more, and it probably isn't even worth throwing at wizards or sorcerers, who are likely to have *shield*.
- *Ray of enfeeblement* is a low-budget quasi–*bestow curse* that has to be sustained with concentration, and whose only saving grace is that it's a ranged spell attack rather than a spell that requires a Wisdom save.
- *Sleep* probably won't take out a single PC at the level where they're likely to encounter even one night hag.

Given the weakness of all these spells (an astonishing level of weakness for a CR 5 creature with 15 hit dice), a lone night hag is not engaging in any epic magical duels. If push comes to shove, its only real asset is its claws. A far superior asset is its ability to keep push from coming to shove in the first place.

A night hag knows that if it's caught before collecting the soul it's after, the mission is a failure, and there's no point in hanging around. All it takes is a light wound (12 damage or more) for the unmasked night hag to cut and run, making its escape via the Ethereal Plane or *plane shift*. Only if somehow chased and cornered does it have any reason to stand and fight, and in order to have the use of Claws in combat, it Changes Shape back to its true form while being pursued if it hasn't done so already.

Elementals

Denizens of planes that are governed not by natural laws but by *ideas about* the natural world, elementals are constituted of *meaning* as much as they are of matter, and they behave in accordance with those ideas, whether summoned as servants by magic or pursuing their own purposes on their home planes. They want what their constituent elements "want" and act as those elements act. When they're threatened, it's a tug of war between preserving their own lives and expressing their natures no matter what.

Elemental Spirits

Elementals are spirits of air, fire, water, and earth, usually summoned to do a spellcaster's bidding. Each is physically powerful in some way, not too bright, able to see in the dark, capable of two melee attacks in a turn, resistant to physical damage from nonmagical weapons, and immune to exhaustion, paralysis, petrifaction, poisoning, and unconsciousness. Beyond that, the elements they're generated from grant them additional powers and influence their manner of movement and fighting.

Elementals are summoned spirits, not evolved creatures. They have no particular survival instinct—on the contrary, they're bound to the will of their summoners and peevish about it, and what they want more than anything is to get back to the plane they came from. If they're destroyed, they get exactly what they want. Consequently, elementals fight to the death with zero concern for damage to themselves. They're also indiscriminate in their target selection and may or may not keep attacking the same opponent round after round.

Air elementals are distinguished by their wicked fast 90-foot flying speed (their only form of movement); their extremely high Dexterity; their resistance to lightning and thunder damage; their immunity to grappling, restraint, and falling prone; and their Air Form and Whirlwind features. Their Strength and Constitution are also high, but the contour of their physical abilities suggests a combat style based on being fast and hard to hit.

From the fact that it recharges, we can infer that the Whirlwind feature is the air elemental's most favored weapon. Air elementals are Large creatures, meaning they take up four 5-foot squares (or three 5-foot hexes). Their Air Form trait allows them to occupy the same space as a hostile creature, and their Whirlwind feature allows them to affect creatures "in the elemental's space," meaning in all the squares (or hexes) they occupy. From the Targets in Areas of Effect table in chapter 8 of the *Dungeon Master's Guide*, we can calculate that a spell whose effect covered the same area as an air elemental would typically be expected to affect two people. Therefore, an air elemental uses this ability whenever (a) it has it available and (b) two or more of its opponents are within a single 10-foot square (or a triangle of three 5-foot hexes).

Whirlwind flings creatures that fail their Strength saving throws up to 20 feet "in a random direction." It's interesting that the text specifies that the direction is random but seems to leave the distance up to the DM's discretion. I'd choose one of these three methods of determining distance and direction:

- Determine the direction randomly, as written, by rolling a d8 for a square map (or a d6 for a hex map) and assigning numbers clockwise, starting with "northeast"; the target moves as far in that direction as it can until it strikes an obstacle (a wall, a piece of furniture, another creature) or reaches the maximum distance of 20 feet.
- Determine the direction randomly, as above, and also determine the distance randomly by rolling 1d4 and multiplying the result by 5 feet.
- Decide both the direction and the distance yourself, for maximum amusement.

When not zeroing in on a cluster of enemies to use its Whirlwind feature on, an air elemental moves continuously in narrowing and widening circles (counterclockwise in the northern hemisphere of your game world, clockwise in the southern), looping through its opponents and making Slam attacks against any two whom it passes over—or, if it passes over only one, Slamming that opponent twice. (Multiattack grants the air elemental two Slam attacks; it doesn't say they must be against the same target, and movement can be broken up between attacks and other actions any way one sees fit.) It uses its full movement each round and couldn't care less about its opponents' opportunity attacks.

Earth elementals are distinguished by their burrowing movement; their extremely high Strength and Constitution and low Dexterity; their vulnerability to thunder damage; their tremorsense, which lets them "see" other creatures by feeling the vibrations they transmit through the ground; and their Earth Glide and Siege Monster traits.

Earth elementals are brutes, engaging opponents directly in melee combat. Although they choose their targets at random, once they've chosen them, they stubbornly stick with those targets, pounding on them until they're subdued, unless their controller directs them to do otherwise. If they're fighting in concert with another creature that makes ranged weapon or spell attacks, and that creature is fighting a target that's taken cover, rather than choose a living target, they may choose to destroy the cover instead. The Siege Monster trait grants them double damage against the cover; Armor Class and hit points for inanimate objects are given under "Objects" in chapter 8 of the *Dungeon Master's Guide*.

Note that the Earth Glide trait allows earth elementals to burrow only through *unworked* earth and stone. It can pass freely and easily through cavern walls or the dirt floor of a peasant's hut, but not through the stone walls or floors of a castle. It can, however, *smash* through stone walls or floors.

Fire elementals are distinguished by their immunity to fire damage, grappling, restraint, and falling prone; and their Fire Form, Illumination, and Water Susceptibility traits. Their Strength is merely average, but their Dexterity and Constitution are very high: They're scrappers. Like air elementals, fire elementals can occupy the same space as one or more opponents, and they use this trait to charge repeatedly through their enemies.

Fire elementals don't necessarily move constantly, like air elementals do; what they try to do is set *everyone* on fire. Both their Fire Form trait and their touch attack ignite creatures and flammable objects. When a fire elemental uses Fire Form to ignite one or more creatures in a space it shares, this does an automatic 5 fire damage to each creature; its Fiery Touch does twice as much damage to each creature it hits, but it requires an attack roll to hit. Against AC 15, it has a 60 percent chance of hitting, for 6 expected damage—slightly higher than Fire Form's.

On the other hand, Fire Form *is not an action*—it's something that just happens as a fire elemental moves. It's not required to stop in a hostile creature's space to set that creature on fire—it sets a creature on fire whenever it first *enters* that creature's space in a turn. It can still leave afterward, and the creature remains on fire. Thus, if it can move 50 feet and pass through every PC along the way, setting each one on fire, that's exactly what it does! And it still gets to make two Fiery Touch attacks, either along the way or afterward! And it can do this *every turn*!

A fire elemental's target selection process looks something like this: Is there someone who's not on fire? If so, can I set them on fire just by rushing past? If so, do it! If not, can I reach them with a Fiery Touch attack at the end of my move? If so, do it. If not, oh, well, maybe next turn. If everyone's on fire, then I'll just stay where I am and keep hitting whoever's in reach with Fiery Touch.

There are two things that fire elementals don't like: water and cold damage. These don't simply hasten fire elementals' return to their home plane—they dilute their essence, and that displeases them. However, they're not smart or wise enough to know for sure whether they should avoid the source of the unpleasant effect or make it a top-priority murderization target. They might do either. Flip a coin.

Water elementals are distinguished by their swimming movement; their resistance to acid damage; their immunity to grappling, restraint, and falling prone; and their Water Form, Freeze, and Whelm features. They have high Dexterity and extremely high Strength and Constitution, a contour that makes them more brute-like than otherwise. And like air and fire elementals, they can occupy other creatures' spaces.

Like the air elemental's Whirlwind, the water elemental's Whelm feature has a recharge, making it the preferred method of attack against any group of two or more opponents clustered within a 10-foot square (or three adjacent 5-foot hexes). One or two of these opponents may end up grappled and drowning. If an opponent is reduced to unconsciousness this way, the water elemental lets go of them—a blessing on solid ground, not so much in open water, as drowning people tend to sink, especially ones weighed down by armor, equipment, and waterlogged clothing.

Water elementals don't rush around the way air elementals do or sweep from opponent to opponent as fire elementals do. If the Whelm feature isn't available to them (or there aren't any clustered opponents to use it against), they make Slam attacks against whoever's within reach, and if no one's within reach, they move only as far as the nearest opponent, then Slam them twice. If they must move farther than 30 feet over dry ground to reach an opponent, they favor clustered opponents over solitary ones.

Unlike fire elementals, which can't stand water or cold damage, water elementals are indifferent to being frozen. It doesn't make them any less watery; it just slows them down. Otherwise, they behave the same.

AZERS

Although they're also beings of elemental fire, lawful neutral **azers** are sober and disciplined, in sharp contrast to chaotic neutral magmins. They loathe being summoned, having once been slaves of the efreets, but they'll cooperate if treated with courtesy and dignity. If not, they'll "work to the contract"—doing what they're explicitly commanded to do and not a whit more.

With exceptional Strength and high Constitution, azers are brute fighters. They're immune to fire and poison damage and the poisoned condition, but they have no resistance to normal nonmagical weapons. Thus, they won't risk an opportunity attack if they ever need to retreat. Their Intelligence and Wisdom are sufficient to make Disengaging a plausible action choice, and they'll take this action when seriously wounded (reduced to 15 hp or fewer) and engaged in melee with more than one opponent. If they're seriously wounded while engaged with only one opponent, they still Disengage unless that opponent seems highly likely to pursue, in which case they Dodge as they retreat instead.

When bound and ordered to fight by its summoner, an azer attacks whomever or whatever it's ordered to attack; as a brute, it's good against front-line fighters and other brutes. Because it carries a shield, it wields its warhammer one-handed. Since it doesn't have darkvision, it uses its own Illumination to see in dim light or darkness, unless it's ordered not to. (Again, how it's treated determines how it uses this trait. If relations with the summoner are good, it anticipates their preference. If relations are bad, it does what *it* wants, until the summoner tells it to do otherwise.)

An azer that breaks free of its summoner's control immediately turns on the summoner if it's been treated poorly, then fights anyone else who tries to intervene, although it won't continue to fight once seriously wounded. At that point, it retreats as described above, to whatever place of safety it can find to hole up in until the summoning spell expires. If it's been treated well, it refuses to follow any more orders after breaking free, but it doesn't attack. Azers summoned using *conjure elemental* can become unbound in this way, whereas those summoned using *conjure minor elemental* simply vanish back to the Elemental Plane of Fire.

Azers encountered on their home plane, being lawful neutral, are indifferent to strangers by default and fight only if attacked or otherwise sorely provoked. In this situation, when one azer is seriously wounded, another azer moves in to cover the wounded azer's retreat. Meanwhile, the wounded azer Disengages or Dodges as described above—and hastens to inform other azers that they're under attack.

WATER WEIRDS, GALEB DUHRS, AND INVISIBLE STALKERS

You'll note that one of the four classical elements, fire, is missing from this group. For some reason, the fifth edition *Monster Manual* doesn't offer a true igneous equivalent to these three creatures, all of which are specifically described as beings that can be summoned from their home elemental planes. The nearest equivalent—which technically can be summoned with *conjure elemental*, though this fact is mentioned nowhere in its flavor text—is the salamander. However, salamanders are neutral evil and, by their description, very much independent agents. Water weirds, galeb duhrs, and invisible stalkers are neutral and (usually) compliant.

Water weirds are guardians, posted by their summoners in pools or fountains to stop trespassers. With very high Strength and Dexterity but merely above-average Constitution, and being invisible while immersed in water, they're ambushers, pouncing on targets and quickly pulling them out of allies' reach. Although they die if removed from the water they dwell in, they're immune to grappling, so the only way to remove them is either *telekinesis* (to hoist them out of it without actually grappling them) or *destroy water* (self-explanatory).

They have only one attacking action, Constrict, which inflicts bludgeoning damage and automatically grapples and restrains a Medium or smaller target on a hit. It also pulls the target 5 feet toward the water weird—read: "into the water."

After a successful Constrict, a water weird "tries to drown" its target. Per "Suffocation" in chapter 8 of the *Player's Handbook*, a water weird is likely to be able to hold a target underwater long enough to drown them only if you rule that the target never gets a chance to take a breath and begins suffocating immediately (see "Cloakers," page 362). But since the water weird's stat block doesn't explicitly say that it can't continue to Constrict the same target, only that it can't Constrict a *different* one, I'd say that this drowning attempt also includes additional Constrict attacks—with advantage, because the target is restrained—until the target either gets away or passes out.

The water weird's movement is particularly relevant to this strategy. It has a 60-foot swimming speed, plus a 10-foot reach. Depending on how much room other creatures have to maneuver around the water weird's basin, it may lie in wait right at the water's edge or 5 feet farther in; the latter is preferable, if feasible. After it first successfully grapples and restrains a target, the water weird immediately drags them as far as possible into the water: up to 30 feet if the target is Medium-size, up to 60 feet if they're Small. Depending on the depth of the water, the water weird will surely pull its victim *down* as well as back. (The larger the body of water, the greater the water weird's advantage.)

If a victim struggles free from a water weird's clutches and tries to swim away, the water weird first moves to within 10 feet of it, then tries to seize them again with another Constrict attack and, if it succeeds, once again drags them down and back as far as it can. Once it's successfully drowned a victim, it rushes back to the water's edge and grabs at another.

Within the constraints set by their summoners, water weirds choose their targets at random, grabbing at anyone within reach. After an unsuccessful attack, a water weird may attack the same target again or switch to a different target. Once it's gotten its pseudopods on a target, however, it singlemindedly attempts to finish that target off before going after anyone else, taking full advantage of its swimming speed to keep unlucky victims from getting away.

Water weirds don't flee or break off attack no matter how much damage they've taken.

Galeb duhrs are also guardians, summoned to protect locations on land. Their lifespan and their patience are for all intents and purposes infinite. Boulderlike in shape as well as texture, they waddle along at a comical 15 feet per round but can double this speed by going into a tuck and roll—and *quadruple* it by doing so on a downhill slope. On top of that, they can bring one or two nearby boulders to life and propel them as their rolling sidekicks, doubling or tripling their attacking power. They use this Animate Boulder feature at the first moment when their presence is known and they're not engaged in melee with any opponent, or when they're moderately wounded (reduced to 59 hp or fewer), whichever occurs first.

Galeb duhrs, with their extraordinary Strength and Constitution, are more suited than water weirds to protracted melee combat; once they engage in melee, they'll remain engaged. However, if they can make a Rolling Charge before their first attack against a target, they will. This forfeits the unseen-attacker advantage on their attack rolls, but the extra damage from Rolling Charge more than makes up for it. It also means that if they happen to finish off every foe they're engaged in melee with, the next target they engage with will be one between 20 and 30 feet away, if possible.

They're also more discriminating about target selection than water weirds are. Since foes with magic weapons can overcome their resistance to bludgeoning, piercing, and slashing damage, they'll steer clear of these targets unless and until they can aim a couple of animated boulders at them at the same time. Otherwise, they and their animated boulders will try to mop up back-line spellcasters, sharpshooters, and skirmishers, since it's most likely to be able to get a rolling start against these, before engaging front-line fighters, who will pose less of a threat if armed with normal nonmagical weapons.

Galeb duhrs also don't flee or break off attack no matter how much damage they've taken. However, they will stop to parley if someone speaks their primordial language, calmly explaining their duty and giving trespassing foes a chance to retreat without further strife.

Airy **invisible stalkers** are hunting dogs rather than guard dogs. Sometimes they're summoned for simple search-and-recover operations; other times, they're evanescent assassins.

Water weirds and galeb duhrs blend in with their surroundings, revealing themselves when they attack, but invisible stalkers blend in with the air itself—they're *always*, as their name indicates, invisible. This means they nearly always make attack rolls with advantage, even when their presence is known; only a PC under the influence of a *see invisibility* or *true seeing* spell, or its equivalent, can negate this advantage. On top of this, their double proficiency in Stealth means that, unless an opponent has exceptionally good passive Perception, they routinely attack with surprise.

Invisible stalkers are savvy assessors of their opponents' capabilities, but they're also constrained by their summoners' commands: If they've been ordered to kill a specific person, *that's* whom they attack, period. If ordered to kill multiple people, however, they can get creative. Spellcasters who do direct damage or cast *banishment* (as opposed to casting spells that impose debilitating effects) are top targets, as is anyone who can see them and anyone with any feature that either grants advantage on attack rolls against them or negates their own advantage.

Invisible stalkers exploit their invisibility and high flying speed by staying on the move constantly and attacking from unexpected directions. A typical invisible stalker turn consists of either movement, two Slam attacks, and more movement; or movement, one Slam attack, more movement, another Slam attack, and still more movement. If possible, an invisible stalker always begins and ends its turn out of any opponent's melee reach. Depending on how its opponents are arrayed, this may mean flying up in the air, 5 or 10 feet above them. Because you have to be able to see a foe to make an opportunity attack against it, as long as the invisible stalker remains unseen, it's exempt.

Invisible stalkers don't like being bound to their summoners' service, but it compels them to fulfill the duties they're assigned—*completely*. That means an invisible stalker assigned to kill a single target won't stop attacking that target once they're down to 0 hp—it keeps attacking until they're *killed*. Once it accomplishes that, it's freed from the spell that bound it, and it vanishes back to its home plane. An invisible stalker sent after multiple targets, however, will try to render all of them unconscious before it proceeds to finish any of them off. Like the galeb duhr and the water weird, an invisible stalker never retreats, flees, or disengages, no matter how much damage it takes.

MEPHITS

Mephits are wicked little critters that maliciously embody the para-elements of dust, ice, magma, mud, smoke, and steam. The *Monster Manual* characterizes them as "tricksters," but every one of them is of neutral evil alignment, not chaotic neutral, so their "trickery" is of a decidedly baleful sort. I don't see any reason why they shouldn't behave as evolved creatures with respect to their self-preservation instinct, but if survival is their number one priority, causing gratuitous harm and annoyance to others is number two.

Mephits aren't tough—half of them are CR 1/4, and the other half are CR 1/2. All of them have low Strength, all of them can fly, and all of them have darkvision (meaning they either live underground or are active primarily at night) and the Death Burst trait, which does *something* when they're killed, although that something depends on the type of mephit. And they all have a simple melee attack, along with a breath weapon that has only a one-in-six chance to recharge, so in all likelihood, they'll get to use it only once. Most (but not all) of them are proficient in Stealth, suggesting that they like to ambush their victims, and their low Strength suggests that they'll usually be encountered in decent-size groups; a lone mephit wouldn't dare pick a fight with more than a couple of enemies at once.

Dust mephits have high Dexterity and average Constitution, indicating a preference for ranged combat. They're vulnerable to fire, so they'll keep their distance from torches and campfires, and the second an opponent casts a spell that does fire damage or brandishes a flaming weapon, they hightail it.

A dust mephit leads with its Blinding Breath, attacking from hiding so as to gain surprise and waiting until it can catch at least two opponents in its 15-foot cone of effect. (If it can get more, so much the better, but if it can get two, it won't delay in order to see whether it can get three.)

What it does on its second round of combat depends on how much luck it had in the first. It will engage a blinded enemy with its claws, but not if there's an unblinded enemy who can intervene. If it can use its Blinding Breath again, it will, but in most cases, it can't. Without an ally to back it up, it simply flies away, using the Dash action to double its movement and satisfying itself with the momentary debilitation of its victim(s). If every enemy is blinded, on the other hand, it seizes the advantage and attacks one with Claws. It's indiscriminate in its selection of targets; it slashes at whoever's closest.

As soon as an enemy shakes off its dust blindness, unless it can use its Blinding Breath again, the dust mephit takes off. It's not bright enough to Disengage and not nimble enough to Dodge as it flees; it simply Dashes. It also flees if its blinded opponent, despite rolling with disadvantage, manages to land a lucky blow and reduce the dust mephit to 6 hp or fewer. Before it does, though, it drops its once-per-day use of *sleep*, in the hope of knocking out its enemy before they can make an opportunity attack against it.

Ice mephits are similar to dust mephits, except that they're also vulnerable to bludgeoning damage, so they'll stay well clear of anyone carrying a blunt weapon. Other than that, their tactics are similar to those of dust mephits. They lead with Frost Breath, again trying to catch at least two enemies in the chill cone. However, since Frost Breath doesn't grant advantage to ice mephits or impose disadvantage on their opponents, they don't follow it up with melee attacks. Instead, they fly around out of reach, waiting for their Frost Breath to recharge, and Readying the Dash action in case an opponent comes within 10 feet so that they can avoid melee engagement. This assumes they're being chased by melee opponents; if they're not, but they're being shot at by a ranged attacker, they Dodge instead. Dealing with both is too much for them. In that instance, they flee.

If an ice mephit takes serious damage (reduced to 8 hp or fewer), it drops its once-per-day *fog cloud* on an area that includes its attacker, then exploits its enemy's blindness to make its escape, since a blinded melee opponent can't make an opportunity attack. Other, less injured mephits won't fly into the fog in order to attack the enshrouded enemy, because they'd be blinded, too: Darkvision doesn't help a creature see in an area heavily obscured by something other than darkness.

Magma mephits have a slightly above-average Constitution to go with their slightly above-average Dexterity, making them skirmishers, more willing than dust or ice mephits to fight up close. Also unlike those two, magma mephits lead with their once-per-day innate spell, *heat metal*, because it has the potential both to enhance their action economy and to impose disadvantage on the enemy's attack rolls. Each magma mephit in the encounter picks an enemy wearing metal armor or wielding a metal weapon and casts *heat metal* to make it glow red-hot. On subsequent turns, if that enemy is still wearing the armor or holding the weapon, it uses its bonus action to deal this damage again.

While they have fewer qualms about engaging in melee than dust or ice mephits do, they do like to have the upper hand, so they engage in melee with Claws only against opponents who either have dropped their weapons, are clinging grimly to red-hot weapons that are burning them, or are wearing armor that's causing them similar discomfort. Against opponents who aren't wearing metal armor and are holding nonmetal weapons, they use their Fire Breath instead, positioning themselves out of immediate melee reach and, if possible, where they can catch at least one other enemy in the cone of effect. Until their Fire Breath recharges, they do their best to stay out of reach of melee attacks, Readying a Dash action in case any opponent comes within 10 feet, or Dodging if they have to avoid ranged attackers but not melee attackers.

Once an opponent has retrieved their no-longer-hot weapon, the magma mephit is done, as it is if it's seriously wounded (reduced to 8 hp or fewer), and it flies away, using the Dash action.

Mud mephits, like magma mephits, are skirmishers. Unlike any of the mephits mentioned so far, they have no innate spellcasting ability that they can use to inconvenience enemies or cover their escape. What they can do, though, is restrain enemies with their Mud Breath (I'm not sure how mud can be *exhaled*, exactly; I feel like this must be more of a mud spew), and this is the feature they lead with.

Like dust mephits, if mud mephits' "breath" weapon doesn't restrain all their opponents, they've got basically nothing, and they have to submerge themselves and scram. (Mud mephits can swim, presumably through mud as well as water, so this, rather than flying, is their best mode of departure.) If they do manage to restrain all their opponents, it's clobberin' time, starting with the nearest restrained enemy.

If an enemy breaks free of their restraint, the mud mephit beating on it isn't fast enough to run away or even swim away; it's pretty much got to resign itself to its fate. Notice that while the preceding three types of mephits are all CR 1/2, mud mephits are CR 1/4, and because of this, I think they'll have to be present in even larger numbers—at least three of them for every two enemies, preferably more—before they'll bother picking a fight in the first place.

Smoke mephits are also CR 1/4, so again, they won't start a fight unless there are at least three of them for every two enemies. They do have innate spellcasting, but the spell they can cast once per day, *dancing lights*, is useless in combat. I'd say they use it only to mess with people they don't want to actually fight but feel like harassing anyway.

If and when they do decide to start a fight, they lead with Cinder Breath, which, like dust mephits' Blinding Breath, can blind opponents in its cone of effect. In all other respects (minus the *sleep* spell, which they don't have), smoke mephits follow the same modus operandi as dust mephits.

Steam mephits are CR 1/4, but they're a little better equipped to hold up once a fight starts than mud and smoke mephits are. They lead with *blur*, which they cast innately, *before* revealing themselves to their victims, and only then let loose with their Steam Breath against their nearest foes—as always, trying to include at least two enemies in the cone of effect.

Because *blur* gives their opponents disadvantage on attack rolls against them, they have less to fear from opportunity attacks, and so, as skirmishers, they use the tried-and-true flier tactic of stationing themselves up in the air, flying down to attack with Claws, then flying back up, out of reach of melee attackers. This provokes an opportunity attack each time they leave their opponents' reach, but as mentioned, this attack is made with disadvantage, and an opponent with Extra Attack doesn't get that additional swing when attacking as a reaction. If their Steam Breath recharges, they're more than happy to use it again, flying down just low enough to do so.

Steam mephits flee when seriously wounded (reduced to 8 hp or fewer), using the Dash action to fly away.

MAGMINS

Magmins are as likely to be the result of a PC's *conjure minor elemental* spell as they are part of a planned encounter, and as long as they're bound to their summoners, they can be ordered around. If one breaks free, however, it immediately runs amok, setting as many things on fire as it can.

With high Dexterity and above-average Constitution, a bound magmin can be employed as a skirmisher, chasing down less armored, more mobile enemies. Since they're typically summoned in groups of four, they can scatter to reach multiple targets, pair off against two targets, or all mob one. When ordered to fight this way, they move at full speed toward their targets, ideally trying to reach a distance of 10 to 30 feet. They also use the Dash action if this won't cause them to overshoot; if it will, they burn (ha) their turn action by setting a nearby flammable object on fire. When they can move to engage from the aforementioned distance, they attack using the Touch action.

Bound magmins are compelled to follow their summoners' orders, and if the order is to attack, they're not at liberty to retreat if their lives are threatened. Consequently, they keep fighting until they're killed, at which point their Death Burst trait causes an incendiary explosion. Other magmins aren't hurt by this—they're immune to fire damage. On the contrary, they're delighted by it, and may spontaneously burst into flame (via the Ignited Illumination trait) in their exuberance.

Uncontrolled magmins, on the other hand, try to avoid other sentient beings. Sentient beings don't burn well. Wood, paper, fabric, and oils burn *great*! Magmins are irresistibly drawn to these materials, using Touch to set them ablaze, and once they've ignited everything within reach that can be ignited, they run off looking for more things to ignite. They don't even fight back: Being resistant to physical damage from nonmagical weapons, they usually won't suffer much injury from an opportunity attack, and they simply Dash away from any foe who manages to close with one of them, using the Touch action instead only when they're cornered, and setting whatever they can on fire until someone catches up and kills them.

Although their Ignited Illumination trait allows them to give off light, they don't need it themselves, having darkvision with the standard range of 60 feet. Thus, this isn't really a combat-oriented trait, unless their *summoner* requires light to fight by. And conversely, if their summoner has darkvision, their ecstatic, reflexive use of this feature will actually negate this advantage, and the summoner may have to order them to shut it off.

GARGOYLES

You might imagine **gargoyles** to be constructs—statues given life—or maybe monstrosities with stony-looking skin, but in fifth edition D&D, they're elementals, creatures of sentient stone. They certainly aren't your typical elemental earth creature: They can fly speedily, and their alignment is chaotic evil, giving them a decidedly destructive and malevolent streak. Lurking amid stony ruins and along stark cliffs, they have no need for sustenance; they hunt and kill out of malice and, perhaps, a desire to give other creatures' bodies back to the earth.

Gargoyles are flying brutes with high Strength and Constitution and no ranged attack. Although they lack any trait that allows them to avoid opportunity attacks, they do have resistance to physical damage from nonmagical weapons (except those made of adamantine), allowing them to hold station in the air between turns, fly in to Multi-attack their targets, then fly back into the air, out of reach of melee attacks. Their targets will get opportunity attacks against them, but these will usually do only half damage.

Although they lack proficiency in Stealth, their False Appearance trait allows them to disguise themselves as statues, gaining the element of surprise against unwitting trespassers. They have darkvision, so their preferred time to attack is after nightfall, but since they're territorial rather than roaming, they don't often get a choice in the matter.

Gargoyles' cruel, malevolent nature drives them to attack the smallest and weakest targets first, although they won't back down if attacked by a stronger opponent. Because they're immune to exhaustion, they aggressively chase down fleeing foes (see "Chases," *Dungeon Master's Guide*, chapter 8). They're also immune to poison damage, the poisoned condition, and petrifaction, but these don't affect its tactics.

A gargoyle retreats, flying away and using the Dash action, when it's seriously wounded (reduced to 20 hp or fewer).

SALAMANDERS

Salamanders are the nearest fiery analogue to water weirds, galeb duhrs, and invisible stalkers, but they're significantly more independent-minded, serving only efreets (and those only reluctantly and resentfully). They have a society of their own, on the Elemental Plane of Fire, and if they're hanging out on the material plane, they're probably doing so against their will.

As fighters, salamanders are shock troops. Their exceptional Strength is coupled with high Dexterity and Constitution (their Con is higher than their Dex, though not significantly so): They can engage in either toe-to-toe slugfests or hit-and-run attacks, but in general they'll favor melee over ranged attacks, because they can do much more damage at close range.

Salamanders are immune to fire attacks, vulnerable to cold attacks, and resistant to physical damage from nonmagical weapons. Thus, they're more cautious around foes who wield magic weapons, as well as spellcasters who sling frost spells. Because of their choleric temperament, however, this caution is as likely to result in focused fire (pun intended) as in avoidance.

The salamander wields a spear, most likely two-handed, since its Armor Class includes no shield or other off-hand weapon. Lacking any clothing or tack, it has no way of transporting any weapon other than the one it holds in its hands—yet another reason why it would rather jab with its spear than hurl it. If it throws that spear at an enemy, it's got no more spear.

Thus, a salamander closes quickly with its foes and immediately Multiattacks with both Tail and Spear. The Tail attack comes first, since a successful hit grapples and restrains its target, thus granting advantage on the follow-up Spear attack. It also grants *automatic* Tail hits on subsequent turns, as long as the target remains grappled—and since a grappled creature is, by definition, touching the salamander, its Heated Body does additional fire damage, which is included in the damage of the Tail attack.

This is pretty much it. A salamander doesn't have high enough Wisdom to target its foes carefully, but it does have high enough Intelligence to switch gears if it realizes someone's using a magic weapon or slinging ice spells. If it's near enough to close with a spellslinger or an attacker with a magic ranged weapon, it charges that enemy and tries to grab them with its tail. An opponent with a magic melee weapon presents a trickier problem. Heated Body still does damage to that opponent whenever they land a hit, but ideally, the salamander would rather not be hit by that weapon at all. How to destroy the wielder while avoiding the weapon?

Thanks to the salamander's Large size and exceptional Strength, an optional rule in chapter 9 of the *Dungeon Master's Guide*, "Action Options," offers a solution: It can use its action to Disarm its opponent, a contest that it has advantage on if its opponent is wielding their weapon one-handed and no disadvantage on if the opponent wields it two-handed. Then, as a free interaction with an object (*Player's Handbook*, chapter 9, "Interacting with Objects around You"), it can snatch that weapon up with one hand or smack it out of reach with its tail. If it's knocked away and the opponent tries to go after it and pick it back up, the salamander can then make an opportunity attack!

Additionally, salamanders speak their own primordial language, Ignan, the common tongue of the Elemental Plane of Fire. A salamander attacked by an enemy with a magic weapon calls out that fact to its allies. If that enemy is disarmed and their weapon smacked away, another salamander may rush to pick it up (or, if it's a *frost brand* weapon, hurl the odious thing far, far away) or attack that same enemy from another direction (see "Optional Rule: Flanking," *Dungeon Master's Guide*, chapter 8).

A salamander's self-preservation instinct kicks in when it's seriously wounded (reduced to 36 hp or fewer). Not quite smart or self-disciplined enough to Disengage but not so dim as to merely flee, the salamander Dodges as it retreats at its full movement speed.

A **fire snake** is a juvenile salamander. It also has the Heated Body trait, Multiattack (Bite plus Tail), and the same damage immunity, vulnerability, and resistance as the mature salamander has. But it's not especially strong, tough, or bright. It fights solely by instinct, and although it's as truculent as its older siblings are, it can't withstand a sustained engagement and has to rely on hit-and-run attacks.

Fire snakes in the company of adult salamanders fight differently from a nest of fire snakes with no big 'uns around. While the adult salamanders do their thing, fire snakes nip at the heels of the salamanders' opponents (again, see "Optional Rule: Flanking"). As soon as an opponent turns around and starts attacking a fire snake, it

ELEMENTALS

Dashes away, without regard for opportunity attacks. If it's not seriously wounded (reduced to 8 hp or fewer), it will then come back and resume attacking as soon as its opponent's attention is occupied by an adult salamander again. However, a group of fire snakes without an adult around attack willy-nilly, using half their movement to close distance with an opponent, Multiattacking, then using the other half of their movement to back away again—again, without regard for opportunity attacks. Any foe who makes an opportunity attack against a fire snake is just asking to get burned anyway.

XORN

The three-legged, radially symmetrical, metal-munching **xorn** have been weirding adventurers out since they first appeared in the AD&D *Monster Manual*. Refugees from the Elemental Plane of Earth, they chow their way through the Underdark, zeroing in on deposits of gems and precious metals—which is to say, treasure. Neutral by alignment, they're not necessarily hostile upon encountering strangers, but they want what they want, and they can smell it on you if you're carrying. And they're as relentless as a rolling boulder.

With exceptional Strength, extraordinary Constitution, and no ranged attack, xorn are brutes by default; all their other abilities are stodgily average. They have proficiency in Stealth, expertise in Perception, and the Stone Camouflage trait; moreover, their Earth Glide trait lets them burrow without disturbing the earth or stone they're burrowing through. They could be fantastic ambush attackers if they wanted, but it's not really their style. First, they're not evil. Second, they don't hunt living things. Third, who needs to sneak up on a pile of coins? It's not going to run away.

Xorn have darkvision and tremorsense, both with a range of 60 feet; they also have the unique Treasure Sense trait, which lets them sniff out "precious metals and stones" within the same range. Thus, if a xorn is trundling through the rock beneath your intrepid adventurers' feet, and it's close enough to feel them marching overhead, it's also close enough to smell whether they're carrying enough treasure to stimulate its interest.

A xorn "attack," therefore, doesn't look quite like any other monster's attack. It pops partway out of the ground, with just its mouth and arms exposed, right next to its target—but instead of Biting or Clawing at its target, it snatches the target's pack, pouch, or purse and begins tearing it apart. (If you need a mechanism for determining whether a xorn can tear a pack off a PC's back, you can use the Disarm action under "Action Options" in chapter 9 of the *Dungeon Master's Guide*. Alternatively, the xorn doesn't have to tear the pack *away*; it can simply tear it *open*.)

If the PCs don't attack once they're no longer surprised, the xorn, as its next action, takes any coins and gems it finds and devours them without hesitation. (Call this the "Use an Object" action, with "use," in this case, meaning "eat.") Round by round, the xorn keeps tearing open containers and eating the goodies inside until none are left, whereupon it leaves peacefully; or until someone interferes, whereupon it does not leave peacefully.

A xorn committed to combat fights dirty. Rather than remain aboveground, out in the open, it descends into the earth—technically without leaving its opponent's reach, since it's still right next to the opponent, just underground!—and sidles over *beneath* the opponent. Then it Hides, using Stone Camouflage to gain advantage on its ability check as it rises just enough to expose its closed mouth to the open air. If the opponent above it, on their own turn, moves more than 5 feet from their square or hex, the xorn uses its opportunity attack to Bite with unseen attacker advantage—as a toothy, gaping maw suddenly appears *in the floor* and chomps down on the opponent's leg.

The next round, if an opponent is still above it, the xorn uses its full Multiattack. It always uses its Bite attack first—if the xorn hasn't given its position away with an opportunity attack, it applies its unseen attacker advantage to the attack action that deals the most damage, and if it has, the order doesn't really matter—then follows up with its Claw attacks. Finally, it uses its movement to pull its arms and mouth back into the ground, where it's untouchable. If no opponent is within reach at the start of its turn, it relocates underneath one. Then, if it has no movement left, it waits; if it has any movement left, it attacks. Each time it dives below the earth, it Hides again the first chance it gets, so that it can breach the surface with its mouth yet still gain unseen attacker advantage on its next Bite.

Smart PCs will Ready their Attack actions to smack the xorn as soon as they see it pop out of the ground again. But a half-buried xorn with only its mouth and arms exposed must be considered to have at least half cover, and a xorn with only its mouth exposed—not its arms— must be considered to have three-fourths cover. These circumstances increase the xorn's already high AC 19 to 21 or 24! Plus, since the xorn has resistance to piercing and slashing damage from non-adamantine, nonmagical weapons, it's going to be confoundedly hard to kill— though somewhat less difficult to drive off, since it retreats back into the earth when seriously wounded (reduced to 29 hp or fewer).

Fortunately, not every xorn goes berserk at the very scent of precious minerals. If it's eaten well recently, a xorn may come all the way up out of the ground and point to a PC's pack with one claw, to the top flap with another, and to its mouth with a third, rather than immediately try to rip the pack away. Unless someone in the party speaks Terran or has a *comprehend languages* or *tongues* spell, however, it may be hard to strike a bargain with a xorn that serves the interests of the party as well as the interests of the xorn, and a xorn that can't get the party to give it the crunchy, sparkly noms it wants may grow agitated and, eventually, hostile.

DJINN

A **djinni** is a soul bound to the elemental essence of air. By default, djinn are chaotic good, but they're also haughty and vengeful, and a party of PCs may find themselves fighting one if it's trying to get payback against someone who once betrayed it. Djinn don't reproduce naturally, so they don't have the same kind of evolved behaviors as creatures that reproduce over generations have, but they are keen to preserve their own existence—not to mention slick hagglers—and will readily parley with anyone they recognize as a major threat.

Djinn have high Dexterity and extraordinarily high Strength and Constitution, an ability contour that suggests a brute fighter but really allows them to fight however they want. They also have high Intelligence and Wisdom and extraordinarily high Charisma, giving them a strong self-preservation impulse, shrewd target selection, the ability to strategize, and most of all, the ability and willingness to seek negotiated solutions to conflict. Their saving throws and damage immunities don't have much bearing on their fighting style, except insofar as they aren't afraid of most spellcasters. You've got to be at the top of your game to beat a djinni that way.

The djinni's triple scimitar Multiattack, which does not only slashing damage but also bonus lightning or thunder damage, is a simple but severe damage dealer. Create Whirlwind is useful for restraining enemies, against whom the djinni then has advantage on its attack rolls.

Most djinni spells aren't oriented toward combat (it's a rare creature that will use *create food and water* to hurl smoked hams), but a few are. *Conjure elemental* can summon an ally whose tactics are described above. *Gaseous form, invisibility,* and *plane shift* offer paths of escape, and *plane shift* can also be used offensively against a single foe. *Major image* can create a distraction. *Thunderwave* becomes formidable when cast by a djinni facing more than one melee attacker, thanks to its spell save DC of 17 and the fact that it can cast it at will.

A djinni will take you seriously if you can inflict a moderate injury on it (reduce it to 112 hp or fewer) or if, somehow, you can preemptively demonstrate your ability to do so. A party of four adventurers who can each reliably deal 12 damage or more per turn—I'm talking probabilistically, meaning that *on average*, each PC will deal 12 or more, taking into account chance to hit against AC 17 and normal distribution of damage die rolls—can probably convey this information by their bearing and conduct alone, as can a party of five who can deal 10 damage or more apiece or a party of six who can deal 8 damage or more apiece. (Do these calculations *before* your session, as part of your prep.)

If a djinn takes the PCs seriously, it will parley with them, seeking a bargain that serves both its own interests and the PCs'. This is assuming, however, that the PCs don't insult it. If they do, it will seek a bargain that serves its own interests and *seems* to serve the PCs' interests as well but actually screws them over. Djinn may be chaotic good by alignment, but they take insolence from no one. The *creation* spell is a good way for a djinni to swindle rude PCs, since the products it "creates"—which can include gold and gems—fall to dust after 10 minutes to an hour. Or it might summon the PCs an elemental "servant" that turns on them once the djinni is safely on its way.

If a fight is unavoidable, a djinni uses Create Whirlwind, its most distinctive feature, immediately at the outset of combat. Depending on the makeup of the opposition, it might Create Whirlwind to capture a cluster of opponents, to restrain its most powerful melee opponent, or to take a potentially bothersome ranged attacker out of play. The djinni then moves the whirlwind around to scoop up multiple opponents until it can't contain any more. Its capacity is substantial: Covering four 5-foot squares (or three 5-foot hexes) and 30 feet in height, it can hold three or four Medium-size enemies in *each* of three "stories." The djinni can also fly, holding itself up out of reach of melee attackers while it's doing this.

Next, the djinni Multiattacks with its scimitar against the most powerful opponent within reach, especially one already restrained by the djinni's whirlwind. If at any time the djinni is being confronted by two or more non-whirlwinded melee opponents, it turns to face as many as it can and casts *thunderwave* to repel them. A spellcaster who's powerful enough to lob a spell past the djinni's defenses and do at least 49 damage to it, and who botches their DC 17 Charisma saving throw, will suddenly find themself *plane shift*ed to the Elemental Plane of Air.

If talk has failed and so has fighting, a djinni bugs out when seriously injured (reduced to 64 hp or fewer), using *gaseous form* or *plane shift*.

EFREETS

Efreets* are genies of fire, elemental beings akin to djinn, but more consistently wicked and malicious. They're strong, cunning, and ruth-

---

* The *Monster Manual* uses the singular "efreeti" and plural "efreet," apparently by analogy to singular "djinni" and plural "djinn," but this is an error. It's true that in Arabic, a single "genie" is called جني *jinnī*, and "genies" as a class are called جنّ *jinn*, but the singular word for a malicious, wily supernatural being is عفريت ʿ*ifrīt*, and the plural is عفاريت ʿ*afārīt*. عفريتي ʿ*ifrītī* is not a noun but an adjective, meaning "fiendish." Instead of "afarit," I use the Anglicized plural "efreets."

less, and they view mortal humanoids as lesser beings fit only for enslavement and other forms of exploitation.

With their extraordinarily high Strength and Constitution, they're straight-up brute fighters. But not dumb ones: Their Intelligence, Wisdom, and Charisma are all high as well. They have proficiency in Wisdom saving throws, along with Intelligence and Charisma, but not in Dexterity or Constitution. Their native Constitution is so high, they needn't worry about making Con saves, but their Dexterity is barely above average for a humanoid, so they're slightly warier of spellcasters than djinn are.

In addition to a double Scimitar attack that does both slashing damage and bonus fire damage with a ferocious +10 modifier to hit, efreets can also Hurl Flame, doing 5d6 fire damage at a range of up to 120 feet. (You can bet that spellcasters, with their lower average Armor Classes and ability to circumvent the efreet's high AC, will be primary targets of this ability.) Both the attack modifier and damage of this ranged attack are lower than those of the efreet's Scimitar melee attack, so an efreet uses Hurl Flame only when a particular ranged opponent is giving it more trouble than any of its melee opponents are—and, moreover, that ranged opponent is more than 60 feet away, out of range of the efreet's flying movement. Within 60 feet, the efreet simply rushes the opponent and attacks with Scimitar.

The efreet's repertoire of spells is similar to the djinni's. Like djinn, efreets can innately cast *gaseous form*, *invisibility*, and *plane shift* once per day each, giving them ways of escaping when seriously injured (reduced to 80 hp or fewer); *plane shift* can be used offensively against a single foe as well. *Conjure elemental* can summon an ally whose tactics are described above, and *major image* can create a distraction.

One thing efreets have that djinn don't is a single daily use of *wall of fire*, which does 5d8 fire damage per turn to all opponents within it or within 10 feet of one side of it. Since the wall is opaque, an efreet can use *wall of fire* to cut itself off from enemy spellcasters and ranged attackers; even better, it can also create a ring-shaped wall with a 10-foot radius around itself, forcing melee opponents to take damage both from its scimitar and from the wall. It's a Large creature with 200 hit points and a flaming scimitar, and it's immune to the fire damage. "I'm not trapped in here with you—you're trapped in here with me!"

Efreets can also cast *enlarge/reduce* up to three times per day. For very brief interactions, efreets can *reduce* themselves to Medium size, making themselves appear as nonthreatening as red-skinned fire devils possibly can, but the spell's duration of just 1 minute indicates that this spell is really meant for combat, not social interaction. (As for using *reduce* offensively, the difficulty is that the best candidates for it are also most likely to succeed on the Constitution saving throw.) More likely, they'll cast *enlarge* on themselves during combat for the additional 1d4 damage they gain with each weapon strike. The question is, when? The effect takes a full action, and the opportunity cost of that action is much greater than 2d4. Becoming a Huge creature rather than a Large creature offers limited advantages, but I can think of one off the top of my head: The target of a grappling attack can be no more than one size Larger than the attacker. Thus, any Medium-size player character crazy enough and strong enough to try to grapple an efreet will find the task simply impossible once the efreet grows from Large to Huge. In short, an efreet will *enlarge* itself when Huge size allows it to avoid an attack or an effect that Large size doesn't.

Efreets are clever and patient fighters that can outlast more fragile opponents and know it. If melee opponents are giving them trouble, they'll Disengage and fly into the air out of their attackers' reach, repositioning themselves so that they can face all those opponents at once without being flanked. From the air, they can Hurl Flame to eliminate or suppress spellcasters and other ranged attackers so that they can then proceed to clobber their melee opponents without distraction.

Efreets don't parley as readily as djinn do, and when they do, they always try to gain an edge or negotiate a loophole that will give them the better end of the bargain. Helping them further their interests in no way guarantees that they'll be inclined to help the PCs further theirs. Efreets readily accept offers of surrender, but surrendering to an efreet invariably means becoming its thrall—and servitude to an efreet may well mean an unplanned sojourn of indefinite duration on the Elemental Plane of Fire.

MARIDS

The "four elements" of air, earth, fire, and water originated with the Greeks, but somewhere along the line, some D&D writer must have read that djinn, in Arab myth, were supernatural beings of air and that efreets were supernatural beings of fire; decided that there had to be corresponding entities of water and earth, too; and shoehorned **marids** into the genies-of-water role, maybe because of the syllable *mar-*, which means "sea" in Latin. In Arabic, however, مارد *mārid* means "defiant" or "rebellious," and it's used to describe all sorts of troublemaking creatures, including not only certain genies but demons and giants as well.

The D&D marid, like its fiery cousin, the efreet, is a brute fighter with extraordinarily high Strength and Constitution but also extraordinarily high mental attributes. Like djinn, marids have proficiency in Dexterity, Wisdom, and Charisma saving throws along with a Constitution high enough to make saving throws easily without proficiency, so they'll have little to fear from spellcasters.

The marid's equivalent of a djinni's Create Whirlwind and an efreet's Hurl Flame is Water Jet, a linear, guaranteed-damage attack that can push enemies away and knock them prone. Based on this feature's 60-foot range, there's not much reason to expect it to affect more than two creatures at once (based on the Targets in Areas of Effect table in chapter 8 of the *Dungeon Master's Guide*), and since the marid can always position itself to line up any two opponents in its sights, is there any reason for it not to use this feature again and again?

Since Water Jet consumes a full action, and since anyone can clear the prone condition on their own turn simply by spending half of their movement speed to get up, there's not much opportunity for a combo here unless the marid is accompanied by other creatures. On the other hand, even disregarding knockdown, a Water Jet aimed at two targets can be counted on to do more damage, on average, than two Trident strikes except in only a handful of plausible cases. In all of these, the defender's Dex save bonus is +8 or greater (+3 or greater with advantage on the save, such as when a barbarian is using the Danger

Sense class feature), and their AC is 12 or less, so you don't even need to look at cases beyond these.

Marids have Intelligence 18. They know, intuitively, which attack will do more damage against which targets. And that's Water Jet, unless its prospective targets are exceptionally nimble *and* those it can poke with a trident are poorly armored.

Water Jet also makes a good "damaging disengage," if the marid wants to reduce its risk of provoking an opportunity attack while repositioning itself. It's good for exploiting the environment by knocking a PC into a hazard, over a precipice, or off the deck of a boat. And if the marid is accompanied by one or more minions, *they* can increase their expected damage by attacking a prone character with advantage.

But there is one thing that may boost the appeal of a Trident attack. I'll get to it in a second.

The marid has the same standard "genie package" of *gaseous form, invisibility, plane shift*, and *conjure elemental*; unlike the djinni and the efreet, it lacks *major image*. It has a few other tricks up its sleeve, though.

Control water is a powerful once-per-day ability that allows the marid to create a whirlpool in a body of water which can catch a PC in its vortex and subject them to bludgeoning damage; to flood an area with any amount of standing water; or to create a 20-foot-high tidal wave and bring it crashing down on its enemies.

Not to be underestimated is *fog cloud*, which the marid can cast at will. It does require concentration, so it can't be cast at the same time as *control water, conjure elemental*, or *invisibility*. But what it can do is heavily obscure an area, blinding the PCs but not bothering the marid at all, since it has blindsight out to a distance of 30 feet. Within that radius, the marid has advantage on melee attack rolls against blinded PCs, while they'll have disadvantage on attack rolls against it, and a barbarian blinded by fog can't use Danger Sense to dodge a Water Jet. Meanwhile, ranged attackers and spellcasters outside the *fog cloud* won't be able to make out anything inside it. With the advantage provided by *fog cloud*, Trident attacks become feasible against moderately armored opponents (up to AC 15), but only if the prospective targets of a Water Jet have the same high Dex save bonuses as mentioned above.

The marid doesn't need to cast *water breathing* or *water walk* on it-self: It's amphibious. But it can cast these on PCs if they can persuade it to do them a favor (the same goes for *create or destroy water* and *purify food and drink*). That will take some doing, however. Chaotic neutral by alignment, marids are haughty and whimsical; their desires change by the moment, and they're quick to take offense. If one takes an extra-special dislike to a particular PC, it may try to *plane shift* them to the Elemental Plane of Water.

If the PCs can reduce a marid to 160 hp or fewer, or if they can reliably deal it 17 damage or more per turn, it will look to strike a bargain, although what it perceives as its interests may strike the PCs as quite eccentric or offensive. If seriously injured (reduced to 91 hp or fewer), it will skedaddle, using *gaseous form, invisibility,* or *plane shift.*

Dao

I include the **dao** only for completeness' sake, because—let's be frank—it's not all that interesting a monster, unless you're running a thematic campaign on the Elemental Plane of Earth. Like the marid, it seems to exist only because someone thought the existence in myth of air and fire genies meant there had to be water and earth genies too. It doesn't even appear to have a source in Arabic folklore. And its afterthought nature shows in its abilities.

Dao are straight-up brutes, lacking the cleverness of their cous-ins, although they still have above-average Intelligence, Wisdom, and Charisma by humanoid standards. They do have proficiency in Intelli-gence, Wisdom, and Charisma saving throws, and their Constitution is extraordinarily high, but they're susceptible to spells that require Dexterity saves, which spellcasters can exploit.

Dao can attack unarmed or with a maul; the latter does greater damage and allows them to knock targets prone, so it's clearly the preferred option. They have no special attack related to their element, only the Sure-Footed trait, which gives them advantage on saving throws against being knocked prone themselves.

Dao have Innate Spellcasting along with the standard genie pack-age of *gaseous form, invisibility, plane shift,* and *conjure elemental,* lacking *major image* but including *phantasmal killer, wall of stone, passwall, move earth,* and *stone shape*. That's a lot of spells, but they don't add up to much. Elsewhere, I've noted *phantasmal killer*'s unfortunate requirement that the target fail two consecutive Wisdom saving throws in order to take any damage at all. For a dao to have about a two-thirds chance of harming an opponent with *phantasmal killer*, the opponent must have a Wisdom saving throw modifier of –3; for a roughly fifty-fifty chance, –1. That's bad enough to lead most dao to the conclusion that the spell doesn't work often enough to bother with. The other earth-related spells in the dao's repertoire don't inflict damage or debilitating conditions. The one possible exception is *wall of stone*, which can be used to imprison an enemy spellcaster.

All roads lead to the conclusion that the sophistication of the dao's tactics doesn't extend beyond:

- Summon an earth elemental to help out.
- If a spellcaster lobs a spell that requires a Dex save, wall them off.
- Pick a nearby target and whack it with this great big hammer.

Dao are seriously injured when reduced to 74 hp or fewer, and at that point, they exit the scene using one of their abundant movement options. If they have nothing else, boy, do they have movement options. They can fly, burrow, and cast *passwall, gaseous form, invisibility,* and *plane shift*. (That last, as I've noted before, can also be used to banish a pesky enemy to another plane, but honestly, I don't believe dao would have that kind of imagination—or, more to the point, the ability to guess accurately whether any enemy has a low enough Charisma to make the effort worthwhile. Then again, they might do it to whomever, simply out of rage or spite, and become even more enraged and spiteful if it doesn't work.)

CONSTRUCTS

Constructs are explicitly *not* evolved creatures—most often, they're magical creations, made from inanimate objects. This means they can behave in whatever manner their creators want them to . . . within limits. Even so, if you're creating an animated object, you presumably want it to function in the most effective manner it can, given the traits you've imbued it with. More exotic constructs are created from logic itself on the plane of pure law, and these beings pursue their goals with unflagging energy—and mechanical rigidity.

ANIMATED OBJECTS

Animated armor is uncomplicated: It's a melee fighting robot, more or less. It has no ability to distinguish between opponents, no ability to adapt, and no self-preservation instinct, so it fights until it's destroyed.

But there is room for *some* flexibility here: Its Multiattack states, "The armor makes two melee attacks." As always, in fifth edition D&D, it pays to read the rules absolutely literally. For instance, on the facing page of the *Monster Manual*, the solar's Multiattack reads, "The solar makes two *greatsword* attacks" (emphasis mine). It specifies the kind of weapon the solar must use when it attacks more than once on its turn. But the animated armor's Multiattack specifies only two *melee* attacks. Grappling and shoving are both melee attacks that can substitute for one attack in an Attack action—or a Multiattack action.

So which is better: to make two Slam attacks, or to attempt to shove an opponent prone, then make a Slam attack, potentially with advantage?

We have to start with the null hypothesis that shove/Slam is no better than Slam/Slam. After all, while shoving the opponent prone does offer advantage on one Slam attack roll, Slam/Slam lets the animated armor make two rolls as well, with the additional possibility that *both* attacks may be hits. Shove/Slam, in contrast, can produce no more than one hit.

Shoving involves a contest between the attacker's Strength (Athletics) and the target's Strength (Athletics) or Dexterity (Acrobatics). The animated armor has no Athletics skill, and its Strength is above average but not exceptional. So it makes sense to use this attack only against opponents with low-to-average Strength *and* low-to-average Dexterity. Who's likely to fit that profile? Supporters, probably—clerics, druids, bards. Certainly not front-line fighters, slippery rogues, or long-range spellcasters. And we've already established, based on the animated armor's lack of intelligence, that it can't differentiate between targets. So unless it's under the direct control of its creator, it's not going to be able to execute a mode of attack that depends on the class of the target.

Similarly, if a target has a high Armor Class, the animated armor's Slam attack might have a low chance to hit, and it might be worth it to try to knock the target prone first. But again, the animated armor can't tell what a target's AC is, unless it's given commands that are simultaneously very specific and very broad, e.g., "Shove standing trespassers wearing metal armor." This is the full extent of the complexity a suit of animated armor can handle—under a *generous* interpretation of its capacity for independent judgment.

That means that if we want to establish a rationale for shove/Slam, we have to look for it not in its likelihood of success but in the payoff—that is, knocking the target prone. What could increase the value of this condition? How about having lots of allies that could also attack the prone target? Imagine a gallery in a haunted castle, with a hall lined with suits of armor on each side, a dozen or so altogether. In a setup like this, shove/Slam might begin to yield some benefit—but grapple/shove might be even better. This combination, if both attacks are successful, can reduce the target's speed to 0, then knock them prone—in effect, a wrestling pin. With a speed of 0, the prone target can't get up, and *all* subsequent Slam attacks have advantage. The heuristic would be simple: Is the target standing or prone? If standing, grapple, followed by shove on a hit and Slam on a miss. Is the target prone? Slam/Slam.

Here's one other angle: Shoving doesn't have to knock a target prone. It can also push the target 5 feet. Say, into a pit.

And one more: Grapple/Slam is also an option. Grappling doesn't confer advantage on attack rolls, but maybe the animated armor is the minion of some other creature; maybe its assigned mission is not to kill but to capture. In this latter situation, Slam/grapple is no better or worse than grapple/Slam.

But these are outlier cases. Most of the time, you'll want to stick with the simple Slam/Slam.

Flying swords are an oddity: Why on earth would they have proficiency in Dexterity saving throws yet use Strength for attack rolls and damage? I feel like a flying sword, *by definition*, ought to be a "finesse weapon." In this case, it would have +4 to hit and deal 1d8 + 2 slashing damage. (If you use this modification, raise the flying sword's challenge rating from 1/4 to 1/2.)

Since they have a flying speed of 50 feet and can hover, a flying sword floats in the air, out of its targets' reach—10 feet should do the trick in most cases—swoops down to attack, then flies back up. Targets will get opportunity attacks against it, but that's an acceptable risk for a construct with AC 17; if enemies are clustered together, however, it attacks from a direction that avoids *additional* opportunity attacks from enemies other than its target. Beyond this, it has no ability—and makes no effort—to differentiate between targets.

A flying sword has no reason not to fight until it's destroyed.

The **rug of smothering** has exceptional Strength, high Dexterity, merely average Constitution, and a movement speed of only 10 feet per round, making it an ambush predator that has to strike fast and hard. Its Smother attack does no immediate damage but grapples, restrains, and blinds its target, then deals damage at the start of the target's turn.

While it's enveloping a target, it can't attack anyone else; meanwhile, all its target's allies will be attacking it (and hurting the target in the process, since half of all damage done to a rug of smothering passes through to whoever's inside it). Chances are, that first attack is the only one it will ever get.

If you want a cheap laugh, you can have the rug Dash away with its prey inside it (at the dizzying speed of 10 feet per round—not 20, because it's dragging a grappled victim), try to Dodge incoming attacks, or even Hide behind another piece of furniture. Playing it more seriously, however, the fact that it restrains its victim means that an ally of the rug of smothering, if one is present, can target that victim with a weapon or spell attack and gain advantage on the roll, or cast a spell requiring a Dexterity saving throw to resist, which the victim will have disadvantage on.

A rug of smothering has no reason not to fight until it's destroyed.

SCARECROWS, HELMED HORRORS, AND SHIELD GUARDIANS

The scarecrow and the helmed horror are much more capable of operating independently than animated objects; the shield guardian, on the other hand, is little more than an anthropomorphic drone.

Scarecrows, unlike animated objects, are brought to "life" by infusing them with the spirits of slain fiends or other evil creatures. They have an odd ability contour, mostly flat but with above-average Dexterity and Charisma. The latter seems to provide only a power source for their Terrifying Glare feature and some modest defense against banishment. The former suggests either a preference for ranged attacks over melee engagement or a reliance on Dexterity for both attack and defense—more on this in a moment.

Scarecrows are vulnerable to fire, and this presents an interesting behavioral wrinkle. Like other constructs, scarecrows must follow the commands of their creators, but unlike most other constructs, the source of their dynamic force is the spirit of a creature that was once alive. Combined with a Wisdom high enough to indicate a normal survival instinct, this suggests that a scarecrow threatened with fire is torn between the instinct to flee and the compulsion to obey its creator. This drives it a little bit haywire, as it tries simultaneously to flee the fire and kill the enemy who brandishes it. In this situation, don't worry about whether the scarecrow's actions make tactical sense. It *should* behave irrationally.

A scarecrow is resistant to physical damage from normal weapons. It also has an effective Claw/Claw Multiattack that can impose the frightened condition, which is disadvantageous to an opponent trying to fight back. Its Claw attacks use Dexterity, not Strength, so the scarecrow is best thought of as a shock attacker, specializing in swift, hard strikes and reluctant to engage in drawn-out combat. On the other hand, even two dice of damage don't amount to much when the dice are d4s. So how can we make this creature an *effective* shock attacker?

The key is Terrifying Glare and the fact that it can impose paralysis, a devastating condition to anyone afflicted by it. A paralyzed opponent is incapacitated and immobile, all attack rolls against them have advantage, and every melee hit from point-blank range is an automatic critical. *That's* what makes the scarecrow a shock attacker: doubled damage dice.

Here's how it all fits together. Using its False Appearance, a scarecrow lurks, motionless, until a target comes within 30 feet of it. It gazes upon that target with its Terrifying Glare. It doesn't even need to raise its head to do this; it can merely swivel its eyes. This is not an "attack" as far as the rules are concerned, so whether it succeeds or fails, it doesn't give away the scarecrow as anything but the straw dummy it appears to be. Also, unlike certain similar saving throw effects—for instance, dragons' Frightful Presence—Terrifying Glare can be attempted on the same target repeatedly if it doesn't work the first time.

The scarecrow uses this ranged non-attack until it succeeds in frightening and paralyzing a target. (If it tries its Terrifying Glare on a target twice and that target makes their saving throw both times, it gives up on that target—it can tell it's not going to work.) Once a target is paralyzed, that's when the scarecrow springs into action: On its next turn, it closes to melee range and Multiattacks, with advantage on both Claw attack rolls. Every hit is a crit—*and* means that the target continues to be frightened until the end of the scarecrow's next turn, so they roll with disadvantage when trying to fight back. (Note, incidentally, that even if a quick-thinking ally of the target casts *lesser restoration* to end their paralysis before the scarecrow attacks, the target is still frightened—*lesser restoration* doesn't remove that effect.)

A scarecrow will spend two turns engaged in melee with a target. After that, if the target's not dead, too bad. At the end of the second turn, the scarecrow retreats its full movement speed (30 feet) from its foe, heedless of opportunity attacks because of its damage resistance. (The opponent can probably close that distance; they also probably won't want to, considering the damage the scarecrow has done already.) This distance gives the scarecrow room to try its Terrifying Glare again, either on the same target or on someone else.

Scarecrows have darkvision, and fighting in darkness emboldens them to attack non-paralyzed, non-frightened creatures, as long as those creatures don't also have darkvision. Against dwarves, elves, gnomes, et al., they stick to their standard glare-first, julienne-later method.

A seriously wounded scarecrow (reduced to 14 hp or fewer) flees, using the Dash action, if doing so doesn't contradict the orders its creator has given it. If its creator has commanded it to fight to the death, it does, hissing and snarling with pain and rage.

A single scarecrow will pose a challenge to a whole party only if it's made up entirely of level 1 characters. Although scarecrows don't have high enough Wisdom to avoid fights in which they're outmatched, if you as the DM want to make a scarecrow encounter interesting for a party of higher-level player characters, make sure it includes more than one scarecrow. You can use the encounter balancing rules in chapter 3 of the *Dungeon Master's Guide* to get a sense of how many scarecrows to throw at them. Personally, I think if you're going to include a scarecrow encounter at all, it should be a Hard encounter. It should have a palpable horror vibe, not a *Scooby-Doo* vibe.

Helmed horrors are much more straightforward. They have a high-Strength, high-Constitution brute profile and a double Longsword Multiattack that complements it. They're no Sun Zi, but they can adjust to adverse circumstances (though they won't proactively try to alter them for their own benefit) and can identify a character's class and assess their weaknesses as accurately as any ordinary observer could. If it's feasible for them to do so, they'll go after glass cannon opponents first.

Helmed horrors can fly at the same speed as they can move along the ground, and if their opponents aren't pushovers, they'll make free use of this ability to station themselves 10 feet up in the air, fly down to attack, then fly back up out of melee fighters' reach. With AC 20, resistance to physical damage from normal weapons, and a decent store of hit points, they're not going to worry about opportunity attacks.

Unless the creator of the helmed horror has some knowledge of the PCs' party and their capabilities, use the default list of spell resistances, or one tailored to the adventure setting. However, if the creator *does* have intelligence on the party, feel free to have the helmed horror resist the spells the PCs lean on most.

Helmed horrors have no reason not to fight until they're destroyed, and the only outward indication of how much damage they've taken will be armor pieces knocked askew and weird, irregular eruptions of light from where they've been hit.

Outwardly, a **shield guardian** looks a lot like a helmed horror or animated suit of armor, although PCs with a discriminating eye might describe them as something more along the lines of an "armor golem." Their ability contour is pure brute, and they wield no weapons, attacking only with their fists. Shield guardians are bodyguards rather than independent sentinels; in a sense, they're not even *creatures* as much as devices employed by those whom they protect. They do only what they're commanded to do. Therefore, you should think of their tactics not as their own but as an extension of the tactics of their controllers. A more malevolent controller may send a shield guardian forth to demolish enemies; one who just wants to be left alone might order it to attack only those who pose a direct and immediate threat.

That being said, a key feature the creator will want to make use of is Shield, which makes the shield guardian function something like a PC fighter or paladin with the Protection fighting style; instead of imposing disadvantage on the attack roll, however, it increases the controller's AC by 2. Aside from this, the shield guardian is a simple melee bot. It's optimized for toe-to-toe combat and really can't do anything else except discharge a stored spell.

Shield guardians aren't resistant to weapon damage, but they do regenerate, regardless of what kind of damage they've taken. They also have the Spell Storing trait, which doesn't require the controller to be conscious to use: "When commanded to do so by the wearer *or when a situation arises that was predefined by the spellcaster* [emphasis mine], the guardian casts the stored spell with any parameters set by the original caster." Thus, the Spell Storing can function as a dead man's switch, activating at the moment the controller loses consciousness or even sometime afterward.

I say "controller" rather than "creator" because the creator of a shield guardian can transfer control to someone else by giving them the amulet to which the shield guardian is bound. Killing the shield guardian presumably destroys the amulet, but killing the controller explicitly doesn't. A character who takes possession of the amulet thereby takes control of the shield guardian.

Shield guardians have no reason not to fight until they're destroyed.

GOLEMS

Golems are living statues, animated through magic. Specifically, according to legend, by hacking the divine power by which life was created; according to the *Monster Manual*, by summoning an animating spirit from the Elemental Plane of Earth. Golems are fashioned to be servants, with great strength, limited intellect, and no free will. A golem severed from the command of its creator may be either inert and harmless (if it could fulfill its last command) or dangerously berserk (if it couldn't).

There are four types of golems in the *Monster Manual*: clay, stone, iron, and flesh. One of these things is not like the others. The flesh

HOMUNCULI

Homunculi are constructs, bound to their creators' will and instructions, but they do have some intelligence independent of their creators. Although they have a high Dexterity, they have little damage-dealing capability and can't really be sent against anyone tougher than a commoner. Nor does their poisonous bite have a high DC to resist, nor do they have any effective way to escape after making a melee attack without provoking an opportunity strike. And they have so few hit points that even a level 1 PC has a good chance of killing one in a single hit.

Thus, the only smart thing for a homunculus to do when attacked is to skedaddle. Since it has not only its own intelligence but the intelligence of its creator behind it, we can give it the benefit of the doubt and assume it's capable of Disengaging, which it does if any foe gets in its face. It flies away at full speed, Dashing if it doesn't have to Disengage. It uses its Bite attack only when inescapably cornered.

golem is, for all intents and purposes, Frankenstein's monster, and of all the types of golems, it has the most unfit vessel for its life force and the most existential angst. The clay golem is the direct conceptual descendant of the Golem of Prague, and the stone and iron golems are stronger variations on this theme.

All golems are straightforward brutes, with exceptional (and in most cases extraordinary) Strength and Constitution and below-average Dexterity. If anything, they're even more brutish than the average brute, because of their immunities to normal weapons and to many debilitating conditions (they can be incapacitated, knocked prone, restrained, or stunned, but not charmed, frightened, paralyzed, petrified, or poisoned). Any variation in behavior comes from their special features.

The most distinctive thing about the **flesh golem** is its Aversion to Fire. A flesh golem that takes fire damage has disadvantage on attack rolls and ability checks until the end of its next turn, so it's going to steer clear of anyone wielding a flaming weapon of any kind, including a torch, or from an uncontrolled open flame, such as a slick of burning lamp oil or alchemist's fire. On its turn, it compulsively moves away from any such flame until there's at least 30 feet between them. It may combine this movement with movement toward some other target, but the distance is nonnegotiable, and if there's no other place or thing that it's specifically moving toward, it moves directly and diametrically away from the flame. This aversion doesn't apply to other "burny" types of damage, such as acid or radiant, just fire—and lightning "damage" actually restores hit points to it, thanks to its Lightning Absorption trait. (It's not *attracted* to lightning, though.)

The second-most distinctive thing about the flesh golem is its Berserk trait. As constructs (i.e., arcane creations from inanimate materials), golems have no self-preservation instinct in the conventional sense. That is, they seek to avoid obvious danger in the course of carrying out their orders—if you tell one to fetch something on the other side of a chasm, it will look for a bridge rather than march straight into it—but if they're ordered to fight, they fight till they're destroyed. Whether controlled or uncontrolled, a seriously damaged flesh golem, rather than flee, simply goes haywire, attacking the nearest creature within its movement range. If there's no one within range, it attacks an object instead.

The golem's creator can talk it down, but aside from that, the only way to stop its berserk rage is, counterintuitively, to heal it back up to its hit point maximum.

The **clay golem** shares the Berserk trait with the flesh golem. In addition, it has the Acid Absorption trait: Acid not only doesn't harm it but *heals* it. Thus, while the flesh golem compulsively avoids fire, once a clay golem observes that one of its foes is dealing acid damage, it compulsively *pursues* that foe. If more than one foe is dealing acid damage, it goes after whichever one is closest.

Clay golems also have the Haste feature, which is a little weird because of how it's written. For the clay golem, Haste is an *action*, which means it can't be taken in the same turn as a Multiattack action. A golem under Haste can Slam as a bonus action, however.

For the sake of comparison, let's look at two different possible clay golem behaviors over the course of two rounds:

- **Multiattack, Multiattack.** In round A, the golem makes two Slam attacks. In round B, the golem makes two more Slam attacks.
- **Haste, Multiattack.** In round A, the golem makes one Slam attack, as a bonus action. In round B, the golem makes two Slam attacks, then a third Slam attack as a bonus action. It also has +2 to its Armor Class and advantage on Dexterity saving throws in both rounds.

Essentially, by using Haste, the golem gains an AC bonus and advantage on Dex saves at the cost of having to put more of its attacking eggs in the second-round basket. Is this a good deal for the golem? D&D's designers must believe it is, because they put Haste on a recharge.

That being said, there's clearly a lot more benefit to forgoing an attack in the first round of combat in exchange for bonuses that apply in the first and second rounds than there is to, say, forgoing an attack in the third round in exchange for bonuses that apply to the third and fourth. A clay golem is much more likely to be able to cash in on an attack delayed until round 2 than one delayed until round 4 or later.

But here's the counterpoint: The clay golem has Intelligence 3. Its behaviors aren't simply mechanical, they're *purely* mechanical. It may not be enough to say that if the clay golem has Haste available to it, it will probably use it, or that it will use it if it seems to make more sense than not using it. We may have to conclude that if the clay golem has Haste available, it *automatically* uses it. (With one somewhat obvious exception: Even if it recharges, it doesn't make sense for a golem to use Haste two turns in a row. Haste offers negligible payoff if the golem doesn't make its three Slam attacks in the subsequent round.)

The **stone golem**'s single unique feature is Slow, which is also a recharge ability. It's limited only by radius, not by number of targets, and applies to essentially every character engaged in melee with the golem, possibly including supporters as well. With a radius of 10 feet, this power pays for itself if it affects just two enemies; against only one, however, it's not worth the cost of the action, because it means giving up a Multiattack. The rule, therefore, is that the stone golem uses Slow when (a) it's available and (b) two or more enemies *who are not already Slowed* are within 10 feet of it.

The **iron golem** has Fire Absorption, which works the same way as the clay golem's Acid Absorption and has the same effect, except with regard to fire rather than acid. It also has Poison Breath, a small-scale equivalent of a dragon's breath weapon. The 15-foot conic area of effect calls for a minimum of two targets; however, with Intelligence 3, the iron golem isn't knowledgeable enough not to use this feature on dwarves or stout halflings. It uses its Poison Breath on the most, nearest enemies, whatever they may be.

As for its weapon attacks, its sword has a longer reach and does more damage; therefore, it always prefers a Sword attack over a Slam attack, unless it's somehow disarmed.

MODRONS

Modrons are constructs, automata with vaguely mathematically inspired bodies, humanoid faces, and in the illustrations of the fifth edition *Monster Manual*, disturbingly full lips. The more advanced the modron, the more it can multitask, and the more authority it has over other modrons. All modrons possess natural armor, above-average Dexterity, 120 feet of truesight, and the traits Axiomatic Mind and Disintegration.

One of the many peculiarities of modrons is that they're denizens of an outer plane, yet their challenge ratings top out at 2. How many *low*-level adventurers are going to travel to Mechanus? I wonder whether these creatures must exist at least primarily for the sake of background decoration. They're not going to pose a challenge to the PCs who encounter them except in great numbers—legions.

The **monodrone** is the simplest, lowest-level modron. It can fly, but it doesn't have any way to avoid opportunity attacks, so the tactic of holding station in the air, flying down to attack, and flying back up is suboptimal. Instead, it uses its flying movement to make ranged javelin attacks over opponents' cover, traverse vertical distance, and ignore difficult terrain. (Not that there's any difficult terrain in Mechanus.)

Although it has average Wisdom, its Intelligence is animal-level: It chooses targets indiscriminately and has no ability to adapt to changing circumstances. Whatever its orders are, it follows them to the letter.

It carries a dagger and a javelin, and it's slightly better at attacking with the former than the latter (+3 to hit vs. +2). So here's a simple formula for monodrone combat: Approach to 30 feet, throw the javelin, then close to melee range and fight with the dagger from that point on. If at any time a monodrone manages to defeat or displace its opponent, retrieve javelin, GOTO 10.

Monodrones have no independent judgment, and since modrons exist in infinite supply, they have no self-preservation instinct. A damaged monodrone follows its instructions until it's destroyed.

Duodrones are only marginally more intelligent than monodrones, and they can't fly. They can attack twice in one action, but they must do so with the same weapon: either two Javelin attacks or two Fist attacks, never one Javelin and one Fist. Like the monodrone, the duodrone has a Dexterity that's slightly higher than its Strength—but unlike the monodrone, the duodrone carries no finesse weapon for melee combat.

For this to make any sense at all, I think a duodrone has to carry several javelins into battle, and the number must be odd (you'll see why in a moment). Historically, in Classical times, soldiers carried three to five javelins onto a battlefield in their off hands or—rarely, and only toward the end of the period—in a quiver. Let's give the duodrone five javelins, because in the illustration, its fingers are long and skinny; it can probably hold a big bundle.

When combat begins, a duodrone approaches to 30 feet and throws two of its javelins. If its opponent closes with it, it uses one of its remaining javelins as a melee weapon; if not, it hurls two more, and at that point it still has one remaining that it can use for melee fighting. A duodrone can fight with its fists, but that doesn't mean it should. A javelin does a bit more damage, so it will prefer to have one left over.

Like the monodrone, a duodrone retrieves its thrown javelins whenever there's a break in the action—but only if it can pick up two that have landed in the same person, place, or thing. Picking up just one javelin would mess up the duodrone's system. Also like monodrones, duodrones don't retreat, no matter how much damage they take.

Nothing distinguishes a **tridrone** from a duodrone except its Multiattack (three attacks, meaning it always wants to carry $3n + 1$ javelins—we'll start it off with seven, since it has *two* extra hands to carry them in) and its near-average Intelligence, which allows it to adapt to a changing situation. Tridrones still won't retreat to save themselves, but they will position and reposition themselves on a battlefield to take advantage of terrain, cover, chokepoints, and other features with potential tactical benefits, and they'll order lesser modrons to do the same. They'll also respond appropriately to obstacles and hazards created by their opponents. However, they lack the Intelligence to *create* tactically beneficial features, obstacles, or hazards themselves; they can only take advantage of ones that already exist.

Monodrones and duodrones aren't intelligent enough to Disengage independently, but with a tridrone on the field to give the order, they can hear it and obey. Tridrones cover the retreat of monodrones and duodrones that have Disengaged to take a new position. Also, it takes at least a tridrone to recognize an attack that does extra damage to constructs, such as a *mace of smiting*. Once an enemy makes such an attack, a tridrone focuses all its attacks on that enemy and orders the other modrons under its command to do the same.

Quadrones are archers whose Dexterity and Multiattack both strongly favor ranged attacking over melee, so unlike tridrones, quadrones lead from the rear, not from the front line. If someone needs to run interference, quadrones order tridrones to do that. To the fullest extent possible, quadrones maintain position between 35 and 80 feet from the nearest opponent, someplace with a good view of the whole battlefield and as much cover as they can get. From there, they rain arrows down upon their foes, at a rate of four shots per turn. Twenty is a good number of arrows to give them.

When a quadrone runs out of arrows, five combat rounds have gone by, and that's enough time for a quadrone to realize that things are not going as they should. At that point, they order a tactical retreat toward a location with more modrons, including more quadrones, with any surviving tridrones in their unit acting as rearguard.

Pentadrones, despite being at the top of the modron hierarchy (as far as the *Monster Manual* goes, at least—we can hypothesize the existence of infinite types of modron), are brute fighters. If you're using a battle grid, remember that pentadrones are Large creatures, so they take up more space.

Pentadrones march right up toward the front line of combat, let loose a cone of Paralysis Gas as soon as they can catch at least three enemies in it (not having the Intelligence to direct it specifically at enemies who look more susceptible to it), then start whaling away with their five arms, targeting those who *haven't* succumbed to paralysis. They leave paralyzed targets to the lesser modrons under their command, which need advantage on their attack rolls more than the pentadrones do and are less equipped to battle those tough enough to make their Constitution saves. They continue attacking with their arms until their Paralysis Gas recharges, at which point they use that weapon again.

Pentadrones, like tridrones, cover the retreat of lesser modrons if such a thing becomes necessary, but even they don't retreat simply because they've taken serious damage. They order a retreat only if combat lasts more than five rounds, at which point the quadrones under their command will have run out of arrows.

When pentadrones lead a battle with other modrons under their command, monodrones, duodrones, and tridrones will forgo their ranged attacks in order to seize the opportunity of attacking a para- lyzed opponent at melee range for the "every hit a crit" benefit. When there's no paralyzed opponent within their movement distance, they go back to their normal javelin-hurling routine, if they have any jav- elins left.

Finally, let's talk about why lawful neutral beings are engaging in combat at all. Lawful evil beings will want to kill trespassers by default, but lawful neutral beings are interested in maintaining order by the simplest, most straightforward methods available, and fighting is rarely simple or straightforward. Their default disposition toward strangers is indifference, not hostility. They'll leave your PCs alone unless and until the PCs break the modrons' rules or start causing a ruckus.

Unfortunately for the offending PCs, modrons aren't equipped with features that would make them good at grappling. They can choose to attack to subdue rather than kill (see "Knocking a Creature Out," *Player's Handbook*, chapter 9), and I think this would be consis- tent with the values of the plane of pure law. Why kill what you can capture and put on trial? Trials are probably the pinnacle of public entertainment in Mechanus.

But also note the fine print on that page: Only *melee* attacks can be nonlethal. Duodrones and, especially, quadrones are optimized for *ranged* combat. Small problems can be dealt with by monodrones that can swarm troublemakers and bring them back as captives. But a problem too large for monodrones will often involve modrons that aren't going to compromise their combat effectiveness to *avoid* killing their enemies. And the modron method of solving problems is simple: Throw more modrons at it. Mechanus never runs out.

Oozes and plants are two creature types with one thing in common: Most of them are more "hazard" than "villain." They tend to lack the necessary mobility, intelligence, and ambition to pose threats beyond their immediate vicinities. There are exceptions, however—and even the non-exceptions should be as threatening as you can make them to the player characters who stumble across them.

OOZES

The fifth edition *Monster Manual* claims that oozes "have no sense of tactics or self-preservation," but I can't buy the second half of that. They may be "drawn to movement and warmth," but even an amoeba will move away from an electric current. Despite the lore that oozes originated as fragments of the demon lord Juiblex, I treat them as evolved beings, akin to slime molds—scavengers that exist as part of the subterranean ecosystem.

The *Monster Manual* lists four types of oozes: the gray ooze, the ochre jelly, the black pudding, and the gelatinous cube. All of them have several things in common: negligible Intelligence and Charisma (the ochre jelly, with Intelligence 2, is the genius of the bunch), low Dexterity and Wisdom, high Constitution, a corrosive pseudopod attack, and 60 feet of blindsight. Also, all but the gelatinous cube are Amorphous and can climb walls.

The **gray ooze** is the weakest and simplest of the four. Its False Appearance allows it to blend in with wet rock, so it's self-evident that this is where a gray ooze lies in wait for its next meal. (Unlike the other oozes, the gray ooze has a +2 Stealth "skill," reflecting its camouflage ability.) When a living being comes within 60 feet of it, it senses the being's presence. If the being is coming toward the ooze, it holds still; if the being moves away from the ooze again, it begins to follow, continuing its slow-motion pursuit for as long as it can do so without having to expose itself (that is, move onto a surface that isn't wet rock). When it finally comes within reach of a living being, it extends a pseudopod and grabs on.

The idea of a gray ooze forming itself into a big fist and whomping somebody is ridiculous to me, so I prefer to interpret its "bludgeoning" attack as *squeezing*: When the ooze gets its pseudopod around a PC's leg, say, it begins to constrict and suck that leg into itself, doing physical and acid damage all the while. It keeps attacking—corroding any metal the target is wearing—until either it takes enough damage to drive it off or destroy it or the PC is completely digested.

By "completely digested," I don't just mean the PC is reduced to 0 hp: I mean that it's *dead*. An unconscious victim may be presumed to be completely engulfed by the gray ooze, but it isn't dead yet, only well on its way. Once the gray ooze has engulfed its victim, it moves away from other living beings at its full movement speed, continuing to "attack" the target inside it. Only when the target has failed three death saving throws (including each time they take damage) are they finally dead.

The gray ooze begins with 22 hp, and its predatory behavior is interrupted when it's reduced to 8 hp or fewer. At this point, it lets go of whatever target it's attacking and Dashes away (potentially exposing itself to opportunity attacks). Of course, Dashing, for an ooze, means traveling a whopping 20 feet per round, and catching up to it will be no problem at all for a vindictive party. So if there's a crack it can slither into, it will.

The **ochre jelly** functions in the same manner as the gray ooze, with only two differences. First, since it has Spider Climb, it prefers to hang on ceilings and drop down on its prey. Second, it can be cut or blasted into multiple smaller ochre jellies.

A full-size, undamaged ochre jelly has 45 hp. Suppose it's approached by a chirurgeon with a scalpel, who neatly slices it in two. The Large jelly isn't damaged by the cut, but it's divided into two Medium jellies, each with 22 hp, and each of those in turn can be divided into two Small jellies with 11 hp each. (Small jellies can't be split.) To force a Large jelly to retreat, it has to be reduced to 18 hp or fewer by non-slashing, non-lightning damage; a Medium jelly must be reduced to 8 hp or fewer; and a Small jelly, 4 hp or fewer. Like the gray ooze, these Dash away at 20 feet per round; unlike the gray ooze, they go straight up the nearest wall to the ceiling, their instinctive place of safety, if there's no crevice to flow into.

A **black pudding** is like a cross between the gray ooze and the ochre jelly—able to corrode weapons and armor like the former and to hang from ceilings and Split like the latter. It spreads itself across the ceiling of a cavern and, rather than drop on its prey, reaches down and gloms onto it with a sludgy pseudopod. A Large black pudding retreats when it's reduced to 34 hp or fewer by non-slashing, non-lightning damage; a Medium pudding must be reduced to 16 hp or fewer; and a Small pudding must be reduced to 8 hp or fewer. Cutting a hanging black pudding in half results in one half that falls to the ground and one that remains stuck to the ceiling. The one on the ground behaves like a gray ooze or ochre jelly, remaining in place until it's absorbed its prey (reduced them to 0 hp), then oozing back up the wall with it to finish digesting it in peace. If a black pudding that's hanging from the ceiling reduces a victim to 0 hp or fewer, it slurps them right up off the ground.

The **gelatinous cube** is always on the move, and it makes no attempt at stealth or surprise. It's a juggernaut, systematically scouring its area for anything it can digest, like a dungeon Roomba. I'd go so far as to suggest that it should *never take the shape of a cube*. The cube shape never made sense, and it only *seemed* to make sense back in the days when every dungeon was drawn on graph paper, at a scale of 10 feet per quarter inch. (I'd like to think we DMs all have enough sense nowadays to draw cavern passages as naturally irregular in width, shape, and direction.) Instead, the "cube" should be an enormous floor-to-ceiling blob, and suicidally curious PCs who walk right up to one should see it constantly extending and withdrawing creepy little pseudopods to sweep out every irregularity in a cavern wall.

Normally, it moves at less than its full movement rate—say, only 5 feet per round—so that it doesn't miss a morsel. When it senses living creatures, however, it approaches at full movement speed to a distance of 25 feet, then waits motionless for one round, counting on its Transparency to let it go unnoticed until they come within reach. If they do, it attacks with surprise. If they maintain their distance, and at least one PC is still 25 feet away or closer at the end of that round, it uses its full 15 feet of movement, then its Engulf action—which includes *another* 15 feet of movement—to absorb its prey. If the creatures move away from it instead, it follows, Dashing if necessary, until either it's 25 feet from them again or it can no longer catch up.

Unlike the other oozes, the gelatinous cube doesn't leave once it's absorbed a victim. It keeps moving forward, Engulfing anyone and everyone in its path. The only thing that will make it reverse direction is reducing it to 33 hp or fewer, whereupon it Dashes away from the PCs. (Woe, then, to any PC who escaped being Engulfed by popping out the *back* of the cube.)

BLIGHTS

In D&D, some plants are "awakened": They possess consciousness and mobility. And, of course, some awakened plants are evil and want to kill you. These are called "blights."

Being plants, they derive nutrients from the soil, so they don't need to kill to eat. They attack strictly out of spite.

Twig blights, found in forests and abandoned settlements in forested areas, are Small and scrappy, with poor Strength but good Dexterity and Constitution. They don't have high mobility, so they compensate with numbers, growing in large patches. They also have proficiency in Stealth and the False Appearance trait, so ambushes are a likely tactic (insert Birnam Wood joke here). They have 60-foot blindsight and are vulnerable to fire.

Whenever a party of adventurers encounters a patch of twig blights, they'll be inert, disguising themselves as ordinary desiccated shrubs. When victims come within reach, they'll attack with surprise (give them advantage on these attack rolls for hiding in plain sight, unless the PCs are watching out for them).

They're cursed beings, not evolved creatures, so they don't have much in the way of survival instinct; they attack until they're destroyed.

They'll follow a foe who tries to retreat, but they won't Dash after one. If their numbers are sufficient to surround an enemy, however, they will. And if attacked with fire, they'll Dash away from the source.

Needle blights, found in evergreen forests, are human-size amalgamations of plant matter and needle-shaped leaves, which they can hurl at opponents. Needle blights may be encountered in groups, but unlike twig blights, they aren't *always* encountered in groups: They have sufficient Strength and Constitution to take on low-level opponents alone. The more suffused with evil influence an area is, however, the greater their numbers. They also aren't ambushers—they have no Stealth skill. They're not concerned with whether they're seen, only with whether they're approached (which they can detect out to a range of 60 feet, with blindsight).

Their Intelligence is animal at best, and while they aren't slow, they also don't move if they don't have to. When a party of PCs comes within 30 feet of them, they attack with Needles; if one closes to within melee range, they attack with Claws. If the melee opponent then moves away, they make their opportunity attacks, but they may not bother to pursue, unless they're trying to chase trespassers out of their part of the forest. They don't flee when wounded and fight until they're destroyed; they're not afraid of fire.

Vine blights, found in forests and jungles, are vaguely humanoid-shaped masses of braided vines that can lash out and grab other creatures. They have some measure of Stealth—not a lot, but enough, when combined with their False Appearance, to blend into their surroundings in dim light. They're not dexterous, though, so while they do ambush victims, they wait until those victims get very close, then use Entangling Plants to restrain them. Finally, they engage restrained opponents in melee, grappling and squeezing them until they drop. They make opportunity attacks against retreating opponents and pursue to the best of their ability, although their movement speed is a less-than-impressive 10 feet. If they can catch a retreating opponent within the 15-foot radius of Entangling Plants, they do.

Vine blights, according to the *Monster Manual* flavor text, are connected to a "Gulthias tree," a fiendish arboreal being for which there's no listing in the *Monster Manual*. The Internet consensus appears to be that a Gulthias tree should be treated as an evil-aligned awakened tree. Awakened trees are Huge brutes with a 10-foot reach; all they really do is smack opponents repeatedly with their branches and run away from fire. They're not that interesting and only slightly challenging. If you're in need of a more formidable opponent, you might rather go with an evil-aligned treant: These have many more hit points and can also hurl rocks.

But given that the original Gulthias, according to the flavor text, was a vampire whose blood was so full of evil potency that it turned the wooden stake that skewered him into an undead sapling, it seems to me that something more is called for, such as a homebrew monster that's part awakened tree/treant, part vampire—maybe that has the Regeneration and Charm abilities, does necrotic damage, or both. Something like this:

GULTHIAS TREE

Huge plant, neutral evil

Armor Class 13 (natural armor)
Hit Points 59 (7d12 + 14)
Speed 20 ft

Str 19 (+4) **Dex** 6 (–2) **Con** 15 (+2) **Int** 10 (0) **Wis** 10 (0) **Cha** 10 (0)

Damage Vulnerabilities fire
Damage Resistances bludgeoning, necrotic, piercing
Senses blindsight 120 ft (blind beyond this radius), passive Perception 10
Languages Common
Challenge 4 (1,100 XP)

Creeping Fog. Within 500 feet of the Gulthias tree, the forest is suffused with a thick miasma that blocks sunlight. The entire area is dimly lit and lightly obscured. A strong wind (at least 20 miles per hour) disperses it.

False Appearance. While the Gulthias tree remains motionless, it is indistinguishable from a normal tree.

Regeneration. The Gulthias tree regains 10 hp at the start of its turn if it has at least 1 hp and isn't in sunlight. If the Gulthias tree takes radiant damage, this trait doesn't function at the start of the Gulthias tree's next turn.

ACTIONS

Multiattack. The Gulthias tree makes two attacks, only one of which may be an Impale attack.

Slam. Melee Weapon Attack: +6 to hit, reach 10 ft, one target. *Hit:* 14 (3d6 + 4) bludgeoning damage. Instead of dealing damage, the Gulthias tree can grapple the target (escape DC 16).

Impale. Melee Weapon Attack: +6 to hit, reach 10 ft, one creature that is grappled by the Gulthias tree, incapacitated, or restrained. *Hit*: 7 (1d6 + 4) piercing damage plus 10 (3d6) necrotic damage. The target's hit point maximum is reduced by an amount equal to the necrotic damage taken, and the Gulthias tree regains hit points equal to that amount. The reduction lasts until the target finishes a long rest. The target dies if this effect reduces its hit point maximum to 0. A humanoid slain in this way and then buried in the ground rises the following night as a vine blight under the Gulthias tree's control.

MYCONIDS

Myconids are vaguely humanoid fungus creatures, categorized by the *Monster Manual* as "plants" in defiance of our current understanding of fungi as less closely related to plants than to animals (really!). Granted, we shouldn't be surprised when anything in D&D defies science—but if, as a DM, you feel like honoring science *and* being perversely difficult toward your players, you might choose to reclassify myconids as beasts, monstrosities, or even aberrations. The last category might fit best, as they're intelligent, but they're certainly not a humanoid intelligence, or even an *animal* intelligence.

As subterranean creatures, all myconids share 120 feet of darkvision, plus the features Sun Sickness, Distress Spores, and Rapport Spores. Sun Sickness penalizes myconids for venturing aboveground during the day: It gives them disadvantage on all ability checks, attack rolls, and saving throws while in sunlight, and if they spend more than an hour out in it, it kills them. (They dry up or something, I guess.) Distress Spores gives them a form of telepathic communication with other myconids, informing them when they're injured. Rapport Spores are interesting: They give *all* living creatures exposed to them the ability to share thoughts over a limited distance. Which is useful, because otherwise myconids have no form of verbal communication.

Myconids are lawful neutral, not evil. Although not automatically friendly, they're not automatically hostile, either; their default disposition is indifferent. But they are lawful, which means that being a troublemaker in their vicinity may provoke a hostile response from them. The more Chaos Muppety your player characters are, the less likely myconids are to appreciate their presence.

Myconid sprouts are, basically, fungus babies, and shame on any PC picking on them. With low Strength and only average Dexterity and Constitution, they'd normally be skirmishers, except that they also have a base movement speed of only 10 feet, so they're not really capable of skirmishing. They certainly won't start any kind of fight unless they outnumber the PCs by a sizable margin—four to one or more. Otherwise, if the PCs show any degree of hostility toward them, they'll simply Dash directly away, which in their case means retreating at the breakneck velocity of 20 feet per round. They won't use their Rapport Spores unless and until they come within 10 feet of a larger myconid. If they're damaged, their Distress Spores will summon other myconids up to 240 feet away (by travel distance—the spores can't pass through walls) to come to their aid.

With a base movement speed of 20 feet, **myconid adults** are faster than myconid sprouts but still slow by humanoid standards. Having only average Strength and Dexterity and slightly above-average Constitution, they're not strong enough to be brutes or agile enough to be skirmishers. They compensate with their Pacifying Spores, which have, roughly, a 25 to 50 percent chance of stunning a single opponent. These aren't great odds, so adult myconids prefer to outnumber their opponents two to one before initiating a fight.

An adult myconid uses its Pacifying Spores as its first action unless another myconid has already done so successfully against the same opponent. If so, its course of action depends on the reason why the myconids are fighting. Counterintuitively, if they were attacked unprovoked, a myconid with a stunned opponent will release Rapport Spores and try to determine its opponents' reason for attacking. But if the myconids are the aggressors, because their opponents have been causing intolerable mayhem, a myconid with a stunned opponent seizes the opportunity to attack with advantage.

Once combat is underway, either because the myconids are the aggressors or because the PCs are determined to reject any peaceful resolution, a myconid with a stunned opponent continues to attack with advantage. A myconid whose opponent has resisted others' attempts to stun it uses its own Pacifying Spores. However, a myconid whose opponent has resisted *its own* attempt to stun it won't try further; it simply attacks with its fists, without advantage. The first myconid to attack a previously stunned opponent on whom the effect has worn off will use its Pacifying Spores again, assuming it has uses left.

An adult myconid's self-preservation instinct kicks in when it's seriously injured (reduced to 8 hp or fewer), but because of its low speed, fleeing is a difficult proposition. It will Dash, but this is less "fleeing" and more "withdrawing"; if its opponents are determined to pursue it, its chances aren't good. If there are enough casualties that the myconids are outnumbered by their opponents, they'll stop attacking, release Rapport Spores, and try to parley. If parley fails, they'll release one final burst of Pacifying Spores, then all Dash away the next round.

A **myconid sovereign** is the guiding mind of a circle of myconids. Myconid sovereigns have above-average Strength and Constitution, suiting them more naturally to the brute fighter style. If the myconids are responding to provocation by chaotic PC behavior, the response will be led by a sovereign.

Myconid sovereigns have a Multiattack action comprising one spore attack (either Pacifying or Hallucinating) and one Fist attack. While Pacifying Spores stun opponents, Hallucinating Spores poison them. What's the difference? A stunned creature automatically fails Strength and Dexterity saving throws, and attack rolls against the creature advantage. A poisoned creature doesn't automatically fail any saving throw, nor do attack rolls against the creature have advantage, but the creature has disadvantage on *its own* attack rolls and ability checks. In either case, the spore target is incapacitated, meaning it can't move or take actions or reactions.

So, wait—if the poisoned target is incapacitated while it hallucinates, if it can't take actions or reactions, what does it matter if it has disadvantage on its attack rolls and ability checks? Technically, it confers disadvantage if a hallucinating creature has to make a skill contest roll that doesn't involve taking an action, such as a Perception check against the Stealth skill, an Athletics or Acrobatics check against being grappled or shoved, or a Wisdom check against Deception, Persuasion, or Intimidation. Shoving an opponent and knocking them prone would then confer advantage on melee attack rolls against that opponent, but that's taking two rounds (and two rolls) to do what Pacifying Spores accomplishes in one. In short, combat-wise, the net effect of Hallucinating Spores is incapacitation, and that's it—any other effect is purely situational and incidental.

From this, we can conclude that if the myconid sovereign is responding to PC mayhem, it's not going to bother to use its Hallucination Spores; it's going to use its Pacifying Spores the same way a myconid adult would. Only if the PCs are the aggressors, and the myconid sovereign isn't sure why, will it resort to its Hallucination Spores, then try to talk the hallucinating opponent into pursuing a different course of action.

I haven't discussed the myconid sovereign's final feature, Animating Spores, aka Create Fungus Zombie. This takes the corpse of a dead humanoid or beast and turns it into a **spore servant**, a slow-moving thrall of the myconids. It fights as a brute, whether or not that style suits it, no longer having access to any ranged attacks, spells, or other class or combat actions it previously possessed.

Note the wording: "It loses any action that isn't Multiattack or a melee weapon attack that deals bludgeoning, piercing, or slashing damage. . . . If the servant has no other means of dealing damage, it can use its fists or limbs to make unarmed strikes." This means a spore servant can't Dash, Disengage, Dodge, Help, Hide, Search, Use an Object (to any degree that requires an action), or Ready another action. Although the *Monster Manual* isn't super clear on the matter, I'd assume that Animating Spores restores the hit points of the spore servant to its former maximum.

Spore servants are, for all intents and purposes, mindless drones, which the myconids can (and will) throw at their opponents indiscriminately, although they do have the common sense to aim spore servants at stunned opponents, in order to give them advantage on their attack rolls. They have no self-preservation instinct (or, for that matter, free will) and will fight until they're destroyed.

SHAMBLING MOUNDS

The **shambling mound** is an old-school classic: Veteran AD&D players will remember the *Monster Manual* illustration that looked like a Christmas tree with a carrot for a nose. Viny quasi-zombies of the swamps and rainforests, shambling mounds are brutes that tramp around indiscriminately ingesting whatever organic matter they come across, vegetable or animal. Also, beating people up.

Oddly for such a large, ungainly creature, the shambling mound has proficiency in Stealth, which I have to attribute to its natural camouflage. Being a plant without normal senses, it's immune to blindness and deafness, along with exhaustion. It has blindsight in a 60-foot radius, is resistant to cold and fire damage (that's one hardy plant), and not only is immune to lightning but actually absorbs the electrical energy and uses it to regenerate.

According to the *Monster Manual* flavor text, shambling mounds don't pursue prey but rather wait for prey to come within reach, but for creatures that must feed all the time—and also have "shambling" in their name—this seems like a dull way to play them. It may not move around much, but why wouldn't a shambling mound be trudging through the woods when the player characters encounter it? Of course, whether it's waiting or walking, it does so as stealthily as it can, in order to gain the element of surprise against its prey.

The tactical combination is neatly laid out in the shambling mound's actions. Its Multiattack lets it make two Slam attacks; if both attacks hit, its target is grappled, and it gets to Engulf in the same turn, blinding, restraining, and suffocating its target. As long as the target remains grappled, the mound shambles away, since it's got what it came for, although it can Slam other opponents who come after it. If the target gets free, the shambling mound repeats its Multiattack against it, or against some other target that happens to be within reach if its original target has run away to a safe distance.

Note that the only sense the shambling mound has to detect the PCs with is its blindsight. Any PC farther than 60 feet from it is effectively invisible to it. If it's struck by a missile weapon or spell effect from outside this range, it doesn't know where it came from, only which side of it hurts. It uses its movement to go in the opposite direction—but if it's hit from multiple directions, and these send conflicting signals about which way it should go, it either averages them out or simply stops moving altogether. On the other hand, if it's attacked from within its blindsight range, it moves *toward* its attackers and tries to whomp them. This goes double for anyone attacking it with lightning damage. It *likes* lightning damage. It will move full speed toward the source, hoping for more, even if that source is beyond its sensory radius.

"If a shambling mound faces defeat before an overwhelming foe, the root-stem can feign death, collapsing the remains of its mound," the *Monster Manual* flavor text tells us. My standard threshold for serious injury is 40 percent of hit point maximum, which in the shambling mound's case means it's been reduced to 54 hp or fewer.

TREANTS

Treants are, of course, ents. I can only assume they're called "treants" for the same reason that the humanoid creatures who are obviously hobbits are called "halflings": an inability to obtain usage rights from the Tolkien estate. (This may also be why D&D has always spelled "worg" with an *o* instead of an *a*, and why a demon obviously inspired by Tolkien's balrog is called a "balor.")

Treants are chaotic good, and good *usually* means "friendly," but not always. Evil displeases them mightily, but so does any kind of civilization encroaching on their turf. Even if one doesn't do anything to hurt them or the trees and forests they care for, they still may get annoyed enough with trespassers to want to teach them a lesson about treading where they oughtn't. In this last case, their primary goal is deterrence, and if they can't drive the trespassers out, they'll attack to subdue, then take out the trash themselves.

Another thing to like about treants is that they're resistant to bludgeoning and piercing damage but not to slashing damage. Anytime fifth edition D&D bothers to distinguish among the three different types of physical damage, it gets a thumbs-up from me. Note also that treants are resistant to *any* kind of bludgeoning or piercing damage, even if it comes from a magic weapon.

With their extraordinary Strength and Constitution and poor Dexterity, treants are brutes. They have a ranged weapon attack in the form of lobbing rocks, but they mostly do this while walking toward someone they perceive as an enemy. Once they get within striking distance, they're all about the Slam attack—which they get two of per turn, thanks to Multiattack.

Treants are vulnerable to fire, but they're not scared of it per se. Rather, it angers them and draws their ire. Only if an opponent deals it at least moderate fire damage (41 or more in a single turn) does a treant get scared and take evasive action. Having decent natural armor and a lot of hit points, it backs off—heedless of opportunity attacks—and hurls a rock at whoever dealt the fire damage when it's at least 30 feet from its former melee opponent(s) but no more than 60 feet from that target. Note that, per "Knocking a Creature Out" (*Player's Handbook*, chapter 9), melee attacks can be declared non-fatal, but ranged attacks are always lethal. Giving a treant a second- or third-degree burn is the one sure way to eliminate any qualms it has about killing people.

Once per day, a treant can Animate Trees, turning two nearby trees into quasi-treants. These aren't the same as awakened trees: They do Siege Monster damage to inanimate objects, and while they're stronger and much tougher, they lack the sentience of an awakened tree. In essence, they're like woody drones directed by the treant which can make only a single Slam attack each turn. (Although the stat block isn't direct about it, a fastidiously literal reading—always a good idea in fifth edition—implies that animated trees don't get a Multiattack.) A treant will Animate Trees only if it feels genuinely threatened, which is to say, if the combat encounter difficulty (as calculated per the "Combat Encounter Difficulty" formula in chapter 3 of the *Dungeon Master's Guide*) is merely Easy or Medium for its enemies, or if they launch a surprise attack and manage to do 41 or more damage to it before it can act.

Generally speaking, treants are loath to fight in the first place. They aren't proficient in any social skill, but their high Wisdom indicates a preference for talking things out and issuing warnings before coming to blows, as well as an ability to size up the level of challenge their opponents present (again, per "Combat Encounter Difficulty"). If their opponents are too difficult to handle alone, they'll issue a booming call for aid, and you can have enough additional treants show up in the third through fifth combat rounds to level the playing field. Again, however, unless their opponents are setting fires or spraying poison or acid willy-nilly, they're going to stick to nonlethal melee attacks as much as possible, then carry their unconscious foes to the nearest edge of the forest (which isn't necessarily where they entered from or where they were going) and huck them a good distance away.

In some instances—for instance, if a group of low-level PCs encounter one of these CR 9 entities—a treant may decide that its opponents aren't even worth pummeling. In this case, remember that you do have the option of having the treant make an ordinary grapple attack to pick an opponent up off the ground. Being Huge creatures, they can carry a Medium or Small PC—or two!—without even being slowed down, as well as order a couple of animated trees to do the same. Then they can march to the edge of their territory, put their opponents down (or toss them, if they've been annoying), give them a pat on the behind, and send them on their way.

All that being said, when a long-lived, peace-loving treant determines that its opponents need to die, not only is it going to start that fight, it's going to *finish* it. Its foes can try to surrender, and maybe it will be moved to accept and stand down. But it's not going to let its own injuries hold it back from what needs to be done, nor will it ever allow itself to be taken as a prisoner. By Rillifane, it will end the threat to itself and its forest home or die trying.

BEASTS

STIRGES

Stirges are flying, bloodsucking parasites. One alone is a pest, but a flock of them constitutes a threat, and this is how they'll nearly always be encountered.

Their Strength is pitiful, but their Dexterity is high. This makes them hit-and-run attackers, or rather hit-and-fly attackers, since they waddle along at a laughable 10 feet per turn but fly at a brisk 40. With a Wisdom of only 8, they're indiscriminate in their target selection, attacking whoever comes closest to them; and with a barely cognizant Intelligence of 2, they know only one way to attack and stick with it regardless of circumstances.

This attack revolves around the use of their Blood Drain feature. Starting from a position in the air above its victim, a stirge dives down to bite with its mosquitolike proboscis. If it hits, it latches on. At the start of each subsequent turn, if its victim hasn't yanked it loose, it automatically drains more hit points from them. Keep track of this number for each stirge individually, because once it's drained 10 hp from its prey, a stirge is sated, and it detaches and flies away at normal speed (potentially incurring one or more opportunity attacks as it departs).

Note the wording of the Blood Drain feature: A stirge detaches after it drains 10 hp "or the target dies"—*not* "or the target falls unconscious." In other words, the stirge keeps slurping up its victim's blood even after they fall to 0 hp. This means an automatic failed death saving throw on the part of the victim ("If you take any damage while you have 0 hit points, you suffer a death saving throw failure. . . . If the damage equals or exceeds your hit point maximum, you suffer instant death"—*Player's Handbook*, chapter 9, "Death Saving Throws"). These little blighters are tenacious—maybe fatally so, for entry-level PCs.

What if a stirge misses its attack? Then it flies back up into the air, holding station about 20 feet above its target, and tries again on its next turn. That's its standard attack cycle: Fly down, attack, then either latch on (on a hit) or fly back up (on a miss).

Stirges aren't bright, but they have *just* enough savvy to know that they get less tasty blood if they have to share a victim. Thus, if the nearest potential target already has another stirge attached to it, a stirge passes it by and attacks the second-nearest target. Only when other stirges have latched on to every other living being in the vicinity do they begin to double and triple up—half an artery is better than none.

Stirges are evolved creatures with a normal survival instinct, but they're also very fragile: Any damage sufficient to seriously injure a stirge is also sufficient to kill it outright. Thus, retreat isn't something you need to concern yourself with when running a stirge encounter—at least, not on the part of the stirges. They'll definitely pursue opponents who try to retreat, though, unless and until they've slaked their thirst for blood. Even though any one stirge may be well fed, every other stirge in the flock is going to want its share, too.

Note that stirges have darkvision, indicating that they'll be encountered primarily at night or underground. They gain nothing from hunting in daylight. Consider them nocturnal.

DINOSAURS

"Sophistication" is not the word that leaps to mind when discussing the battle tactics of dinosaurs. Most of these ancient beasts are dumb brutes, with extraordinary Strength and Constitution and rock-bottom Intelligence. They fall into two main categories, plus one variation:

- *Plant-eaters.* These tend to be peaceful unless spooked. They may lash out if you invade their space, and they'll defend themselves if cornered, but most of the time, they'll mind their own business. If attacked, they'll usually run.
- *Meat-eaters.* These are predators that will hunt, kill, and eat any creature smaller than themselves. If they're hungry—and they usually are—you can count on them to chase and attack anyone and anything they might construe as food.
- *Flying meat-eaters.* These behave like their landbound kin, but the fact that they can fly adds an aerial wrinkle to their attack pattern.

The fifth edition *Monster Manual* contains stat blocks for six dinosaurs: allosaurus, ankylosaurus, plesiosaurus, pteranodon, triceratops, and tyrannosaurus rex.

I'll look at these by dietary group, from lowest challenge rating to highest within each. Think of this as the dinosaurs' pecking order, as any meat-eating dinosaur will attack and eat another dinosaur of a smaller size and lower CR, while a higher CR plant-eater, although it won't actually attack other plant-eaters with lower CRs, may yet decide to muscle in and chase them off if the grazing in an area is especially good.

The **ankylosaurus** is a Huge (elephant-size) dinosaur covered with knobby, bony horns and sporting a clublike tail. Its speed is only 30 feet, and it will run only from single predators its own size or larger. Smaller predators get whacked with the tail. It never occurs to the ankylosaurus that running away might give it a better chance of surviving against one or more smaller predators than bludgeoning them with its tail will, even if it's seriously wounded.

The **triceratops**, also a Huge dinosaur, is deceptively fast, having a movement speed of 50 feet per turn. Its hide is thick but not armored; its neck is guarded by a large bony shield plate. The distinctive features that give this beast its name are the three horns on its snout and forehead, with which it can charge an enemy like a rhinoceros. It uses its

Trampling Charge feature to gore and flatten any enemy smaller than a tyrannosaurus, then Stomps on its prone foe for good measure. The triceratops can use its Stomp *only* against prone creatures; in other situations, it uses its Gore attack.

The advantage provided by Trampling Charge is so good for the triceratops that it will run from enemy to enemy in order to keep using it, switching opponents whenever a prone enemy gets up from the ground, indifferent to opportunity attacks. Of course, this is effective only if its enemies are more than 20 feet apart from one another. If they all cluster up, this tactic doesn't work anymore, and the triceratops just Gores everything in sight.

A seriously wounded triceratops (reduced to 38 hp or fewer) flees the scene using the Dash action. It will also Dash away from a tyrannosaurus as soon as it sees one.

The **pteranodon**, not to be confused with the pterodactyl (for which no stats are provided), is a Medium (human-size) flying carnivore. However, its preferred diet is fish and seafood, so it won't mess with creatures on land, including other dinosaurs and your PCs.

Suppose, though, that your PCs are shipwrecked and flailing around in the water, or just out for a swim, in an area populated by pteranodons. In that scenario, the Small members of your party might get dive-bombed by a pteranodon hungry for lunch—or a flock of them. The pteranodon has the Flyby feature, meaning that you don't get an opportunity attack when it flies out of your reach, and its flying speed is a zippy 60 feet per turn, so the standard flying-predator tactic of hovering 30 feet in the air, diving to attack, then flying back up suits it perfectly. Pteranodons don't expect to be attacked back, so they fly away when only moderately wounded (reduced to 9 hp or fewer).

The **allosaurus** is a Large (cattle-size), *very* fast hunter that runs down its prey like a big cat. Its primary method of attack is to charge toward its targets and land claws-first on the back of its prey (the Pounce feature). If it succeeds in knocking its target prone, it gets a bonus Bite attack. It then tries to devour its target on the spot, using Bite until they're dead. The allosaurus is a brute, with extraordinary Strength and exceptional Constitution; it must be seriously wounded (reduced to 20 hp or fewer) even to *consider* backing off. No matter what, after knocking a target prone with Pounce on a prior turn, it's going to try to take at least one more bite. If and when it does abandon its meal, unlike other dinosaurs, it Disengages (a function of instinct, not discipline, plus its overall intimidating presence) before retreating.

The Large **plesiosaurus** hunts close to shore, but it's most at home in the water, where it has a 40-foot swimming speed, rather than on land, where its speed is a more plodding 20 feet per turn. In addition to its swimming speed and its Hold Breath ability, the plesiosaurus is the only dinosaur with proficiency in Stealth, so its strategy can be summed up in two words: water ambush. The plesio hides beneath the surface of the water, watching for the movement of other creatures. When one comes within range, *om nom nom*. The plesio's Bite action is its only attack, but it does three dice of damage, which isn't paltry. A brute like the allosaurus, the plesio isn't going to be deterred from its dinner by merely moderate wounds; rather, when reduced to 47 hp or fewer, it substitutes a grapple attack for its Bite attack and tries to drag its prey underwater. Then, even if its prey wriggles loose from its jaws, it continues to make Bite attacks while its prey tries to swim back to shore—and the plesiosaur is almost certainly the faster swimmer. Only when seriously wounded (reduced to 27 hp or fewer) does the plesiosaur finally give up, drop its prey, and withdraw to deeper waters.

Finally, the thunder lizard you've been waiting for: the Huge **tyrannosaurus rex**. Exceeded in size only by the brontosaurus (which has no stat block in the *Monster Manual*), exceeded in ferocity by none, the tyrannosaurus is shockingly fast (50 feet per round) and has extraordinary Strength and Constitution. Its speed allows it to chase down pretty much anything—or anyone—it feels like snacking on, and it can grapple and restrain a target on a successful Bite attack. The sole drawback to its kit is that it must use its Multiattack on two *different* targets: a Bite attack against an opponent in front of it, and a Tail attack against an opponent beside or behind. If you have to choose, you definitely would rather get hit by the tail.

The tyrannosaurus chooses its prey before charging and striking—like other predators, it goes after the easiest target in sight, i.e., the young, the old, the weak, the isolated, and the oblivious—and it sticks with its choice. There are so few things in nature that can hurt it significantly, it doesn't even *realize* when it's moderately wounded. When it's seriously wounded (reduced to 54 hp or fewer), it Dashes off with any restrained victim still in its jaws, inflicting additional Bite attacks as it runs.

Flying Snakes

You could be forgiven for getting the **flying snake** confused with the couatl, since they seem to come from the same source material. The easy way to think about it is that the flying snake is the cute, undomesticated wild version, while the couatl is the powerful, otherworldly, people-size version. Or, in Scholastic Aptitude Test format, couatl : flying snake :: angel : titi monkey.

Flying snakes, by and large, avoid combat. First, they're unaligned, so they have no evil intent to drive them. Second, they're *very* low in Strength. Usually, this indicates a preference for fighting in numbers, but snakes are predominantly solitary, not social. (Note that the *Monster Manual* contains no "Swarm of Flying Snakes" entry.) A flock or nest of flying snakes would be a rare thing, perhaps the result of control by some more powerful being with an affinity for reptiles.

Their Dexterity is exceptional, their Constitution merely average, and they have just 5 hp. If they attack at all, such as if a player character surprises one or stumbles across a nest of its eggs, it's a shock strike: one hit, then fly away as fast as possible. They can do decent enough damage with this strike—their teeny fangs do just 1 piercing damage, but they deliver 3d4 worth of toxic venom—to make them a legitimate threat to entry-level adventurers.

If a group of them are being controlled by a more powerful being, it can use them as a sort of aerial ranged weapon attack by having them hold station 20 to 30 feet up in the air between attacks, fly down to bite, then fly back up out of reach. Thanks to their Flyby feature, they don't incur opportunity attacks when they fly out of their foes' reach.

They also have a swimming speed, although they're not amphibious, so rather than swimming *through* the water, they're more likely slithering across the surface of it.

A flying snake under the control of another being will attack until that being tells it to stop attacking, so survival instincts don't apply. A flying snake in control of itself will flee after just one strike—or before striking at all—and doesn't need to wait until it's injured, unless it's guarding a nest of eggs. In that case, it flees after taking any hit that does 3 or 4 damage. Any more than that would kill it.

ACKNOWLEDGMENTS

First and foremost, I'm indebted to my wife, Jen C. Marshall, for asking me whether I'd run a Dungeons & Dragons group for her and some of her coworkers, leading me to pick up the fifth edition D&D rulebooks and discover just how much the game system had changed—for the better—since I'd played it last.

Next, I want to thank the current and former members of that group—Jen (Tola Illvidri), Ginny Barrett (Paris Camembert), Kay Brown (Tilda Forgeborn), Jeremy Cozad (Kukl), Mattías Darrow (Cull Dowercap/Tobac Sigured), Sam Luchsinger (LeGuardeus Masters), Chelsea Ball (Shava), Seaghan Brien (Thesselus Elsulmun), and Laurel Sallack Macupa (Dorris)—for their enthusiasm and their patience as they learned the rules and I relearned them, and Jeremy especially for three and a half years of hosting our weekly sessions in his home. We're telling some great stories together, and I look forward to telling many more.

I also thank my friend and fellow DM Steve Long, for helping me set up my blog, *The Monsters Know What They're Doing*, and my first DM, Julian Jackson—whose epic imagination I can never hope to equal, a shortcoming I've learned to make up for with obsessive verisimilitude—for thirty years of friendship and innumerable hours of shared gaming experience. Special thanks go to my editor, Jeremie Ruby-Strauss, for curbing my verbosity and spotting my mistakes; and to Umair Kazi of the Authors Guild and my colleague Paul Rapp for helping me navigate the waters of the publishing industry for the first time. Thanks are due as well to Wizards of the Coast for its transformation and revival of the world's most popular tabletop role-playing game.

Finally, a huge shout-out to the readers of *The Monsters Know What They're Doing*, whose enthusiastic comments have kept the project going since 2016. I wasn't sure a demand existed for tactical analyses of monster behavior, but you've shown me that not only is there demand for it, there's a *hunger* for it. Thanks for letting me feed you.

—K.A.

INDEX